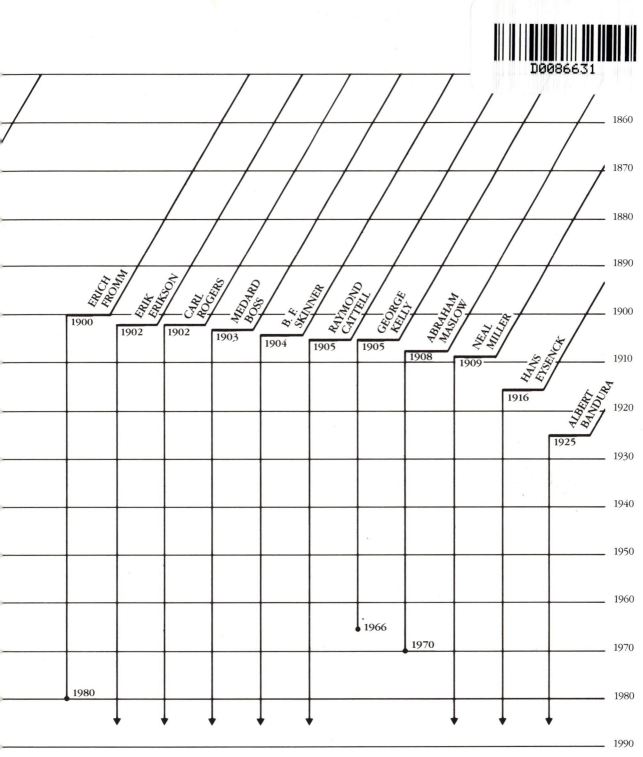

Introduction to Theories of Personality

Introduction to Theories of Personality

CALVIN S. HALL
Santa Cruz, California

GARDNER LINDZEY
*Center for Advanced Study in the
Behavioral Sciences, Stanford, California*

JOHN C. LOEHLIN
University of Texas at Austin

MARTIN MANOSEVITZ
University of Texas at Austin

with the assistance of
VIRGINIA OTIS LOCKE

JOHN WILEY & SONS
New York   Chichester   Brisbane   Toronto   Singapore

Cover painting: Paul Klee,
            ''Senecio.'' Basel,
            Public Art Collections/Art Resource.

Text Design: Edward A. Butler
Production Supervisor: Miriam Seda
Copy Editor: Salley Ann Bailey
Photo Researcher: Flavia Rando
Photo Editor: Stella Kupferberg

ISBN 0–471–08906–0

Printed in the United States of America

20 19 18 17 16 15

Printed and bound by R.R. Donnelley & Sons, Inc.

Preface

Introduction to Theories of Personality represents an effort to make the personality text that defined the field—Hall and Lindzey's *Theories of Personality*—more accessible to the beginning psychology student. *Theories of Personality* (first edition, 1957) was addressed largely to an audience of seniors and graduate students—although its total sales of more than 700,000 copies make clear that it has been used in many undergraduate classes at various levels. Commonly, today, beginning students of personality are sophomores, sometimes freshmen, and their background in psychology is often limited. *Theories of Personality*, which assumes some acquaintance with the major areas of psychological study and research, has presented the beginning student with a formidable task. With this fact in mind, we have prepared a shortened and simplified version of that text, one in which some of the more difficult sections have been revised or eliminated and in which a lively program of teaching aids is presented to stimulate students' learning of the material as well as their further exploration of the theorists' original work.

Introduction to Theories of Personality resembles its parent in many ways. It describes and interprets the major theories of human personality, introducing the student to the main ideas of each theorist. It discusses research generated by each theory, examines representative studies, and indicates the theory's significance for current personality research. It presents each theory sympathetically, thus allowing students to see in a positive way what that theory can accomplish. In a final section of each chapter the theory is critically evaluated.

In several ways, this new book also differs from its predecessor. First, there have been some changes in the theories presented: some deletions, a few additions, and some shifts in emphasis. Second, by careful selection, the text has been reduced in length, and some reorganization has permitted a presentation that should be easier for the student to follow. Third, many teaching aids have been incorporated into the book—boxed inserts, figures, tables, summaries, and a glossary. Finally, a considerable amount of updating has been done.

Our primary criterion for theorist inclusion remains the influence a theory has had or continues to have on personality research. This criterion has led us, for example, to continue to discuss the influential theories of Kurt Lewin, B. F. Skinner, and Neal Miller and John Dollard, even though many current personality texts do not. Accounts of some other theorists whose work is of less influence on current personality research have been deleted (for example, Andras Angyal) or treated briefly in boxed inserts (for example, Kurt Goldstein). The growing interest in cognitive approaches led us to add a presentation of the work of George Kelly (Chapter 8). And we have included, in Chapter 11, a brief section on behavior genetics, a field of study that has attracted increasing interest among personality investigators. The important theory of Albert Bandura is featured in a new chapter (Chapter 15) that covers contemporary social learning approaches to personality, including the work of Martin Seligman and Walter Mischel.

The book is arranged in four major sections, reflecting the psychodynamic, humanistic, trait or dispositional, and learning theory approaches to personality. This new arrangement should facilitate instructors' use of the book in courses of varying lengths; for example, an instructor may assign only some chapters from each part in a briefer course.

Other suggestions will be found in the instructor's manual that accompanies the text. Within each chapter the book again follows generally in its predecessor's footsteps. We begin with an introduction to the salient features of a theory. The chapter then discusses the theory's treatment of the structure, or enduring aspects, of personality and follows this with its handling of personality dynamics, or motivation and change in personality. Next is a section on personality development. The chapter then explores the kinds of research that the theory has produced. Finally, we discuss various critiques of the theory and offer a brief evaluation.

At the end of each chapter of *Introduction to Theories of Personality* is an itemized summary that recapitulates the chapter's important points and a set of suggestions for further reading. Instructors using the book in a two-semester course may find the latter section helpful in supplementing the text with additional material. Added within chapters are boxed inserts of various kinds: biographical sketches of the theorists, illustrative research studies, and discussions of important concepts or methods. In addition, the text has been illustrated with many figures and tables. Although we have used a simpler writing style in this new book, the scholarly character of the original text has been carefully maintained. We have aimed throughout for clarity, simplicity, and economy of presentation.

Like *Theories of Personality*, this book is designed primarily for use in such courses as personality, theories of personality, or introduction to personality. The book may also be used, however, in courses such as abnormal psychology or developmental psychology. Inasmuch as it is designed to be comprehensible to the student who has had only an introductory course in psychology, it is suitable not only for the general liberal arts student but for students in such other fields as educational psychology, special education, social work, nursing, and psychiatry.

We would like to acknowledge the assistance of several people who have done much to make this volume possible. We thank Professor Gordon Bear of Ramapo College for his constructive reviews of each chapter of the book. We are grateful to the many Wiley staff members who have contributed their talents to the project: we especially wish to thank Mark Mochary, Stella Kupferberg, Susan Goodall, and Miriam Seda. G. L. is grateful for the use of the facilities of the Center for Advanced Study in the Behavioral Sciences and, in particular, for Joyce McDonald's judicious and patient execution of many tasks associated with completion of the book. We wish also to thank Elizabeth McGehee Parella for her meticulous typing of the manuscript.

All these and many others have helped, but most of all we acknowledge the contributions of those whose ideas and work we present in the pages to follow.

Contents

Introduction to Theories of Personality

Chapter one

1.

Come, begin.
    HAMLET

Introduction to Personality Theory:
A Framework for Comparison

This book offers the reader an organized, concise summary of the major theories to which students of human personality subscribe. Each chapter outlines the salient features of a theory, discusses relevant research, and appraises the theory in terms of its strengths and its weaknesses.

In this first, introductory chapter we begin by considering the meaning of the term "personality" and examining the nature of "theory." Then, armed with a rough idea of what a personality theory is, we explore the role that personality theory has played, since its formal debut in the late nineteenth century, in the overall field of psychology. Next, taking a further step toward defining personality theory, we examine some specific features that distinguish it from other kinds of psychological theory.

This background review sets the stage for our consideration of the major issues in modern personality theory on which theories generally take a particular stance. These "dimensions of personality theory" give the reader a framework for understanding and comparing the theories we examine throughout the book. We conclude the chapter with a brief exploration of the general strengths and weaknesses of personality theories, considering how such theories may help or hinder us in our quest to understand human beings and their highly complex behavior.

WHAT IS PERSONALITY

How often have you heard someone say, "Bill hasn't got much personality" or "Cindy has a terrific personality"? These and similar statements represent one common popular usage of the word **personality.** This sense of the term has mostly to do with the impression an individual makes on others—it refers to his or her social skills, charismatic qualities, and the like. As the foregoing examples suggest, this use of the term tends to be highly **evaluative.** We are saying essentially that a person is or is not attractive, interesting, pleasant—in short, that a person is or is not someone we want to be with.

A second, almost equally common popular use of the term personality is somewhat more **descriptive**. In this usage, the term is combined with an adjective such as ''aggressive'' or ''easygoing''; thus, ''Jack has a very aggressive personality'' or ''Melissa has an easygoing personality.'' Here personality is described by an individual's most outstanding characteristic—it is thus defined by the most salient impression the person makes on others.

Psychologists, as you will discover in this book, tend to take much broader and more complicated views of personality. The word personality has a wealth of different meanings in psychological writings, as Gordon Allport (1937) demonstrated in his survey of the literature (see also Chapter 10). Of the almost 50 different definitions of personality revealed by Allport's study, we will examine just a few here.

Some theorists see personality as defined essentially by the reactions of other people. Termed **biosocial** by Allport, this view suggests that a person's ''social stimulus value'' is his or her personality. As in the popular views of personality just mentioned, the person is what others think he or she is. According to a contrasting, **biophysical** definition, personality has an organic, or inherent, component. It is linked to specific qualities of the person that can be described and measured objectively, such as physique (see, for example, William Sheldon's theory of the somatotype, Chapter 11).

A ragbag, or **omnibus**, definition lists every concept considered of importance in describing the person, whereas an **integrative** definition holds that personality is what gives order and congruence to the many different behaviors in which a person engages. On the latter view, personality is organization, or pattern.

Personality is seen by some as centered on the individual's effort to adjust to his or her environment. For others, personality designates the things about the person that are unique—the things that set him or her apart from others. And for still other theorists, personality represents the essence of the person. That is, personality is what a person ''really is''—it is what is most typical, most deeply characteristic of the person.

Throughout this book, the reader will meet definitions of personality like those just described, as well as many others. It is important to keep in mind that no one of these definitions is *the* definition of personality. A particular personality theorist defines personality so as to include those aspects of human functioning central to his or her theory. In addition, different definitions of personality may overlap. Thus a particular theory could define personality in a way that is integrative

and biosocial, centered on adjustment, and concerned with the essence of a person. Another theory might also be biosocial in emphasis but omnibus in form and focused on individual differences.

WHAT IS A THEORY?

A theory is commonly thought to be something that exists in opposition to a fact. That is, it is viewed as an hypothesis about what is true, a speculation about reality; it is something that is not *known* to be true. In general, a theory is thought to be capable of being confirmed or disconfirmed when sufficient data have been collected and analyzed. In our view, however, theories themselves are neither true nor false. It is only their implications, or their derivations, that can be proven or disproven.

HOW ARE THEORIES CONSTRUCTED?

A theory is a set of ideas that the theorist creates; it is not something "given" by nature or by the data. It is an arbitrary choice of a particular way of representing the events in which one is interested. In this sense, it is as creative as the novelist's plot or the artist's sketch, differing only in the kinds of data it employs and in the way its usefulness is judged.

Because a theory is created by a theorist, it rests on no ultimate principle; it is simply one way of looking at a given set of objects or events. Rather than true or false, a theory is useful or not useful, depending on whether the predictions it generates turn out to be verifi-

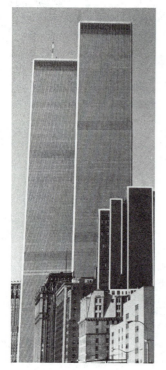

On the left we see two tall, rectangular buildings. On the right, the gradual convergence of the vertical lines carries the eye upward: the buildings seem to reach toward the heavens. Just as these pictures show us different aspects of the World Trade Center's twin towers, so two personality theories may illuminate different aspects of the person: a Skinnerian view, for example, may stress objective behavior; a Jungian view may emphasize the striving for transcendence.

able. Thus, although we cannot specify how a theory is to be created, we can specify how it should be evaluated.

WHAT CONSTITUTES A THEORY?

In its ideal form, a theory consists of (1) a cluster of assumptions that are relevant to the topic under investigation and systematically related to each other and (2) a set of empirical definitions that relate the assumptions to the world of observable events.

The first requirement means, for example, that the assumptions made in a theory of audition must have something to do with the process of hearing; those made in a theory of perception must bear on the perceptual process. Such assumptions may be very general or quite specific. For example, one theory may assume that all behavior is motivated, whereas another may assume that an increase in anxiety will interfere with motor performance.

A theory's assumptions not only must be stated clearly; they must be explicitly related to each other. If the theory is to be logically consistent, it must have a **syntax**, or a set of rules for systematic interaction among assumptions and their embedded concepts. Without such rules, it is impossible to make sense of empirical data. For example, suppose we add to our assumption that increased anxiety interferes with motor performance the assumption that increased self-esteem will, on the other hand, enhance such performance. Before we can investigate either of these assumptions, we need to define the relationship between anxiety and self-esteem. Otherwise, in situations where anxiety and self-esteem may both be changing, we will be unable to interpret changes in motor performance.

Empirical definitions, or as they are often called, **operational definitions**, attempt to specify operations that we can use to measure relevant variables. It is by means of these definitions that the theory comes in contact with observational data, or the real world. Empirical definitions need to be as exact as present information permits. At the same time, researchers must maintain a certain amount of flexibility in formulating definitions, lest fruitful paths of inquiry be obscured. For example, if we were to define anxiety simply as measurable physiological change in, say, heart rate or respiration, we would be missing other phenomena that characterize this unpleasant emotion, such as poor concentration, agitation, and fear.

WHAT DOES A THEORY DO?
First and most important, a theory must lead us to observe both new data and relations among these data. Thus a theory should lead to a systematic expansion of the available knowledge about a particular phenomenon. Moreover, deriving from the theory empirical propositions (hypotheses, predictions) that can be tested by observations should stimulate this expansion of knowledge.

The basic function of any science is to discover stable and demonstrable relations among events, and it is the function of a theory to further this process in a systematic manner. The theory produces empirical propositions that, when tested, allow us to accept or reject or modify the theory. The **usefulness** of a theory has two major aspects: **verifiability** is the theory's capacity to generate predictions that are confirmed by data; **comprehensiveness** is the theory's capacity to produce predictions that cover the range of empirical events the theory purports to deal with.

Related to the notion of a theory's usefulness is its **heuristic** influence. A theory not only generates research in a systematic way, producing specific propositions that lead to specific studies; it may generate research simply by suggesting general ideas or by arousing disbelief and resistance. Sigmund Freud's and Charles Darwin's theories, for example, aroused both interest and strong resistance and were at least as important for the broad new paths of investigation they opened up as for the specific, testable propositions they generated.

The second important thing a theory must do is permit us to incorporate known empirical findings within a logically consistent and reasonably simple framework. Thus, ideally, a theory should enable us to organize and integrate everything known about a given set of phenomena. For example, an adequate theory of psychotic behavior should be able to arrange the bizarre symptomatic phenomena of schizophrenic and other psychotic disorders in an understandable and logical framework. (The psychotic disorder, or **psychosis**, is a mental disorder that seriously disrupts a person's life, interfering with relations with other people, with normal emotional expression, and with intellectual functioning.) Such a theory should be able to account for such matters as the age, sex, and geographical distribution of people exhibiting psychotic behavior, the responsiveness of such people to various kinds of drug treatments, such people's relationships in families, and the like.

Theories are guided, and to some degree controlled, by what has been observed and reported to date. Some empiricists have held that theories are simply after-the-fact rationalizations of what the investigator has already reported. To maintain that view, however, is to miss the main function of a theory, which is to point out or suggest new and as yet unobserved relations.

A third contribution of a theory is that it enables the investigator to identify the important issues to be studied. In this sense, the theory is a set of blinders; it prevents the scientist from being dazzled or overwhelmed by the full complexity of natural events and enables him or her to abstract from these events efficiently and systematically. To abstract and simplify is a natural means of coming to understand the events we study, but if we do this without the guidelines provided by an explicit theory, we are likely to be influenced by implicit assumptions and attitudes of which we may be quite unaware. Theories force us to articulate our assumptions for our own benefit, at the same time making them accessible to other investigators.

THEORY AND PARADIGM

The **paradigm**, a kind of grand theory or super model, is a concept brought into scientific usage by the historian of science, Thomas Kuhn (1962). A paradigm provides a compelling way of looking at problems and solutions for a whole area of scientific research. For example, the well-known paradigms of Copernican astronomy or Newtonian physics represented ways of approaching particular aspects of the world that were revolutions in scientific thought. Paradigms, according to Kuhn, occur within prescribed areas and are so astounding and so convincing yet at the same time so conducive to further exploration and discovery that they become universally accepted, at least until they are replaced by further such sweeping revolutions. As this book demonstrates, in the psychology of personality, we do not yet have a true paradigm. There are many more or less systematic ideas about the nature of personality, but so far none has gained a position of real dominance.

PERSONALITY THEORY AND THE HISTORY OF PSYCHOLOGY

We have said that personality is defined by the particular concepts a theorist uses to describe or understand human behavior. And we have said that a theory is composed of a set of assumptions about certain empirical phenomena, together with the empirical definitions needed to move from theory to concrete reality. Combining these statements, we can define personality theory initially as a set of assumptions about human behavior, together with appropriate empirical definitions. And we should add to this definition the prescription that a personality theory should ideally be comprehensive; that is, it should be able to deal with or make predictions about behavioral events that fall within the scope of its definition of personality.

Let us flesh out this rather abstract discussion by considering some of the ways in which personality theory both resembles and differs from other psychological theories. This review will set the stage for our exploration of nine basic issues, or dimensions, on which the theories discussed in this book can fruitfully be compared with each other.

INFLUENCES OF OTHER TRADITIONS ON PERSONALITY THEORY

Personality theory has ancient roots, tracing its origins to conceptions of human nature and behavior advanced by such classical scholars as Hippocrates (Greek physician; about 460–377 B.C.), Plato (Greek philosopher; about 427–347 B.C.), and Aristotle (Greek philosopher; 384–322 B.C.). Personality theory today reflects not only these earliest foundations but the contributions of many great thinkers over the more than 2000 years that have intervened.

We cannot explore here all the threads that make up the tapestry of personality theory. Throughout this book, you will find occasional references to the influences on specific personality theories of the thinking of some of the world's outstanding scientists and philosophers. Here, however, we will content ourselves with examining a few relatively recent sources of influence on personality theories in general.

Of the many fields of inquiry that have influenced the development of personality theory, four have had particularly far-reaching implications for this field of study. The tradition of **clinical observation** that began with Jean-Martin Charcot (French neurologist and psychiatrist; 1825–1893) and includes, of course, Sigmund Freud (Chapter 2) has done more to determine the nature of personality theory than any other single factor. The **Gestalt tradition**, whose followers were

Here the painter Raphael has depicted Plato and Aristotle, who were both early theorists of personality, in earnest dialogue.

convinced that human behavior could be studied only as a unit, not as a collection of small elements, has contributed an important theme to modern personality theory. **Experimental psychology** in general and **learning theory** in particular have brought increased concern with properly controlled research, a better understanding of theory construction, and a more carefully detailed account of how behavior is modified. Finally, the **psychometric tradition**, with its focus on individual differences, has brought increasing sophistication to the measurement of behavior and the analysis of data.

As the reader will see, the four main parts of the present book provide a grouping of personality theorists that is based essentially on the shared influences of these four traditions. The first part of the book, with a focus on the psychodynamic process, consists of theorists primarily of the clinical tradition (Freud, Erikson, Jung, Adler, Horney, Fromm, and Sullivan). In the second part, with its focus on the person's experience of self and world, a number of the theorists show an influence of the Gestalt and related traditions (Maslow, Rogers, Binswanger and Boss, Lewin, and Kelly); several were influenced by the clinical tradition as well.

In the third part of the book, focusing on enduring characteristics of the person, a strong influence of the psychometric tradition is evident, affecting all the theorists in varying degrees (Cattell and Eysenck most strongly, but also Murray, Allport, and Sheldon). Influences of the clinical and Gestalt traditions are found again in this group.

Finally, in the fourth group of theorists, focusing on learning and the environment (Skinner, Miller and Dollard, and Bandura), the influence of the tradition of learning theory and experimental psychology is strong, although some of the other influences play a role as well.

DISTINCTIVE FEATURES OF PERSONALITY THEORY

Personality theories probably differ from each other almost as much as theory and research in personality differs from theory and research in other areas of psychology. Most personality theories, however, share at least some qualities that distinguish this area of inquiry from the broad field of psychology.

To begin with, there are significant differences between the streams of influence that determined the early paths of general psychology and personality theory. Darwin's work and the many nineteenth-century developments in physiology clearly influenced both areas of endeavor, but during the twentieth century, the major factors influencing each area have been distinguishably different.

Psychology gradually came into being in the late nineteenth century as the offspring of philosophy and experimental physiology. The study of personality, however, evolved directly out of the theory and practice of medicine. Thus, out of its need to understand the troubled, or ''abnormal,'' person, personality theory from its very beginnings led rapidly to practical applications. The early giants in the study of personality, such as Sigmund Freud (Chapter 2) and Carl Jung (Chapter 4), were practicing physicians who dealt with the so-called disorders of the mind; they were psychotherapists.

Whereas, personality theorists worked almost exclusively with clinical data, experimentalists derived ideas and models from the natural sciences. Experimental and learning approaches to psychological theory derived from the study of such things as perception and memory—how human beings acquire information, store it, and so on. Such names as Herman von Helmholtz (1821–1894), Wilhelm Wundt (1832–1920), and later, John B. Watson (1878–1958) appear in the annals of this subdiscipline of psychology.

It is not surprising that these nineteenth-century leaders of academic psychology engaged in research somewhat removed from everyday practicalities. These investigators worked in universities where they were free to follow their own intellectual inclinations and to define what was significant largely by their own interests. In contrast, the early personality theorists, faced with patients' daily problems of life, magnified by neurosis or worse, were forced to derive formulations that at least attempted to deal with the common emotions and conflicts that hampered, disabled, and even killed fellow human beings. (The person with a **neurosis**, or neurotic disorder, generally functions normally but experiences such distressing symptoms as excessive anxiety or vague aches and pains.)

In general, then, personality theories tend to be quite **functional** in orientation. The issues with which they are concerned are more centered on matters that crucially affect the survival and general welfare of the organism than are many of the issues examined by experimentalists. For example, the personality theorist may investigate the role of childhood trauma in adult adjustment, while the experimental psychologist examines the speed with which a memory search is carried out. Both efforts add to our knowledge about human beings' structure and function and ultimately to our capacity to survive, but the contribution of the experimentalist, as you can see, is somewhat remote from the well-being of any particular person.

We do not mean to suggest that the path so commonly taken by personality theory will necessarily lead more efficiently to a comprehensive and useful theory of human behavior than the path selected by experimental psychology. Although to the average observer it may seem that the issues personality theorists have dealt with are the most central and most important, it remains to be seen whether tackling these problems head on will advance the science of psychology more rapidly than will approaches that place greater emphasis on rigor and the study of limited domains of behavior.

Personality theorists have often been rebels; they have rebelled against accepted theory and normative problems and against established methods and techniques of research. Previously outside the mainstream of academic psychology, personality theory could more easily question or reject assumptions that were widely accepted by academic psychologists. This freedom, however, was often accompanied by lack of discipline or lack of interest in the systematic and organized formulations of traditional scientists.

Until recently, for example, motivation held relatively little interest for experimental psychologists. Personality theorists, however, have customarily assigned a crucial role to the **motivational process**. William McDougall (1871–1938) wrote that the single most important area of psychology was that which dealt with ''the springs of human action, the impulses and motives that sustain mental and bodily activity and regulate conduct'' (McDougall, 1908, p. 2).

For the personality theorist, only the study of the **whole person** can lead to an adequate understanding of human behavior. The functioning person must be studied in natural surroundings, with each behavioral event considered in relation to all of the person's other behavior. This is a natural outcome of the clinical approach, where whole persons present themselves for treatment.

More than almost any other psychological theory, personality theory functions as an **integrative force**, bringing together and organizing the varying findings of specialists. For example, the experimentalist may know a lot about motor skills, auditory perception, and responses to stress but relatively little about the way these functions work together when, say, a young woman drives a car while arguing with her boyfriend. The personality theorist, on the other hand, is interested in how the whole person behaves as he or she uses these various functions. For example, the personality theorist may ask whether the person's early childhood experience affects his or her response in the present situation. Has the person acquired sufficient self-esteem to entertain others' ideas without becoming angry or defensive? Has the person learned to modulate his or her behavior so as to be able to perform a task satisfactorily in the presence of other, unrelated concerns?

The personality theorist has often been viewed, a bit romantically, as the person who will put together the jigsaw puzzle produced by psychology's many different disciplines. As the reader will see, however, some personality theorists themselves focus on limited aspects of human behavior. The grand theory—psychology's paradigm—seems still to be off in the distance.

DIMENSIONS OF PERSONALITY THEORY

Each of the theories that we discuss in this book makes a number of basic assumptions about human behavior. These assumptions reflect the theorists' positions on some major issues that confront modern personality theory. Examples of such issues are the degree to which people are motivated by conscious or unconscious forces and the relative influence on human behavior and personality of heredity and environment.

Each of the issues examined here represents a set of beliefs about human behavior that tend to fall along a continuum. Although in general each issue can be seen as a choice between one of two opposing views of personality structure and functioning, most theorists take a position that is not wholly in favor of one extreme or the other. We will see, for example, that whereas William Sheldon (Chapter 11) puts great emphasis on the hereditary factors in human behavior, and B. F. Skinner (Chapter 13) strongly emphasizes environmental factors, for most theorists—including Sheldon and Skinner—both heredity and environment exert important influences on the developing and functioning human being.

CONSCIOUS VERSUS UNCONSCIOUS.   The question of whether human behavior is controlled by rational processes of which we are aware—**conscious** processes—or by irrational factors of which we are unaware—**unconscious** processes—is an important issue. For some theorists, like Sigmund Freud (Chapter 2), Carl Jung (Chapter 4), or Karen Horney (Chapter 5), it is the unconscious determinants of behavior—accessible to awareness only under special conditions—that are the most important. Other theorists, like Carl Rogers (Chapter 6), Kurt Lewin (Chapter 8), or Gordon Allport (Chapter 10), tend to emphasize the influence of conscious factors on behavior. Most theorists admit the existence of both conscious and unconscious factors but accord somewhat more influence to one or the other. A common position of middle-ground theorists is that unconscious determinants are of particular significance in people whose behavior is disturbed, or ''abnormal,'' whereas conscious determinants play a dominant role in normal people.

ACQUISITIONS VERSUS PROCESS OF LEARNING.   For some theorists, like B. F. Skinner (Chapter 13), Neal Miller and John Dollard (Chapter 14), and Albert Bandura (Chapter 15), the **learning process**, or the way in which behavior is modified, holds the key to all behavioral phenomena. For others, however, like Henry Murray (Chapter 9), Gordon Allport (Chapter 10), or R. B. Cattell (Chapter 12), it is the **acquisitions**, or structures, of personality—the outcomes of learning—that are of greatest interest. No theorist denies the significance of learning in human behavior, but theorists generally tend to emphasize either the learning process or its resulting acquisitions.

HEREDITY VERSUS ENVIRONMENT.   The question of the relative importance in human behavior of genetic, or **hereditary**, factors and **environmental** factors has concerned students of behavior for as long as people have thought about why human beings behave as they do. Almost no one will deny that hereditary factors have some implications for behavior, but many personality theorists insist that the major behavioral phenomena can be understood without calling on factors that are genetic and biological.

Many American psychologists have tended to favor some branch of environmentalism. Rogers (Chapter 6) and Bandura (Chapter 15), for example, place very little emphasis on hereditary factors. As we will see in Chapter 11, however, current research in the area of behavior genetics tends to support the notion that inherited tendencies do exert an appreciable influence on human personality. Theorists such as Sheldon (Chapter 11) and Hans Eysenck (Chapter 12) have placed considerable emphasis on such tendencies.

PAST VERSUS PRESENT.   For some personality theorists, like Freud (Chapter 2) and Erik Erikson (Chapter 3), an important key to adult behavior is to be found in events that have taken place in the earliest years of development. For such theorists, events that occur in the remote **past**, in infancy and childhood, may be of greater overall importance than contemporary events in explaining behavior. For other theorists, such as Lewin (Chapter 8) and Allport (Chapter 10), behavior can be understood and explained largely by reference to events occurring in the **present** or the immediate past.

HOLISTIC VERSUS ANALYTIC.   A number of theories hold that human behavior is understandable only in terms of the context in which it occurs. This **holistic** view subsumes two related notions. First, everything people do is assumed to be related not only to everything else they do, but to their entire physiological and biological functioning. Thus the person is an organic whole, not to be understood if studied piece by piece. Second, behavior can be understood only with reference to the "field," or the environmental context, in which it occurs.

Theorists who emphasize field, or organismic views, such as Abraham Maslow (Chapter 6), Lewin (Chapter 8), or the existentialists Ludwig Binswanger and Medard Boss (Chapter 7), generally feel that although one may study separate aspects of behavior, one must continually relate the objects of one's investigation to other aspects of the person. These theorists feel that one cannot permanently split off an aspect of behavior for study because behavior is so intricately interrelated.

On the other hand, some theorists, like Skinner (Chapter 13), Miller and Dollard (Chapter 14), or Bandura (Chapter 15), hold that the proper approach to behavior is **analytical**. These theorists believe that the best way to understand behavior is to begin with small, discrete units of behavior, such as reflexes or habits, and then build up to more complex analyses. Such theorists hold essentially that the scientific methods of physics and the other natural sciences are wholly appropriate to the study of human personality.

PERSON VERSUS SITUATION.   For years theorists have lined up on either side of the so-called **person–situation** debate, the issue of whether behavior is to be seen largely as a product of the person and his or her own inner processes or as a product of the situation or environment in which the person exists. Most theorists today subscribe to some form of the interactionist view stressed by Henry Murray (Chapter 9), which holds that person and situation are both critically important in determining behavior. Some theorists, however, still find themselves at one or the other pole of this issue. Skinner (Chapter 13), for example, locates all causal factors ultimately in the environment, whereas followers of Binswanger and Boss (Chapter 7) often locate the major determinants of behavior within the person.

Related to the person–situation issue is the question of how important sociocultural factors are in human behavior. Some theorists, such as Erich Fromm (Chapter 5), strongly emphasize the role of such factors in shaping and controlling behavior. Other theorists, like Sheldon (Chapter 11), place much more emphasis on internal biological determinants of behavior. The most extreme examples of an emphasis on sociocultural factors are to be found among anthropological and sociological theorists, but some personality theorists who, like Fromm (Chapter 5), Horney (Chapter 5), and Harry Stack Sullivan (Chapter 5), hold that internal dynamic factors are crucial determinants of behavior also stress the importance of sociocultural influences.

PURPOSIVE VERSUS MECHANISTIC.   For some theories of personality, such as Alfred Adler's (Chapter 5), purpose and goal seeking are essential and central aspects of behavior. On this view, human behavior is basically **purposive**, or teleological, in nature; throughout life, people continue to set and to strive for specific goals. For other theorists, however, seeking and striving are merely the way behavior looks to the behaver; the underlying driving forces lie in the individual's past.

Theories like Skinner's (Chapter 13), which do not hold purpose to be central in determining behavior, are often called deterministic or **mechanistic**. Mechanistic views hold that we can explain events wholly in terms of their antecedents; that is, in terms of other events that have preceded the events in which we are interested. This position assumes that behavior can be accounted for in terms of physical laws and principles comparable to those that have proven so successful in the natural sciences.

Many theorists maintain intermediate positions. Among the theorists who claim that human beings' behavior is purposive, most allow that behavior is also influenced by past events. Jung (Chapter 4), for example, maintains that both purposive and mechanistic views are necessary for a complete understanding of human personality.

A FEW MOTIVES VERSUS MULTIPLE MOTIVES.   For a few theorists, only one or two motivational concepts are considered necessary to explain all behavior. For example, for Maslow and some other holistic theorists, the self-actualization motive reigns supreme. For George Kelly (Chapter 8), the expansion of a person's knowledge system is the all-important directive force in human behavior. For most theorists, however, behavior is impelled by a number of distinct motives—sometimes a relatively small number, sometimes a fairly large number. Murray (Chapter 9), for example, defines some 20 basic needs, and for some theorists, like Lewin (Chapter 8) or Allport (Chapter 10), the number of motives is theoretically limitless.

Theorists also differ in terms of the amount of attention they pay to primary or innate motives as opposed to secondary, or acquired, motives. In general, theorists who tend to focus primarily on hereditary causes of behavior, such as Freud (Chapter 2), are more interested in primary motives. Those who, like Miller and Dollard (Chapter 14), find the environment the most significant cause of human behavior and focus on the learning process tend to see acquired motives as being of greatest importance.

NORMAL VERSUS ABNORMAL.   Some theorists—particularly those discussed in the first part of this book—have considered the study of abnormal, or psychologically disturbed, behavior a key means of understanding the normal person. Other theorists, such as Allport (Chapter 10) or Cattell (Chapter 12), focus on the normal or mentally healthy person in deriving their theories of human psychological functioning. Theorists who find pathological behavior a proper subject of study tend to hold that all behavior exists on a continuum and that normal and abnormal thus differ only quantitatively, not qualitatively. Theorists who feel that it is inappropriate to apply to normal people principles of behavior derived from the study of persons who are more or less seriously disturbed generally tend to see a qualitative difference between normal and pathological functioning.

The reader will find it helpful to consider the issues we have discussed in the preceding sections as he or she proceeds through the book. Figure 1.1 provides a useful summary of these discussions.

PERSONALITY THEORY: STRENGTHS AND WEAKNESSES

We have defined personality theory as a set of assumptions about human behavior, together with the empirical definitions required, first, to move from the abstract statement of the theory to the empirical observations and, second, to test and/or support the theory. And we have said that personality theory should be relatively comprehensive; that is, it should be able to deal with or make predictions about a wide range of human behavior.

Do the personality theories that we examine in this book meet these qualifications? Hardly. Some go farther than others toward fulfilling these requirements, but in general, existing personality theories do not look much like ideal theories, either in structure or in function.

In the first place, most personality theories are not very explicit; it is hard to get at their specific basic assumptions. In general, they are not presented in a straightforward, orderly manner. Many are put forward in descriptive language that seems intended more to persuade by its rhetoric than to convince by its precision and capacity to predict behavior.

Lack of clarity results in a frequent confusion between what is assumed and what is stated empirically and thus open to test. Remem-

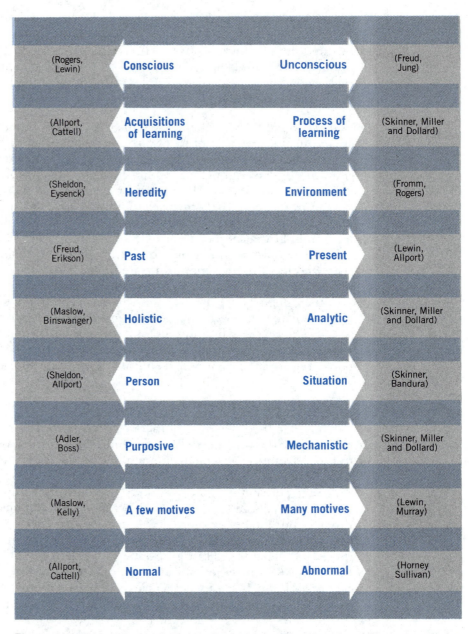

(Rogers, Lewin)	**Conscious**	**Unconscious**	(Freud, Jung)
(Allport, Cattell)	**Acquisitions of learning**	**Process of learning**	(Skinner, Miller and Dollard)
(Sheldon, Eysenck)	**Heredity**	**Environment**	(Fromm, Rogers)
(Freud, Erikson)	**Past**	**Present**	(Lewin, Allport)
(Maslow, Binswanger)	**Holistic**	**Analytic**	(Skinner, Miller and Dollard)
(Sheldon, Allport)	**Person**	**Situation**	(Skinner, Bandura)
(Adler, Boss)	**Purposive**	**Mechanistic**	(Skinner, Miller and Dollard)
(Maslow, Kelly)	**A few motives**	**Many motives**	(Lewin, Murray)
(Allport, Cattell)	**Normal**	**Abnormal**	(Horney, Sullivan)

Figure 1.1 Dimensions of personality theory. Most theorists fall at some point along the continuum of each dimension. Although the theorists given as examples (in parentheses) tend to emphasize the poles with which they are associated here, few do so to the exclusion of the opposing poles.

ber that it is only the derivations from a theory that are subject to test. Because the theory itself is to be judged only in terms of how successfully it generates verifiable propositions, it is particularly important that we be able to distinguish between theory and derivations.

Lack of explicitness can also prevent derivations from being generated with a high degree of consistency. That is, different people using the same theory may arrive at different and conflicting derivations. This situation may come about also because most personality theorists tend to offer after-the-fact explanations rather than to make new predictions about behavior. One might assume that when a theory is stated mathematically, different people using it independently would arrive at very similar formulations. However, no theory has really advanced very far toward the ideal of mathematical notation. Lewin's (Chapter 8) system, for example, which has made some attempts in this direction, has been seriously criticized, and his mathematical formulations have been little used.

The vivid and highly literary mode of description used by such theorists as Binswanger and Boss (Chapter 7) makes it very difficult for anyone who wants to use their theories to be sure of just what he or she is grappling with. Most of the other theories we will discuss are also cast in verbal form, but within the realm of verbal description, theorists vary considerably with respect to the clarity of their exposition.

Given these weaknesses of personality theories, what indeed are their value? What function do personality theories serve for the person who uses them? At the very least, they serve to point in a general way toward the kinds of research that can be considered important, by stating a particular cluster of concepts and assumptions about behavior. In addition, they tend to identify particular variables that are important in the exploration of delimited areas of inquiry. For example, a student of the relationships between physique and temperament might find in Sheldon's (Chapter 11) identification of major dimensions of each a useful starting point. Many investigators have found Allport's (Chapter 10) "traits" and Murray's (Chapter 9) "needs" useful guides in studying personality. Thus, even if a theory does not provide an exact proposition for test, it will orient the theorist toward certain problem areas and indicate what particular variables might be of central importance.

Even though personality theories are far from perfected, they are still a considerable step forward from the thinking of the naïve observer. They are better than "no theory," for "no theory" is actually implicit theory. If we should decide to "forget about" theory and simply focus on empirical data, we would actually be using implicit theory, personally determined and probably involving inconsistent assumptions about behavior. These unidentified personal assumptions would determine what we would study and how. A theory forces us to make explicit the rules we are following. Only in this way can our work be evaluated and supported or refuted.

The bottom line in the evaluation of personality theories is their heuristic value. However vague and poorly developed a theory, if it can be shown to generate significant research, the chances are that it has something important to say about human behavior. It is not always easy to agree on just what *is* important research, and it is not always easy to determine just what aspect of a theory has led to a particularly fruitful line of investigation. In fact, however, personality theories have often been highly provocative. They have led to a great deal of research, even though relatively little of it has been the result of formal derivation.

Perhaps these theories' greatest single asset is their ability to stimulate curiosity, stir doubts, encourage us to think about the important issues they raise, and keep us trying to evolve more precise statements for test. Whether one or another of them will prevail or whether portions of various theories will eventually be found to fit together in ways we do not see now it is impossible to tell. Each is a concerted, often passionate, effort to understand human behavior, and all have been formulated by people whose learning is extensive, not only in the area of personality but in other subdisciplines of psychology—such as clinical, developmental, social, or experimental psychology—as well as in many more or less closely related fields—such as anthropology, sociology, neurophysiology, medicine, philosophy, history, literature, religion, and computer science.

Skinner's observation that although in 2500 years we have learned an enormous amount about our environment we have learned relatively little about ourselves forces us to reflect on the fact that in this long period of time, we have not yet learned to control or eliminate the worst of humankind's ills, such as poverty, crime, and war. We can only hope that as varying disciplines continue to contribute their special learning to the broad base of knowledge about human behavior, we will come closer and closer to the day when the crucial connections will be made and an integrated theory will evolve. As in any science, we can only work toward that resolution by examining every lead that appears fruitful and by giving every reasonable hypothesis a fair trial. The researcher who can entertain a wealth of ideas for a time and then pursue the few that seem most promising stands a good chance of benefiting from the years of thoughtful endeavor that have gone into the framing of such ideas.

So it is for the reader of this book. It is our hope that you will read each of the succeeding chapters with an open mind, giving each theorist your total if temporary allegiance as you explore a theory. Then, particularly if you are going on in psychology and personality, by all means choose a theory. Give it your total commitment, and make it work for you. Even if it turns out not to be your final choice, you will have gained a great deal. In demonstrating the theory to be unproductive, you will have learned much about the facts of behavior and about opposing views, and you will be able to make a far more sophisticated second choice.

Now it is time to begin our story. Each of the four major parts of this book is introduced by a brief discussion of how the group of theories in that part range themselves with respect to our nine dimensions of personality theory. An accompanying chart orients the reader with respect to this discussion as well as to the subsequent chapters. And each individual chapter summarizes the important features of a given theory, discusses relevant research, and evaluates the theory. The last chapter reviews all of the theories presented in the book, comparing them in terms of the personality theory dimensions and examining their ability to generate research. In addition, our final chapter describes some current research trends and considers the future development of personality theory.

SUMMARY

1. In popular usage, ''personality'' tends to have an evaluative connotation. It is a measure of a person's social skills or the reflection of his or her most outstanding characteristic.

2. Psychologists' definitions of personality—which include the **biosocial**, **biophysical**, **omnibus**, and **integrative** definitions—are a function of each theorist's view of the structure and functioning of human personality.

3. A theory comprises a set of assumptions, arrived at by convention, about a particular phenomenon or event, and a set of empirical definitions that tie abstract theory to concrete observations. A theory's assumptions must be relevant to the topic under study and related to each other. Empirical definitions must be as precise as present information permits.

4. The basic function of a theory is to discover stable and demonstrable relations among events, or variables. A theory must lead to the observation of new data and of relations among such data, and it must also allow for the incorporation of known empirical findings within a consistent and reasonably simple framework. It must enable the investigator to select and isolate the important issues to be studied.

5. Theories are judged by their **usefulness**, including their **verifiability** and **comprehensiveness**, and by their **heuristic** influence, or their capacity to generate, in an informal way, new and significant inquiry.

6. A **paradigm** is a grand theory, or super model, that is unprecedented and universally accepted and that provides model problems and solutions in a particular tradition of scientific research. As yet, personality psychology has no such paradigm.

7. Personality theory's roots are in the fifth century B.C., but personality theory as we know it today began to evolve in the late nineteenth century out of the clinical work and observations of Jean-Martin Charcot, Sigmund Freud, and others; Gestalt psychology; experimental and learning theory; and the psychometric tradition.

8. The chief difference between personality theory and other psychological theories lies in their separate lines of development, the former out of medicine and the need for immediate therapeutic application, the latter out of academic interests and pursuits. As a result, personality theory is more functional in nature than experimental psychology. It serves as an integrative force, uniting findings of the various subdisciplines of psychology and attempting to provide a unified picture of how a whole person behaves.

9. By remaining outside the mainstream of academic psychology, personality theory has long enjoyed the freedom to question or reject assumptions widely accepted within the general field of psychology. At the same time, it has often lacked rigor as well as interest in traditional scientific methods.

10. Personality theories can usefully be understood and compared in terms of nine basic issues that confront modern theorists: **conscious** versus **unconscious** determinants of behavior, **acquisitions** versus the **process** of learning, **heredity** versus **environment**, **past** versus **present**, **holistic** versus **analytic** approach, **person** versus **situation**, **purposive** versus **mechanistic** views, a few versus **multiple motives**, and **normal** versus **abnormal** behavior. Most theorists take positions that fall somewhere on the continua along which these dimensions of personality theory lie, but some strongly emphasize one or the other of the stated poles.

11. Few personality theories fulfill the requirements of an ideal theory, such as explicitness, a clear distinction between assumptions and empirical derivations, and consistency of derivations. However, theories do draw some limits about what is considered important to study, and they provide some guidance to the exploration of such delimited areas.

12. Personality theories are better than ''no theory,'' which is actually implicit theory, for implicit theory cannot be judged, supported, or refuted.

13. Most important is a theory's **heuristic** value—if it generates significant research, it probably has something meaningful to say about human behavior. And if a theory simply generates ideas by arousing curiosity, doubt, or enthusiasm and by generally making us think about important issues, it cannot be said to be without value.

SUGGESTED READING

The reader will find interesting discussions of the development of contemporary personality theory in Allport, *Pattern and Growth in Personality* (1961); Boring, *A History of Experimental Psychology* (1950); and Murphy and Kovach, *Historical Introduction to Modern Psychology* (1972). The current status of theory and research in the many areas of personality psychology is summarized periodically in volumes of the *Annual Review of Psychology*. Recent articles in this publication include Helson and Mitchell, ''Personality'' (1978); Loevinger and Knoll, ''Personality: Stages, Traits, and the Self'' (1983); and Rorer and Widiger, ''Personality Structure and Assessment'' (1983). Highly personalized accounts of the lives and work of many of these theorists are contained in recent volumes of Boring and Lindzey, *A History of Psychology in Autobiography* (1966), and Lindzey, *A History of Psychology in Autobiography* (1973, 1980).

Other helpful introductions to the field of personality psychology include Geen, *Personality: The Skein of Behavior* (1976); Maddi, *Personality Theories: A Comparative Analysis* (1980); and Mischel *Introduction to Personality* (1981).

The reader interested in the methodology of science will find it useful to examine Kuhn, *The Structure of Scientific Revolutions* (1962); Suppe, *The Structure of Scientific Theories* (1974); and Turner, *Philosophy and the Science of Behavior* (1967).

Part 1   Focus on Psychodynamic Forces

In this first part of the book we discuss seven theorists: Sigmund Freud, the founder of psychoanalysis (Chapter 2), and Erik Erikson, Carl Jung, Alfred Adler, Karen Horney, Erich Fromm, and Harry Stack Sullivan (Chapters 3–5), all of whom started out within the psychoanalytic framework but departed from it to formulate their own distinctive views. Because all six of these theorists are primarily psychotherapists, their theories of the person tend to focus on the psychodynamic forces—such as anxiety and defense mechanisms—that are presumed to underlie much human behavior.

Like the charts that introduce the next three parts of the book, and like the summary chart in Chapter 16, Figure 1 is not to be regarded as a final statement of where this part's theorists stand with respect to each of the nine dimensions of personality theory that we presented in Chapter 1. Few theories are stated with optimal precision, theorists sometimes change their views, and not all dimensions are relevant to all theories. Thus, many theorists could be moved up or down a notch on these charts, depending on which aspect of the theory one chooses to emphasize. Skim Figure 1 lightly at this point, but return to it after you have studied the theories in this part and ask yourself, which theorists would I place differently? Why?

In general, Figure 1 suggests that the theorists in this first group tend to emphasize unconscious rather than conscious determinants of behavior, what is learned rather than how it is learned, the abnormal rather than the normal, the past rather than the present, and a relatively small number of basic motives. Most of these theorists are intermediate in respect to the holistic–analytic and purposive–mechanistic dimensions, and they give roughly equal emphasis to person and situation. Freud and Jung tend to emphasize hereditary factors; Horney, Fromm, and Sullivan particularly stress the social and cultural determinants of personality.

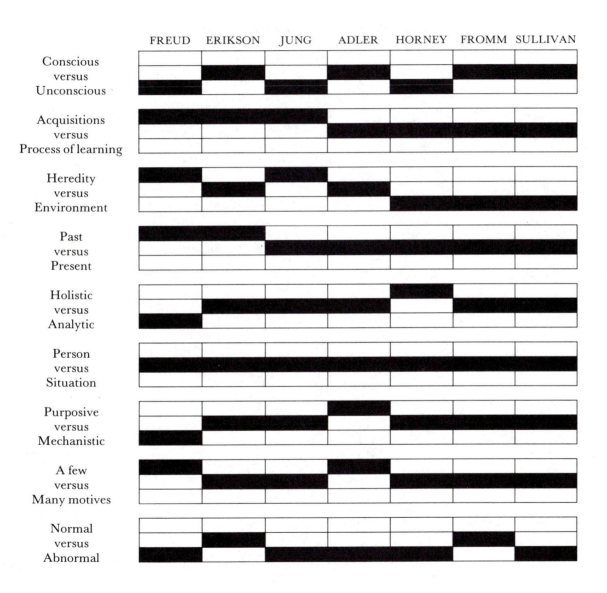

Figure 1   Psychodynamic theorists and the personality theory dimensions.

27

Chapter two

2.

*He perceived that the ultimate secret of
power was . . . understanding.*
ERNEST JONES

Classical Psychoanalysis: Sigmund Freud

Windows were open for the first time since fall, and a breeze moved delicately around the room, bringing the suggestion of newly green branches and the littlest flowers of early spring.

The faculty committee on appointments were sitting around a small conference table covered with resumés and reprints of journal articles.

"I know it's hard to concentrate on this today, but we've got to make a decision about our new staff member." The chair of the meeting paused and looked down a list he was holding. "Has everyone seen all six of these people now for a personal interview?"

Everyone nodded assent.

"Okay, then—how about Jim Brown? Bob, you saw him last, I think. What's your thought?"

Bob turned back from the window, tapping his pipe in the ashtray, and replied, "I liked the guy, Paul. Despite his beauty"—he grinned—"he's not dumb. He's bright and competent. I particularly liked his teaching style in the graduate seminar. I think he'd be a fine addition to the faculty. I vote yes."

"Thanks." Paul turned to the department's award-winning researcher. "Lisa, what do you think of Jim's research?"

"He's quite creative, Paul," Lisa picked up one of the reprints. "For example, this last study has never been done before. It's very thoughtfully worked out. His design is good, and he presents a tight argument. I have some quibbles with his methodology, but in general I'm extremely impressed." The little breeze curled around her, and she glanced out the window briefly. "Yes," she said, "I vote for him too. I think Jim would be an excellent bed." She gasped, and her eyes widened in horror. "I mean *bet*!" Then she and everyone laughed.

Sigmund Freud, who explored the unconscious for over forty years and established its great significance in mental and emotional functioning, often began a lecture to a new audience with an account, like the foregoing, of a **parapraxis**, or a slip of the tongue. Such slips, which we all make from time to time, are excellent examples of how the mind operates simultaneously at different levels, or in different ways. Slips of the tongue also illustrate how matters over which we have some conflict may be related to the unconscious mind but find sudden—and sometimes embarrassing—expression. In the foregoing anecdote, it is clear that while the researcher was consciously evaluating the candidate's work she was also unconsciously considering other equally interesting aspects of the man.

What is the **unconscious**? It is that area of our experience that is not normally accessible to us either because its contents never were conscious (traces of events that happened before we had language, when we were infants) or because its contents have been repressed, or pushed out of awareness, because they are in some way threatening to us. For example, a woman may ''forget'' that her friend is chronically late for appointments until each time it happens because she is afraid that if she expresses her anger, the friend will become angry too.

How does unconscious material come into awareness? You have just seen one of the ways: sometimes unconscious thoughts erupt into consciousness quite unexpectedly. More often, however, unconscious material remains hidden away until it finds expression in our dreams or fantasies (where it is usually disguised) or in our conscious associations to material in our dreams. As we begin to try to understand our dreams and to relate events in them to ideas and events in the real world, the unconscious thoughts that underlie dream images may come to awareness.

Sigmund Freud, in proposing his theory of the unconscious, found himself in opposition to the mainstream of nineteenth-century thought. Many scientists and philosophers felt that the then new science of psychology should attend to the conscious mind, analyzing its contents or exploring its active processes—such as sensing, thinking, and imagining; others felt that because mind was an abstraction, only behavior could properly be studied. For Freud, however, the mind was like an iceberg: the small part of the iceberg that we see represents the conscious mind; the great mass below the water represents the unconscious urges, passions, and repressed ideas and feelings that control conscious thought and action.

Many before Freud—Friedrich Nietzsche, Gustav Fechner, and Pierre Janet, among others—had speculated on the nature of mental contents that are outside awareness (Whyte, 1962). Freud, however, gave the unconscious a central place in his theory of human behavior, which was the first comprehensive personality theory to be formulated. Freud's work made him one of the most influential yet, as we will see, controversial figures of modern times. Whether or not one agrees with Freud's theories and methods, it is clear that, like Charles Darwin, Karl Marx, and Albert Einstein, he helped to shape twentieth-century thought.

BOX 2.1 — Sigmund Freud (1856–1939)

From the time he was very young, Freud wanted to be a scientist. He had an "overpowering need to understand some of the riddles of the world in which we live and perhaps even to contribute something to their solution" (Freud, quoted by Jones, 1961, p. 22). The theories of Darwin soon attracted him, and he drew inspiration as well from a romantic essay of Goethe's in which the German poet suggests not only the beauty but the meaning and purpose of Nature (Jones, 1961).

The best entrée to the world of science in nineteenth-century Europe was a medical degree, so after being graduated from high school (*gymnasium*) summa cum laude, Freud entered the University of Vienna medical school. When, toward the end of his studies, he began to work in the laboratory of the famous German physiologist, Ernest Brücke, he thought he had achieved his goal, for eventually becoming a full professor or even chairman of Brücke's Institute of Physiology seemed a reasonable expectation. Soon, however, Freud had to face the fact that the institute's rate of pay was impossibly low and that other staff members were not much older than he and thus unlikely to retire to make room for him. Moreover, Freud was a Jew, another factor that at that time limited his opportunity for advancing to his goal. By 1882, Freud had met and fallen in love with Martha Bernays, and he wanted very much to marry her and start a family. Since he had no money, he could not afford the luxury of a scientific career, and he concluded that he would have to adopt a practical calling. Thus, although he had already achieved some notoriety for his investigations of the nervous system, he took up the practice of medicine, specializing in nervous disorders, and became affiliated with Vienna General Hospital.

Freud soon began to specialize in neurology, and in 1885 he spent a year in Paris, where he studied with Jean-Martin Charcot, the French neurologist and psychiatrist. Freud was greatly impressed with Charcot's revolutionary views on hysteria and particularly with Charcot's demonstration, by means of hypnosis, that hysterical symptoms had a psychogenic origin. Only a few years earlier Freud had been fascinated by Josef Breuer's discovery of a new method of treating hysteria in which patients described the first appearance of their symptoms at some length. Frequently, the symptoms then disappeared. Gradually, Breuer's method, Charcot's discoveries, and Freud's own experience with neurotic patients (in those days, neurologists often saw people who complained of "nervous" difficulties that today would be termed "neurotic") crystallized, and Freud began to evolve his theory of the unconscious and his unique method of free association (see page 51).

Although it would still be a few years before he could devote himself exclusively to the development of psychoanalytic theory and method, Freud had now effectively achieved his earlier goal. As he wrote to a friend in 1896, "I am now on the way to satisfying [my longing for philosophical knowledge] by passing over from medicine to psychology" (Jones, 1961, p. 221). Psychology had become Freud's "dominating passion," and one of his primary aims was to develop, out of psychopathology, a new science of "normal psychology."

The battle was far from over, however. Because many of the theories Freud began to propose—such as those of infantile sexuality and universal incestuous desire—were so startling, Freud spent many early years in professional isolation. The world of medicine rejected his views, offering him little but criticism and contempt. Nevertheless, with a small group of followers—which included Carl Jung and Alfred Adler, who eventually broke away and formulated their own theories of psychoanalysis (see Chapters 4 and 5)—Freud founded the International Psycho-Analytic Association and continued to work and to write.

In 1909 Freud was invited by G. Stanley Hall, psychologist and president of Clark University, to come to the United States to lecture at the university's twentieth-anniversary celebration. According to Jones (1961), when Freud accepted his honorary doctorate, describing it as the "first official recognition of our endeavors," he was visibly moved by this evidence of respect after so many years of ostracism.

Throughout his long and dedicated career, Freud always found time to spend with his wife and their five children, both in Vienna and at their summer vacation spots. (Anna Freud, his youngest daughter and closest associate in his last years, became a psychoanalyst in her own right—see page 71.) Freud's one personal extravagance was his passion for antiquities—as Jones (1961) points out, his interest "ever turned to the matter of origins and beginnings." Thus when he trav-

In his consulting room in Vienna, Freud offered his patients not only the comfort of his famous couch but a veritable museum. These antiquities from Greece, Rome, and other ancient civilizations kept silent company with Freud's patients as the latter delved into their own buried histories.

eled, on occasion, to Italy, Greece, and other European countries, he always brought back statues and other relics of ancient civilizations.

Freud's last trip away from his lifelong home of Vienna, however, was undertaken in tragic circumstances. In 1938 he and his family barely escaped the Nazi terror, moving permanently to London. By this time, Freud was in constant torment from cancer of the palate and jaw, and he lived only a year longer. Despite 16 years of this inexorable disease, Freud had maintained an amazing vitality. At age 70, he had made major changes in some of his most fundamental concepts: in *The Ego and the Id* (1923), he completely revised his theory of the structure and functioning of the mind, delineating for the first time the intricate relations among id, ego, and superego. And even in his last book, *An Outline of Psychoanalysis*, written when he was 82, there are occasional hints, according to James Strachey, Freud's translator and editor, of entirely new developments in the making.

Freud's influence on the layperson has been considerable for he focused, in his work, on topics that are familiar to everyone, and his ideas have often challenged beliefs that people have about themselves and about others. Freud's continuing and significant impact on psychology is evidenced, for example, in a recent survey of clinical psychologists (Norcross and Prochaska, 1982) in which about 30 percent of the respondents said that their theoretical orientation was psychodynamic. (It is true that many psychodynamic theories differ considerably from Freudian theory. However, such theories can be said to be derivatives of Freud's approach, inasmuch as they either accept and build on many of his basic postulates or take specifically opposing views.) No other theoretical orientations were represented by a percentage response as high: indeed, 30 percent is a somewhat higher figure than those reported in any of several earlier such surveys.

WHAT MAKES UP PERSONALITY?

The personality, for Freud, consists of three major systems: the id, the ego, and the superego. Roughly, the id represents uninhibited impulses, the superego the voice of conscience, and the ego rational thinking. Suppose that you give up an exciting concert weekend out of town to help a friend with a paper, only to have the friend take off for the weekend himself. Your first impulse may be one of rage, with thoughts of physical violence; that is your id operating. Then you may feel guilty and ashamed of such thoughts; your superego has taken over. Eventually, you may decide to tell your friend that you are angry and that he has been inconsiderate and selfish; that is your ego, mediating between the raw impulses of your id and the punitive injunctions of your superego.

THE ID

The **id** is the original personality system out of which the ego and superego develop. At birth, the id is composed of everything psychological that is inherited. As life unfolds, the id continues to represent the inner world of subjective reality. It is entirely unconscious and has no direct knowledge of the external world.

As the oldest and basic component of personality, the id is in close touch with bodily processes, and it derives from them the psychic energy that powers the operations of all three systems. The id is often referred to as the "reservoir" of psychic energy.

The id operates by the **pleasure principle**: it tries to obtain pleasure and avoid pain. For the id, pleasure means a state of relative inactivity, or of low energy levels; pain means the tension that is brought about by excitation, or increases in energy. Thus when stimuli create tension, the id tries to reduce or eliminate the tension and to return the organism to a low energy level.

To achieve its aims, the id has two processes at its command. **Reflex actions**—inborn automatic reactions like blinking—enable it to deal with simple forms of excitation and usually work immediately. To handle complex stimuli, the id must use what is called the **primary process**, a more complicated psychological procedure in which the id forms an image of something that can reduce or remove the tension. For example, the hungry baby pictures food or its mother's nipple.

The process of forming an image of a tension-reducing object is called **wish fulfillment**. The nighttime dream is one of the best examples of wish fulfillment; other examples are daydreams and psychotic hallucinations. You may wonder how frightening dreams and images can fulfill wishes: a wish can conflict with and be overcome by a fear, or wishes of different personality systems may conflict. For example, a dream of being thrown into prison and finding that one is wearing one's lover's jacket might reflect a conflict between a wish for intimacy and a fear that the lover will destroy one's freedom.

Simply forming an image of something, of course, does not satisfy a need: the baby cannot suck at an imaginary nipple. Thus, it must develop ways of distinguishing images from the objects in reality that they represent and of securing those objects. it is to achieve this end that the ego and its chief means of operation, the secondary process, come into being.

THE EGO

The **ego** evolves out of the id to enable the organism to deal with reality. Since the baby's picture of food does not satisfy its hunger, the baby must learn to match that image with real food—it must convert the image into an actual perception. The id cannot perform this function; only the ego can distinguish between things in the mind and things in the external world.

The ego is said to obey the **reality principle**, which requires that action be delayed until the ego can determine whether something has existence in objective reality. Thus the ego temporarily suspends the pleasure principle, which demands immediate action, and by means of the **secondary process**—realistic thinking—delays action until it finds a need-satisfying object.

The secondary process involves **reality testing**. That is, the ego makes a plan for satisfying a need and then tests the plan to see if it works. Suppose, for example, that you are about to take an exam. The primary process leads you to think of the ''A'' that you want and the grade-point average you need for graduation; the secondary process ensures that you will decide what material you must know for the exam, study that material, and then test yourself to see if you have learned it. Clearly, for the organism to be efficient, the ego and the secondary process must control cognitive functioning.

Called the ''executive'' of the personality because it chooses the stimuli to which we respond and decides what instincts to satisfy and when and how, the ego nevertheless derives its power from the id, and its ultimate purpose is to forward the id's aims. But the ego must also meet the demands of the third and last personality system to develop, the superego.

THE SUPEREGO

The **superego** evolves out of the ego and represents parental values, or the society's standards as the parents have interpreted them. Gradually the child incorporates the behaviors its parents approve into its **ego ideal** and those its parents disapprove into its **conscience**. These two subsystems of the superego then reward the child with feelings of pride for approved behaviors and punish it with feelings of guilt for disapproved actions. Thus, self-control replaces parental control.

Like the id, the superego is nonrational. It demands perfection rather than simply one's best. And it punishes one with equal harshness whether one *does* something "bad" or only thinks it. But the superego is also like the ego because it tries to control the id's impulses. In its main functions—inhibiting the id, forcing moral goals on the ego, and seeking perfection—it opposes both id and ego and tries to impose its own views on the personality.

As you review this section and study the summary in Table 2.1, remember that the id, ego, and superego are not to be thought of as mannikins that operate the personality. They are just names for systems of psychological structures and processes that obey certain principles. Ordinarily, these systems work together as a team, under the guidance of the ego. But when serious conflicts arise among them, we may see abnormal behavior.

THE DYNAMICS OF PERSONALITY

Freud saw the human organism as a complex system that uses the energy it derives from food for such various purposes as breathing, physical movement, perceiving, and remembering. He assumed that physiological energy and **psychic energy**—the energy that powers psychological activities like thinking—could each be transformed into the other. The id was the point of contact between the energy of the body and that of the personality.

INSTINCTS AS PSYCHIC ENERGY

An **instinct** is a psychological representation of a bodily need; it is a wish to fulfill a physiological need. For example, the hunger instinct derives from a nutritional deficit in body tissues, and it is represented mentally as a wish for food. Instincts are quantities of psychic energy, and all the instincts together make up the total amount of energy available to the personality.

CHARACTERISTICS OF INSTINCTS.   Instincts have four important features: a source, an aim, an object, and an impetus (see Figure 2.1).

TABLE 2.1   *The Three Systems of the Personality*

ID	EGO	SUPEREGO
Original system. Contains instincts and provides psychic energy for operations of all three systems. Knows only the inner world; has no knowledge of objective reality.	Develops out of id to deal with external world. Obtains energy from id. Knows both inner world and objective reality.	Develops out of ego to serve as moral arm of personality. Represents internalized parental values. Divided into conscience (which punishes "wrong" behaviors) and ego ideal (which rewards "right" behaviors). Like id, does not distinguish between subjective and objective; hence, thoughts are as punishable as deeds.
Follows pleasure principle and operates by primary process. Aims solely to distinguish between pleasure and pain so as to obtain only pleasure and avoid pain.	Follows reality principle and operates by secondary process. Aims to distinguish between fantasy and reality so as to satisfy organism's needs. Must coordinate demands of id, superego, and external world. Aims overall to maintain life and see that species is reproduced.	Aims to distinguish between right and wrong and to see that person obeys moral strictures. Demands perfection.
Seeks immediate instinctual gratification.	Delays instinctual gratification until it can be achieved without conflict with superego or external world.	Inhibits instinctual gratification.
Is nonrational.	Is rational.	Is nonrational.

Freud said that throughout life, the **source** of an instinct—the bodily need it represents—remains constant, unless it is changed or eliminated by physical maturation. Similarly, an instinct's **aim**—the fulfillment of the need—remains constant over time.

The **object** of an instinct includes everything that one has to do to obtain that object. Thus the object of the hunger instinct may include shopping for food, cooking it, and serving it. Unlike source and aim, the object of an instinct may vary a good deal. This is because psychic energy can be displaced: when something we want is not available—because it is absent or because obstacles prevent us from obtaining it—we can shift our interest to something else. And if the second choice is also unavailable, we can displace energy again and so on until we find an object that satisfies our need.

An instinct's **impetus**—the reflection of the force or intensity, of a need—is rarely the same. For example, if you have had a good breakfast you may want only a sandwich for lunch, but if you have

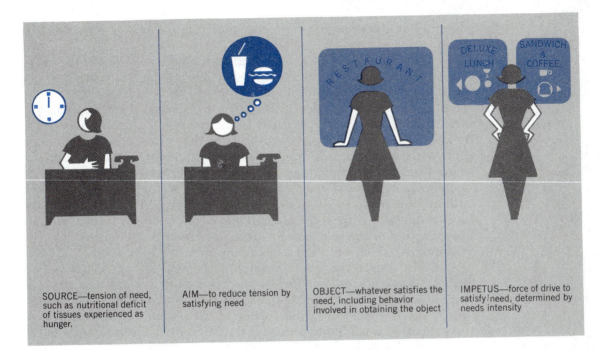

SOURCE—tension of need, such as nutritional deficit of tissues experienced as hunger.

AIM—to reduce tension by satisfying need

OBJECT—whatever satisfies the need, including behavior involved in obtaining the object

IMPETUS—force of drive to satisfy need, determined by needs intensity

Figure 2.1   An instinct has four features: The hunger instinct as an example.

eaten nothing since yesterday, you may want a full meal.

You will recall that the id, which seeks only pleasure, finds tension painful. Freud's model of the instincts is a **tension-reduction** one: an organism's behavior is activated by irritants, or increases in tension, and is quieted by actions that dispel the tension. Thus, an instinct's aim is essentially **regressive** (''going back'') in that it seeks to return the person to the (relatively quiet) state that existed before the instinct was aroused.

Of all the instinct's characteristics, the capacity to displace energy from one object to another is the most significant. Indeed, this capacity is the single most important feature of personality dynamics. It accounts for the apparent plasticity of human nature and the remarkable versatility of our behavior. Almost all of our interests, preferences, habits, and attitudes represent energy displacements from earlier objects. We will have more to say about this crucial concept later in the chapter.

CLASSES OF INSTINCTS.   Rather than enumerate the instincts, Freud proposed two general categories: the life instincts and the death instincts. The **life instincts**—for example, hunger, thirst, and sex—are in the service of survival and reproduction; they preserve both the individual and the species. The energy of the life instincts is called **libido.**

In the earliest years of his work, Freud devoted almost exclusive attention to the sex instinct (see Freud, 1905a). It is important to understand that this instinct involves not just the desire for and enjoyment of genital sexual pleasure but pleasure derived from many bodily areas. Thus, the word "sensual" sometimes describes what Freud is talking about as well as if not better than the word "sexual." Not one but many bodily needs trigger sexual and sensual desires. Each of these needs is linked with an **erogenous zone**, which is a sensitive region of the body or skin—such as the mouth or the genitals—in which stimulation tends to occur, producing tension. Manipulation of the area reduces or dispels the tension and produces pleasurable feelings. The concept of the erogenous zone is integral to Freud's theory of development, which we will discuss a little later.

The **death instincts**, sometimes called the **destructive instincts**, work in less apparent ways than the life instincts. As a result, we know very little about them except that in time they achieve their aim: everyone does eventually die. On the basis of a nineteenth-century theory that all living processes tend to return to the stability of the inorganic world, Freud (1920a) proposed that all human beings have a wish—which of course, is usually unconscious—to die: "the aim of all life is death" (p. 38). However, he did not identify the bodily sources of the death instincts and did not name their energy.

As important derivative of the death instincts is the **aggressive drive**. It is to keep from destroying themselves, Freud said, that human beings engage in violent and destructive behaviors. In order to preserve the organism, the life instincts generally counter the death instincts and turn their energy outward, against other people. Some of this energy is channeled into substitute, acceptable activities such as controlling the environment or watching such aggressive sports as hockey or wrestling. And some finds (weakened) expression in self-punishment, such as the actions of the superego.

Every action is overdetermined, or derived from several motives (Freud, 1933b). Thus, life and death instincts may work together as, for example, in eating, which is life preserving but includes the destructive acts of biting, chewing, and swallowing. Or the life instincts may neutralize the death instincts: people may use mastery to obtain the objects of their love. The instincts may also conflict, as when a person feels both love and anger toward another. And sometimes the death instincts get the upper hand: love can take on a sadistic aspect.

In his well-publicized correspondence with Einstein on the subject of war and pacifism, Freud (1933b) suggested that the life instincts, in the form of "emotional ties" among people, should be enlisted against the human propensity for war. Yet he expressed doubt that such ties, unsuccessful in the past, would be able to prevent future conflict. His pessimism reflected his underlying belief that people were not capable of controlling their impulses and finding acceptable outlets for them (Hall and Lindzey, 1968).

HOW ENERGY IS DISTRIBUTED AND USED

The term **personality dynamics** refers to the way the personality changes and grows and thus to the way psychic energy is distributed and used by the id, ego, and superego. The amount of energy that is available to the personality is limited, and the three systems must compete for it. Thus unless new energy is added to the total structure, if one system becomes stronger, the other two become weaker.

THE FLUID ENERGY OF THE ID.   At first, the id has all the personality's energy and uses it, as we have seen, in reflex actions and wish fulfillments, under the direction of the primary process. It **cathects**, or invests energy in, objects that appear to it to gratify its needs. But because the id cannot distinguish between subjective and objective, its energy is very fluid—it is easily displaced from one thing to another. A hungry baby will put into its mouth anything it can see and grasp—its fingers, a corner of its blanket, a plastic toy. But when such investments of energy in objects—called **object cathexes**—fail to satisfy the organism's needs—in the case of the hungry baby, fail to reduce hunger—energy is diverted from the id's purely subjective processes to the logical and objective processes of the ego.

THE EGO'S EXPANDING ENERGY STORE.   The ego, which has no energy of its own, gradually acquires more and more of the id's energy because it is more successful than the id in reducing tensions and thus satisfying the organism's needs. This success of the ego is due to its ability to make use of a very important mechanism, called **identification**, by which the ego matches the id's mental image with an actual perception. Whereas the id believes that its image of a desired object and that object in reality are the same, the ego knows that image and real object are different and that the image must be conformed to the reality.

The concept of identification is of great significance, for all cognitive advances consist in making one's mental representations of the world into more accurate pictures of the world as it really is. When the baby succeeds in conforming its mental image of food to the actual milk-giving nipple, its ability to satisfy its needs is greatly increased.

The ego eventually monopolizes the store of psychic energy because every time it succeeds in obtaining an object and satisfying a need, the energy that the id had invested in an image of that object flows to the ego. Of course, any time the ego fails to satisfy the instincts, the id may reassert its power.

Because the ego is so efficient, it accumulates extra energy that it can invest in a variety of objects and activities. It devotes a portion of this energy to developing fundamental psychological processes such as perceiving, discriminating, and reasoning. But some of the ego's energy must go into the creation of restraining forces, or **anticathexes.** These forces are usually used to keep the id from acting impulsively or irrationally, but they can be used against the superego as well if its demands become too oppressive. If either the id or the superego threatens to get out of hand, the ego can protect itself with what are called defense mechanisms; we will discuss these a little later.

Last but not least, the ego as the executive of the personality uses energy to coordinate the activities of all three systems. It tries to create harmony within the personality so that transactions with the environment can be made smoothly and effectively.

THE ENERGIZING OF THE SUPEREGO.   Like the ego, the superego acquires energy through identification. Very early the baby invests energy in its parents, on whom it is completely dependent for the satisfaction of its needs. As the child grows, the parents transmit society's values, as they have interpreted them, to the child through rewards and punishments. To retain the parents' love and approval, the child learns to match, or identify, its behavior with its parents' standards. It invests energy in their ideals and prohibitions. Thus, by tapping into the person's original investment of energy in his or her parents, the superego gains access to the id's energy reservoir.

This little boy's attempt to match his father's feat with the barbell suggests that he has adopted his father's values of physical health and strength.

The channeling of instinctual energy into the ego and superego begins the complicated interplay of driving forces (cathexes) and restraining forces (anticathexes) that constitutes the dynamics of personality. The id has only driving forces, but the ego and the superego use energy both to forward and to frustrate the instinctual aims. To govern the personality wisely, the ego must check both the id and the superego yet have enough energy left over to deal with the external world. If the ego fails to become strong enough, it will be unable to acquire enough energy from the id, and the result may be maladjusted behavior. If the id retains control of a great deal of the energy, the person may be impulsive (act rapidly, apparently without thinking), self-indulgent, or even violent and destructive. And if the superego obtains an excessive amount of energy, the restraining forces of the conscience may tie the person up in moral knots while the forces of the ego ideal may set such high standards that the person is greatly inhibited and develops a depressing sense of failure.

ANXIETY

Anxiety is a key variable in almost all theories of personality. The result of conflict, which is an inevitable part of life, anxiety is often seen as a major component of personality dynamics. Freud's analysis of anxiety in terms of both normal and abnormal functioning had great impact on later theorists, and it has continued to influence many, many clinicians.

Much of personality functioning involves dealing with the external world. The world of reality may provide us with or deprive us of supplies like food; it may offer us security or threaten our very lives. It can disturb as well as comfort and satisfy, and when we are not prepared to cope with threats, we may become afraid or anxious.

Freud (1926b) conceptualized three types of anxiety: neurotic and moral anxiety are both derived from **realistic anxiety**, which is essentially fear of real dangers in the external world. Both neurotic and moral anxiety have their genesis within the person. **Neurotic anxiety** is said to develop often out of early childhood experience in which parental training and behavior is harsh and/or uncaring. When we are neurotically anxious, we are afraid of the (imaginary) punishment we will receive from (imaginary) parental or other authority figures for satisfying our instinctual impulses—just as our parents once punished us. **Moral anxiety** is aroused when we violate our incorporated parental standards. When we are morally anxious, we are afraid of being punished by our superegos—or by our consciences, to be exact.

Neurotic and moral anxiety may sound somewhat similar to you. How do imaginary punishment and imaginary parents differ from one's conscience? The difference lies essentially in the degree of control the ego exerts. Often in moral anxiety one is rational and capable of thinking a problem through; the superego is exerting its demands, but the ego is able to withstand them and to decide on a course of action. In neurotic anxiety, however, people are often in such distress—sometimes even in panic—that they cannot think clearly; the id prevents them from distinguishing between what is imaginary and what is real. Neurotically anxious people almost believe that some external force will actually punish them; that is, they often behave as if they believed this. Morally anxious people usually know that is is their own inner dictates that are causing them distress.

Anxiety of any kind is a signal to the ego that danger is imminent and that, unless appropriate measures are taken, the ego may be overpowered. Anxiety motivates us to do something—to flee the external danger, to inhibit the instinctual impulse, or to obey the voice of conscience. When the ego cannot cope with anxiety by rational methods, it must use unrealistic defensive measures.

HOW PERSONALITY DEVELOPS

Freud was probably the first psychological theorist to focus on personality development and to stress the roles of infancy and early childhood in forming the person's character. Freud's conception of personality development may well be one of the most important contributions of psychoanalytic theory to contemporary personality theory and developmental psychology.

Freud believed that after about the end of the fifth year of life, growth and change in personality consisted largely of elaborating the basic structure formed in the first years of the child's existence. Paradoxically, Freud rarely studied young children directly; he based his theory on his work with analytic patients whose mental explorations so often led them back to early childhood experiences.

For Freud, personality development is essentially the learning of new ways to reduce tension. As the child grows, it experiences increasing tensions from four major sources: physiological growth processes, frustrations, conflicts, and threats. As the person moves through five stages of development that are based to a considerable degree on physiological changes—we discuss these stages on pages 47–51—the important processes of identification and displacement, as well as a variety of defense mechanisms, can help him or her deal with these increasing tensions.

IDENTIFICATION

One way of reducing tension is to imitate, or identify with, people who are more successful in gratifying their needs than we are. The earliest models we choose in this process of **identification** are our parents. Later we may identify with teachers, athletes, rock stars, and others. Usually we are not conscious of our identifications, and we do not have to identify totally with another person; mostly we incorporate only those features that we think will help to achieve our goal. It is often hard to tell just which characteristics of a person account for his or her success, however, so we may have to try several before we find the one that works.

Because we are accustomed to the notion of imitating other people, the form of identification we are now discussing is a little easier to understand than the form we considered earlier, by which the ego and superego acquire the id's energy. But you can see the relationship between these concepts. When the ego identifies a mental image with a real sensory impression or perception, it makes something that is internal conform to something external. When the child forms its superego by creating its own moral standards as copies of its parents' standards, it also conforms something internal to something external. When we identify with others whom we admire and respect, we make some of our own characteristics (internal in the sense that they belong to us) like those of others (who are external to us).

The process of identification is of great significance in both the dynamics and the development of personality. Not only do we acquire new information by conforming our mental images with what is actually out there in reality; we save a great deal of time and energy by adopting behaviors, attitudes, and styles that demonstrably work for other people. If we had to learn how to reduce tension solely by our own trial and error, we might never develop sufficiently to function as independent beings.

DISPLACEMENT

The second major means by which the personality develops is the **displacement** of energy. As we have already seen, when the organism is barred from obtaining the original object of an instinct, it seeks another object—it displaces energy from one to the other. If the way to the new object is also blocked, displacement continues until something is found to relieve the tension.

The source and aim of an instinct, you will recall, remain constant. However, throughout many displacements, the object may vary greatly. For example, the goal of a young musician was to study with Andrés Segovia and become a classical guitarist. Unfortunately, this young person could not afford the expense of studying with such a great artist and in another country. So she joined a rock group with whom she had played informally. But although she and the group liked her playing, she was not really satisfied. She left the group and began taking lessons again. By chance one day she began giving lessons her-

In this detail from Leonardo da Vinci's Adoration of the Magi *we see one of the artist's many portraits of the Madonna. If Freud was right in his interpretation of da Vinci's life, Mary's loving gaze at her child reflects da Vinci's longing for intimacy with the mother he lost.*

self to another young musician she met at a concert, and she decided then to become a teacher of classical guitar.

Substitute objects are rarely if ever as tension reducing as original ones, and the less they resemble the originals, the less tension is reduced. As displacements pile up, Freud said, they create a pool of undischarged tension, and the search for better ways of reducing tensions continues. Teaching did not satisfy the young musician quite as performing would have done; eventually she played occasional duets with her students and formed a small group for informal concerts. According to Freud, human restlessness and the variability of human behavior result from this continuing search for better ways of reducing tension.

Civilizations have developed, Freud believed, because human beings have diverted energy from primitive object choices to socially acceptable pursuits (1930). Displacements that produce social and cultural achievements are called **sublimations**. Freud observed, for example, that Leonardo da Vinci's many paintings of the Madonna were the sublimated expression of his longing for intimacy with his mother, from whom he was separated when very young (1910).

Clearly, the displacement of psychic energy is of great significance in the development and functioning of personality. If we could not redistribute our energy, we would be destroyed by our frustrations. And we would miss out on the great variety of interests, values, and attachments that characterize the adult human personality.

DEFENSE MECHANISMS

In the course of development the ego sometimes confronts tensions it cannot handle. Impulses, memories, thoughts, feelings—all can arouse excessive anxiety and force the ego to defend itself by extreme measures. These **defense mechanisms** of the ego are mental processes that have as their goal the reduction of anxiety and that share two particular characteristics: they operate unconsciously, and they deny, falsify, or distort reality.

As we pointed out earlier, the concept of the unconscious was integral to Freud's theory of the mind, and it is crucial to his notion of the ego's defense mechanisms. The ego uses its restraining forces (anticathexes) to effect **repression**, or the forcing out of conscious awareness of memories, thoughts, and ideas that arouse anxiety. Although repression is a very powerful mechanism, repressed material sometimes pushes its way through to awareness or finds expression in some disguised form. When repression alone fails to control the threatening material, it is joined by additional defense mechanisms—the other chief ones are **projection**, **reaction formation**, **fixation**, and **regression**—which in one way or another deny reality or alter one's perception of it. Table 2.2 illustrates the operation of all these defensive measures.

All these defense mechanisms develop because the infant's ego is too weak to cope with environmental demands: it needs help in warding off stimuli and reducing tension. Almost all people develop defense mechanisms; some use of these measures is quite normal. In time, however, if used excessively, defense mechanisms can only interfere with psychological development because they prevent one from dealing with the world realistically. They waste energy that can be used more effectively. And if they fail, the resulting anxiety can pose serious difficulties for the person.

Defense mechanisms tend to persist when the ego does not develop the strength to cope without them. But the ego may fail to gain strength because so much of its energy is tied up in its defenses. How does the ego break out of this vicious circle? The ego grows through the interaction between changes in the organism itself, particularly changes in the nervous system, and changes in the organism's environment. The circle can be broken early by ensuring that a child has the opportunity to learn, step by step, how to deal with stresses and challenges. It can also be broken later, by helping adult neurotics who did not learn in this gradual way, when they were children, to do so now and to learn that what threatened their young and weak egos no longer poses a realistic threat.

TABLE 2.2   The Ego's Principal Mechanisms of Defense

DEFINITION AND AIM	OPERATION	EXAMPLES
REPRESSION The purposeful but unconscious forgetting of something. Repression occurs when a memory, thought, or feeling (object cathexis) that arouses anxiety is forced out of consciousness by a restraining force (anticathexis). **Aim:** To deny or falsify existence of threat to ego's safety.	Repression is necessary for normal personality development and used to some extent by everyone. But it is dangerous because it can place entire areas of emotional life out of the person's reach. Often repression alone is not enough, and the ego must call on other means of controlling a threatening impulse. The latter may be allowed expression in disguised form: as *displacement* (a shift to another object), as an *hysterical symptom* (physical difficulty without an underlying physical basis), as a *psychophysiological disorder* (physical difficulty with both physical and psychological bases), or as a *phobia* (extreme and unrealistic fear of something). Or the impulse may be avoided by means of another defense mechanism.	Because a young man fears his sexual impulses, he is unable to recall the explicit sexual scenes he saw in a recent movie. *Repression + displacement:* A girl is afraid to express anger toward her parents and instead is rebellious and hostile to her teachers. *Repression + hysterical symptom:* After the plane he was flying crashes and his best friend and copilot is killed, a pilot cannot see, even though tests show no physical problem. *Repression + psychophysiological disorder:* Psychoanalysis reveals that a woman who has developed severe migraine headaches typically represses anger and goes along with others rather than assert her own needs. *Repression + phobia:* A man is frightened of things made of rubber. His father once punished him severely for breaking his little brother's prized rubber balloon. Rubber now triggers memories of that event and of the man's old wish that his brother would die.
PROJECTION Attribution to others of one's own unacceptable impulses. **Aim:** To eliminate thoughts and feelings that arouse anxiety; to convert neurotic or moral anxiety into realistic anxiety, which is easier to deal with.	Projection avoids admitting one's own sexual or aggressive impulses by insisting that it is others who have such desires. It substitutes a lesser for a greater danger; one can escape an external danger but not an internal one. Projection may also enable a person to express threatening impulses under the guise of self-defense.	A woman who cannot face her great anger toward her parents and other authority figures believes that her colleagues are trying to undermine her. She argues with everyone at a staff meeting and then accuses her boss of being hostile to her and planning to fire her.

TABLE 2.2

DEFINITION AND AIM	OPERATION	EXAMPLES
REACTION FORMATION Adoption of attitudes and behaviors that are opposite to one's true thoughts and feelings. **Aim:** To hide thoughts and feelings that arouse anxiety.	Typically, reaction formation masks negative feelings (e.g., anger, hate) with positive ones (e.g., love, affection). But sometimes it masks positive feelings with negative ones. In general, reaction formation can be distinguished from honest feelings by its exaggeration and its compulsive character. It may satisfy an original impulse; for example, excessive love can smother.	A woman has always envied her friend and feels second best but is afraid to compete. Instead, she lavishes affection and attention on her friend, generally preventing her from leading her own life. A man is very much attracted to a woman but, because he fears to lose his independence, is hostile and argumentative when they meet.
FIXATION[a] Focus on concerns of a particular stage of development long after one should have moved to the next. **Aim:** To avoid the frustrations and dangers of new situations.	Fixation leads a person to remain fixated on an old way of life, clinging to what is familiar, because of fear of failure or of being unable to cope with the demands of a new situation.	At age 7, a child still sucks his thumb and is frightened of going anywhere without his mother.
REGRESSION[a] Resumption of behaviors that were appropriate to an earlier stage of development. **Aim:** To get help in facing a traumatic event.	Regression involves retreating, under stress, to earlier stages of development, during which others were available to help and the person felt secure.	After a fight with her husband that leads to talk of divorce, a young woman returns to her parents' home, where she allows her parents to baby her and cater to her every whim.

[a]In general, people do not fixate or regress completely. Immature but isolated forms of behavior persist, tending to emerge when people are thwarted or frustrated.

STAGES OF DEVELOPMENT

For Freud, the first few years of life are decisive in the formation of personality. According to Freud's model of development, between birth and the age of 5 or 6, the child passes through three stages—the **oral**, **anal**, and **phallic** stages—in each of which development proceeds out of changes and growth in specific impulses and needs. During the **latency** stage, which comprises the next five or six years, impulses tend to be repressed. The sudden and considerable changes of adolescence reactivate the impulses, and then, as things quiet down, the person moves into the final, **genital** stage, the stage of maturity.

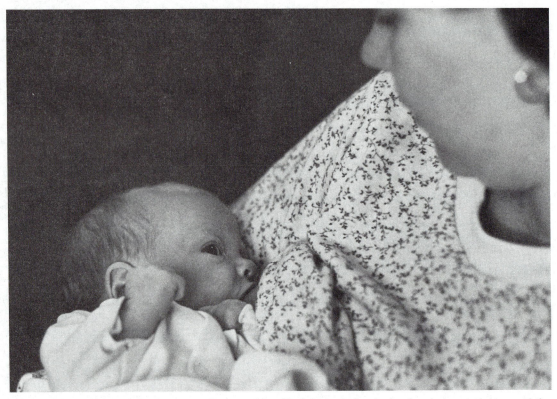

In the Freudian oral stage of development, eating is the dominant activity, and the baby must rely on those who care for it to fulfill all of its needs.

ORAL STAGE. The theme of the **oral stage**, which usually lasts through the first year of life, is eating, an activity that stimulates the lips, mouth, and throat. When the teeth appear, biting and chewing are added. These two modes of activity—incorporating and biting food—are the prototypes for such later character traits as acquiring knowledge or collecting things (**oral incorporation**) and the heavy use of sarcasm or argumentativeness (**oral aggression**).

This stage is particularly characterized by feelings of dependency. The baby relies totally on others for care and protection. Dependency feelings tend to persist to some degree in most of us, arising in later life whenever we feel anxious or insecure.

ANAL STAGE. Expelling feces relieves uncomfortable pressure created by the accumulation of digested food. During the **anal stage**, which lasts from about 1 to 2 years of age, toilet training forces the child to learn to postpone the pleasure of relieving anal tension.

Depending on parental attitudes and methods, this training may have far-reaching effects. For example, if parents are overly strict, the child may rebel and hold back its feces, becoming constipated; this tendency is the prototype of such later traits as stinginess and stubbornness (**anal retentiveness**). Or the child may vent its rage by expelling feces at inappropriate times, later showing traits like disorderliness, destructiveness, or cruelty (**anal expulsiveness**).

PHALLIC STAGE.   During the **phallic stage**, which in general begins at about age 2 and lasts till 5 or 6, children become preoccupied with their genital organs. Masturbation—the stroking and manipulation of one's sex organs—produces great sensual pleasure. At the same time, there is an intensification of sexual longing in children for their parents that initiates an important series of changes in the objects in which children invest energy. The most important development of this stage is the appearance of the Oedipus complex, with its accompanying phenomena of castration anxiety (in boys) and penis envy (in girls).

As you can see from Box 2.2, the Oedipus complex—the child's sexual attraction to its parent of the opposite sex and hostility toward its parent of the same sex—comes about and is resolved through the interplay of a number of driving and restraining forces (cathexes and anticathexes). This interplay leads eventually to the child's identifying with its same-sex parent, converting sexual to nonsexual love for its opposite-sex parent, and, generally, choosing as sexual partners peers of the opposite sex.

Freud assumed that every person is inherently bisexual—that we inherit tendencies of the opposite sex as well as of our own and are attracted to both sexes. In general, masculine tendencies predominate in males and feminine tendencies in females, so that most people identify with their own sex and choose opposite-sex partners. Homosexual impulses usually remain latent, finding expression in partial identifications with opposite-sex parents. For example, a heterosexual man, married, and with a family, may express such a partial identification with his mother—an artist—in his choice of a career in music.

LATENCY STAGE.   Fear of parental retaliation leads to the repression of the child's sexual longings, and roughly between the ages of 5 and 12, children move into the **latency stage**, when sexual and aggressive impulses of the earlier stages (**pregenital impulses**) are in a subdued state. During this stage, the child develops the capacity for sublimation and begins to feel concern for others. With the onset of puberty and its physiological changes in the reproductive system, the pregenital impulses are revived, and the person begins the adaptations that culminate finally in the stabilizing of the personality in the next stage.

BOX 2.2   The Oedipus Complex

Freud named the **Oedipus complex** for the legendary king of Thebes whose unwitting murder of his father and marriage to his mother form the dramatic nucleus of Sophocles' play *Oedipus Rex*. According to Freud, between the ages of about 2 and 5 the child develops a sexual attraction to its opposite-sex parent and a hostile, or aggressive, feeling toward its same-sex parent: the boy wants to possess his mother, replacing his father; the girl wants to possess her father and displace her mother.

The Oedipus complex evolves differently in males and females. Both boy and girl begin by loving their mother, because she satisfies their needs, and by resenting the father as a rival for the mother's affections. The boy imagines that his father and (stronger) rival will cut off the boy's genitals as punishment for desiring the mother. It is often the mother's specific threats of such an event, designed to keep the boy from masturbating, that arouse this fear. Sometimes the father resents the mother's attention to the son and becomes harsh and punitive toward him. Frequently, the boy believes that his fear is confirmed when he first sees the female genitals, which seem to him to be the result of the operation he dreads. **Castration anxiety** (the fear of being castrated) then forces the boy to repress both his desire for his mother and his hostility toward his father. By identifying with his ri-

val and father, he gets at least vicarious satisfaction of his sexual impulses toward his mother. At the same time, he represses his dangerous feeling for her and converts it into tender affection. The boy's Oedipus complex is then said to have been "resolved." Freud's (1909) famous case involving a troubled young boy, referred to as "Little Hans," provided some support for his theory of the Oedipus complex.

The female Oedipus complex is more complicated. Freud proposed that when the girl discovers that a boy has a protruding sex organ whereas she has only a cavity, several important things happen. To begin with, the girl believes that her lack of a penis is her mother's fault. As a result, the girl's love for her mother changes to anger and hostility, and the girl chooses her father as a sexual object because he has the penis she wants and she hopes to share it with him. **Penis envy**, the female counterpart of castration anxiety, is both the belief that one has been deprived of this valued organ and jealousy of those who possess it. Thus, whereas the boy's fear that he will be castrated leads to the resolution of his Oedipus complex, the girls' belief that she has already been castrated leads her *into* the Oedipus complex—the sexual attachment to her father and resentment of her mother. According to Freud, the girl's Oedipus complex is dissolved only gradually as she begins to realize the impossibility of pos-

sessing her father and to displace her feelings for him to other men. And as this happens, her resentment of her mother abates, and she begins to identify with her.

In both males and females, attitudes toward the opposite sex and people in authority are conditioned largely by the development and resolution of the Oedipus complex. And it is the resolution of this complex that causes the superego—which Freud termed the "heir" of the Oedipus complex—to undergo its final development. The boy's superego incorporates the prohibitions and ideals of his father's superego and becomes the bulwark against incest and aggression.

The female superego is weaker than the male superego, Freud said. This is because the resolution of the female Oedipus complex is such a long-drawn-out process and because the complex is not so strongly repressed in the girl as in the boy (the girl, Freud said, retains some attachment to her father). Not surprisingly, psychologists and feminists have taken issue with Freud's conception of female psychology. Alfred Adler and Karen Horney (see Chapter 5) were among the first to offer opposing theories, and although one feminist writer (Mitchell, 1974) has come to Freud's defense, a number of authors have continued to protest his theories of feminine psychology and sexuality (see, e.g., Wesstein, 1971; Chesler, 1972).

GENITAL STAGE.   In the **genital stage**, which begins at about age 12 and carries the person through adolescence and onward, people begin to love others for altruistic motives. The driving forces of the earlier stages are narcissistic, or self-oriented. Children obtain pleasure by stimulating their own bodies and are interested in other people only as sources of additional pleasure. Gradually, as people participate in group activities and prepare for work, marriage, and raising a family, they become transformed from pleasure-seeking, self-centered infants into reality-oriented, socialized adults. The selfish impulses of the earlier stages are fused and synthesized with the altruistic impulses of the present one. The reproduction of the species, the main biological function of the genital stage, is promoted by the psychological changes from total self-interest to concern for others.

You will find a survey of the stages of development and their significant dynamics in Table 2.3.

RESEARCH EMPHASES AND METHODS

Freud was trained in the methodology of nineteenth-century science. He had done formal research in the fields of neuropathology and histology, and he was familiar with the new experimental movement in psychology. Nevertheless, in his studies of the human mind, he did not use laboratory techniques; he never attempted to test his concepts and theories in controlled, empirical investigations. His theories were based, rather, on the painstaking analysis of data that consisted principally of the words and actions of the patients he treated for psychological difficulties. Because he saw patients, typically, for long periods of time, the data available to him for study were extensive, and he was meticulous and highly self-critical in ensuring that in each single case all the pieces fit together—that his analysis of the data was logical and internally consistent.

We will look here at the two fundamental techniques of psychoanalysis, free association and the analysis of dreams. After considering Freud's case studies and his own self-analysis—which was an important contribution to his theories—we will have a few words to say about current research on psychoanalytic concepts.

FREE ASSOCIATION

Freud evolved his unique method of **free association**—out of a technique devised by a friend and colleague, Josef Breuer, for the treatment of hysteria. (**Hysteria** is a broad term for a variety of psychological disturbances in which repression is the chief defense mechanism. In a common form of hysteria, physical pain and disability are experi-

TABLE 2.3   *Freudian Stages of Development*

STAGE/ ZONE OF ACTIVITY	APPROXIMATE AGE PERIOD	IMPORTANT DYNAMICS
Oral (mouth)	0–1	Eating is the infant's chief waking activity. The emphasis on taking things into the mouth, eating, sucking (oral incorporation), or biting and chewing (oral aggression) is prototypical of later character traits such as acquisitiveness or aggressiveness.
Anal (bowels)	1–2	Toilet training is ordinarily the child's first encounter with discipline and external authority. Expelling feces (anal expulsion) or holding feces back (anal retention) are prototypical of later character traits such as irresponsibility and stinginess.
Phallic (penis)	2–5	The increase in sexual urges leads to development of the Oedipus complex. In males, incestuous love for the mother and hostility toward the father are followed by fear of being castrated (castration anxiety) by the father. Fear leads to resolution of the complex through identification with the father and conversion of sexual love for the mother into tender affection.
		In females, love for the mother becomes hostility when the female discovers that she has been castrated (she has no penis, only a cavity) and assumes that it is her mother who has somehow brought about this unhappy state of affairs. Desire for and envy of the penis (penis envy) lead the female to choose the father as a sexual object. The complex is resolved only gradually in females through maturation and realization of the impossibility of possessing the father.
Latency	5–12	Dynamic activity is said to be repressed. Feelings of shame and disgust as well as esthetic and moral ideals, built up gradually, restrict sexual energies. Such energies are diverted to other needs, notably education and the beginnings of concern for others. The capacity for sublimation develops.
Genital (genitals)	12 on	Altruistic love (unselfish love of others) joins the self-love of the first three (pregenital) stages. Interest in others solely as providers of pleasure to the self becomes real altruistic concern for their welfare. The need for reproduction of the species underlies sexual attraction, socialization, vocational planning, and preparation for marriage and raising a family.

Bertha Pappenheim (1859– 1936) was the famous "Anna O." who, as a patient of Freud's colleague Breuer, inspired the well-known technique of free association.

enced despite the absence of any clearly established organic disorder.) Breuer, in turn, had developed his technique with the help of his patient, the now famous "Anna O." (in reality, Bertha Pappenheim, who became one of the world's first social workers and a strong supporter of women's causes; see Jones, 1961). One day, when this patient related the details of how one of her symptoms first appeared, to Breuer's and her astonishment, the symptom disappeared. She continued to describe the genesis of her symptoms, calling the method the "talking cure," and when Freud learned of it from Breuer, he was fascinated by its apparent potentialities.

Unlike the "talking cure," however, free association requires that patients relate not only the origins of their symptoms but everything and anything that comes into their awareness. Freud's method, in its classical form, requires that the psychoanalyst refrain from interrupting the patient's flow of speech. The analyst comments or asks questions only to encourage the patient when he or she pauses or seems blocked. This prescription has given rise to the common, much joked about picture of the analyst who remains impassive in the face of the patient's wildest productions. Some analysts of the strict Freudian school still adhere to a pattern rather like that, but today many are far more active and responsive. And indeed, Freud himself—as you can see from Box 2.3—was often a very active and empathic participant in the therapy process.

Underlying the technique of free association are three basic assumptions: first, that everything we say and do not only has meaning but is related to everything else we have said and done; second, that unconscious material crucially affects our behavior; and, third, that unconscious material can be brought into meaningful awareness by encouraging the free expression of our thoughts as they occur. The assumption is that by this technique, associations between real events and mental images (memories, dream images) will lead to the uncovering of repressed, unconscious material. Thus, free associations are not really ''free'' but are specifically connected in a causal chain, and their flow is determined by the unconscious processes active within the person at the time. According to Freud, although a patient will block out certain topics and attempt to evade or disguise others, eventually the person's chains of associations will lead the listener to an understanding of the person's mental and emotional conflicts.

DREAM ANALYSIS
The technique of **dream analysis** developed naturally out of the requirement that patients talk about everything that came to their minds. Freud's first patients spontaneously recalled their dreams and gave associations to them. When Freud perceived the richness of the material produced by dreams and their associations, he began to examine his own dreams and found the same wealth of information. As a result of these insights, he formulated his famous theory that the dream is the fulfillment of a wish and the expression of the most primitive workings and contents of the human mind (Freud, 1900).

The dream is created by the primary process. In sleep, when the ego is relatively weak, unconscious thoughts and impulses try to find expression. But the ego manages to disguise this material; that is why the dream's wish is not always immediately apparent and why the analysis of a dream is often difficult.

The interpretation of dreams makes up a significant portion of the psychoanalytic process, for it offers an important avenue to the unconscious material that, in Freud's view, forms the bedrock of human psychological functioning. Indeed, for Freud, the dream was ''the royal road to the unconscious.'' A topic that has fascinated all people throughout the ages, dream interpretation continues to be the subject of investigation by both clinicians and researchers.

CASE STUDIES
The vast amount of raw material from which Freud fashioned his theory of personality will never be known. Freud published very few ac-

BOX 2.3   Katharina's "Uncle"

Enjoying the view from the summit of a mountain he had just climbed during a vacation in the Alps, Freud was approached by a young woman with a request for a professional consultation. It seemed he could not escape the neuroses, even, as he put it, "at a height of over 2000 meters"!

In Freud's account of this brief therapy session (Breuer and Freud, 1895), he altered an important fact: the 18-year-old Katharina was not the niece of the man described here as her uncle—she was his daughter. Thirty years passed, however, before Freud felt he could reveal the truth about this young woman's experience with a sexually abusive, perhaps alcoholic, father.

To Freud's initial question as to the nature of her complaint, Katharina replied,

"I have so much difficulty in breathing. Not always, but sometimes it catches me so that I believe I am choking."

Surmising that she was actually describing an anxiety attack, Freud said,

"Sit down and describe to me how such a state of 'difficulty in breathing' feels."

"It suddenly comes upon me. There is first a pressure on my eyes. My head becomes so heavy and it hums so that I can hardly bear it, and then I become so dizzy that I believe I am falling, and then my chest begins to press together so that I cannot get my breath."

"And do you feel nothing in the throat?"

"The throat becomes laced together as if I choked."

"And you feel nothing else in the head?"

"Yes, it hammers as if it would split."

"Yes, and doesn't that frighten you?"

"I always feel, 'Now I must die,' and I am otherwise courageous. I go everywhere alone, into the cellar and down over the whole mountain, but on the day that I have this attack, I do not trust myself anywhere. I always believe that someone stands behind me and suddenly grabs me."

Freud concluded that Katharina was describing an hysterical attack that included a component of anxiety. He discovered that during the attack, Katharina would see a face that she did not recognize. He learned that she had her first attack when she was at an inn on another mountain that her "aunt" (actually her mother) was then managing. He decided to hazard a guess, based on previous cases in which he had seen young women experience anxiety at the first contact with the world of sexuality.

"If you do not know it, I will tell you what I believe is the cause of your attacks. At that time, two years ago, you had seen or heard something which embarrassed you much, something that you would rather not have seen."

"Heavens, yes, I caught my uncle with my cousin Francisca! . . . My uncle, the husband of my aunt, . . . at that time kept an inn with my aunt on the mountain. Now they are divorced, and it is my fault that they are divorced because through me it be-

came known that he had something to do with Francisca."

"Yes, how did you come to discover this?" . . .

"Two years ago, two gentlemen once came up the mountain and wanted to get something to eat. My aunt was not at home and Francisca, who always did the cooking, could not be found anywhere. Nor could we find my uncle. We looked for them everywhere until Alois, my cousin, said, 'In the end Francisca will be found with father.' . . . We went to the room where my uncle lived and that was locked. That seemed peculiar. Then Alois said: 'On the path there is a window from which you can look into the room.' . . . I looked in, the room was quite dark, but then I saw my uncle and Francisca, and he was lying on her."

"Well?"

"I immediately left the window and leaned against the wall and got the difficulty in breathing which I have had since then. My senses left me. My eyes closed tight and my head hammered and hummed."

Katharina then told Freud that she did not understand what frightened her. He encouraged her to recall what went through her mind at the time of the incident, but she said she was so frightened that she forgot everything. She was able to say that the face she continued to see was "horrible" and that of a man. But she could go no further.

She then related that after the incident she was dizzy again and stayed in bed for three days, vomiting continuously. Freud inferred that her vomiting might have signified disgust and asked,

"*If you vomited three days later, I believe you felt disgust when you looked into the room.*"

"*Yes, I surely was disgusted,*" she said reflectingly, "*But at what?*"

"*Perhaps you saw something naked. How were these two persons in the room?*"

"*It was too dark to see anything and both of them had their clothes on. Yes, if I only knew at what I was disgusted at that time.*"

Freud again encouraged Katharina to say what came to her mind, and she then revealed that she told her "aunt" of her discovery because she sensed some change in the latter. Angry scenes followed, and eventually her "aunt" decided to leave her "uncle" with Francisca—who had become pregnant—and took Katharina and the other children with her to begin managing another inn.

Then Katharina began to relate several incidents that had occurred two or three years before the traumatic event she had just described, in which her "uncle" made sexual advances to her as well as to Francisca. Once, when she and her "uncle" were sharing a room at an inn, she retired early while he continued to drink and play cards. She awakened suddenly to "feel his body."

She jumped up and reproached him: "*What are you up to, uncle? Why don't you remain in your bed?*" He attempted to joke about it, and said, "*Go, you stupid goose, be quiet. You don't even know how good this is.*" "*I don't want anything good from you. You don't even let me sleep.*" She remained standing at the door, ready to flee out to the path, until he stopped and fell asleep.

Katharina then described several other occasions when she had to defend herself against her "uncle" when he was very drunk. She also told Freud of two more incidents involving apparent sexual activity between her "uncle" and Francisca.

After she finished these . . . stories she stopped. She looked as if changed. The sulky, suffering features were vivified, her look was cheerful. . . . Meanwhile, the understanding of her case dawned upon me; what she related last, seemingly without any plan, explains excellently her behavior at the scene of the discovery. At that time she carried with her . . . experiences which she recalled, which she did not understand, and which did not help her in drawing any conclusion. At the sight of the pair in the act of coitus, she immediately connected the new impression with these . . . reminiscences, she began to understand and simultaneously to reject. [After] . . .

a short period . . . came the vomiting as a substitute for the moral and physical disgust. With this the riddle was solved. She was not disgusted at the sight of the two but at a reminiscence which this sight awakened in her and explained everything. This could only be the memory of the nightly attack when she "felt her uncle's body."

"*Now I know what you thought at the time that you looked into the room*" [Freud said]. "*You thought, 'Now he does with her what he wished to do with me on that night and the other time.' It disgusted you, because you recalled the feeling how you awakened in the night and felt his body.*"

"*It is very probable*" [Katharina replied] "*that this disgusted me and that I thought of it at that time.*"

Now Katharina was able to say that the hallucinated face was that of her "uncle." During the quarrels with her "aunt," her "uncle" had expressed rage toward Katharina, saying that the divorce was Katharina's fault. He had threatened her with physical harm on several occasions; when he saw her, his face would become "tense with rage," and he would run at her with raised hand. She "always had the greatest anxiety that he might grab" her. "The face which I then always saw was his face in a rage."

counts of patients' analyses, partly because he feared to reveal material that would enable people to recognize a particular person. Each of the cases described in Table 2.4 was presented primarily to illustrate a particularly important analytic concept. Whether these four case histories were the actual empirical sources for the concepts they exemplify or whether they were simply good examples we do not know. However, these studies do reveal the type of material Freud collected, the techniques he used, and the way he thought. Thus, if you want to become familiar with the way in which Freud worked, you should read one or more of these original case studies.

CURRENT PSYCHOANALYTIC RESEARCH

In the years since Freud's death, a number of experimental tests of psychoanalytic propositions have been undertaken. Several experiments from two ongoing research programs are described in Box 2.4. In each case, the results confirmed the hypotheses, and in fact the results of the many experiments performed in these two programs have quite consistently confirmed psychoanalytic concepts (Silverman, 1976). However, not all attempts to verify Freudian hypotheses have been successful. We will have more to say about this in the next section.

EVALUATION

Freud's ideas are challenging. His conception of the individual was both broad and deep. A penetrating observer, he was disciplined yet bold and original in his thinking. Above all, his theory has the virtue of trying to portray people, with all their physical and psychological attributes, living partly in the world of reality and partly in a world of fantasy, moved by forces of which they have little knowledge, beset by conflicts and inner contradictions, and capable of rational thought and action yet, by turn, confused and clearheaded, frustrated and satisfied, hopeful and despairing, selfish and altruistic. For many, Freud's picture of the human being has an essential validity.

Nevertheless, no other psychological theory has been subjected to such searching—and often bitter—criticism. The only comparable case in modern science is that of Darwin, whose evolutionary doctrine shocked Victorian England. Initially, colleagues and laypeople alike reacted very negatively to Freud's ascribing sexual and destructive wishes to the baby, attributing incestuous urges to everyone, and explaining human behavior generally in terms of sexual motivation. In recent years, Freudian theory has been criticized as painting too bleak a picture of human nature. It is often characterized as lacking suffi-

TABLE 2.4   *Some of Freud's Most Famous Cases*

CASE	CONCEPTS ILLUSTRATED	COMMENTS
Dora (1905a)	Hysterical symptoms as reflections of repressed sexual impulses; use of dream analysis in revealing repressed material	Dora, an 18-year-old young woman, was experiencing depression, fatigue, and other physical problems. She was enmeshed in complex interrelationships that involved her parents, her father's mistress, and the latter's husband, who had made advances to Dora. Freud presents detailed analyses of two of Dora's dreams, in which verbatim accounts of her associations and his interpretations give a remarkably clear picture of dream analysis technique.
Little Hans (1909a)	Theory of infantile sexuality, including Oedipus complex and castration anxiety	Five-year-old Hans feared a horse would bite him if he went out into the street. Hans's physician–father treated him with Freud's guidance. In this case, which includes many verbatim accounts, from the father's notes, of dialogues between him and Hans, Freud demonstrates that Hans's phobia was an expression of phallic-stage dynamics.
Schreber (1911)	Relationship between paranoia (delusional state, usually involving ideas of persecution by others) and latent homosexuality	Schreber, an appeals court judge, wrote an account of his own illness, which had been diagnosed as paranoia. He believed he was the Redeemer and was being transformed into a woman. Freud's analysis, based solely on Schreber's written account, shows that these delusions were related and that the motive for both was latent homosexuality. Freud hypothesizes that the basic conflict in paranoia (at least in males) is homosexual desire. By reaction formation, the person turns this threatening desire into hate and then projects that hate: "I love him" becomes "I hate him" and then "He hates me and is persecuting me."
Wolf Man (1918)	Child's reaction to primal scene (child's real or fantasied observation of parental sexual intercourse); effects of castration anxiety on later life	"Wolf Man," a young man in his twenties, incurred a gonorrheal infection that reawakened a long-repressed castration anxiety. He became depressed and unable to function independently. Freud analyzes this man's childhood neurosis and interprets a frightening dream of wolves that the Wolf Man had in childhood as a reaction to the primal scene.

BOX 2.4   Testing Freudian Concepts in the Laboratory

Since the mid-1960s, psychologists at New York and Michigan State universities have had under way two research programs that are considered models of theoretical and experimental sophistication. These studies were designed to test a number of hypotheses derived from the general psychoanalytic notion that heightened conflict over unconscious sexual and aggressive desires can lead to ''abnormal'' behavior.

AGGRESSION AND INDEPENDENCE

At New York University's Research Center for Mental Health, Silverman (1976) and his associates have used **subliminal stimulation** (the presentation of stimuli below the threshold of perception) to examine the effects of unconscious conflicts on people with depressive or schizophrenic symptoms. With a **tachistoscope** (an instrument that provides a very brief exposure of visual material), the experimenter shows subjects a picture of a printed message so quickly—usually for .004 second—that they cannot tell what it is. Although subjects are not consciously aware of what they have seen, they apparently register the material in some way, for it has been shown repeatedly that such material affects subsequent behavior.

Silverman's group proposed that if the psychoanalytic postulate that depression results from turning one's unconscious aggressive feelings toward others against oneself were correct,

subjects' depression should be deepened if their unconscious aggressive wishes were activated. (Psychoanalysis holds that depression masks anger and aggression. Freud had proposed not only that the aggressive drive was self-destruction turned outward but that if the drive met obstacles it could be turned back against the self.) These researchers thus showed depressed persons aggressive pictures or messages—for example, a snarling man holding a dagger or a phrase like CANNIBAL EATS PERSON—and asked subjects to rate their feelings before and after these presentations. Then, in other sessions, they showed the same subjects neutral stimuli—for instance, a picture of a person reading or a phrase like PEOPLE ARE WALKING—again asking for before and after self-ratings.

As predicted, subjects' depressive feelings became more intense after ''seeing'' aggressive material but did not change in response to neutral material. In order to be sure that the increased depression was a specific response to the aggressive material, the experimenters also studied the effects of showing stimuli designed to arouse other feelings. Again, they found that depression increased only in response to aggressive material.

Silverman and his co-workers also showed that reducing unconscious conflict led to a decrease in abnormal symptoms. When they presented the message MOMMY AND I ARE

ONE to people who had been diagnosed schizophrenic, their subjects' symptoms became milder; this did not happen when they presented neutral messages. One of the many theories about the dynamics of schizophrenia proposes that people whose behavior is schizophrenic have very conflicted relationships with their mothers. The theory suggests that such people have failed to achieve normal independence and thus both desperately need and fear or hate their mothers. According to Silverman (1976), the oneness suggested by the MOMMY message warded off subjects' hostile feelings toward their mothers, implied that subjects could have unlimited mothering, and decreased subjects' anxiety at being separated from their mothers.

Recently, Silverman (1983) has summarized his continuing research and that of his students using the method we have described, now termed **subliminal psychodynamic activation**. Silverman describes additional interesting findings and discusses some controversial issues raised by the failure of some studies to confirm his own early findings.

OEDIPAL CONFLICT

In one of the many studies carried out by Reyher and his associates at Michigan State University (Sommerschield and Reyher, 1973), male college students were hypnotized and then told a story in which they were nearly seduced by very attractive older women. This story was designed to activate unconscious Oedipal conflicts. Under hypnosis, the subjects were told that they would not remember anything about the story and that after they had awakened they would have strong sexual feelings when certain words were mentioned.

As predicted, when presented with the critical words, the subjects reacted with such signs of disturbance as sweating, trembling, and confusion. When asked to rate their feelings, they described themselves as guilty, ashamed, or disgusted. The presentation of neutral words had no effect.

You may wonder what would happen if one showed the various stimuli used in the New York University and Michigan State experiments in such a way that subjects could perceive and understand them consciously. The answer is nothing. Apparently unconscious wishes can be stirred up only by something that is also outside conscious awareness. Presumably our defenses keep us from responding consciously to material aimed at unconscious conflicts, just as they keep us from being aware of such conflicts.

cient humanism and as failing to take account of positive phenomena, such as joy and self-actualization.

By far the most serious criticisms of psychoanalytic theory have been those directed at Freud's lack of scientific method. His failure to carry out or report his research in a systematic way makes it very difficult to evaluate his work. As we saw in the last section, others have begun to test Freudian concepts by means of controlled experimentation. It may be many years, however, before we will be able to make final judgments about Freud's concepts and theories. For now, we need a way of at least tentatively assessing the usefulness of his postulates, the validity of his conclusions.

How do we evaluate a program of scientific investigation? As we indicated in Chapter 1, a theory must enable us to predict future events. In addition, a theory's concepts must be capable of being operationalized, or related to specific empirical variables that can be distinguished from other variables and that are subject to measurement and tests for significance. Research related to the theory must be controlled; that is, variables other than those under direct examination must be kept from influencing research findings. And research must be capable of being replicated, or repeated, by someone else, in exactly the same fashion.

To **predict** future events, a theory must provide a set of relational rules by which one can formulate such expectations. It must enable us to say, for example, that if A happens, B will happen also, or, conversely, that if A does not happen, B will not happen either. But Freudian theory is essentially descriptive. It does not provide rules for connecting events. We cannot specify precisely what connects traumatic experiences with guilt feelings, repression, and dreaming or the formation of the superego with the Oedipus complex.

Freud's theories are often couched in rather vague terms. His theory of the death instincts, for example, is not well articulated—recall that he neither identified the origin of these instincts nor named their source of energy. As we saw in the last section, one can **operationalize** the concept of the unconscious as subliminal perception, or the mind's apparent ability to respond to stimuli that are below the threshold of awareness. But there are no satisfactory empirical referents for the death instincts. Suicide, drug addiction, and other self-destructive behaviors that might be seen as evidence of such instincts can be and have been explained in other ways. For example, the traditional psychoanalytic explanations for chronic alcoholism have included fixation at the oral stage, repressed rage because of early deprivation, and regression to a dependent state. Today, however, researchers are increasingly impressed with the possible biological—perhaps genetic—bases of alcoholism and other drug addictions. Thus, at present, it is unclear what contribution ''death instincts'' might make to our understanding and explanations of addictive behavior.

Some of Freud's concepts are difficult to test because they are difficult to refute. If an hypothesized phenomenon can have two quite opposite results, one cannot easily disconfirm it. For example, emphasis on anal retention (fixation at the anal stage) may lead a person to be stingy. However, through reaction formation, such a person might also become overly generous.

Freud's theory does not suggest how we are to **measure** such things as the interplay of driving and restraining forces (cathexes and anticathexes). For example, how can we judge the strength of the ego? How weak must the ego be for it to be overridden by an instinctual impulse? Without such specifications, no laws can be derived.

Moreover, because Freud did not quantify his data, we cannot weigh the statistical significance of his findings. How often, for example, did he find an association between paranoia and latent homosexuality? Or between the primal scene and adult instability? How many cases of a particular type did he study? What were the socioeconomic, occupational, ethnic, and religious backgrounds of his patients? What were his criteria for assigning cases to particular clinical categories—that is, hysteria, paranoia, and so on?

Freud also failed to **control** for the influence of variables other than those he was specifically observing. For example, as feminist writers have pointed out, he took no note of the sociocultural factors that undoubtedly contributed to the grave discontent of many of his women patients. Instead, he ascribed their distress to envy of the penis.

The objectivity of Freud's observations has been questioned from other points of view. Freud acknowledged, for instance, that he did not keep verbatim records of what went on in analytic sessions. He believed that notetaking would distract both patient and therapist. Thus, he worked from notes made some hours later, claiming that he remembered what was significant and forgot what was trivial. Modern experiments on the reliability of testimony, however, suggest that distortions and omissions of various kinds might well have crept into his records.

Some critics point out that Freud's "observations" may have been based on preconceived notions. For example, they ask, did his own admitted "Oedipal" conflict (Jones, 1961) lead him to find incestuous wishes in others? Did he infer unconscious (and thus unfulfilled) incestuous desires in people because he was loathe to recognize the not uncommon fact of incest and the sexual abuse of children? Did his preoccupation with death from the time he was 40, as well as his own experience of cancer, contribute to his postulation of the death instincts (Fromm, 1973)?

Finally, because Freud gives us only his conclusions and does not present his original data systematically or describe his line of reasoning or methods of analysis, it is almost impossible to **replicate**, or repeat, his investigations according to his original design. It is not surprising, then, that other researchers have often arrived at quite different conclusions and that there are many interpretations of what are presumably the same phenomena.

How can modern science deal with the problems inherent in Freudian theory and methods? The theory certainly does not lack predictive intent. Freud's overriding concern was to discover the reasons for the behavior he observed—to uncover the origins of things and the continuing, forward-moving connections between them. What the theory lacks is a systematic means of identifying the specific links in the causal chains Freud postulated and thus of validating the conclusions he drew. The theory needs better operational definitions and clear specifications as to the conditions under which such chains of causation operate.

As more and more research is carried out, we can expect that psychoanalytic concepts will be better articulated and clearly related to empirical phenomena. Those concepts that prove incapable of such clarification will probably be discarded. Freud himself performed this sort of operation, often dropping an idea or theory when further observations failed to confirm it.

With respect to the problem of systematic recording, modern electronics have greatly lessened the likelihood that record keeping will be a distraction during therapy sessions. And a few trained psychoanalysts who are primarily scientific investigators have begun to examine actual recorded therapy sessions in an effort to validate the objectivity of analytic observations (see, e.g., Malcolm, 1981).

Although the studies at New York and Michigan State universities that we have already discussed generally support Freudian hypotheses, other research efforts have failed to confirm psychoanalytic theory. And writers who have surveyed the literature on psychoanalytic research evaluate such research quite differently. Eysenck (Eysenck and Wilson, 1974), for example, is a relentless foe of Freudian theory and finds no evidence at all for its validity. On the other hand, Kline (1972) and Fisher and Greenberg (1977) conclude that the balance between supportive and disconfirming research is clearly in Freud's favor. Fisher and Greenberg affirm the "basic soundness of Freud's thinking" in half a dozen conceptual areas. They also propose revisions in some parts of his theory and point out that many concepts have yet to be examined.

We need continuing and creative research on a wide range of Freudian concepts, and to achieve this, we will need more effective cooperation between psychoanalysis and psychology. Although the two disciplines have common roots in experimental physiology and philosophy, they were long kept apart by psychology's distaste for the psychoanalytic method, which shunned scientific principles and techniques, and the fact that psychoanalysis was interested in the unconscious workings of disturbed people's minds whereas psychology focused on the normal mind's conscious processes. Gradually, however, a number of factors have brought the two fields closer to each other and perhaps as psychoanalysis becomes more interested in the experimental approach, we will see a truly broad-based attempt at validating the claim of psychoanalysis to be a science of personality. In any event, if you decide to go on in the field of personality, keep in mind the importance, underlined in Chapter 1, of understanding a theory before trying to critique or modify it. Although the criticisms we have discussed here are valid ones, others that you will discover are not. Like other theories, Freud's has often been distorted, both by critics and by well-meaning adherents. It is a challenging task to fully comprehend his theory but for the serious student a task well worth the effort.

In summary, there is no question that the work of Sigmund Freud has had an enormous effect on modern life. In identifying major problems of personality structure and functioning that continue to interest theorists and researchers, Freud made a highly significant contribution to the psychology of personality. Even if some aspects of Freudian theory are incorrect, we cannot overlook the broad, general influence the theory has had on other theorists, researchers, and psychotherapists. Right or wrong, Sigmund Freud certainly set personality psychology on fruitful paths of inquiry, and for that alone we must be very grateful.

SUMMARY

1. The **id** is the oldest system of the personality. It provides the psychic energy for all three systems. It knows only the subjective inner world, and it operates by the **pleasure principle** and the **primary process**.

2. The **ego** represents rational thinking. It tries to conform the id's mental pictures to objective reality. The ego operates by the **reality principle** and the **secondary process**.

3. The **superego** represents moral standards. Its **conscience** punishes wrong behaviors, and its **ego ideal** rewards right behaviors.

4. An **instinct** is both a quantity of psychic energy and a wish to fulfill a bodily need. All instincts together equal the personality's total energy.

5. The **life instincts**, such as hunger and sex, seek to preserve the individual and the species; the **death instincts** embody the organism's wish to die. The **aggressive drive** is self-destruction turned against other people.

6. The id **cathects**, or invests psychic energy in, any object that seems to gratify its needs. The ego invests energy only in real need-satisfying objects. It uses excess energy to develop other psychological processes and to restrain the id and the superego. The superego invests energy in building and maintaining moral standards.

7. **Realistic anxiety** is the fear of a real danger in the external world. **Neurotic anxiety** is the fear of punishment from an imaginary external source. **Moral anxiety** is the fear of self-punishment, or of one's conscience.

8. Personality development is the learning of new ways to reduce tension. By **identification**, the child learns to copy others' successful behavior. By **displacement**, it learns to transfer energy from blocked objects to those that are attainable.

9. The ego attempts to deal with excessive anxiety by means of **defense mechanisms—repression**, **projection**, **reaction formation**, **fixation**, and **regression**—that operate unconsciously and deny or distort reality.

10. The personality develops through **five stages: oral**, **anal**, **phallic**, **latency**, and **genital**. The self-oriented dynamics of the first three stages are crucial to character formation. They lead, after a fourth period of relative calm, to the appearance, in the fifth stage, of the mature, socialized adult.

11. Freud's theory is based on the words and actions of the patients he saw in treatment. His two principal techniques for gathering and interpreting the data were **free association** and the **analysis of dreams**.

12. Freud's published **case histories** illustrate some of his important concepts.

13. The most serious criticisms of Freudian theory are those that call it to task for its failure to employ scientific method. Freud's constructs are not always clearly framed so that they have clear empirical referents. His observations were neither recorded nor made under con-

trolled conditions. Thus they were subject to the influence of extrane-
ous variables, including his own biases, and they are not readily
subjected to quantification or tests for significance. It has been very
difficult, as a result, to replicate Freud's observations according to his
exact design, and his theory has been considered by many to be more
descriptive than predictive.

14. Beginning in the late 1940s, however, psychologists have been
making serious efforts to establish the validity of psychoanalysis
through scientific procedures. Several recent surveys of such research
have found considerable support for a number of Freud's conceptions.
And recently, some psychoanalysts have begun to use laboratory techniques to investigate aspects of Freudian theory, for example, analyzing taped records of actual analytic sessions.

SUGGESTED READING

Hall's *A Primer of Freudian Psychology* (1954) ofers an expanded yet succinct
version of the material presented in this chapter. If you wish to explore psychoanalytic theory in depth, you should also read some of Freud's own works.
These are contained in the 24-volume *Standard Edition of the Complete Psychological
Works of Sigmund Freud* (1953–1974). Many of the monographs and books we will
suggest to you are also available in paperback editions.

Freud often addressed a new audience by describing slips of the tongue
and other mistakes that betray unconscious material. *The Psychopathology of Everyday Life* (1901), probably the most popular of all Freud's writings, contains many
examples of such errors.

The *Introductory Lectures on Psycho-analysis* (also titled *A General Introduction to
Psycho-analysis*, 1917) focus particularly on the analysis of dreams and Freud's
general theory of the neuroses. The *New Introductory Lectures on Psychoanalysis*
(1933a) present Freud's later thinking on many aspects of his theories, including
the structure of personality, anxiety, the instincts, dreams, and feminine psychology. Together, these two sets of lectures provide an excellent introduction to
Freudian theory.

Freud considered *The Interpretation of Dreams* (1900) his greatest work, re-
marking, as late as 1931, that "it contains . . . the most valuable of all the discoveries it has been my good fortune to make." A book not just about dreams but
about the dynamics of the human mind, it is heavy reading but well worth the effort. It is Freud's earliest major work, predated only by Breuer and Freud's *Studies in Hysteria* (1895), which describes Breuer's "talking-cure" method and the origin of Freud's technique of free association.

All of Freud's published case histories are fascinating to read. You may
particularly enjoy exploring the case of the "Wolf Man," because the patient's
own account of his analysis with Freud is now available in a volume that also contains Freud's original case history (see Gardiner, *The Wolf Man by the Wolf Man*,
1971). You might also want to look at the case of the "Rat Man" (1909b; *Standard Edition*, Vol. 10), whose many **obsessions** (unavoidable ideas) revolved
around his sexual desires and his relationship with his dead father; or the case of a

female homosexual (1920b; *Standard Edition*, Vol. 18), in which Freud sets forth his very forward-looking ideas on the origins and development of homosexuality.

After you have read some of Freud's own work, you may want to examine some of his critics' comments. Many writers, both within and outside the psychoanalytic camp, have explored one or another specific Freudian concepts. More inclusive appraisals, however, may be found in three works cited earlier: as we noted, Eysenck and Wilson, *The Experimental Study of Freudian Theories* (1974), find no value in Freudian theory. In contrast, Fisher and Greenberg, *The Scientific Credibility of Freudian Theories and Therapy* (1977), and Kline, *Fact and Fancy in Freudian Theory* (1972), find evidence both for and against psychoanalytic concepts. The last three writers underline the great contribution of psychoanalytic theory to the study of human behavior and call for continuing and broadened research on Freud's many theories and concepts.

Ernest Jones's three-volume *The Life and Work of Sigmund Freud* (1953, 1955, 1957) is the definitive account of Freud's long life; a one-volume version, edited and abridged by Trilling and Marcus (Jones, 1961), is also available. Jones, who was an English psychoanalyst and a member of Freud's original group of followers, remained an associate and friend for 40 years; he played an important role in Freud's escape from Vienna in 1938 and in his move to London. Jones was one of the last people to see Freud before Freud died.

In recent years a number of other biographical treatments of Freud's life have been written; one of the latest is Clark, *Freud: The Man and the Cause* (1980).

Chapter three

3.

There is in every child at every stage a
new miracle of vigorous unfolding
which constitutes a new hope and a
new responsibility for all.

ERIK ERIKSON

Contemporary Psychoanalytic Theory:
Erik Erikson and Others

In this chapter we will be concerned with some of the changes that have been made in Freud's theory of personality since his death in 1939. Freud himself often modified and extended his theory, and the origins of many changes in psychoanalytic thought, both his own as well as those made by others, can be found in some of his earliest writings. Many psychoanalytic writers have sharpened and amplified Freudian theory and have applied it to an increasingly broad range of situations. Some have used techniques other than the psychoanalytic session—for example, the direct observation of children—to test psychoanalytic propositions. And some have led psychoanalytic theory in different directions: the so-called ego psychologists have freed the ego from its bond with the id, with the result that psychoanalytic theory has made fresh and creative advances.

Until the 1920s, Freud rather ignored the ego, focusing his energies on the exploration of the unconscious. Then in 1921, in a book entitled *Group Psychology and the Analysis of the Ego* (Freud, 1921), and again two years later in *The Ego and the Id* (Freud, 1923), he began to devote more attention to the theory of the ego and the structures of personality. In the later book he presented his definitive account of the interacting systems of the personality—id, ego, and superego—offering an entirely new perspective on the structure and function of the mind. The ego was clearly subservient to the whims of its two companions, but it was also entrusted with many important functions, such as reality testing and the control of motor behavior. Thus, Freud seemed almost to contradict his earlier view that the ego is the weakest of the three mental agencies. After his daughter Anna Freud (1946) endorsed the "fresh direction" in Freud's thinking, the study of the ego became a more legitimate enterprise, and other psychoanalytic theorists began to feel free to explore the ego and its operations in greater depth.

Our chief focus in this chapter will be on the contributions of Erik Erikson, whose work, perhaps better than that of any contemporary figure, represents both the theory of ego functioning and the elaboration and extension of classical psychoanalytic concepts. For Erikson, the ego approaches the world in a creative fashion, adapting to the circumstances in which it finds itself or devising ways to change those circumstances. Erikson's psychosocial theory of development builds on but modifies and greatly expands Freud's own developmental theory.

But before we consider Erikson's theory and concepts, let us examine briefly the views of several theorists who have contributed substantially to the new ego psychology: Anna Freud, Heinz Hartmann, and Robert White. Anna Freud, opened the door to this new line of thought, but she continued to believe that psychoanalysis must investigate all three of the personality systems equally. It was Heinz Hartmann (1958, 1964) who really launched the new ego theory. Hartmann emphasized the ego's adaptive functions—which Freud had already suggested in his concept of reality testing—and showed how the ego's defenses could serve healthy as well as maladaptive purposes. After Hartmann read his groundbreaking paper presenting this view at the Vienna Psychoanalytic Society in 1937, others went on to elaborate the concept of an independent ego and evolved significant modifications of their own. One such theorist is the Harvard psychologist Robert White, who developed the idea of "effectance motivation," a drive or motive source that leads human beings to develop their capabilities and master their environment.

THE PSYCHOANALYTIC TRADITION AND EGO PSYCHOLOGY

One of major innovations of ego psychology was the incorporation into the theory of the effects of the external environment. That is, the development and functioning of the ego results not only from internal processes but also from external events. Early experiences with adults charged with the responsibility of caring for the infant set the stage for later developments in the child's behavior. Such early experiences with caretaking persons (termed, in ego psychology, **objects**) affect the child's later ability to become independent and to interact comfortably with other people. **Object relations** is the term given to these relationships with other people.

Ego psychology helped psychoanalysis to become more interpersonal and social than earlier formulations that emphasized inner processes had allowed. Ego psychology theory, sometimes also referred to as "object relations theory," widened the horizons of psychoanalytic theory by proposing that gratifying and nurturing interactions with adults as well as frustrating and depriving ones could affect the child and its future style of interacting with people, both in adolescence and in adulthood. These theorists did not reject the importance of the id or the superego. Actually, by giving emphasis to the ego, they brought it more into balance with the other personality structures.

ANNA FREUD: THE EGO AS EQUAL PARTNER

Among Anna Freud's important contributions to ego psychology were her efforts to integrate new findings and theory in child psychology into the psychoanalytic treatment of the child. She studied nursery school children as well as children who were in psychoanalytic treatment at her Hampstead Clinic. Thus her writings reflect theory and practice that evolved from working with both normal and disturbed children.

Anna Freud had an enormous influence on the first generation of child psychoanalysts; she trained and worked with many of the most prominent early child analysts, including Erik Erikson, whom we also discuss in this chapter. Anna Freud's writings have had a significant impact on child psychoanalytic treatment, on the education of children, ānd on techniques of child rearing.

We will discuss two of Anna Freud's most important contributions to personality theory (see also Dyer, 1983): her approach to the understanding of child development and her elaboration of the defense mechanisms. Anna Freud believed that the child's development should be considered in a broader context than had been customary and that inquiry should not be limited to such phenomena as sexual and aggressive behavior. She proposed that each child be evaluated along several **developmental lines**, or dimensions of human functioning, each outlined as a sequence in the child's maturation leading, in general, from dependence and self-orientation to self-mastery and healthy relations with others. Using these developmental lines, both the level and the sequence of a child's development can be assessed. By taking this perspective of advancement along a developmental line, it is possible to assess each individual child's progression from infancy to maturity. An example of a developmental line is presented in table 3.1. Other developmental lines include the progression from suckling to rational eating, which starts with nursing and advances to self-determination of eating; and from wetting and soiling to bowel–bladder control.

Anna Freud's contribution to the description of the **defense mechanisms** expanded Sigmund Freud's original conception. As you will recall, in Chapter 2, we discussed 5 defense mechanisms (see pages 45–47). Anna Freud (1946) outlined 10 defense mechanisms: regression; repression; reaction formation; isolation; undoing; projec-

TABLE 3.1   An Example of a Developmental Line

FROM EGOCENTRICITY TO COMPANIONSHIP

- A selfish, self-focused outlook on the world; other children either are not noticed at all or are perceived only in their role as destroyers of the mother-child relationship and as rivals for parental love.

- Other children are related to as lifeless objects, as if they were toys to be handled, pushed around, and sought out and discarded, as the mood dictates; no response, either positive or negative, is expected from them.

- Other children are related to as partners in carrying out a specific task like playing a game, building with blocks, destroying something, or causing mischief of some kind; the length of the partnership is determined by the task and thus is secondary to it.

- Other children are related to as partners and as people in their own right, independent of any particular activity; the child can admire, fear, compete with, love, or hate them, identify with their feelings, acknowledge and respect their wishes, and share possessions with them on a basis of equality.

Source: A. Freud (1965, pp. 78–79).

tion; introjection; turning against the self; reversal; and sublimation, or displacement. At times, Anna Freud discussed additional mechanisms of defense, and some writers have developed yet other useful catalogs of defense mechanisms. Anna Freud also made significant contributions to the theory of how defenses develop. She explored the relations between developmental level and choice of defense, and she was one of the first to focus on the normal, adaptive functions served by some defense mechanisms—their capacity to be useful in the child's adjustment to the external world.

HEINZ HARTMANN: THE AUTONOMOUS EGO

Heinz Hartmann is widely acknowledged as the father of ego psychology. Following Freud's (1937) statement that "id and ego are originally one," Hartmann postulated that both id and ego emerged out of an early, undifferentiated phase. Each system has its origin in inherent predispositions, and each has its own independent course of development. The ego, according to Hartmann, is not motivated solely by instinctual—that is, sexual and aggressive—objectives; in Hartmann's view, outer reality is also a determining factor in ego functioning. The ego is autonomous and seeks actively to adapt to the world around it.

Hartmann suggested that ego defenses could serve healthy purposes as well as combat dangerous instincts. The ego is not always in conflict with either id or superego; it operates often in a "conflict-free" sphere in which it pursues such processes as perceiving, remem-

BOX 3.1   Anna Freud, Heinz Hartmann, Robert White

Anna Freud.

Heinz Hartmann.

Robert White.

Anna Freud (1895–1982), the youngest of Sigmund Freud's six children, became her father's companion, confidante, and colleague. Trained as a teacher and as a psychoanalyst, Anna Freud specialized throughout most of her career in child analysis. In London, from the late 1930s, she directed a complex of services for children that included both treatment and education at the nursery–kindergarten level. The author of several books and over a hundred papers, Anna Freud contributed to all fields concerned with the child, including pediatrics, medicine, education, and the law, and her awards and honorary degrees were numerous.

Heinz Hartmann (1894–1970) took his M.D. degree at the University of Vienna and began his career at the Psychiatric and Neurologic Institute in Vienna. Hartmann underwent his training analysis (all classical psychoanalysts must undergo psychoanalysis with another analyst) with Sigmund Freud and then served as an instructor and training analyst at the Vienna Psychoanalytic Institute. After brief periods in Paris and Lausanne, Hartmann moved, with his wife and two sons, to New York, where he opened a private practice and joined the faculty of the New York Psychoanalytic Institute. Hartmann was president of the International Psycho-Analytical Association for a number of years as well as editor of the *Internationale Zeitschrift für Psychoanalyse.*

Robert W. White (1904–   ) obtained his B.A., M.A., and Ph.D. at Harvard University, where he became chairman of the Department of Social Relations and director of the Harvard Psychological Clinic. At Harvard, where he remained till his retirement, White was a colleague of Gordon Allport (Chapter 10), Erik Erikson (this chapter), and Henry Murray (Chapter 9). In spite of their close association, all of these personality theorists worked relatively independently of each other, and their theories developed along rather different lines. White has also been interested in personality assessment, in psychotherapy—specifically, in patient–therapist interaction—and in psychopathology. His classic text in abnormal psychology, *The Abnormal Personality*, is at this writing in its fifth edition. White now lives in Marlborough, New Hampshire, where he continues to write and study.

bering, thinking, and problem solving in adapting to one situation or another. Thus, its defenses may sometimes be used to deal with non-pathological conflicts between different ego processes or aims.

Hartmann's important contribution to ego psychology lies in his effort to describe the ego and its development in broader terms. The ego, for Hartmann, was more responsive to reality, or the external world, and functioned independently of the id. Thus, Hartmann's conception, in which the ego served to help the person adapt and cope, could account for nonpathological functioning in a manner that Freudian theory could not. Hartmann's work also contributed to making psychoanalytic theory more appealing to psychologists, who were interested in exploring such ego processes as perception, memory, and thinking.

ROBERT W. WHITE: THE EGO'S NEED FOR COMPETENCE

Robert White's influential writings expanded on the psychoanalytic theory of the id and its drives and rejected the idea that the sole motivation for behavior was drive reduction and the satisfaction of biological needs. According to White (1959), the muscles, and the brain, the eyes, and other sensory organs require activity for growth and health. Thus, human beings seek stimulation; they do not remain passive or strive exclusively for a lessening of drives. As examples of human drives toward stimulation, White describes the play of the infant and toddler, defining a new motive that he calls **effectance motivation**: "Effectance thus refers to the active tendency to put forth effort to influence the environment" (1963, p. 185). When efforts of this sort are successful, the person feels competent. **Competence**, one of the most important concepts in White's (1959) theorizing, is the ability of a child, adolescent, or adult to deal with the world, both animate and inanimate, in a successful manner, permitting the organism to grow, to mature, and to survive the challenges of life.

White's approach to the ego and his expanded conception of the ego led him, necessarily, to revise the psychosexual stages of personality development (White, 1960). Motives and drives that were not solely biological needed to be included in each stage so as to allow for other aspects of personality development. In the phallic stage, for example, White emphasizes not only the Freudian conception of the Oedipus complex but the child's developing competence in its use of imagination and fantasy. This competence is associated with growing language and communication skills as well as with the experience the child gains of the world as a function of its increasing mobility. In revising the psychosexual stages, White, like Erikson—whom we discuss next—has established a wider conceptual scheme for understanding both successful and deficient personality development.

ERIK H. ERIKSON

Many feel that Erik H. Erikson has breathed new life into psychoanalytic theory. Although some of his concepts differ from Freud's, Erikson has elaborated the structure of psychoanalysis and has reformulated its principles in the light of new discoveries and changing concepts. Erikson maintains that he has remained faithful to Freud's theory and that his contributions, which extend and elaborate psychoanalytic ideas, are not inconsistent with the fundamental tenets of Freudian psychoanalysis.

Erikson, like Anna Freud, Hartmann, White and other contemporary ego analytic theorists, is a good deal more concerned with the ego than with the id and superego. Erikson sees the ego as representing "man's capacity to unify his experience and his action in an adaptive manner" (1963, p. 15), and he makes the ego the master rather than the slave of the other two systems.

Erikson has built on Freud's concept of developmental stages, extending his own scheme through the entire life cycle, from birth to death. Erikson accepts the basic biological–sexual dynamics postulated by Freud. One of Erikson's major contributions, however, has been to emphasize the importance of the individual's interaction with the social environment in shaping personality; the ego has "roots in social organization" (1963, pp. 15–16).

A NEW, CREATIVE EGO

Building on and extending the work of Sigmund and Anna Freud and Heinz Hartmann, Erikson describes an ego that has creative qualities. It not only strives actively to adapt to its environment but finds creative solutions to each new problem that besets it. Even when thwarted, the ego responds with vigor, for it has a basic strength and flexibility.

One of Erikson's greatest contributions is his argument that the ego's nature is determined not only by inner forces but by social and cultural influences. Erikson's research in American Indian cultures, along with his observations of other cultures in European countries and in India, has permitted him to evolve quite a flexible theory of development, one that is neither culture specific nor time bound.

Many of the "ego qualities" that, as we will see, emerge in each stage of development reflect the influence of social and cultural factors. Although Erikson believes that such qualities as "basic trust" and "initiative" exist in rudimentary form in early stages, he maintains that they develop and mature only through experience with the social environment.

As a practicing psychoanalyst, Erikson sees the vulnerability of the ego, its irrational defenses, and the fateful effects on it of trauma, anxiety, and guilt. And he is keenly aware of the effects on the individual of restrictive or uncaring surroundings. But Erikson sees the ego as being adaptable and creative and as having some autonomy. Moreover, his external world is more favorable than Freud's. It is not entirely inhibitory and punitive but sometimes encourages and supports the individual. Thus Erikson sees the ego as being capable—sometimes with a little help from a therapist—of dealing effectively with its problems.

A PSYCHOSOCIAL THEORY OF DEVELOPMENT

In conceptualizing his eight-stage theory of development, Erikson turned to embryology (the division of biology that deals with the development of the organism from conception to birth) for the principle of **epigenesis**. According to this principle, a new, living organism develops out of an initially undifferentiated entity that is somehow programmed to develop all the organism's parts in sequence.

Erikson proposes that, just as our physical parts develop and grow, in a specific order, from a genetic design, so too do our egos, our psychological characteristics, evolve out of an earlier "ground plan." Although each positive ego quality that the ego acquires throughout the eight-stage life cycle—trust, autonomy, initiative, and so on—exists at birth in some form, it first becomes salient at a clearly specified time. For example, in the first stage of the life cycle, the baby may show something like autonomy as it "angrily tries to wriggle [its] hand free when tightly held" (Erikson, 1959, p. 53), but it is not until the second stage that the baby is ready and able to really assert itself and that those who care for it are ready to make their demands known.

The ego quality that emerges at each succeeding stage of life depends and builds on qualities developed in earlier stages. For example, if we trust ourselves and others (stage I), we can acquire autonomy (stage II)—we can feel safe being responsible for ourselves and can rely on others to encourage us yet allow us the space we need.

Erikson includes both psychosexual and psychosocial aspects of growth and change in his developmental scheme. His **psychosexual** components are modeled on Freud's developmental stages but differ from these in several ways. For example, Erikson places great emphasis on puberty and adolescence, which in his scheme precede the "genital" stage of adulthood.

But Erikson is most interested in the **psychosocial** component of development. He shows, in a framework of successive **psychosocial crises**, how each ego quality emerges in response to both the inner "ground plan" and the social environment and how it must establish and maintain itself against the challenge it confronts. By "crisis," Erikson means a turning point, a time when both potential and vulnerability are greatly increased, so that things may go either well or badly. For example, the crisis of the fourth stage pits the ego quality of indus-

BOX 3.2   Erik H. Erikson (1902–   )

Erik Erikson freely admits that his own life has probably influenced his theories in various ways. It does seem likely, at least, that Erikson's early feelings of confusion and alienation contributed to his famous concept of the identity crisis.

Erikson was born in Germany of Danish parents who separated before his birth. For many years, Erikson assumed that his German stepfather, a pediatrician, was his actual father; he never met his real father.

Because of his Danish background, Nordic looks, and Jewish heritage (his father was Christian, his mother and stepfather were Jewish), Erikson was not fully accepted by his schoolmates. His Jewish peers nicknamed him "the goy" (a Yiddish term for "gentile"), and his non-Jewish acquaintances considered him a Jew (Coles, 1970, p. 180).

At graduation from *gymnasium* (high school), Erikson "felt at a loss, out of place, and out of joint" (Coles, 1970, p. 14). He thought that he wanted to be an artist, but he was not ready to settle down. He began to wander through Europe, sketching and making extensive notes about everything he saw. After a year he enrolled at an art school but soon resumed his travels. Again he entered a school of art; not long after, he exhibited some of his woodcuts and etchings.

Erikson was 25 when he found what he really wanted to do. In 1927 he began to teach, in Vienna, at a small progressive school for American children. Many of the children's parents—and some of the children too—had come to Vienna to be analyzed by Freud or by one of his followers, and eventually Erikson met Freud and his family. Soon Erikson enrolled at the Vienna Psychoanalytic Institute and began a personal analysis with Anna Freud. Erikson was considered one of the institute's brightest and most promising students. He trained in both adult and child psychoanalysis, and he was graduated in 1933.

Like so many European professionals and academicians, Erikson was acutely aware of the worsening political climate of the 1930s. (Adolf Hitler, who was advocating the destruction of the Jews, became chancellor of Germany early in 1933; in 1934, the Austrian chancellor was murdered by the Nazis, and four years later Nazi Germany invaded and annexed Austria.) Thus, in 1933 Erikson moved to the United States, bringing with him his wife, the former Joan Serson—a Canadian-American who had come to Vienna to research the history of dance—and their children, Kai and Jon (their third child, Susan, was born in America). Settling in Boston, Erikson opened a private practice and became the city's first child psychoanalyst.

Erikson had been given appointments at the Harvard Medical School and at Massachusetts General Hospital, and he soon affiliated also with the Harvard Psychological Clinic and the Judge Baker Guidance Center, a pioneering clinic for the treatment of emotionally disturbed children. At Harvard, Erikson met many scholars whose ideas helped to shape his own—anthropologists like Margaret Mead, Gregory Bateson, and Ruth Benedict and psychologists like Henry Murray (Chapter 9) and Kurt Lewin (Chapter 8). As a member of Murray's research team, Erikson wrote a section in Murray's (1938) *Explorations in Personality* on the use of play in personality analysis.

From Harvard, Erikson moved to the University of California at Berkeley, where he wrote his first important book, *Childhood and Society* (1950, rev. 1963). Later, in protest at the university's dismissal of faculty members who refused to sign a loyalty oath or to give any information about their political affiliations, Erikson resigned his own position. (He stated that he was not a communist but refused nevertheless to sign the oath.) His letter of resignation, reprinted in Coles (1970), is an eloquent affirmation of his faith in the power of knowledge and of his belief that the freedom to entertain ''deep and often radical doubts'' is crucial to the development of adaptive, creative thinking. (The univer sity later reinstated Erikson and the others whom it had dismissed; it also offered Erikson a new post.)

After resigning from the University of California, Erikson moved to the Austen Riggs Center for psychoanalytic training and research, in Massachusetts, where he continued to explore the special problems of youth and began his studies in psychohistory. In 1960 he returned to Harvard as professor of psychology and remained there until his formal retirement in 1970. During this second period at Harvard, Erikson established his now famous course on ''The Human Life Cycle.''

At present, Erikson lives near San Francisco, where he serves as a consultant to Mt. Zion Hospital and the University of California's Health and Medical Sciences Program. He continues his theoretical pursuits; in addition to expanding on topics that he has addressed previously, he is now also emphasizing new areas of concern, such as adulthood and aging.

try against the challenge of possible inferiority: during the early school years, children are especially quick to master new skills, yet they are also particularly susceptible to feeling inferior if they fail.

Ego qualities are not ''achieved'' once and for all, nor are they acquired by forever overcoming challenges. ''What the child acquires at a given stage is a certain *ratio* between the positive and the negative which, if the balance is toward the positive, will help him to meet later crises with a better chance for unimpaired total development'' (Erikson, 1959, p. 61). The basic conflicts remain, and the human personality ''to remain psychologically alive, must resolve these conflicts unceasingly'' (p. 51); for instance, our trust in ourselves (self-confidence) may be challenged repeatedly throughout life as we try new and risky things. And we need a portion of some negative qualities to survive; for example, if we were totally trusting (stage I) of everyone and everything, we would be vulnerable to many dangers. If we were incapable of feeling guilt (stage III), we would be unable to learn responsible behavior toward other people.

In the sections that follow and in Table 3.2, which is presented now to give you an overview of the stages and their sequence, note that although the order of the stages is fixed, their timetable is not; a given individual may pass through these stages at either a faster or a slower pace. Thus, although we have indicated approximate age ranges for each of the eight stages, both in the text and in the table, the reader is warned not to take these age ranges as gospel. Erikson himself has tended to avoid indicating specific age periods, for he is concerned lest his developmental scheme be taken as inflexibly decreeing that, for example, a child *must* learn basic trust by his first birthday or that a young person *must* achieve her identity by the age of 20.

TABLE 3.2 *The Eight Stages of Development*

STAGE AND APPROXIMATE AGE RANGE	PSYCHO-SEXUAL ASPECT	PSYCHO-SOCIAL CRISIS	VIRTUE	MAJOR DEVELOPMENTS
I Infancy 0–1	Oral–Sensory	Trust versus Mistrust	Hope	The mother–baby relation lays the foundation for trust in others and in oneself, but it also presents the challenge of mistrust in others and lack of confidence in self. Hope is the enduring belief that one can achieve one's needs and wants.
II Early childhood 1–3	Anal–Muscular	Autonomy versus Shame, Doubt	Will	Learning self-control establishes a sense of independence, but the child may also develop shame and doubt about his or her capacities to operate autonomously. Will is the ability to make free choices and to control and apply oneself.
III Play age 3–6	Infantile Genital, Locomotor	Initiative versus Guilt	Purpose	Mobility and curiosity encourage the development of initiative in mastering the environment, but feelings of guilt over aggressiveness and daring may arise. Purpose is the ability to set and pursue goals confidently and without fear of punishment.
IV School Age 6–12	"Latency"	Industry versus Inferiority	Competence	Learning to control one's imagination and to perform school work develops industry, but children may also develop feelings of inferiority if they fail or think they fail to master tasks. Competence is the exercise of physical and intellectual capacities in the completion of work.
V Adolescence 12–20	Puberty	Identity versus Identity Confusion	Fidelity	A sense of uniqueness as a person, a desire for a meaningful role and place in society, and efforts to define self and goals lead to the development of a sense of identity. But puberty, physical growth, the necessity of leaving childhood, and uncertain values make this transition the most difficult of all, and the adolescent may become confused over who and what he or she is and wants to be. Fidelity, the capacity to be loyal to people and ideals, both results from and strengthens identity.

TABLE 3.2   (Continued)

STAGE AND APPROXIMATE AGE RANGE	PSYCHO-SEXUAL ASPECT	PSYCHO-SOCIAL CRISIS	VIRTUE	MAJOR DEVELOPMENTS
VI Young Adulthood 20–30	Genitality	Intimacy versus Isolation	Love	The wish to unite one's identity with those of others leads the person to seek intimacy, but a shaky identity may make one avoid relations with others and lead to isolation. Love is the capacity for mutual devotion in sharing relationships.
VII Adulthood 30–65		Generativity versus Stagnation	Care	The need to create things—children, ideas, products—leads to generativity; if this need is not expressed, the personality risks stagnation and impoverishment. Care is the capacity to care for and guide what has been generated—one's children, projects, and so on.
VIII Mature Age 65 +		Integrity versus Despair	Wisdom	Review of one's life, with a feeling of satisfaction that that life has had order and meaning within a larger order, leads to integrity; doubts and unfulfilled desires may produce despair and meaninglessness. Wisdom preserves and passes to others the accumulated knowledge and experience of the years.

Source: Erikson (1959, 1963).

Note also in Table 3.2 that the psychosexual aspects of Erikson's first four stages appear analogous to Freud's oral, anal, phallic, and latency stages. As already noted, Erikson extends psychosexual dynamics beyond the purely biological. Thus, for example, in the first stage, he discusses the baby's openness to and eagerness for all kinds of sensory stimulation; he does not limit this ''oral–sensory'' stage to experiences involving the mouth. For Erikson, social experience as well as genetic endowment influences the organism's development and functioning.

Notice too that Erikson places quotation marks around the term ''latency,'' indicating that he considers it a kind of shorthand expression for what he prefers to describe as the ''long delay of physical sexual maturation.'' In addition, Erikson describes a stage of ''puberty'' separate from the stage of ''genitality'' first described by Freud. Erikson has not yet specified additional psychosexual aspects beyond genitality, but it may be that his current study of adulthood and aging will produce such new formulations.

Table 3.2 has been designed not only as an overview but as an aid to the consolidation of what readers have learned. Thus, you may want to return to this table after you have read the entire section on the stages of development.

TRUST VERSUS MISTRUST. At the beginning of the first year of life, the baby spends most of its time eating, eliminating, and sleeping. Its ability to do all these things in a peaceful and relaxed way signals the appearance of the first ego quality, a sense of **basic trust**. As the baby spends more and more time awake, it becomes familiar with a growing number of sensual experiences that coincide with feeling good. The baby's mother becomes a familiar presence, and the baby learns that it can trust her to care for its needs.

The baby also learns that although its mother goes away, it can rely on her to return. This knowledge enables the baby to trust itself— to trust its ability to cope in its mother's absence. And every time its mother does return, the baby's certainty that she would come back is confirmed and strengthened. The baby's beginning ability to trust itself and the correlation of its inner beliefs with outer reality provide the baby with the first, rudimentary sense of ego identity.

In the best of circumstances, Erikson (1968) says, the gradual but inevitable separation of mother and baby as the baby matures seems to introduce a "dim but universal nostalgia for a lost paradise" (p. 101). This feeling of having been somehow deprived is prototypical of the **basic mistrust** that also evolves during this stage. Throughout life, trust must be strong enough to maintain itself against the powerful sense of having been abandoned. A sound relationship with the mother that "combines sensitive care of the baby's individual needs and a firm sense of personal trustworthiness' is the essential ingredient in a lasting sense of trust (Erikson, 1963, p. 249).

As the baby learns that its trust in its parents is justified, it learns that **hope**, the first virtue to arise, is something that can be realized. And, gradually, it learns which hopes are possible and which are not; it learns to abandon useless hopes and to focus on those that can be fulfilled.

AUTONOMY VERSUS SHAME AND DOUBT. The crisis that pits a spirit of **autonomy** against a tendency to feel ashamed and doubtful of one's own powers generally occurs during the second and third years of life. As it begins to be highly mobile and self-propelled, the child must learn what it may and may not do. Its constant pursuit of new experiences leds it into a head-on conflict with two demands: that it submit to being controlled by others and that it learn to control and modulate itself.

As people move through Erikson's eight stages of development they gain new qualities and learn new skills, and each new quality or skill builds on those acquired earlier. Having learned, as a baby, to trust others, as well as himself (Stage I), the toddler has the courage to stand, and later walk, on his own (Stage II). The schoolchild can apply herself to her studies (Stage IV) because she has learned to trust her own ability, to take initiative, (Stage III), and to rely on the caring and rewarding characteristics of others. The teenager (Stage V) who has learned trust and application to a task can confidently confront the dual tasks of establishing an identity and finding a place in the world of her peers. Young parents, who have found their own identities and have developed a capacity for intimacy (Stage VI) can turn their creative energies to nurturing and teaching others (Stage VII). Older people (Stage VIII) can give expression to all they have learned and experienced as they also explore new areas, such as poetry-writing.

Erikson, like Freud, sees toilet training as an area in which these demands are strongly felt. For Erikson, however, elimination is only one of many spheres in which the child confronts challenges to its need to assert itself. Exploring the contents of kitchen cabinets, walking without holding its mother's hand, staying up late—in these and many other of its endeavors the child must submit its will to others.

Gradually, the child learns that controlling itself gives it a feeling of pride and that failing to do so brings feelings of **shame** and **doubt**. Although the parents encourage and support the child in the experience of new situations and thus promote freedom of self-expression, they also resort to shaming techniques to tame the child's willfulness. Too much shaming may lead the child to rebel or leave it with a lasting sense of insecurity.

The virtue of **will** develops out of the child's earliest efforts at self-control and its observations of the superior will of others. The capacity to make free choices and to restrain and apply oneself increases gradually as the child gains in powers of attention and in the ability to manipulate things, to move about on its own, and to talk.

INITIATIVE VERSUS GUILT.   In the third stage, roughly the fourth and fifth years of life, the ego quality of **initiative** enables the child to plan and set about tasks. The child is eager to learn and learns quickly. It begins to master skills and tries hard to perform well.

The danger in this stage is the development of **guilt**. The child has already begun to learn what is forbidden, but its ambitions are unlimited and it may become aggressive and manipulative in trying to achieve its goals. Its growing capacities may lead it to dare too much.

Sexual fantasies in particular may arouse guilt. Remember that in the Freudian system, this is the time of the Oedipus complex. For Erikson, however, the greater significance of this period lies in its manifestation of the general conflict between the generations. As the child develops a "sense of moral responsibility" (superego), it experiences severe conflict between the inner urges that propel its growth and the parental guidelines that it is now expected to make its own.

The difficulty of the child's task may be increased by the tendency of its superego to be more restrictive than its parents intended. Or the child may develop lasting resentment if it finds its parents "trying to get away with the very transgressions" the child now cannot tolerate in itself (Erikson, 1963, p. 257). As it gives up some of its hopes and fantasies, Erikson says, the child may suppress an "inner powerhouse of rage" (1963, p. 257).

The virtue of **purpose**, which is the courage to pursue goals without fearing punishment or guilt, develops through play, which is now the child's major activity and, according to Erikson, vitally important for its development. In play, the child learns to master reality by repeating difficult situations and tasks and by finding out what things are for and experimenting with how to make them work. By imitating adults in its play, the child learns to anticipate future roles.

INDUSTRY VERSUS INFERIORITY.   More or less equivalent to the Freudian period of latency, between the ages of 6 and 12, the fourth stage of life is ''only a lull before the storm of puberty'' and ''socially a most decisive stage'' (Erikson, 1963, p. 260). A sense of **industry** develops as the child learns to control its lively imagination and to apply itself to formal education. Indeed, ''such is the wisdom of the ground plan that at no time is the child more ready to learn quickly and avidly, to become big in the sense of sharing obligation, discipline, and performance'' (Erikson, 1968, p. 122). Gradually, its interest in play is surpassed by a concern to produce and to learn how to use the tools of work. The danger in this stage is that if the child fails—or is made to feel that it has failed—to master the tasks of school and home, it may develop a lasting sense of **inferiority**.

It is only through the child's application to work and its development of a sense of industry that the virtue of **competence**—''the exercise of dexterity and intelligence in the completion of tasks'' (Erikson, 1964, p. 124)—emerges. The child needs instruction and methodology, but it is important that it apply its intelligence and abounding energy to some undertaking—school, chores at home, manual skills, art, sports, or whatever—lest it develop the feeling of being less able than others.

IDENTITY VERSUS IDENTITY CONFUSION.   At this point, at the onset of the teens, Erikson's model of psychosocial development greatly expands and deepens the Freudian portrayal of the life cycle. It is in this fifth stage of the cycle, which for Freud marked the person's entry into the final, adult (or ''genital'') stage of life, that the young person, according to Erikson, is just beginning to form an identity. During this stage, which lasts from puberty, at about age 12, to the end of the teens and sometimes a bit beyond, adolescents begin to sense their individuality. They become aware that they have the strength to control their own destinies and feel the need to define themselves and their goals. Adolescents want to take their place in society, whether in more or less conventional roles or in roles that challenge established ways. This, then, is a time for making plans.

But it is also a time of more radical change than ever before. ''Genital puberty floods body and imagination with all manner of impulses, . . . intimacy with the other sex approaches and is, on occasion, forced on the young person, and . . . the immediate future confronts one with too many conflicting possibilities and choices'' (Erikson, 1968, pp. 132–133). Among these choices, the most difficult,

Erikson (1968) says, is that of an occupation. Suddenly one has to make, for oneself, decisions that have long-term consequences.

It is not surprising, then, that adolescents often experience **identity confusion**. They are enormously conflicted about whether and how to give expression to their strong sexual urges. They want to make important decisions but feel unprepared. They desperately want to participate in society but are afraid of making mistakes and of being misled. Thus they are self-conscious and often embarrassed, and their behavior is inconsistent. At one moment they may withdraw for fear of being rejected or disappointed; the next minute they may abandon themselves in an intimate relationship or a cause.

Often disturbing to parents and others is a teenager's development of a **negative identity**—a sense of being potentially bad or unworthy. Usually, the young person deals with such a negative identity by projecting it onto others: "They're the ones who are bad, not me." But sometimes the adolescent embraces a negative identity: one young woman, the daughter of a school superintendent, dropped out of high school but continued to hang around the school grounds, occasionally being arrested for vandalism of school property. Some young people look for their identities in counterculture movements that espouse values that are completely opposite to the values they were taught at home.

Adolescents often overidentify with heroes—such as rock stars—or form cliques that confer a kind of collective identity on them and in which they stereotype themselves, their ideals, and their enemies. These behaviors are part of their effort to understand themselves and to formulate values.

Stereotyping and projecting undesirable characteristics can lead to prejudice, discrimination against others, and even crime. However, the capacity to distinguish between good and bad is also part of the readiness for ideological involvement.

As they explore ideologies, adolescents experience the human need to belong to some particular kind of people. They begin to test for the sort of group they want to be part of, be it ethnic or religious or designed to renew or change the social structure.

In their identifications and cliques, adolescents test their capacities for loyalty, and it is the ability "to sustain loyalties freely pledged in spite of the inevitable contradictions of [other] value systems" (Erikson, 1964, p. 125) that Erikson calls **fidelity**. To be faithful to one's values, one needs to be developing a pretty firm sense of identity. At the same time, fidelity supports a continuing sense of identity: the more one adheres to one's values, no matter how they may be challenged, the more certain one becomes of one's identity.

Some young people in this age group are not ready to resolve their identity crisis and need a period of delay. Erikson has called such a period a **psychosocial moratorium**, by which he means a time during which adult commitments are postponed. How such moratoriums are expressed in different societies at different times is an interesting topic in itself. In our present culture, they frequently comprise periods of "dropping out," as youths prepare themselves to make the kinds of decisions they must about their future adult roles.

INTIMACY VERSUS ISOLATION.   In the sixth stage, the years of young adulthood—roughly the twenties—people are ready and eager to unite their identities with those of others. Young adults seek relationships of **intimacy**—friendships and working relationships as well as loving, sexual relationships. They are ready to develop the strengths they will need to fulfill commitments to others, even though commitment may call for sacrifice and compromise.

Earlier sexual encounters are little more than efforts to define a person's own sexual identity; "each partner is really trying only to reach himself" (Erikson, 1968, p. 137). But now true sexual genitality can develop. With a firm sense of identity, the person is ready to share himself or herself in a trusting relationship.

Isolation, the danger of this stage, is the inability "to take chances with one's identity by sharing true intimacy" (Erikson, 1968, p. 137). A shaky identity may combine with a fear of responsibility to prevent an individual from forming any really close relationships.

It is only after people have developed a solid sense of who they are and what they want their lives to be that they can develop this stage's virtue of **love**. According to Erikson, love is a "mutuality of devotion" that overcomes the inevitable antagonisms between people who differ in personality, experience, and roles.

GENERATIVITY VERSUS STAGNATION.   The seventh stage, which encompasses the years of adulthood—from about ages 30 to 65—sees the development of **generativity**, the "concern for establishing and guiding the next generation" (Erikson, 1968, p. 138). In general, this means that adults want to have children to whom they can transmit their values. More broadly, generativity includes productivity and creativity. Human beings also need to generate products and ideas, and some people fulfill the "parental drive" in this way rather than by raising children. By not giving expression to the need for generativity, one risks **stagnation**, in which the personality becomes impoverished and regresses into self-concern.

Care is the "widening concern for what has been generated" (Erikson, 1964, p. 131). It is the need to look after others and to teach them. Teaching fulfills our need to feel that we are important to others; it also helps to keep us from becoming overly concerned with ourselves. Care and teaching ensure that a culture will survive. The experience and knowledge that each of us accumulates is thus preserved and protected.

INTEGRITY VERSUS DESPAIR.   When people have guided, cared for, and taught others, they reach the eighth and last stage—which begins at about age 65—in which the ego quality of **integrity** appears. They perceive that their lives have had an order and a meaning within a larger order. They can see that others have lived differently, but they are prepared to defend the dignity of their own life-styles.

One creates one's own life-style within the culture or civilization in which one lives. Thus, the integrity of one's life-style becomes, in a sense, one's inheritance from oneself. Quoting the Spanish dramatist and poet, Pedro Calderón de la Barca, Erikson (1963) says that integrity is the "patrimony" of the soul (*el honor es patrimonio del alma*). That is, we inherit our integrity from ourselves; our integrity reflects all that we have been and done and achieved.

The danger is that in contemplating the ups and downs of one's life and the nearness of death, one may feel **despair**. One may feel that one's life has been without meaning and that there is now no time to go back and begin again.

But if integrity outweighs despair, one acquires the virtue of **wisdom**, which maintains and conveys the integrity of accumulated knowledge. Although older people function somewhat more slowly, they may retain a playfulness and a curiosity that they can use to sort out and integrate their experience. They can represent to the young a feeling of completeness that can counteract the feeling of being helpless and dependent, of being finished with life.

RITUALIZATION, RITUAL, AND RITUALISM: SOCIOCULTURAL ASPECTS OF DEVELOPMENT

Erikson (1966, 1977) has further elaborated his psychosocial stages of development in his formulation of what we might call the sociocultural phenomena of ritualization, ritual, and ritualism. These phenomena develop according to Erikson's epigenetic principle, and they add important new dimensions—again, of both strength and weakness—to his developmental scheme.

Each developmental stage is characterized by a **ritualization**, a somewhat playful, culturally patterned way of doing something in interaction with others (Erikson, 1977). The ritualization is an agreed-upon interplay between at least two persons; it is repeated "at meaningful intervals and in recurring contexts," and it has adaptive value for both participants (Erikson, 1966, p. 602). The earliest ritualization, which we will discuss in a moment, is the encounter between the mother (or the mothering person) and her baby.

In adulthood, the ritualization becomes the **ritual**, an activity engaged in by a community of adults to mark an important event of a recurring nature. The ancients, for example, celebrated the summer and winter solstices. We mark events in the life cycle such as baptism, coming of age, graduation, and marriage with special rites. The clearest example of ritual is probably found in religious activity: people renew or affirm their faith by attending prescribed "services" on a regular basis; holy days are marked by special rites. But, as we will see, rituals abound in everyday life. The mother–baby ritualization we have described evolves into the adult ritual of encounter with another person.

Ritualizations integrate the young into society by teaching them to fulfill their needs in ways that are acceptable to the culture. Ritualizations ensure young people's belongingness in their culture by drawing them into a shared vision of how things should be; they replace infantile omnipotence with a sense of power shared with others, and they deflect feelings of unworthiness to outsiders, who do not know the "right" way of doing things. Ritualizations help to prepare the young to become ritualizers themselves, and they provide a foundation for the identity that will be sealed in adolescence.

Two qualities that are also characteristic of play, as Erikson (1963) defines it, give the ritualization its playful aspect. The ritualization gives the child the opportunity to create models of reality and then to master that reality by experiment and planning. In addition, the ritualization, as simply the forerunner of the formal ritual, allows a certain amount of freedom to the participant (the playing person, according to Erikson, must be able to choose what he or she does without compulsion and to do it without feeling limited in time and space). At the same time, because adults, who are the agents of ritualization, strongly encourage the child to take part, the ritualization does contain some elements of compulsion.

The ritualization can be distorted into a **ritualism**, in which a person's attention becomes focused exclusively on self. Ritualisms lead people to become more concerned with their own performance than with their relations with each other or with the meaning of what they do.

Ritualisms are not playful, for they are performed compulsively. Like the ritualizations from which they are derived, they tend to be culturally patterned; within a given culture, ritualisms labeled aberrant, deviant, or abnormal do show similarities. Nevertheless, ritualisms can be quite idiosyncratic.

Ritualisms often involve other people but, in a sense, they deny the existence of others. The person dominated by ritualisms zeros in almost exclusively on his or her own needs and wishes; it is impossible for such a person to interact with others in a mutually satisfying way.

INFANCY. Most mothers (in Western cultures, at least) do certain things each time they approach their babies: they gaze at their babies, touch and cuddle them, check to see if anything is hurting them. And babies generally respond by gazing back, nestling, making sounds of pleasure, and so on.

As the mother talks to her baby and calls it and herself by name, and as the baby responds, the existence and importance of both baby and mother are affirmed. Such "mutuality of recognition" is an important element in ritualization. Each time mother and baby meet, the bond between them is strengthened. Ritualizations are thus also a way of overcoming the ambivalence that characterizes all human relations: in affirming positive bonds, the importance of negative feelings may be diminished.

Erikson calls the ritualization of infancy **numinous**, to suggest that the baby's sense of its mother's presence has a degree of awe, or mystery. The numinous is a sort of "sense of a hallowed presence" (Erikson, 1977, p. 89). In adulthood, it is experienced most often in the ritual of **encounter with another person**, where it is seen as mutual respect. The numinous can also be found in reverence for an admired leader.

In this first stage of life, developing trust includes the realization that no one is perfect. If the baby learns to accept its mother's occasional absence, and if the mother accepts the baby's behavior, good and bad, the adult will allow both self and other to fail from time to time. If people do not trust themselves and others, however, they can be caught up in an unending search for perfection in which the numinous ritualization is distorted into blind worship, or the ritualism of **idolism**. People may idolize others because they do not trust themselves, or they may idolize themselves because they do not trust others.

CHILDHOOD. In the **judicious** ritualization, the child begins to judge right and wrong in itself and others. This ritualization becomes the adult ritual of the **courtroom trial** in which innocence and wrongdoing are assessed.

Learning to judge people means learning to distinguish between "us" and "them," and in this stage we can see the beginning of prejudice, or **pseudospeciation**. The human being has a built-in tendency to think of the "subspecies" to which he or she belongs—family, class, tribe, nation—as "*the* human species" (Erikson, 1968, p. 41). A sense of irreversible difference between one's own and other "kinds" can attach itself not only to evolved major differences among human populations but to small differences that have come to loom large (Erikson, 1977). In the form of ingroup loyalties, pseudospeciation can contribute to human beings' highest achievements; in the form of outgroup enmities, it can express itself in clannishness, fearful avoidance, and even mortal hatred.

The ritualism of **legalism** is sticking outwardly to moral or legal principles without any true sense of moral responsibility. As Erikson (1977) points out, courtroom proceedings, which must establish legal guilt and deter potential crime, are often far removed from the "subjective processes which make a person feel morally liable" (p. 97).

PLAY AGE.   In the **dramatic** ritualization, the child draws from its own fantasies, and from the fantasy world of books and other sources, to create small plays in which good characters conquer evil ones. Thus, the child plays out the question of what it dares to do and what will bring guilt. The major adult ritual that derives from this ritualization is the **theater** and other **dramatic forms**.

The danger here is the ritualism of **impersonation**, which is a negative kind of role playing. A person may even assume a role that risks "mortal danger to the self and others" (Erikson, 1977, p. 102), such as that of a delinquent or a drug abuser.

SCHOOL AGE.   In the **formal** ritualization, the child's learning of the proper way to perform tasks gives it a sense of quality and craftsmanship. This prepares the child for the adult ritual of **work**. All work, whether it be finishing wood or designing a space laboratory, has a formal methodology, a correct standard of performance.

Formalism is a striving for perfection in which the person becomes concerned almost exclusively with the doing itself rather than with the substance of the activity or its outcome. An extreme example of this ritualism is the obsessive handwashing engaged in by certain neurotics.

ADOLESCENCE.   From here on, Erikson does not specify the rituals that derive from given ritualizations. Clearly, ritualization and ritual occur closer and closer in time as one moves through the life cycle, and one might almost say that in the last four stages, the ritualization describes the ritual. Nevertheless, here and in Table 3.3, we have suggested some specific rituals for the last four stages, and you may want to try thinking of others. (Note that because the "three R's" outlined in Table 3.3 evolve throughout Erikson's eight developmental stages, column 1 essentially repeats column 1 of Table 3.2. The two tables can usefully be studied together.)

The adolescent ritualization of **ideology** is a "solidarity of conviction" that integrates earlier ritualizations into a coherent set of ideas and ideals. A firmly held ideology provides a general pattern for life and prepares one to become a ritualizer in the lives of others.

Some rituals that might be traced to this ritualization would be events that affirm one's chosen way of life, such as ceremonies of graduation and investiture (e.g., being ordained in a church or sworn into office) or promotion.

TABLE 3.3   Erikson's Three R's

STAGE	RITUALIZATION	RITUAL	RITUALISM
I Infancy	Numinous	Encounter with another person	Idolism
II Childhood	Judicious	Courtroom trial	Legalism
III Play Age	Dramatic	Theater, other dramatic forms	Impersonation
IV School Age	Formal	Work	Formalism
V Adolescence	Ideology	Affirming important life choices	Totalism
VI Young Adulthood	Affiliation	Being with others	Elitism
VII Adulthood	Generational	Caring for others	Authoritism
VIII Mature Age	Integral	Affirming one's legacy, wisdom	Sapientism

Source: Erikson (1966, 1977).

The ritualism of this stage is **totalism**, the insistence on certain "truths" within a narrow, closed system of ideas. Like idolism, totalism involves blind worship but of a system of beliefs rather than of a specific person.

YOUNG ADULTHOOD.   The **affiliative** ritualization reflects the fact that as we love, maintain friendships, and work, we share ourselves with others. Marriage is probably one of the best examples of a ritual of affiliation, and it may be followed by such rituals as a couple's way of being with one another at the day's end (e.g., discussing the day's events over a drink or jogging together for a half hour), taking a vacation, or celebrating an anniversary. Other rituals of this stage might include regular social activities (e.g., playing racquetball with a friend once a week) and ceremonies of initiation into organized groups.

The ritualism of **elitism** can be seen in the formation of exclusive groups. Elitism can be based on almost any interest or concern; it need not involve specific ideology, as does totalism.

ADULTHOOD.   In the **generational** ritualization, the adult—as parent, teacher, producer, healer—acts as a transmitter of values. Related rituals might include the giving of gifts or rewards for good performance in school or visiting grandparents and other relatives on special holidays or in the context of family reunions.

The ritualism that may develop in this stage is **authoritism**: people may seize and use authority without either justification or concern for those who are ruled.

MATURE AGE.   In the **integral** ritualization, the old personify wisdom and affirm "the meaning of the cycle of life" (Erikson, 1977, p. 112). A ritual of this stage—not without its negative connotations—is retirement from the official labor force. Other rituals might be the counterparts of those of the preceding stage—visits with children, grandchildren, and other relatives. The last rituals are probably those of dying and death.

For the older person who has not achieved integrity, there is the danger of a last ritualism: **sapientism**, the pretense of being wise, may be adopted to hide a lack of wisdom, perhaps a feeling of despair.

RESEARCH EMPHASES AND METHODS
Like other psychoanalytic theorists, Erikson has based many of his conceptions on his therapeutic work. His research and writing on identity, for example, is well grounded in clinical observation and experience. Erikson's theories, however, are also derived from his observations of ordinary young people—adolescents as well as young children, the latter in play situations that Erikson first used in child psychotherapy. His conceptions are informed as well by his studies of the lives of historical figures and by his sociocultural studies, space precludes our discussing the latter here.

PLAY IN THERAPY AND RESEARCH.   Erikson was one of the first child analysts to make extensive use of play in therapy. His early use of toys—building blocks, dolls, and so on—in helping a child to express its deepest concerns has encouraged the use of this sort of technique by many other child analysts. And he has paraphrased Freud—who called dreams the "royal road to the unconscious"—in asserting that play is the "royal road" to understanding the young ego's efforts to make sense of its experience. Children, Erikson says, often reveal their concerns more clearly in play than in words. In one of his few published case studies, for example, Erikson describes how 3-year-old Sam, who believed that he had made his grandmother die, kept building things that looked like coffins with his blocks. When Erikson suggested to Sam that maybe he was afraid he would die too, Sam was able to release his terrifying feelings.

Erikson's success with play in therapy led him to put together a standard set of toys and blocks that he used in several studies of ordinary young people. Best known is his study of a group of 300 10-to 12-year-old children, half boys and half girls, who were part of a University of California long-term (longitudinal) developmental study (Erikson, 1963, pp. 97–108). Erikson wanted to see how the children's "play" might correlate with other information about their lives, and he asked each child to make "an exciting scene out of an imaginary moving picture" (p. 98) and then to tell a story about the scene.

An unexpected finding was that the children's scenes revealed gender differences (see Fig. 3.1). Most girls placed human dolls in arrangements of furniture that looked like rooms. A few girls used blocks to enclose their scenes with low walls. Girls' scenes were generally calm but occasionally disrupted by a male doll or an animal rushing in and causing an uproar.

Boys used many blocks to build complex structures that usually included high towers. Boys' scenes had a lot of action. Traffic moved or jammed up in streets, police directed or halted the traffic, and animals and Indians moved about.

Noting that the girls' constructions tended to focus on calm "inner space" while the boys' scenes emphasized active "outer space," Erikson suggested that the "ground plan" of the body—that is, anatomic and physiological sex differences—seemed to influence this use of space. But, he pointed out, the play scenes were probably also influenced by traditional concepts of sex roles (Erikson, 1963, p. 106).

A number of critics (e.g., Caplan, 1979) have attacked these conclusions. In general, behaviorists and social learning theorists prefer an explanation of the children's constructions that invokes the kinds of toys that girls and boys are given and the kinds of activities in which they are encouraged from early on (see Maccoby and Jacklin, 1974). Feminist critics agree with this view, insisting that the observed differences can be due only to social and cultural influences (see, e.g., Millet, 1970). Erikson (1975) maintains, however, that behavior is always determined jointly by biological, psychological, and sociocultural factors.

PSYCHOHISTORY.   Psychohistory is the study of the lives of historical figures by means of both psychoanalytic techniques and historical methods of analysis. Although Freud examined the lives of several important figures (see, e.g., Freud, 1910, 1928, 1939), it was Erikson who really established this form of study, with essays on Adolf Hitler, leader of Nazi Germany, and Maxim Gorky, the Russian writer, first published in 1950 (Erikson, 1963). Erikson's best known studies are of the German religious reformer Martin Luther (Erikson, 1958) and Mohandas K. ("Mahatma") Gandhi (Erikson, 1969), the originator of the concept of nonviolent revolution and an early architect of India's independence. In 1970 Erikson's book on Gandhi won a Pulitzer prize and the National Book Award.

Life History versus Case History.   There is a major difference between what we hope to learn in studying the case history of a troubled person, on the one hand, and the life history of a famous figure, on the other. As Erikson's developmental scheme shows, all human beings confront conflicts throughout life. In analyzing a person in trouble, we

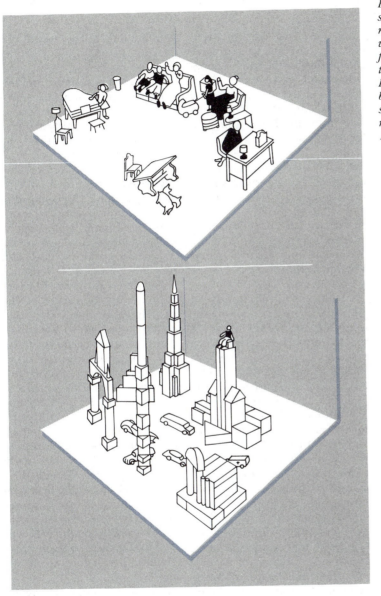

Figure 3.1   Children's play constructions. The scenes most commonly created by girls were rooms with furniture, in which human figures sat or engaged in such activities as playing the piano (a). Boys most often constructed buildings, high towers, and streets through which traffic moved busily (b). (From Erikson, 1963, pp. 100, 102, figures 6, 7.)

start with the knowledge that something has caused him or her to "fall apart"—to be unable to function adequately in some area of life. Our concern is to discover the conflicts that have caused the person's difficulties and, by finding ways to resolve these conflicts, to help the person get himself or herself together again.

BOX 3.3   Erikson's Gandhi

Invited to give a seminar on the human life cycle, in Ahmedabad, India, the city in which Mohandas K. Gandhi (1869–1948) came to prominence, Erik Erikson began to be newly aware of the role that "Mahatma" Gandhi had played in the labor relations of that city and of the significance of that role for Gandhi's rise to national leadership. ("Mahatma" means "great-souled"; it is a title given someone considered to be a wise and selfless leader.) As Erikson came to know people who had known and either supported or opposed Gandhi, he began to sense that the strike Gandhi led in 1918, in which he embarked on his first public fast, had a special meaning in Gandhi's development both as a person and as a leader of his country.

In *Gandhi's Truth* (1969), Erikson suggests that the months that led up to the Ahmedabad strike encompassed an identity crisis of proportions rivaling Gandhi's earlier identity crisis in South Africa, when his first encounter with racial prejudice was instrumental in changing him from a somewhat rigid, British-trained barrister to a passionate advocate of human rights. In 1918 Gandhi was 49, and he had returned to India only a few years earlier from more than 20 "sweet and bitter" years in South Africa, where he had evolved his concept of *satyagraha* (literally, "truth force"; more familiarly, "passive resistance" or "militant nonvio-

lence") and had put it to test, making, over the years, some small gains for the Indian population of South Africa.

Now, nearly a quarter of a century after the first major shift in the direction of his life, Gandhi was back in his own country. For some years, he had been advocating home rule for India, but the events leading up to and following the Ahmedabad "Event," as Erikson terms it, occasioned another major shift in him: he became no longer a loyalist, but a nationalist.

Gandhi perceived in the social and political climate of Ahmedabad in 1918 an opportunity to test on Indian soil his method of *satyagraha*, which involved putting one's whole self, including one's physical body, on the line to protest wrongs and seek their redress. Living conditions in Ahmedabad, a highly industrialized city, were bad. Sanitary measures were practically nonexistent, and many people lived in floorless lean-tos. The *monsoon* (a periodic wind that brings heavy, long-lasting rains) caused flooding, and it was impossible to ensure a supply of clean water. When an epidemic of plague broke out, mill owners offered a special "plague bonus" to workers who would stay in the city. One group of workers, who were not likely to leave because they were better paid than some and well settled in their homes, were not offered this bonus. This group threatened to strike and were locked

out by the mill owners. The lockout turned into a strike, and when the workers, who with Gandhi's support had initially stood firm, appeared disillusioned at their lack of success in moving the mill owners, Gandhi declared that he "would not take any food" until the increase the workers had requested was granted.

In his book, Erikson discusses Gandhi's early relations with his parents and suggests that Gandhi's closeness to his mother and his conflicts with his father may well have affected later turns in his life, such as his embracing of the principles of *satyagraha* and *ahimsa* (not only refraining from doing violence to another person but respecting the other person's "truth") and his vow of sexual abstinence, made in his early thirties. At the same time, Erikson points out, whereas we may want to know why neurotic people have been unable to work through early conflicts and get on with their lives, in the case of an historical figure, a leader, we want to know how the person did manage to work through such conflicts and in fact use them in accomplishing all that he or she has.

Although Gandhi was greatly troubled about his decision to undertake his first public fast and went through much agonizing self-inquiry even after the decision was made (for example, he felt that by fasting he was forcing the mill owners to give in out of pity rather than out of respect for the workers' rights), in the end he maintained his position. Four days later, the mill owners agreed to arbitration. Although the immediate gains from the strike were small, among its longer-lasting results were the creation of an industry-wide Board of Arbitrators and the foundation of the Ahmedabad Textile Labor Association. By 1967 the Ahmedabad textile workers had risen from being among the lowest paid in the country to being the highest paid (*The Statesman*, quoted in Erikson, 1969, p. 420).

Concluding his description of the Ahmedabad strike and fast, Erikson writes that by the time Gandhi's own account of it appeared in the *Bombay Chronicle*, he had recovered (from both the fast and his doubts about the rightness of it) and

had already chaired a meeting in Ahmedabad on the situation of indentured labor in the Fiji Islands, *had on March 22 inaugurated the Kheda Satyagraha by addressing 5000 peasants in Nadiad, and had traveled to Delhi to meet the Viceroy's Private Secretary in order to discuss the release of the Ali brothers, two prominent Muslim rebels. This, then, is the difference between a case history and a life-history: patients, great or small, are increasingly debilitated by their inner conflicts, but in historical actuality inner conflict only adds an indispensable momentum to all superhuman effort (Erikson, 1969, p. 363).*

When we study historical figures, however, we start with the knowledge that such individuals have changed the world in significant ways. This time we are interested in how these people have kept themselves together in spite of crises. We want to know how they have been able to transcend their conflicts and to inspire others either to acts of positive social change, as in the case of Gandhi and Luther, or of violence and destruction, as in the case of Hitler.

It follows that case histories and life histories examine specific kinds of conflict from different points of view. For example, suppose a man cannot hold on to a job because he refuses to accept others' authority. He lacks the initiative to develop and implement ideas of his own yet rebels against his boss's direction and then feels guilty. We will want to know why this man has been unable to resolve the conflict of authority (Oedipal conflict) and has apparently failed to develop autonomy and initiative.

When Erikson studied Gandhi, on the other hand, he was much less interested in why Gandhi's Oedipal conflict went unresolved than in how it was that Gandhi was able to act out his conflict of authority in such a way as to lead others in rebellion (see also Box 3.3). Millions of Indians followed his leadership to work for freedom from British rule.

Rules for Psychohistorical Studies. Erikson (1975) has laid down some strict rules for carrying out psychohistorical studies. He points out, for example, that one must pay close attention to when—that is, in what developmental stage of life—the subject of such a study made a particular statement and to how that statement fits in with the continuity of the person's life. One must also look carefully at what was going on in the world around the person at the time of his or her statement and at how contemporary events fit into the historical process.

Erikson also points out that psychohistorians run the risk of projecting their own needs and conflicts on the subjects of their study. Although he does not specify that the psychohistorian should be analyzed—as a psychoanalyst must be—he does seem to suggest that a personal analysis would help the researcher to become more aware of his or her own conflicts and of how they might influence the psychohistory.

Erikson is somewhat ambivalent about this new "industry" of psychohistorical analysis. Courses are now being taught at various universities, books have been published, and entire journals are devoted to the subject. Erikson's concern about all this activity is well founded, for the historian may well lack adequate training in psychology and psychoanalysis and the psychologist may lack adequate training in history. All too often, this set of circumstances leads to the production of psychohistorical works that are bad psychology, bad history, or, in some cases, both!

RESEARCH ON IDENTITY.   Many psychologists have been intrigued by Erikson's ideas on identity formation. James Marcia (1980), for example, and his students have published many studies that use an interview method devised by Marcia for evaluating identity status. In men, the interview assesses decision making and commitment regarding selection of an occupation, as well as religious and political beliefs. With women, the interview focuses on attitudes toward sexuality, in addition to religious and political beliefs. (In his early studies in the 1960s, Marcia did try to use the same parameters with both men and women. He reports, however, that for women, at least at that time, selection of an occupation did not appear to be as meaningful a category of response as were attitudes revolving around the expression of sexuality.) Based on their interview data and a set of specific scoring methods, to be quite reliable, Marcia and his co-workers are able to assign young people to four distinct identity statuses: identity achievement, foreclosure, identity diffusion, and moratorium. This four-category system seems to be an improvement on the simpler two-category system, of identity versus identity confusion, first proposed by Erikson.

According to Marcia, **identity achievement** comes about when the person has experienced a period of crisis but has resolved the crisis and made a commitment to, for example, certain occupational goals. People in the **foreclosure** status have made firm commitments but have not experienced a period of crisis. These young people often make their commitments on the basis of parental models. Persons in the **identity diffusion** status may or may not have experienced a crisis period but have as yet made no decisions or commitments. People in the **moratorium** status are in the midst of Erikson's "identity crisis"; they have not yet made firm commitments, but they are in the process

TABLE 3.4   *Marcia's Identity Status Categories*

IDENTITY STATUS	CRISIS	COMMITMENT
Identity achievement	Resolved	Made
Foreclosure	None experienced	Made
Identity diffusion	May or may not have been experienced	None made
Moratorium	In process	Vague signs evident

Source: Marcia (1980, Table 1).

of doing so. Table 3.4 summarizes Marcia's view of these four identity statuses.

Using this method of classifying people as to identity status Marcia (1980) has studied such personality variables as anxiety, self-esteem, authoritarianism, interactional style, moral reasoning and autonomy, and the development and change over time in identity status. As one might anticipate, there has been a good deal of debate about gender differences in identity formation and other identity processes. Future work may clarify some of the controversial issues. Clearly, identity is a key personality process for both men and women, and the college-age years are probably, for most people, the most critical for this important developmental process (Waterman, 1982). Erikson's seminal ideas on identity formation have stimulated a considerable amount of interest and research activity among personality psychologists. As Waterman, reviewing much of the recent research, concludes, ''The basic hypothesis embodied in Erikson's theory of identity development—that movement from adolescence to adulthood involves changes in identity that can be characterized as progressive developmental shifts—fares very well in empirical studies'' (1982, p. 355).

EVALUATION

Of the theories discussed in this chapter, it is Erikson's by far that has stimulated the greatest amount of research. Erikson's influence on personality psychology has been deeper and broader than has that of any of the ego psychologists. In general, the latter have contributed only minitheories; they have not provided the detailed or comprehensive portrait of the person that Sigmund Freud, Erik Erikson, and others whom we will study later in the book have offered.

Anna Freud's work is highly regarded by clinicians and teachers, especially by those concerned with children. The impact of her endeavors on education and on child psychotherapy will continue to be felt for some time. Her work, in general, however, has failed to stimulate much empirical research. Although her students clearly display her influence in their writings, they do not seem to be making original contributions or extending her work into new areas of personality study.

Heinz Hartmann's great contribution lies in his having liberated psychoanalysis from the psychology of the id, giving the ego room to function, and making it more accessible to psychological study. Hartmann clearly played a very important role in the early days of ego analytic theorizing when his fresh and bold ideas added a significant new dimension to our understanding of the structure of personality. His conceptions, however, have been absorbed into the ego analytic work of many theorists and clinicians; his own contribution was a partial one.

Robert White's ideas have interested psychologists in research on topics that had long been neglected, such as curiosity, exploration, and competence. His emphasis on these aspects of ego functioning expanded Sigmund Freud's original ideas and made the human being less a creature of solely biological drives. White's ideas continue to provide research impetus to psychologists. And they have greatly widened the array of phenomena that can be studied from a psychoanalytic point of view.

These three ego psychologists—Anna Freud, Hartmann, and White—have made important contributions to personality psychology. The influence of Anna Freud and of Hartmann has in general been felt most strongly in the area of clinical practice; White has had a greater impact on the mainstream of academic psychology.

Erik Erikson is highly regarded not only in academic and professional circles but in society at large. Unlike Sigmund Freud, Erikson is not a controversial figure. He has rarely taken strong issue with others' viewpoints, and, although his own work has been criticized on several grounds, he has never suffered the bitter kinds of attack made on Freud.

Psychologists find Erikson's theory of development and his concepts of identity and the identity crisis particularly attractive. In general, they prefer his emphasis on the psychosocial aspects of development to Freud's focus on psychosexual dynamics. Psychologists, psychoanalysts, and many others admire Erikson greatly for the acuteness of his observations, his sensible interpretations, and his deep compassion for everything human.

Four major criticisms of Erikson's work have been made. First, some writers view Erikson as being just as overly optimistic as, they think, Freud was excessively pessimistic. Erikson (1975) denies this charge, pointing out that for each psychosocial stage he posits a crisis and a specific negative ego quality (mistrust, shame, and so on) that denotes a lifelong source of potential anxiety. It is true, however, that

Erikson gives relatively little space in his writings to specific discussions of anxiety. And he tends to focus on its positive aspect: without anxiety, he says, "there is no human strength" (Erikson, 1975, p. 259).

Erikson is clearly as interested in the resolution of conflicts as he is in failure and breakdown. Unlike earlier psychoanalytic writers who focused almost exclusively on psychopathology, Erikson feels there is much to be gained from studying the growth and development of people who are not patients. In this approach, he is not alone, as you will see when we discuss such theorists as Abraham Maslow and Carl Rogers.

A second criticism is that Erikson has watered down Freudian theory, sacrificing the id and the unconscious to the ego and the conscious mind. This is not really a criticism of Erikson's theory but rather a complaint that he differs with Freud—who never claimed to have the ultimate measure of truth. Some think Erikson differs so greatly from Freud that he should not be considered a Freudian, but most observers do not hold this view.

A third criticism charges Erikson with supporting the status quo in suggesting that the individual must adjust to the ways of the society in which he or she grows up. What Erikson actually says is that we find our identity within the possibilities offered by our particular society and that these may include either stability or change. And Erikson's profound interest in people who have radically changed the societies in which they lived (e.g., Gandhi and Luther) makes it seem rather unlikely that he intends to advocate simply accepting one's lot.

A final and somewhat more serious criticism attacks the empirical bases of Erikson's theories. No one questions the amount and variety of his data; it is the use of these data that is at issue. With the exception of his studies of young people's play constructions, Erikson has not supported his hypotheses by means of controlled experimentation. In general, his concepts are based on personal observation, which cannot help but be somewhat subjective.

On the plus side, Erikson's overall psychosocial theory of human development is very appealing to psychologists, who generally prefer it to Freudian developmental theory. His ideas have been widely disseminated in other disciplines as well, notably education and educational psychology.

More important, Erikson's formulations provide a rich source of hypotheses for empirical test. As we have seen, for example, researchers are finding support for Erikson's theory in investigations of identity formation and identity status.

Erikson has emerged as one of the most highly regarded contemporary psychoanalytic theorists, and he has attracted the attention of many personality researchers. It seems likely that his thought will influence personality theory and research for a long time to come. Today, when behavioral and social scientists are increasingly focusing on problems of adulthood and aging, Erikson (1982) has turned his attention to these later stages of the life cycle. This current emphasis of Erikson's is as timely as was his highlighting of adolescent identity concerns before and during the height of the youth culture.

SUMMARY

1. Sigmund Freud modified and reshaped his theories throughout his life; his followers have continued this process and have applied Freudian theory in an increasingly broad range of situation.

2. The development of **ego psychology** brought about a major change in psychoanalytic thinking. After Freud himself began to devote more attention to the ego, others began to undertake serious study of the ego and its functions, emphasizing the ego's adaptive and creative aspects.

3. Ego psychology gave rise to the school of psychoanalytic thought known as **object relations theory**, which emphasizes the ways in which early relations with other people affect personality development.

ANNA FREUD

4. The **developmental line** provides a way of assessing a child's progress from dependence toward self-mastery in a number of areas of human functioning.

5. The ego makes use of 10 **defense mechanisms**: repression; projection; reaction formation; regression; isolation; undoing; introjection; turning against the self; reversal; and sublimation, or displacement. Choice of defense may be related to developmental level, and some defenses serve normal, adaptive functions.

HEINZ HARTMANN

6. The ego is motivated both by instinctual drives and by factors in the external world. The ego is not always in conflict with the id or the superego but functions in a **conflict-free sphere** where it pursues such processes as perceiving, remembering, thinking, and problem solving. The ego serves an important function in helping the person adapt to and cope with the external world.

ROBERT WHITE

7. The ego is motivated not only by the need to satisfy biological drives but by the need to explore, to learn, to master the environment.

8. **Effectance motivation** explains this human need for stimulation and activity. Making successful efforts to influence the environment

gives the person a sense of **competence**, which permits the person to grow and to meet life's challenges.

ERIK ERIKSON

9. The ego develops in response to both inner forces and the social environment. It is adaptive and creative, and it strives actively to help the person cope successfully with his or her world.

10. The **psychosocial theory of development** outlines a life cycle of eight stages, in each of which a positive **ego quality** (such as **basic trust**) must outweigh a negative one (such as **basic mistrust**) to permit the development of a **virtue** (such as **hope**).

11. By the principle of **epigenesis**, each new ego quality evolves at a different stage but is present in a "ground plan" at birth. And each ego quality and virtue depends on the development of each quality and virtue that has preceded it.

12. Although in each stage a balance is struck between positive and negative ego qualities, the individual continues to confront each of the conflicts described repeatedly throughout his or her life cycle.

13. Each stage is also characterized by a **ritualization** (such as the mother–baby interaction) that prepares the way for an adult **ritual** (such as the encounter with another person). But a ritualization may be distorted into a **ritualism** (such as blind worship of another).

14. In support of his psychosocial theory, Erikson has undertaken three primary types of research. Using **play** situations that evolved out of his therapeutic work with children, he has observed numbers of young people. And he has created the **psychohistory**, the examination of the life of a famous figure in history. He has interpreted all this research as supporting his theory, and his psychohistorical studies have served to illustrate it.

15. Researchers have elaborated Erikson's conception of identity formation, proposing four categories of **identity status**: **identity achievement**, **foreclosure**, **identity diffusion**, and **moratorium**. Research findings have given some support to the validity of these categories.

16. In general, the ego psychologists Anna Freud, Heinz Hartmann, and Robert White are seen as having made highly significant contributions to the advancement of psychoanalytic thinking but as not having created comprehensive theories of personality of their own.

17. Erikson has been criticized for neglecting the negative aspects of personality functioning, for having sacrificed some important aspects of Freudian theory such as the id and the unconscious, and for failing to support his hypotheses with controlled experimentation. On the other hand, many psychologists greatly prefer Erikson's psychosocial

theory to Freud's developmental theory. And, most important, Erikson's theory has provided a rich source of hypotheses for study; some of his conceptions are finding support in the research of a number of investigators.

SUGGESTED READING

The reader who would like a more detailed understanding of the ego psychology school of thought may want to look at Rapaport, ''A Historical Survey of Psychoanalytic Ego Psychology'' (1959), or Blanck and Blanck, *Ego Psychology* (1974).

Anna Freud's best known work is *The Ego and the Mechanisms of Defense* (1946), in which she expands on Sigmund Freud's formulations of the defense mechanism. Her *Normality and Pathology in Childhood: Assessments of Development* (1965) outlines her concept of the developmental line and discusses the use of developmental lines in working with both normal and disturbed children. A. Freud, *Introduction to Psycholoanalysis: Lectures for Child Analysts and Teachers* (1974) will acquaint you further with Anna Freud's thinking, and the application of her thought in the area of the law as it relates to the child is described in Goldstein, Freud, and Solnit, *Beyond the Best Interests of the Child* (1973). Lustman, ''The Scientific Leadership of Anna Freud'' (1967), and Dyer, *Her Father's Daughter: The Work of Anna Freud* (1983), offer biographical material and analyses of Anna Freud's scientific contributions.

Hartmann's *Ego Psychology and the Problem of Adaptation* (1958) is a revised and expanded version of his important 1937 paper in which he first presented his innovative ideas on the nature and functioning of the ego. For the student who wishes to explore Hartmann's works, two other books may be of interest: Hartmann, *Essays on Ego Psychology: Selected Problems in Psychoanalytic Theory* (1964), and Hartmann, Kris, and Lowenstein, *Papers on Psychoanalytic Psychology* (1964).

Robert White's important concepts of effectance motivation and competence are discussed in his ''Motivation Reconsidered: The Concept of Competence'' (1959), ''Competence and the Psychosexual Stages of Development'' (1960), and ''Ego and Reality in Psychoanalytic Theory: A Proposal Regarding Independent Ego Energies'' (1963). You may find *The Enterprise of Living: Growth and Organization in Personality* (1972) interesting to examine, as well as White's best known work on personality growth and functioning, *Lives and Progress* (1975). You may also want to look at White and Watt, *The Abnormal Personality* (1981).

Erik Erikson has described his psychosocial theory of development in greatest detail in *Identity and the Life Cycle* (1959), *Childhood and Society* (1963; first published in 1950), and *Identity: Youth and Crisis* (1968). These books also outline his conception of the ego, and the last of these books focuses particularly on ego identity and the identity crisis. *Insight and Responsibility* (1964) examines the virtues that appear in each developmental stage, and *Toys and Reasons* (1977) presents Erikson's conception of ritualization and ritualism.

In *Life History and the Historical Moment* (1975), Erikson discusses the psychohistory, and his *Gandhi's Truth* (1969) and *Young Man Luther* (1958) are probably the best examples of his work in this field. In view of Erikson's observation that many factors including one's intellectual persuasion and training may affect one's interpretation of a life, you may find it interesting to examine Domhoff's *Two Luthers: The Orthodox and Heretical in Psychoanalytic Thinking* (1970), which compares two quite different yet essentially Freudian views of Luther: Erikson's book and Norman O. Brown's *Life against Death* (1959). For some shorter works you might look at Erikson's essays on Adolf Hitler (Erikson, 1963) Maxim Gorky (Erikson, 1963), George Bernard Shaw (Erikson, 1968), William James (Erikson, 1968), and Thomas Jefferson (Erikson, 1974).

We noted earlier that Erikson's studies of people who radically changed society somewhat belie the criticism that he advocates sticking to the status quo. In this connection, you might like to read *In Search of Common Ground: Conversations with Erik H. Erikson and Huey P. Newton* (K. T. Erikson, 1973), recorded and edited by Kai T. Erikson, the well-known sociologist and Erikson's older son.

Two biographical studies of Erikson have been written. In *Erik H. Erikson: The Growth of His Work* (1979), Robert Coles, psychiatrist, former student of Erikson's, and later colleague, offers a fully rounded portrait of the man and his work. In *Erik H. Erikson: The Power and Limits of His Vision* (1976), Paul Roazen, who has also written a biographical study of Freud, examines some of the differences between Erikson's and Freud's theories.

Chapter four

4.

Our picture of the world only tallies with reality when the improbable has a place in it.

CARL G. JUNG

The Analytical Psychology of Carl Jung

"Tom's quite an **extravert**, don't you think?"

"No, that's just his **persona**. Actually, he's an **introvert**. He pretends to be sociable—smiles—laughs a lot—makes small talk. But he's really a very private person."

"Well, I think he's awfully attractive."

"*I* understand him—I know what he needs."

"What are you—some sort of **earth mother**?"

"Well, I guess I do need to take care of people."

"*I* don't want to take care of Tom—I want to play with him—he can take care of *me*."

"That's **the child** in you."

"No, come on—sometimes he's very paternal. He takes a puff on that pipe of his, you know, and then delivers some very profound thought—"

"That's when he's playing **wise old man**. But he can be so vulnerable—so, almost, feminine. Sometimes he seems to really feel what I feel—it's his **anima**, I guess. . . ."

All the terms emphasized in this imaginary conversation represent concepts developed by Carl G. Jung, the founder of analytical psychology. Like Freud, Jung was influenced by nineteenth-century developments in science and philosophy, such as the application of evolutionary theory to the understanding of human beings, the findings of archeology, and the comparative study of peoples of different cultures.

But Jung differed from Freud in a number of very important ways. (For an account of their relationship, see Box 4.1.) First, Jung rejected Freud's emphasis on the importance of sexuality, contending that the human being's sexual needs are only one part of his or her makeup—important, to be sure, but no more so than, say, the need to eat, the need for a spiritual life, or the need for specific religious experience.

BOX 4.1   The Reluctant Crown Prince

In the early years of the century, Sigmund Freud and Carl Jung learned of each other's work, and each perceived support for his ideas in the work of the other. Perhaps it is not so surprising, then, that when they met for the first time, in March 1907, they talked virtually nonstop for 13 hours!

The personal and professional relationship between these two giants of modern psychology lasted for 6 years. They corresponded on a weekly basis and visited one another from time to time, and Freud began to see Jung as his "crown prince" and successor (Freud was the older by about 20 years). But there were early hints of the coming discord; in one of his first letters, Jung expressed his reservations about Freud's "sexual theory" (McGuire, 1974, pp. 4–5).

Jung was also troubled by what he considered Freud's lack of understanding of spirituality—by Freud's insistence on seeing all evidences of humankind's "higher nature" as nothing but repressed sexuality. Freud could not agree with Jung's conception of a collective unconscious, even though Freud did accept the idea of the "racial memory" (see, e.g., Freud, 1916, 1919). And Freud termed "bosh" what Jung felt were evidences of parapsychological phenomena.

There were still other problems. Jung was, by his own confession, "a solitary" (Jung, 1961 p. 41), and Freud's calling him his successor "embar-

rassed" him. Jung's theoretical differences with Freud made it impossible for Jung to "uphold [Freud's] views properly" (p. 157). And Jung did not want to be "burdened . . . with the leadership of a party" (p. 157). He was concerned only, he said, with "investigating truth" (p. 158).

In 1909 Freud and Jung traveled together to lecture at Clark University (Worcester, Massachusetts). At dinner, on the first leg of this trip, Jung talked excitedly about the discovery in certain areas of northern Germany of "peat-bog corpses," the remains of prehistoric human beings whose bodies had been preserved by the acids in the bog water. Suddenly, Freud fainted. When he was revived he remarked that it was clear from Jung's conversation that Jung had death wishes toward Freud. It is reported that Freud had similar strong reactions on subsequent occasions when Jung held forth on topics related to death, the suggestion being that Freud suspected Jung of wanting to usurp his power.

On the trip to Clark, Freud and Jung analyzed each other's dreams, and when Jung, endeavoring to interpret one of Freud's dreams, asked Freud to disclose more details of his private life, Freud refused, saying, "I cannot risk my authority!" Jung (1916) says that "at that moment he lost it altogether"; Jung felt that Freud was placing authority above truth.

Freud saw himself as the fa-

ther figure in this relationship and Jung as the victim of a father complex. Reassuring Jung, on one occasion, Freud begged him to "rest easy, dear son Alexander, I will leave you more to conquer than I myself have managed, all psychiatry and the approval of the civilized world, which regards me as a savage!" (McGuire, 1974, p. 300). (Freud referred to Alexander the Great, 356–323 B.C. Suspected of murdering his father, Philip, Alexander greatly expanded Philip's empire.) But Jung's inner view of an aspect of himself had always been that of a "wise old man," and Jung was not about to tolerate playing son to father Freud, no matter how great a future might thereby be envisioned.

Jung was certain that his *Symbols of Transformation* (1911–1912) would cost him Freud's friendship, and perhaps it did. In this book, among other things, Jung presented his own view of what Freud had labeled the "Oedipus complex" (see Box 2.2). Jung's view differed from Freud's in significant ways. For example Jung believed that mother–father–child dynamics were an expression of spiritual or psychological needs and bonds rather than exclusively sexual desires.

The correspondence between Freud and Jung began to show a growing touchiness, and in January 1913, after Freud analyzed a slip of the tongue made by Jung and thereby aroused the latter's ire, Freud proposed to Jung that "we abandon our personal relations entirely" (McGuire, 1974, p. 539). In the fall, Jung relinquished his editorship of the *Psychoanalytic* *Yearbook*. The following April he resigned as president of the International Psycho-Analytical Association, and a few months later he withdrew as a member. The break was then complete. Freud and Jung never again saw one another.

Jung disagreed with Freud's mechanistic view of the world; for Jung, human behavior is conditioned not only by what has happened in the past but by what people envision will happen in future—by their aims and aspirations. Jung's view is as purposive as it is mechanistic: both past events and anticipated future ones can cause human behavior. This perspective leads Jung to conceive the meaning of life rather differently from Freud. For Freud, human beings are involved, essentially, in an endless repetition of instinctual demands and the attempt to satisfy or repress them; for Jung, people are engaged in constant, creative development.

A unique feature of Jung's theory is his emphasis on the racial, or phylogenetic, origins of personality. (**Phylogeny** refers to the evolution of a genetically related group of organisms. The phylogenetic origins of personality lie in the individual's inheritance, through memory traces, of the past experiences of the human race.) The foundations of personality, Jung holds, are archaic, primitive, innate, unconscious, and universal. His archetypes (see pages 114–117), some of which we have already encountered—the persona, the earth mother, the child, the wise old man, and the anima—are universal images, or thought-forms, inherited from past generations, that predispose people to perceive and respond to the world in particular ways.

DEFINITION OF PERSONALITY

For Jung, the personality, or **psyche** (from the Greek for "spirit" or "soul"; now also "mind"), embraces all thought, feeling, and behavior, conscious and unconscious. The psyche guides us in adapting to our social and physical environment.

The psyche is from the beginning a unity. According to Jung, we are born with wholeness, or with the potential for wholeness, and what we experience and learn serves to fulfill this potential. We strive to elaborate this fundamental unity while at the same time to preserve it by ensuring harmony among all its elements. The ultimate goal of life is the optimal development of the person's wholeness: "Personality is the supreme realization of the innate idiosyncrasy of a living being. it is an act of high courage flung in the face of life, the absolute affirmation of all that constitutes the individual, the most successful adapta-

BOX 4.2   Carl Gustav Jung (1875–1961)

Growing up in a small lakeside town in Switzerland, Carl Jung was torn between his interest in science and his strong philosophical bent. He was fascinated by the natural world and by the findings of archaeology, but he was drawn also to the contemplative life, perhaps in part because of his immersion in the world of religion—his father and several uncles were pastors in the Swiss Reformed Church.

When Jung entered the University of Basel, in 1895, he was forced to make a choice. He recounts, in *Memories, Dreams, and Reflections*, that two dreams he had in succession cast the die for science and that he then chose to study medicine, largely because it offered a way of earning a living. (Like Freud, he lacked the money necessary at that time for a career in the pure sciences.) Preparing for his last exams several years later, Jung read a textbook on psychiatry by Richard von Krafft-Ebing (German neurologist and early sexologist; 1849–1902), and suddenly his future became clear to him: "Here alone [in psychiatry] the two currents of my interest could flow together. . . . Here was the empirical field common to biological and spiritual facts. . . . Here at last was the place where the collision of nature and spirit became a reality" (Jung, 1961, p. 109).

In 1900 Jung became an assistant at the Burghölzli Mental Hospital, in Zurich, which was then directed by Eugen Bleuler (Swiss psychiatrist and authority on schizophrenia; 1857–1939). Under Bleuler's direction, Jung began to study word association and schizophrenia, and it was through his writings on these topics that Jung first made contact with Sigmund Freud (see Box 4.1).

When the ill-fated relationship between Jung and Freud came to an end, in 1914, Jung entered upon "a period of inner uncertainty" (1961, p. 170). He had already given up his position at the Burghölzli to devote more time to his own work, and now he resigned his instructorship at the University of Zurich as well. For a while he could do nothing more than see his regular therapy patients. He devoted much of his time to analyzing his own dreams and visions, in a sometimes frightening exploration:

The unconscious contents could have driven me out of my wits. But . . . the knowledge [that] . . . I must help my patients, I have a wife and five children . . . these were actualities which made demands upon me and proved to me again and again that I really existed, that I was not a blank page whirling about in the winds of the spirit. (Jung, 1961, p. 189)

Jung's family—his wife, the former Emma Rauschenbach, and his son and four daughters—were a "joyful reality" and the base to which he could always "return" from his journeys into a "strange inner world" (Jung, 1961, p. 189).

Jung, in 1918, with his wife, Emma, and four of their children. Emma Jung was a disciple of her husband's and followed his theories in her own practice of psychotherapy.

ential books, *Psychological Types* widely, seeking to understand the mentalities of other cultures. What he learned about contrasting customs, myths, and religious beliefs and practices eventually found its way into his voluminous writings.

What was Jung like? A big, strong man, he appeared quite outgoing, and a hearty laugh punctuated his sometimes slangy speech. As much as he enjoyed discussions with colleagues and students, however, Jung needed often to be alone with his thoughts and his books. All his work, all his creative activity, he felt, originated in his first period of retreat, when he "dedicated [himself] to service of the psyche," and he continued to probe his unconscious throughout his life. It was, he said, his "greatest wealth" (Jung, 1961, p. 192).

After several years, Jung resumed his research and writing, (1921). He began to travel producing one of his most influ-

tion to the universal conditions of existence coupled with the greatest possible freedom for self-determination" (Jung, 1934a, p. 171).

ENDURING FEATURES OF PERSONALITY

The personality is composed of a number of systems that operate on three levels of consciousness. The ego operates on the conscious level. The complexes and the archetypes operate normally on the level of the personal unconscious and the unconscious, respectively. The attitudes and functions operate on all levels of consciousness. In time, conscious and unconscious are synthesized within the person through the operation of the self, the most important archetype of all.

CONSCIOUSNESS AND THE EGO

Consciousness appears early in life, perhaps even before birth. Gradually, consciousness becomes differentiated from the infant's general, or gross, awareness of stimuli. We can see consciousness becoming increasingly specific in babies as they begin to recognize people and objects about them. For example, the baby learns to distinguish among individual members of its family and to differentiate these familiar faces from the unfamiliar faces of strangers. According to Jung, one of the first products of this process of differentiation is the ego.

As the organization of the conscious mind, the **ego** plays the important role of gatekeeper; it determines what perceptions, thoughts, feelings, and memories will enter consciousness. If the ego were not so selective, we would be overwhelmed by the experiences that would crowd into our minds. By screening experiences, the ego attempts to maintain a coherence within the personality and to give the person a sense of continuity and identity.

THE PERSONAL UNCONSCIOUS AND ITS COMPLEXES

What happens to experiences that the ego does not admit? Nothing that has been experienced disappears; such experiences are stored in the **personal unconscious** (similar to Freud's "preconscious"). Experiences that have been suppressed, or forgotten, as well as those that failed to make a conscious impression, fill the personal unconscious. For the most part, these contents are within easy reach of consciousness; for example, during a lecture, you may not be aware of an angry exchange of words you had with a friend just before the hour began, but you can easily recall the argument when the class is over.

Within the personal unconscious, a group of ideas may cluster together to form what Jung called a **complex**. Jung discovered the complex through his research on word associations (see page 133). Finding that people often had difficulty producing associations to particular words and to words related to those words, Jung reasoned that the personal unconscious must contain groups of associated feelings, thoughts, and memories that have strong emotional content. Thus, any word that touched on such a cluster might cause an unusual response. For example, a person might take an unusually long time to respond to a particular word. Or the record of a person's physiological response, such as heart rate, might show a sudden change at the moment at which a particular word was read.

The word *complex* has become part of our everyday language. When we say that someone has a complex, we mean that the person is so preoccupied with something that it influences almost all his or her behavior. This is essentially what Jung meant when he said, "A person does not have a complex; the complex has him." When some one idea or set of ideas so obsesses a person that it interferes with his or her normal everyday functioning, it almost seems as if it is the complex that is in control and not the person. For example, a young woman with a serious inferiority complex was obsessed with the notion that she was less competent, less talented, and less attractive than other people. She was so convinced of her inferiority to others that she did poorly in school, had only a few friends, and was only rarely able to express her own needs and wishes.

Mild complexes guide and color all of our lives. In general, complexes are unconscious, although related elements may become conscious from time to time. Some complexes may lead to outstanding achievements. For example, Napoleon's obsession with power enabled him to build an enormous empire. Michelangelo's obsession with beauty produced great and lasting works of art.

What causes a complex to develop? At first, Jung held that early childhood experiences were responsible. Questioning whether such experience could create the powerful force that a complex often exerts, however, he was led to discover contributing factors within a deeper level of the psyche, the collective unconscious.

THE COLLECTIVE UNCONSCIOUS

The collective unconscious is one of Jung's most original and controversial conceptions. When he introduced this notion—that our evolutionary past provides a sort of blueprint not only of our bodies but of our personalities, a blueprint carried in a so-called collective unconscious—the scientific world was still reeling from the impact of Freud's revelations about the role of the unconscious in human psychic functioning. Jung's ideas, like those of Freud, met great resistance and skepticism.

In Jung's theory, the **collective unconscious** is composed of **primordial images**—thought-forms or memory traces from our ancestral past—not only our human past but also our prehuman, animal ancestry. These images are a record of common experiences that have been repeated over countless generations. For example, because human beings have always had mothers, an image of the mother exists in our collective unconscious. And this image, which is quite separate from our personal experience of our mothers, is universal. Because of our common evolutionary history, and because we all have similarly constructed brains, all peoples share essentially the same collective unconscious. (Because we live in widely varying cultures, however, these images do vary in form and content.)

Jung emphasized that we do not inherit specific memories or ideas; he was not advancing a theory of acquired characters such as that proposed by Jean Lamarck (French naturalist; 1740–1829). What we inherit is a predisposition or potentiality for certain ideas. Human beings are born with the potential to see the world in three dimensions but become able actually to do this through experience and training. Similarly, Jung said, we are born with the potential to perceive, think, and feel in many particular ways, and this potential is fulfilled by our personal experience.

The unconscious—both personal and collective—can be of great help to us: "It has at its disposal all subliminal contents, all those things which have been forgotten or overlooked as well as the wisdom and experience of uncounted centuries" (Jung, 1943, p. 114). But if we ignore the unconscious, it can disrupt our lives. As we have seen, a complex can interfere with effective functioning. Similarly, neglected contents of the collective unconscious may find expression in such things as phobias, delusions, and other symptoms of serious psychological disturbance. The most powerful system of the personality, the collective unconscious may in such situations overthrow both the ego and the personal unconscious (Jung, 1936, 1943, 1945).

ARCHETYPES.   The collective unconscious contains an almost unlimited number of images, or thought-forms, but Jung focused on several that contain a particularly great amount of emotion. These **archetypes** (original models on which other, similar things are patterned) are, like all primordial images, "*forms without content*, representing merely the possibility of a certain type of perception and action" (Jung, 1936, p. 48). Yet they have great strength, carrying as they do the weight of thousands of years of human experience.

It is the archetype that joins with a person's early experience to form the center of a complex and that gives the complex the power to attract other experiences to it. Consider the archetype of power, for example. Throughout their existence, human beings have been exposed to innumerable examples of great natural forces—swift-flowing rivers, waterfalls, floods, thunder, lightning, hurricanes, forest fires, earthquakes, and so on. An archetype of energy, or power, has evolved out of these experiences—a predisposition to perceive and to be fascinated by power and a desire to create and control power. The child's fascination with electronic toys, the young person's preoccupation with cars, the adult's obsession with releasing the hidden energies of atoms have their roots in this archetype of energy.

Jung identified and described many archetypes—birth, rebirth, death, power, magic, unity, the hero, the child, God, the demon, the wise old man, the earth mother, and the animal, to name just a few. We will describe the archetypes that are most important in shaping personality and behavior: the persona, the anima and the animus, the shadow, and the self. The self archetype is particularly crucial to the development and functioning of the personality. It was, Jung said, the most important result of his studies of the collective unconscious. The ultimate, unifying system of the personality, the self powers the important processes of individuation and transcendence (see page 132) by which the person strives for self-realization.

The Persona.   The **persona** is the mask, or facade, that people exhibit publicly. It reflects our perception of the role society expects us to play

Jung might well see evidence of the archetype of energy, or power in our current fascination with white water rafting.

in life. It also reflects the way we wish to be seen by others. Actually, the persona may comprise a number of masks; for example, a man may appear reserved and unemotional in his work and tough and competitive at tennis but warm and demonstrative with his family.

The persona is necessary for survival, for it helps us to control our feelings, thoughts, and behavior. If people identify completely with their persona, however, it can lead them to become alienated from themselves and from their true feelings.

The Anima and the Animus.   The persona may mask another important archetype: the **anima** (in men) and the **animus** (in women). Everyone, Jung said, has qualities of the other sex, not only physiological characteristics, such as sex hormones, but feelings, attitudes, and values. The anima reflects the ''feminine'' side of the male psyche—feelings and emotionality; the animus reflects the ''masculine'' side of the female psyche—logic and rationality.

The anima and the animus can help men and women understand and respond to one another, but they can also cause misunderstanding if people project them without regard for others' real qualities. For example, if a woman's animus emphasizes athleticism, she may misinterpret a man's artistic interests as weakness. If a man's anima stresses gentleness, he may misinterpret a woman's competitive spirit as aggression.

Jung's concept of the anima and animus, although it tended to focus on traditional views of what is masculine and feminine, presaged current thought on such topics as androgyny and women's—and men's—liberation. Jung felt strongly that men must express the female aspects of their personalities and that woman must express the male aspects of their personalities. If they do not, he asserted, these traits will remain unconscious and undeveloped, and as a result the unconscious itself will be weak and immature.

The Shadow.   The **shadow** archetype reflects the animal instincts that human beings have inherited in their evolution from lower forms of life (Jung, 1948d). The shadow is probably the most powerful and potentially the most dangerous of all the archetypes. Yet because it represents strong emotions, spontaneity, and the creative urge (recall the Freudian id), it is also the source of all that is best in human beings.

When the ego and the shadow work together, the forces of the shadow are channeled into useful behavior, and the person feels full of life and vigor. But if adequate outlets are not provided for the shadow, the individual may become self-destructive or destructive of others.

The shadow represents basic instincts and as such is the source of realistic insights and adaptive responses that have survival value. These qualities can be very important to the person in situations that require immediate decisions and reactions, when there is no time to evaluate things and to consider the most appropriate response. If the shadow has been allowed to individuate, its reactions to threats and dangers may be very effective. If it has been repressed, however, the person may be overwhelmed by the situation and unable to take action.

The Self.   The concept of wholeness is a crucial feature of Jung's psychology, and it is the archetype of the **self** that motivates the person toward this wholeness. The self archetype expresses itself through various symbols, the chief one being the ''magic circle,'' or **mandala** (Sanskrit for ''circle''), the emblem of complex unity that you can see illustrated in Figure 4.1 The mandala, a circular form that often contains a multiple of four, or a ''quaternity,'' is found in numerous Eastern religions (e.g., in Tibetan Buddhism it assists meditation and concentration), and it appears in many other cultural and historical contexts. The circle symbolizes oneness, or wholeness. The multiple of four may have different meanings: the four directions; the four ancient elements of fire, water, earth, and air; the Trinity and the Holy Mother; and so on.

The self becomes the midpoint of personality around which all other systems cluster. It directs the process of individuation, through which the useful and creative aspects of the unconscious are made conscious and channeled into productive activity. If we picture consciousness with the ego as its center, Jung said, we can think of the process of

Figure 4.1   A Tibetan mandala of the type used in meditation.

assimilating the unconscious into the conscious as involving the shift of
the center of the personality from the ego—which is at the center of
consciousness—to a point midway between the conscious and unconscious. This new point then becomes the location of the self, and this
new balance, between the conscious and the unconscious, "ensures for
the personality a new and more solid foundation" (Jung, 1945,
p. 219, and see Figure 4.2).

Although the self archetype is present from birth, it does not appear until middle age. The difficult task of achieving self-realization
requires great discipline, effort, and wisdom and, as we will see, it is
rarely, if ever, completely accomplished.

SYMBOLIZATION.   A symbol is a visible sign of something invisible: it
is something that stands for or suggests something else. For Jung, the

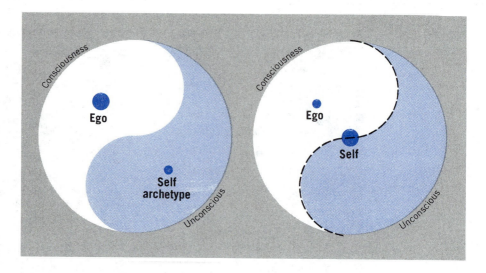

Figure 4.2   The evolution of the self as the center of the personality. a indicates that in the early years of life, the unconscious is relatively inaccessible to consciousness (solid dividing line). The self here is small and unconscious; the ego is large and at the center of both consciousness and the personality. b indicates that as the personality matures, the unconscious is assimilated into consciousness (broken dividing line). The self becomes the center of the personality, shifting to a point midway between the conscious and the unconscious and surpassing the ego in importance.

symbol was even more than this, and his writings on symbolism in religion and alchemy (a medieval science known generally for having dealt with the transmutation of base metals into gold but also concerned with the evolution of the human spirit) fill 5 of the 18 volumes of his collected works. Indeed, probably the two most important concepts of Jung's philosophy are the archetype and the symbol.

Symbols are the outward expressions of archetypes. Because the latter are deeply buried in the collective unconscious, they can express themselves only through symbols. It is only by analyzing and interpreting these symbols—which appear in dreams, fantasies, visions, myths, art, and so on—that we obtain any knowledge of the collective unconscious and its archetypes.

A symbol operates in two major ways. In its retrospective sense, guided by the instincts, the symbol may simply represent an impulse that for some reason cannot be satisfied. For example, dancing may be symbolic of the sex act. In this sense, symbolization is somewhat like sublimation (see page 123).

In their prospective sense, guided by the ultimate goals of humankind, symbols express stored-up wisdom, both racial and individually acquired, that is applicable to the future. Thus, they represent levels of development that are ahead of humanity's present status. Jung held that a person's destiny, the highest evolution of his or her psyche, was marked out by symbols: the symbol "represents an attempt to elucidate, by means of analogy, something that still belongs entirely to the domain of the unknown or something that is yet to be" (Jung, 1916, p. 287).

ATTITUDES AND FUNCTIONS: JUNG'S PSYCHOLOGICAL TYPOLOGY
With the exception of the ego, all the aspects of the personality that we have talked about so far function almost exclusively at the unconscious level. There are two important aspects of personality, however, that operate at both levels of consciousness; these are the **attitudes**, introversion and extraversion, and the **functions**, thinking, feeling, sensing, and intuiting.

INTROVERSION AND EXTRAVERSION.   The two major **attitudes**, or orientations, of personality are introversion and extraversion. The person characterized by **introversion** is oriented toward subjective experience—he or she tends to focus on the inner, private world where reality is represented as it is perceived by the person. The person characterized by **extraversion** is oriented toward objective experience; such a person tends to spend more time perceiving the external world of things, events, and other people than thinking about his or her perceptions.

In general, people characterized by introversion are introspective and preoccupied with their own, internal affairs. They often appear aloof, reserved, even unsocial. People characterized by extraversion are concerned with their interactions with other people and the world around them. They appear active and outgoing and take an interest in the external world.

In this section, as is common practice, we will use the terms "introvert" and "extravert." Note, however, that by each of these terms we mean a person in whom one or the other attitude is dominant, not exclusive. As we will see, in the Jungian system, both introversion and extraversion are a part of every individual's makeup. These two attitudes oppose each other, however, and one tends to rule the personality; the other tends to be repressed and unconscious. Thus, the unconscious of the introvert is extraverted; the unconscious of the extravert is introverted.

Dreams regularly provide an outlet for the expression of the unconscious aspects of personality. And, not uncommonly, one's unconscious attitude may find expression in extreme circumstances. Behavior in such circumstances may be rather primitive and crude, because unconscious processes are not as well developed as conscious ones. For example, a man who is normally a "private person," reserved, scholarly, and focused on his work, may suddenly face tragedy—the death of his wife. He may startle friends and acquaintances by behaving in ways "unlike" him, such as calling them up at odd hours, getting drunk or stoned, talking wildly about quitting his job, and the like.

Or a woman who seems a typical extravert—who meets people with warmth and enthusiasm and whose job involves her in constant interaction with new people—suddenly becomes moody, contrary, and unsocial. You wonder, What on earth can be eating her? She is facing an important career decision, and having to think about it and to consider all its ramifications is making her very uncomfortable. Her unconscious introversion has become active and is in conflict with her normally dominant extraversion.

THINKING, FEELING, SENSING, INTUITING.   As in the case of the attitudes, one function is normally dominant and conscious, whereas the remaining functions are nondominant and usually unconscious. There are four psychological functions: thinking, feeling, sensing, and intuiting.

Thinking, an intellectual function, seeks to connect ideas with each other so as to understand the nature of the world and to solve problems. **Feeling**, an evaluative function, accepts or rejects ideas and objects on the basis of whether they arouse positive or negative feelings; it gives human beings such subjective experiences as pleasure, pain, anger, and love. Thinking and feeling are **rational** functions because they require judgments; one must decide, for example, whether ideas are connected or whether something is pleasing or distasteful.

Sensing involves the operation of the sense organs—one senses by seeing, hearing, touching, tasting, and smelling as well as by responding to sensations from within one's own body. Thus, sensation provides one's perceptions of oneself and of the world around one. **Intuiting** is a kind of perception by way of the unconscious, or the subliminal. When one has an intuition about something, one has a "hunch" about it: an art dealer discovered an old painting in an antique shop and, though she could find no obvious clue to the painting's origin, she "knew" it was by an old master—she "felt" it in her "bones."

Sensation and intuition are **nonrational** functions. They respond directly to stimuli, present or unknown—they are not produced by thought or evaluation. These two functions are not necessarily contrary to reason or evaluation—they simply have nothing to do with such processes.

The way the four functions operate may be clarified by the following example. Suppose that four friends have been traveling in the U.S. Southwest, and at daybreak they stand at the rim of the Grand Canyon. One person experiences a sense of awe, grandeur, and breathtaking beauty; she is dominated by her feeling function. Another person, dominated by the sensing function, sees the canyon as it is, as his photographs will later portray it. A third person, whose thinking function rules her, attempts to understand the canyon in terms of geological theory and principles. And as the fourth person, who is ruled by intuition, gazes at the canyon, he experiences it as a mystical phenomenon whose great significance is only partially revealed.

Although all four functions operate in everyone, not all four are equally well developed. Usually one, called the **superior** function, is dominant and conscious. One of the other three functions usually acts in an **auxiliary** capacity to the superior function; if the latter is prevented from operating, the auxiliary function automatically takes its place. The least developed of the four functions, the **inferior** function is repressed and unconscious and expresses itself in dreams and fantasies. This function is also served by an auxiliary function.

Because thinking and feeling are both rational functions, they tend to oppose each other; thus, neither can be an auxiliary for the other. Suppose that a person's superior function is thinking; his inferior function will then be feeling. Either of these rational functions can be served by one of the nonrational functions. Thus, for example, this person may use information obtained from sensation as an aid in thinking. Or, using intuition, he may achieve hunches and insights that he can then think through.

Ideally, it would be advantageous to have all attitudes and functions equally developed and available for use, but that is not the way it works. Although the psyche tries to achieve such harmony and balance as it strives for self-realization, there are always inequities among its various components. As the attitudes and functions combine to produce the eight psychological types described in Box 4.3, one attitude and one function tend to dominate in a given individual. Still, the other attitude and the other functions are always present, and it is important to keep this in mind as you study Jung's types. Jung cautioned that he did not intend by his concepts to put people ''into this box or that'' (1968, p. 19).

There is considerable psychological literature on Jung's conceptions of introversion and extraversion. A number of tests have been constructed (e.g., the Myers–Briggs Type Indicator, Myers, 1962; and the Eysenck Personality Inventory, Eysenck and Eysenck, 1964). Hans Eysenck (Chapter 12) made extraversion one of his primary dimensions of personality, and other researchers have studied Jung's typology (see Ball, 1968; Gorlow, Simonson, and Krauss, 1966; Shapiro and Alexander, 1969). Tests that assess the four functions in conjunction with the two attitudes have also been constructed (see Gray and Wheelright, 1964; Myers, 1962).

INTERACTION AMONG PERSONALITY FEATURES
The personality features that we have described interact in three ways—they may oppose each other, compensate for one another, or

BOX 4.3   Jung's "Psychological Types"

Jung stressed that everyone has his or her own unique pattern of attitudes and functions, and he insisted that his conception of eight basic "psychological types" was intended simply to help in classifying his data. Unfortunately, despite Jung's repeated warnings, psychologists and others have tended to regard the eight "types" that we will describe here as fixed categories into which all people are supposed to fit.

As you read the brief sketches of these "types," keep in mind that although ordinarily one attitude tends to dominate, most people have characteristics of both introversion and extraversion. And although a person tends to use one or two functions more than the others, all four are present in the psyche. Thus, no one you know will precisely fit any one of the eight categories, but you will recognize in friends and acquaintances many of the characteristics described. Figure 4.3, a mandala of the eight types, will help you review the material on each.

INTROVERSION–THINKING

We might find introversion and the thinking function dominant in, for example, philosophers. People with this combination of dominant attitude and function may appear emotionless and distant because they tend to value (abstract) ideas more than (concrete) people. They want to pursue their own thoughts and are not particularly concerned about having their ideas accepted by others. They may be stubborn, inconsiderate, arrogant, and stand-offish.

EXTRAVERSION–THINKING

Primarily extraverted thinking people—scientists and researchers, for example—tend to appear impersonal, even cold or haughty; they, like introverted thinking types, repress the feeling function. Objective reality is the ruling principle for such people, who not only abide by their constructions of reality but expect everyone else to do so too.

INTROVERSION–FEELING

Introverted feeling people experience intense emotions but keep them hidden. Such people may be writers and artists, expressing their intensity only in their art. They may give the impression of inner harmony and self-sufficiency, but their feelings may erupt in sudden emotional storms.

EXTRAVERSION–FEELING

For extraverted feeling people, feelings change as frequently as the situation changes. Such people may be actors. They tend to be emotional and moody but also sociable and sometimes showy. They tend to form intense but shortlived attachments to others.

INTROVERSION–SENSATION

The introverted sensing person tends to become immersed in his or her own psychic sensations and to find the world uninteresting in comparison. Such people may often appear calm and self-controlled, but they may also be rather boring because of their relative deemphasis on thoughts and feelings. They may try to express themselves through art, but their emphasis on a nonrational function may result in failure to communicate.

EXTRAVERSION–SENSATION

Extraverted sensing types may be businesspeople—they are often realistic, practical, and hardheaded. They tend to accept the world as it is without giving it much thought. They may be "sensuous" people—pleasure loving and thrill seeking. They often live for the sensations they derive from their experiences. Such people may also be susceptible to compulsions and addictions of various kinds.

INTROVERSION–INTUITION

Dreamers and prophets but also visionaries and cranks are often introverted intuiting types. Isolated in a world of primordial images whose meaning they do not always understand, such people may be unable to communicate effectively with others. They tend to be impractical, but they may have brilliant intuitions that others can adopt and elaborate.

EXTRAVERSION–INTUITION

Inventors and entrepreneurs are often extraverted intuiting types. Such people seem always to be looking for new worlds to conquer. They can be very good at promoting new enterprises, but their interest is not sustained. Novelty keeps these people going, and they may have difficulty holding onto anything—ideas, jobs, people.

Assessing someone's psychological type requires estimating the relative strength of attitudes and functions and judging also whether each is conscious or unconscious. Usually, this sort of assessment can be made only through long-term study or analytic treatment, but efforts have been made to shorten the process by devising tests—lists of questions about preferences, interests, habitual behaviors. For example, a preference for a solitary walk in the country over going to a party might indicate introversion; a preference for soaking in a hot tub over studying astrophysics might suggest the sensing function.

How do attitude and function preferences develop? According to Jung, inborn factors—as yet unknown to us—manifest themselves very early in life. These are the primary determining influences, although modifications may be made by parental and other social factors. Parents and children are often of different types, and frequently a child is pressured to conform to a parent's orientation. An extraverted thinking trial attorney, for example, may clash with his introverted sensing son, who wants to be an artist; an introverted feeling novelist may fail to understand her extraverted intuiting daughter, who wants to develop her own business.

Efforts to change children's "types," if apparently successful, often lead to later neurosis. Parents, Jung said, should respect a child's psychological type and should encourage a child to develop in the direction of its own inner nature. Much parent–child conflict, he thought, could be traced to incompatibility of character types.

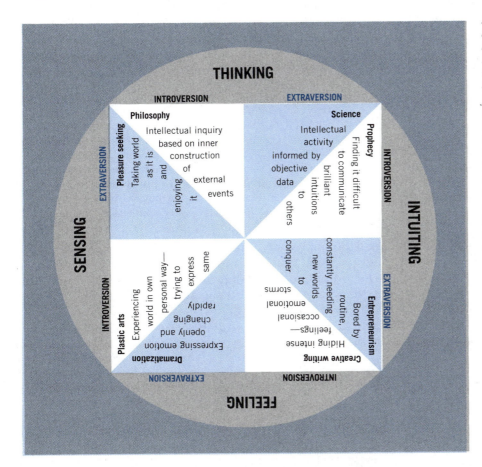

Figure 4.3 The attitudes and functions. The circle, as in all mandalas, represents the unity of the person. The four functions make up the "quaternity" here. The two attitudes represent the tension of opposites. The presence of all attitudes and functions indicates that all exist within the person, whether conscious or unconscious.

join together in a synthesis. Common to most personality theories is the principle of **opposition**—the notion that the personality contains polar, conflicting tendencies. For Jung, tension is the essence of life; without it, there would be no energy and thus no personality. Opposition exists everywhere in the personality—ego opposes shadow, introversion opposes extraversion, thinking opposes feeling, and the anima or animus may oppose the ego (as well as compensate for it).

Must the personality be in conflict and turmoil always? No, for polar elements also attract and complement each other. By the principle of **compensation**, the psyche is prevented from becoming neurotically one sided. In general, compensation occurs between the conscious and the unconscious; what appears dominant in conscious functioning is compensated for by a dissimilar, repressed characteristic. For example, if a conscious attitude is frustrated in some way, the unconscious attitude will assert itself. In sleep when one cannot exercise one's preferred attitude, the unconscious attitude takes over and expresses itself in dreams. And an archetype may have a compensatory relation to the conscious mind. The anima and animus provide men and woman with, respectively, their feminine and masculine characteristics.

Finally, according to Jung, the personality strives constantly for the union of opposites. It strives for **synthesis** of contrasting features so as to form a balanced, integrated personality. We will see shortly how, through the transcendent function, the personality may succeed in achieving such integration.

PERSONALITY DYNAMICS

For the interactions we have just discussed to occur, energy—motive power—must be generated. What is this energy, and where does it come from?

Jung proposes that the personality is a relatively closed system. That is, it must be dealt with as a unitary system, more or less self-contained, and apart from any other energy system. The personality can take in new energy from biological processes or other, external sources, such as the individual's experiences. It expends energy in psychological work—the work of keeping the personality functioning. The effect that energy drawn into the system has on personality functioning depends on the nature of that energy and on the nature of the existing energy in the system.

PSYCHIC ENERGY

The energy of the personality is called psychic energy (Jung, 1948c). This energy, or "life energy," as Jung also refers to it, is manifested consciously as many sorts of striving, desiring, and willing as well as by such processes as perceiving, thinking, and attending. Because the personality is not a totally closed system, it does not reach a steady state of equilibrium; it is always in motion. The dynamics of this constant movement maintain a balance between a condition of too little input of new energy and too much. If the personality system were a totally open system and continually took in new energy, it would be chaotic; if it were totally closed and took in no new energy, it would soon stagnate. People who are healthy (in psychological terms) strike a balance between complete chaos and utter boredom.

Psychic energy originates in the experiences a person has. In a manner of speaking, experiences are digested and converted to psychic energy. Just as the body continuously uses physical energy to run its machinery—even when we sleep our hearts beat and we breathe—the personality is also always consuming energy—in our sleep some important psychological events, such as dreaming, take place.

Jung holds that there is some kind of reciprocal action between physical energy and psychic energy, but he does not specify the nature of this action. In any event, psychic energy is a hypothetical construct; it cannot be measured directly. It finds expression in such psychological activities as attending, feeling, wishing, willing, and striving and in such potential forces as dispositions, attitudes, and tendencies.

PSYCHIC VALUES

A **psychic value** is a measure of the amount of psychic energy committed to a particular psychic element. For example, a person who values beauty highly will expend a great deal of energy in surrounding herself with beautiful objects, traveling to places where beauty can be found, and so on. On the other hand, a person who places a high value on power will consign a great deal of energy to activities that increase his sense of strength and control.

Although we cannot determine the absolute value of the psychic energy invested in something, we can assess its value relative to other values. We can ask people, or observe, which of two things they prefer; we can measure the relative amounts of time that people spend on one or another activity or interest; we can place obstacles in people's paths to various goals and see how long they persist in trying to overcome the obstacles; or we can record the relative frequencies with which people dream of different themes. Thus, if a man, says he would rather read *Playboy* than *Foreign Affairs*, if we observe him to spend more time dating than studying, if in a lab experiment he works harder to get the attention of a woman than to win a game of chess, and if his recorded dreams deal with sexual themes more often than any other—we may assume that he places a high value on sex.

TABLE 4.1   *Assessing Unconscious Values*

METHOD	DESCRIPTION
Observation and deduction	Observing behavior and making inferences. For example, we observe that a woman introduces her mother into almost every conversation, adopts her mother's interests, spends time with her mother's friends, prefers to read about mothers and daughters: all these signs suggest a mother complex.
	If a complex appears only in disguised form, we may have to analyze disparate elements of behavior and deduce the underlying cause. For example, we observe that a man is submissive but also that he always gets his way. A power complex—a need to control others—may be exerting itself in this man through his subtle manipulation of others.
Complex indicators	Noting or looking for such disturbances of behavior as a slip of the tongue or a blockage of memory. Calling his wife by his mother's name may betray a man's mother complex. Forgetting her friend's name (Tod) when about to introduce him to someone because the name resembles the German word for death (*Todt*) may suggest a woman's death complex
Emotional reaction	Presenting a person with lists of words or phrases and recording reactions such as response time or physiological response patterns. A significantly delayed response may indicate that a word has touched off a hidden complex with which that word is associated, and an uncharacteristic physiological response (e.g., rapid pulse) may confirm the emotional arousal.

Assessing the strength of unconscious values is particularly difficult; it involves evaluating the ''constellating power'' of a complex. What is this power? It is, essentially, the ability of the nucleus of a complex to attract other things to it. Thus, for example, a nucleus of ''strong leader'' that informs a power complex may draw to it such associations as assuming responsibilities, getting one's decisions accepted by others, and continually seeking respect and admiration. Each new experience is assimilated into the complex. Table 4.1 describes three specific methods for measuring the power of a complex.

EQUIVALENCE AND ENTROPY

Jung based his view of psychodynamics on two principles derived from the laws of thermodynamics (the science of the relation of heat energy to energy of other kinds and, particularly, the convertibility of heat energy to mechanical energy and the revere). Jung's principle of **equivalence**, like the first law of thermodynamics, holds that energy is conserved; that is, it is never lost from the personality system. If the energy consigned to a particular element of personality decreases, an equivalent amount of energy will appear elsewhere in the system—energy is transferred from one element to another. For example, as a child's interest in building blocks declines, her interest in playing soccer may increase.

What determines the direction in which energy flows? Why does it go, say, from the ego to the self? The principle of **entropy**, like the second law of thermodynamics, holds that energy tends to flow from a stronger (hotter) to a weaker (colder) element. For example, as people mature and become increasingly able to assimilate material from their unconscious, energy flows from the (strong, conscious) ego to the (initially weak, unconscious) self.

The aims underlying both these principles are stability and equilibrium. According to equivalence, the amount of energy in the system must remain the same; according to entropy, the energy consigned to the various elements within the system must remain in balance. Because the personality is only a relatively closed system, it can never be in perfect balance. Ideally, however, the point can be reached where each of the personality's elements contributes effectively to its functioning.

It is a general rule of Jungian psychology that any one-sided development of personality creates conflict and tension and that an even development of all the constituents produces harmony and contentment. Because a weak system will always attempt to improve its status at the expense of a strong one, a personality in which one element is overdeveloped is under constant pressure to develop other, weaker aspects.

THE USES OF ENERGY

Psychic energy is used for two general purposes: the preservation of life and the development of cultural and spiritual activities. As people become more efficient at satisfying their basic, biological needs, they have more energy for the pursuit of cultural interests.

By what mechanisms are these purposes advanced? Jung discusses two important concepts in this connection. **Progression** is ''the daily advance of the process of psychological adaptation'' (Jung, 1948b, p. 32). It is the person's continual adjustment to or attempt to modify the environment. **Regression** is ''the backward movement'' of psychic energy (p. 33) or the rise in value of psychic processes concerned with inner, usually unconscious, needs. When the conscious ego is adjusting satisfactorily to both the demands of the environment and the needs of the unconscious, energy follows a progressive movement; opposing forces are united in a harmonious flow. When a frustrating situation interrupts this forward movement, however, energy may regress into the unconscious.

Regression is not necessarily bad, for it may help the ego to find a way around an obstacle. Regression may uncover useful knowledge in the unconscious—knowledge and wisdom of the person's own as well as his or her racial past. Regression occurs regularly in dreams, which are important revelations of unconscious material.

A biologist, at loggerheads with the chief of his laboratory, dreamed one night of his father, with whom he had felt very competitive. Then, not long after, he dreamed of an old chieftain who welcomed a young man into tribal society after the youth had performed an intricate ritual with materials given him by the old man. On awakening, the biologist suddenly saw a way to get his chief's approval and support: he based his research proposal on earlier research of the chief's, which he had forgotten. Jung might say that the biologist regressed temporarily into his unconscious, where memories of his father and the archetype of the wise old man helped him see past the obstacles he confronted.

Sublimation means the displacement of energy from instinctive and less differentiated processes to those that are more differentiated and that emphasize cultural and spiritual aims. Suppose, for example, that a woman enters a religious order and forsakes the expression of her sexuality and her procreative powers, devoting herself instead to the work of prayer, meditation, and caring for others. Energy has been withdrawn from the sex drive and invested, or sublimated, in other, spiritual forms of expression.

Suppose, on the other hand, that a man's sexual energy is blocked in its expression because he is terrified of intimacy with another person. Because energy cannot just disappear, if no outlet for it is found, **repression** will occur and it will retreat into this man's unconscious. If it builds up there to too great an extent, it will begin to flow toward the conscious mind (ego), where it will disrupt rational processes and possibly find expression in some other outlet. Then this man may, for example, undertake to have the local high school library purged of all modern literature that discusses premarital sexual activities, birth control, abortion, and other similar topics. He may become utterly preoccupied with his effort, making irrational speeches about it to the school board and engaging in other such excessive behaviors.

THE DEVELOPMENT OF PERSONALITY

Jung does not offer a fully articulated theory of development, and his stages of development are only loosely formulated (see Box 4.4). He assigns an important role in development to heredity, making it re-

BOX 4.4   The Stages of Life

Jung did not elaborate his concept of the stages of life as Freud elaborated his psychosexual stages of development and Erikson his psychosocial stages of the life cycle. Moreover, Jung was clearly much more interested in the third stage—"middle age"—than in any other. It is in this stage that the important process of individuation (see page 132) culminates and the person begins to turn from material concerns to things of the spirit.

CHILDHOOD

Jung (1909b) observed that young children frequently have emotional difficulties. He points out, however, that such difficulties almost always reflect "disturbing influences in the home" (Jung, 1928, p. 54). Until children enter school, they lack the continuity of consciousness that comes with a sense of personal identity. According to Jung, children live enclosed in a psychic atmosphere provided by their parents, and their psychic life is governed by instincts. Except for the order in behavior brought about by these instincts—eating, sleeping, and so on—the child's life would be anarchic and chaotic if it were not programmed by the parents.

At the same time, Jung says, it is a mistake to interpret children who are "peculiar, obstinate, disobedient, or difficult to handle" as willful or seriously disturbed. In such cases, "we should always examine the parental milieu, its psychological conditions and history. Almost without exception we discover in the parents the only valid reasons for the child's difficulties" (1928, p. 54).

YOUTH AND YOUNG ADULTHOOD

A "psychic birth" takes place at puberty, accompanying the physiological changes that occur then and the eruption of sexuality. This stage marks the formal psychic differentiation of child from parents (Jung, 1931). Suddenly the personality faces many decisions and must make many adaptations to social life. If the person is adequately prepared, Jung says, the transition from childhood activities to a vocation can be reasonably smooth. If the person is stuck in illusions of childhood, however, or has built up unrealistic expectations, he or she can have a multitude of problems. For example, a young man who planned to become a pilot may discover that his visual acuity is inadequate for the demands of such a job. If he cannot then shift his aims he may experience considerable distress.

Not all problems encountered in this second stage are external, like that of choice of a vocation. Inner difficulties, caused by the sexual instinct or by oversensitivity and insecurity, may arise. And somewhere deep within us (the child archetype is responsible), we want to remain children, to stay in the period when we had no real problems and no responsibilities. Still, the tasks of the second stage have more to do with extraverted than with introverted values. People must be able to make decisions, overcome barriers, and achieve satisfactions for themselves and others. They must "lend [themselves] to the attainable," even though this means "renouncing all [their] other psychic potentialities" (Jung, 1931, p. 394).

MIDDLE AGE

Beginning somewhere between the ages of 35 and 40, people begin to feel the need for spiritual values, a need that is always part of the psyche but that is pushed aside early in life because materialistic interests must then take precedence. By middle age people have adapted themselves more or less successfully to the environment—they are established in vocations, they are married, they have children, and they have become participants in community and civic affairs. Suddenly, however, they may find themselves at a loss, questioning the meaning and purpose of their lives. They no longer need to invest their energies in the endeavors that have brought them success, and the consequent loss of values may create a vacuum in their personalities. They need new values that will broaden their horizons beyond purely materialistic considerations. Middle age is a time for self-realization. The person needs, through contemplation and meditation, "to understand the meaning of his individual life . . . to experience his own inner being" (Jung, 1935, p. 50).

Jung was one of the first personality theorists to try to understand the psychology of the middle years. It is likely that his own experience of self-exploration and of setting a new course, with new values and goals—which occurred when Jung was about 40—had a great deal to do with his interest in this period of life.

Another factor in Jung's interest in this period was doubtless the fact that many of his patients were in this age bracket. They were often people who had achieved considerable success and recognition, both professionally and socially, but for whom life had lost its zest and its meaning.

OLD AGE

This period held little interest for Jung. He believed that childhood and old age were similar: in both stages, the person functions largely in the unconscious. The child has not yet formed a consistent, reasoning, conscious ego; the old person, Jung said, sinks gradually into the unconscious, finally vanishing within it.

Jung felt that because the belief in life after death is common to religions of all kinds, there must be a reason for it. As one possibility, he suggested that psychic life may go on after physical death so that the psyche may achieve self-realiza-

tion. (As we will see, self-realization can never be fully attained in life, for perfection is beyond the reach of anyone.) This idea is based on the Buddhist notions of **karma** (a force generated by one's actions that, in its ethical consequences, determines one's destiny in the next life) and **rebirth**: until one's karma is fulfilled, it may be, Jung (1961) suggests, that one continues to return to three-dimensional existence. Perhaps, he says, when a person's karma is at last fulfilled (presumably, after several lifetimes), the psyche may attain what Buddhism calls **nirvana** (a state of oblivion in which pain, suffering, and all external reality cease to exist).

sponsible for the biological instincts that serve the purposes of self-preservation and reproduction. (These instincts are inner impulsions to act in certain ways when particular tissue conditions arise.) In this view, of course, Jung (1929, 1948b) does not differ from modern biologists. What is unusual about his view—and not in accord with modern biology and psychology—is his insistence that in addition to the biological instincts, we inherit ancestral "experience" in the form of archetypes.

THE WHY OF PSYCHIC EVENTS

Jung's approach to explaining why things happen is more variegated than Freud's. Freud, as you will recall, held a deterministic or **mechanistic** position; for him every event was caused by something that had occurred in the past. Jung put forward a **purposive** view, which explains the present in terms of the future. On this view, people's behavior is assumed to be determined by their future purposes, or goals. Jung believed that both viewpoints—the mechanistic and the purposive—are necessary for a complete understanding of personality; the present is determined not only by what has occurred in the past but also by what it is hoped or expected will occur in future.

Jung suggests that a purely mechanistic view is likely to produce resignation and despair in people, for it makes them prisoners of the past. They are not really free to set goals or make plans because what has already happened has immutably determined what will happen. The purposive view, on the other hand, gives people a feeling of hope and something to live and work for.

Few theorists today would argue with Jung's dictate that, in our quest for understanding, we look at both the past and the future. Rare, however, is the theorist who is willing to embrace Jung's third explanatory principle—the principle of **synchronicity**—which invokes neither past nor present causes. This principle holds that events may occur together in time and may appear to be related but may neither cause nor be caused by each other.

To Jung, experiences of mental telepathy, clairvoyance, and other such paranormal phenomena suggested that there is another kind of order in the universe besides that described by causality, and he applied this principle to his concept of the archetype. The archetype does not cause either a mental or a physical event, Jung said; rather, it possesses a quality that ''permits'' synchronous events to occur. Jung's principle seems an improvement on the notion that a thought can actually cause something to happen, a belief held by some students of **parapsychology** (the study of psychological phenomena that appear not to follow known principles of nature), but it is just as difficult as that notion to support. As an example of synchronicity, Jung (1961) relates the following story:

> *After several therapy sessions with a depressive patient who was about to return to his home in another city, Jung told this man that he should get in touch with Jung immediately if ''he observed his spirits sinking.'' One night, after having spent an evening that was ''curiously restive and nervous,'' Jung lay awake for some time. Then, after a brief period of sleep, he awoke with a start and had the feeling that someone had come into the room. He turned on the light, looked about the room and down the hall but found nothing—''it was still as death.'' Certain that someone had entered the room, he tried to think back to the moment of awakening and recalled that it had been with a feeling of dull pain, as though something had struck my forehead and then the back of my skull.'' The next day brought a telegram, saying that Jung's patient had fatally shot himself; a little later came the news that the bullet ''had come to rest in the back wall of the skull.'' (Adapted from Jung, 1961, pp. 137–138)*

This and other similar events contributed to Jung's fascination with the paranormal, a fascination that he never succeeded in getting Freud or indeed many others to share. A considerable amount of research has been devoted to explaining ''synchronous'' events, and in general such events are deemed statistical flukes. However, phenom-

ena and occurrences that seem to be related to such emotionally significant events as physical harm to or the death of people we know will
doubtless interest researchers for some time to come.

INDIVIDUATION AND THE TRANSCENDENT FUNCTION
Individuation and transcendence are the superordinate processes by
which human begins develop, throughout their lives, in the direction
of a stable unity. Guided by the archetype of the self, thee processes
lead human beings to strive toward making more and more of the unconscious conscious, toward differentiating all their component aspects—ego, anima or animus, shadow, and so on—to the fullest possible extent, and toward integrating all these aspects into a harmonious
whole.

Individuation and the transcendent function are closely bound
up with each other, for they are both processes for coming to terms
with the unconscious (see, e.g., Jung, 1943). **Individuation**, however, is responsible for more analytic processes—separating, differentiating, and elaborating various aspects of personality—and the
transcendent function is responsible for more synthetic processes—
integrating unconscious with conscious material, integrating systems
within themselves, and integrating the systems overall into an effectively functioning whole.

Repressive and regressive forces in the personality may oppose
the operation of these two processes, but the push toward wholeness is
very strong. This unconscious desire is often expressed in dreams,
myths, and other symbolic representations. One of its most common
symbols is the mandala, which we have already encountered (see page
117). According to Jung, the drawing or painting of mandalas can
have a therapeutic effect, and many of his patients produced such
paintings spontaneously.

According to Jung, no one can avoid the powerful influence of
the unity archetype, although just what form its expression will take
and how successful it will be in realizing its aim varies from person to
person. The goal of complete differentiation, balance, and unity has
rarely if ever been reached, Jung observed, except perhaps by Jesus
Christ or Buddha.

RESEARCH EMPHASES AND METHODS
Jung drew the data on which his theories are based from many different sources: clinical and experimental research, dreams and visions of
normal people and patients, myths and fairy tales, primitive life and
customs, anthropology, history, literature, the arts, the religions of
both East and West, astrology, parapsychology, and alchemy. Jung

found symbolic, archetypal material in all these disparate sources, no matter what part of the world they came from, and he drew very convincing connections between these materials, to demonstrate their meaningful operation in people's lives.

Jung held that his discoveries were factual, not speculative; his concepts, he said, were "merely names for *facts*" (Jung, personal communication, 1954). Many readers, however, find Jung's "facts" highly speculative indeed. American psychologists, in particular, find unacceptable the comparative research methods used by Jung and his followers because these methods lack controls for bias and chance factors and fail to employ systematic techniques of quantification. Such controls and techniques are essential if researchers are to estimate reliability, establish validity, and replicate studies.

Initially, however, many American psychologists were attracted to Jung because of his experimental (and properly controlled and quantified) studies using the word association test. Derivatives of this work have a relatively established place in American psychology today. We will look briefly at this research topic before discussing the studies that occupied Jung most of his life, the exploration of the collective unconscious and its archetypes.

COMPLEXES: THE WORD ASSOCIATION TEST

Sir Francis Galton (English scientist and the first student of individual differences; 1822–1911) is credited with being the first to study word associations, in his effort to explicate the learning process. Wilhelm Wundt (German scientist and founder of experimental psychology, 1832–1920) formally introduced this type of research into experimental psychology. It was Jung, however, working under Bleuler's direction, who first used word associations to study the emotional content of the mind.

As mentioned earlier, Jung (1909a) regularly found that certain words and phrases elicited unusual responses in his subjects, and he hypothesized that such responses were clues to mental contents that were otherwise inaccessible. In Jung's **word association test**, the experimenter read a standard list of words one at a time to a subject who was instructed to respond to each word, as read, with the first word that came to mind. The time the subject took to respond to each word was measured with a stopwatch.

Because various physiological functions are involved in emotional arousal, Jung began to measure several of these functions while subjects were responding to his word list. A pneumograph, connected to a band strapped around the chest, measured the strength and duration of the subject's breathing. A psychogalvanometer, using electrodes applied to the skin, measured changes in the skin's electrical conductance, changes that are due primarily to fluctuations in the amount of sweating.

Jung proposed that when a particular word elicited a delay in verbal response time and/or a significant alteration in breathing or skin conductance, a complex had been tapped. Suppose, for example, that the word *wood* caused a young woman to have difficulty responding, to breathe rapidly, and to give evidence of heightened skin conductance. We might assume that a hidden complex had been touched off. After more words, such as *school, jacket,* and *beard,* triggered similar responses, and after further inquiry, we might discover that the young woman had been attacked some time before by a bearded man wearing an unusual type of jacket in a wooded area near the school where she taught. If she had never mentioned this incident before, we might infer that the trauma of it drew out archetypal material having to do with sexual attack and that the terror the event aroused was so great that the entire incident was repressed into her unconscious.

Jung used his word association test in working with patients as a way of getting quick clues to important complexes. Today psychologists and others occasionally use similar tests in clinical diagnostic settings. Jung also used his technique to investigate some instances of thievery at the University of Zurich, and his reports of this and other similar work (see, e.g., Jung, 1905) were read with interest by many, including persons involved with law enforcement. Today the method has been adapted for use in the detection of lying and criminal activity. It is also occasionally used in studies of interests and attitudes.

ARCHETYPES: ANALYSIS OF DREAMS AND OTHER UNCONSCIOUS MATERIAL

Jung's search for evidence in support of his concept of the archetype led him to investigate many obscure and complex subjects, including, as we have said, the medieval science of alchemy. Repeatedly he found in such sources symbols and expressions that were the same as, or closely paralleled, symbols that appeared in his patients' dreams and fantasies. A growing accumulation of such conjunctions convinced Jung that there are universal ideas, or thought-forms, that can have come down to people only as some sort of inborn or racially inherited quality.

For Jung, as for Freud, dreams were the clearest expression of the unconscious mind. "Dreams," Jung wrote, "are impartial, spontaneous products of the unconscious psyche . . . . They show us the unvarnished natural truth" (1934b, p. 149). However, he said, not all dreams are equally useful. Many—the "little" dreams—are concerned with relatively unimportant preoccupations. The dreams that particularly interested Jung were the "big" dreams—those that occur when the unconscious is seriously disturbed by something, often with some failure of the ego to deal satisfactorily with the external world. Such dreams are **numinous** (Jung's term for an intensely moving experience)—strange and uncanny.

For Freud, you will recall, the dream represented a repressed wish. For Jung (1948a), the dream was an effort to further the project of developing the personality. Dreams serve the process of individuation either by compensating for the neglected, and thus undifferentiated, aspects of the psyche or by sketching out plans for future achievements or solutions to problems. In the normal person, conscious and unconscious levels are of about equal importance. When the conscious attitude is "more or less adequate," the dream is simply compensatory. But when a person's conscious attitude is "unadapted both objectively and subjectively," the dream is informed by "a guiding, prospective function" that can help the conscious mind make more satisfactory adaptations (Jung, 1948a).

Jung found it useful to analyze material from the unconscious as expressed not only in dreams but in fantasies purposely conjured up in waking life. Remember that in Freud's free association method, the dreamer focuses on a dream element and gives successive associations, which usually move increasingly away from the element itself. In Jung's method of **amplification**, however, the dreamer—and the analyst—"stand by" the dream element, giving multiple associations directly to it. Jung believed that a true symbol has many aspects and that to understand the meaning of a symbol for a patient, both patient and therapist must contribute all they can.

Jung's writings contain numerous examples of this method as applied to dream analysis as well as to other archetypal materials. For example, exploring the archetypal notion of unity, Jung (1951a) examines in great detail the symbol of the fish, which, he says, is one of the oldest of all symbols, appearing in inscriptions from the Babylonian and Phoenician cultures.

Using his **dream series** method, Jung analyzed every dream in the context of those that preceded and followed it. For him, a person's dreams occur in a "coherent series in the course of which the meaning gradually unfolds more or less of its own accord" (1944, p. 12). It is, Jung said, as if we had not just one book before us but many, each throwing light on the unknown terms. Once we have read all the books, we can decipher the difficult passages in each one.

Jung's method here is one of internal consistency, an approach that you will recall Freud relied upon in constructing his theory of personality. The idea is that if all the separate interpretations make sense when put in juxtaposition, the chances are good that each one by itself is accurate. This method is often used in psychology when researchers must work with subjective, nonquantifiable material like dreams, stories, and fantasies.

A third method of analysis unique to Jung is that of **active**

"I've followed this way and I've followed that way, and the
way to go turns out to be my way."

Drawing by Dedini; © 1982 The New Yorker Magazine, Inc.

imagination, a kind of introspection that produces material that is
"part dream, part vision, or dream mixed with vision" (Jung, 1951b,
p. 190). Subjects are asked to concentrate their attention on an elusive
dream-image or on a spontaneous visual image conjured up consciously and at will and to observe the changes that take place in it.

Among the instances of active imagination that Jung (1951b)
records is a series of nondreams described by a woman patient. She begins:

*I saw a white bird with outstretched wings. It alighted on the figure of a woman,
clad in blue, who sat there like an antique statue. The bird perched on her hand,
and in it she had a grain of wheat. The bird took it in its beak and flew into the
sky again. (p. 191)*

In this case, active imagination included having the patient elaborate
on her image in a painting. Her depiction of the woman she had visu-
alized as having large breasts suggested to Jung that this female image
represented the patient's mother.

EVALUATION

Jungian psychology has many proponents throughout the world, and institutes for the training of Jungian analysts and for the treatment of patients have been established in a number of cities. Followers of Jung such as Gerhard Adler (1948), Micheal Fordham (1947), Sir Herbert Read (1945), Esther Harding (1947), and Jolande Jacobi (1959) have continued to explore Jung's theories and to elaborate many of his concepts.

What influence has Jung's theory of personality had on the development of scientific psychology? Except for the word association test and his concept of introversion–extraversion, Jung's formulations have had relatively little visible impact on psychological research, largely because neither Jung nor his followers have attempted to quantify these formulations.

Jung's conception of introversion–extraversion has lent itself rather well to procedures that are susceptible of quantification. Questionnaire items, for example, can be rated, scored, and analyzed statistically, and as we have noted, there is considerable literature on this topic.

Jung, however, has probably been criticized more roundly by experimentalists than even Freud. Not only did Jung hold the comparative method a perfectly acceptable scientific tool, but he refused to be bound to theory:

> Theories in psychology are the very devil. It is true that we need certain points of view for their orienting and heuristic value; but they should always be regarded as mere auxiliary concepts that can be laid aside at any time. We still know so very little about the psyche that it is positively grotesque to think we are far enough advanced to frame general theories. We have not even established the empirical extent of the psyche's phenomenology: how then can we dream of general theories? No doubt theory is the best cloak for lack of experience and ignorance but the consequences are depressing: bigotedness, superficiality, and scientific sectarianism. (Jung, 1946, p. 7)

Probably the most serious assault on analytical psychology has been made by Edward Glover (1950), the British psychoanalyst, who who ridiculed the concept of the archetype, insisting that such "thought-images" can be accounted for in terms of experience alone. Indeed, many have criticized Jung for this apparent doctrine of acquired characters. He, of course, argued that he did not postulate actual inherited thoughts or behaviors, only the potential for them. But it is, at least as yet, impossible to distinguish between an inherited thought and an inherited potential for a thought, neither of which can be shown to have a basis in concrete reality.

Until recently, at least, Jung's influence on psychology has probably been more indirect than direct, and it is, unfortunately, difficult to evaluate the indirect effects of a theory. Sometimes ideas occur more or less spontaneously in the minds of a number of people at about the same time, owing to the prevailing intellectual climate. For example, both Adler (Chapter 5) and Jung emphasized the purposive nature of the human being. Did one influence the other? Did one or the other or both influence subsequent views? Did their theories and others' come about as a reaction to the extreme mechanism of nineteenth-century science? Again, Jung's idea of self-realization is certainly echoed in the work of Horney, Allport, Rogers, and Maslow—to name only psychologists discussed in this book—but Jung is rarely credited with developing this conception, and we have no way of knowing how other theorists came by it.

What Jungian theory needs is for more hypotheses derived from it to be tested experimentally. Some efforts have been made to test Jung's approach to the analysis of dreams (Bash, 1952; Dallett, 1973) as well as his theory of symbolization (Melhado, 1964; Meier, 1965). And his conceptions of the attitudes and functions have received a fair amount of attention. Helson (1973, 1982) shows a special sensitivity to the complexity of Jung's ideas and to the demands of empirical research. Her studies have focused particularly on cognitive–affective style in personality in relation to Jung's psychological types. Carlson (Carlson, 1980; Carlson and Levy, 1973) has also focused on the psychological types, studying variations among types in such things as memory and social perception.

Although psychologists have been reluctant to embrace Jungian theory, Jung's influence outside the field has been considerable. Many writers in the areas of history, literature, philosophy, and religion have acknowledged their indebtedness to Jung. Some examples are the historian Arnold Toynbee, the writers Philip Wylie and Hermann Hesse, and the author and critic Lewis Mumford. The field of religion has accorded Jung particular respect; he was invited, for example, to give the Terry lectures on "Psychology and Religion" at Yale (Jung, 1938).

When all is said and done, Jung's theory of personality, as developed in his prolific writings and as applied to a wide range of phenomena, stands as one of the most remarkable achievements in modern thought. The originality and audacity of Jung's thinking have few parallels in recent scientific history, and no one other than Freud has opened more conceptual windows into what Jung would call "the soul of man." Certainly Jung's ideas merit the closest attention from any serious student of psychology.

SUMMARY

1. The personality, or **psyche**, is a unity that includes all thought, feeling, and behavior, whether conscious or unconscious.

2. The **ego**, the organization of the conscious mind, screens experiences for admission to **consciousness**.

3. Forgotten, suppressed, or rejected experiences are stored in the **personal unconscious**.

4. A **complex** is a group of ideas that cluster together in the personal unconscious.

5. The **collective unconscious** is composed of primordial images, or **archetypes**, inherited from our racial, and even animal, past. Its contents can be helpful but, if ignored, can interfere with effective functioning.

6. Four archetypes are of great importance in shaping the personality: the **persona**, the **anima** and **animus**, the **shadow**, and the **self**. The self gradually becomes the center of the personality and guides the person toward self-realization.

7. **Symbols**, which are the outward manifestations of archetypes, often represent the wisdom of the collective unconscious.

8. The **introverted** attitude reflects a focus on an inner, private world. The **extraverted** attitude reflects a focus on the external world of things, events, and people. **Thinking** and **feeling** are opposing, **rational** functions; **sensing** and **intuiting** are opposing, **nonrational** functions.

9. The attitudes, functions, and the eight **psychological types** they make up have been studied by a number of researchers since Jung.

10. **Psychic energy**, or **life energy**, is derived from the individual's experiences, and it powers activities such as attending, thinking, willing, and striving.

11. A **psychic value** is a measure of the energy committed to a particular psychic element.

12. Psychic energy follows the principles of **equivalence** and **entropy**: the amount of energy in the personality system stays the same, and within the system energy remains in balance.

13. Psychic energy pursues its two purposes of preserving life and developing cultural and spiritual activities through progression, regression, sublimation, and repression. In **progression** and **sublimation**, energy moves forward; in **regression** and **repression**, it retreats to the unconscious.

14. Of the four **stages of life—childhood, youth and young adulthood, middle age**, and **old age**—the second, which emphasizes adap-

tation to social and economic requirements, and the third, in which the person turns from material to spiritual concerns, are the most important.

15. Causality lies both in the past (**mechanism**) and in the future (**purposivism**). **Synchronicity** may explain the occurrence of events that do not follow natural laws.

16. Individuation and the **transcendent function** both involve making what is unconscious conscious and lead to self-realization.

17. The **word association test**, which permits us access to important unconscious material, is used in clinical diagnostic settings as well as in the detection of crime.

18. Dreams, which are the clearest expression of the unconscious, compensate for neglected aspects of the psyche and outline future plans or solutions to problems.

19. Jung has been criticized for his use of the comparative method of research, his general neglect of controlled experimentation, and his concept of the collective unconscious. His influence on scientific psychology to date has been largely limited to his word association research and his conceptions of introversion–extraversion and the psychological types. His purposive view of personality functioning and his concept of self-realization have probably influenced other theorists, and many of his ideas have wide acceptance in a variety of disciplines.

SUGGESTED READING

The best guide to Jung's writings, most of which are contained in the 18 volumes of his *Collected Works* (1953–1978), is Jung's semiautobiographical work, *Memories, Dreams, and Reflections* (1961). This book, essentially an inner, spiritual revelation, will help you to understand Jung's thinking.

Hall and Nordby, *A Primer of Jungian Psychology* (1973), offer an excellent introduction to Jung's theory and work. Judicious selections from Jung's voluminous writings are offered by Campbell, *The Portable Jung* (1971), and Storr, *The Essential Jung* (1983).

One of Jung's last statements of his views is contained in his essay ''Approaching the Unconscious'' (1964). This essay, intended for the general reader, is a very clear presentation of one topic that concerned Jung: self-realization through the unfolding of the unconscious.

Jung's psychological types are described in some detail in Chapter 10 of *Psychological Types* (1921). His work on the word association test is briefly summarized in ''The Association Method'' (1909), in *Experimental Researches*, Volume 2 of his *Works*. In that same volume you will find a wealth of interesting material on Jung's studies of word association and the psychophysical response.

The symbolism of the mandala is discussed at some length in *The Archetypes and the Collective Unconscious*, Volume 9, Part I, of the *Collected Works*, and

Jung's approach to the study and interpretation of dreams is explored in the fourth part of *The Structure and Dynamics of the Psyche*, Volume 8 of the *Works*. You may find it interesting to see how Jung applied his vast learning and powers of insight to issues of current concern, in "Flying Saucers: A Modern Myth of Things Seen in the Skies" (1958).

Jung was accused of collaborating with the Nazi regime during World War II, and in this connection, you may find it interesting to read his accounts of several of his own, premonitory dreams that seemed, at least in retrospect, to foretell both world wars and to express his concern about German aspirations; see, for example, *Letters: 1906–1950*; Part III of *Civilization in Transition*, Volume 10 of Jung's *Collected Works*; and *Memories, Dreams, and Reflections* (1961). Stern, in *Jung: The Haunted Prophet* (1976), has written rather critically of Jung in this regard, whereas followers of Jung such as Jaffé (1971) and Cohen (1975) have insisted that Jung was misrepresented.

Both Jung (1961) and Freud (1914, 1925) have written about their relationship, as have others (Dry, 1961; Jones, 19055; Weigert, 1942), and almost all the letters the two men exchanged have been published (McGuire, 1974). Jung's writings on Freud and psychoanalysis appear in *Freud and Psychoanalysis*, Volume 4, and in *Psychology and Religion: West and East*, Volume 15, of his *Works*.

Biographical material on Jung can be found in a number of books (Bennett, 1961; Dry, 1961; Fordham, 1953; Hannah, 1976; Jaffé, 1971; Stern, 1976; Wehr, 1971; van der Post, 1976; von Franz, 1975), but none of these can be regarded as a definitive biography. Jung's own statement, in *Memories, Dreams, and Reflections*, remains our best source of information on his life. Jaffé, *C. G. Jung: Word and Image* (1979), has produced a very beautiful book of pictures and accompanying biographical text, and a collection of Jung's letters has been published by Princeton University Press (1973, 1975).

Chapter five

5.

There is no absolute truth, but what comes closest to it is the human community.

ALFRED ADLER

All of us retain the capacity to change . . . as long as we live.

KAREN HORNEY

Every man carries within himself all of humanity.

ERICH FROMM

Everyone is much more simply human than otherwise.

HARRY STACK SULLIVAN

Interpersonal Dynamics: Alfred Adler, Karen Horney, Erich Fromm, and Harry Stack Sullivan

Nineteenth-century scientific thought conceived of the human being as a biological creature whose transactions with the world served three purposes: individual survival, species survival, and evolutionary development. On the basis of Charles Darwin's proposal that some individuals are better equipped for these purposes than others, many scientists began to focus their attention on questions of individual variation and the adaptive qualities of psychological processes.

Toward the end of the century, however, the new disciplines of sociology and anthropology began to study the human being in varying environments, and the view that personality may be shaped more by social circumstances than by biological factors became prominent. Gradually, a number of Freud's followers withdrew their allegiance to classical psychoanalysis and began to fashion their own theories along the new, *social* psychological lines.

Alfred Adler, regarded by many as the first psychoanalyst to see the human being as essentially a social creature, developed a theory in which the need for superiority and the need to relate to others were primary. Karen Horney, who was first and foremost a clinician, fashioned a theory that sees the person as adopting one of several interpersonal styles of behavior in an effort to solve basic conflicts. Erich Fromm was deeply interested in socialist thought and adopted an approach to personality that emphasized socioeconomic and cultural variables. Harry Stack Sullivan was probably more independent of psychoanalytic doctrine than the others, and his "interpersonal theory of psychiatry" was profoundly influenced by his study of sociology and anthropology.

Each of the four theories discussed in this chapter has its distinctive assumptions and concepts, but there are many parallels among them (see, e.g., Ansbacher and Ansbacher, 1956; James, 1947; Munroe, 1955). Human beings, in their view, are essentially conscious, rational creatures whose potentials for both self-realization and cooperation with others need only be supported and encouraged.

143

According to Alfred Adler, "the problems of life are [always] social" (Ansbacher and Ansbacher, 1956). For Freud, the essential components of a healthy life were the abilities "to love and to work." For Adler, healthy functioning meant not only loving and working but feeling a communality with other people and being concerned for their welfare.

Adler's theory of personality made a number of significant contributions to psychology. The "first of the ego psychologists" (Marmor, 1972), Adler pioneered in the development of a psychology in which consciousness is by far the more significant portion of the personality. Like the ego psychologists, Adler conceived of a self that searches actively for experience that will enhance its own development and, in the absence of such experience, seeks to create it. Adler's concept of the person as primarily a social being was greatly influential in the development of social psychology, a discipline that began to evolve in the early part of this century. And, in contrast to Freud, Adler held that the human being's need for sexual satisfaction is only one among many basic needs; it is the way we organize, plan, and carry out all our life's activities, Adler said, that determines how we will express our sexual needs, not the other way around.

As we explore the main features of Adler's theory, we will be talking essentially about personality dynamics. Adler insisted that "all [life] is movement" (Ansbacher and Ansbacher, 1956, p. 195), and he preferred not to think in such terms as structure or developmental stages. Such conceptions, he felt, tend to reify, or make concrete, things that are abstract. Structural terms interfere with our understanding of the flow of human behavior. In his view of the person as a feeling, thinking, purposeful creature, operating in a social environment, Adler is an intellectual forebear of humanistic and phenomenological theories such as those of Abraham Maslow and Carl Rogers (Chapter 6), of the field theory of Kurt Lewin (Chapter 8), and of cognitive theory like that of George Kelly (Chapter 8).

FICTIONAL FINAL GOALS

Adler's concept of human motivation was quite opposite to Freud's. For Adler, our behavior is determined by our perceptions of what we hope to achieve in the future, not by what we have done—or what has been done to us—in the past. Psychological phenomena, he said, cannot be explained by "instincts, impulses, experiences, traumata," but only by "the perspective in which [such phenomena] are regarded, the individual way of seeing them, which subordinates all life to the final goal" (Adler, 1930, p. 400).

BOX 5.1   Alfred Adler (1870–1937)

Alfred Adler, with his son Kurt and daughter Alexandra, on a lecture trip, Berkeley, California, 1936. Kurt Adler and Alexandra Adler, psychiatrists like their father, continue his work at New York City's Alfred Adler Mental Hygiene Clinic.

Alfred Adler was born in a suburb of Vienna to a middle-class Jewish family, the second of six children. Growing up in a neighborhood where people of varying backgrounds lived, Adler spent much of his childhood playing and fighting with peers who included Jewish and non-Jewish children of both the middle and lower classes. It seems likely that his lifelong concern with the social aspects of personality had its roots in this early experience.

Adler apparently decided quite early to become a doctor—both his own early bout with rickets and a younger brother's death may have been influential in this decision—and he attended the University of Vienna, receiving his medical degree in 1895. He specialized in ophthalmology and then practiced general medicine for a time before turning to psychiatry.

In 1902 Adler met Sigmund Freud, and for the next nine years Adler was a charter member of the Vienna Psychoanalytic Society, of which he became president in 1910. Adler's theories were increasingly at variance with those of Freud and other society members, however, and in 1911 he resigned his post and left the society (Adler, 1978; Ansbacher and Ansbacher, 1956; Colby, 1951; Jones, 1955, 1961).

Adler then formed his own group, which he called the Society of Individual Psychology, and soon attracted followers throughout the world. Today Adlerian groups are represented in many countries; in the United States, the North American Society of Adlerian Psychology has branches in New York, Chicago, and Los Angeles. Alexandra Adler and Kurt Adler, two of the four children born to Adler and his wife, the former Raissa Timofeyevna Epstein, are both practicing psychiatrists associated with the Alfred Adler Mental Hygiene Clinic in New York City.

In 1935, after numerous visits to the United States, Adler settled permanently in New York City, where he became professor of medical psychology at what is now the Downstate Medical Center, State University of New York. He continued to travel abroad to lecture, consult, and give clinical demonstrations, and it was on one of his trips that he collapsed and died, apparently of a heart attack.

Adler's manner was not imposing, but he apparently was a dynamic speaker to whom audiences responded with enthusiasm. According to his biographers, although he enjoyed these encounters, he derived even greater pleasure from informal meetings with students and colleagues, in coffeehouses, where discussions often went on for hours. Paying as much attention to the beginning student as to the mature scholar, and listening as much as he himself talked, Adler was his own best example of social interest in action.

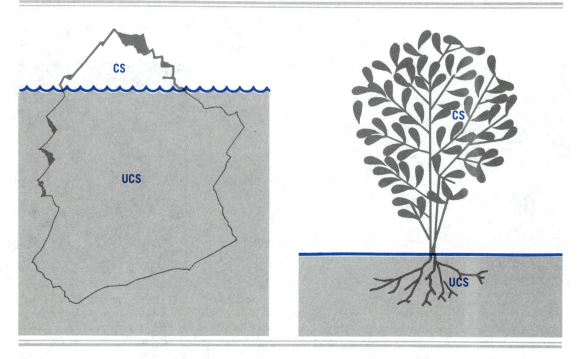

Figure 5.1   The Freudian and Adlerian concepts of the mind. The psychoanalytic view is classically represented by an iceberg, most of which is concealed beneath the surface; the unconscious, for Freud, is the larger part of the mind. Adler's view can be represented by a jade tree, which has a small root system and a luxuriant growth above the ground; for Adler, the larger portion of the mind is conscious.

Adler theorized that to guide our behavior we create **fictional final goals**. These goals are ''fictional'' because they are not necessarily based on reality. Rather, they represent our ideas of what is possible based on our subjective interpretation of the world. Because, as we will see, human beings' primary drive is to become better—bigger, stronger, more skilled, and so on—the goals they set themselves are expressions of ideal states, expressions that help in dealing with the environment. For example, the statement ''All men are created equal'' is not true, yet it can serve to guide the behavior of people who want to make it true.

It is important to understand that fictional final goals do not exist in the future as part of some universal plan—they do not represent fate. They are our own personal creation, and they exist subjectively, here and now, as ideas that exert great influence on our behavior. For example, if we believe that virtuous people go to heaven and those who are evil to hell, we are likely to conform our behavior to the standards that parents and other authority figures have given us.

OVERCOMING INFERIORITY AND BECOMING SUPERIOR:
THE GREAT UPWARD DRIVE

For Adler, the human being is motivated by one primary urge—the urge to overcome the feeling of inferiority and to become superior. Thus, our behavior is determined essentially by the future that we envision—by our goals and expectations. Pushed by feeling inferior, pulled by the desire to be superior, we spend our lives trying to become as nearly perfect as possible.

Inferiority, for Adler, means feeling weak and unskilled in the face of tasks that need to be completed. It does not mean being inferior to another person in a global sense, although it does imply that we compare our specific abilities with those of others who are older and more experienced. Adler's concept of **superiority** is very like Jung's notion of transcendence and is the forerunner of self-realization, or self-actualization, proposed by Horney, Maslow, and others. Again, by this concept, Adler does not mean being better than others or winning out over them. By striving for superiority, Adler means continually trying to become something better—to become nearer and nearer to one's ideal goals.

It is the feeling of inferiority that gives birth to the striving for superiority, and together they make up the "great upward drive" that pushes us continually to move "from minus to plus, . . . from below to above" (Adler, 1930, p. 398). This drive, according to Adler, is innate and is *the* drive that powers all other urges.

The feeling of inferiority, Adler said, is quite normal: all of us begin life as small, weak creatures. Throughout life, feelings of inferiority arise constantly as we meet new and unfamiliar tasks that must be mastered. These feelings are the cause of all improvement in human behavior. The child, for example, who is learning to skate and keeps falling feels inferior because she is not (yet) a good skater. The child's feeling motivates her to keep practicing until she can skate well. The 40-year-old adult who earns a promotion feels inferior in his new position until he learns how to handle the new assignment. Each time we confront a new task, our initial awareness of inferiority is overcome as we achieve a higher level of functioning.

Certain conditions such as pampering and neglect—we will discuss these later—may lead a person to develop an inferiority or a superiority complex. These two complexes are closely related. A **superiority complex** always hides—or compensates for—a feeling of inferiority, and an **inferiority complex** often conceals a feeling of superiority. For example, a person who is arrogant and boastful and tries to dominate people who are in some way weaker than himself may be demonstrating a superiority complex. In reality, the person feels inadequate, but by calling attention to himself and by pushing other people around, he can pretend to be superior. A person who is continually depressed and discouraged may develop excuses for not striving for self-improvement and thereby obtain special services from others. This person may actually feel entitled to these services because of a hidden sense of superiority and the belief that all her troubles are really not her fault.

Believing as he did that the overarching motive of every person, man and woman, child and adult, is to become strong, competent, achieving, and creative, Adler was one of the earliest supporters of equality for the sexes. By his concept of the **masculine protest**, which referred chiefly to ''manifestations in women protesting against their feminine role'' (Ansbacher and Ansbacher, 1956, p. 49), he proposed that rather than wish to be a man, as Freud had suggested, a woman wishes for the qualities and privileges regarded in our culture as male, such as strength, courage, independence, success, sexual freedom, and the right to choose a partner for oneself.

SOCIAL INTEREST

Adler's concept of social interest is not easy to define. His original term *Gemeinschaftsgefühl* can be—and has been—translated in many different ways, and the broader meaning of the concept is still debated. For present purposes, we will define **social interest** as a caring and concern for the welfare of others that continues, throughout life, to guide a person's behavior.

Although the capacity for social interest is inborn, Adler said, it is too small or weak—at least at this point in the evolution of the human being—to develop on its own (Ansbacher and Ansbacher, 1956). As a result, it is the responsibility of the mother, as the ''first other person whom the child experiences,'' to develop this innate potentiality in the child. If the mother does not ''help the child extend his interest to others,'' the child will be unprepared to meet the problems of living in society. Adler believed that in this situation, the educational system or some form of therapy had to substitute for parental training; see Box 5.2.

According to Adler, it is social interest that enables a person to strive for superiority in healthy ways and the lack of it that leads to maladaptive functioning:

All failures—neurotics, psychotics, criminals, drunkards, problem children, suicides, perverts, and prostitutes—are failures because they are lacking in social interest. They approach the problems of occupation, friendship and sex without the confidence that they can be solved by cooperation. The meaning they give to life is a private meaning. No one else is benefited by the achievement of their aims. . . . Their goal of success is a goal of personal superiority, and their triumphs have meaning only to themselves. (Ansbacher and Ansbacher, 1956, p. 156)

BOX 5.2   Teaching Social Interest

Reasoning that adult maladjustment could be reduced if faulty early training in social interest could be corrected, Adler became very interested in what today is often referred to as the field of community mental health. In 1919 Adler was invited to lecture regularly at an adult education institute in Vienna (the *Volksheim*), and by 1922 he had begun to establish child guidance clinics in the school system.

Such clinics were not new, but Adler was the first to conduct therapeutic sessions that included not only a problem child but the child's parents, teachers, and other interested people. These public demonstrations were an early form of family, or group, psychotherapy.

Adler further reasoned that although it was not possible to reach all problem children directly, he could reach them by "teaching" their teachers. He saw the educational system as being responsible for encouraging the development of social interest in children, especially in cases where parental training had failed or was absent. His ideas coincided with those of Vienna's school board, which had undertaken to reform the school system after the end of World War I. Adler was invited to join the faculty of the municipal teachers' college (the Pedagogical Institute) and lectured there beginning in 1924. A little later, an experimental school based on Adlerian principles (Adler himself was not connected with this school) was established in Vienna. This school was closed for political reasons in the 1930s, but it reopened after World War II (Adler, 1979, pp. 376–377).

The concept of social interest explains how it is possible for all people to struggle for superiority at once. Ultimately, social interest consists of people striving for the "perfection" of society as they strive for their own individual "perfection." In this sense, "social interest is the true and inevitable compensation for all the natural weaknesses of individual human beings" (Adler, 1929, p. 31). Our striving to overcome our particular inferiorities leads us to struggle to improve society as a whole. The state of perfection toward which we all strive is one in which individual and society live, love and work together harmoniously.

Clearly the notions of social interest and striving for superiority are closely interwoven. The healthy human being, according to Adler, at the same time that he strives for his own superiority helps others to achieve their goals. In a letter to his oldest daughter and her new husband, Adler made marriage a model for society: "married life is a task at which both of you must work, with joy. . . . Fill yourselves with the brave resolve to think more about each other than about yourself, and always try to . . . make the other's life easier and more beautiful. Don't allow either of you to become subordinate to the other. No one can stand this attitude" (Adler, 1978, p. 340). For healthy people and a healthy society to develop, Adler said, there must be a constant interplay between concern for oneself and concern for the other.

Like many other psychologists (and personality psychologists—see, e.g., Lewin, Chapter 8, and Allport, Chapter 10), Adler was con-

These volunteer workers on a new "farm" in New York City's South Bronx—an area of both devastation and renewal—illustrate one of Adler's most important conceptions: that in our common struggle for strength and competence, we can create a better society.

cerned with problems of discrimination, ethnic prejudice, and hostility among nations:

The honest psychologist cannot shut his eyes to social conditions which prevent the child from becoming a part of the community and from feeling at home in the world, and which [tend to make him] grow up as though he lived in enemy country. . . . The psychologist must work against [excessive] nationalism . . . against wars . . . against unemployment . . . and against all other obstacles which interfere with the spreading of social interest in the family, the school, and society at large. (Ansbacher and Ansbacher, 1956, p. 454)

STYLE OF LIFE

By his concept of the **style of life**, Adler sought to explain the uniqueness of the person. Everyone has goals, feels inferior, strives to be superior, and does or does not color this striving with social interest. But everyone does these things in a different way. The style of life is our unique way of seeking the particular goals we have set in the particular life circumstances in which we find ourselves.

For Adler, as we have noted, the most salient characteristic of life was movement. For the sake of discussion and analysis, one can "freeze" movement and talk about such things as a thought, a feeling, an act (Adler, 1979, p. 118). But such "frozen moments" can be understood only if they are returned to the stream of life—they must always be interpreted in the context of a person's ongoing style. For example, suppose you see a classmate running and playing with a group of children. If you freeze the movement, you see joy and laughter. But you know that this young woman's brother, to whom she was very close, has just died. You wonder how she can be so uncaring. When you learn that for some years she and her brother had worked together with groups of less advantaged children, the frozen moment suddenly fits the style of her life: in tribute to the dead man, his sister is going on with their work.

There are as many styles of life as there are people in the world. For example, one person may seek to become superior in physical strength and ability, and another may strive for intellectual achievement. According to Adler, each of these persons will arrange his or her life to fit the particular end goal and a particular way of striving for it. Thus, the first person may play soccer and baseball in school and basketball in college. She may become a firefighter, go on camping trips with her husband and children, and lead a scout troop. The second person may read and study alone much of the time. A Phi Beta Kappa in college, he may become a microbiologist, pursue a career in cancer research, and encourage his children's interest in science.

By the age of 4 or 5, attitudes and ways of perceiving are pretty much fixed—the style of life is set. The style of life is not simply determined by the child's "intrinsic ability" (heredity) and "objective environment"; it is formed by the child out of his or her *perception* and *interpretation* of both of these basic elements. Quite early,

the line of direction is established and the individual becomes definitely oriented. . . . The individual's apperceptions are from then on bound to fall into a groove. . . . The child will not perceive given situations as they actually exist, but under the prejudice of his own interests. . . . The interpretation [of experience] always accords with the original meaning given to life. Even if this meaning is very gravely mistaken . . . it is never easily relinquished." (Ansbacher and Ansbacher, 1956, p. 189)

Thus, the style of life does not ordinarily change. Concrete expressions of the style may vary (as in the examples we have given), but unless the person recognizes "faults and errors" and purposely changes the direction in which he or she is going, the basic style remains the same (Ansbacher and Ansbacher, 1956, p. 397).

THE CREATIVE POWER OF THE SELF

The **creative power of the self** is the essential principle of human life. It is the "third force" that ultimately determines human behavior (Adler, 1978; Ansbacher, 1971). According to Adler, heredity gives us "certain abilities," and the environment gives us "certain impressions." These two forces, in combination with the way in which we experience and interpret our heredity and environment, make up the "bricks" we use in our own "creative" way to construct our particular attitudes toward life and our relations with the outside world (Adler, 1935, p. 5).

Adler's concept of the creativity of the self clearly reflects his antimechanistic view of personality: the human being is not the passive recipient of experience but an actor and initiator of behavior. This concept underlines Adler's view of personality as dynamic rather than static: the person is constantly moving through life, actively interpreting and using all experience. And it supports his notion that personality is unique: each person creates his or her own particular personality out of the raw material of heredity and experience.

RESEARCH EMPHASES AND METHODS

Like Freud, Adler was a clinician, not an experimentalist. Many researchers have explored Adlerian concepts, particularly his notion of birth order, but Adler's own research consisted primarily of observations and inferences drawn from his work with therapy patients and with problem children in the school setting.

THE RELATION OF PERSONALITY TO BIRTH ORDER.   Adler's **birth order** theory is based on his belief that heredity, environment, and individual creativity combine to determine personality. Adler pointed out that each child in the family is born with a different genetic inheritance and into a different social setting and that each child interprets its situation in a different way. Thus it is important to look at both the similarities among people born into the same **ordinal position** (first, second, third, etc.) and at the differences in the ways such people interpret their experience. For example, the first-born child, who receives undivided parental attention and concern until displaced by a sister or brother, may become a responsible adult who is similarly protective of others or an insecure person lacking in social interest. Just how first-borns will develop depends on a number of factors, including their genetic inheritance (e.g., developmental disability can alter patterns of interrelating), their preparation for the arrival of siblings, and their unique interpretation of their particular experience. Thus, although there is a general tendency, Adler believed, for first-, middle-, and later-born children as well as only children to exhibit the qualities

Although we can see a "family resemblance" among the members of this large family, each child probably has very different personality characteristics. For Adler, characteristics of the oldest, the middle, the youngest, or the only child might be influenced by genetic factors as well as by such factors as whether an oldest child was still at home when younger children were born or whether two siblings were separated by few or many years. One thing we can be certain of—no member of this family could feel like an only child!

outlined in Table 5.1, any individual child may demonstrate quite different characteristics.

Initially, Adler's birth order theory was given little credence (see, e.g., Jones, 1931). Over the years, however, researchers have explored its predictive power in a wide range of settings. They have looked at such phenomena as relation of birth order to a person's desire or distaste for human contact in anxiety-provoking situations (e.g., Schachter, 1959) and the effects of birth order on a person's intellectual development (e.g., Zajonc and Bargh, 1980). A fair number of studies offer some support for Adler's various proposals; other studies, however, do not support his theory (for reviews of the literature, see Vockell, Felker, and Miley, 1973; Ernst and Angst, 1983). The present consensus seems to be that birth order is at least one of the factors that influence personality, and the concept continues to stimulate research.

EARLY MEMORIES. For Adler, a person's **earliest memory** unerringly expressed his or her style of life: "It offers an opportunity to see at one glance what he has taken as the starting point for his develop-

TABLE 5.1   Adler's Ideas on Personality Characteristics as a Function of Birth Order

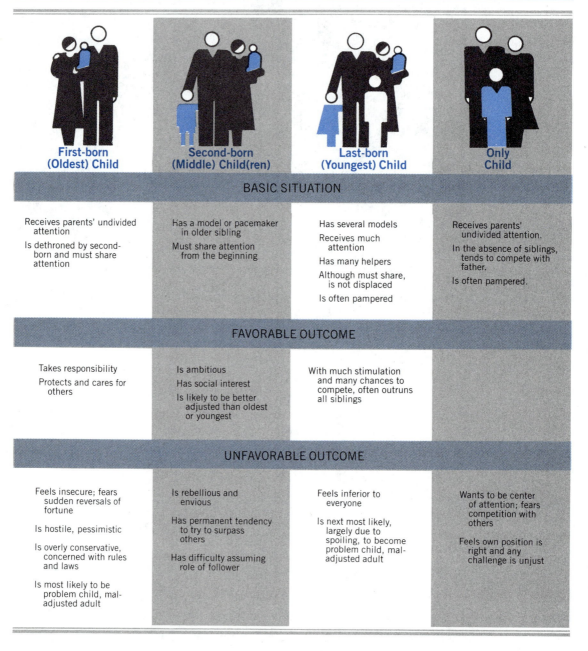

	First-born (Oldest) Child	Second-born (Middle) Child(ren)	Last-born (Youngest) Child	Only Child
BASIC SITUATION	Receives parents' undivided attention Is dethroned by second-born and must share attention	Has a model or pacemaker in older sibling Must share attention from the beginning	Has several models Receives much attention Has many helpers Although must share, is not displaced Is often pampered	Receives parents' undivided attention. In the absence of siblings, tends to compete with father. Is often pampered.
FAVORABLE OUTCOME	Takes responsibility Protects and cares for others	Is ambitious Has social interest Is likely to be better adjusted than oldest or youngest	With much stimulation and many chances to compete, often outruns all siblings	
UNFAVORABLE OUTCOME	Feels insecure; fears sudden reversals of fortune Is hostile, pessimistic Is overly conservative, concerned with rules and laws Is most likely to be problem child, mal-adjusted adult	Is rebellious and envious Has permanent tendency to try to surpass others Has difficulty assuming role of follower	Feels inferior to everyone Is next most likely, largely due to spoiling, to become problem child, mal-adjusted adult	Wants to be center of attention; fears competition with others Feels own position is right and any challenge is unjust

Source: Adapted from Ansbacher and Ansbacher (1956); Adler (1931).
Note: Individual family configurations often create variations in these patterns. For example, if siblings are separated by many years, each person may show some of the characteristics of an only child. And if two later-born siblings are separated from others by a number of years, the older may take on some of the qualities of the first-born, the younger qualities of the second-born. Why Adler failed to say anything positive about the only child's situation is not known. One recent study (Feldman, 1978), however, found only children to be better adjusted than first-borns.

ment'' (Ansbacher and Ansbacher, 1956, p. 351). For example, a young woman told Adler that when she was 3 years old, her father bought ponies for her and her older sister and that while her sister ''triumphantly'' led her pony down the street, her own pony went too fast for her and dragged her ''face downward in the dirt.'' According to Adler, this memory reflected the young woman's feeling of being second best to her sister. The young woman's style of life was in fact characterized by driving ambition coupled with deep feelings of insecurity and fear of failure.

Adler always began a course of therapy by asking for the person's earliest recollection, and he used this method also with groups, finding it an easy and economical way of investigating personality. Without ignoring the importance of unconscious material, Adler found that some of the most revealing psychological phenomena were reflected in people's conscious memories. Moreover, he pointed out that all memories in some way express the style of life. There are no ''chance'' memories, for we choose to remember things that we feel have an important bearing on our life situations.

FAULTY LIFE-STYLES.   Adler held that maladaptive life-styles were the product of one of three conditions of early childhood: organic infirmity, pampering, or neglect. Children with **physical or mental infirmities** bear a heavy burden and are likely to feel inadequate in meeting the tasks of life. With parental understanding, however, such children may develop strengths to compensate for their weaknesses.

Children who are **pampered** fail to develop social interest and instead expect society to conform to their self-centered wishes. Children who are **neglected** (or rejected) become enemies of society and are dominated by the need for revenge. Both pampering and neglect can contribute to what Adler called the **pampered style of life**. According to Adler, a person with such a style is one who wants to be pampered, not necessarily one who actually is or has been pampered (Ansbacher and Ansbacher, 1956, p. 242). The pampered person expects ''to receive without giving'' (p. 369); such a person does little or nothing for other people and either manipulates or forces others into satisfying his or her needs.

According to Adler, pampered individuals are potentially the most dangerous of all people in society. Adler's major effort in the areas of both therapy and education was directed, through encouraging parents and teachers to develop children's social interest, toward preventing or correcting what he termed the evils of pampering. Interestingly, today a number of people are focusing on the "narcissistic personality disorder," which in some ways resembles Adler's "pampered" style of life (see, e.g., Kohut, 1971).

KAREN HORNEY

Karen Horney is concerned with the person in the totality of his or her experience and functioning; her approach to personality is a holistic one (Kelman, 1971). That is, she subscribes to the belief that the separate aspects of personality can be studied only in their relations to each other and to the personality as a whole. Physicochemical, emotional, and cognitive events; social, cultural, spiritual, and moral factors; intrapsychic and interpersonal processes—all are part of Horney's picture of the human being.

Although Horney (pronounced "horn-eye") described the well-functioning person (Horney, 1945), as a therapist, she was more concerned with the so-called neurotic individual. She believed that a warm and loving home could enable a person to avoid neurotic anxiety and conflict. Like Erich Fromm, however, she also believed that certain aspects of our society create such intense conflict in people that they may also need plenty of "good breaks" to cope with the challenge of becoming a healthy person.

Initially, Horney was influenced by Freudian thought, but she drew also from Jung and, especially, Adler. She eagerly exchanged ideas with peers and colleagues and often acknowledged that contemporaries such as Fromm and Harry Stack Sullivan had contributed to her thinking. Early on, Horney stated that her formulations were not "meant to be the beginning of a new psychoanalytic 'school' " (1939, p. 11) but, according to Munroe (1955), Horney's concepts and theory differ "so radically" from contemporary Freudian thought that it is difficult to see clearly the parallels between the two.

Horney herself declared that "nothing of importance in the field of psychology and psychotherapy has been done without reliance on Freud's fundamental findings, (1939, p. 18). Most significant, she believed, were his doctrines that (1) all psychic processes and events are causally determined (i.e., everything occurs for a reason, rather than at random); (2) all behavior may be determined by unconscious motivation; and (3) the motivations that drive us are emotional, nonrational forces.

BOX 5.3   Karen Horney (1885–1952)

Karen Horney was born in Hamburg, Germany, of a Norwegian father and a Dutch–German mother. As a child, Horney was close to her mother, an intellectual and strong-willed woman, and often resented her father, a sea captain, who was given to tyrannical rages. Yet she also admired her father and accompanied him on several long voyages.

Horney decided at age 12 to study medicine and, with the support of her mother and brother, persuaded her father to allow her to prepare for this career. She entered the University of Freiburg in 1906, and the next 10 years were eventful ones: While pursuing her M.D. (University of Berlin, 1915), she married Oskar Horney, a successful businessman; gave birth to their three children, Brigitte, Marianne, and Renate; and was psychoanalyzed by Karl Abraham, one of Freud's first followers.

Until 1920 Horney worked at a neuropsychiatric hospital near Berlin and practiced privately. When the Berlin Psychoanalytic Institute opened its doors that year, she was one of its six instructors, and she remained with the institute until 1932, when Franz Alexander invited her to become his associate director at the Chicago Psychoanalytic Institute.

Two years later Horney moved to New York City, where she joined the New York Psychoanalytic Institute (NYPI). She soon was part of a group that included Erich Fromm (whom she had known since Berlin days), Harry Stack Sullivan, Margaret Mead, John Dollard, Paul Tillich, Ruth Benedict, Erich Maria Remarque, Abraham Maslow, Clara Thompson, Harold Lasswell, and Medard Boss. Psychologists, anthropologists, sociologists, philosophers, writers—they met often in the evenings, sometimes sharing professional ideas, sometimes singing or playing games.

It was in 1923 that Horney presented her first challenge to Freudian concepts in a paper that dealt with the notion of penis envy, and by 1941 she had published two books that clearly stated her argument with Freudian thought and outlined her own theories. She had also gained quite a student following, and in the spring of that year, the membership of the NYPI voted to disqualify her as a teacher of beginning students because she was "disturbing" the students with her radical ideas. In a dramatic moment, Horney rose and walked out of the meeting, followed by Thompson and several others, and they all marched down the street singing, "Let my people go!" Shortly thereafter, Horney and several colleagues founded the Association for the Advancement of Psychoanalysis, which gave birth to what is now known as the Karen Horney Psychoanalytic Institute and Center. Fromm, Sullivan, and Thompson were members of the new association and institute at the outset but left two years later as the result of some internecine warfare that, ironically, mirrored Horney's own split with the NYPI (see also Box 5 4).

In all, Horney wrote five books developing her theories of personality and psychotherapy, and she published many papers and articles as well. She lectured at the New School for Social Research (New York City) annually and taught and supervised students at her own institute. Several years before her death, from cancer, she became interested in Zen philosophy, and she began studying Japanese theories of personality and therapy.

On the other hand, Horney felt that Freud's theory was too mechanistic and biological and that, as a result, it was incapable of describing the full range of human motivation and behavior. Freud's minimal concern with interrelations between people, she felt, led to many errors, chief among which was an incorrect emphasis on sexual motivation and conflict: security, not (sexual) pleasure, is the prime motivating force in human personality functioning. Horney also insisted that aggressive or destructive behavior is not, as Freud suggested, inborn but is, rather, a means by which people try to protect their security.

In 1923, Horney first challenged Freudian theory (Horney, 1967b), attacking Freud's concept of "penis envy." This concept underlies the doctrine that woman is basically inferior to man and that a girl's discovery that she lacks a penis is often the beginning of a neurotic refusal to accept a lesser role in life. Both Adler and Horney were early supporters of the notion that "penis envy" is largely symbolic of women's wish for equal status and power with men.

ANXIETY AND CONFLICT

According to Horney, all of us experience what German philosophers called the *Angst der Kreatur* ("creature anxiety")—the knowledge that in the face of the vast and uncontrollable forces of nature, we are essentially helpless and vulnerable. We first experience this very normal type of anxiety when we are infants. Loving guidance in our early years helps us learn to cope with threatening situations, but without such guidance, we may develop what Horney called basic anxiety and basic hostility and, eventually, neurotic distress.

BASIC ANXIETY AND BASIC HOSTILITY.   **Basic anxiety**, a derivative of fear, is the "insidiously increasing, all-pervading feeling of being lonely and helpless in a hostile world" (Horney, 1937, p. 89). Basic anxiety is always accompanied by **basic hostility**, a derivative of anger, which is the predisposition to anticipate harm from others and thus to distrust them. Together, anxiety and hostility lead people to believe that they must always be on guard to protect their security.

Both anxiety and hostility tend to be repressed, or put out of awareness (see also Chapter 2): to show fear exposes one's weakness; to show anger risks punishment and the withdrawal of love and security. What may set in quite early, then, is a cyclical process that Horney called the **vicious circle:** basic anxiety leads to excessive need for affection, including demands for unconditional love; when these demands are not met, the person feels rebuffed and hostility intensifies; but hostility must be repressed lest the person lose what love and security are offered; failure to deal with powerful emotions creates a diffuse rage and intensifies anxiety and hostility; as a result, the need for affec-

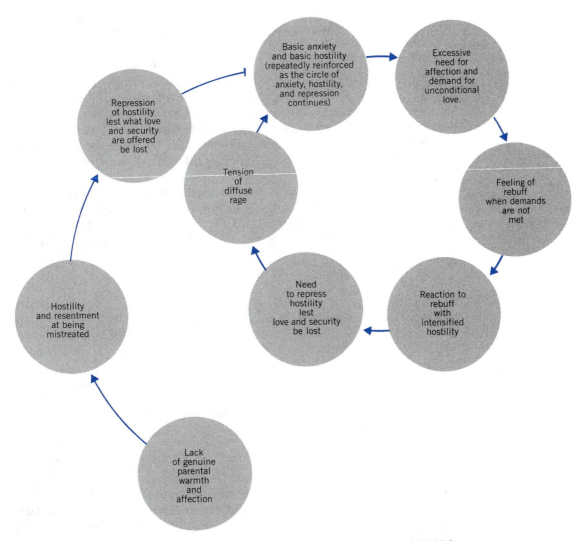

Figure 5.2   The basic vicious circle. (Based on Horney, 1937.)

tion is increased—and the circle begins again (see Figure 5.2). The notion that the psychologically troubled person becomes locked into a circle of intensifying distress and unproductive behavior is fundamental
to Horney's theory of neurosis.

CONFLICT.   Conflict between opposing forces is inevitable in human
functioning:

*It is not neurotic to have conflicts. At one time or another, our wishes, our inter-
ests, our convictions are bound to collide with those of others around us. And . . .
conflicts within ourselves are an integral part of human life. . . . We may have to*

decide between desires that lead in opposite directions . . . [or] between wishes and obligations . . . [or] between two sets of values.'' (Horney, 1945, p. 23)

In addition, cultural values in and of themselves are often in conflict. For example, our society encourages us to be competitive and to strive for achievement and superiority, but it also admonishes us to care for others and to put their interests before our own. In a ''civilization [that] is in a stage of a rapid transition, where highly contradictory values and divergent ways of living exist side by side, the choices the individual has to make are manifold and difficult'' (Horney, 1945, p. 24).

If the normal person is subject to so much conflict, what of the neurotic? Basic anxiety and basic hostility are formed out of a conflict between the need for security and the need to express fundamental emotions and thoughts. The person with basic anxiety thus begins life with what is a conflict of truly crushing proportions: the need to survive versus the need to be.

ATTEMPTS AT COPING

To cope with basic anxiety, people develop a number of strategies. They create and strive to actualize an idealized self-image by attaining perfection, or ''glory''; they develop a ''pride system'' to support the idealized image, as well as a set of impossible standards of behavior, or ''shoulds''; and they try to disown, or ''externalize,'' things in themselves with which they cannot cope. All these efforts can produce ''alienation from self.''

THE IDEALIZED SELF-IMAGE AND THE SEARCH FOR GLORY.   Because they feel inferior, people with basic anxiety develop an **idealized self-image**—an imaginary (and largely unconscious) picture of the self as the possessor of unlimited powers and superlative qualities. The **actual self**, the person one is in everyday life, is often despised because it fails to fulfill the requirements of the idealized image. We have all heard people berate themselves for some minor error: ''What an idiot I am— how could I have done such a stupid thing?'' Horney suggests that only people who secretly believe in their own perfection (or potential for perfection) are so intolerant of their imperfections.

Underlying both the idealized self and the actual self is the **real self**, which is revealed only as a person begins to shed the various techniques developed to deal with basic anxiety and to find ways of resolving conflicts. The real self is *not* an entity but a ''force'' that impels growth and self-realization (Horney, 1950, p. 158).

In a **search for glory**, the person tries to fulfill the idealized self-

Drawing by Stevenson; © *1984 The New Yorker Magazine, Inc.*

image. A formulation quite similar to Adler's "superiority striving," the search for glory can be distinguished from normal striving for achievement in three ways: neurotic strivings are **compulsive**—the person *must* strive to be first; they are **indiscriminate**—the person must be first in *all* situations; and they are **insatiable**—*no* amount of success is ever enough.

THE PRIDE SYSTEM.   The **pride system** is composed of two phenomena that inevitably accompany each other; neurotic pride and self-hate. **Neurotic pride** is false pride because it is invested in things that support the idealized self-image—such as being stronger or more intelligent than everyone else. The feeling of inferiority that underlies the idealized self-image, along with the constant failure of the actual self to live up to this image, produces **self-hate**, or self-criticism. Every failure increases both the person's self-hate and his or her need to maintain pride in the idealized self—another vicious circle.

THE "SHOULDS."   In a further effort to support the idealized self-image, people develop **shoulds**, a set of demands on self that are "altogether too difficult and too rigid" (Horney, 1950, p. 65). Some demands are plainly fantastic: a student in the last year of college was writing a senior paper, doing a research project, serving as president of the student association, writing a column for the campus paper, playing clarinet at a local club, and attempting to carry on an extensive social life. When he blew up over a minor grammatical error in his column, his friend asked him what he was trying to prove.

The shoulds are based on the assumption that everything should be done easily, no matter what other facts affect the doing. For example, a professor of art history felt that she should be able to write an article on an obscure Romanian painter within a few days and was thrown into a depression because the writing did not flow. She ignored the fact that before starting to write, she needed to do some research, organize her thoughts, consider whether she had something to say, and make a clear outline.

EXTERNALIZATION.   Like projection (see Chapter 2), **externalization** lets people deny thoughts and feelings that they find distressing and impute them instead to other people. Externalization is a somewhat broader concept than Freud's, however, for it suggests that people may experience as originating outside the self not just distressing phenomena but everything in life. That is, people may not only attribute their failures to the actions of others; they may also attribute their successes to luck, their good mood to the weather, and so on. (The notion that people vary in terms of the degree to which they believe they control their own lives has been explored by Rotter in his work on locus of control; see Chapter 15).

ALIENATION FROM SELF.   Each of the coping efforts discussed in this section both reflects and promotes **alienation from self** (more vicious circles at work). For example, the idealized self-image is totally unlike the actual self, and externalization is a denial of the actual self. Alienation from self has far-reaching effects on one's personality and life. To begin with, if people believe that others are responsible for their difficulties, they can neither respond to others' friendly feelings nor express such feelings themselves. In addition, the more energy goes into the pride system, the less is available for the constructive drive toward self-realization. Finally, the pride system prevents people from assuming responsibility for themselves: if a person cannot recognize that she is the instigator of her own behavior, she will be unwilling to bear the consequences of that behavior and she will not recognize that only she can do something about the difficulties that have resulted from it.

NEUROTIC "SOLUTIONS" TO CONFLICT:
HORNEY'S MODEL OF INTERPERSONAL STYLES

According to Horney (1945, 1950), people relate themselves to others in three basic ways: they move toward others in self-effacement, seeking affection; they move against others in expansion, seeking dominance; and they move away from others, in resignation, seeking detachment. As human beings develop, they learn to use first one and then another of these interpersonal styles. Although eventually people usually come to prefer one style over the others, they are capable of expressing all three of these competing styles from time to time.

People who have never conquered basic anxiety and basic hostility, however, cannot tolerate conflict. As a result, they early adopt and adhere rigidly to one particular style, which becomes their "solution" to neurotic conflict (Horney, 1950). As we examine these three styles, you may find Table 5.2 helpful in clarifying how the attempts at coping we have discussed find expression in each style.

SELF-EFFACEMENT.   It is common to find that the person whose style is one of **self-effacement** grew up "under the shadow" of someone, such as a preferred sibling or a parent, who demanded utter devotion (Horney, 1950). Such a person learns early to defer to others in the hope that they will offer help, protection, and love.

Self-effacing people do nothing that could anger others and rarely assert their own needs openly. They may exaggerate feelings of helplessness and suffering, however, to obtain others' concern. Their idealized self-image emphasizes lovableness, and their shoulds include being totally good, unselfish, and long-suffering. Such persons' claims are that everything should be done for them because they are so loving and never angry or mean. They are enormously proud of their goodness but criticize themselves for not being as good and kind as they "should" be. When they are not reassured by approval from others, they may redouble their efforts to gain such approval, and if they meet with further disappointments, another vicious circle is set in motion.

EXPANSION.   People who adopt the style of **expansion**, Horney (1950) suggests, seek to dominate others and to achieve their own aims at all costs. Their contempt for others may be quite open, or it may be masked by a pretense of friendliness. Their motivating force is the determination to overcome every obstacle.

There are three types of expansion. **Narcissistic** people appear highly self-confident and have no conscious doubts of their own talents and skills. Often, Horney says, such people were favored (Adler would say "pampered") children. They are sometimes loving and generous but only in anticipation of return favors. When they cast their bread

TABLE 5.2   Interpersonal Styles and Coping Attempts

	INTERPERSONAL STYLES		
COPING ATTEMPTS	SELF-EFFACEMENT MOVING TOWARD OTHERS, SEEKING LOVE	EXPANSION MOVING AGAINST OTHERS, SEEKING DOMINATION	RESIGNATION MOVING AWAY FROM OTHERS, SEEKING TO AVOID RELATIONSHIPS
Idealized self-image	Good, generous, loving, unselfish, sympathetic, kind, humble, self-sacrificing	All-powerful, invincible, needing no one's help; intellectually, physically, morally superior	Independent, self-sufficient, resourceful, self-contained, free of desires and passions, true to oneself, unique
Search for glory	Perfect love; surrender to someone who will take over one's life; Christlike perfection; martyrdom	Absolute control; to be on top and better than everyone; triumph and vengeance	Freedom; perfect serenity—absence of troubles, irritations, upsets
Sources of pride	Being good, kind, lovable (consciously denied but shown in hypersensitivity to being criticized)	Intellectual powers, vigilance, ability to outwit others, justice, foresight, planning, being above hurt and suffering	Wisdom, being "realistic," detachment, stoicism, self-sufficiency, independence, resistance to coercion, being above competition
Sources of self-hate	Inferiority, stupidity, weakness; being unlovable, unwanted	Fallibility; need for love, spontaneity, joy of living	Inertia, failure to accomplish anything, sense of futility
Shoulds	Develop any love relationship into one of perfect harmony, make partner love one; not waste time on self; not strive for more than one has	Accomplish any task; handle any situation; solve any problem, no matter how complex; conquer everything by sheer will; always be right	Forgo all pleasure; not become attached or emotionally involved with anyone; not have to change; not have to adjust to anyone else's needs
Externalization	Of anger, hostility, and self-hate, by seeing others as accusing or critical of self, or by suffering and thus making others feel guilty	Of fear, anxiety, and helplessness, by calling others frightened, and weak; of own fallibility, by pointing out others' stupidity and errors	Of need to control and make demands on others, by seeing others as demanding submission and as interfering with one's life

Source: Adapted from Horney (1942, 1945, 1950).

upon the waters, they expect it to come back buttered—thickly!

Perfectionistic people base their feelings of superiority on high intellectual and moral standards. They externalize their failures, constantly finding others stupid and immoral and generally at fault. Having such high standards can give these people a feeling of mastery, but because they can tolerate no imperfection, being forced to admit their own errors may release self-hate.

Arrogant-vindictive people have quite commonly had "particularly bad human experiences," such as humiliation, neglect, or brutality (Horney, 1950, p. 202), and they are convinced that other people are dishonest and malevolent. They are highly competitive and proud of their ability to outwit others. Such people's self-hate, according to Horney, is of especial intensity, which accounts at least in part for their unrelenting efforts to hurt others. They dare not show the tiniest weakness lest they be overwhelmed by their feelings of self-condemnation.

RESIGNATION.   **Resignation** is potentially the most destructive of all the neurotic "solutions," for it means withdrawing from the interpersonal field and thus from life itself. (The extreme of this style is found in psychosis.) Horney (1950) suggests that in some way, the early environment of resigned people made excessive demands on them to fit in and threatened to engulf them without regard for their individuality.

Resigned people may engage in many varied activities but without depth or commitment. They may say, do, and even think what is expected in their particular environment, for the sake of others' opinions. When one tries to connect with such people in some way, one realizes the shallowness of their adaptation. Erich Fromm, discussing a similar personality—which he labeled the "marketing" type (see page 169)—postulated a permanent defect in the person's capacity to experience real emotional distress. Horney disagreed, finding that in time such people revealed in therapy, "deeply buried sadness, self-hate and hate for others, self-pity, despair, anxiety" (1950, p. 289); they are not defective, she insisted, but engaged in a determined flight from inner life.

Although, as we have seen, Horney suggested childhood factors that may cause the adoption of particular styles, she probably would have been quick to say that there are always exceptions to a rule. Thus, a child whose egocentric parent denies its rights as an individual does not always become a resigned type; a child who has been physically abused and deeply hurt psychologically does not necessarily become an expansionist, arrogant–vindictive type. Other factors in the child's early life—and probably biological factors as well—may influence his or her development. A child raised in apparently benign circumstances may develop neurotic difficulties. Or a child raised in an unhealthy situation may, by his or her own hook, rise above the situation.

Horney's picture of the neurotic person, locked into vicious circles of fear, anger, anxiety, and frustration, has a certain face validity. Most of us occasionally get caught up in such circular processes: for example, your anxiety about writing an important paper may make you procrastinate, which may make you feel guilty, which may make you more anxious, and so on. However, a "lucky circle" may start as soon as you are able to work constructively on a problem (Horney, 1937, p. 226). Attaining insight and trying new ways of behaving increase self-confidence, and greater self-confidence lessens the need to do the things that perpetuate the old, vicious circles.

ERICH FROMM

In his theory of personality, Erich Fromm attempted to combine the very different views of Freud and Karl Marx (1818–1883)—not Marx the political and economic theorist but Marx the social theorist and philosopher. Fromm believed that many of Freud's discoveries, such as the role of the unconscious in human behavior, were of "extraordinary significance" for the understanding of human personality. But he felt that Freud was wrong on a number of counts, particularly in his emphasis on the functioning of the individual rather than the interrelations between individual and society and in his insistence on the sexual origin of behavior.

Fromm could be called a Marxian personality theorist. He himself, however, preferred the label of "dialectic humanist," by which he meant to convey his concern with human beings' unceasing struggle for dignity and freedom in the context of their need for connectedness with each other.

THE CONDITIONS OF HUMAN EXISTENCE

For Fromm, the most significant phenomenon of human existence was the duality of human nature. As a member of the animal kingdom, the human being has certain physiological needs. As the only animal that possesses self-awareness, however, the human being is also set apart from nature. According to Fromm (1973), our self-awareness, reason, and imagination have made us "the freak of the universe." We are subject to the physical laws of nature. Our bodies tie us to nature, and we cannot rid ourselves of them. At the same time, our minds push us to challenge nature in ways that no lower animal can do. Thus, we are always aware of our limitations, but we also transcend them.

BOX 5.4   Erich Fromm (1900–1980)

Erich Fromm, who was born in Frankfurt, Germany, obtained his Ph.D. degree in 1922 from the University of Heidelberg, where he studied psychology, sociology, and philosophy. After graduation, Fromm trained at the Berlin Psychoanalytic Institute, where he met and married his first wife, Frieda Fromm-Reichmann. The two analysts then helped to found and run the Psychoanalytic Institute in Frankfurt.

In 1933 Fromm accepted an invitation to join the staff of the Chicago Psychoanalytic Institute; shortly thereafter, he established a private practice in New York City. There he renewed his friendship with Karen Horney, whom he had known in Berlin, and met Harry Stack Sullivan. Both Fromm and Sullivan were members of Horney's American Institute of Psychoanalysis when it was first established. Soon, however, dissension among institute members developed over whether Fromm, who lacked the M.D. degree, should be allowed full membership; some members wanted to secure an affiliation for the institute with a medical college. Horney herself, who had been a close friend of Fromm, evidently deserted him in this conflict, and Fromm quit the institute, taking Sullivan and Clara Thompson with him. Fromm later joined with Sullivan and others in founding the William Alanson White Institute and remained a faculty member there until his death.

Fromm taught at a number of other institutions, including Columbia, New York, Michigan State, and Yale universities, and the New School for Social Research (New York City). In 1949 he joined the faculty of the National Autonomous University of Mexico, where he built the medical school's department of psychoanalysis. Fromm also founded and directed the Mexican Psychoanalytic Institute, and he continued for many years to commute to New York to engage in other professional activities. In 1976 he moved, with his third wife, Annis Freeman Fromm, to Switzerland, where he later died, at the age of 79.

Fromm was a person of enormous intellectual curiosity, and he read and studied widely throughout his life. At 72 he was still taking courses in fields new to him, such as neuroanatomy. Fromm was a prolific writer, and his more than 20 published books have received the thoughtful attention of both academicians and laypeople.

THE EXISTENTIAL DILEMMA.   The inherent conflict between our animal limitations and our human possibilities constitute what Fromm calls the **existential dilemma**. On the one hand, we struggle to be free, to master the environment and our animal nature; on the other hand, freedom enslaves us by alienating us from our roots in nature. The child who struggles for autonomy may feel lonely and helpless without its parents; the society that struggles for freedom may feel even more endangered by isolation from other nations. Freedom thus becomes a burden. One may be free, but for what? To face life alone.

What is the answer to this dilemma? One can escape the burden

TABLE 5.3   The Uniquely Human Needs

FREEDOM VERSUS CONNECTEDNESS	UNDERSTANDING AND ACTIVITY
Relatedness–rootedness The need to join with other loving beings, to be part of something, to belong. The human being's irrational desire to maintain his or her first relationship, with the mother, must be translated into a feeling of solidarity with others. The most satisfying relations are based on love, caring, responsibility, respect, and understanding of the other.	**Frame of orientation** The need to make sense of the world. One's frame may not be "true," but it must provide some cohesive way of grasping and interpreting the environment.
Transcendence The need to rise above one's animal nature—to move from being a creature to being a creator. It is only when the need to create is thwarted that the need to destroy arises.	**Frame of devotion** The need for a goal, for direction and purpose. The human being, without instincts but with a brain that allows him or her to think of many possibilities, needs an object of "ultimate concern"—a basis for values and a focal point of all strivings.
Unity The need to remedy the existential split between one's animal and nonanimal natures. Only the effort to become fully human—by sharing in love and work with other human beings—can bring about unity.	**Excitation–stimulation** The need to exercise the nervous system—to make use of the brain's capacities. Human beings need not only simple stimuli (e.g., food) but activating stimuli (e.g., a poem or a principle of physics) that elicit not just one-time reactions but active, productive, continuing response.
Identity The need to develop a sense of individuality. This goal can be achieved through identifying with others (e.g., slave with master, citizen with country, worker with employer) or through individual creative effort.	**Effectiveness** The need to realize one's existence—to counteract the sense of "powerlessness" and to exercise one's competence.

Source: Adapted from Fromm (1955, 1968, 1973).

of freedom, Fromm says, by submitting to outside authority, but then one acquires a new bondage. (For example, Germany's Nazi regime at first seemed to some to offer security to an economically unstable society. In time, of course, it destroyed millions of people and enslaved everyone). Or—Fromm's prescription—one can unite with other people in the spirit of love and shared work, thereby creating *mutual* bonds and responsibilities and a better society.

HUMAN NEEDS.   In seeking the answer to the existential problem, human beings have developed needs that represent their specifically human characteristics. (Physiological needs, such as food, drink, and sex, essentially reflect our animal nature.) Four of these needs—**relatedness–rootedness**, **transcendence**, **unity**, and **identity**—reflect very clearly our dual needs to be a part of something and to be autonomous. A second set of needs—a **frame of orientation**, a **frame of devotion**, **stimulation–excitation**, and **effectiveness**—involve our needs to make sense of the world in which we live, to have a purpose (or goal), and to exercise our unique characteristics. Table 5.3 describes each of these needs.

THEORY OF SOCIAL CHARACTER

Human character develops, according to Fromm, out of the need to substitute something for the animal instincts human beings have "lost" in their climb up the ladder of development. Lower animals are governed primarily by instinct. The human infant, however, is born not only helpless but with minimal instinct; thus, it must *learn* how to behave. Character, which has stability over time, enables the human being to function in a world of ever-impinging stimuli without having constantly to stop and consider what to do. For example, the frugal person does not have to think about whether to save or to spend; such a person, we say, saves "instinctively"—his or her character leads to behavior that is almost automatic.

How does character develop? According to Fromm (1955), it is shaped by the "social arrangements" under which human beings live. As we will see, Fromm's character types are somewhat similar to Freud's, but they are not produced by early channeling of sexual energies; they derive, instead, from societal pressures to behave in certain prescribed ways.

SOCIAL CHARACTER TYPES. Fromm did not always clearly relate later versions of his theory of **social character** to earlier ones, but one important concept can be traced through most of his writings—his concept of the positive, life-affirming orientation, **productiveness**, as opposed to **nonproductiveness**, the negative, life-denying orientation.

Fromm first divided the nonproductive orientation into four categories—**receptive** (passively receiving things—food, drink, love, ideas, material goods, help), **hoarding** (gathering, ordering, keeping, and protecting things), **exploitative** (taking the things one wants from others by force or cunning), and **marketing** (adapting constantly to external demands and, thus, lacking self-identity). Later, he indicated that each of these four categories is on a continuum that stretches between productiveness and nonproductiveness:

Every human being, in order to survive, must be able to accept things from others, to take things, to [preserve], and to exchange. . . . Only if his way of ac-

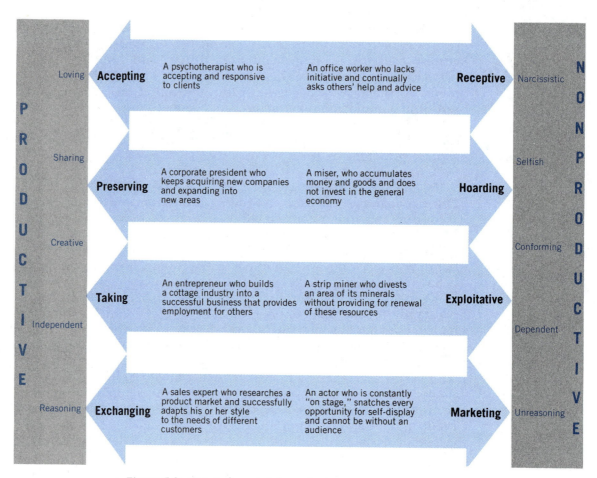

Figure 5.3   Fromm's social character types

quiring things and relating himself to others is essentially nonproductive [do these abilities] turn into the craving to receive, to exploit, to hoard, or to market. (Fromm, 1970, p. 78)

Thus, each of the four types may combine with either the productive or the nonproductive orientation. (In addition, two or more of the types may combine with each other; the most common combinations, as you might imagine, are receptive–hoarding and exploitative–marketing.) And, since no one is totally productive or totally nonproductive, people may fall at any point on a particular continuum. Figure 5.3 indicates the relationships between the two orientations and four character types and offers some examples of how they may combine.

CHARACTER AND SOCIETY.   The receptive orientation, according to Fromm, developed in a society in which power was centered in the

This painting from the fifteenth century Book of Hours, a collections of prayers and lessons for the layperson, shows peasants at work in a French nobleman's fields. According to Fromm, people who lived as slaves in a feudal society where the very few wielded absolute power developed a receptive, or passive/dependent, character.

hands of a few—the feudal or the master–slave society. The exploit-ative orientation developed in the context of piracy and the robber baron mentality. The hoarding orientation developed along with the exploitative orientation in the eighteenth and nineteenth centuries and was localized in the growing middle class, which found security in the "preservation of what had been acquired" (Fromm, 1974, p. 88). The marketing orientation is the product of present-day society in which entrepreneurial opportunities are reduced and in which, to get ahead, people must fit themselves into large organizations and play whatever roles are in demand.

How does society mold character? It is the task of parents and educators to make children *want* to act as they must in order to keep a given society going. In our capitalistic system, for example, children must be taught the value of saving so that capital will be available for an expanding economy. In communist China, children must be taught to put the needs of society above their own so that the goals of the state can be achieved.

But society also warps and frustrates people by demanding be-havior that is contrary to their nature. Fromm believed that both capi-talist and communist societies turn people into robots by making them wage slaves and by isolating them from the meaning and product of their labors. He was particularly critical of modern, consumer-ori-ented societies that constantly create new needs in people. He ques-tioned whether all humankind's desires should necessarily be satisfied and suggested that if there were fewer material possessions to be ob-tained and less incentive to obtain them, people would be free to fulfill themselves in more creative ways.

The society Fromm advocated—which he called "humanistic communitarian socialism"—was one "in which man relates to man lovingly, in which he is rooted in bonds of brotherliness and solidar-ity" (1955, p. 362). In such a society, the human being would gain a sense of self and would be able to create rather than destroy. Fromm believed that each person had to participate more actively in govern-ment. He proposed what he labeled "humanistic management," in which individual citizens would meet in small groups to debate politi-cal and social issues and to recommend government policy (a system that would resemble the New England town meeting). Fromm's views have met with considerable criticism (e.g., Schaar, 1961). You may want to consider whether you agree with a common assessment—that although Fromm's ideas sound good, many of his proposals are un-workable.

RESEARCH ON SOCIAL CHARACTER

In 1957, with the primary purpose of testing his theory of social char-acter, Fromm undertook the study of a small Mexican village that since the early years of the century had undergone rapid change. To a society already modified by revolutionary land reforms, twentieth-century technology and industrialization were bringing further alterations in class structure. The village's two original classes, the landowners and the landless workers, were joined by a third class of merchants and entrepreneurs who took the initiative in introducing the products of technology to the villagers. The members of this new class, who had been rather a disliked minority, became the symbols of progress and the leaders of the community.

Fromm and his colleagues (Fromm and Maccoby, 1970) employed various techniques to assess the character of their subjects, the village members. They used a detailed interview to elicit information on the conscious level and two projective tests—the Rorschach and the TAT—to tap unconscious material. (The Rorschach, or ''ink blot,'' test asks people to describe what they see in a series of ambiguous designs. The TAT, or Thematic Apperception Test, devised by Henry Murray, asks subjects to tell stories to a series of pictures; see also Box 9.3.) The findings of this study tended to support Fromm's social character theory. Each of the three classes displayed a typical character consistent with its distinctive socioeconomic conditions.

The **productive–hoarding** landowners were wedded to the traditional values that accompany the practice of small-scale agriculture—authority, responsibility, and preservation of tradition. The **nonproductive–receptive** landless workers were submissive to authority, religious yet fatalistic, and they accepted their relative powerlessness. The **productive–exploitative** entrepreneurs had adapted to the new, industrializing society and valued education, technology, and social mobility.

HARRY STACK SULLIVAN

Harry Stack Sullivan was the first native-born American to develop a major theory of personality. Like many other theorists, Sullivan began by studying Freud, but he soon found himself disagreeing with many Freudian concepts. The school of thought Sullivan evolved—known as the **interpersonal theory of psychiatry**—holds that personality is ''the relatively enduring pattern of recurrent interpersonal situations which characterize a human life'' (Sullivan, 1953, p.111). Personality, in Sullivan's view, is a hypothetical entity that can be conceived of only in the context of interpersonal behavior. Throughout life, each of us operates in a social field; from our very first day on earth, we are involved in interaction with others. Even when we are alone, others are present in our thoughts, our feelings, our fantasies.

BOX 5.5   Harry Stack Sullivan (1829–1949)

Born in Norwich, New York, and raised on neighboring farms, Harry Stack Sullivan was the only surviving child of Irish Catholic parents whose own parents had immigrated from Ireland. Sullivan's early years were not happy ones, according to all accounts. Evidently, his father was a distant person and his mother a complaining, semi-invalid; neither gave Sullivan much affection. In addition, living on an isolated farm, Sullivan had no friends of his own age until he entered school, where he was again disadvantaged as the only Catholic child in what was then a very "Yankee Protestant" community (Chapman, 1976).

Despite these handicaps, Sullivan was a superior student, valedictorian of his class and winner, in 1908, of a scholarship to Cornell. Something happened in his first year at Cornell, and he was dismissed for poor grades. The many varying accounts of what this something was reflect in part, Sullivan's own conflicting statements about his early history. Whatever did happen—a schizophrenic episode is the possibility most often mentioned—Sullivan weathered it, and by 1917 he had obtained his M.D. degree.

In 1921 Sullivan was offered an appointment at St. Elizabeth Hospital, in Washington, D.C., where he began, apparently for the first time, to work with the psychiatrically disabled. According to Chapman (1976), this was the turning point in Sullivan's career. The theories of personality and of psychopathology that he began to evolve out of his own working experience were also strongly influenced by his association with the psychiatrists William Alanson White, of St. Elizabeth's, and Adolf Meyer, of the Johns Hopkins University Medical School. Both men had studied Freud but had developed, and encouraged in others, quite eclectic views.

After serving on the staff of Sheppard and Enoch Pratt Hospital (near Baltimore) for several years, Sullivan decided to open a private practice in New York and moved to that city in 1931. During the eight years he spent in New York, Sullivan became friends with Karen Horney and Erich Fromm, and they and others met often for both professional and friendly conversation.

In 1936 Sullivan returned to the Washington, D.C., area where he helped to found the Washington School of Psychiatry and the journal *Psychiatry*, which he edited for the rest of his life. Later, he was instrumental in founding the William Alanson White Institute of Psychiatry, in New York City.

According to most of those who knew him, Sullivan was a private and lonely person. He was "generous to the point of imprudence" (Chapman, 1976), giving money to friends in need and opening his home to anyone needing a place to stay. Yet most of the time he apparently lived almost reclusively (Perry, 1982). In social situations, he could be gracious and charming, but on occasion he was quiet and withdrawn. At professional meetings, he was often impatient and argumentative, and he not infrequently lost his temper in anguished efforts to convince others of the crucial importance of his interpersonal perspective.

The first truly American psychiatrist and the founder of an important new school, Sullivan was a person of vivid contrasts. He attracted students, colleagues, and friends, and his work continues to exert wide influence, particularly in the fields of psychiatry and clinical psychology.

DYNAMICS OF PERSONALITY

Sullivan conceived of the human being as an energy system, one of whose primary concerns is to reduce the tensions created by needs. These tensions, and the behaviors the organism uses to dispel them, are experienced in three cognitive modes, or ways of perceiving and thinking.

TENSION.   Tension occurs on a continuum that ranges from absolute relaxation, or **euphoria**, to absolute tension, as in terror. There are two main sources of tension: physicochemical needs, such as for food or drink, and anxiety, which results from threats to security.

Satisfying a need dispels tension. Failure to satisfy needs, if prolonged, may lead to a state of **apathy**. By being held in abeyance, so to speak, the needs are lessened in force, and tension is lowered.

Needs are satisfied by **energy transformations**, or behaviors—physical actions, or mental operations such as perceiving, remembering, and thinking. These behaviors are conditioned largely by the society in which a person is raised. Except for basic physiological needs, there are no innate motivators of human behavior. People learn to behave as they do through interactions with others.

Anxiety, which for Sullivan is the "first great educative influence in life," is transmitted to the infant by its mother. (Sullivan often spoke of the **mothering one**, a term that, for him, included any or all of the baby's primary caretakers.) If the mother herself is anxious, she will express this disturbance in her look, her tone of voice, or in other ways. In time, the baby tries to avoid whatever seems to create anxiety; when it cannot, it may escape by means of **somnolent detachment**, or falling asleep.

Dealing with anxiety is not so simple as dealing with physicochemical needs. Eventually, it involves one of Sullivan's most important concepts—the self-system—which we will discuss a bit later.

MODES OF EXPERIENCE.   In his unique conception of cognitive functioning, Sullivan postulated three types of experiencing that evolve as the organism grows and matures. **Prototaxic**, or undifferentiated, experience begins at birth. All the infant knows are momentary states. It has no awareness of "before" or "after" or of itself as an entity separate from the rest of the world. Thus, its experience is infinitely connected and yet disconnected—it is all of one piece, but it is not integrated into any logical sequence. While elements of prototaxic experience—that is, simple sensations—may persist as components of later mental life, experiences that are predominantly prototaxic are rather rare in adulthood (Sullivan, 1953).

About the beginning of the second year, when the baby begins both to distinguish events and to recognize their common features, it moves into **parataxic**, or associational, experiencing. In this mode, the baby often connects events just because they occur together or because they are similar in some small detail. For example, if a baby is fed applesauce for the first time with a spoon that has just been washed in boiling water, it may reject the food. Thereafter, it may reject applesauce because it expects the original burning sensation, not because of any quality of the food itself.

Parataxic experiencing and thinking, in Sullivan's view, occupy a bigger place in adult cognitive functioning than we may sometimes like to acknowledge. For example, a person may walk into a room of people who continue to talk as they turn to look at him and have the momentary feeling that everyone is talking about him. A woman may think her friend is angry with her because he seems distant when in actuality his behavior has nothing to do with her and everything to do with his fear about an impending shakeup in his company.

The third and highest level of cognition is the **syntaxic**, or logical, mode, in which realistic thinking predominates. According to Sullivan, the earliest successful use of language ushers in this mode. When, somewhere between a year and a year-and-a-half, children begin to learn words that are generally accepted as describing given events, they have begun to think syntaxically. This learning is made possible by **consensual validation**—achieving a consensus, or agreement, about something with other people and then validating it, or establishing it as true, by repeated experience.

All three modes of experience can occur throughout life. Normally, however, the syntaxic begins to dominate between the ages of about 4 and 8 or 10.

ENDURING ASPECTS OF PERSONALITY

Sullivan insisted on the dynamic nature of personality, often deriding concepts "such as superegos, egos, ids, and so on" (1953, p. 167). Nevertheless, he gave an important place in his theory to several aspects of personality that clearly have stability over time: the dynamism is a habitual pattern of behavior; the personification is an image of the self or of another; the self-system, which evolves largely to cope with anxiety, has characteristics of both dynamism and personification.

THE DYNAMISM.   A **dynamism** is a specific and recurrent pattern of behavior that characterizes a particular person. It may involve a particular zone of the body, serving to satisfy basic needs of the organism, such hunger or sex. For example, the dynamism of eating involves the mouth; the dynamism of sexual desire (Sullivan's term is **lust**) involves primarily the genitals.

The dynamisms that are distinctively human are those that have no particular bodily zone but, rather, characterize our interpersonal relations. They are habitual reactions toward other people and may take the form of feelings, attitudes, or overt actions. For example, a child who typically hides behind his mother when a stranger appears shows a dynamism of fear. A girl who is habitually cruel to playmates exhibits a dynamism of malevolence. By far the most important of the distinctively human dynamisms is the self-system, which we will discuss shortly.

PERSONIFICATIONS.   A **personification** is an image—of oneself or of another person—that one builds up out of experiences with either need satisfaction or anxiety. Interpersonal relations that involve satisfaction tend to build positive images; those that involve anxiety build negative ones. For example, the first personifications the baby develops are of the **good mother**—out of its experience of being nursed and cared for tenderly—and the **bad mother**—out of its experience of the mother's anxiety or anger. Remember that the baby experiences prototaxically—thus, it does not connect these two ''mothers.'' Eventually, however, these and other personifications fuse into one complex image of ''mother'' that incorporates more realistic, consensually validated features.

The personification of the mother is followed by personifications of other people who are close and significant. These early pictures of others are rarely accurate descriptions because they are formed in order to understand and respond to people in fairly isolated situations. However, these images tend to persist throughout life and to influence our attitudes toward many other people. For example, a lawyer who has personified her father as mean and dictatorial may react angrily to being overruled by a judge, another older man in a position of authority. It is easy to see how the transfer of early personifications can interfere with interpersonal relations in adult life.

As the infant begins to differentiate itself from its environment, it forms personifications of itself as well as of others. The personification of **good-me** develops from experiences that are rewarding, beginning with satisfying feeding. The personification of **bad-me** develops out of experiences of anxiety brought about by the mother's anxiety or by disapproval or punishment. Like the separate personifications of the mother, good-me and bad-me are ultimately fused into one image of the self.

A third self-personification, the **not-me**, evolves out of experiences that entail very intense anxiety, such as severe physical or mental abuse. Because such experiences are so terrifying, everything about the self that is connected with them is **dissociated** from the rest of the personality, or put out of awareness. The not-me represents these dissociated aspects of the self and is accompanied by what Sullivan called

uncanny, or weird and somewhat dangerous, emotions. The not-me is never integrated into the personality but is maintained as a separate system encountered by so-called normal people only in an occasional nightmare. People suffering serious mental disturbance, however, may encounter the not-me as "most spectacularly real" (Sullivan, 1953, p. 162).

THE SELF-SYSTEM.   The **self-system** comes into being to avoid or minimize anxiety. The self-system also represents the personification of the self, or what we are talking about when we say "I" or "me" or "my" (Sullivan, 1953, pp. 165, 167). Thus the self-system has essentially two components—the self-protective aspect that engages in **security operations** and is the first to develop, and the aspect that represents the self as an entity—the **personified self**—which comes into being after the more rudimentary images of good-me and bad-me have been formed (Sullivan, 1953, p. 168). Figure 5.4 outlines the steps through which the self-system develops.

Because anxiety arises very early—in the very first interpersonal relationship, between mother and baby—it quickly becomes imperative for the baby to develop some way of coping with it. The defense of sleep (somnolent detachment), which we have already discussed, has obvious limitations, and the baby begins to evolve other ways of escaping anxiety. One way is to conform its behavior to parental wishes or demands. Another is to avoid perceiving the troubling stimulus in the first place: by **selective inattention**, the child simply fails to notice what it does not want to, or cannot, cope with. Thus the self-system comes to control the content of awareness—"that is, what we know we're thinking about"—to a very great extent (Sullivan, 1953, p. 234).

Selective inattention can be helpful in life because "there is no need of bothering about things that don't matter, things that will go all right anyway" (Sullivan, 1953, p. 233). But if we ignore things that do matter, the self-system becomes isolated from the rest of the personality. Because the self-system protects us from anxiety, we tend not to interfere with it. Gradually, it may exclude more and more information, and as a result we may fail to learn new things, to profit from experience. Most important, we may fail to develop **foresight**, the ability to anticipate events and to direct our behavior in adaptive ways.

Although the self-system serves the useful purpose of reducing anxiety, it also interferes with our ability to live constructively with others. In general, the more experience people have with anxiety, the more inflated the self-system becomes and the more separated from the rest of the personality. The self-system may prevent the person from making objective judgments of his or her own behavior, and it may gloss over obvious contradictions between the image it holds of the per-

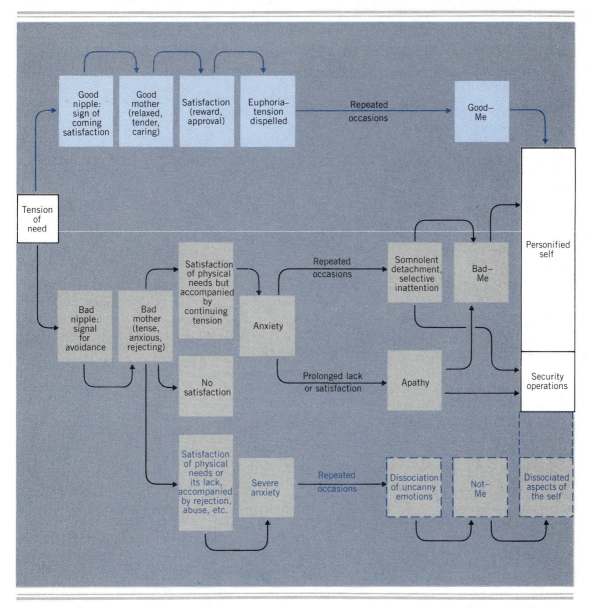

Figure 5.4   The development of the self-system. The self-system suggested here is a so-called normal one; the part devoted to "security operations" is rather limited, and the area given to "dissociated aspects of the self" is very small. Presumably in a nonnormal self-system, both of these portions would increase in size; the security operations portion might be the largest of the three in a neurotic self-system; the area of dissociated aspects might be the largest in a psychotic self-system. See the text for additional discussion of how the self-system develops. (Based on Sullivan, 1953.)

son, or the personified self, and the way the person appears in his or her interactions with others. Nevertheless,

   . . . *however truly the self-system is the principal stumbling block to favorable*

TABLE 5.4 Sullivan's Developmental Stages

	PERIOD*	MAJOR ACHIEVEMENTS	NEGATIVE DEVELOPMENTS
Infancy	From birth to articulate speech (0 to 18 months)	Beginning to organize experience; learning to satisfy some of one's own needs	Security operations of apathy and somnolent detachment
Childhood	From speech to the need for peer relationships (18 months to 4 years)	Learning through identifying with parents; learning to sublimate (or to substitute one need satisfaction for another)	"As if" performances; rationalizations; preoccupations Malevolent transformation
Juvenile Era	From need for peer relationships to need for a chum (4 to 8 or 10 years)	Learning to cooperate and to compete with others; learning to deal with authority figures	Stereotypes Ostracism Disparagement
Preadolescence	From need for chum to onset of puberty and sexual needs (8 or 10 to 12 years)	Learning to love another as well as, if not better than, oneself	Loneliness
Early Adolescence	From puberty to the establishment of a stable pattern of sexual behavior (12 to 16 years)	Integration of needs for intimacy and sexual satisfaction	Unsatisfying patterns of sexual behavior
Late Adolescence	From establishment of sexual pattern to development of an adult repertory of social, vocational, and economic activities (16 to the early twenties)	Integration into adult society Self-respect	Inaccurate personifications Restrictions of living
Maturity	(early twenties on)	Consolidation of achievements of each preceding stage	

*Age ranges are approximations. Sullivan was not precise about the timing of all stages. Chapman suggests that age periods may vary by as much as two or three years and that transitions are never abrupt.
Source: Adapted from Chapman (1976) and Sullivan (1953).

changes in personality . . . that does not alter the fact that it is also the principal influence that stands in the way of unfavorable changes in personality. . . . [The self-system] is always before us, whether we regret it or praise it. . . . [It] is simply tremendously important in understanding the vicissitudes of interpersonal realities. (Sullivan, 1953, pp. 169–170)

PERSONALITY OVER TIME: THE DEVELOPMENTAL EPOCHS
Sullivan viewed personality as evolving through six clearly differentiated stages: infancy, childhood, the juvenile era, preadolescence, early adolescence, and late adolescence. Table 5.4 presents a brief overview of these stages that will help you review after you have read the discussion in this section. Sullivan's theory of development, which is based on social determinants, shares some characteristics with Erikson's ''psychosocial'' conception; it is quite unlike Freud's scheme, which was based on the unfolding of the sexual drive.

INFANCY.   During the period of **infancy**, which extends from birth to the appearance of articulate speech, the baby's chief concern is obtaining food. Thus, the first object in the environment that it focuses on is its mother's (or the bottle's) nipple. The nipple, as representative of the mother, acquires various images, the most important of which are the **good nipple** of the relaxed, tenderly caring mother—a sign of impending satisfaction—and the **bad nipple**—of the anxious mother—a signal for avoidance. These concepts eventually become translated into the personifications of the good and bad mother.

During this stage, the baby makes the transition from the prototaxic to the parataxic mode of cognition. As it learns to differentiate its body from the environment, it begins to make coordinated movements, such as those involving eye and hand and hand and mouth. By the end of the ninth month of life, the baby has begun to organize some of its experience and has learned some ways of satisfying its own needs—for example, by thumbsucking. Experiences of tension and anxiety may call out the dynamisms of apathy and somnolent detachment, which contribute to the development of the self-system.

CHILDHOOD.   The beginnings of articulate speech and of learning in the syntaxic mode usher in the stage of **childhood**, which extends to the appearance of the need for peer relationships. The development of language permits, among other things, the fusion of different personifications. For example, the good and bad mothers are integrated into one image of a person called ''mother.'' By the end of this period, good-me and bad-me have also become integrated, as the self-system acquires a more coherent structure.

During this period, children learn to hide aspects of their behavior that they believe will bring about anxiety or punishment. For example, they learn to rationalize, or to give plausible reasons, for things they have done or propose to do. And they engage in what Sullivan calls **as if** performances: by **dramatization**—basically a healthy device and common to all of us—they play at being grown up, learning, through identifying with their parents, how to behave in acceptable ways. For example, a child may pretend to be her own parent and punish her doll for some behavior her parents have disapproved. Or, through **preoccupation**, children may learn to concentrate on a single activity that enables them to avoid dealing with something that distresses them. For example, a child may try to avoid the anxiety aroused by his parents' bitter arguments by preoccupying himself with his music collection.

If these devices are used in moderation, they can help the child grow and develop. If children are subjected to a great deal of anxiety, however, they may increasingly use as if behaviors to protect themselves from the dangers of being involved with other people, and they may develop the **malevolent transformation**, the feeling that one "lives among enemies."

Expressions in adulthood of the malevolent transformation range from mild suspicion and distrust to paranoid behavior. For example, a man may have relatively few close relationships, consider himself a "loner," and keep to himself when in distress. Or a woman may really believe that others are trying to do her in and take action to prevent this, such as lining her clothes with aluminum foil to ward off the harmful rays others are beaming at her.

It is during childhood that one develops the capacity for sublimation, or the **unwitting** (Freud would say, "unconscious") substitution of a socially acceptable thing or activity for something else that causes anxiety or otherwise gets one into trouble. The substitution does not fully satisfy the original need but, because it wards off anxiety, it is chosen over the thing one really wants to do. For example, the child who wants to play with its feces may learn to play with other small objects, such as toy cars.

THE JUVENILE ERA.   The **juvenile era** lasts through most of the grade school years and up to the appearance of a strong need for an intimate companion. The most significant development of this stage is the great leap forward in socialization. Children learn cooperation, competition, and the meaning of group feeling. They acquire experience with authority figures outside the home. Their opportunities for the consensual validation that supports syntaxic thinking are greatly expanded.

Significant negative developments in this period are the learning of stereotypes, ostracism, and disparagement. **Stereotypes** are shared personifications that are handed down from generation to gen-

About the age of 10 or 11, having a chum—someone to share one's thoughts, dreams, and activities—is crucial, Sullivan said, to the development of healthy interpersonal relations. With such an intimate friend of one's own sex, one learns both self-respect and respect for others, and one learns to care for another as much as for oneself.

eration. Examples are the "absentminded professor," the "dumb blonde," the "crooked politician," or the "blood-thirsty general."

Children may experience **ostracism**, or forcible isolation, by being assigned to or falling into an outgroup in juvenile society. Because the latter society reflects the larger one, differences among individuals tend to lead to the formation of groups that are either "in" or "out" in respect to general esteem and influence.

Disparagement, or putting other people down, can have disastrous effects, particularly in adult life. Usually learned from parents, who speak slightingly of people whom they dislike or with whom they feel competitive, this way of bolstering one's own self-esteem is not only self-deceptive but very destructive of good interpersonal relations: "One of the feeblest props for an inadequate self-system is the attitude of disparaging others, . . . the doctrine that if you are a molehill then, by God, there shall be no mountains" (Sullivan, 1953, p. 309).

PREADOLESCENCE. This very brief period, lasting only until the onset of puberty, is of enormous importance. Preadolescence marks the beginning of the capacity for close relationships with others that are characterized by real equality and mutual caring. The young person needs a **chum**—an intimate companion of the same sex, someone in whom to confide and with whom to collaborate in trying to understand and solve the problems of life. The chum's happiness and "feeling of worthwhileness'' become as important as, if not more important than, the child's own feeling of well-being.

Sullivan suggests that through the chumship, the young person may be able to overcome problems formed in earlier stages such as the malevolent attitude or the tendency to disparage. Having a chum teaches the child that one person can offer another tenderness, caring, and respect. As a result, there is no need to anticipate hostility or to attack others' self-respect. Without a chum, Sullivan said, preadolecents may become the victims of a desperate loneliness that is worse than anxiety, and they may be seriously handicapped in approaching the tasks of adolescence.

EARLY ADOLESCENCE.   The physiological changes of puberty lead to the development of sexual desire (**lust**) and usher in the period of **early adolescence**, which ideally culminates with the establishment of a satisfactory pattern of sexual activity. Many of the problems that arise during this period reflect conflicts among three basic needs: security, or freedom from anxiety; intimacy, now ordinarily with someone of the opposite sex; and sexual satisfaction. For example, if parents and other family members criticize or ridicule the young person's choice of a love object, the need for intimacy may collide with the need for security. Or, if the need for intimacy does not shift from chumship with someone of the same sex to closeness with someone of the opposite sex—as the beginning of sexual drives normally dictates—the young person may have difficulty establishing a satisfactory pattern of sexual behavior. Such a development may also lead to the establishment of a homosexual orientation.

LATE ADOLESCENCE.   **Late adolescence** lasts until the young person has been initiated into the satisfactions and responsibilities of adult social living and citizenship. During this period, more and more experience occurs in the syntaxic mode. Whether someone goes to work in a machine shop or attends college, he ''is bound to broaden his acquaintance with other people's attitudes toward living, the degree of their interdependence in living, and the ways of handling various kinds of interpersonal problems'' (Sullivan, 1953, p. 299).

If people arrive at late adolescence with inflated self-systems, anticipating anxiety in many areas of life, they are likely to experience one or more of the unfortunate occurrences of this period such as the consolidation of **inaccurate personifications** and various kinds of **restrictions of living**. The latter include unrealistic views of the self, stereotypical notions of others, and anxiety-avoiding behaviors that diminish one's freedom. For example, if one typically avoids all discussion of philosophical issues because of the fear that one is insufficiently informed, one will lose the opportunity to gain ''useful educative and consensual validating experience with others'' (Sullivan, 1953, p. 306).

A final achievement of this period is self-respect, which is a prerequisite for respecting others. Generally, Sullivan pointed out, we disparage others, or put them down, for having qualities that we are anxious about or ashamed of in ourselves. Thus, he said, when we can respect ourselves, we can respect others as well.

MATURITY.   Sullivan had relatively little to say about **maturity**, but he did suggest that each of the significant achievements of the earlier stages will be ''outstandingly manifest in the mature personality'' (Sullivan, 1953, p. 310). Thus mature adults will have learned to satisfy important needs; to cooperate and compete with others; to sustain relationships with others that are both intimate and sexually satisfying; and to function effectively in the society in which they live. Among these achievements, Sullivan (1953, p. 310) clearly considered intimacy to be the most important: mature people are ''quite sympathetically understanding of the limitations, interests, possibilities, anxieties, and so on of those among whom they move or with whom they deal.''

RESEARCH METHODS AND EMPHASES

Sullivan, like most of the theorists we have discussed so far, developed his theory largely on the basis of his clinical work. However, viewing personality as a function of interpersonal interaction rather than made up of complex internal processes, he tied his hypotheses and conclusions very closely to the behavior of people in real-life situations. Much of his therapeutic work, for example, was done in hospital settings where the social interactions among patients and staff were part of both diagnosis and treatment.

RESEARCH ON SCHIZOPHRENIA.   Much of Sullivan's clinical work focused on the problems of people diagnosed as schizophrenic. He was enormously talented in making contact with and understanding such people, and he used this talent in studying and treating those whom other professionals had for years relegated to the back wards of mental institutions. Sullivan insisted that such patients were not hopeless cases and that they could be treated successfully if the therapist was willing to be patient, understanding, and observant.

In 1929, at Sheppard and Enoch Pratt Hospital, near Baltimore, Sullivan set up a special ward for male schizophrenic patients that was isolated from the rest of the hospital and staffed by male attendants whom he chose and trained. (Female staff members were not allowed on the ward because Sullivan believed that male schizophrenics have particular difficulty dealing with women whom they perceive as being powerful and in command.) According to Chapman (1976, p. 47), at the end of a year, it was found that these patients had done much better than others with similar diagnoses; about 80 percent had improved. Moreover, the psychiatrist who ran this ward for an additional year using Sullivan's model reported a 75 percent recovery or improvement rate (Sullivan, 1962, pp. 290–291). Nevertheless, it is not known whether many patients recovered entirely; there was, unfortunately, no follow-up at later intervals, as is customary in such research today (Chapman, 1976).

PROBLEMS OF RACIAL INTEGRATION AND WORLD PEACE.   In the late 1930s, Sullivan was asked by the black sociologist Charles S. Johnson to participate with him in a study in Tennessee of the personality problems of southern, rural, black youth. Subsequently, E. Franklin Frazier, also a black sociologist, asked Sullivan to collaborate in studying black youth in "border" states (Kentucky and the District of Columbia). Sullivan's contributions to these two studies can be found in the published accounts of each researcher (Frazier, 1940; Johnson, 1941). In respect to the first study, Sullivan (1964) noted that he could not find anything "either general or unique" in the black youth's personality except an almost ubiquitous fear and distrust of whites. According to Perry (1964), in an article on anti-Semitism, written about the same time, Sullivan noted that the only general characteristic of Jews that he was able to detect was that they have been taught to expect "at least covert anti-Semitism." Thus for Sullivan, the problem always came down to how people view and interact with each other.

Believing that his views could contribute to improving relations among nations, Sullivan became involved, after the end of World War II, in a series of conferences and meetings under the auspices of United Nations member agencies. Scientists representing different disciplines and countries met together to attempt to formulate some ideas of how nationalistic aggression might be controlled and better international understanding achieved.

Until his death in 1949, returning from a meeting of the World Federation for Mental Health, Sullivan devoted considerable time and energy to the cause of world peace. He also wrote several articles in which he applied his theories to the problem of growing international tensions.

EVALUATION

Adler, Horney, Fromm, and Sullivan invested personality with social dimensions that are as important as, if not more important than, the biological dimensions framed by Freud's instinctivist position. These theorists focused their attention on the second element in the nature–nurture controversy and found that human beings are not by nature fearful and destructive. People are made anxious by the conditions under which they live—unloving or hostile parental behavior, economic and social injustice, and so on. And they become destructive when their basic needs are frustrated, not out of some fundamental drive to destroy themselves or others.

On the other hand, by their focus on environmental–social factors, these theorists, critics say, may have alienated human beings from their biological heritage.

Adler tells us that weakness is intolerable, but he never tells us why; others talk glibly of ego needs without saying why so passionate a demand for status should exist. . . . This is rather like discussing a theory of famine without first explaining why people need to eat. There is no reason why the neo-Freudians should not concern themselves with interpersonal relations, but that does not absolve them from the necessity of considering the biological foundations from which they arise. (Brown, 1961, p. 185)

By reducing personality to the system of the ego and its defenses, critics claim, the socially oriented theorists have ignored the crucial past and present sources of behavior in the human being's physicochemical makeup. Today, when research is turning up more and more evidence of the physiological substrates of behavior, this criticism seems particularly significant (see, e.g., Eysenck, 1967).

Of course, neither Adler, Horney, Fromm, or Sullivan denied the contribution to human personality of biological factors. They all agreed that the baby is born with certain tendencies and predispositions, and that it is the interaction between nature and nurture that determines how personality will evolve and function. And Freud, his defenders point out, did not rule out the influence of the social environment; had he done so, he could hardly have evolved concepts such as the ego, the superego, and the Oedipus complex. Nevertheless, it is clear that the orthodox Freudians place more emphasis than do the socially oriented theorists on the human infant's "special needs as a little animal." (Munroe, 1955, p. 415)

Many critics find the four theorists of this chapter excessively idealistic about humankind. Franck (1966), for example, says that people's propensities are ethically neutral and that the view of personality advanced by the socially oriented theorists reflects their own normative preconceptions rather than scientific inquiry.

Compared with Freud's darker moments, the social–psychological theorists may indeed seem optimistic and melioristic (believing that the world tends to become better and that human beings can help make it better). But they are hardly extravagantly so. More typical is Horney's statement that human beings are essentially neither good nor bad but possess ''evolutionary constructive forces'' to whose urgings they may or may not respond. Interestingly, despite psychology's lack of enthusiasm for Adler's own concept of social interest, related topics, such as altruism, cooperation, and other kinds of proscial behavior keep appearing in the literature (see, e.g., Bach and Torbet, 1982; Etzioni, 1982; Mayeroff, 1971; Sarason, 1974).

Some critics also call these four theorists to task for not having explained just how personality is molded by the social environment. That is, except perhaps for Sullivan, they seem to have neglected the specific details of the learning process, which has been of such central concern to American psychology over the years. Adler and Fromm, for example, say that parents, and often teachers, must train the child to live in society, but they do not specify *how* the child should be so trained. Is it enough just to expose the child to certain conditions of social living? Is there some kind of fairly automatic stamping in and out of behaviors that are socially approved or disapproved? Or does the child mainly use cognitive capacities to perceive, understand, and decide what to do?

Finally, as with Freud, Erikson, and Jung, critics point out the socially oriented theorists' neglect of systematic research. Adler, Horney, Fromm, and Sullivan were all practicing pychotherapists and built their theories of personality largely on their observations and inferences in the therapy setting. Thus, for the most part, it remains to others to explore their concepts in controlled experimentation.

SUMMARY

ALFRED ADLER

1. The person is a socially oriented, self-consciou being that seeks actively to develop itself.

2. The primary human motive is the need to overcome **inferiority** and achieve **superiority**.

3. To guide their behavior, people create **fictional final goals** that represent not reality but what is possible.

4. The **style of life,** the person's unique way of striving for superiority, is fairly set by the age of 4 or 5, although it can be changed by purposeful action.

5. Conditions such as **organic infirmity**, **pampering**, or **neglect** may produce an **inferiority** or **superiority complex** and a maladaptive life-style.

6. The human being's potential for **social interest** must be developed by the parent or the educational system.

7. The **creative power of the self** is what enables the person to use inherited abilities and the forces of the environment to construct his or her particular attitude toward life and relations with others.

8. The ordinal position, or **birth order**, of each child in a family influences the child's personality characteristics.

9. People's **earliest memories** often reveal the genesis of their style of life.

10. The goal of all human beings is to live, love, and work harmoniously with others.

KAREN HORNEY

11. Human personality is the totality of a person's experience and functioning, including physical, psychological, spiritual, social, cultural, and moral factors.

12. Freud's theory is too mechanistic and biological, and it mistakenly gives first place to sexual motivation.

13. The keystone of female psychology is not **penis envy** but the need for power and equality of status and opportunity.

14. Parental mistreatment in early childhood may produce **basic anxiety** and **basic hostility**, which lead to **vicious circles** of intensifying distress and maladaptive behavior.

15. **Conflict** is inevitable in human life, but people with basic anxiety and hostility cannot tolerate it and develop neurotic ways of trying to deal with it: they develop an **idealized self-image,** they **search for glory**, they evolve **neurotic shoulds**, they **externalize** what is unacceptable, and they acquire **neurotic pride** and **self-hate**. All these lead to **alienation from the self**.

16. The three basic ways of relating to others are **self-effacement, expansion**, and **resignation**. Most people prefer one style over the others, but normal people express all three from time to time. Neurotic people cling rigidly to one style of interaction in an effort to avoid conflict.

17. Success in dealing with problems may lead to increased self-confidence, which leads to more success.

ERICH FROMM

18. Human beings struggle continually for dignity and freedom, yet they also experience a strong need for connectedness with one another.

19. The **existential dilemma**, the conflict between the human being's animal, or physiological, needs and the special needs of the self-aware human being, can be solved by uniting with other people in love and work.

20. Needs that are peculiarly human are of two types—those that re-

flect the existential dilemma and those that reflect an overall need to make sense of the world and to work toward a goal.

21. The four dimensions of social character are **accepting–receptive**, **preserving–hoarding**, **taking–exploitative**, and **exchanging–marketing**. Each of these dimensions exists on a continuum that stretches from **productive** to **nonproductive**.

22. Society molds character through the training of the child by parents and educators, but it also warps and frustrates people by isolating them from the meaning of their work and by constantly creating new needs.

23. In the **humanistic communitarian socialist** society envisioned by Fromm, people would relate to one another in brotherliness and would participate more actively in governing themselves.

24. In his study of a Mexican village, Fromm used projective tests as well as other methods to reveal the development of social character.

HARRY STACK SULLIVAN

25. Personality can be conceived of only in the context of interpersonal behavior; people do not exist apart from their relations with others.

26. The human being is an energy system that must satisfy needs and dispel tension by means of **energy transformations**.

27. **Anxiety**, an extreme degree of tension, requires special methods for its dissipation: two important methods are **somnolent detachment** and **selective inattention**.

28. Cognitive functioning occurs in three modes: **prototaxic**, **parataxic**, and **syntaxic**. **Parataxic distortion** interferes with logical thinking. **Consensual validation** facilitates logical thinking and learning.

29. Three personality characteristics are relatively stable over time: the **dynamism**, the **personification**, and the **self-system**. One component of the self-system engages in **security operations**; the other represents the **personified self**, which is the integration of the **good-me** and **bad-me**. The **not-me** is the dissociated aspect of the self.

30. Personality evolves through six stages: **infancy**, **childhood**, the **juvenile era**, **preadolescence**, **early adolescence**, and **late adolescence**. Important developments are the **malevolent transformation**, **stereotypes**, **ostracism**, and **disparagement**.

31. Although Adler, Horney, Fromm, and Sullivan, by focusing their attention on the environment of the person, gave personality a social dimension, critics have taken them to task for neglecting human beings' biological heritage. These theorists, with the possible exception

of Sullivan, have also been criticized for neglecting the specific details of the learning process and for failing, to any great extent, to explore their conceptions in controlled experimentation. Adler, Horney, Fromm, and Sullivan have been criticized for being excessively idealistic about humankind, although in general they propose that people possess the potential for either good or evil. Current psychological literature does reflect an ongoing concern with various forms of prosocial behavior.

SUGGESTED READING

ALFRED ADLER

Probably the best introduction to Adler's theory is *The Practice and Theory of Individual Psychology* (1927). You may also want to look at one of Adler's brief statements of his approach: "Individual Psychology" (1930) or "The Fundamental Views of Individual Psychology" (1935). The three books edited by Heinz and Rowena Ansbacher, however—*The Individual Psychology of Alfred Adler* (1956); Adler, *Cooperation Between the Sexes* (1978); and Adler, *Superiority and Social Interest* (1979)—provide the clearest and best integrated sources of information on Adler's theories.

According to the Ansbachers (Adler, 1978), Adler's most important book is *The Neurotic Constitution* (1912). They warn, however, that "the existing translation . . . is quite inadequate" (Adler, 1978, p. 416). Adler's own literary style was apparently not the smoothest and, to make matters worse, before the Ansbachers began to translate and edit his writings, he was poorly represented in English. Although his works are often difficult to follow, they are worth the effort.

Schachter's *The Psychology of Affiliation* (1959) is an impressive demonstration of birth order effects. For an idea of the wealth of research generated by this concept, you may want to examine Vockell, Felker, and Miley, "Birth order literature 1967–1972," (1973), and Ernst and Angst *Birth Order: Its Influence on Personality* (1983). In addition to birth order, other Adlerian concepts such as social interest and the style of life continue to generate theoretical discussion and research. An examination of some issues of *Individual Psychology* (formerly, *The Journal of Individual Psychology*) will give you an idea of the kinds of studies being pursued in these areas.

Three biographical works have been written on Adler: Bottome, *Alfred Adler: A Biography* (1939); Orgler, *Alfred Adler: The Man and His Work* (1963); and Sperber, *Masks of Loneliness: Alfred Adler in Perspective* (1974). In addition, a brief biographical essay by Carl Fürtmuller appears in Ansbacher and Ansbacher, *Superiority and Social Interest*.

KAREN HORNEY

The best introduction to Horney's thought is her first book, *The Neurotic Personality of Our Time* (1937). *New Ways in Psychoanalysis* (1939), which sets forth Horney's specific arguments with Freudian theory, also contains her latest formal statement on the psychology of women. *Feminine Psychology* (1967a), a collection of Horney's earlier papers, describes her theories in much greater detail.

Self-analysis (1942), Horney's pioneering self-help treatise, is said to be based very largely on her own self-analysis. *Neurosis and Human Growth* (1950) contains Horney's last and most sophisticated presentation of her theory.

Many of Horney's early papers were written and published in German, but you can find more recent essays in issues of the *American Journal of Psychoanalysis*. Rubins, *Karen Horney: Gentle Rebel of Psychoanalysis* (1978), gives a sympathetic account of her life and work, and her own diaries—*The Adolescent Diaries of Karen Horney* (1980)—offer an intriguing glimpse of her as a young woman.

ERICH FROMM

Fromm's first important book, *Escape from Freedom* (1941), which was written under the shadow of the Nazi regime, shows why that form of totalitarianism was able to appeal to an insecure people. To understand Fromm's intellectual background, you may want to examine *Marx's Concept of Man* (1961) and follow it with *Beyond the Chains of Illusion* (1962), in which Fromm attempts to synthesize Freud's and Marx's views.

Fromm wrote over 20 books, among the most famous of which are *The Sane Society* (1955) and *The Art of Loving* (1956). One of his last books, *The Anatomy of Destructiveness* (1973), explores the issue of whether human aggression is instinctive or learned, and *To Have or to Be?* (1976) discusses the two opposing orientations that form the basis for Fromm's theory of social character. A brief biographical sketch of Fromm appears in the introduction to Funk, *Erich Fromm: The Courage to Be Human* (1982), in which the author, Fromm's editor and translator, discusses Fromm's work.

HARRY STACK SULLIVAN

Sullivan published one book during his lifetime: *Conceptions of Modern Psychiatry* (1947). Because he kept detailed notebooks and had many of his lectures recorded, his editors at *Psychiatry* were able to put together five more books, which include also articles originally published in *Psychiatry* and in other books and journals. *The Interpersonal Theory of Psychiatry* (1953) offers the single most complete account of Sullivan's theory and, with *The Fusion of Psychiatry and Social Science* (1964), provides the best source for understanding his concepts. *The Psychiatric Interview* (1954), required reading in many medical schools and clinical psychology programs, is applicable, as Sullivan said, not just to psychotherapy but to such things as employment interviewing and guidance counseling.

Blitsten, *The Social Theories of Harry Stack Sullivan* (1953), and Mullahy, *The Beginnings of Modern American Psychiatry: The Ideas of Harry Stack Sullivan* (1973), have written at length on Sullivan's theory; Mullahy has written five other books on Sullivan. And two biographies of Sullivan have appeared: Chapman, *Harry Stack Sullivan: His Life and Work* (1976), and Perry, *Psychiatrist of America* (1982). (Perry was managing editor of *Psychiatry* while Sullivan was alive and is the chief editor of all Sullivan's posthumously published works.) In 1978 *Psychiatry* published the "Harry Stack Sullivan Colloquium," which contains some interesting reminiscences by colleagues of Sullivan's.

Part 2   Focus on the Experiencing Person

In this second part of the book we discuss six theorists who tend to place great emphasis on the way in which a person experiences his or her world. Abraham Maslow and Carl Rogers (Chapter 6) emphasize the person's striving for self-actualization. Ludwig Binswanger and Medard Boss (Chapter 7) have been heavily influenced by the philosophical movement of existentialism. Kurt Lewin and George Kelly (Chapter 8) are in many ways quite different from each other, but they agree on the idea that the way in which a person constructs and evaluates his or her world is the central fact to be considered in interpreting that person's behavior.

These six theorists are less under the influence of Freud and psychoanalysis than the theorists discussed in the first part of the book. Although all except Lewin are or were psychotherapists and hence concerned to some degree with psychological disturbance, they tend on the whole to take a broader and sunnier view of human nature than the psychoanalysts. The theorists in the present group tend to be relatively more concerned with normal people in their day-to-day functioning, and even with the peaks of human experience.

Again, you may wish to skim Figure 2 briefly, returning to it after reading about the theories. On the whole, the theorists in this part of the book tend to view human beings as purposive and motivated largely by conscious factors. They tend to place more emphasis on environmental than on hereditary influences and to see people as influenced by factors in the present.

In general, these theorists take an interactionist position with respect to person and environment, and they tend to be more conerned with normal than with abnormal functioning. Their positions on the issue of motivation range from Maslow's and Rogers's proposal of a sole, self-actualization motive to Lewin's suggestion that there are as many motives, or needs, as there are specific and distinguishable human cravings. These theorists offer a holistic and humanistic perspective, viewing the person as a whole organism that interprets experience consciously and purposefully.

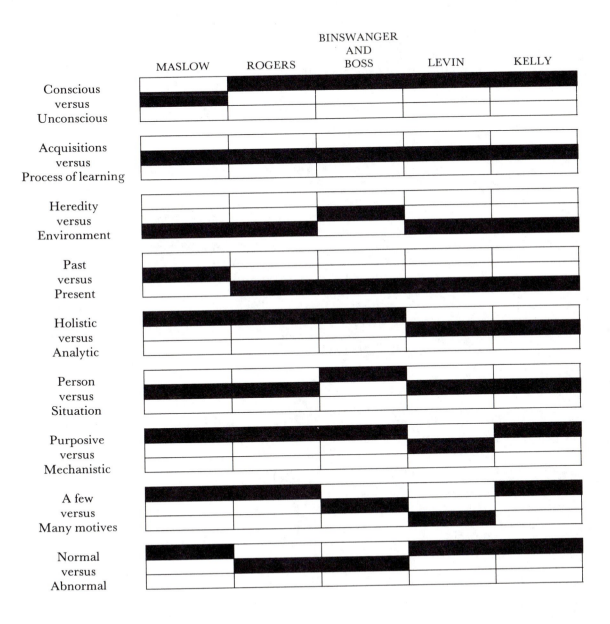

Figure 2   Humanistic-cognitive theorists and the personality dimensions.

Chapter six

6.

Self-actualization is intrinsic growth of what is already in the organism, or more accurately, of what is the organism itself.

ABRAHAM MASLOW

I get great pleasure out of facilitating the development of a person.

CARL ROGERS

Holism and Humanism: Abraham Maslow and Carl Rogers

Ever since René Descartes (French philosopher and mathematician; 1596–1650) split the human being into two separate but interacting entities—body and mind—philosophers, psychologists, physicians, and others have been trying to put the organism back together again—to treat it as a unified, organized whole. The holistic, or organismic, viewpoint, as expressed in the field of medicine, holds that in any illness, whether physical or mental, both mind and body must be treated. A holistic theory of personality focuses on the whole organism as a unified system rather than on separate traits, drives, or habits.

Holism, which traces its roots back to Aristotle (Greek philosopher; 342–322 B.C.), Baruch Spinoza (Dutch philosopher; 1842–1677), and William James (American psychologist and philosopher; 1842–1910), is related to the Gestalt movement that evolved in Germany just before World War I. Holism asserts that the organism always behaves as a unified whole, not as a series of differentiated parts. Mind and body are not separate entities but parts of a single unity, and what happens in a part affects the whole. Conversely, the laws of the whole govern the functioning of its parts. Thus, one must discover the laws by which the whole organism functions in order to understand the functioning of any component. Table 6.1 summarizes the principal features of the holistic viewpoint as it bears on personality theory.

Although most contemporary personality theorists adopt a more or less holistic orientation, the theorists we discuss in this chapter—Abraham Maslow and Carl Rogers—differ from others such as Sigmund Freud (Chapter 2), Carl Jung (Chapter 4), Henry Murray (Chapter 9), and Gordon Allport (Chapter 10) in that they identify themselves also with the humanistic movement in modern psychology. **Humanism** asserts the overall dignity and worth of human beings and their capacity for self-realization. Humanistic theorists oppose what they see as the

TABLE 6.1   Important Features of the Holistic Perspective

1. The normal personality is characterized by unity, integration, consistency, and coherence. Organization is the natural state, and disorganization is pathological.

2. The organism can be analyzed by differentiating its parts, but no part can be studied in isolation. The whole functions according to laws that cannot be found in the parts.

3. The organism has one sovereign drive, that of self-actualization. People strive continuously to realize their inherent potential by whatever avenues are open to them.

4. The influence of the external environment on normal development is minimal. The organism's potential, if allowed to unfold by an appropriate environment, will produce a healthy, integrated personality.

5. The comprehensive study of one person is more useful than the extensive investigation in many people of an isolated psychological function.

pessimism and despair of the psychoanalytic perspective and the ''robot'' conception of human beings offered by behaviorism. Such theorists believe that we contain within ourselves the potential for healthy and creative growth and that if we are willing to accept responsibility for our own lives, we will realize this potential, overcoming the sometimes constricting influences of parental training, education, and other social pressures. Humanism

stands for respect for the growth of persons, respect for differences of approach, open-mindedness as to acceptable methods, and interest in exploration of new aspects of human behavior. . . . It is concerned with topics having little place in existing theories and systems; e.g., love, creativity, self, growth, organism, basic need-gratification, self-actualization, higher values, being, becoming, spontaneity, play, humor, affection, naturalness, warmth, ego-transcendence, objectivity, autonomy, responsibility, meaning, fair play, transcendental experience, peak experiences, courage, and related concepts. (Maslow, 1964, pp. 70–71)

ABRAMAM H. MASLOW

It was Abraham Maslow who christened the humanistic school the ''third force'' in American psychology, the first two being psychoanalysis and behaviorism. Maslow himself moved through all three of these perspectives. He began, as he put it, as a ''monkey man'' (Hall, 1968), writing his doctoral dissertation under Harry Harlow at the University of Wisconsin on dominance as a determinant of social and sexual behavior in rhesus macaque monkeys. Maslow's interests in Freudian theory and in the Gestalt and organismic viewpoints began to grow, however, and his studies in philosophy convinced him that the salvation of the human being was not to be found in either behaviorism or psychoanalysis.

BOX 6.1   Abraham Harold Maslow (1908–1970)

Abraham Maslow was born and brought up in Brooklyn, where his parents had settled after emigrating from Russia. The family was poor at the outset but gradually moved to a middle-class neighborhood, as Maslow's father, a manufacturer, became increasingly successful.

Maslow describes his mother as not being "nice" and says he had little affection for her. He describes his father as a "nice" man but as one who did not understand Maslow's own intellectual interests. An uncle, a male cousin of about Maslow's age, and Maslow's cousin Bertha Goodman were important caring figures in his early years. At 16 Maslow knew he was in love with Bertha, and he married her in 1928, after four year of courtship. They had two daughters, Ann and Ellen, and Maslow has said that the birth of his first child changed his life: "I looked at this tiny mysterious thing and . . . felt small and weak and feeble before all this. I'd say that anyone who had a baby couldn't be a behaviorist" (Hall, 1968, p. 56).

Maslow attended the City University of New York (then City College) and Cornell University for brief periods but earned all his degrees at the University of Wisconsin, where he was Harry Harlow's first Ph.D. student. When he first arrived at Wisconsin, Maslow was full of enthusiasm for Watson and his theories of behavior. After his initial work with monkeys, Maslow did some parallel studies with human beings, finding many similarities (Maslow, 1968). One day in 1941, just after Pearl Harbor was attacked by Japan, Maslow says, he gave up everything he was "fascinated with in a selfish way." He had a "vision of a peace table, with people sitting around it, talking about human nature and hatred and war and peace and brotherhood." He felt that

we didn't understand—not Hitler, not the Germans, not Stalin, not the communists. We didn't understand any of them. I felt that if we could understand them we could make progress. . . . That moment changed my whole life and determined what I've done ever since. Since [then] I've devoted myself to developing a theory of human nature that could be tested by experiment and research. I wanted to prove that human beings are capable of something grander than war and prejudice and hatred. (Hall, 1968, p. 54)

In his theory of metamotivation, or the metaneeds, Maslow tried

to develop an entering wedge, the ba-

sis for an ideology that all human beings can accept. There should be no boundaries. What we need is a system of thought—you might even call it a religion—that can bind human beings together. A system that would fit the Republic of Chad as well as the United States, a system that would supply our idealistic young people with something to believe in. They are searching for something they can put all that emotion into. (Hall, 1968, p. 65)

Clearly, Maslow had broad concerns that went beyond the confines of his early training and work. As he said, "My adventures in psychology have led me in all sorts of directions, some of which have transcended the field of conventional psychology" (Maslow, 1971, p. 3).

Two years before he died, when asked what he would say to a young, self-actualizing psychologist who wanted to know the most important thing he or she could do in this time of social crisis, Maslow said, "I'd tell him to get to work on aggression and hostility. . . . Time is running out. A keystone to our understanding of the evil which can destroy our society lies in this new understanding" (Hall, 1968, p. 57).

In 1951, after 14 years on the faculty of Brooklyn College, Maslow became chairman of the psychology department at Brandeis University. In 1969 he moved to Menlo Park, California, where he became a resident fellow at the Laughlin Foundation. He suffered a fatal

heart attack in June of the following year.

Maslow was president of the
American Psychological Association from 1967 to 1968, and he
was Andrew Kay Visiting Fellow at La Jolla's Western Behavioral Science Institute in
1961–1962. He was a prolific
writer and teacher, much loved
by his students and held in
warm regard by colleagues. He
was generous in his work, often
giving credit to those whose
ideas he admired or used; his
works are full of references to
such predecessors as Adler and
Horney and such contempo-
raries as Carl Rogers.

At some point Maslow asked himself how psychologies based on
the study of people whose mental capacities were, for one reason or another, less than normal could possibly tell us anything very meaningful
about the majority of people who were, he felt sure, healthy and creative. He felt that psychology had only a "pessimistic, negative, and
limited conception" of human beings and that it had dwelt far more on
human frailties than on human strengths, seeking to explore people's
sins while neglecting their virtues. Psychology saw the person as continually, and desperately, trying to avoid pain rather than as actively
seeking pleasure and happiness. Where is the psychology, Maslow
asked, that takes account of gaiety, exuberance, love, and well-being
to the same extent that it deals with misery, conflict, shame, and hostility? Psychology, he said, "has voluntarily restricted itself to only
half of its rightful jurisdiction, and that the darker, meaner half."

Just as theories of the person had neglected an enormous area of
personality functioning, mechanistic science as represented by behaviorism, Maslow felt, was not adequate to a study of the whole person.
The humanistic science he proposed would not substitute for mechanistic science but would serve to complement it, dealing with questions of value, individuality, consciousness, purpose, ethics, and "the
higher reaches of human nature."

WE ARE BASICALLY GOOD, NOT EVIL

To begin with, human beings, according to Maslow, have an essential
psychological structure analogous to their physical structure: they
have "needs, capacities, and tendencies that are genetically based."
Some of these characteristics are typical of all human beings; others
are "unique to the individual." These needs, capacities, and tendencies are essentially good or, at least neutral; they are not evil. This notion of Maslow's was a novel one, for many writers had assumed that
some human needs or tendencies are bad or antisocial and must be
tamed by training and socialization (e.g., the theologians' positing of
original sin; Freud's concept of the id).

Second, healthy and desirable development involves actualizing
these characteristics, or fulfilling the person's potentialities. The person matures "along the lines that this hidden, covert, dimly seen es-

*Drawing by Dana Fradon. ©
1984 The New Yorker Maga-
zine, Inc.*

"We do pretty well when you stop to think that people are basically good."

sential nature dictates, growing from within rather than being shaped
from without'' (Maslow, 1954, p. 340).

Third, Maslow suggests, psychopathology generally results
from the denial, frustration, or twisting of our essential nature. On
this view, what is good? Anything that promotes self-actualization.
What is bad, or abnormal? Anything that frustrates or blocks or denies
the human being's essential nature. It follows that psychotherapy or
therapy of any sort is a means by which people can be restored to the
path of self-actualization and development along the lines dictated by
their inner nature (Maslow, 1954).

A good deal of clinical evidence and some research evidence as
well, Maslow says, suggests that it is reasonable to assume an ''active
will toward health, an impulse towards growth or towards the actualization of human potentialities'' (1967b) in almost every human being.
This inner nature is both weak and strong: it is ''delicate and subtle
and easily overcome by habit, cultural pressure, and wrong attitudes
toward it'' (Maslow, 1968, p. 4). But if it is denied, it goes under-
ground where it continues to press for expression, probably even in the
''sick,'' or poorly adjusted person.

MOTIVATION: A HIERARCHY OF NEEDS

Maslow formulated a theory of human motivation in which the human
being's many varying needs are seen as arising in a hierarchical fashion. That is, certain basic needs, such as hunger and thirst, must be

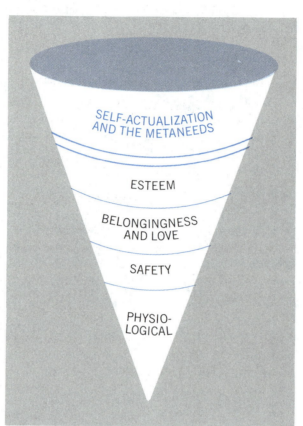

SELF-ACTUALIZATION
AND THE METANEEDS

ESTEEM

BELONGINGNESS
AND LOVE

SAFETY

PHYSIO-
LOGICAL

Figure 6.1 Maslow's hierarchy of needs. It is only when the needs in the smaller circles—beginning with the physiological needs—are relatively satisfied that the metaneeds can be fulfilled.

satisfied before other needs, such as self-esteem, can even be felt, let alone fulfilled. The **basic** or **deficiency** needs are those that arise from some clear lack, or deficit, within the person. Once the deficiency needs are more or less satisfied, the **metaneeds**, or **growth** needs, arise out of the human being's need to pursue goals, to continually go beyond, to become something better, rather than just to be, or to continue to exist. Let us begin with the most basic needs of all, those for physiological satisfaction such as food and drink. Figure 6.1, which represents Maslow's need hierarchy graphically, will help you to see the relation of the various need categories to each other as we go along.

PHYSIOLOGICAL NEEDS. Some **physiological needs** are homeostatic in nature (attempting to maintain a balance among disparate elements). For example, through its intake of food and water, the body attempts to maintain many kinds of equilibrium in the blood and the body tissues such as content of salt, sugar, protein, and other substances.

In some cases an underlying somatic base can be demonstrated for a physiological need—for example, those of hunger, thirst, and fatigue. Temporarily, and up to a point, one can satisfy some of the physiological needs by other activities that do not seem related. For example, one may stave off hunger pangs and thus "satisfy" the need by drinking water or smoking cigarettes. Eventually, however, a true bodily need will demand appropriate satisfaction or the body will die. Conversely, sometimes psychological needs may be disguised as physiological ones; for example, it has been suggested that a person who feels unloved may interpret this feeling of lack as a physiological need and eat to fulfill it.

When the body has an absolute, unsatisfied need for food, all other needs will be pushed into the background, and all the organism's capacities will be put into the service of hunger satisfaction. The urge to write poetry, an interest in American history, the wish for a car or even for a new pair of shoes will, in the extreme case, be forgotten, or become of secondary importance. For the person who is extremely and dangerously hungry, no other interest exists but food. Such a state may even change a person's view of the future; for the seriously hungry person, freedom, love, community feeling, respect, philosophy, and so on may all be waved aside and the person may think if only he or she is guaranteed food for the rest of life, happiness will be complete. But once hunger is satisfied, the person will immediately begin to think of other needs.

SAFETY NEEDS.   The next set of needs to become prominent, once the physiological needs are reasonably well gratified, are the **safety needs**—the needs for security, stability, protection, structure, order, law, limits, freedom from fear and anxiety, and so on. The human expression of these needs is seen most clearly in the infant's uninhibited responses—crying, screaming, and jerking convulsively—to being handled roughly, startled by loud noises or bright lights, or just inadequately supported by a parent. Like severe hunger, severe pain—from an illness, from parental anger and dissension, or from being neglected or abused—may change the child's whole view of the world. The world may become a place of terror and darkness.

Children seem to thrive best when their lives have some organization and structure. Psychologists and educators have found that permissiveness within limits, not unrestricted permissiveness, is both preferred and needed by children. Most people in our society, children and adults alike, prefer a "safe, orderly, predictable, lawful, organized world" that they can count on, in which "unexpected, unmanageable, chaotic, or other dangerous things do not happen" and in which they have "powerful parents or protectors" to shield them from any harm that does arise (Maslow, 1970, p. 41). Children who are brought up in

For Maslow, the need to belong, to feel part of and close to a larger group, is a very basic need. Being members of this extended family may indeed help these people to "keep the faith," as their family crest exhorts them to do.

loving, unthreatening homes do not ordinarily react with panic to sudden or unexpected dangers, and the ''healthy and fortunate adult'' in our society is generally satisfied in his or her safety needs. It is in the economic and social underdog or the neurotic individual that we can see the safety needs clearly.

Often we see the safety needs in such simple things as a desire for a job with tenure and benefits, a savings account, and insurance of various kinds. Science, philosophy, and religion, Maslow says, are partially motivated by the safety needs, but, as we will see, these phenomena have other motivations as well.

BELONGINGNESS AND LOVE NEEDS.   When people's physiological and safety needs are fairly well met, they will strive with great intensity to achieve affectionate relations with others—family, friends, sweetheart, spouse, children. People have **belongingness and love needs**; they need roots, origins. They need to feel part of a home and family, a circle of friends and neighbors, a group of working colleagues. They need to feel that they belong somewhere instead of being transients or newcomers. Maslow suggests that we have a ''deeply animal tendency to herd, to flock, to join, to belong'' (1970, p. 44) that has been frustrated ''by our [society's] mobility, by the breakdown of traditional groupings, the scattering of families, the generation gap, the steady urbanization and disappearance of village face-to-faceness and the

Self-respect and the respect of others comprise the fourth level in Maslow's need hi-erarchy. As this little girl learns to master tasks and develops a feeling of compe-tence, she will build self respect; as she receives appreciation and praise from those who care for her, her self-respect will be strengthened and she will become confi-dent of the esteem of others.

resulting shallowness of American friendship'' (p. 44). The many T-groups (''sensitivity training groups,'' in which people explore their reactions to each other) and other personal growth and encounter groups that exist today may be motivated in part, he suggests, by a need to overcome feelings of alienation and loneliness that stem from these changes in the structure of our society.

Maslow notes that the thwarting of the belongingness and love needs is found at the core of most forms of psychopathology. Thus, he appears to suggest that it is the lack of psychological intimacy with oth-ers, not the frustration of one's sexual desires, that is basic in the pic-ture of maladjustment. Cautioning that ''love is not synonymous with sex,'' he points out that sexual behavior is multidetermined—by sex-ual needs, by love and affection needs, and by other needs.

ESTEEM NEEDS.   There are two sets of **esteem needs**. The first set en-compasses the needs for strength, mastery, competence, self-confi-dence, and independence. The second set comprises the needs for prestige, in the sense of the respect offered us by other people; status; fame; dominance; importance; dignity; and appreciation.

According to Maslow (1970), ''Satisfaction of the self-esteem needs leads to feelings of self-confidence, worth, strength, capability, and adequacy, of being useful and necessary in the world. But thwart-ing of these needs produces feelings of inferiority, of weakness, and of helplessness'' (p. 45). Maslow (1970) seems to suggest that the second set of esteem needs derives or should derive from the first; that is, ''the most stable and therefore most healthy self-esteem is based on *deserved* respect from others rather than on external fame or celebrity and unwarranted adulation'' (p. 46). It seems that achieving adequacy, mastery, and competence and developing confidence in the face of the world and independence of thought and judgment makes for a sound basis for the esteem of others (Maslow, 1970, pp. 45–46).

NEED FOR SELF-ACTUALIZATION.   When all four of the basic, or deficiency, needs we have discussed have been satisfied, the growth need of **self-actualization** arises: ''A new discontent and restlessness will . . . develop unless the individual is doing what he individually is fitted for. A musician must make music, an artist must paint, a poet must write''—in short, what people can be they must be (Maslow, 1970, p. 46).

In framing his concept of self-actualization, Maslow (1970) has acknowledged his debt to Kurt Goldstein, an early organismic theorist who has made significant contributions to personality theory (see Box 6.2). The concept of self-actualization actually has numerous relatives, as Maslow points out. Among these are Jung's concepts of the self archetype, Adler's creative power of the self, Horney's self-realization, Rogers's notion of the evolution and growth of the self.

The specific form that the self-actualizing takes varies greatly from person to person. For example, it may lead one person to become a master bricklayer, another person to invent new electronic devices, a third to establish as service for the poor, a fourth to become an ideal parent, and so on. It is at this level, Maslow says, that individual differences are greatest.

The Metaneeds.   The need for self-actualization is the umbrella need, so to speak, that subsumes 17 **metaneeds**, or **being-values** (see Table 6.2, on p. 210). Some of these metaneeds are concerned with knowing and understanding—for example, the needs for truth, justice, and meaningfulness—and others with an aesthetic need—for example, beauty, order, simplicity, perfection.

Some of the metaneeds are so crucial, Maslow says, that they are almost basic needs: for example, justice, fairness, honesty, and social order, as well as the freedoms to speak out, to express oneself, to do what one wants (as long as it harms no one), to investigate and seek information, and to defend oneself. In addition, there must be no threat to our cognitive capacities, the tools with which we satisfy our needs—our abilities to perceive, to remember, to learn. The use of these capacities in satisfying the deficiency needs is in a sense nega-

BOX 6.2   Kurt Goldstein's Organismic Theory

Kurt Goldstein (German-born neurophsychiatrist and research scientist; 1878–1965) developed his organismic theory of the personality on the basis largely of his many years of work with brain-injured soldiers. From his studies of these men, Goldstein concluded that the most important fact about the human personality is that it functions as a whole, a unity. He found no evidence in his patients for the localization of brain function that other researchers had reported. Goldstein insisted that, when damage occurred to any part of the brain, the effects were generalized and that recovery of function had to be seen from that perspective.

The brain is so constructed, Goldstein said, that damage to any part is often compensated by some new organization of function. For example, one brain-injured man who could differentiate light and dark but could not recognize even the simplest form learned to read by tracing the borders between the dark spots of the letters and the light area of the background.

Now most scientists who study brain and central nervous system functioning—currently a very active area of research—subscribe to a position that combines holistic and localization views. Certain areas of the brain have been discovered to be centers for particular behaviors and functions. However, it has also been recognized that there is some substitutability among parts of the brain.

After founding and directing an institute for the study of brain-injured individuals in Germany for some 15 years, Goldstein traveled, with his wife and three daughters, to the United States, where he continued his work in neuropsychiatry. He was associated with a number of universities and medical schools, including Columbia, Tufts, and Brandeis universities, and the New School for Social Research. Based in New York City, he commuted weekly to Brandeis, where he became acquainted with both Andras Angyal and Abraham Maslow; Maslow has acknowledged Goldstein's influence on his own work. In 1938 and 1939, Goldstein was invited to give the William James lectures on philosophy and psychology at Harvard University.

ENDURING ASPECTS OF PERSONALITY

Goldstein emphasized three enduring aspects of personality: the figure–ground relation, the distinction between natural and unnatural figures, and the distinction between concrete and abstract behavior.

Following the Gestaltists, Goldstein said that the primary organization of organismic function is represented by the **figure–ground relation**. A figure is anything that emerges from or stands out against a background—it occupies the center of one's attention (see Figure 6.2). For example, when you are reading a book in the library, reading is the figure that stands out against a ground of twisting your hair, chewing your pencil, hearing others talk, and so on. If a classmate asks you about yesterday's lecture, listening to him speak will emerge as the new figure. What causes one or another figure to emerge? The requirements of the task in which the organism is engaged. Thus, when you are studying, you must read; when you wish to hear a friend, you must attend to what he or she says.

A second aspect of personality is the distinction between natural and unnatural figures. **Natural figures** represent preferences of the person, and the behavior they involve is both appropriate and flexible. **Unnatural figures** represent tasks imposed on the person, and the behavior involved is rigid and mechanical. For example, a little boy told his mother he had learned a song in Sunday School about a cross-eyed bear named "Gladdy." When the

Figure 6.2   An ambiguous Gestalt. When you perceive this design as a vase, the white portion (figure) has form and appears to come forward, while the gray portion (ground) appears formless and seems to recede. When you perceive the design as two profiles, the reverse takes place: what was ground becomes figure; what was figure becomes ground. From Kendler, 1963.

puzzled mother inquired further, she discovered that the song was "Gladly the Cross I'd Bear"! Learning the words of a song without understanding their meaning is an imposed, mechanical, and thus unnatural figure.

One of Goldstein's important yet controversial contributions to the study of personality is his conception of abstract versus concrete behavior. In **concrete behavior**, the person perceives some stimulus object or event and reacts to it as it appears at the moment. In **abstract behavior**, the person not only perceives and reacts to the stimulus but thinks about it, considering what it means, how it is related to other stimuli, how it can be used, and so on. This distinction between concrete and abstract functioning, which came to be the primary topic of Goldstein's research, continues to engage the research interest

of those studying brain–behavior relations.

PERSONALITY DYNAMICS

Goldstein's three main dynamic concepts are equalization, self-actualization, and coming to terms with the environment. He postulates a fairly constant supply of energy, distributed more or less throughout the organism, which represents the "average" state of tension. When a stimulus changes this tension, the organism tries to return to its average state. Eating when hungry and stretching when cramped are familiar examples of this process. The principle of **equalization** explains the consistency, coherence, and orderliness of behavior. Environmental influence and inner conflict can result in disequilibrium, but in an adequate environment, the organism will remain more or less in balance.

For Goldstein, what seem to be different drives, such as hunger, sex, power, achievement, and curiosity, are simply manifestations of the one overarching motive or purpose of life, **self-actualization**. A need of any kind is a deficit state that motivates replenishment, which is a form of self-actualization. Self-actualization is more than this, however; it is also the creative trend of human nature—the principle by which the organism becomes more fully developed.

Goldstein emphasizes the inner determinants of behavior, but he recognizes the importance of the **environment**, or the objective world, as a source both of disturbance and of necessary supplies by which the organism fulfills its destiny. A normal, healthy organism, Goldstein says, is one "in which the tendency toward self-actualization is acting from within and overcomes the disturbance arising from the clash with the world, not out of anxiety but out of the joy of conquest'' (Goldstein, 1939, p. 305).

RESEARCH

Goldstein's most important research explored abstract and concrete ˜behavior. Convinced that the most important and most common result of damage to the brain was the impairment of the abstract function, Goldstein and his associates developed a number of tests for diagnosing such impairment (see, e.g., Goldstein and Scheerer, 1941, 1953). Although other clinical tests have since been devised for this purpose, the significance of Goldstein's contribution remains undiminished: it was he who first pointed out the importance of measuring this aspect of human psychological functioning.

EVALUATION

Goldstein has been criticized for not being sufficiently holistic—for not including the environment in his concept of the person. Few organismic theorists agree with Angyal (1941), who held that person and environment are inseparable, but most are more willing than Goldstein to see the organism as a differentiated component of a larger system, a system that includes the environment.

Goldstein has also been called to task for not distinguishing clearly between what is inherent in the organism and what has been put there by the culture. At the same time, he has been criticized for putting too much emphasis on maturation and not enough on learning (e.g., Katsoff, 1942). His concept of self-actualization has been criticized as being too general in character to be useful in making predictions (e.g., Skinner, 1940); Maslow's concept, modeled to some extent on Goldstein's, suffers the same criticism. Goldstein has also been criticized for exaggerating the importance of the abstract attitude in psychological functioning. Last but not least, critics have objected to Goldstein's attempt to understand the normal personality by studying brain-injured people. In spite of the foregoing, Goldstein's views have had considerable influence on contemporary psychology.

---

tive—we are then using them to avoid unpleasant or distressing conditions. It is important, Maslow (1970) said, to consider the positive uses of cognitive capacities; the metaneeds that involve satisfying curiosity, knowing, understanding, and explaining are positive impulses to use these capacities. Maslow cites many kinds of evidence for the existence of these positive impulses to intelligent activity, such as the demonstration of curiosity in animals, the natural and unfailing curiosity of the child, the many instances of people pursuing knowledge at great risk to themselves (e.g., Galileo), the fact that the psychologically healthy people Maslow studied were attracted to the unknown and bored by the familiar, and cases of psychotherapy in which symptoms such as boredom and depression disappeared when people took on new activities or tried new lines of endeavor.

The metaneeds have no hierarchy but are equally potent; they can fairly easily be substituted for each other. According to Maslow, they are as inherent in human beings as are the basic needs, and when they are not fulfilled, the person may fall prey to metapathologies, such as apathy, boredom, discouragement, humorlessness, alienation, selfishness, hatred, loss of zest, despair.

TABLE 6.2   *The Metaneeds or Being-Values*

NEED/VALUE	SYNONYMOUS OR RELATED CHARACTERISTICS
Truth	Honesty, reality, nakedness, simplicity, richness, essentiality, "oughtness," beauty, purity, clean and unadulterated completeness
Goodness	Rightness, desirability, "oughtness," justice, benevolence, honesty
Beauty	Rightness, form aliveness, simplicity, richness, wholeness, perfection, completion, uniqueness, honesty
Wholeness	Unity, integration, tendency to oneness, interconnectedness, simplicity, organization, structure, order, synergy
Dichotomy-transcendence	Acceptance, resolution, integration or transcendence of dichotomies, synergy
Aliveness	Process, spontaneity, self-regulation, full functioning, changing yet maintaining, expressing one's essence
Uniqueness	Individuality, noncomparability, novelty, quality of being like nothing else in the world
Perfection	"Just rightness," completeness, state in which there is nothing beyond, nothing superfluous, nothing lacking
Necessity	Inevitability, requirement that something be just exactly as it is
Completion	Totality, ending, finality, fulfillment
Justice	Fairness, "oughtness," necessity, inevitability
Order	Lawfulness, rightness, perfection of arrangement
Simplicity	Honesty, essentiality, state in which there is nothing extra or superfluous
Richness	Differentiation, complexity, intricacy, state in which nothing is missing or hidden and everything is equally important
Effortlessness	Ease, lack of strain, grace, perfect and beautiful functioning
Playfulness	Fun, joy, amusement, gaiety, humor, exuberance
Self-sufficiency	Autonomy, independence, quality of not needing anything other than itself in order to be itself, self-determining, living by its own laws

Source: Maslow (1971, Table 3, pp. 308–309, 1968, p. 83).

Why People Forego the Metaneeds.   According to Maslow, on average, the need for self-actualization is only 10 percent satisfied. Why do people deny their need for self-actualization—draw back from it? Because personal growth ''can bring another kind of fear, of awe, of feelings of weakness and inadequacy. . . . And so we find another kind of resistance, a denying of our best side . . . of our highest potentialities, of our creativeness. In brief this is the struggle against our own greatness, the fear of hubris'' (Maslow, 1968, p. 61; *hubris* is exaggerated pride that brings about retribution).

> *The person who says to himself, ''Yes, I will be a great philosopher and I will rewrite Plato and do it better'' must sooner or later be struck dumb by his grandiosity, his arrogance. . . . He compares his knowledge of his inner private self with all its weakness, vacillation and short-comings, with the bright, shining, perfect, and faultless image he has of Plato. . . . (What he doesn't realize is that Plato, introspecting, must have felt just the same way about himself, but went ahead anyway, overriding his doubts about himself). (Maslow, 1971, pp. 37–38)*

People must learn to manage the integration of humility and pride that is necessary for creative work (Maslow, 1968). They need to be able to embrace being-values, or metaneeds, not only in others but also in themselves. They need, Maslow said, to be able to exclaim, ''Extraordinary! Extraordinary!'' as Aldous Huxley did at all sorts of events. They need to look at the world with innocence, awe, and fascination, yet they must proceed, calmly and unafraid, to do the great work they must. They need to accept feeling small, weak, and unworthy and then go on to do all they can.

We may fear the godlike in ourselves, Maslow says. The dangers and responsibilities of being a leader, of being out front and alone, may make us reluctant to recognize great talents in ourselves. Creative people, he says, attest to the need for courage in the moment of creation (Maslow, 1968, p. 61).

Maslow liked to demonstrate what he called the **Jonah complex** to students: ''Which of you in this class,'' he would ask, ''hopes to write the great American novel, or to be a Senator, or Governor, or President? Who wants to be Secretary General of the United Nations? Or a great composer? Who aspires to be a saint, like Schweitzer perhaps? Who among you will be a great leader?'' Generally, Maslow says ''Everybody starts giggling, blushing, and squirming until I ask, 'If not you, then who else?' '' Maslow's point was that training to be less than you are capable of being—believing that you are unlucky and insignificant and fearing to assert yourself, like Jonah—can lead only to unhappiness, never to self-actualization. (Jonah was asked by God to warn the citizens of Nineveh to repent of their evil ways. When Jonah ignored God's request and set sail for Tarshish, God sent a storm,

Sally Ride, first American woman in space with her fellow astronauts on the space shuttle Challenger as they make final preparations for their June 1983 flight. According to Maslow, to move toward self actualization—to embrace the being values, or metaneeds—people must be able at once to look with humility at the world in its awe-inspiring magnitude and yet to proceed, with courage, to do the work they must. The astronauts have often expressed this kind of wonder and fascination with the universe they explore at great risk at the same time that they calmly carry out the tasks before them.

and Jonah found himself in the belly of a whale. Maslow's interpretation—and there are many—of this biblical story is that Jonah was punished because, out of feelings of unworthiness, he refused his call to greatness.)

According to Maslow, we often countervalue greatness: "We surely love and admire all the persons who have incarnated the true, the good, the beautiful, the just, the perfect, the ultimately successful. And yet they also make us uneasy, anxious, confused, perhaps a little jealous or envious, a little inferior, clumsy" (1968, p. 35). Whether or not they intend to, "great" people make us aware of our own lesser worth. If this is unconscious and we do not know why we feel so, we may attribute the cause to them (project it) and think that they are trying to make us feel inferior. Hostile countervaluing is the result.

Some feeling of awe in the face of greatness is "right," Maslow says. It is suitable to feel so in the presence of the highest and best. But even if we are conscious of what is going on, we may still shy away from it. You have heard people say, "It's just too much," or "I can't stand it," or "I could die." "Delirious happiness cannot be borne for long. Our organisms are just too weak for any large doses of greatness, just as they would be too weak to endure hour-long sexual orgasms" (Maslow, 1971, p. 37). Thus, the Jonah complex is "partly a justified fear of being torn apart, of losing control, of being shattered and disintegrated, even of being killed by the experience" (p. 37).

QUALIFICATIONS OF THE NEED HIERARCHY MODEL.   There are exceptions to the foregoing rules of Maslow's hierarchical model. For example, in some people, esteem needs may come before the need for love and affection; in a few (probably rare) others, the creative need may take precedence over everything else.

If a person has never been deprived of the basic needs he or she may tend to undervalue these needs, not recognizing their importance until a sudden catastrophe occurs, and then be unable to cope. On the other hand, having been secure in the basic needs may give a person the strength to withstand great deprivation. Or constant deprivation from early on may toughen one to meet conflicts and obstacles.

No one is ever 100 percent satisfied in all basic needs. On average, Maslow suggests, people's physiological needs are about 85 percent satisfied, their safety needs about 70 percent, love and belongingness needs about 50 percent, esteem needs about 40 percent, and, as we have noted, self-actualization needs about 10 percent. Also, one does not have to satisfy one basic need completely or even nearly so for another need to arise. For example, if physiological needs are only 10 percent satisfied, a higher need may have to remain totally unsatisfied. If physiological satisfaction rises to 25 percent, however, another need may achieve 5 percent satisfaction. If physiological needs are 75 percent satisfied, a higher need may be 50 percent satisfied, and so on.

HOW IS PERSONALITY ORGANIZED?

For Maslow, the primary unit of personality is the personality syndrome. Maslow's use of the term "syndrome" here is both similar to and different from the use of this term in medicine. As in medicine, the term describes a collection of interrelated characteristics that occur together. In Maslow's usage, however, the term acquires a hierarchical notion: the **personality syndrome** is an "organized, interdependent, structured group of symptoms" (1970, p. 303).

In studying two particular syndromes, the self-esteem and the security syndromes, Maslow has used what he calls **holistic–analytic methodology**. This method of study emphasizes both the whole organism, or person, and the subparts thereof. Maslow recognizes that to examine such subparts, one must become temporarily analytic—one must be willing, for a time, to take a somewhat segmental approach. But, as a holistic theorist, he insists that one must continually return to viewing the organism as a whole, exploring the ways in which the subparts studied interact in the organization and dynamics of the complete person.

Using his holistic–analytic methodology, Maslow arrived at the following definition of the personality syndrome:

[The personality syndrome] is a structured, organized complex of apparently diverse specificities (behaviors, thoughts, impulses to action, perceptions, etc.)

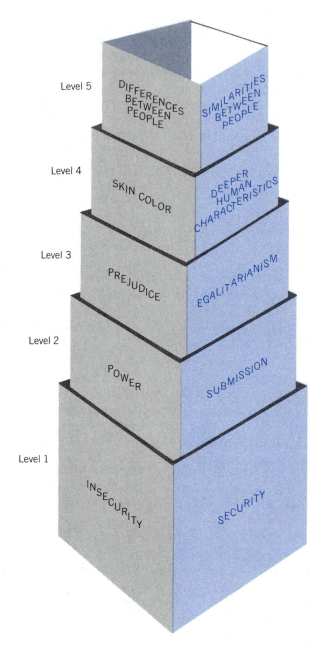

Figure 6.3   The personality syndrome and its subsyndromes.

which, however, when studied carefully and validly are found to have a common unity that may be phrased variously as a similar dynamic meaning, expression, "flavor," function or purpose. (Maslow, 1970, p. 303)

Maslow admits the global nature of this definition, but he cautions that, as we examine the syndrome's components, we must keep in mind that each small element is contained within the larger unit—the personality syndrome. He suggests that we think of a nest of boxes, each smaller box fitting into a slightly larger box and so on until the entire nest of boxes, each containing and being contained, comprises a whole (see Fig. 6.3).

Consider Maslow's analysis of the security personality syndrome. He begins with the level of the syndrome itself, Level 1, and extends the analysis to five levels:

Personality Syndrome	Level 1	Security—Insecurity
Subsyndrome	Level 2	Power—Submission
Sub-Subsyndrome	Level 3	Prejudice—Egalitarianism
Sub-Sub-Subsyndrome	Level 4	Skin Color—Deeper Human Characteristics
Sub-Sub-Sub-Subsyndrome	Level 5	Emphasis on Differences Between People—Emphasis on Similarities Between People

Each lower level (lower number) is contained within each higher level (see also Figure 6.3). By studying the interrelated components at different levels, one can detect the way personality is organized in a given individual.

Maslow also suggests that personality syndromes like self-esteem, security, and intelligence can be studied together. For example, a person who is high in self-esteem and also high in security may express her self-esteem in such a way that she does not offend or threaten others. But someone who is high in self-esteem and low in security may express his self-esteem in a manner that makes him appear contemptuous of others.

The notion of subsyndromes as nested boxes and the notion of personality syndromes themselves as being related to each other are both compatible with Maslow's effort to avoid splitting human beings apart and breaking them up into small, unrelated, and disconnected elements that are situation specific. Maslow's holistic method of study is designed to avoid the pitfalls of the traditional linear approach and the existing mathematical and statistical models that he feels are inadequate for research on personality.

SELF-ACTUALIZING PEOPLE: THE PEAK EXPERIENCE AND THE B- AND D-REALMS

Maslow believed that the study of "crippled," or neurotic, people could produce only a "crippled" psychology. As a result, he undertook to study people who had realized their potentialities to the fullest. Using clinical research methods, in which one studies individual people and then makes judgments about them, Maslow required that in each subject there be "an absence of neurosis, psychopathic personality, psychosis, or strong tendencies in these directions" (1970, p. 150). He also required evidence of self-actualization, which included "the full use of an exploitation of talents, capacities, potentialities, etc." (p. 150). According to Maslow,

This criterion implies also gratification, past or present, of the basic needs for safety, belongingness, love, respect, and self-respect, and of the cognitive needs for knowledge and for understanding, or in a few cases, conquest of these needs. This is to say that all subjects felt safe and unanxious, loved and loving, respect-worthy, and respected" (Maslow, 1970, p. 150).

The specific technique Maslow used in studying his subjects is called **iteration**. Like the mathematical procedure, in which repeating a cycle of operations leads to results that more and more closely approximate the desired result, Maslow's technique involved obtaining information about a subject through such means as interviews or biographical statements, using the data gleaned to further refine the concept of self-actualization, conducting additional interviews to check on these data as well as to discover additional facts, further refining the concept, and so on.

In his studies of living people, such as Eleanor Roosevelt and Albert Einstein, and of famous figures in history, such as Abraham Lincoln, Walt Whitman, and Ludwig Beethoven, Maslow evolved holistic pictures of his subjects. He did not produce the quantitative data that are more typical of personality research. On the basis of his holistic–clinical studies, Maslow compiled a catalog of characteristics that describe self-actualizing people; these are summarized in Table 6.3.

PEAK EXPERIENCING.   In the course of his research, Maslow discovered that among those he viewed as self-actualizing people, the "mystic experience" that William James (1936) had described was a common occurrence. In such experiences, there were

feelings of limitless horizons opening up to the vision, the feeling of being simultaneously more powerful and also more helpless than one ever was before, the feeling of great ecstasy and wonder and awe, the loss of placing in time and space with, finally, the conviction that something extremely important and valuable had happened, so that the subject [was] to some extent transformed and strengthened even in his daily life by such experience. (Maslow, 1970, p. 164)

Maslow christened these occurrences **peak experiences**. Box 6.3 offers an example that Maslow might have termed peak experiencing.

Maslow began to study the peak experience, asking subjects to

TABLE 6.3   *Characteristics of Self-Actualizing People*

SELF-ACTUALIZERS—

Are realistically oriented.

Accept themselves, others, and the natural world as they are.

Are spontaneous.

Are problem-centered rather than self-centered.

Have an air of detachment and a need for privacy.

Are autonomous and independent.

Have a fresh rather than stereotyped appreciation of people and things.

Have generally had profound mystical or spiritual, although not necessarily religious, experiences.

Identify with humankind; possess Adler's *Gemeinschaftsgefühl* (social interest).

Tend to have profoundly intimate relationships with a few specially loved people rather than superficial relationships with many.

Have democratic values and attitudes.

Do not confuse means with ends.

Have a philosophical rather than hostile sense of humor.

Are highly creative.

Resist conformity to the culture.

Transcend the environment rather than just cope with it.

Source: Maslow (1970, pp. 153–174).

Anna Eleanor Roosevelt (1884–1962), lecturer, writer and wife of the 32nd president of the United States, Franklin Delano Roosevelt. For Maslow, a truly self-actualizing person, Mrs. Roosevelt pursued her humanitarian concerns by serving on committees and with organizations whose purpose was to advance the general cause of human freedom and welfare. Here she confers with a colleague at the United Nations.

BOX 6.3   Peak Experiencing: An Eye Opener

It may be true that to be a young man in his late 20s and never to have discovered eye contact until last weekend is to be a little slow. I will not make any excuses; I have been a little slow. Not that I was shifty-eyed—I did not glance, avert my eyes, then glance again; I simply did not look at all. But the point is that a number of good things have been happening in my life recently, so I felt good enough about myself and about where I happened to be at the moment—Third Avenue between 54th and 55th—to suddenly begin looking strangers in the eye and allowing them to look back into mine. It happened on the sidewalk and in stores with, I would say, about half the people I passed; sales-clerks, parking attendants, mothers with babies, even a se-curity guard. Half of us were not initiated; half of us were.

Since this discovery I have enjoyed remembering all those new eyes, all the writhing warmth that was right there just waiting to be acknowledged. It is hard for me to grasp the fact that such intimacy is available between any pair of eyes that has courage enough to encounter another pair of eyes. Dis-covering eye contact ranks as one of the major thrills of my life, right up there with learn-ing to tell time in a flash of com-prehension one day in second grade; staying up all night for the first time and seeing how short it really is; flying the At-lantic for the first time and see-ing how small it really is; hav-ing a girl touch me for the first time; beating my uncle at chess for the first (and last) time; watching my child being born at 4 A.M. then, all day, under-standing that nearly everyone has children; buying a house in the morning and walking the land in the afternoon and skat-ing by myself on my own pond for hours under a full moon that night; putting on a snorkel and mask and discovering that be-neath the black tabletop surface of the ocean there are vast, un-ending tea parties of activity; or trying on a pair of contact lenses and for the first time glimpsing in sharp focus what my adult self looks like without glasses.

It has made my week. I have been in a great mood the whole time, thinking about the word "eye." I have enjoyed writing it down and seeing how stirring it looks on the page, and "oeil," too—it is even more open and unblinking in French. All week I have enjoyed realiz-ing that certain types of art and music and writing have eye contact and certain types do not, and that I will be looking for the difference now. I have enjoyed acknowledging how much common beauty there is in eye contact, especially when walking across Third Avenue with the sun behind me so that the approaching irises are lit up in different colors and take on the texture of lion fur. I have enjoyed thinking that establish-ing eye contact with strangers from now on will bring a cer-tain amount of peace to my daily encounters, whereas pre-viously there has been a certain amount of chaos, a certain amount of thrashing about for the simple reason that I did not know eyes felt at home looking at other eyes, that that was where eyes *belonged*. And for the first time I feel ready to meet my mother's eyes, to hold her gaze, to see what I already know somehow: that her eyes are greyish-blue and small and have grown old and want to lean on me and partake of my strength. The funny thing is that this does not make me sad; it makes me almost so excited that I can't stand it. I cannot wait to see her and give her strength. I cannot wait to get out and see some more sales-clerks and find out what they are up to and walk the sidewalk again and share whatever this thing is that is going on.

Source: Copyright © 1980 by the New York Times Company. Re-printed by permission. The fore-going essay by Daniel Rose, 1980 O. Henry prize winner, appeared in the July 27, 1980 *New York Times* under its original title of "Wake Up to an Eye Opener."

think of the most wonderful experience or experiences of their lives—
"happiest moments, ecstatic moments, moments of rapture, perhaps
from being in love, or from listening to music or suddenly 'being hit'
by a book or a painting, or from some great creative moment'' (1968,
p. 71). He found that people undergoing peak experiences felt more
integrated, more at one with the world, more in command of their own
lives, more spontaneous, less aware of space and time, more percep-
tive, more self-determined, and more playful.

A peak experience may have many lasting effects on the person.
Maslow emphasizes seven such effects:

- The removal of neurotic symptoms.
- A tendency to view oneself in a more healthy way.
- Change in one's view of other people and of one's relations with
  them.
- Change in one's view of the world.
- The release of creativity, spontaneity, and expressiveness.
- A tendency to remember the experience and to try to duplicate it.
- A tendency to view life in general as more worthwhile.

THE B-REALM AND THE D-REALM.   For Maslow, the person relates to
the world in two modes: the D-realm and the B-realm. The distinction
between these two modes of experience is an important one and one
that affects a number of psychological functions, such as cognition,
motivation, and the formation and pursuit of values.

In the **deficiency**, or **D-realm**, the person is concerned with
satisfying the basic needs for survival; that is, the person strives to
overcome or avoid deficiency in needs such as food, drink, shelter.
When these and other basic needs and motives are satisfied, the person
becomes concerned with **being**, or with needs within the **B-realm**,
such as growth motivation, self-actualization, and enhancement of his
or her existence.

In addition to distinguishing D- and B-motives and needs,
Maslow distinguishes between the kinds of cognition that characterize the two realms (see Table 6.4). Although one might think that
B-cognition is the more desirable, Maslow cautions that D-cognition is
needed as well. Indeed, B-cognition alone may be detrimental to the
person; for example, it may interfere with necessary action or lead to
feelings of guilt for being true to oneself but not to others.

ENCOURAGING SELF-ACTUALIZATION
Maslow has not offered a formal theory of personality development.
Concerned, rather, with the development of self-actualization, he has

TABLE 6.4   *Some Characteristics of D-Cognition and B-Cognition*

IN D-COGNITION—	IN B-COGNITION—
Things are seen as dependent on other things, as incomplete.	Things are seen as whole, complete.
Some aspects only of things are attended to; simultaneous attention is given to other, related or causal factors.	Things are attended to exclusively and seen intensely, with total investment.
Something is seen as a member of a class, an instance, a sample.	Something is seen per se, in and by itself, not in competition with anything else.
Things are seen as relevant to human concerns, in terms of their usefulness, dangerousness, and the like.	Things are seen as irrelevant to human concerns.
Things become less interesting; familiarity leads to boredom.	Things become richer by repeated experiencing.
The perceiver experiences not the object alone but object-tied-with self; the ego is the centering point of experience.	The perceiver becomes so absorbed that self disappears; experience is organized around the object rather than the ego.
Things are seen as means to other things.	Things are seen as ends in themselves, as intrinsically interesting.
Things are seen as discrete and mutually exclusive, often with antagonistic interests.	Dichotomies, polarities, conflicts between things are seen as necessary and yet as transcended by a superordinate whole.
Inner and outer worlds are perceived as being more dissimilar.	Inner and outer worlds are perceived as being more similar.
Objects are perceived as normal, everyday, nothing out of the ordinary.	Objects are often perceived as sacred, holy, very special.
Serious things are seen as quite different from amusing things; humor is hostile or absent.	The world and self are often seen as both amusing and poignant; the comic and the tragic are fused; humor is philosophical.

Source: Maslow (1971, pp. 200–265).

offered ideas on how the individual can self-actualize and on how, through education, our society can encourage self-actualization. In his book, *The Farther Reaches of Human Nature*, for example, Maslow (1971) discusses ways that self-actualization can be encouraged in schools. In his view, the typical goal in classroom learning is to please the teacher. Instead, he proposes, students should be helped to find their own identities; to discover their vocations, their fates, and their destinies, and to derive sets of values.

TABLE 6.5   Eight Ways to Self-Actualize

1. Experience things fully, vividly, selflessly. Throw yourself into the experiencing of something: concentrate on it fully; let it totally absorb you.

2. Life is an ongoing process of choosing between safety (out of fear and need for defense) and risk (for the sake or progress and growth): make the growth choice "a dozen times a day."

3. Let the self emerge. Try to shut out external clues as to what you should think, feel, say, and so on, and let your experience enable you to say what you truly feel.

4. When in doubt, be honest. If you look into yourself and are honest, you will also take responsibility; taking responsibility is self-actualizing.

5. Listen to your own tastes. Be prepared to be unpopular.

6. Use your intelligence. Work to do well the things you want to do, whether that means finger exercises at a keyboard; memorizing the names of every bone, muscle, hormone, and so on in the human body; or learning how to finish wood so it looks and feels like silk.

7. Make peak experiencing more likely: get rid of illusions and false notions; learn what you are not good at and what your potentialities are not.

8. Find out who you are, what you are, what you like and don't like, what is good and what is bad for you, where you are going, what your mission is. Opening yourself up to yourself in this way means identifying defenses—and then finding the courage to give them up.

Source: Maslow (1973, pp. 250–252).

Schools should teach that life is precious, Maslow says, and they should encourage peak experiencing. They should give children a sense of accomplishment, and one way to bring this about is to encourage children to help those younger and weaker than they are.

Schools should "refreshen consciousness so that we are continually aware of the beauty and wonder of life" (Maslow, 1971, p. 183). And they should satisfy the child's "basic psychological needs" (security, belongingness, esteem). Clearly, in Maslow's view, personality syndromes and the development of personality are affected in important ways by the experience each child has in school and in society.

A person who can develop the ability to satisfy basic needs can then proceed to self-actualization and the B-values, or metaneeds. Maslow (1973) discusses eight ways to self-actualize, which are summarized in Table 6.5.

The notion of development, or evolution, is inherent in the very conception of self-actualization. Thus, despite Maslow's failure to provide a specific developmental theory, he has been much concerned, as Table 6.5 highlights, with the rational, cognitive processes that are an essential part of self-actualization.

How does the development of personality in some people go awry such that they do not self-actualize? If the growth-oriented, self-actualizing tendency in the human being is so strong, how does it get denied, blocked, frustrated? According to Maslow, Freud's greatest discovery was that "*the* great cause of much psychological illness is the fear of knowledge of oneself—of one's emotions, impulses, memories, capacities, potentialities, of one's destiny" (1968, p. 60). Our fear is defensive, Maslow says, in that it serves to protect our self-esteem, our love and respect for ourselves. "We tend to be afraid of any knowledge that could . . . make us feel inferior, weak, worthless, evil, shameful" (p. 60). The need for self-esteem must be satisfied before the person can move toward self-actualization. Thus any feelings of uncertainty can presumably make one overprotective of one's self-esteem and thus close off growth and change.

Human beings also become miserable or neurotic or fail to self-actualize because, through ignorance and social pathology, the environment prevents them from achieving normal growth. When people are destructive and violent, Maslow asserts, it is not because these qualities are natural to them but because their inner natures have been twisted or frustrated. Here again Maslow stresses the role of society. Just as society can foster self-actualization in the individual, so it can thwart personality development in such a way as to inhibit self-actualization.

CARL R. ROGERS

It is for his method of psychotherapy, originally called nondirective or client-centered therapy, and his pioneering research on the therapy process that Carl Rogers is best known in the world of psychology. Partly because it is tied to psychology rather than to medicine, client-centered therapy has become quite popular among clinical psychologists and other psychological counselors. In addition, because it is fairly easy to learn and does not require long years of training and personal analysis, and because clients are often benefited after only a few therapy sessions, the Rogerian method has become widespread among other people in the helping professions—for example, educational counselors, guidance counselors, and social workers.

Rogers was one of the first psychotherapists to invite the researcher (by way of tape recordings) into the sanctum of the therapy session. Roger's courage in opening his own sessions with clients to the scrutiny of others was unparalleled in the early 1940s, and it is largely due to his work that we have begun to learn something about the nature of psychotherapy and the processes by which it operates.

Therapy is not our concern here, of course, but we will be interested in Rogers's therapeutic method because, like Freud, he developed his personality theory out of clinical experience. Box 6.5, which discusses Rogers's therapy technique, indicates that such important

BOX 6.4   Carl R. Rogers (1902–)

The middle child in a large, close-knit, religious family, Carl Rogers was born in Illinois, where he grew up first in the suburbs and then on a farm. His parents were "masters of the art of subtle and loving control," he writes (Rogers, 1967b). "I do not remember ever being given a direct command on an important subject, yet such was the unity of our family that it was understood by all that we did not dance, play cards, attend movies, smoke, drink, or show any sexual interest" (p. 344).

Rogers's early interest in natural science—the study of moths—led easily to a beginning specialization, at the University of Wisconsin, in agriculture. When he was a sophomore, his interests turned toward religion, and the following year a trip to China and the Philippines with the World Student Christian Federation helped to crystallize Rogers's religious and philosophical thinking. He attended Union Theological Seminary, in New York City, where students, he writes, were so encouraged to think for themselves that some of them—including Rogers— "thought their way right out of religious work" (Rogers, 1967b, p. 354). Rogers transferred to Teachers College of Columbia University, where he obtained his degree in clinical and educational psychology in 1931.

Interning at the Institute for Child Guidance, Rogers found the institute's emphasis on "an eclectic Freudianism" helpful in that "different shades of psychoanalytic thinking and other psychiatric and psychological views" were expressed. "Alfred Adler lectured to us, for example, and shocked the whole staff by thinking that an elaborate case history was not necessary" (Rogers, 1967b, p. 357).

In 1928, with his wife Helen (Elliott) and two small children, David and Natalie, Rogers moved to Rochester, New York, where he joined the staff of what was later to become the Rochester Guidance Center. The center offered diagnostic and treatment services to delinquent and underprivileged children referred by the courts. For nine years Rogers directed these services, and it was with some reluctance that he left his directorship in 1940 to accept an academic position, a full professorship at Ohio State University.

As Rogers began to teach what he had learned about treatment and counseling to graduate students, his ideas on these topics began to crystallize. In 1940, when he gave a talk at the University of Minnesota and presented some of the main ideas of the theory that he was developing, he was surprised at the reaction of his audience, for he had not anticipated the controversy that his ideas would stir up.

In 1945 Rogers accepted a professorship at the University of Chicago, where he directed the Counseling Center, elaborated his client-centered—later person-centered—method of psychotherapy, and conducted formal research on therapy (Rogers, 1951; Rogers and Dymond, 1954). In 1957 Rogers moved to the University of Wisconsin where, for seven years, he held appointments in the departments of psychology and psychiatry. At Wisconsin, he endeavored to apply his theory and technique of psychotherapy in working with people with schizophrenic disorders. This work was not as fruitful as his earlier work at the University of Chicago, in which he had worked with college students. In 1964 Rogers moved to La Jolla, California, where he joined the staff of the Western Behavioral Sciences Institute and later helped to found and became a resident fellow of the Center for Studies of the Person.

Rogers has received many honors throughout his career, including one of the American Psychological Association's first Distinguished Scientific Contribution awards and its first Distinguished Professional Contribution award. From 1946 to 1947 he served as president of the APA. Rogers has traveled widely, and many of his writings have been translated into other languages. He and his colleagues have conducted programs and workshops in many countries, including Japan, Brazil, and Poland. In recent years, Rogers in his writing has shifted his concern from the individual person to marriage and other dyads (1972), groups (1970), society (1977), and reflections on the changes in his own thinking over the years (1980).

Rogerian concepts as the self developed through the therapeutic process and also suggests how Rogers's evolving theory helped him to refine and elucidate his therapeutic techniques.

ENDURING ASPECTS OF PERSONALITY

Perhaps because he is primarily concerned with the ways in which the personality changes and grows, Rogers does not emphasize the structural aspects of personality. Nevertheless, two constructs are of fundamental importance to his theory: the organism and the self.

THE ORGANISM.   The **organism** is the physical creature with all its physical and psychological functions. It includes both the phenomenal field—which we will explain in just a moment—and the self. The organism is also the locus of all experience, and experience is everything potentially available to awareness that is going on within the organism at any given moment. That is, experience includes one's perception of events that occur within one's physical body as well as one's perception of events that occur in the external world. The totality of experiences—both conscious and unconscious—constitutes the **phenomenal field**. One's phenomenal field "can never be known to another except through empathic inference and then can never be perfectly known" (Rogers, 1959, p. 210). It is important to note that behavior is a function not of external reality or of stimuli in the environment or in the person but of subjective reality, or the phenomenal field.

The great unanswered question of phenomenology is, What enables people to separate fact from fiction in their subjective world? Corollary questions are, How can people differentiate between a subjective, or perceived, image that is not a correct representation of reality and one that is? What is "true" reality? Can there be, is there, an impersonal standard of reality?

For Rogers, the only way to differentiate, to test reality, is to check the correctness of the information on which one's hypothesis is based against other sources of information. A very simple example can be seen most everyday: not being absolutely certain which of two shakers contains salt, you shake the one with the larger, more numer-

BOX 6.5   Person-Centered Psychotherapy

In person-centered psychother-apy, the therapist must be able to enter into ''an intensely per-sonal and subjective relation-ship'' with the client, not as a physician relating to a patient and expecting to diagnose and cure, nor as a scientist to an ob-ject of study, but as one person to another. (Rogers's model of psychotherapy probably is still best known as ''client-cen-tered'' therapy, but in recent years he has rechristened it ''person-centered'' to reflect his abiding concern with the growth of all *persons*.) Note that from the very beginning, Rog-ers used the term ''client'' in preference to ''patient.'' No matter what the client's behav-ior or expressed thoughts or feelings, the therapist must feel him or her to be a person of ''unconditional self-worth ''—a person of value and not a ''sick'' person who has come for ''treatment,'' as the medical model of psychotherapy sug-gests.

Therapists must be genuine and not hide behind some de-fensive facade; they must let the client know their own feelings. Therapists must be able to let themselves go in understanding clients; that is, they must be willing to experience the world as their clients do, to sense ''what it feels like to be the cli-ent at each moment of the rela-tionship.'' Therapists must be comfortable in such a relation-ship, even though they may not know where it will lead, and satisfied with providing a cli-mate in which clients are free to be, or to become, themselves.

The gradual realization that they are accepted uncondition-ally by the therapist allows cli-ents to explore increasingly strange and unknown feelings in themselves. In this way, they become acquainted with parts of their experience that have been kept out of awareness be-cause they were too threatening to the self. Feeling safe in the relationship with the therapist, clients can experience these feelings fully, and as they do so, they realize that these feelings are not alien but are parts of them and parts that it is all right to acknowledge. Thus they learn that they do not have ''to fear what experience may hold but can welcome it freely as a part of [their] changing and developing [selves]'' (Rogers, 1961, p. 185).

Rogers, like other theorists we have studied—particularly Jung, Adler, Horney, and Maslow—conceives of the per-son as oriented toward positive growth and as tending to work toward self-actualization and fulfillment for self and others. Rogers has particularly empha-sized the importance of the self-concept in psychotherapy. A key concept of his is congru-ence, the notion that becoming aware of and accepting one's true feelings and experience can lead to greater congruence between one's self-concept and one's actual experience (1959). Complete congruence, if achieved, should produce a fully functioning person.

Rogers has come to view the therapeutic process as a model of all interpersonal relations, and this has led him to formu-late a general theory of inter-personal relationships that can be summarized as follows:

If we assume that

1. Two people are minimally willing to be in contact,
2. Each is able and minimally willing to receive communica-tion from the other, and
3. Contact continues over a pe-riod of time,

we can hypothesize that the greater the degree of congru-ence of experience, awareness, and communication in one per-son, the more this relationship will show a tendency toward ''reciprocal communication with a quality of increasing con-gruence; a tendency toward more mutually accurate under-standing of the communica-tions; improved psychological adjustment and functioning in both parties; mutual satisfac-tion in the relationship'' (Rog-ers, 1961, p. 344).

Note that only one person in the relationship needs to experi-ence congruence for change to occur in the other. You can see how such a model might be ap-plied in a number of areas; in fact, Rogers has used it in analyzing family relationships (Rogers, 1972), education and learning (Rogers, 1969), en-counter groups (Rogers, 1970), and group tension and conflict (Rogers, 1977).

ous holes over your hand. If the particles that fall are white, not black, you conclude that they are salt. Thus, you use direct sense information to supplement the information stored up from past experience. The definitive test would involve tasting the particles; a particular kind of taste sensation would define them as salt, not white pepper or sugar.

THE SELF. Gradually, through experience, a portion of the phenomenal field becomes differentiated—this is the **self**. The self of the self-concept is the ''organized, consistent conceptual gestalt composed of perceptions of the characteristics of the 'I' or 'me' and the perception of the relationships of the 'I' or 'me' to others and to various aspects of life, together with the values attached to these perceptions'' (Rogers, 1959, p. 200). The self is a fluid, changing Gestalt, and it may be in or out of awareness.

The self is a central construct in Rogers's theory. In addition to the **self as it is**, also called the self-structure, there is an **ideal self** that comprises what the person would like to be or holds out as a goal for individual development and achievement.

It is **congruence** or incongruence between the self and the organism that determines maturity, adjustment, and mental health. When the symbolized self—the interpretations of the perceptions of I–me and the I–me relationship with others—matches the actual experience of the organism—that is, when the person's perceptions and interpretations reasonably accurately reflect reality as it tests or is perceived and interpreted by others—the self and the organism are said to be congruent. When there is not such a match, self and organism are incongruent; in such situations, people feel threatened and anxious, behave defensively, and think in rigid and constricted ways.

Rogers's chief concerns are how incongruence develops and how self and organism can be made more congruent. Related issues are the degree of congruence between subjective reality (the phenomenal field) and external reality (the world as it is) and between the self as it is and the ideal self. As we might expect, if the discrepancy between self as it is and the ideal self is great, the person is dissatisfied and maladjusted.

PERSONALITY DYNAMICS

For Rogers, the organism has one single motivating force—the **self-actualizing drive**—and one single goal in life—to become self-actualized. There are many needs, but all are subservient to this basic tendency of the organism to maintain and enhance itself. Two of the most important needs are the need for the **positive regard of others** and the need for **self-regard**. These needs are learned in infancy, when the baby is loved and cared for and receives positive regard from others.

Actualizing itself along lines laid down by heredity, the organism becomes more differentiated, expanded, autonomous, and socialized as it matures. There is a forward movement in the life of every person, and it is this force on which the therapist relies in effecting an improvement in the functioning of his or her client.

For this forward movement to operate, the person must be able to discriminate between progressive and regressive behavior, that is, behavior that leads to self-actualization and behavior that blocks or impedes it. Choices must be clearly perceived and adequately symbolized, that is, represented in awareness. No inner voice tells us which path is the one of progress; we have to know this before we can choose. But once we know, Rogers says, we always choose to grow and self-actualize rather than to regress.

THE DEVELOPMENT OF PERSONALITY

Rogers does not offer a "stage" theory of personality development. He is interested in the ways in which others' evaluations of us can lead to discrepancies between what we actually experience and the way we perceive, or misperceive, that experience.

According to Rogers, if parents' evaluations of children are exclusively positive, such discrepancies will not arise. But such evaluations are typically both positive and negative, and they set conditions under which children feel either worthy or unworthy. Experiences that are followed by feelings of unworthiness tend to be excluded from the self-concept, and this results in a self-concept that does not fit the experience of the organism: the child "values an experience positively or negatively solely because of these conditions of worth . . . taken over from others, not because the experience enhances or fails to enhance his organism" (Rogers, 1959, p. 209).

A very simple example can be seen in the little girl whose self-concept is that of a good girl, loved by her parents, and who is fascinated with trains and talks about becoming a diesel engineer and eventually president of a railroad. Her parents, who are traditionalists, are sufficiently liberated to want her to have a profession but not liberated enough to let her choose a type of work still so exclusively the province of men, and they strongly disapprove of her interests. As a result, the child has to revise her self-image and values somehow. She may decide that she's a "bad" girl for not wanting what her parents want; she may decide that her parents do not like her; or she may decide that she really is not interested in railroading after all.

Any of the foregoing choices will distort the child's reality, for she is not bad, and her parents do like her, and she does want to become an engineer. Her self-image will then get out of step with her actual experience. And, Rogers says, if she denies her "true" values by making the third choice—of giving up her interest—and if she continues to do this sort of thing as other values of hers are undervalued or disapproved by others, her self will end up divided against itself. She will feel as if she does not really know what she is and what she wants, and she will be tense, uncomfortable, and out of sorts.

If denial becomes a style, the person reaches the point where organismic experience that does not fit the distorted self-concept is felt as threatening and produces anxiety. The person becomes increasingly uncomfortable, and to avoid recognition of these threatening experiences, he or she may do such self-destructive things as projecting the unwanted feelings onto others (e.g., thinking others are angry when actually one is angry oneself) or putting himself or herself down, in order to maintain the conviction of self-worthlessness (e.g., rationalizing a promotion by saying, ''The boss just felt sorry for me'' or minimizing the achievement by saying, ''I don't deserve it'').

And this incongruity between organismic and self experience not only hurts the person but interferes in his or her relations with other people. The incongruity may be perceived by others as puzzling. Worse, the tendency on the part of the person to project negative feelings such as anger—because the condition of denying one's organismic experience makes one uncomfortable and unhappy—means that the person's expectation that others will be angry and hostile leads him or her to appear hostile to others.

What is the answer to this split between self and organism? Under conditions in which there is no threat to the self-structure, the split can be either prevented or healed: when parents raise children with love, children accept all experience as part of the self; when therapists accept people who, as children, have not experienced such unconditional love, these people are enabled to accept hitherto threatening experiences and to revise their self-structures. The self-awareness and self-acceptance that are facilitated either by early training or through therapy are correlated with healthy adjustment.

A side effect of being able to accept and assimilate all sorts of experience is that one becomes more understanding of other people. Thus if people are brought up in a warm and positive atmosphere or later, through therapy, are offered such an atmosphere, they are likely to accept others in all their strengths and weaknesses and to be more tolerant of others' behavior. Rogers believes that this notion of being able to perceive and accept ''into one consistent and integrated system'' all one's sensory and visceral experiences has social implications ''such as to stretch the imagination'' (1951, p. 522). Greater understanding of others and greater acceptance of them as individuals could form the basis, he believes, for the gradual elimination of international strife.

Another prerequisite for avoiding or healing the breach between

In this group therapy session, as you can see, Carl Rogers and the other partici-pants wear microphones. Rogers pioneered in the recording of psychotherapy ses-sions, first in the individual therapy hour and later in the group therapy setting.

self and other is to develop a **continuing valuing process** rather than, or as a replacement for, a value system. For Rogers, a system is some-thing that is fixed, static; a process is something that is taking place. Any fixed set of values will tend to prevent one from responding openly and reacting effectively to new experience. To adjust appropri-ately to the changing conditions of life, people must be flexible and must continually review and reevaluate their experience.

RESEARCH EMPHASES AND METHODS

As we have said, Rogers pioneered in the scientific investigation of counseling and psychotherapy. For a long time it was felt that invading the privacy of the therapy session with audio and video recording or with the presence of live observers watching through one-way windows and the like would jeopardize the welfare of the client. Rogers showed, however, that recording therapy sessions, with the client's permission, has no harmful effect on the therapy itself. As a matter of fact, both cli-ent and therapist quickly come to ignore the microphone and behave quite naturally.

Some therapists may also have been reluctant to permit record-ing or observation of their sessions because they were hesitant about having their work scrutinized by others. Audio and/or video recording of an actual session naturally preserves both the therapist's accurate judgments and helpful interventions and his or her errors and mis-judgments. Rogers, by recording his own sessions with clients and making the transcripts public, set an example for others. His willing-ness to look at himself and his own work encouraged other therapists to do the same—to learn from their work and to grow as therapists and as people. Today even the psychoanalytic session is opening to scientific investigation, and the literature contains many examples of research on the nature, the processes, and the outcome of psychotherapy (see e.g., Rogers, 1967a, 1975; Rogers and Dymond, 1954; Shlien and Zimring, 1970; Truax and Mitchell, 1971; Wexler and Rice, 1974).

Rogers and his associates have taken many empirical approaches to the study of personality. They have used the Rorschach test (see page 173) and the Thematic Apperception Test, or TAT (see Box 9.2; also see Rogers, 1967a). They have also used the Minnesota Multiphasic Personality Inventory, or MMPI, and various other personality assessment devices. (The MMPI is a self-report questionnaire in which answers to 550 true–false statements about oneself result in scores on 10 scales that measure such things as anxiety, depression, rebelliousness or conformity, and degree of sociability.) Rogers's principal research approaches, however, fall into three general categories of methodology: content analysis, rating scales, and Q-technique.

CONTENT ANALYSIS.   **Content analysis** is a procedure in which extracts from the record of a person's verbalizations are studied and tabulated. It involves recording, classifying, and counting a person's statements—typically, in the therapy hour—in order to examine various hypotheses or propositions about the nature of personality. Using content analysis procedures, the nature of a person's self-concept and the changes that occur in it during therapy can be seen (see, e.g., Rogers, 1967a).

Porter (1943), pioneering in an early application of content analysis to Rogerian therapy, showed that this method yielded reliable results in the study of counseling interviews. And the notion of change in the self-concept was studied by Rogers's student Raimy (1948), who classified references to the self in six categories (positive or approving, negative or disapproving, ambivalent, ambiguous self-references; reference to external objects and persons; and questions) and analyzed records of 14 therapy cases, each of which had between 2 and 21 therapy sessions. Raimy's study showed that at the start of therapy, clients' self-references were preponderantly disapproving or ambivalent; as counseling progressed, fluctuations in self-approval occurred, with mounting ambivalence. At the conclusion of counseling, clients judged improved were making a preponderant number of self-approving statements, whereas those who had not improved were still being ambivalent and disapproving of themselves. Studies modeled on Raimy's have obtained similar results (see, e.g., Seeman, 1949).

Another hypothesis explored by content analysis is the notion, mentioned earlier, that people who are more accepting of themselves are also more accepting of others. Some studies have reported data

RATING	DEGREE OF CONGRUENCE
1	A discrepancy between the way the therapist experiences the client and the way the therapist communicates with the client, verbally and nonverbally, is clearly evident.
2	The therapist communicates information to the client in response to questioning, but the therapist's response has a phony, or "half-truth" quality. The therapist appears to be avoiding, hedging, and generally uneasy.
3	The therapist does not contradict his or her feelings about the client but neither does he or she communicate these exact feelings to the client. The therapist is acongruent.
4	The therapist communicates information to the client spontaneously, or in response to questions, openly and easily. He or she admits areas of ignorance and makes no attempt to "fool" the client.
5	At any given moment, the therapist communicates his or her feelings about the client openly and freely, whether they are positive or negative, without trace of defensiveness or retreat into professionalism.

Figure 6.4 A scale for assessing congruence in the psychotherapist. (Rogers, 1967a.)

that mildly support this idea (see, e.g., Medinnus and Curtis, 1963). Other studies (e.g., Gordon and Cartwright, 1954) have failed to turn up any evidence that changes in feelings about the self produce or are followed by changes in feelings toward others. Wylie (1978) concludes that although the available evidence tends to support the hypothesis that self-acceptance is associated with acceptance of others, most studies are so seriously flawed that the findings must be regarded as equivocal.

RATING SCALES.   A principal contribution by Rogers and his collaborators in recent years is the measurement of process and change during psychotherapy by the use of **rating scales**. The rating scale Rogers has devised consists of a series of statements that qualify the characteristic to be measured by describing the relative strength or weakness of that characteristic on a continuum of 5, 7, or 9 points. As an example, Figure 6.4 shows the congruence scale developed by Kiesler (Rogers, 1967a) that assesses the degree to which the therapist's organismic experience and self-concept are unified, thus enabling him or her to respond to the client without defensiveness.

Although Rogers agrees that therapy outcome must be assessed, he feels that more can be learned about therapeutic effectiveness by studying the attitudes and behavior of the therapist in relation to

RATING	RELATIONSHIP QUALITY
1	*Relationship refused.* The client appears clearly to reject a relationship with the therapist or to fail to see either the desirability or the likelihood of a close relationship in the therapy setting (e.g., the client may declare that he or she will not come to another session)
2	*Relationship accepted physically only.* The client does not specifically reject the relationship but gives no sign of considering it desirable or even possible (e.g., the therapist may say that he or she would like to get to know the client better or to understand something the client has just said better, but the client does not take the therapist's statements seriously).
3	*Relationship partially or intermittently accepted.* At times and on some levels, the client indicates acceptance of the relationship but other moments or other signs indicate the opposite (e.g., the client may corroborate the meaningfulness of a statement by the therapist but may not discuss that thought or feeling again).
4	*Relationship fully accepted.* Therapist and client are "parallel"—that is, they express the same relationship quality—and together in what they are doing, what they assume is happening, and the way they see the value and purpose of this interchange. Nonparallel interchanges are assumed to be momentary only.
5	*Relationship as part of therapy.* Therapist and client are parallel and together, and the client indicates that what goes on in therapy affects not only his or her thoughts, feelings, and behavior in the hour but his or her entire self, or inner processes.
6	*Relationship fully established.* Therapist and client no longer need to explore their relationship; the relationship is simply there. Therapy can be terminated at any time that therapeutic content is considered to have been satisfactorily dealt with.

Figure 6.5   A scale for assessing the quality of the therapist–client relationship. (Rogers, 1967a.)

changes in the client. The scale in Figure 6.4 may be used for this purpose, as may the scale in Figure 6.5 that assesses the quality of the therapist–client relationship. In an ambitious study of psychotherapy with state hospital patients diagnosed schizophrenic, Rogers (1967a) used a number of rating scales, which were filled out by therapists, patients, and independent judges who saw only excerpts from therapy session transcripts. The findings of this study are too complex to detail here, but among the most important discoveries was a negative correlation between the therapists's evaluation of the therapeutic relationship and patients' and judges's evaluations of it. Rogers comments, "It is a sobering finding that our therapists—competent and conscientious as they were—had overoptimistic and, in some cases, seriously invalid perceptions of the relationships. . . . The patient . . . or [the judge] turned out to have more useful perceptions'' (1967a, p. 92). Exploring these findings, Rogers and his associates discovered that the mediating factor in this surprising turn of events appeared to be therapy outcome. That is, in cases in which the outcome was favorable, therapist and client–judge ratings *were* similar; it was in the cases of relatively unsuccessful therapy that therapist and client–judge assessments were so discrepant.

Q-SORT.   In their investigations of the self-concept, Rogers and his associates turned to the work of the British psychologist, William Stephenson, for a method of data collection. Stephenson (1953) had developed a procedure he called ''Q-technique,'' which included a sophisticated methodology and statistical operations as well as data collection procedures. It was the latter that interested Rogers, and he adapted these procedures for his use as the method of Q-sort.

Q-Sort Procedure.   The **Q-sort** enables one to study a person's notions about himself or herself systematically—although it can be used for other purposes as well. In Q-sort, a person is given a packet of cards or slips of paper that contain various statements and is asked to sort these statements into a prearranged distribution along a continuum from those most characteristic of the person doing the sorting to those least characteristic.

Q-sorts can be performed in many ways, depending on the specific question the investigator wants to examine. For example, people may be asked to sort statements so that they describe them as they are now, as they would like ideally to be, as they were at the age of 10, as they think their parents see them, and so on. Items for the Q-sort can also be made up in different ways. They can reflect a particular theory of personality, or they may reflect statements made in actual therapy sessions or items already created for other personality inventories. Correlational methods, analysis of variance, or factor analysis may be used to analyze the data obtained from a Q-sort.

The Problem of Defensiveness.   One serious problem with Q-sorts— and with other self-rating devices—is that of **defensiveness**. People do not always give totally accurate pictures of themselves, for they want to look good both to themselves and to others. Thus they may give answers that actually reflect denial, rationalization, projection, hostility, and the like (Haigh, 1949). Whether such defense is conscious or unconscious is in question: psychoanalytic investigators, of course, hold that defenses operate unconsciously; others, such as Haigh (1949), assume that most defensive behavior is intentional deception designed to save face.

Several studies (Cole, Oetting, and Hinkle, 1967; Friedman, 1955; Havener and Izard, 1962) have indicated that a high correlation between the self and ideal-self conceptions is not an adequate criterion of adjustment. At least two forms of serious maladjustment—paranoid schizophrenia and antisocial behavior—may produce self and ideal-self sorts that are highly congruent, almost as congruent as the sorts of presumably normal subjects. People who are only mildly neurotic, however, may have very incongruent concepts of self and ideal self.

Chodorkoff (1954) undertook an interesting study in which subjects' own self-descriptions were compared with the assessment of independent judges—based on such data as Rorschach and TAT protocols and word association test scores—and with a measure of perceptual defense.

The subjects—30 college students—sorted 125 statements into 13 piles, from most to least characteristic of them. Their adjustment was assessed by means of judges' ratings and the Rorschach data. Finally, judges had biographical information, word association test data, and TAT protocols, and they made a Q-sort for each subject with the same 125 items the subjects themselves had used. The perceptual defense measure involved exposing neutral and threatening words for increasingly longer periods—starting, of course, with periods too brief to allow clear, conscious perception—and measuring the difference between the recognition thresholds for each type.

Chodorkoff's findings confirmed this study's three original hypotheses:

1. The greater the agreement between self-description and description by others, the less perceptual defense the subject showed.
2. The greater this same agreement, the more adequate was the subject's personal adjustment.
3. The better the person's adjustment, the less perceptual defense he or she displayed.

EVALUATION

Abraham Maslow, a leader of humanistic psychology and an active and productive contributor to the study of personality, presented a theory that is highly attractive to many psychologists. It tries to deal with vital and contemporary human concerns. Some critics feel, however, that in Maslow's theory it is difficult to tell where the scientific leaves off and the inspirational begins. Humanistic psychology in general, they suggest, is more a secular replacement for religion than a scientific psychology.

Some critics claim that the humanists' empirical gifts to psychology have not equaled their speculative contributions. Others accuse the humanists of accepting as true what is still hypothetical, of confusing theory with ideology, and of substituting rhetoric for research.

Nevertheless, Maslow's theory has turned out to be one of the most provocative of the holistic or organismic, theories. Writing in 1970, Maslow said that his theory had been

quite successful in a clinical, social and personological way, but not in a laboratory and experimental way. It has fitted very well with the personal experience of most people, and has often given them a structured theory that has helped them to make better sense of their inner lives. . . . Yet it still lacks experimental verification and support. (Maslow, 1970, p. xii)

A major problem with Maslow's theoretical concepts is that they overlap considerably. As a result, it is difficult to discuss one concept or collect research data on it without getting involved with others. Maslow encouraged others to test his ideas and respected their efforts. His own work was rather informal and clinical–descriptive, but it provided a rich source of ideas.

Rogers, like Maslow, is a leader of the ''third force'' in psychology, and it is in large part because of his work that the humanistic approach is as strong and influential as it is. His optimism, his faith in the inherent goodness of human beings, and his steadfast belief that troubled people can be helped without either the long-drawn-out probing of psychoanalysis or the laboratory trappings of behaviorism are attitudes that have attracted many people.

Rogers's person-centered theory and his emphasis on the self have stimulated an enormous amount of research. Not all empirical findings are favorable to his theory nor is all research on the self attributable directly to Rogers, but no one has been more influential than he in providing an intellectual tradition in which research on the self could flourish.

To Rogers also can be attributed the beginnings of true research on the psychotherapeutic process. Rogers's own openness has encouraged others to, in a sense, open the doors of their consultation rooms, so that data from psychotherapy sessions can be recorded and then scientifically studied. Rogers has stimulated his own students as well as a number of other psychologists to study the therapeutic process.

Psychologists' main criticism of Rogers's theory is that it is based on a naïve type of phenomenology (see, e.g., Smith, 1950). Rogers has been criticized for ignoring the unconscious, whose importance in human behavior has been attested to by psychoanalytic investigations for more than 80 years. Rogers insists that self-reports, contrary to prevailing views, are adequate to reveal the person; he insists there is no need to probe, analyze dreams, or excavate psychic layer upon layer.

Rogers, however, clearly conceives of an organism that has many experiences of which the person is not aware. The very notion of congruence presupposes that there are "unsymbolized" organismic experiences that must be brought into useful awareness. The distinction between psychoanalytic repression and these "unsymbolized" experiences, then, is a very fine one. Perhaps the essential difference between Rogers's position and the psychoanalytic one is that Rogers believes it is possible to prevent repression from ever occurring—by giving a child unconditional positive regard—or to eliminate it entirely—by giving a client in therapy the same unconditional positive regard. The psychoanalyst, on the other hand, says that no amount of unconditional positive regard is sufficient to overcome repression; even under the most favorable conditions, a part of one's experience remains unconscious.

Rogers recognizes the dilemma in which defensive behavior places person-centered theory, but he is not about to jettison a viewpoint that he feels has been so fruitful. At the same time, as we have seen, he has not hesitated to employ methods other than the self-report to study the personality—projective tests, inventories like the MMPI, even physiological measurements. He has not changed his view expressed some 30 years ago, that he prefers "to live with [the dilemma of defensive behavior] until we understand it more deeply and perhaps can develop more sensitive theories as well as the instruments to deal with it" (Rogers and Dymond, 1954, p. 431).

SUMMARY

1. According to the **holistic**, or **organismic**, viewpoint, the organism is a unified whole, functioning according to laws that cannot be found in the parts of which it is comprised. The organism has one sovereign drive, that of **self-actualization.**

2. The **humanistic** viewpoint sees people as neither inherently "bad" (psychoanalysis) nor robotlike (behaviorism) but as having the potential for healthy and creative growth. Humanism stands for an open-minded approach and methods and for the exploration of new aspects of human behavior.

ABRAHAM H. MASLOW

3. Maslow, a founder of the **"third force"** in psychology, stressed the study of the positive, healthy, creative aspects of human beings.

4. According to Maslow, the human being's basic needs, capacities, and tendencies are good or neutral, not evil, and healthy development means actualizing these tendencies. It is denial or frustration of this essential nature of the human being that leads to psychopathology.

5. The human being's needs are arranged in a hierarchy: each set can be fulfilled only when the preceding sets have been (relatively) satisfied. **Physiological** needs must be satisfied first, followed by the needs for **safety, love and belongingness, esteem,** and **self-actualization.** Esteem needs may be for self-esteem or for the esteem of others. The need for self-actualization subsumes 17 **metaneeds,** or **being-values,** which involve knowing, understanding, and aesthetic concerns among others.

6. Metaneeds involve the positive rather than the negative use of cognitive capacities; they involve seeking happiness and fulfillment rather than avoiding pain. The metaneeds are equally potent; any one may substitute for another.

7. Self-actualization is rather rare because people have difficulty balancing pride and humility, because they fear the responsibilities of being leaders, because they are jealous of ''great'' others and feel less worthy, and because intense pleasure or happiness may become almost unendurable.

8. The order in which needs are satisfied may vary, and one need does not have to be 100 percent fulfilled for another, higher need to achieve some satisfaction.

9. The **personality syndrome** is an organized, interrelated group of characteristics that occur together. At levels of increasing specificity, the subsyndrome appears at Level 2, the sub-subsyndrome at Level 3, and so on. Personality syndromes combine to produce particular personality characteristics. Two important syndromes are the security and the self-esteem syndromes.

10. Holistic–analytic methodology involves studying the complete organism, or person, and its subparts, alternately examining the subparts and exploring the way these subparts interact in the organization and dynamics of the whole.

11. Self-actualizing people, those who have realized their potentialities to the fullest, have been studied by the method of **iteration.**

12. The **peak experience** is a mystical experience of intense feeling and sensations, both psychological and physical. Aftereffects may include such things as changes in one's view of the world and one's relations with others and the release of creativity.

13. Experience, including motivation, cognition, and values, occurs in the **D-realm** and the **B-realm**, both of which are necessary for survival. When deficiency needs are satisfied, being needs, or metaneeds, become prominent.

14. People can fail to self-actualize because they fear becoming aware of their own weaknesses. Society can also impede self-actualization or encourage it: schools should help satisfy children's basic psychological needs of security, belongingness, and esteem and should teach them how to self-actualize.

CARL R. ROGERS

15. Carl Rogers's theory of personality owes much to his unique, **person-centered**—earlier, **client-centered**—**approach** to psychotherapy. This approach—which stresses genuineness, or congruence, in the therapist and the therapist's unconditional and warm acceptance of the client as he or she is—is widely used in the helping professions.

16. The two important enduring aspects of personality are the **organism** and the **self**. The organism is the locus of all experience. The self is a portion of the **phenomenal field**, which is the totality of experience. The self is an ever-changing entity, and it may be in or out of awareness.

17. The organism has one motivating force—the **self-actualizing drive**—and one single goal in life—to become self-actualized.

18. Discrepancies between the organism and the self arise out of others', particularly parents', negative evaluations of a person. Continued distortions of a person's experience by others' evaluations can lead to self-destructive behavior.

19. The split between self and organism can be prevented if parents raise children with love and affection. It can be healed if therapy provides the **unconditional positive regard** to the person who lacked this acceptance in childhood.

20. It is **congruence** between the organism and the self that determines maturity, adjustment, and mental health. Congruence requires the continual review and revision of one's values. It also makes people more understanding of others and more tolerant of others' behavior.

21. Rogers pioneered in studying the nature and processes of psychotherapy by tape recording therapy sessions.

22. Rogers has used **content analysis** to study the changes in a person's self-concept that occur in therapy.

23. Rating scales have been used to study the quality of the therapeutic relationship. The evidence suggests that clients and independent judges sometimes assess this relationship more accurately than do therapists.

24. Q-technique is used to study people's ideas about themselves. **Defensiveness**—which derives from the need to look good to oneself and to others—may affect Q-sort studies.

25. Maslow has been criticized for failure to support his conceptions adequately with laboratory and experimental research, and he readily admits this shortcoming. His theory, nevertheless, has provided a rich source of ideas for researchers in the field of personality.

26. Rogers's theory has been criticized primarily for insisting that conscious self-report is adequate to reveal the person and for continuing to hold this view despite the problems caused for it by the phenomenon of defensive behavior. Rogers's theory, however, has stimulated a great deal of investigatory activity. And Rogers broke important ground in initiating research on the psychotherapeutic process.

SUGGESTED READING

ABRAHAM H. MASLOW

Toward a Psychology of Being (1968) is one of Maslow's more popular books and you may find it a helpful introduction to his approach. *Motivation and Personality,* first published in 1954 and revised in 1970, is Maslow's definitive work. It contains the gist of his much reprinted, germinal paper on "A Theory of Motivation" (1943), and it covers most of his major contributions to the study of personality. This book also includes reports on Maslow's innovative studies of self-actualizing people.

Being-values, or the metaneeds, and the peak experience are discussed extensively in *Toward a Psychology of Being* as well as in *Religions, Values, and Peak Experiences* (1964). Maslow's ideas on his version of utopia can be found in "Eupsychia: The Good Society" (1961). And if you are interested in his ideas about self-actualization in industry and management, take a look at *Eupsychian Management* (1965).

Biographical material on Maslow can be found in Lowry, *A. H. Maslow: An Intellectual Portrait* (1973a); Goble, *The Third Force: The Psychology of Abraham Maslow* (1970); and Wilson, *New Pathways in Psychology: Maslow and the Post-Freudian Revolution* (1972). Lowry has also edited Maslow's journals, in *The Journals of Abraham Maslow* (1979), and he has collected some of Maslow's important papers in *Dominance, Self-esteem, Self-actualization: Germinal Papers of A. H. Maslow* (1973b). In *Abraham H. Maslow: A Memorial Volume,* Bertha Maslow offers a complete bibliography of her husband's writings.

CARL R. ROGERS

The informal statement of Rogers's theory of personality contained in one of his most famous books, *On Becoming a Person* (1961), may be your best introduction to Rogers's thinking. Rogers's personality theory was first outlined formally in *Client-Centered Therapy: Its Current Practice, Implications, and Theory* (1951) and further elaborated in "A Theory of Therapy, Personality and Interpersonal Relationships as Developed in the Client-Centered Framework" (1959).

After you have read the chapter in this book on B. F. Skinner (Chapter 13), you may find it interesting to read the "debate" between Rogers and Skinner reprinted in Evans, *Carl Rogers: The Man and His Ideas* (1975).

Rogers's *A Way of Being* (1980), which includes some early papers as well as new chapters, focuses on both personal and professional experiences, relationships, thoughts, and activities. This book, in which "client centered" becomes "person centered," represents the culmination of Rogers's shift from "talking simply about psychotherapy" to talking "about a point of view, a philosophy, an approach to life, a way of being, which fits any situation in which *growth*—of a person, a group, or a community—is part of the goal'' (Rogers, 1980, p. ix).

If you are interested in seeing how Rogers and others are able, by studying the records of therapy sessions, to point to evidence of what a client's self-picture is and of what changes occur in it during therapy, you should look at Rogers, *Counseling and Psychotherapy: Newer Concepts in Practice* (1942); Rogers and Dymond, *Psychotherapy and Personality Change: Coordinated Studies in the Client-Centered Approach* (1954); and/or Snyder and others, *Casebook of Nondirective Counseling* (1947).

Wylie, *The Self-concept.* Vol. 1: *A Review of Methodological Considerations and Measuring Instruments* (1974), contains a critical and comprehensive survey of self-ideal-self, Q-sort studies. Wylie's second volume, *Theory and Research on Selected Topics* (1978), offers a critical review of psychotherapy studies.

Rogers's autobiography appears in Boring and Lindzey, *A History of Psychology in Autobiography* (1967b).

Chapter seven

7.

Daseinsanalysis starts with the observation of facts so simple that many contemporary philosophers and psychologists, accustomed to complicated speculations, have a hard time grasping them.

MEDARD BOSS

In short, instead of reflecting on something we should let the something speak for itself.

LUDWIG BINSWANGER

Existential Psychology: Ludwig Binswanger and Medard Boss

Shortly after World War II, a popular movement known as existentialism arose in Europe and quickly spread to the United States. Among its most articulate spokespersons were the French philosopher, novelist, and playwright Jean Paul Sartre and the French-Algerian novelist Albert Camus. Existentialism became something of an intellectual fad and was taken up by a heterogeneous assortment of the avant-garde—artists, writers, intellectuals, clergy, university students, and dissidents and rebels of various sorts.

Underlying this popular movement was, however, a serious philosophical tradition, whose most notable ancestral figure was Søren Kierkegaard (Danish philosopher and theologian; 1813–1855). The existential psychology we will discuss in the present chapter arose out of the merging of this tradition with phenomenology, a school of thought founded in Germany in the early 1900s.

Existentialism seeks to understand human beings as they exist in the world; it stresses the freedom and responsibility of the individual. **Phenomenology** is the study of the data of immediate experience; psychologists using this approach place great stress on how the individual perceives his or her world. Phenomenology has often been employed to investigate the phenomena of such psychological processes as perceiving, learning, remembering, thinking, and feeling. Existential psychology, however, has used phenomenology to study phenomena and processes generally regarded as belonging to the sphere of personality, such as the choices a person makes that define his or her life-style.

This chapter focuses on Ludwig Binswanger and Medard Boss, two Swiss psychiatrists, whose adaptation of the work of the German philosopher Martin Heidegger (1889–1976) to the study of human personality was seminal in the development of modern existential psychology. Other influential figures in contemporary existential psychology include James Bugental

(1965), Viktor Frankl (1969), R. D. Laing (1968), Rollo May (1969), E. W. Straus (1966), and Adrian Van Kaam (1966). A number of theorists discussed in this book have been influenced by the existentialist movement; included in this group are Erich Fromm (Chapter 5); Abraham Maslow, and Carl Rogers; Kurt Lewin (Chapter 8); and Gordon Allport (Chapter 10).

WHAT IS EXISTENTIAL PSYCHOLOGY?

The quality of revolt that characterizes existential psychology arises from the protest of the early existentialists first against German idealist philosophies and later against the tendency to treat human beings as objects to be calculated, manipulated, and controlled. The existentialists feared that this trend would sap human beings' ''capacity for decision and individual responsibility'' (May and Basescu, 1968, p. 77).

Existential psychology differs from other psychological systems in several very fundamental ways. First, it rejects the concept of causality as it is understood in the natural sciences. According to existential psychology, there are no true cause–effect relationships in human existence—there are only sequences of actions and experiences, and one cannot derive causality from mere sequence. What happens to the child, therefore, is not the cause of the adult's behavior, although the child's and adult's experiences may have similar meanings.

For the existential psychologist, causality has no meaning in human behavior except in the form of motivation. For example, suppose that a gust of wind closes a door; we can say that the wind has caused the door to shut. Suppose, however, that a person closes the door. We could say that the pressure exerted by her arm on the door has caused it to close, but this would miss the essential character of the person's experience. From her point of view, she closes the door purposefully because she knows that doing so will mute the noise from the street, prevent rain from coming in, and so on. And the act of shutting the door requires that she understand where to place her hand, what it means to pull or push something, and other principles of effective behavior. Thus, motivation and understanding, not cause, are the operative principles in the existential analysis of behavior.

Second, existential psychology is firmly opposed to the dualism of mind and body, which requires that we explain experience and behavior in terms of things external to them, such as environmental stimuli or bodily states. As Straus (1963) has put it, it is the human being that thinks, not the brain.

Third, existential psychology does not include the notion of an unconscious mind and refuses to admit any other hidden explanation of human behavior. Phenomena are what they are; they are neither facade nor derivative of something else. It is the business of psychology

BOX 7.1 Ludwig Binswanger (1881–1966)

Ludwig Binswanger was born and spent his entire life in Kreuzlingen, Switzerland, where for some 50 years he served as chief medical director of the Bellevue Sanatorium. He was the most renowned member of what might well be called a psychological dynasty: his father and grandfather, both psychiatrists, preceded him in heading Bellevue; his uncle and two of his brothers were psychiatrists; his son became chief psychiatrist at Bellevue after Ludwig retired; Ludwig's daughter is a psychologist; and a grandnephew is a psychiatrist.

After undertaking studies in Germany, at Heidelberg and elsewhere, Ludwig Binswanger received his M.D. from the University of Zurich in 1907, studying under Eugen Bleuler (the famous director of the Burghölzli clinic; see Chapter 4) and with Carl Jung. Like Jung, Binswanger was one of the first Swiss psychiatrists to become a follower of Freud, and although Binswanger, like Jung and others, broke away from Freudian psychoanalysis, he maintained a close friendship with Freud until the latter's death (see Binswanger, 1957). The two corresponded but met only rarely; one of the last occasions was Freud's eightieth birthday celebration, at which Binswanger gave an address.

In 1906 Binswanger took a position at the Burghölzli where, you will recall, Jung was also employed. Two years later, Binswanger began working at Bellevue; he was made medical director of the sanatorium in 1910. He continued to work at the clinic until he retired in 1956 at the age of 75.

Binswanger and his wife, the former Herta Buchenberger, maintained a lifelong residence on the grounds of Bellevue where they raised their six children. Tall, handsome, and quite imposing, Binswanger could often be seen taking one of his long walks about the sanatorium grounds. He traveled abroad very little, restricting his visits mainly to Zurich and Vienna. Binswanger served as president of the Swiss Psychiatric Association from 1926 to 1929.

Binswanger's main intellectual influence was Martin Heidegger, whom he knew. He also derived some ideas from Martin Buber (1958). Although Binswanger and Heidegger were not always in philosophical agreement, they remained on good terms, and Heidegger was present at a ceremony held to honor Binswanger only a short time before Binswanger's death.

to describe or explicate phenomena as carefully and as fully as possible.

Fourth, because of its denial of unseen forces, existential psychology is suspicious of theory: theory implies that something not visible is producing what *is* visible. Moreover, theory, as a preconception, prevents us from being completely open to the world; such openness is necessary to understand the truth of experience.

Finally, existential psychology vigorously opposes regarding a person as a thing, like a stone or a tree, to be managed, controlled, shaped, or exploited. People are free, and they are responsible for their existence. Technology, bureaucracy, and mechanization have led to

BOX 7.2 Medard Boss (1903–)

Medard Boss was born in St. Gall, Switzerland, but moved when he was very young to Zurich, where he has lived and worked ever since. Abandoning an early interest in art, Boss decided to pursue a career in medicine, and he studied at the University of Zurich, as well as in Paris and Vienna, receiving his M.D. degree from Zurich in 1928. While he was in Vienna, he was analyzed by Sigmund Freud.

After completing his studies, Boss became assistant to Eugen Bleuler at the Burghölzli clinic in Zurich. Then, four years later, Boss undertook further psychoanalytic training in London and Germany with several prominent psychoanalysts, including Ernest Jones (Freud's principal biographer), Karen Horney, and Kurt Goldstein.

Returning home, Boss went into private practice. And he and several other psychotherapists began a series of monthly meetings at the home of Carl Jung.

The year 1946 was a turning point in Boss's intellectual life, for he met and became acquainted with Martin Heidegger. As a result of their close association, Boss developed his ideas on existential psychology, or *Daseinsanalysis*.

Since 1947, Boss has been a lecturer in psychiatry at the University of Zurich and a training analyst at the Burg-

hölzli psychiatric clinic. He was a professor of psychotherapy at the University of Zurich from 1954 to 1973, and he is honorary professor at the University of Cuyo in Mendoza, Argentina. Boss is president of the Daseinsanalytic Institute for Psychotherapy and Psychosomatics in Zurich. For a number of years he was president of the International Federation for Medical Psychotherapy, and he is now honorary president of this organization. He is also a member of the Indian Psychiatric Society and of the Royal Medico-Psychological Association, in England. Boss was given the "Great Therapist Award," by the American Psychiatric Association in 1971.

Boss (1965) has traveled to India twice and has been much influenced by his encounter with Eastern wisdom. Currently Boss resides in Zurich, with his wife, the former Gertrud Wissler.

the alienation and fragmentation of the human being—in short, to the dehumanization of people.

Freedom, however, and responsibility for one's own existence do not, to the existential theorist, necessarily imply optimism or hope. Indeed, the existential psychologist is as concerned with death as with life. Dread and the threat of nothingness loom large, and guilt is an inescapable feature of human existence. Becoming a human being is a tough project, and few achieve it fully.

Some of the ideas expressed in the foregoing paragraphs may seem familiar to you. We have indeed encountered similar thinking, in Chapters 5 and 6. Maslow and Rogers have stressed the need for openness to the world, and Adler and Rogers particularly deemphasize the role of the unconscious in human behavior. Horney and Fromm spoke with conviction about alienation and dehumanization, and you will recall Fromm's argument in *Escape from Freedom* (1941) that the freedom

The theme of the 1936 Charlie Chaplin film, "Modern Times," was the dehumanizing character of modern technology. Here the "little man," trying desperately to keep up with the assembly line, is swept into the machinery.

and independence that we so eagerly seek often bring with them intolerable burdens of responsibility and isolation.

DASEIN: BEING-IN-THE-WORLD

Dasein (literally in German, "there-being") is a central existentialist concept derived from Heidegger. *Dasein,* generally translated as **"being-in-the-world,"** is the whole of human existence. To be in the world, to "be there," *is* human existence. This fundamental concept of existential psychology is not a property, an attribute, or a part of a person—like an ego or an anima—but the whole of the person's existence. Human beings have no existence apart from the world, and the world that we can know has no existence apart from human beings. People are "the luminated realm into which all that is to be may actually shine forth, emerge, and appear as a phenomenon" (Boss, 1963, p. 70).

A **phenomenon** is a "shining forth" of immediate reality—it *is* reality. Nothing more basic lies behind it or is required to explain it. In existential or *Dasein* analysis, one tries to describe what is in one's experience as accurately as language permits. In *Dasein* analysis, one

TABLE 7.1   *Existential World-Regions*

Umwelt (''around-world'')	The environment, or the ''natural world''; one's physical surroundings, landscape
Mitwelt (''with-world'')	The world of one's relationships with his or her fellow human beings; the world of interpersonal relations
Eigenwelt (''own-world'')	The self's relation to itself; includes the *thought-world* (the psychological self) and the *body-world* (the bodily self)

Source: Binswanger (1958a); May and Basescu (1968).

does not probe for concealed meanings; to the extent that people are open to perceive and respond to what is in their experience, the meanings of objects and events will be revealed to them.

Being-in-the-world does not allow for the person and the environment to be two separate things. It does not talk about person and environment interacting but instead about the person's mode, or manner, of being-in-the-world within three primary world-regions: the biological or physical surroundings, or *Umwelt;* the world of other people, the human environment, or the *Mitwelt;* and the person himself or herself, both the psychological and the physical (bodily) self, the *Eigenwelt* (see also Table 7.1). Box 7.3, a description of a young woman in terms of her being-in-the-world in these world regions, will give you an idea of the meaning of the three regions and the way they are used in existential analysis. You will note that the writing style is very different from that used by theorists we have studied so far; this is because in existential psychology, there is almost a complete absence of the traditional technical terminology of psychology and often a reliance upon a somewhat poetic vocabulary. Existentialism has always had strong ties with literature and indeed regards literature as psychology, albeit about fictional persons.

MODES, EXISTENTIALS, AND WORLD-DESIGN

There are a number of different **modes** or ways in which being-in-the-world is expressed. According to Binswanger (1963), two people may operate in a **dual** mode: ''I'' and ''Thou'' become ''We.'' A **plural** mode describes a world of formal relations with others, competition, and struggle. A person we might call a ''loner'' expresses a **singular** mode of existence, whereas someone who chooses to bury himself in a crowd expresses the mode of **anonymity**. Most people have many modes of existence: the task of existential psychology is ''to understand the totality of man's experience of himself in *all* his modes˜ of existence'' (Binswanger, 1963, p. 173).

BOX 7.3   Being-In-The-World for Ellen West

In "The Case of Ellen West," Binswanger (1958a) describes a young woman who spent most of her adult life in and out of medical and psychiatric treatment. Ellen's last referral was to Binswanger's sanatorium, where she spent her final months, committing suicide at the age of 33, three days after being discharged. Ellen West's disturbance may well have had a constitutional basis, for a number of her relatives became psychotic and two of her uncles committed suicide. Ellen's symptoms included an obsession with hunger and eating that alternated with bouts of self-starvation.

In summarizing Ellen's modes of being in the three world-regions, Binswanger clarifies the meaning of these regions and shows how they are used in existential analysis. His account here is based on his own observations and interviews with Ellen, on her past medical and psychiatric records, and on Ellen's own writings, which consisted of poems, letters, diaries, and a detailed written account of the course of her illness.

The quoted passage that follows shows Binswanger's attempt to capture the flavor of Ellen West's world. The references to holes, walls, fog, weeds, worms, and the like reflect the imagery in her poems, dreams, and fantasies. The references to longing for freedom, to eating, and to the dread of being fat represent some of this woman's main motivational concerns.

If . . . we attempt to summarize . . . the individual features and phenomenal forms of [Ellen's] mode of being-in-the-world within the various world-regions . . . we shall . . . do best to start out from the landscape-world [Umwelt]: the being-limited and being-oppressed showed itself here as darkening, darkness, night, cold, ebbtide; the boundaries or limits as moist fogwalls or clouds, the emptiness as the Uncanny, the longing for freedom (from the hole) as ascending into the air, the self as a hushed bird. Within the world of vegetation, the being-restricted and being-oppressed showed itself as wilting, the barriers as suffocating air, the emptiness as weeds, the longing for freedom as urge to grow, the self as withered plant. Within the world of things we found

the being-restricted in the hole, cellar, tomb; the barriers in walls, masonry, fetters, nets; the longing for freedom in the vessel of fertility, the self in the discarded husk. . . .

Within the Mitwelt *being-restricted is seen as being subjugated, oppressed, impaired, and pursued; the emptiness as lack of peace, indifference, joyless submission, seclusion, loneliness; the barriers as fetters. . . .*

Within the Eigenwelt *as thought-world, we recognized being-restricted in cowardice, indulgence, giving up of high-flown plans; the barriers in accusing, jeering ghosts or specters encircling and invading from all sides, the emptiness in being-ruled by one single idea, even as Nothingness; the self in the timid earthworm, the frozen heart, the longing for freedom as desperation. Finally, within the* Eigenwelt *as body-world, we found the being restricted or oppressed in being fat, the barriers or walls in the layer of fat against which the existence beats its fists as against walls, the emptiness in being dull, stupid, old, ugly, and even being dead, the longing for freedom in wanting-to-be-thin, the self as a mere tube for material filling-up and re-emptying.* (Binswanger, 1958a, pp. 328–329)

For Boss, following Heidegger, there are certain characteristics, called **existentials**, that are inherent in every human existence. Among these, the most important are spatiality; temporality; existence in a shared world; and mood, or attunement. Table 7.2 describes these existentials as well as two more that we will discuss in somewhat more detail later: guilt and mortality.

World-design is Binswanger's term for the all-encompassing pattern of a person's mode of being-in-the-world. The world-design determines both how people will react in specific situations and what

In the existentialist "dual mode" of being-in-the-world, when two people are seen to operate as one, "I" and "Thou" become "We."

kinds of character traits they will develop. It is reflected in everything the person does.

The world-design may be broad and expansive or, as is typical in neurotic patients, it may be narrow and constricted. For example, Binswanger describes one patient whose world-design was constructed around the need for continuity. Any disruption of continuity produced great anxiety in this young woman; once she fainted when the heel of her shoe fell off. Separation from her mother also evoked a great deal of anxiety in this woman, for it meant a break in the continuity of their relationship.

Note that a psychoanalytic view would be likely to regard this woman's reaction to the loss of a heel as symptomatic, or symbolic, of her fear of separation from her mother. Binswanger, however, sees both events as expressive ways of relating to the world; he sees neither as a derivative or displacement or cause of the other.

Binswanger suggests that the more varied the world-design, the better off the person; threat in one area may be compensated by refuge afforded in another. Healthy people may, for example, be able to express different aspects of themselves, living in different, though connected, "worlds," in their occupations, their home lives, and their hobbies.

TABLE 7.2   *Boss's Existentials*

	DESCRIPTION
Spatiality of existence	Openness and clearness in one's relation to another; not to be confused with physical space. Existentially, one may be more open and clear to a distant friend than to one's next-door neighbor.
Temporality of existence	Having time or not having time for doing something in particular; not the same thing as clock or calendar time. The notion of available rather than measured time. Time may be expanded, as in "I am going to spend next year going round the world," or contracted, as in "I have only a minute to spare." Temporality also expands or contracts to include more or less of the past and future, as we recall or anticipate things.
Human existence in a shared world	Human existence is always a sharing of the world with others; it is private only in certain pathological conditions. Human beings coexist in the same world. Mutual openness to the world permits the same phenomena to shine forth in the same meaningful ways to all human beings.
Mood, or attunement	A very important existential, mood determines the degree to which we are open to the world and thus what we perceive and respond to. Openness illuminates different phenomena from time to time. For example, if we are anxious, we will be attuned to threats and dangers; if we are happy, we will be attuned to satisfying relationships and events.
Guilt	Existential, or primary, guilt begins at birth. We are responsible for carrying out all the possibilities for living of which we are capable, and because every choice, decision, and act is a rejection of other possibilities, our guilt—for not carrying out those possibilities—can never be totally assuaged.
Mortality	Mortality confers on us the responsibility for making the most of every moment of our existence and for fulfilling that existence to the best of our ability.

Source: After Boss (1963, pp. 40–48).

HUMAN POTENTIAL AND THE GROUND OF EXISTENCE

When existential psychologists speak of **authenticity**, they are referring to a person's realization of the full possibilities of his or her being. It is only by actualizing one's potentialities that one can live an **authentic** life. When we deny or restrict the possibilities of our existence or permit ourselves to be dominated by others or by our environment, we are living an inauthentic existence. And as human beings, we are free to choose either sort of life.

There is, of course, some limit as to what human beings can freely become. One limitation is the **ground of existence** onto which a person is thrown. The conditions of this **thrownness**, or the way in which one finds oneself in the world, constitute the basis from which one must develop one's life. Persons who have been thrown into existence on different grounds may aspire to the same ultimate goals but, given their different starting places and the different constraints on their movement, they will take different routes to these goals. The concept of "thrownness" is a broad one and can encompass a host of the background particulars of any individual's existence: his physical and mental capacities, the social position of his family, the era in history in which he was born, how his parents treated him when he was young, and so forth.

An authentic existence must rest on recognizing the ground of one's existence; an inauthentic existence results from shutting oneself off from one's ground. The punishment for inauthenticity is guilt. People who block themselves off from the ground of their existence do not "stand autonomously" in their world; they do not take their existence upon themselves but entrust themselves to alien powers and make these powers "responsible" for their fate (Binswanger, 1963).

BEING-BEYOND-THE-WORLD

In authentic existence in the dual mode, that is, in the shared love of two persons, Binswanger suggests that existence can shift to a new level, a **being-beyond-the-world**. In this form of existence, life takes on a timelessness and a security—in Binswanger's (1958a) phrase, a "homeland and eternity"—beyond that which can be found in the ordinary forms of being-in-the-world (p. 269).

Binswanger contrasts being-beyond-the-world and being-in-the-world: "Here the present no longer means . . . a decisive resolution of the situation, but a meeting of I and Thou in the eternal moment of love. This is no longer a case of being-able-to-be, but of a being-allowed-to-be . . . of the grace of being We" (p. 312).

A person whose world-design is constricted by anxiety and guilt and who finds his or her existence dominated by the singular mode may have very little experience of being-beyond-the-world. Even for such an individual, the dual mode may shine through to some degree: "There is scarcely a human being in which no germ of love may be discovered" (p. 313). Ironically, however, this very glimpse of the possibility of being-beyond-the-world may serve to exacerbate the loneliness, guilt, and impoverishment of such a person's existence.

EXPLAINING THE EVOLUTION OF A HUMAN EXISTENCE

We have said that existential psychology rejects the notions of causality, mind–body dualism, and separation of person and environment. According to this view, a human individual is not an object set in motion by drives and energies and directed by instincts and needs. Existential psychology rejects a motivational theory as such. Nevertheless, existential psychology is very centrally concerned with matters that a traditional psychology would call "motivational" or "dynamic." Existential analyses place great emphasis on the time dimension of experience; on purpose, choice, and change; and on how present experience takes account of the past and dynamically transforms itself toward its future.

This central concern of existentialism with the temporal dimension of being-in-the-world is reflected in the title of Heidegger's major work: *Being and Time* (1962). We have already noted the great emphasis placed by the existentialists on the notion of choice—clearly a motivational concept. Binswanger and Boss often portray in detail, in their case histories, the disturbances or distortions of the temporal dimension that occur in the worlds of their patients. Often such worlds are found to be deficient in their futures. Patients may feel that their existence is stagnant—that their present is dominated by their past and that there is no place forward to go.

How do the existentialists take into account specific motives, such as hunger, fatigue, and sex? Basically, they point to differences in a person's experienced worlds when he or she is hungry, say, or sleepy, or sexually aroused. In the world of a hungry person, things that can be eaten or that are associated with eating stand out. Boss treats such sharpenings or colorations of experience under the concept of **mood**. A person's mood of sexual excitement provides one pattern of **attunement**, or **world-openness**, at a given moment; the mood of hunger provides a different one.

CHOICE, GUILT, DREAD

Why, given that people are free to choose, do they so often suffer from anxiety, depression, and other more disabling disorders? There are two reasons why people suffer unhappiness, boredom, alienation, emotional distress. First, being free to choose does not guarantee that one will make wise choices. We may choose to live authentically or inauthentically; each choice is made freely, but the consequences are quite different. Second, human beings can never transcend their existential guilt, which consists in their failure to fulfill all the possibilities of which they are capable in life.

To avoid **unwise choices**, we must be aware of the possibilities of our existence, and to be aware of these possibilities, we must remain open, so that these possibilities will disclose themselves. But our possibilities are not unlimited; we cannot by whim be anything we want to be. We have our ground of existence, remember, to reckon with. This ground—our thrownness in the world—sets some limits on our behavior. It does leave us free to make choices and, of course, if we make these unwisely we will reap the consequences.

The other cause of human distress, **existential guilt**, is present in everyone's life—no one can escape it, for in realizing certain possibilities, one must inevitably deny others. Guilt is "an inherent part of human existence; it can never be expunged either by Freudian psychoanalysis, Jung's analytic psychology, or Daseinsanalysis" (Boss, 1977, p. 54).

Accompanying guilt is something else no one can avoid: the dread of **Nothingness.** According to Heidegger, Nothingness is a presence within Being of non-Being. It is the constant threat that one will lose one's being, or become nothing. It is always there, fearful, uncanny, beckoning. Death is the absolute Nothingness, the threat of total dissolution of being-in-the-world. But the deaths of possibilities are also deaths, little deaths, small intrusions of non-Being into Being. Thus, anyone who is fully and deeply aware of life will always have some sense of existential dread, of the shadow of Nothingness or non-Being lying at the back of even the sunniest Being.

BECOMING: THE DEVELOPMENT OF THE INDIVIDUAL

The most important developmental concept in existential psychology is that of **becoming.** Existence is always in the process of becoming something new, for the person's goal is to become completely human—to fulfill all the possibilities of being-in-the-world. Even though this is an endless and hopeless project, it is one's responsibility to do the best one can. To refuse to become is to lock oneself in a constricted and darkened room; this is what the neurotic and the psychotic have done. Most people, however, make some progress in actualizing their possibilities.

The important existential of **mortality** is what confers on human beings the responsibility for making the most of every moment of existence and for fulfilling that existence to the best of their abilities. Indeed, human existence might be called a "being-unto-death"; the knowledge of death leaves us no choice but to live in some sort of permanent relationship to it.

Existential psychology has sometimes been accused of being solipsistic (**solipsism** is the notion that the self is the only thing that exists and that the self can know only itself), largely because of its emphasis on the individual's experience. However, existential psychologists hold that the becoming of a person and the becoming of the world are a co-becoming because a person is in-the-world. People disclose the possibilities of their existence through the world, and the possibilities of the world are, in turn, disclosed by the people who are in it. As one grows and expands, so will the other; if one is stunted, the other will also be stunted.

Existential psychology does not emphasize genetic or learning or physiological explanations of human behavior. Explanations of these kinds are not so much wrong as they are beside the point. According to Boss, such explanations can be formulated only after we understand present phenomena in their own right. And then, he suggests, such explanations will add nothing essential to our knowledge. Although we may sometimes act today as we did as children—because we perceive that a present encounter has the same meaning as one that occurred in childhood—our motivation is still based on our present being-in-the-world.

Existential psychologists always consider a person's being-in-the-world from an historical point of view. However, they do not usually divide being-in-the-world formally into specific stages, such as infancy, childhood, and adolescence. Existential psychology recognizes that there are differences in the mode of existence at different ages—between the infant and the adult, for example—along with a fundamental continuity.

This kind of historical continuity, however, is not the cause and effect known to physics:

Nothing that happens to a child . . . is capable of producing and maintaining any pattern of behavior in this causal sense. The experiences of childhood can only limit *and* distort *the carrying out of inborn possibilities of relating to the world. They cannot cause and produce the relationships themselves. (Boss, 1963, p. 243)*

We must ask of a patient, not so much how he may have acquired a certain neurotic behavior in childhood, but "what is keeping him a prisoner of his neurotic behavior patterns right now?" Thus, history is not unimportant, but it is only important as it is reflected in the present, and it is in the present that it must ultimately be dealt with.

Ideally, being-in-the-world should be open to past, present, and future all at once. The temporality of existence expands or contracts to include more or less of the past and the future: when we recall something, the emphasis is on the past; when we look ahead to something, the emphasis is on the future.

RESEARCH EMPHASES AND METHODS

Existential psychology uses the phenomenological method in studying human existence. In this method, experience is described in concrete, everyday words and as it appears immediately in awareness. The phenomenological investigator does not look for discrete elements of experience or of consciousness but attempts to explicate the "givenness" of any experience.

For example, in the following quotation from the opening paragraph of Wolfgang Köhler's *Gestalt Psychology*, (1947) the author describes his immediate world:

A blue lake with dark forests around it, a big, gray rock, hard and cool, which I have chosen as a seat, a paper on which I write, a faint noise of the wind which hardly moves the trees, and a strong odor characteristic of boats and fishing. . . . There is still more in this world: for instance, my hand and fingers as they lightly move across the paper. Now, when I stop writing and look around again, there is also a feeling of health and vigor. But in the next moment I feel something like a dark pressure somewhere in my interior which tends to develop into a feeling of being hunted—I have promised to have this manuscript ready within a few months. (1947, pp. 3-4)

An existentialist's analysis of this phenomenological report might note the openness of the speaker to the *Umwelt* of lake and trees and the *Eigenwelt* of his own bodily sensations. There is the feeling of health and vigor, suggestive of a freedom to act and choose, but in the next moment, the "dark pressure" of the promise to complete the manuscript; a commitment made has limited the speaker's possibilities to act in other ways.

VALIDATING PHENOMENOLOGICAL ANALYSIS

Typically, in phenomenological analysis, the investigator describes and explicates the verbal reports and observed behavior of a subject or patient. There are two techniques for validating such phenomenological explications: intrasubjective and intersubjective validation. In **intrasubjective validation**, the technique most frequently used in existential case studies, validity is established by the observation of consistency among several explications of the same behavior in a variety of situations. This is obviously a limited form of validation, for the repeated detection of a particular theme in the case material of a given person might sometimes reflect the preoccupations of the observer as much as those of the person observed.

In the second validating technique, **intersubjective validation**, several trained phenomenologists independently describe the same phenomenon and then compare their results.

On the whole, however, existential theorists have not greatly concerned themselves with the formal apparatus of scientific validation, preferring to rely on the conviction carried by their analysis of particular cases. Examples of such cases may be found in Boxes 7.3 and 7.4.

BOX 7.4   The Dream as a Mirror of Life

The contention of the existential psychologist that dreaming and waking are not entirely different spheres of existence, that each can mirror the other, is nicely illustrated by a series of dreams reported by a patient of Boss over the course of three years of therapy (Boss, 1957, pp. 113–115). In the dreams of this patient—an engineer in his forties who complained of depression and sexual impotence—the changing conditions of his life were faithfully reflected in the changing nature and content of his dreams.

For the first half year of therapy, this man dreamed exclusively of machinery and other material objects. No people, animals, or even plants ever appeared in his dreams; his mode of existence in both waking and dreaming appeared dry, mechanical, even lifeless. About the time he began to dream about plants, trees, and flowers, the depressing meaninglessness of his life had begun to disappear. Near the end of the first year, insects—usually, though, of a dangerous and harmful type—appeared frequently in his dreams, to be followed by toads, frogs, and snakes. The first mammal to appear in the engineer's dreams was a mouse; next came a rabbit, and then a wild pig. Pigs remained a favorite dream animal for a time, then their place was taken by lions and horses. By this time the engineer's sexual potency had returned to full strength.

This man's first dream of a human being occurred two years after the beginning of therapy: he dreamed of an unconscious woman swimming under a sheet of ice. Six months later he dreamed that he was dancing with a very passionate woman and that he fell in love with her.

At the outset of this man's therapy, his mode of existence, both in waking and in dreaming, was that of a machinelike robot. He showed no awareness of the full reality of existence, of his being-in-the-world with people—including his wife—or animals or even plants. Instead of disclosing and luminating the full, rich world of existence, his *Dasein* was constricted, mutilated, and concealing. As his therapy progressed, however, his openness to the world increased, and this opening up was reflected at the same time in both his waking and his dreaming life.

DASEINSANALYSIS OF DREAMS

For the existential psychologist, the **dream** is another mode of being-in-the-world. Dreaming and waking are not entirely different spheres of existence and, in fact, the mode of existence portrayed in a dream often mirrors the person's mode of existence in waking life and vice versa (see Box 7.4). Neither sphere is reducible to the other: they are two autonomous modes of being in which the person exists alternately. There are, of course, significant differences between them. Events in the waking sphere are relatively connected and are shared with other people; events in the dream sphere are disconnected and unique to the dreamer.

If the meaning and content of dreams and waking life are so similar, why do we need to examine dreams with particular care? Because each mode of existence may bring out clearly certain aspects of a person's being that, in another mode, are only dimly glimpsed. Thus, waking experience may help us to understand dreams, and dreams may help us to understand waking experience. According to Boss (1977), one must ask three basic questions about a dream:

1. What is the dreamer's being-in-the-world open to during the dream; that is, what phenomena (people, animals, objects) appear in the dream?

2. What is the dreamer's emotional response to these phenomena—fear, anger, happiness, sadness, indifference?

3. What is the dreamer's (dreaming) response to the phenomena—flight? attack? embrace?

Answers to these questions provide a basis for an existential analysis of a dream (again, see Box 7.4).

Just as it denies the significance of unconscious thoughts and wishes, existential psychology dispenses with the Freudian notion of symbolism. According to Boss, "Dream phenomena are . . . always just what they are as they shine forth; they are an *un*covering, and *un*veiling and never a covering up or a veiling of psychic content" (1963, p. 262). For example, in one experiment, Boss (1957) hypnotized several women and suggested to each that she would dream that a man who loved her approached her, naked, with the intent of making love. Three of the subjects, who had healthy attitudes toward sex, had pleasant, openly erotic dreams. Another woman, who had a number of neurotic conflicts, including a fear of sex, dreamed of being attacked by a coarse man in uniform carrying a pistol. A Freudian analysis would probably suggest that the uniform symbolized the dreamer's need to cover the man's nakedness and that the pistol symbolized the erect penis. Boss, however, says neither uniform nor gun are symbols. The uniform expresses the dreamer's narrow, hidden, anxious mode of existence; the pistol expresses the dreamer's feelings of threat and danger; in waking life she was afraid of guns. The objects and events of the dream express the dreamer's attitudes; they do not *stand for* other, hidden objects, as symbols. Thus, says Boss, dreams are revelations of existence and not concealments.

EVALUATION

Both psychoanalysis and existential psychology have philosophical roots, but the former is based firmly in nineteenth-century scientific positivism, whereas the latter has continued to maintain close relations with philosophy. Like psychoanalysis, existential psychology was born in Europe, nurtured there by practitioners in the field of medicine, and exported to the United States. Unlike psychoanalysis, however, existential psychology had an almost immediate impact on the thinking and practices of a number of American psychologists, owing in large part to changes in the complexion of American psychology that occurred over the first 50 years of this century.

When Freudian theory first arrived in the United States,

around 1910, American psychology was highly academic. By 1950, when the work of the existential psychologists began reaching U.S. shores, many psychologists were involved in clinical and other applied work and were finding that much of what they had learned in graduate school was not useful in their everyday jobs. Many felt that psychology had been straightjacketed by behaviorism and that it had lost sight of the person and of human values. Existentialism was thus seen as offering a basis for a humanistically oriented psychology.

One criticism of existential psychology advanced by "scientific" psychology centers on the former's insistence that people are free to make choices about their lives. If this were true, say the behaviorists and other deterministically oriented scientists, prediction and control would be impossible, and experimentation, as we know it, would be of limited value.

Existential psychologists might be inclined to reply that the sort of narrow, dehumanized experimentation carried on in many psychological laboratories *is* of limited value in understanding real-life behavior. But their more fundamental response is that "scientific" psychologists are missing the point—they have their determinism in the wrong place. Brain physiology may be looked at deterministically in detail. That is one enterprise. Human experience may be examined carefully as it occurs. That is another enterprise. A deterministic chemistry and physics may be useful in the first enterprise. But in the second, to ignore the variations in different human worlds in the sense of freedom would be to overlook one of the most central features of the phenomenon being studied.

The second perspective does not necessarily deny the possibility of the first. Binswanger, for example, remarks: "In this context we do not say: mental diseases are illnesses of the brain (which of course they remain from a medical–clinical viewpoint). But we say in the mental diseases we face modifications of . . . being-in-the-world" (1958b, p. 195).

Another point on which American experimental psychology and existential psychology differ is the latter's insistence that human beings are unique among the creatures of the earth. Because a person is not an animal like other animals, it is unacceptable to generalize the findings of experimentation with animals to human beings. Existential psychology appears, thus, to reject the doctrine of evolution and its central concept of the continuity of species. Existential psychology maintains that, although people do have a ground of existence, or inheritance, they, unlike other species, are free to make of this ground pretty much what they choose.

Existential psychology has also been criticized for using a high-flown, poetic, and esoteric language, more akin to literature than to science. And indeed, such writings as "The Case of Ellen West" (Box

7.3) are dense with complex and allusive language and literary and classical references. A writer who uses the four elements of earth, air, fire, and water as fundamental categories in his analysis (as Binswanger does on occasion) makes modern scientists understandably nervous as to whether such a writer is one of them. But, of course, Binswanger would reply that to use the elements of modern chemistry as a reference scheme to order the dreams and fantasies of Ellen West would be genuinely bizarre, whereas the ancient four-element scheme is deeply ingrained in human thinking and lends itself naturally to this purpose.

Finally, some American psychologists are troubled by what they see in existential psychology as an ethical–religious concern, inappropriate to a science. Some existential psychologists actually use concepts such as ''God'' and thereby arouse fears that they are trying to sneak religion into psychology.

Boss writes that he hopes existential psychology will never develop into a theory in the modern meaning of the natural sciences. All that existential psychology can contribute to psychology, Boss says, ''is to teach the scientists to remain with the experienced and experienceable facts and phenomena, to let these phenomena tell the scientists their meaning and their references, and so do the encountered objects justice'' (Boss, personal communication). Existential psychology may not be able to resist becoming a theory, for the human being is a theorizing creature. In any event, this new way of studying and comprehending human beings has made a clear contribution to the study of human personality. Whether existential psychology survives, solidifies into a theory, or withers way, it has brought a fresh perspective to old issues and a new excitement to many psychologists concerned with understanding the lives of individual human beings.

SUMMARY

1. **Existential psychology** traces its roots to **existentialism** and **phenomenology**; it studies human existence through phenomenological analysis.

2. Ludwig Binswanger and Medard Boss, the chief architects of modern existential personality psychology, were greatly influenced by the philosopher Martin Heidegger.

3. Existential psychology rebelled against scientific determinism, rejecting causality, mind–body dualism, and the concept of the unconscious. It also avoids theory and the manipulation and control of human beings for scientific purposes.

4. Existential psychology places great emphasis on human beings' **freedom of choice**.

5. *Dasein*, or **being-in-the-world**, is the whole of the person's existence. It is understood by studying the phenomena of immediate experience.

6. The person's mode of being-in-the-world is expressed in three world-regions: the *Umwelt*, or physical environment; the *Mitwelt*, or human environment; and the *Eigenwelt*, or psychological and bodily self.

7. The **modes** of being-in-the-world include the **dual**, **plural**, and **singular** modes and the mode of **anonymity**.

8. Human existence is characterized by certain **existentials**, among the most important of which are spatiality, temporality, existence in a shared world, mood, guilt, and mortality.

9. The **world-design** is the person's all-encompassing mode of being in the world. It includes the person's reactions and the kinds of traits he or she will develop. A person's world-design can be broad and varied, or it may be narrow and constricted.

10. The person achieves **authenticity** through realizing the possibilities of his or her existence.

11. Although human beings have freedom of choice, they are limited by their **ground of existence**, or their **thrownness**. Shutting oneself off from one's ground leads to inauthenticity and guilt.

12. Human beings relate past and future to their present in the **time dimension** of their being-in-the-world. Their worlds take on different characteristics as different **moods**, such as moods of hunger or fatigue, become dominant.

13. Unhappiness and distress are caused by unwise choices and by **existential guilt**, the inescapable failure to fulfill one's every possibility.

14. The **dread** of non-Being is another inescapable accompaniment of human existence.

15. Existence is always in process of **becoming**; the person's goal is to become completely human, authentic. Refusal to become leads to neurosis and psychosis.

16. **Intrasubjective validation** relies on consistency among the investigator's observations as analyzed by an investigator, to establish the validity of phenomenological analysis. **Intersubjective validation** compares the observations of several trained investigators in validating such analysis.

17. Dreams and waking life often share the same mode of existence. However, the Dasein of dreams may reveal material not clearly perceived in waking life, and the Dasein of waking life may reveal material that does not appear in dreams.

18. Dreaming is not symbolic; dream phenomena do not cover up psychic contents but instead reveal them.

19. Existential psychology has been criticized for insisting that people are free to be what they want, for being too close to philosophy and insufficiently scientific, for rejecting the doctrine of evolution and insisting that human beings are unique, for being literary and esoteric, and for seeming to inject an inappropriate religious–ethical concern into psychology. On the other hand, existential psychology offers an approach to the study of human behavior that attempts to stay free of preconceptions and hypotheses and to adhere as closely as possible to concrete data. It has been welcomed by many as a basis for a humanistically oriented psychology.

SUGGESTED READING

In coming to understand existential psychology, you may find it helpful to explore the concept of existentialism as outlined in Barrett's *Irrational Man: A Study in Existential Philosophy* (1962). Heidegger's *Being and Time* (1962), one of the most influential—and most difficult—books in modern philosophy, sets forth his ontology, or philosophy of existence. For a brief, scholarly discussion of phenomenology, you may want to look at MacLeod's ''Phenomenology: A Challenge to Experimental Psychology'' (1964).

Existential psychology is discussed by May in *Existential Psychology* (1969), in several introductory chapters in *Existence: A New Dimension in Psychiatry,* edited by May, Angel, and Ellenberger (1958), and by Van Kaam in *Existential Foundations of Psychology* (1966).

Ludwig Binswanger's major work is *Grundformen und Erkenntnis Menschlichen Daseins* (1964). Unfortunately, rather little of Binswanger's work has been translated into English. As a result, many American readers are limited to Binswanger's (1958a, b, c) three chapters in *Existence* and to the collection of hispapers, introduced by Jacob Needleman, in *Being-in-the-World: Selected Papers of Ludgwig Binswnager* (1963).

Binswanger's most famous case study, ''The Case of Ellen West,'' appears as a long chapter in *Existence.* You may find it interesting also to read Carl Rogers's chapter on ''Ellen West—and loneliness'' in *A Way of Being* (1980), in which Rogers offers his views on how this young woman might have been treated, perhaps with better success.

A number of Medard Boss's writings have been translated into English. The best introductions to Boss's thought are offered by his *The Analysis of Dreams* (1957), *Psychoanalysis and Daseinsanalysis* (1963), and *Existential Foundations of Medicine and Psychology* (1977). The latter offers the most mature statement of Boss's position.

If you are interested in exploring the argument over the relative merits and deficiencies of phenomenology and behaviorism, you should look at Wann's *Behaviorism and Phenomenology: Contrasting Bases for Modern Psychology* (1964). B. F.

Skinner, Carl Rogers, and others offer some spirited discussion in this book.

Spiegelberg's *Phenomenology in Psychology and Psychiatry* (1972) gives an historical account of the phenomenological movement. It contains chapters on both Binswanger and Boss and relates their ideas to those of other important figures in the existential and phenomenological traditions.

Chapter eight

8.

The Personal World: Kurt Lewin and George Kelly

Kurt Lewin helped restore the analysis of subjective experience to scientific respectability, insisting, in the 1920s, that human beings can be understood only through knowledge of their "life spaces," their own personal worlds. Lewin's approach set the stage for other, similar views, such as those of George Kelly, the other theorist discussed in this chapter. Kelly particularly emphasized the knowledge-seeking aspect of human personality, seeing the human being as an amateur scientist, curious, exploring, theory building. Although Lewin's and Kelly's theories of the person are quite different—for example, Lewin emphasizes motives, but Kelly does not—they share the overall view that the way we represent our worlds to ourselves is of prime importance in the makeup and functioning of our personalities.

KURT LEWIN'S FIELD THEORY

The physical sciences like physics and chemistry have often influenced the course of newer sciences like psychology by providing them with new ways of thinking about the things they study. So-called field theories in physics provide an example. Such nineteenth-century European scientists as Michael Faraday, James Maxwell, and Heinrich Hertz made spectacular progress in the understanding of electrical and magnetic phenomena by developing mathematical ways of representing continuous "fields" of influence, such as the magnetic field around an electric current flowing in a wire. This understanding led to such practical devices as electrical motors and generators. Somewhat similar field notions underlie the more recent "unified field theories" of physics that attempt to use field ideas to unify such disparate phenomena as gravitation and the relations among subatomic particles.

It is hardly surprising, then, that some psychologists have sought to adapt ideas of this kind to the understanding of psychological concepts. The movement known as Gestalt psychology (see also Chapter 6) represented one such effort. Much of the work of the Gestalt psychologists focused on such topics as perception and problem solving, and the details of how they adapted "field" ideas to address such psychological problems need not concern us here. However, one psychologist loosely affiliated with the Gestalt group, Kurt Lewin, was deeply concerned with issues of personality, motivation, and social behavior. Lewin's field theory of personality will be considered in the first part of this chapter. Although Lewin himself was quite interested in the mathematical aspects of his theory, for the most part we will not need to be: most of the theory's essential ideas can readily be communicated in words or simple diagrams.

Although Lewin's theory has some fairly abstract aspects, the reader should not think that he was a remote, ivory-tower theorist. On the contrary, his broad interests and lively imagination led him to deal with a wide variety of human concerns. For example, he initiated what has come to be known as "action research"—research whose objective is the changing of social conditions, and he founded the science of group dynamics, the study of the way groups form, function, and change.

STRUCTURE OF PERSONALITY

Lewin called the psychological field of his theory the life space. A person's **life space** is the total set of facts that, at a given instant, affect his or her behavior. A person's life space might include, for example, his perception of himself in his particular physical and social environment; his needs, wishes, and intentions; his memories of particular past events and his imaginings about future ones; any emotions he might be feeling; and so forth.

Consider, for example, the life space of a particular young man sitting in a particular college classroom on a particular spring afternoon. His life space includes some general sense of who he is, of what the classroom is like, and of where he is sitting in the room. Rather prominent features of his life space include the attractive young woman in the next seat and his intention to ask her to have a cup of coffee with him after class. His life space also includes the professor (to whom he is paying no particular attention at the moment). The evidence for this is the fact that the professor's presence is affecting his behavior: the young man is silent rather than chatting with his pretty neighbor. His life space does not, however, include the elaborate distinctions about early European history that the professor is making, as will become evident on the upcoming quiz. Our young man's life space may also include imagined events, such as a softball game scheduled for later that afternoon. He may imagine himself coming up to

BOX 8.1   Kurt Lewin (1890–1947)

The second in a family of four children, Kurt Lewin was born in Mogilno, Poland, then a village in Prussia. Although Lewin's father was a leader in the community, where he farmed and owned the general store, he moved his family to Berlin when Kurt was 15 so that the Lewin children could obtain better schooling.

After completing his secondary education, Kurt Lewin enrolled at the University of Berlin, where he studied psy-chology under Karl Stumpf, the well-known experimental psychologist. Lewin received his doctorate in 1914 and then served in the German army during World War I. When he returned to Berlin, he joined the faculty of the Psychological Institute and remained there for some years.

In the early 1930s, while on a visiting professorship at Stanford University, Lewin decided to settle in the United States and brought his wife, the former Gertrud Weiss, and his four children to this country. After spending two years at Cornell University, Lewin became a professor at the University of Iowa where, with a group of graduate and postdoctoral students, he pioneered in action research and the study of group dynamics.

In 1945 Lewin moved, with some of his students, to the Massachusetts Institute of Technology, where he founded and was the first director of the Research Center for Group Dynamics.

Lewin was a person of enormous energy who threw himself into everything he did and "imparted his excitement about problems of psychology to his collaborators, students and colleagues alike, [drawing] them into his own life pattern of intense hours of work relieved by almost equally intense hours of play and discussion" (Heider, 1974, p. 485). At the end of these discussions—which often continued for hours and in which membership shifted as people came and went—no one could say who was the source of a particular idea. However, "there was no doubt in anyone's mind that Lewin was the indispensable member. . . . His willingness to grant an enthusiastic hearing to even the most adventurous speculation supplied the ferment that made each participant rise above himself" (Dembo, quoted in Marrow, 1969, p. 27).

bat and hitting a home run to win the game—as well as the affections of the young lady in the next seat.

The life space of anyone at any given moment is divided into regions. The young woman constitutes one such region in our young man's life space, the baseball game another, the professor yet another. The young man himself is also represented by a region in his life space. Each of these regions may in turn be further subdivided.

The mathematical approach that Lewin uses to deal with life spaces is based on the branch of mathematics known as **topology**, which focuses on the connections among things, their part–whole relations, and so on, rather than on such matters as their size and shape. Thus in studying the diagrams in this chapter, the reader should focus

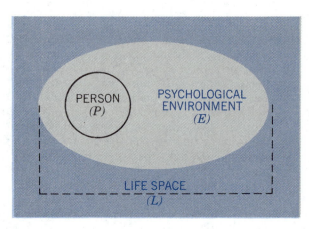

Figure 8.1   The life space. Person and psychological environment make up the life space (P + E = L).

on the connectedness and communications among regions rather than on the rather arbitrary shapes and dimensions used to represent these regions on the printed page.

The most basic subdivision of the life space is between the person and the psychological environment (Figure 8.1). We will consider each of these important subdivisions in turn.

THE PERSON.   Lewin usually represented the **person** as an enclosed circle, indicating that the person is an entity set apart from everything else in the world and yet included within that world. Enclosing the circle in a (larger) ellipse indicated that the person is both differentiated from and included within the life space, which, as we will see, comprises everything within the ellipse.

The person not only is separated from the environment but is differentiated within himself or herself. As Figure 8.2 indicates, Lewin sees the person as divided into two main regions: the **perceptual–motor region,** on the periphery of the circle, represents the perceptual and motoric aspects of the person; in the center, the **inner-personal region** represents the motivational aspects.

Note the use in Figure 8.2 of both thin and heavy lines for boundaries between the **cells** or subregions of the inner-personal region. A very important quality of a boundary line is its **permeability**, or the relative ease with which the areas on either side of the boundary can influence each other. Figure 8.2 suggests that not all cells are equally accessible to each other. For example, cells *d* and *c* representing, say, this particular person's needs for academic achievement and sexual gratification, are psychologically independent of one another, but *c* and *b* (*b* represents the need for affection) mutually interact. And cell *a,* representing, say, a fear of high places, is essentially walled off from the rest of this person's motivational system.

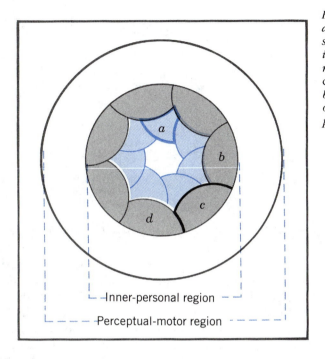

*Figure 8.2 The differenti-
ated person. The inner-personal region is subdivided
into cells. Heavy lines surrounding a and portions of
c and d indicate inaccessi-
bility between these and
other cells; see text for explanation.*

THE PSYCHOLOGICAL ENVIRONMENT.   The **psychological environment** is represented by surrounding the circle that represents the person with an ellipse. The area within the ellipse but outside the circle is
the psychological environment, and the total area within the ellipse, as
we have said, constitutes the life space (see Figure 8.1).

As Figure 8.3 indicates, the psychological environment, like the
person, is divided into regions. Notice that again, some boundaries are
permeable (thin lines) whereas others are impermeable (heavy lines),
indicating that certain areas of our worlds can influence others
whereas certain other areas cannot. For example, region *C,* representing, say, this person's family, is not accessible to regions *A, B,* or *D,*
representing possible activities with friends.

THE LIFE SPACE.   One of Lewin's best-known equations, $B = f(P, E)$,
or $B = f(L)$, states that behavior is a function of both person and environment, or of the life space. The **life space** is composed of the person
plus the psychological environment, and it contains everything that
must be known if one is to understand the immediate behavior of a
person.

What about the environment external to a person's life space—
the world as it physically exists or is perceived by others? For a full understanding of the life space itself, we need to understand the relations

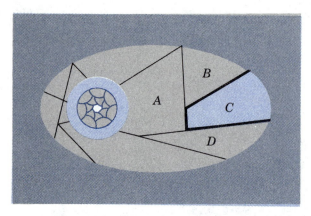

Figure 8.3   The differentiated environment. C represents an area of experience that is not accessible to areas A, B, or D; see text for explanation.

between it and what Lewin called the **foreign hull**, the area beyond the life space.

In the first place, things that exist or occur in the foreign hull can materially influence the psychological environment. Similarly, a person's behavior can produce change in the physical world. Because of this reciprocal influence, the boundary between the foreign hull and the psychological environment is said normally to be permeable.

The concept of the permeability of the boundary between the life space and the outer world is important in Lewin's theory, for it implies that long-term prediction of behavior from a knowledge only of the present lifespace is usually not possible. Because something in the outer world may change the whole course of events in the life space—a chance meeting, an unexpected telephone call, an accident of some sort—the psychologist can at best understand a person's immediate life space and its implications for how he or she will begin to act. Prediction of the outcome of the action will depend on prediction of events in the foreign hull, which may require use of the laws of physics and sociology, as well as one's knowledge of the life spaces of other people.

Regions of the life space.   There are as many regions in the life space as there are separate psychological facts in existence at any moment in time. For example, if the fact of feeling hungry is the only one that exists at present, a person's inner-personal area will have just one cell, for hunger. But suppose a person—let's call him Joe—is anticipating meeting a friend, Julie, for dinner. Joe's psychological environment may contain a region for eating dinner, a region for being with Julie, and perhaps a region for driving his car. At dinner, Joe and Julie discuss a research project, a conflict Joe is having with a colleague, a book on ethics Julie has just read, the news about a nuclear accident, and their feelings about whether they want to get married. Now the regions of Joe's life space (and of Julie's) are greatly expanded—*P* would have to include cells not only for hunger and social contact but for achievement need, competition and power, intellectual interest, fear, and love; E would include regions for eating dinner, being with a friend, driving to a restaurant, discussing professional activities, working through personal conflicts, examining ideas about morality, considering ways to prevent nuclear disaster, and exploring intimate thoughts and feelings with another, cared-for person.

Each cell or region of the life space is occupied by a separate **fact.** For Lewin, a fact can be almost anything, either sensed or inferred—thirst, a chair, another's concern—and it can be empirical, phenomenal, hypothetical, dynamic. As we will see, the facts of the inner-personal region are called "needs," and the facts of the psychological environment have a dynamic property called "valence." Each need occupies a separate cell in the inner-personal region, and each valenced object occupies a separate region in the psychological environment. An **event** is the result of an interaction between two or more facts, that is, cells or regions. For example, when a person moves from one region to another in the life space, this is an event, because (at least) three facts are involved—the starting region, the destination region, and the person who moves.

How do regions influence each other?   When one inner-personal cell influences another, it is said to communicate with the other. However, changes in the psychological environment often occur by means of the **locomotion**, or movement, of the person from one region to another. Lewin drew this distinction to point out that the person is a unity and that elements of the person, though they can be in touch with each other, cannot be said to move from one area to another. The person himself or herself, however, can indeed "move" from one area of interest, concern, or activity to another.

Locomotions may be physical movement, or they may be changes in the focus of attention. In fact, a great many of the locomotions that particularly interest the psychologist concern alterations in the focus of one's perceptual and attentional processes.

Remember our student listening to a lecture that did not interest him much? In his life space, he may hardly be in the classroom region; at a given moment, he may be in the softball region of his psychological environment, mentally playing a game. If his neighbor whispers to him about an upcoming rock concert, he may easily "move" into the rock concert region. In fact, he may spend very little time in the classroom region during the entire class hour.

Communication and locomotion are events, inasmuch as they involve interaction between two or more facts. Three principles govern the derivation of events (see Table 8.1). The first has already been stated: the principle of **relatedness** says that an event is always caused

TABLE 8.1   *Principles That Define an Event*

PRINCIPLE	EXPLANATION
Relatedness	Two or more facts interact.
Concreteness	Facts must actually exist in the life space. Potential or possible facts, which do not yet exist, cannot cause present events.
Contemporaneity	Facts must be contemporaneous; only present facts can produce present behavior. Facts that no longer exist cannot create events in the present.

Source: Lewin (1936).

by the interaction of two or more facts. The second, the principle of **concreteness,** says that only facts that actually exist in the life space can have effects. Facts in the foreign hull cannot cause behavioral events unless and until they affect the life space. And the closely related principle of **contemporaneity** says that only present facts can produce present behavior. Facts of infancy or childhood have no bearing on present behavior unless they have somehow remained in existence throughout the years (Lewin, 1936). But although the actual events of the past or potential events of the future cannot determine behavior today, our attitudes, feelings, and thoughts about past and future are a part of our present life space and may considerably influence our conduct. Thus, the present life space must be representable as containing a psychological past and a psychological future (Lewin, 1951).

LEVELS OF REALITY.   According to Lewin's concept of **levels of reality**, reality consists of actual locomotions, and unreality consists of imaginary locomotions. Moreover, there are degrees of reality or unreality. For example, a person may change her job or work out a problem; she may plan a new project or a vacation; or she may daydream about becoming president of her company. Each of these activities takes place at a different level of reality; planning or thinking about something occurs at some intermediate level between the most realistic performance and the most unrealistic fantasizing.

The reality–unreality concept applies to the person as well as to the psychological environment. For example, an inner-personal cell may actually affect the motor area or it may do so only in imagination. Thus, a person may say aloud, to another person, what is on his mind, or he may only think or daydream about doing so.

PERSONALITY DYNAMICS

Structural representations of the life space tell us what the life space looks like at a given point in time, but they do not tell us what it looks

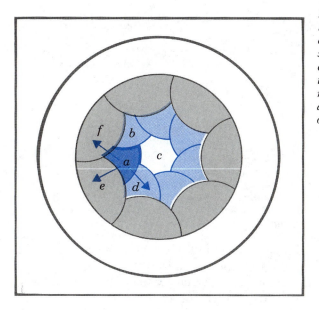

Figure 8.4 Diffusion of tension. Tension may be diffused from system a *to systems* d, e, *and* f, *but because the boundaries between* a, b, *and* c *are impermeable, tension can be diffused to the last two cells only indirectly, via* d *and* f.

like when the person begins to behave. To understand behavior, we need dynamic concepts.

ENERGY, TENSION, AND NEED.   For Lewin, as for many others, the person is a complex energy system. The energy that performs psychological work is called **psychical energy.** What creates this energy? Briefly, an increase of tension in one part of the system (person) relative to the rest of the system produces disequilibrium, and the system's effort to equalize the tension within its parts produces psychical energy. When the system is successful, the output of energy stops and the system comes to rest.

In Lewin's field theory, **tension** describes the state of one system relative to the state of surrounding systems; in the person, tension refers to the state of one inner-personal cell relative to the states of other inner-personal cells.

For Lewin, tension has two important properties. First, it tends to become equalized; that is, if system *a* is in a high state of tension and systems *b, c,* and *d* are in a state of low tension, tension will tend to pass from *a* to *b–d* until the four systems are in a state of equal tension (compare Jung's principle of entropy).

A second important property of tension is its tendency to exert pressure on the boundary of the system in which it is contained. If that boundary is permeable, tension will flow readily to other systems. If it is impermeable, however, diffusion will be impeded. As Figure 8.4 shows, a given region shares its boundary with more than one other region. Here, region *a* shares its boundary with regions *b–f*. Note that

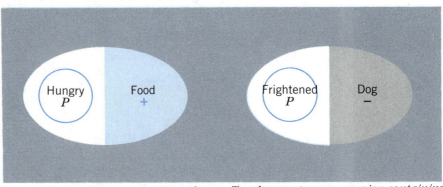

Figure 8.5   Positive and negative valences. To a hungry person, a region containing food has a positive valence; to a person who fears dogs, a region containing a dog has a negative valence.

the boundary of *a* shared with regions *b* and *c* is impermeable, but the portion of *a*'s boundary shared with regions *d–f* is permeable. Thus, tension from *a* will move easily to *d–f* but not to *b* and *c*.

What causes tension to increase in one region? The arousal of a need. A **need** can be a physiological condition, such as hunger, thirst, or sex; it can be a desire for something, such as a job or a lot of money; or it can be an intention to do something, such as complete a task or keep an appointment. For Lewin, need is equivalent to such terms as motive, wish, drive.

According to Lewin, there are as many needs as there are specific and distinguishable cravings. One can have a need for sex. One can have a need for an enchilada. Or one can have a need to hear the third movement of Bartok's Concerto No. 2 played by Weissenberg. Lewin attempted neither to list all needs nor to reduce all needs to one general one. He felt that far too little was yet known about needs to systematize them in any way. In his system, only the needs that exist currently, that are actually producing effects in the preset situation, are important. For example, everyone is capable of feeling hungry, but it is only when the need for food is disturbing a person's equilibrium that that need must be taken into account.

Quasi-needs are specific intentions, often shaped by social factors (Lewin, 1951). The specific needs just described—for sex, enchilada, or Bartok's piano concerto—are examples of quasi-needs; they have evolved out of people's interactions with other people and with aspects of the culture in which they live.

Needs change as a result of the many small and large social groups a child belongs to, or wants to belong to, or wants not to belong to. Parents' advice or demands and peers' urging affect or are interwoven with other socially induced needs. The culture in which we grow up affects practically every one of our needs and all of our behavior.

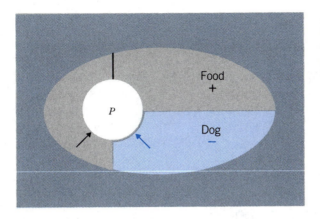

Figure 8.6 Vectors and valences. A positive valence results in a vector that pushes the person in the direction of an object; a negative valence results in a vector that pushes the person away from an object.

ACTION.   We have seen how tension is created and how it affects different systems within the person. We might guess that when accumulated tension presses on the boundary between the inner-personal and motor regions of the person action would result. Not so, says Lewin, at least not directed action; two other concepts are required to connect motivation, in the inner-personal sphere, with purposeful behavior, in the psychological environment.

Valence.   A **valence** is the value for the person of a region of the psychological environment. A region with a positive valence contains a goal object that will reduce tension; for example, for a hungry person a region that contains food will have a positive valence (see Fig. 8.5a). On the other hand, for a person who fears dogs, a region that contains a dog will have a negative valence (Fig. 8.5b).

Basically, valences are determined by needs; the value of food depends on the degree of one's hunger. However, other factors also affect valences. For example, even for a hungry person, certain foods may have a negative valence if they are things he or she does not like.

Vector.   A person acts, or performs a locomotion, when a sufficiently strong force is exerted upon him or her. Borrowing from physics and mathematics, Lewin calls such a force a vector. **Vectors**, represented by arrows, are psychological forces that impinge on the person, tending to make him or her move in a certain direction (see Fig. 8.6).

The direction and strength of a vector are a function of the positive or negative valence of one or more regions in the psychological environment. That is, if one region of the environment is positively valenced (e.g., contains desirable food), a vector pointing in the direction of that region will impinge on the person (Fig. 8.6). If a second region is negatively valenced (e.g., contains a feared dog), another vector will impinge on the person, pushing the person away from that

BOX 8.2   The Dynamics of Conflict

Lewin (1935, 1951) described psychological conflict as occurring in a field of psychological forces. These forces, or vectors, represent the direction and strength of the tendency to change, and the combination of a number of forces, called the **resultant force,** leads the person to move (psychologically or physically) in one direction or another depending on the valence, or value for the person, of particular areas of the life space. The valence, in turn, depends to a great extent on need, although other factors affect valence as well.

There are several kinds of forces. **Driving forces** lead to movement, or locomotion, of some sort. **Restraining forces,** which represent physical or social barriers to movement, do not lead to locomotion but influence the effect of driving forces. **Forces corresponding to a person's own needs** reflect a person's wish to do one thing or another—go to a movie, eat a certain food, and the like. **Induced forces** correspond to the wishes of another person, such as a parent or a peer. Finally, **impersonal forces** are those that appear to reflect neither the person's wishes nor those of a specific other person; they are "matter-of-fact demands."

Lewin defines a conflict situation as one in which "forces acting on the person are opposite in direction and about equal in strength" (1951, p. 260). He proposes several types of conflict situations. The first

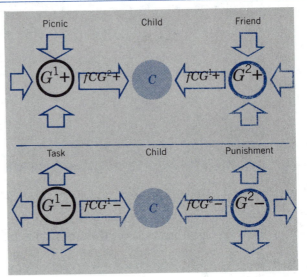

Figure 8.7   Conflict between two positive goals (a) *and two negative goals* (b). *(After Lewin, 1951, p. 261.)*

type involves a conflict between two or more driving forces: a person "is located between two positive or negative valences which are mutually exclusive" (p. 261). For example, a child may have to choose between two positively valued activities—playing with a friend or going on a picnic. Or a child may find herself between two negative valences—doing a certain disagreeable task or being punished. Lewin represents these two situations as in Figure 8.7. In panel *a,* a force fCG^1+ is pushing the child (C) in the direction of the first, positive goal, the picnic, while another force fCG^2+ pushes toward the second goal, playing with a friend. In the second figure, one force fCG^1- pushes the child away from the first negative goal—the unpleasant

task—and another force fCG^2- pushes the child away from the second negative goal—being punished. According to Lewin, in the first situation, the child will try to reach both goals if possible. In the second situation, the two negative valences produce a resultant force in the direction of "leaving the field" altogether; the child may run away from home (temporarily, one hopes) to escape the disagreeable alternatives.

Where a positive and a negative driving force conflict, Lewin says, there is typically a point at which the two forces are equal in strength, and the person may be caught wavering around that point until one force becomes dominant. Suppose, he says, that a young child is trying to seize a toy boat from the waves on the seashore

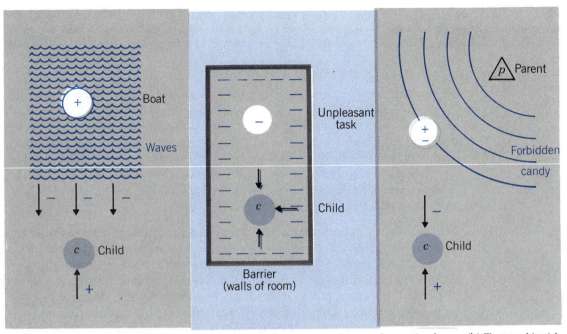

Figure 8.8   Other forms of conflict. (a) *Equilibrium between positive and negative forces.* (b) *Trapped inside a barrier with an unpleasant task.* (c) *A negative valence induced by a powerful parent.*

(Fig. 8.8*a*). The force propelling the child toward the boat is strong, but the force leading him to retreat from the waves may be greater. Because the waves have a limited range of effect, the negative valence of the waves decreases rather rapidly as the child retreats; the force pushing him toward the boat does not decrease so rapidly. Thus, there is a point of equilibrium relatively near the goal at which the child moves first in one direction and then in another. But the balance of forces may shift. If a wave knocks the child over, he may give up the boat; if his father says, "I told you it was time to go—you'll have to leave the boat," the child may brave the water and grab his boat.

In the second type of conflict

situation, a driving force and a restraining force conflict with each other. Most commonly, a person is prevented by a barrier from reaching a goal or from leaving a field of negative valence (Fig. 8.8*b*). Based on experiments with children, Lewin says that a child typically tries to go round or over or in some other way to negotiate such a barrier in order to reach the goal object or to avoid the negative situation. When such efforts fail, the barrier often acquires a negative valence of its own. The child is then less and less likely to approach the barrier and eventually leaves the field. The child may return and try again, but if failure persists, leaving the field eventually will be permanent. Frequently, Lewin says, a state of "high

emotional tension" results from unsuccessful efforts to negotiate a barrier that prevents one from leaving a negatively valenced field.

In a third kind of conflict situation, any one of the situations we have discussed may reflect the opposition of two forces representing the person's own needs, the opposition of two induced forces, or the opposition of an "own" and an induced force. Of particular interest is the last situation; for example, if a child's (*C*) own need is opposed by the wish of its parent (*P*), who is more powerful than the child, *P* can "create induced driving or restraining forces . . . which correspond to *P*'s will" (Lewin, 1951, p. 268, and see Fig. 8.8*c*). The child may attempt to rebel or to undermine the power of the parent, at least in the area of the conflict. But if this effort is unsuccessful, the child may direct its aggressiveness toward peers or other objects. Or it may give up resisting "if the suppressive power of the leader is too great" (p. 268).

region (Fig. 8.6). If several other vectors were involved in our example of positive valence—say, if the person were tired as well as hungry and the food needed preparing, or the person had to attend an important meeting and had no time to stop for lunch—the resulting locomotion would be the result of all existing vectors. Such situations often involve psychological conflict, a topic on which Lewin initiated empirical research (see Box 8.2) and on which Neal Miller and John Dollard greatly expanded, as we will see in Chapter 14.

Locomotion. When we talked about locomotion in the section on structure, we noted that Lewin's concept of locomotion more often than not referred to psychological rather than physical movement— that is, to shifts in a person's focus of attention or thoughts. To illustrate Lewin's concept of locomotion, however, we will use an example of behavior that entails both psychological and physical movement.

Suppose that a child looks into a store window, sees a display of candy bars, and wishes she had some candy. According to Lewin, the sight of the candy arouses a need, and the need does three things: it releases energy, thereby arousing tension in an inner-personal region— the candy-wanting system; it gives a positive valence to the region in which the candy is located; and it creates a force or vector that pushes the child in the direction of the candy.

If the child can simply enter the store and buy the candy, the situation can be represented by Figure 8.9a: the vector will push her to cross the permeable boundary into the positively valenced candy region. But suppose that the child has no money; then the boundary becomes impassable, as in Figure 8.9b. She may get as close to the candy as possible, even putting her nose against the store window, but she will be unable to reach it.

Now suppose that the child decides to ask her father for money to buy the candy. The intention to get money from her father is, according to Lewin, a quasi-need. Figure 8.10a shows what happens if the child's plan works: the child reaches the candy by way of her father. But suppose her father refuses her request; then she may decide to see if a friend will loan her the money. Figure 8.10b describes this second situation: the impermeable boundary around the father—his refusal to give the child the money—stops the path started by vector 1; vector 2 then pushes the child on a path that leads through the permeable boundary to the friend, who is willing to lend her money, and from there to the candy.

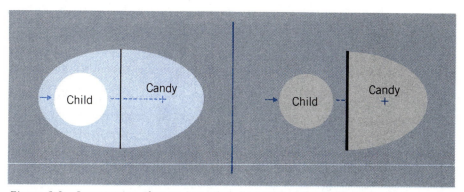

Figure 8.9   *Locomotion, free or impeded. In panal a, the child, pushed by a vector, easily crosses the permeable boundary to obtain the candy, which has a positive valence. In panel b, the child is stopped by an impermeable boundary, representing lack of money.*

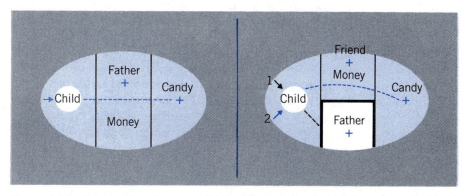

Figure 8.10   *Locomotion, free or redirected. In panel a, the child, again pushed by a vector, freely passes through permeable boundaries, obtaining money from her father and buying candy. In panel b, the child, pushed by vector 1, is stopped by her father's refusal of money, represented by an impermeable boundary. Vector 2 pushes the child toward a friend who loans her the money to buy the candy.*

RESTRUCTURING THE ENVIRONMENT.   The psychological environment is a very fluid concept. Because the dynamics of the environment can change in at least three different ways (see Table 8.2), there are numerous possibilities for altering it.

Every locomotion changes the life space in some way. And remember that locomotion can be either psychological or physical. In the example of the child and the candy, her actual approach to her father and friend and her walking into the store are physical motions, but her thinking about how to get the candy and her shift to seeing her friend rather than her father as the means to the candy are locomotions of a cognitive nature.

TABLE 8.2   *Restructuring of the Psychological Environment*

FOCUS OF CHANGE	DESCRIPTION
Valence	A region may change quantitatively, becoming more positively or more negatively valenced; or it may change qualitatively, going from positive to negative, or vice versa. New regions may appear, old ones disappear.
Vector	Vectors may change in strength, direction, or both.
Boundary	Boundaries may become firmer or weaker and appear or disappear as regions change.

Having provided so many ways in which to restructure the environment, Lewin seems clearly to stress dynamics in his picture of personality. Any one of his diagrams should be seen as analogous to one frame of a filmstrip (recall Adler's ''frozen moment''). Thus, to represent the behavior of a human being over the course of one day, we might have to draw many hundreds of such diagrams.

MAINTAINING EQUILIBRIUM. As you might guess, in Lewin's tension-reduction system, an important goal of psychological processes is to maintain the person in a state of **equilibrium** (recall the theories of Freud, Jung, Sullivan). The accumulation of tension in one inner-personal cell can lead to a number of events: when a boundary can no longer resist the pressure from such a region, there may be a breakthrough of energy into the motor region that will produce agitated behavior, such as a tantrum or an explosion of violence. If the boundary between the inner-personal and motor regions is fairly permeable, tension may be dissipated, little by little, in restless activity.

By far the most prevalent—and most effective—method of returning to a state of equilibrium is through an appropriate locomotion in the psychological environment—one that brings the person into the region of a satisfying goal object. But tension may sometimes be reduced and equilibrium restored by a substitute locomotion, one in which satisfying another need discharges the tension from the first need system. For example, if you are very angry about something but cannot express your anger lest you be fired, you may express a related need—the need to engage in vigorous physical action—by, say, some strenuous exercise like swimming 100 laps.

Finally, tension may be reduced to some extent by purely imaginary locomotion. We can gain a kind of vicarious satisfaction from merely daydreaming about what we would like to be and do.

It should not be thought, however, that a tendency toward equilibrium means that the person is likely to ''run down'' completely, to equalize all tensions in the inner-personal regions. Lewin makes it clear that in complex systems, coming to equilibrium means not a loss of tension but a balancing of internal tensions (1935, p. 58ff.). As we will see in the next section, a main feature of psychological development is the creation of the kind of internal structuring that ensures a psychological equilibrium of balanced tensions, not one that is tension free.

DEVELOPMENT OF PERSONALITY

Lewin's is a purely psychological theory. As a result, when he discusses development, he does not deal with an issue that has intrigued many other theorists—the nature–nurture issue. Lewin neither rejected the role played by heredity and maturation in the individual's development nor thought these influences insignificant. He did feel that psychology had been too focused on typical or average patterns of development and that it had neglected the psychological development over time of individual life spaces.

Development, for Lewin, is concrete and continuous; age scales and developmental stages, he felt, were not really helpful in understanding psychological growth. Concepts such as differentiation, organization, and integration were more useful, Lewin felt, in describing behavioral change.

BEHAVIORAL CHANGE. According to Lewin (1951), a number of important behavioral changes occur during development. The variety of our activities, emotions, needs, relationships, and so on increases as we grow older. (This variety may begin to decrease late in life.) Moreover, as we grow, we gain freedom of movement, and time becomes extended. Young children are pretty much creatures of the present, but as people mature, they begin to think about the past, to plan for the future and, thus, to incorporate in their current life spaces a time perspective somewhat longer than just a few minutes, an hour, or a day.

With age, the person also gives evidence of important changes in organization. For example, a very young child can maintain a relationship with only one other child at a time, but an older child or an adult can interact with people in groups. Also, behavior becomes hierarchical; whereas a young child may play with blocks without any clearly articulated purpose, an older child may see such play as instrumental in gaining approval or in competing successfully with another child.

Behavior can also become more complicated; young children generally do one thing at a time, and, because they are easily distracted, they often fail to return to a task when interrupted. An older child can be crayoning while talking to a friend, interrupt his activity to do an errand for his parents, return to crayoning, answer the phone and continue to crayon, and so on.

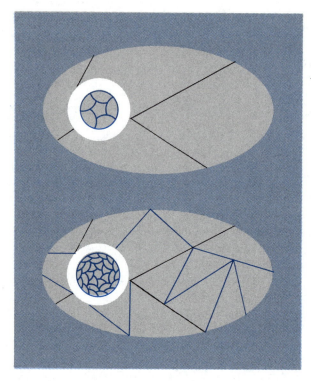

Figure 8.11   Development and differentiation. Panel a depicts the life space of a young child with relatively few inner-personal cells and environmental regions. Panel b depicts an adult's life space with many cells and regions, representing highly differentiated systems of needs, activities, and experience.

We know that the infant's behavior typically involves diffuse reactions of the entire body. Lewin called this kind of mass activity **simple interdependence**, meaning that for the infant, tension systems are interchangeable. That is, whatever the source of tension—hunger, thirst, wetness, fear—tension spreads evenly throughout the organism, resulting in this mass activity.

With increasing maturity comes **organizational interdependence**, in which independent actions become organized hierarchically, and separate activities or needs are combined and integrated into larger wholes. Building a treehouse, for example, requires the individual to bring together a great many separate activities—drawing a plan, gathering materials, doing the carpentry, perhaps supervising the work of friends, and so on.

Finally, as we mature, our ability to distinguish reality from fantasy improves. Increasing realism of perception is particularly noticeable in the area of social relations. For example, a small child may view others' behavior largely in terms of its own wishes and needs. An older child, however, understands realistically that other people have plans and purposes of their own that affect their behavior.

An increasing tendency to ''economize'' our actions, Lewin

"Mommy will see you later. Mommy has to go to law school now."

Drawing by Weber. © 1982 The New Yorker Magazine, Inc.

says, is evidence of maturity. Striving to accomplish maximal results with minimal effort in any task requires adjusting one's life space to the real characteristics of the external physical and social environments, and such behavior is far more typical of adults than of children.

DIFFERENTIATION AND INTEGRATION.   Differentiation, one of Lewin's key concepts, serves to explain the increasing variety of behavior, the freedom of movement associated with the ability to do more different things, the expansion of time, and the distinction between what is real and what is not real. Lewin defines **differentiation** as an increase in the number of parts of a whole. The number of regions, or cells, in the inner-personal sphere multiplies with age, and the number of regions in the psychological environment also increases (Fig. 8.11*a, b*).

In learning to distinguish reality from unreality, we learn to distinguish not only between the true and the false but between different degrees of possibility and probability. Thus, whereas the small child may perceive simply that Mommy is here or not here, the older child may understand that Mommy won't be home until late because she has class on Tuesday evenings or that Mommy has just stopped by a neighbor's and will probably be home soon.

As differentiation proceeds, many new boundaries are created. In general, boundary strength increases with age. This accounts for the lessening in distractibility and the growing ability to engage in complicated behavior patterns. The child is much more subject to influence from his or her environment than is the adult and can thus discharge tensions more readily and directly.

Differentiation and increasing separation among regions can account for many of the observed changes in behavior, but they cannot explain the fact that behavior may also become increasingly organized and integrated with age. Indeed, they would seem to suggest quite the opposite. It is the concept of organizational interdependence, already mentioned, that explains how different regions of P and E, despite their increased autonomy, become organized in hierarchical fashion so as to work together to produce integrated behavior. The easy substitutability of regions for each other disappears, and a whole hierarchy of dominant–subordinate relationships becomes established, wherein region a rules region b, b rules c and d, and so on. For example, an infant may play with a doll in a simple way, as by pounding things with it. An older child may engage in play with dolls that involves a complex hierarchy of goals and subgoals. Father may go to the office, mother may dress the children. Dressing the children may include subgoals, such as dressing Mary and dressing George. Dressing George may include the subgoals of putting on George's shirt, his pants, and his shoes. Putting on George's shoes may require finding them. And so forth. Each of these subgoals involves setting up a temporary quasineed, or intention, and coordinating these in such a way that when all the subgoals of a higher goal are satisfied, the higher goal is satisfied as well.

RESEARCH EMPHASES AND METHODS

Lewin carried out many studies of his own, taking the lead in formulating empirical tests of many of his basic hypotheses. Perhaps his most significant contribution, however, lay in his influence on his students and colleagues as well as on subsequent generations of psychologists. According to de Rivera (1976), Lewin thought best in interaction with others, and in long, intense discussions—that sometimes lasted many hours—he was the catalyst, generating theories and ideas for research that were reflected in the work of many different people.

We cannot begin to do justice here to the many areas of research generated by Lewin's theories but will describe one example to give some flavor of his work. One of the first research programs Lewin and his associates launched was one to explore and, it was hoped, to support Lewin's concept of **tension systems**. The nearly 20 empirical studies produced in this program by Lewin's earliest students and published between 1926 and 1934 in the *Psychologische Forschung*, the journal of experimental psychology launched at the University of

Berlin, were considered a "major revolution in psychological research" (Marrow, 1969, p. 40).

The revolutionary character of this research lay in its having successfully subjected to laboratory experiment, for the first time, some of the properties of the personality's inner structural and dynamic features. The key to this success was Lewin's ingenuity in devising simple experimental operations linked to his theoretical concepts.

One such series of experiments used the procedure of **task substitution** to study the relations among tension systems (Lewin, 1935). The basic idea is this. A child is working at a task, say, building a house with blocks. According to Lewin's theory, a tension system has been set up in the child; a quasi-need, which has been activated in his inner-personal region, leads him to work toward the completion of the task. Suppose now that we interrupt the child's activity, give him some crayons, and ask him to draw a picture of a house. We have now set up a new tension system, for the drawing task. The two systems, being somewhat similar, can be presumed to be in some degree of (internal) communication with one another. How much? We can tell by allowing the child to complete the second task and then seeing whether he spontaneously resumes the first. For according to the theory, if the cells representing the two intentions are in close communication with one another, the draining of tension from the second will also tend to drain the first, and there will be relatively little tension left to lead to a resumption of the first task. On the other hand, if the two cells are relatively isolated from one another, completing the second task will have little nor no effect on the leftover tension of the first, and the child should tend to resume block building after completing the drawing.

We thus have a simple means of studying a feature of the inner-personal region that is far removed from direct view: the permeability of the boundary between two inner-personal cells. We can also examine various factors that influence this permeability.

A typical task-substitution experiment was carried out by one of Lewin's students, Käte Lissner (1933). Lissner studied the ways in which the similarity of the second task to the first appeared to affect the communication between tension systems. She showed that the more similar the second task was to the first, the more effective a substitute it was for it, and the less frequently spontaneous resumption of the initial task occurred. Lissner also showed that if the experimenter, in giving her instructions, made a distinction between the tasks, emphasizing that the second was different from the first, the child was more likely to resume the original task than if no such distinction was made. Presumably the experimenter's instruction increased the firmness of the boundary between the inner-personal regions corresponding to the two intentions. Lissner also investigated the variable of task difficulty and found that if the substitute task was easier than the initial task, it was a less effective substitute than if it was more difficult. Presumably, performing an easy task involved less tension-reduction and so was less effective in reducing the leftover tension from the original task.

Another of Lewin's students, Wera Mahler (1933), looked at still another variable: the degree of reality of the second task. Mahler, for example, interrupted children in the middle of drawing a picture. Some were then asked to state to the experimenter how they would finish the picture; others were asked only to imagine how they would finish it. Fewer of the first group of children resumed the original task. Apparently, the greater the degree of reality of the second task, the greater the contact between the two corresponding tension systems.

As a final example, Köpke (cited in Lewin, 1935) used the task-substitution procedure to test a specific hypothesis of Lewin's about a certain group of mentally retarded children. Lewin hypothesized that these children not only were less internally differentiated than normal children but had firmer boundaries between their inner-personal regions. If this were true, there should be less substitutability among tasks for these children. And this was what Köpke found, to a striking degree. When the original task was to draw an animal on red paper, and the (very similar) substitute task was to draw the same animal on green paper, the retarded children, unlike normal children, nearly always went back to the original task after completing the substitute task.

GEORGE KELLY'S THEORY OF PERSONAL CONSTRUCTS

A clinical psychologist is testing a client. She gives him a number of 3" by 5" cards on which she asks him to write down the names of various people: "A teacher you liked." "A teacher you disliked." "Your wife (or present girlfriend)." "An employer or supervisor under whom you worked and whom you found it hard to get along with." "Your mother." "Your father." "A neighbor with whom you get along very well." "A person of your own sex whom you would enjoy having as a companion on a trip." "The most intelligent person whom you know personally." "A girl you did not like when you were in high school." And so on, until the client has written down the names of a couple of dozen people with whom he has had various kinds of relationships during his life.

Then the psychologist picks out a set of three of the cards—perhaps the wife, mother, and girl the client did not like in high school—and says: "Now I would like you to tell me something about these three people. In what *important way* are two of them alike and different from the third?" She records his response, picks out another set of three cards, and again asks for a way in which two of the people are alike and different from the third. Then she picks out another combi-

BOX 8.3   George Alexander Kelly (1905–1967)

Born on a Kansas farm and raised on a homestead in eastern Colorado, George Kelly had rather irregular early schooling. When his parents could spend a few weeks in town, Kelly attended school, but most of the time he studied at home. When Kelly was 13, he tried commuting to the nearest high school, but his parents finally decided to send him to school in Wichita. From that point on, Kelly, who was an only child, lived away from home most of the time.

By the time Kelly was graduated, in 1926, from Park College with a B.A. in physics and mathematics, he had begun to develop an interest in social problems. When he enrolled the next fall at the University of Kansas, he undertook a master's program in educational sociology and wrote his thesis on workers' distribution of leisure-time activities. During the next two years, Kelly took an assortment of jobs. He taught in a labor college; he conducted speech classes for the American Bankers Association and an Americanization class for prospective citizens; he taught at a junior college in Iowa—where he met Gladys Thompson, a fellow teacher, who later became his wife; he studied more sociology; and he spent a few months as an aeronautical engineer. Then, in 1930, on an exchange fellowship in Edinburgh, he obtained the Bachelor of Education degree. Returning to the States, he began the study of psychology, and in 1931, he was awarded the Ph.D. degree from the State University of Iowa.

For three years, Kelly taught at Fort Hays State College in Kansas, where he developed a program of traveling clinics that brought clinical psychology services to the schools in the state. During World War II, he served in the Aviation Psychology Branch of the Navy's Bureau of Medicine and Surgery. After that, in 1945, he became an associate professor of psychology at the University of Maryland. In 1946, he became professor and director of clinical psychology at Ohio State University, where a few years later he published his major work, *The Psychology of Personal Constructs*. (1955).

Kelly served as president of both the clinical and the consulting divisions of the American Psychological Association, and he also headed the American Board of Examiners in Professional Psychology. In 1960–1961, according to Thompson (1968), Kelly and his wife traveled around the world on a project funded by the Human Ecology Fund and designed to apply the personal construct theory to international problems.

In 1965 Kelly accepted the Riklis Chair of Behavioral Science at Brandeis University. He died before he was able to finish his work on a book of his collected papers, a book since completed by Maher (1969).

nation of three cards, and asks again. She repeats this process perhaps 30 times.

The psychologist is a follower of George Kelly, and her procedure is designed to obtain information about her client's "personal constructs." If her client says that his mother and the girl he did not like in high school are alike, and different from his wife, because "they were both bossy and she is nice," then "bossiness–niceness" is a personal construct of this client, a dimension that he uses to categorize his world. It is personal because it is the person's own construct, a feature of his own idiosyncratic way of sorting out the people and events he encounters. It is a construct because it is something he has created, something he actively imposes on the world to make sense out of it, not information he has passively absorbed from it.

THE STRUCTURE OF PERSONALITY

George A. Kelly, in his major work, *A Psychology of Personal Constructs* (1955), states his basic theory in the form of a fundamental postulate and 11 corollaries (see Table 8.3). We will not find it necessary to explicate all these in detail, but it is worth considering the fundamental postulate briefly:

A person's processes are psychologically channelized by the way in which he anticipates events. (Kelly, 1955, p. 46)

The first part of this statement, "A person's processes are psychologically channelized," indicates what the theory is about: the way in which an individual's activities are directed. The second part indicates the kind of explanation given: the person "anticipates events" by means of his or her system of personal constructs.

The personal construct system is the main structural feature of Kelly's personality theory. It is also, as we will see later, the main dynamic feature, and, as Kelly treats it, its development is more or less synonymous with personality development.

The **personal construct**, the basic unit of Kelly's theory, is the means by which people **construe** or interpret the events of their worlds. "A construct is a way in which some things are construed as being alike and yet different from others" (Kelly, 1955, p. 105). One of the ways in which the client in our example perceived women was that some are "bossy" and some are "nice." Personal constructs have a number of distinctive characteristics. They are, for example, **dichotomous**, or bipolar: good–bad, tall–short, strong–weak, friendly–hostile, and the like. Kelly always wants to know not just what things a person sees as going together but what things are placed in contrast to what other things: "In what way are two of these people alike and different from the third?"

A construct also has a **range of convenience**. It applies to some things and is irrelevant to others. Thus the construct "tall–short" has people and ladders within its range of convenience but not (at least for most people) the time of day or the weather.

Personal constructs may or may not be verbalized. Sometimes people can state clearly a basis on which they make judgments of people or events. Often, however, the nature of a construct must be inferred from vague or fuzzy statements, and sometimes it cannot be put into words at all but can only be inferred from a person's behavior.

TABLE 8.3   The Fundamental Postulate and Its Corollaries

FUNDAMENTAL POSTULATE

A person's processes are psychologically channelized by the ways in which he anticipates events.

COROLLARIES

Construction corollary. A person anticipates events by construing their replications.

Individuality corollary. Persons differ from each other in their constructions of events.

Organization corollary. Each person characteristically evolves, for his convenience in anticipating events, a construction system embracing ordinal relationships between constructs.

Dichotomy corollary. A person's construction system is composed of a finite number of dichotomous constructs.

Choice corollary. A person chooses for himself that alternative in dichotomized construct through which he anticipates the greater possibility for extension and definition of his system.

Range corollary. A construct is convenient for the anticipation of a finite range of events only.

Experience corollary. A person's construction system varies as he successively construes the replications of events.

Modulation corollary. The variation in a person's construction system is limited by the permeability of the constructs within whose ranges of convenience the variants lie.

Fragmentation corollary. A person may successively employ a variety of construction subsystems which are inferentially incompatible with each other.

Commonality corollary. To the extent that one person employs a construction of experience which is similar to that employed by another, his psychological processes are similar to those of the other person.

Sociality corollary. To the extent that one person construes the construction processes of another, he may play a role in a social process involving the other person.

Source: Kelly (1955, pp. 103–104).

Although personal constructs are definitely cognitive—that is, they have to do with a person's knowledge of the world—they are by no means purely so. They are the basis of evaluations of and emotional responses to people and events. Thus, they have motivational and emotional aspects as well.

An important characteristic of personal constructs is their **permeability**. A construct is permeable to the extent that it can take on new objects and events. A completely impermeable construct would be one that referred to only a fixed set of things or events. For example, if "edible–inedible" is an impermeable construct for a man, he may have trouble if he travels to a country where eating habits differ from his own. If "the right way–the wrong way" of doing things is an impermeable construct for a woman, she is apt to have difficulties cooperating with fellow workers on a task.

ORGANIZATION OF PERSONAL CONSTRUCTS. By various means, people organize their constructs into a **personal construct system**, a process that makes it more likely that constructs will be used with some consistency. For example, a person's construct of ''good–bad'' may be at a higher level of generality than his or her construct of ''intelligent–stupid.'' For this person, all intelligent things are good, and all stupid things are bad, but not vice versa—there are many good and bad things that are outside the range of convenience of the ''intelligent–stupid'' construct. In another kind of organization, some constructs may refer directly to other constructs in the system. For this person, an ''evaluative–descriptive'' construct may have both ''good–bad'' and ''intelligent–stupid'' within its range of convenience (toward the ''evaluative'' end).

Naturally, the degree of organization of personal construct systems is always less than perfect. Inconsistencies inevitably arise as the system develops and changes over time. People may differ in the extent to which their personal construct systems are coherent or fragmented, and a particular individual may also vary in this respect over time.

PERSONAL CONSTRUCTS IN INTERPERSONAL BEHAVIOR. The basic purpose of an individual's constructs, as stated in Kelly's fundamental postulate, is to permit the anticipation of events. For most of us, many of the most critical events involve the behavior of other people. A key corollary to the fundamental postulate is what Kelly calls the ''sociality corollary'':

> *To the extent that one person construes the construction processes of another, he may play a role in a social process involving the other person. (1955, p. 95)*

That is, to the extent that Tony can grasp how Carla sees the world, he can take part in social roles with her, whether this involves a friendly conversation, getting her to dominate him, or selling her insurance. The concept of role is of central importance in personal construct theory: **role** is defined as ''a psychological process based upon the role player's construction of aspects of the construction systems of those with whom he attempts to join in a social enterprise'' (Kelly, 1955, p. 97).

It is not assumed that the people participating in social roles necessarily have similar construct systems or even that they are correct in their construing of each others' constructs, although both these conditions are likely to facilitate successful behavior in social roles. The essential feature of role behavior is that people use their constructs to anticipate how other people will construe events.

PERSONALITY DYNAMICS AND DEVELOPMENT

Kelly on occasion has mused on the question of whether personal construct theory could properly be labeled a dynamic theory:

> *Generally I have claimed that it is completely nondynamic. It is utterly innocent of any forces, motives, or incentives and, so far as I have been able to observe, all the other gremlins have been properly exterminated. But then, I may be quite mistaken about this, because I start with the assumption that something is going on, rather than the traditional assumption that the world is filled with a number of things that must be prodded into action by forces. And, since I assume that we start with a process, I am struck with the disturbing thought that personal construct theory may be the only truly dynamic theory available to psychology. So you can take your choice; this is either an all-out dynamic theory or an all-out nondynamic theory. I don't really much care which point of view you take, just so you take one or the other and not something in between. (Kelly, in Maher, 1969, p. 217)*

Kelly's bantering tone notwithstanding, it would seem that insofar as his theory sees the person as inherently active, always in process, always using the construct system to anticipate events, it can be considered a dynamic theory. Kelly is very clear, however, that he is against the notion of motives that are *separate*:

> *I am afraid I am the fellow who has said that motivation—or psychodynamics—is the kind of explanation we resort to when we don't want to bother to understand a person. We simply say that man does what he does not as an expression of his construction of the world, but because he has been pushed into it by the agents which inhabit his psyche. (Kelly, in Maher, 1969, p. 218)*

There is another feature of personal construct theory that, in addition to the postulate of an inherently active person, has important implications for dynamics, or the kinds of changes a personal construct system undergoes over time. This feature is expressed by the principle of **elaborative choice**, which holds that the choices a person makes are such as to move the construct system in the direction of a greater ability to predict: "We assume . . . that whenever a person is confronted with the opportunity for making a choice, he will tend to make that choice in favor of the alternative which seems to provide the best basis for anticipating the ensuing events" (Kelly, 1955, p. 64).

Such improvement of prediction may for some people take the form of a constriction and sharpening of the construct system, to enable it to predict better and better within a limited range of situations.

For others, it may take the form of a broadening of the system's scope and a widening of the range of situations in which predictions can be made. In either case, the particular path taken is the one that seems most likely to enhance the future ability of the construct system to anticipate events. Judgment regarding this path is, of course, made from within the construct system as it exists, and such judgment may be wrong—the choice may turn out to have an effect quite other than anticipated.

Stating his general view of motivation, Kelly remarks that

in our assumptive structure we do not specify, nor do we imply, that a person seeks "pleasure," that he has special "needs," that there are "rewards," or even that there are "satisfactions." In this sense, ours is not a commercial theory. To our way of thinking, there is a continuing movement toward the anticipation of events, rather than a series of barters for temporal satisfactions, and this movement is the essence of human life itself. (Kelly, 1955, p. 68)

"MAN-AS-SCIENTIST."   By emphasizing human beings' use of a personal construct system to predict and control events, Kelly points out that his theory can explain his own behavior as a scientist in the same way that it explains his subject's or client's behavior as a person. Kelly suggests that there is something rather patronizing—perhaps even absurd—about the psychologist who assumes that one set of principles governs his or her behavior and an entirely different set governs the behavior of everyone else. By making both scientists' and other human beings' lives center around a search for understanding, prediction, and control—by saying that every person is in his or her own way a scientist testing hypotheses about the world—Kelly neatly avoids this dilemma.

ANXIETY AND GUILT.   For personal construct theory, **anxiety** is "the recognition that the events with which one is confronted lie outside the range of convenience of one's construct system" (Kelly, 1955, p. 495). In other words, one becomes anxious when one's ability to construe and predict events is threatened with failure. The degree of anxiety will reflect the seriousness with which the situation is perceived: Does it appear that some slight patching up of the construct system may be able to deal with the problem, or is it possible that a fundamental defect has been uncovered?

The anxiety-proneness of a personal construct system may be related to the permeability of its constructs. A person with relatively impermeable constructs, if confronted with new events, will in general be less able to accommodate them than will a person with more permeable constructs.

In personal construct theory, anxiety then, arises from a perceived inadequacy of the personal construct system. **Guilt**, on the other hand, is related to role. Roles, it will be remembered, involve the construing of the constructs of others. Kelly distinguishes a class of roles, **core roles**, that are basic to the maintenance of an individual's identity. A child's role vis-à-vis his parents, for example, may have this character. Guilt results from perceived failure in a core role.

Suppose, says Kelly, that a man is walking across a busy street, holding the hand of his little girl and watching the traffic. He inadvertently steps into an open manhole, with the result that he breaks a leg, cracks several ribs, and loses the sight of his left eye. He will undoubtedly have a considerable reaction to this event. However, Kelly says, one thing is clear:

> *His feelings are quite different from what they would be if he had allowed his child to step into that open manhole, fracture her little leg, crack several ribs, and lose the sight of her left eye. . . . Moreover, the difference cannot be attributed merely to the fact that it is against the law of Moses to drop your children into open manholes, or that the clergy generally take a dim view of that sort of mistake, or that it tends to be counterrevolutionary. The difference is pretty much a matter of the fact that the man's mistake has seriously involved someone other than himself. And more than that, it has involved someone to whom he, in his role as a parent, is deeply committed. (Kelly, in Maher, 1969, p. 177)*

PSYCHOLOGICAL DEVELOPMENT.   For Kelly, a discussion of psychological development requires no radically new concepts. Psychological development simply reflects the evolution of the personal construct system. However, certain kinds of constructs may be especially important in childhood. One of these is the use of a particular person to define a construct. Father may stand for authority, for example, or Mother for social belongingness.

Constructs that develop before the child is competent with language may present special problems later in life. Such constructs are often highly permeable, showing themselves in a variety of situations, and they may serve as core role constructs. At the same time, because of their ancient and preverbal character, the person is not aware of their existence or of the extent of their influence. For example, a woman may often be amazed to discover the degree to which her role constructs governing her relationships with men are affected by her preverbal constructs originally defined by the way she construed her father.

Kelly places no special emphasis on heredity in his theory. Presumably, it is responsible for people having some of the initial properties they have, but Kelly does not discuss this. He does have some comments on learning:

Learning is assumed to take place. It has been built into the assumptive structure of the system. . . . Learning is not a special class of psychological processes; it is synonymous with any and all psychological processes. It is not something that happens to a person on occasion; it is what makes him a person in the first place. . . . One may say that learning has been given a preeminent position in the psychology of personal constructs, even though it has been taken out of circulation as a special topic. In the language of administrators, it has been "kicked upstairs." (Kelly, 1955, p. 75ff.)

RESEARCH EMPHASES AND METHODS

The spirit alone of Kelly's theory of man-as-scientist should encourage empirical exploration of his constructs. His very notion that human beings are constantly construing their worlds should give us an incentive to examine the "range of convenience" of Kelly's own constructs. And no doubt this has happened. The most immediate stimulus to the considerable volume of empirical research arising from personal construct theory, however, seems to have been Kelly's invention of a measurement device, the Role Construct Repertory Test, or "Rep test," as it is popularly referred to.

Recall the brief scene with which we opened our discussion of Kelly. The clinical psychologist was using a version of the Rep test designed for individual clinical testing. Other versions have been developed for group testing. A popular variant for research is the "repertory grid," in which the columns of a rectangular matrix represent people and the rows represent personal constructs.

For example, the repertory grid has been used by Bieri and his co-workers to assess the complexity of an individual's construct system. Such cognitive complexity has been related to a number of phenomena of social perception and clinical judgment. Box 8.4 describes one such study.

Research has been carried out with the Rep test on a variety of topics in clinical, social, and personality psychology. There has been research, for example, on how evidence that fails to confirm people's constructs affects them, on how the personal constructs of schizophrenics differ from those of normal people, and on how matches and mismatches between the personal construct systems of psychotherapists and their clients affect the success of psychotherapy. A number of studies have focused on Kelly's conception of social role—the construing of another's constructs. These studies have involved interactions between husbands and wives, friends, and strangers.

It is a curious fact that although Kelly's theory arose in the American Midwest and bears many marks of its origin, personal construct research has caught on more in Europe, particularly in Great

BOX 8.4   Cognitive Complexity and Prediction

According to personal construct theory, people's construct systems develop in the direction of making them better able to predict events. James Bieri reasoned that this should mean that people with better differentiated personal construct systems should be more accurate at predicting other people's behavior than would those whose personal construct systems were less well differentiated. He tested this hypothesis in an experiment (Bieri, 1955).

Bieri measured the complexity of his subjects' construct systems by means of a version of Kelly's Role Construct Repertory Test (described below). He then measured their ability to predict behavior by having them predict how two of their classmates would fill out a questionnaire concerning a variety of social situations. The questionnaire contained 12 multiple-choice items like the following:

You are working intently to finish a paper in the library when two people sit down across from you and distract you with their continual loud talking. Would you most likely:

 a. Move to another seat
 b. Let them know how you feel by your facial expression
 c. Try to finish up in spite of their talking
 d. Ask them to stop talking

The cognitive complexity measure was obtained as follows. The subjects (22 female and 12 male college students) filled out a 12×12 role construct repertory grid. That is, the names of 12 persons were listed by the subject along the top of the grid, and 12 combinations of three of these were used to arrive at constructs that were listed as labels of the 12 rows. Then the subject went through and marked other people in each row who were also describable by the construct.

A person received a high score for cognitive complexity if his or her construct system classified people in many different ways, as shown by a great variety of patterns of marks on the rows of the grid. A low score meant that a construct system wound up classifying everybody pretty much the same way.

Subjects had also filled out the behavior prediction questionnaire for themselves, so it was possible for Bieri to break the correct predictions down into those cases where the subject had accurately predicted the other person's behavior when it was different from his

or her own and those cases that could have been got right without the use of personal constructs at all if subjects simply decided how they would behave themselves and said that the other person would do the same thing.

And the results?

On the whole, Bieri's prediction was supported. The subjects who obtained higher cognitive complexity scores were significantly more accurate predictors ($r = .29$). Moreover, this accuracy was obtained by correct prediction of differences from themselves ($r = .35$), not of the identical behavior ($r = .02$). A tendency to judge incorrectly that the other person would act like oneself went with low cognitive complexity ($r = -.40$). The ability to predict the behavior of classmates was apparently not just a matter of a person's general intelligence. A verbal intelligence measure available for most of the subjects only had correlations in the range .01 to .12 with the prediction task.

Personal construct systems, in at least this case, seem to behave in the way that Kelly's theory says they should.

Britain, than it has in the United States. Since Kelly's death, several volumes on personal construct research have been published by British and Canadian psychologists (see, for example, Adams-Webber, 1979; Bannister and Mair, 1968; Stringer and Bannister, 1979).

Lewin was intensely interested in the dynamics of group interaction. Encounter groups, whose origins is traced to Lewin's early work, often help people learn to communicate better and thus to interact in more satisfying ways.

EVALUATION

Kurt Lewin's influence on many areas of psychology, including both personality and social psychology, has been great. There is little question that in the latter area, his has been one of the most seminal minds in the history of the field. The application of his field theory in such areas as group dynamics and action research has led to a tremendous amount of investigatory activity and has established whole new fields of endeavor. Lewin, for instance, helped found the National Training Laboratories in Bethel, Maine, out of which the sensitivity training, or T-group, movement developed. And the origins of the encounter group have been traced to a workshop for community leaders on interracial tension conducted by Lewin in 1946 (Burton, 1974).

Lewin's influence can be seen in many subsequent research endeavors in social psychology. For example, Rokeach's (1960) work on the open and closed mind uses Lewinian concepts such as that of differentiation. Festinger's (1957, 1964) theory of cognitive dissonance makes use of Lewinian ideas about conflict and decision making and the change that takes place after decisions are made. And Heider's (1958) work on social perception and interpersonal relations draws on Lewin's field theoretical approach and his use of topology.

Other areas of psychology have shown a strong Lewinian influence as well. In motivational psychology, Atkinson's theory of achievement motivation (Atkinson, 1964; Atkinson and Feather, 1966) is an extension and elaboration of Lewin's work on level of aspiration. Lewin's treatment of conflict has heavily influenced subsequent writers (e.g., Miller and Dollard—see Chapter 14). The whole field of ecological or environmental psychology (Barker, 1968; Mehrabian and Russell, 1974) has arisen in part because of Lewin's call for an investigation of the relationship between the life space and its "foreign hull."

Lewin's field theory has not been without criticism, however. Some of this criticism has been focused on its general characteristics as a theoretical structure; some has been directed to more specific issues.

What are the primary criticisms?

Several writers have suggested that Lewinian life space diagrams can be drawn only after the fact—that they are in effect descriptions of what is already known and have little, if any, predictive power (e.g., Brolyer, 1936–37; Garrett, 1939; Lindzey, 1952; London, 1944). According to this view, there is a loose metaphorical or illustrative relationship among the ideas, the mathematics, the diagrams, and the empirical data rather than a tight and rigorous one. Spence remarks, "Lewin sets up a most attractive program for theory. Taken in conjunction with his interesting experiments, the illusion is nicely created that there is some connection between them" (Spence, 1944, p. 54 fn).

Lewin agrees that predictive theory is better than merely descriptive theory, although he suggests that a theory of the latter kind that integrates a diversity of known facts may be of considerable scientific value. He points, moreover, to the nonobvious predictions tested in his own research and that of his students as evidence that his theory does indeed have predictive power (Lewin, 1951, p. 20).

A second criticism of Lewinian theory is that it fails to specify clearly the relation of the life space to the external environment (Brunswik, 1943; Cartwright, 1959; Leeper, 1943; Tolman, 1948). According to several critics, because Lewin fails to conceptualize clearly how the external environment produces change in the life space, and vice versa, his field theory risks falling into the trap of subjectivism. Lewin replies that he does take into account aspects of the objective environment that affect the life space at any given time. Both in his experimental investigations and in his action-oriented research, he has provided many examples of how external events can come to modify life spaces. In fact he pioneered in an area of investigation that he called "psychological ecology," which studies the way in which the constraints of the external world affects the psychological environment (see Lewin, 1951, Chapter 8).

A third criticism, voiced particularly by those for whom the person is a product of heredity, maturation, and learning, faults Lewin for failing to take the person's past history into account (Garrett, 1939; Leeper, 1943). Lewin denies that field theory is not interested in development or in historical problems or in the effect of previous experience. He feels that his principle of "contemporaneity," that only current events can influence behavior, has been widely misunderstood to mean that field theorists are unconcerned about the effects of previous experience: "Nothing can be more mistaken" (Lewin, 1951, p. 45). Lewin points to his strong, continuing interest—and that of his students—in developmental problems and stresses the frequent necessity of using past-history information in inferring the present state of someone's life space.

On the positive side, much can be said in favor of Lewin's theory. We have already mentioned its impressive ability to generate empirical research, although the distinction between the theory's direct effects and Lewin's remarkable personal influence on students and colleagues is difficult to draw here.

Lewin's theory had an important and timely historical influence on theorizing about personality. For one thing, Lewin clearly recognized that to encompass the vital aspects of human behavior, a theory would have to be multidimensional in scope—it would have to be a field theory, embracing a network of interacting variables rather than the pairs of variables that an oversimplified stimulus–response (S–R) psychology was emphasizing in the 1920s and 1930s. The fact that the student of today has the option of studying human psychology from more than just the S–R approach owes much to Lewin's pioneering work.

Lewin also helped to make a subjective frame of reference scientifically respectable at a time when a narrow behaviorism was the dominant voice in psychology. His concept of the life space and of the psychological environment as distinct from the external environment was a most important contribution. It reminded people that human beings are not robots, simply responding to stimuli according to their programs, but feeling, thinking, cognizing creatures, motivated by psychological needs, intentions, hopes, and aspirations and behaving both selectively and creatively.

Lewin's influence also led to a great increase in naturalistic research, that is, research performed in more or less natural settings—children at play, workers in factories, people of all ages engaged in various sorts of group activities. Here, some of the artificiality of the laboratory experiment could be avoided and the validity of a hypothesis could be tested with minimal manipulation of human subjects.

In summary, the power of Lewin's field theory lies more in the influence it has had than in its formal completeness or its mathematical development. It has spurred research in many areas of psychology. It has opened doors to new ways of looking at personality and new methods of investigating such central topics as motivation, emotion, and psychological development. "Lewin's basic notions . . . have a wealth of implicit meaning which has not been exhausted, and they are therefore still full of promise for further development" (Heider, 1959, p. 119). This view remains valid. Lewin's theory of the person in a psychological environment is still very much alive.

George Kelly's theory has been significant both as a theory of personality and (by means of the Rep test) as a stimulus to personality research. It focused on human beings' understanding of their world at a time when cognitive approaches were becoming increasingly attractive to psychologists. Like Lewin's theory, however, it has not escaped criticism.

Perhaps the most frequent criticism of Kelly's theory has been that it shortchanges the emotional and motivational aspects of human existence. In an early appraisal, Jerome Bruner said of the theory that it "fails signally . . . in dealing convincingly with the human passions" (1956, p. 356). Bruner found personal construct theory more persuasive in dealing with "the post-adolescent peer group of Columbus, Ohio" than with the heights and depths of human experience. Carl Rogers also noted a "lack of any sense of depth" in Kelly's discussion of psychotherapy, and an impression that for Kelly therapy is seen as "almost entirely an intellectual function" (1956, p. 357ff.). W. A. Russell argues that Kelly's theory of the individual as simply active fails to explain the fact that the individual's activity level varies immensely and, thus, "ignores a decade or more of significant evidence on the effects of arousal change" (1969, p. 432). As the sole explanation of the direction of behavior, expansion of the construct system via the principle of elaborative choice is seen by critics as inadequate (Bruner, 1956; Russell, 1969). Although it may not be absolutely impossible to deal with self-limiting human behaviors—suicide, to take an extreme case—under this principle, it is surely not easy.

Other critics have argued that Kelly's theory fails to provide a complete analysis of behavioral processes. Personal constructs are held to be key determinants of behavior, but the details of how such constructs are acquired are not well specified. Mischel (1971), for example, argues that Kelly needs also to clarify the conditions under which one of a person's constructs rather than another is applied in a given situation. Mischel also points to difficulties posed for personal construct theory by cases in which behavioral changes appear to precede cognitive changes—the latter cannot then be used as explanations of the former.

A third kind of criticism that has been made of personal construct theory faults it for its insularity. Bruner comments, "With respect to ancestry, Professor Kelly seems to care little for it" (1956, p. 356). Bruner mentions Piaget, Sullivan, Allport, and Lewin as among theorists whose relations to Kelly's work might have been profitably discussed. The tendency toward a narrow orthodoxy among many of Kelly's followers has also been commented on (e.g., Russell, 1969; Rosenberg, 1980; Funder, 1981). "With few exceptions the main role of personal construct theory has been to use it, more or less unquestioningly, as a framework for formulating hypotheses and interpreting findings. . . . History tells us that the more successful theories and ideologies are those that generate controversy, modification, and branching rather than orthodoxy and reverence" (Rosenberg, 1980, p. 899).

Or one can look at the other side of the coin and emphasize the virtues of these vices. One can see Kelly's work as a bold and original theory, penetrating to the heart of psychological problems in a radical new way for which much traditional obsessing over the details of learning and motivation is simply irrelevant. Kelly has always maintained that any theory, including his, does some things better than others. It is after all by what a theory can do within its "range of convenience," not by what it does not do, that, in Kelly's view, it should be judged.

Kelly has been amused by attempts to classify personal construct theory:

> *I have been so puzzled over the early labeling of personal construct theory as "cognitive" that several years ago I set out to write another short book to make it clear that I wanted no part of cognitive theory. The manuscript was about a third completed when I gave a lecture at Harvard University with the title, "Personal Construct Theory as a Line of Inference." Following the lecture, Professor Gordon Allport explained to the students that my theory was not a "cognitive" theory but an "emotional" theory. Later the same afternoon, Dr. Henry Murray called me aside and said, "You know, don't you, that you are really an existentialist."* (in Maher, 1969, p. 216)

In placing Kelly in a chapter with Kurt Lewin we have expressed our own view that Kelly's most distinctive feature is the emphasis that he shares with Lewin on the person as an active constructor of his or her own unique world. We recognize, of course, that Kelly might well choose to add our act of classification to his catalog of misguided attempts to pigeonhole personal construct theory. Nevertheless, he can hardly fault us for using our own personal construct system to make sense of this mysterious and significant object that we have encountered.

SUMMARY

KURT LEWIN

1. Field theory sees behavior as a function of the currently existing field, or **life space**, which is composed of the person plus the psychological environment.

2. The **person** is divided into an **inner-personal** region, representing motivational aspects of behavior, and a **perceptual–motor** region.

3. The **psychological environment**, the environment as it affects behavior, is also divided into **regions**, representing values, activities, and other areas of the person's experience.

4. The life space is surrounded by the **foreign hull**, the objective, physical world. Events in this world affect behavior only by way of the changes they make in the life space.

5. Communication among regions is affected by several properties of regions, the most important of which is the **permeability** of their boundaries.

6. There are as many regions in the life space as there are **facts** in existence at a given time, and the life space changes constantly in number of regions, strength or weakness of boundaries, and so on.

7. An **event** is the interaction of two or more currently existing facts; only present facts can determine present events.

8. **Psychical energy** is created by the buildup of tension in one system vis-à-vis others and the consequent disequilibrium. **Tension** has two properties: it tends to become equalized, and it tends to exert pressure on the boundary of the system in which it is contained.

9. Tension increases as a result of the arousal of a **need**, and there are as many needs as there are distinguishable cravings. **Quasi-needs** are momentary intentions that are often shaped by social factors.

10. Tension leads to action, when there exists a goal object with a positive **valence** and a **vector** that pushes the person toward that goal object.

11. With age, according to the principle of differentiation, behavior becomes more varied, freer in movement, more time extended, more organized, more hierarchical, and more complicated. The infant is governed by **simple interdependence**, in which tension systems are interchangeable; the adult is governed by **organizational interdependence**, in which behavior is integrated and organized hierarchically.

12. Connections among inner-personal regions were studied by Lewin and his students in a series of experiments using the method of **task substitution**.

GEORGE KELLY

13. Personal construct theory's **fundamental postulate** states that people's behavior is directed by the ways in which they anticipate events in the world around them.

14. People interpret events by means of the **personal construct**, in which things are seen as being alike and yet different from others.

15. Personal constructs are **dichotomous**; they have a **range of convenience**; they are **permeable** or **impermeable**; they have cognitive, motivational, and emotional aspects; and they may or may not be verbalized.

16. The **personal construct system** gives consistency and order to a person's constructs.

17. The **sociality corollary** of the fundamental postulate states that to the extent people can construe each other's construction processes, they can interact with each other. In such interactions they fulfill **social roles**.

18. Human beings are the active constructors of their worlds rather than passive reactors to forces, internal or external, that are more powerful than themselves.

19. Through **elaborative choice**, people make choices so as to move their construct systems in the direction of a greater ability to predict events.

20. The same principles of prediction and control govern the scientist's and the ordinary person's behavior.

21. Anxiety arises when the person's ability to interpret and predict events is threatened with failure. It is more likely to arise when a person whose constructs are relatively impermeable is confronted with new events.

22. Guilt arises from the perceived failure in a **core role**, such as the role a father plays in respect to his child.

23. Early constructs may be defined by specific people (father = authority). Preverbal constructs may come later to govern a person's behavior without his or her being aware of them.

24. Learning and motivation are basic aspects of personality constructs, not separate processes.

25. The **Role Construct Repertory Test**, which measures a person's own idiosyncratic way of sorting out the people and events he or she encounters, has been used in research in clinical, social, and personality psychology.

26. Although Kurt Lewin's influence is seen today in many areas of social psychological research, his personality theory has been criticized for being descriptive rather than predictive, for not clearly stating how the life space interacts with the external environment, and for not dealing specifically with the effects of heredity, maturation, and learning. Lewin's field theory did focus attention on the multidimensionality of behavior and, with its concept of the psychological environment, it restored the subjective analysis of experience to respectability. The theory opened new doors, making it possible to investigate many psychological issues for the first time.

27. George Kelly's theory has been criticized for neglecting the emotional and motivational aspects of human behavior, for failing to specify the ways in which personal constructs are acquired and applied, and for tending to shun the use of other relevant theories and conceptions, adhering narrowly to its own framework. Personal construct theory is, however, a bold and original theory. Its most distinctive feature is its emphasis on the person as an active constructor of his or her unique world.

SUGGESTED READING

A selection of papers from the German phase of Lewin's career were published in English under the title *A Dynamic Theory of Personality* (1935). *Principles of Topological Psychology* (1936) is a systematic treatment of Lewin's structural theory of the person and the environment in the life space. *Field Theory in Social Science* (1951) and *Resolving Social Conflicts* (1948) are collections of papers from the American phase of Lewin's career. The 1951 book contains the more general papers on his field theory; the 1948 volume contains papers addressed more to social issues: cultural change, conflict, and intergroup relations.

A good idea of the quantity and variety of research developing from Lewin's ideas can be obtained from the article on him by Lippitt in the *International Encyclopedia of the Social Sciences* (1968) or from Duetsch's article on "Field Theory in Social Psychology" in the *Handbook of Social Psychology* (Lindzey and Aronson, 1968). And a good description and analysis of Lewinian field theory may be found in a chapter by Cartwright (1959).

Tolman, "Kurt Lewin" (1948), offers a brief appreciation of Lewin's life and career, written at the time of Lewin's death. More recently, Marrow, *The Practical Theorist: The Life and Work of Kurt Lewin* (1969), has written a biography that also deals in some detail with Lewin's field theory and his professional work in general.

A pleasant way to start reading George Kelly is to browse among the selected papers published under the title *Clinical Psychology and Personality* (Maher, 1969). A number of these were originally presented as talks rather than as formal publications, and several are quite entertaining. For a brief but a more systematic presentation of the theory, see Kelly, "A Summary Statement of a Cognitively Oriented Comprehensive Theory of Behavior" (1970). Another chapter-length presentation of the theory, by a former student of Kelly's is Sechrest, "The Psychology of Personal Constructs: George Kelly" (1963).

The serious student of Kelly's work will of course want to read at least some part of Kelly's major work, *The Psychology of Personal Constructs* (1955). Volume 1 describes the theory and the Role Construct Repertory Test and will be of most general interest. Volume 2 largely treats specific clinical topics.

Reviews of the research generated by Kelly's theory are available in Bannister and Mair, *The Evaluation of Personal Constructs* (1968); Stringer and Bannister, *Constructs of Sociality and Individuality* (1979); and Adams-Webber, *Personal Construct Theory: Concepts and Applications* (1979). A recent summary of this research may be found in a chapter by Adams-Webber, ''Personal Construct Theory: Research into Basic Concepts'' (1981), and a short description of variants of the repertory grid appears in a chapter by Fransella, ''Repertory Grid Technique'' (1981).

Brief biographical sketches of George Kelly may be found in Maher's 1969 book and in an obituary by Thompson (1968).

Part 3   Focus on Enduring Characteristics

This third part of the book considers the work of five distinctive theorists. It explores the broad and versatile theories of Henry Murray (Chapter 9) and Gordon Allport (Chapter 10), the biologically rooted theory of William Sheldon (Chapter 11), and the factor theories of Raymond Cattell and Hans Eysenck (Chapter 12). These theorists tend to focus on stable, enduring features of the personality; they are sometimes called trait or type theorists. Although several (Murray, Cattell, and Eysenck) have had clinical training and experience, all are primarily academic psychologists.

All five theorists have been influenced by the psychometric tradition stemming from Sir Francis Galton, with its concern for accurate measurement of the ways in which individuals differ from one another in personality characteristics. And in fact all five have devised important psychological tests or measurement procedures that have been used extensively in psychological research and assessment, both by the theorists themselves and by others.

Once more, you will probably wish to review Figure 3 more carefully after reading about the theories. Even a brief glance at the chart, however, suggests that the theorists considered in this part of the book are concerned with stable characteristics of personality, either the acquisitions of learning or hereditary factors. They emphasize the person over the situation or take an interactionist view, and they tend to call upon a fairly considerable number of motives to explain behavior. On the whole, they tend to look at normal rather than abnormal behavior, although most of these theorists have studied abnormal behavior in one context or another and have made use of such work in formulating their theories. As you can see from the chart, on the remaining dimensions of personality theory, this group represents a variety of positions.

Figure 3   Trait–type theorist and the personality dimensions.

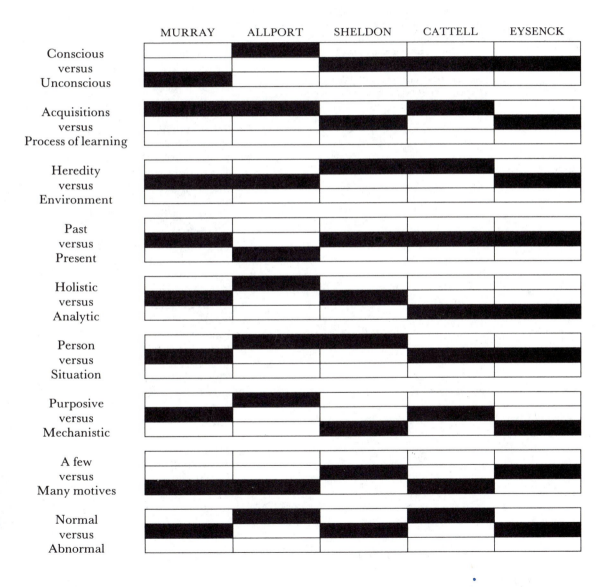

Chapter nine

9.

To study human nature patiently, to arrive at understanding, to gain some mastery; there would be little hope in the enterprise if it were not for the history of science, the steady, unassertive, conquering pace of disinterested observation, experiment, and reflection.

HENRY A. MURRAY

Personology: Henry Murray

Henry A. Murray has brought a particularly varied and complex background to the study of the human personality. A former surgeon and a research biochemist, he is an experienced psychoanalyst and an academic psychologist, and he holds a place in literature as an expert on the life and work of the author Herman Melville. "Not since William James has there been an American psychologist so versatile" or one who has written with such "verve and boldness" (Adelson, 1981).

In the 1930s, Murray coined the term **personology** to describe the branch of psychology that studies individual "human lives and the factors that influence their course" (1938, p. 4). Firmly convinced that to understand the meaning of any single process of personality one must have some grasp of the whole, Murray has emphasized the need for "systematic full length studies of individuals." He has repeatedly pointed out the meaninglessness of much data obtained in the vacuum, as it were, of the laboratory, insisting that we will make little progress as long as we study the person primarily out of context and under contrived conditions.

Murray's conviction that each segment of human behavior must be understood in conjunction with the rest of the functioning person has led him to present a theory that is strongly holistic. Unlike some other holistic theorists, however, Murray includes within his basic unit of study the environment in which the person functions, and he has developed an elaborate set of concepts to represent environmental forces. In emphasizing the interaction between the person and his or her environment, Murray anticipated by some 30 years the "interactionist" position now widely held by investigators who until recently had argued hotly for one side or the other of the "person–situation debate".

Murray's clinical background has contributed to his belief in the importance of describing the complexity of each individual case, and he has evolved extensive systems (taxonomies)

309

for classifying data. At the same time, he has devised ways to select and define variables that are central to understanding the person. Murray was one of the first investigators in academic psychology to give serious audience to psychoanalytic thought and to attempt to translate Freudian and Jungian concepts into testable hypotheses. Thus, he has contributed greatly to finding empirical support for concepts and theories that originated in the psychoanalytic, or psychotherapeutic, setting.

Murray has always taken as self-evident the essential uniqueness of each person and, indeed, of each behavioral event. Every piece of behavior "leaves behind it some trace of its occurrence . . . [for example,] the germ of an idea, . . . a more affectionate attachment to some person, a slight improvement of skill," and as a result, "by scarcely perceptible gradations," the person changes from day to day (Murray and Kluckhohn, 1953, p. 10). Thus each time people meet, they are unique and so is their interaction.

Although his clinical training and experience often required him to focus on what is not normal, Murray, in his lifelong study of personality has been concerned primarily with the normal individual. As he puts it, examining only the "aberrant or neurotic features" of people is like studying only the criminal and radical elements within a country; neither method produces an accurate picture, either of the human being or of society at large (Murray, 1938).

Probably the most distinctive feature of Murray's theory is its emphasis on a highly complex system of motivational concepts. Within this scheme, past and present factors both carry weight in determining behavior, and unconscious motivation figures importantly.

Unlike most of the theorists we have studied so far, Murray has consistently emphasized the links between psychological events and underlying physiological processes. Today, as neurophysiology, biochemistry, and related disciplines uncover more and more information about the role of the central nervous system in psychological functioning, Murray's insistence on regarding the brain as the locus of personality seems prophetic.

A DEFINITION OF PERSONALITY

According to Murray, personality is an abstraction formulated by the theorist and not simply a description of a person's behavior. That is, personality is a formulation based both on observable behavior and on factors that as yet we can only infer from what is observable.

Despite its essentially abstract nature, Murray's conception of personality assumes that there are central organizing and governing processes in the individual, processes whose function it is to integrate the conflicting forces to which the person is exposed, satisfy the person's needs, and plan for the attainment of the person's goals. Person-

BOX 9.1   Henry A. Murray (1893–   )

Henry A. Murray seemed to be heading for a career in research biology and biochemistry when he spent three weeks with Carl Jung that literally changed his life: " 'The great floodgates of the wonder-world swung open,' and I saw things that my philosophy had never dreamt of. Within a month a number of bi-horned problems were resolved, and I went off decided on depth psychology. I had *experienced* the unconscious, something not to be drawn out of books" (Murray, 1940, p. 153).

Born and raised in New York City, Murray took his undergraduate degree at Harvard and then enrolled at Columbia College of Physicians and Surgeons. After he was graduated, in 1919, at the head of his class, he spent two years in a surgical internship. Eventually, he decided against a career in surgery, however, in part because of an early and inadequately

treated visual problem. Having obtained a master's degree in biology, he did embryological research at what is now Rockefeller University and then took a Ph.D. in biochemistry at Cambridge (England). It was during his Easter vacation in 1925 that he traveled to Zurich to meet Carl Jung.

Shortly after Murray returned to the United States, he was offered an assistantship by Morton Prince, who had just founded the Harvard Psychological Clinic. Despite Murray's lack of formal training in psychology, Murray was soon made director of the clinic, and until the outbreak of World War II, he presided over an intensely creative theoretical and empirical enterprise. In an effort to investigate and to formulate a theory of the human personality, Murray gathered about him a group of able students and scholars from a variety of fields. Erik Erikson (Chapter 3) was among the scholars who contributed to the work of *Explorations in Personality* (1938), a partial record of the generativity of this era, and many of today's prominent figures in the field of personality—Robert R. Holt, Gardner Lindzey, Donald W. MacKinnon, Saul Rosenzweig, R. Nevitt Sanford, M. Brewster Smith, Silvan S. Tomkins, and Robert W. White, among others—were students or close associates of Murray's. These people carried away not only the insights generated in their joint endeavors but the spirit

and love of creative thinking and exploration. They are probably the largest cluster of influential contemporary personality psychologists associated with any single theorist.

From 1943 to 1946, as a lieutenant colonel in the Army Medical Corps, Murray established and directed an assessment service for the Office of Strategic Services. His organization had the difficult task of screening candidates for dangerous and secret missions by evaluating emotional stability, capacity to withstand stress, and interpersonal skills. In 1946 Murray was awarded the Legion of Merit for his work.

Returning to Harvard in 1947, Murray lectured on clinical psychology in the new Department of Social Relations. Within two years, he had established the Psychological Clinic Annex, where he continued, with colleagues and students, to pursue his research on personality.

In 1961, just before his formal retirement, Murray received the Distinguished Scientific Contribution award of the American Psychological Association, and in 1969 the APA presented him with its Gold Medal award for a lifetime of contribution to the field. The Henry A. Murray Research Center for the Study of Lives was established in 1979 at Radcliffe College.

Murray was married for 45 years to Josephine Rantoul, and the couple had one child, Josephine Lee Murray, who is a pediatrician. Several years after his first wife's death, Murray married Caroline C. Fisher, and he lives at present in Cambridge only two blocks from William James Hall, where he continues his study on the life and work of Herman Melville.

ality must reflect not only the enduring and recurrent elements of behavior but also what is novel and unique. And personality must reflect the functioning of the person over an entire lifetime: the individual events in the person's life can be understood only as they relate to the person's past, present, and anticipated future.

Finally, Murray strongly emphasizes the importance of linking psychological processes and events with the structures and functioning of the brain, even though we do not yet know precisely how these things are connected. For Murray, the phenomena that make up personality are absolutely dependent on central nervous system functioning; as he says succinctly, "No brain, no personality" (Murray, 1951a, p. 267).

ENDURING ASPECTS OF PERSONALITY

Consistent with his view of the person as operating within a field of forces, Murray sees personalities as in a state of flux. Thus, like some of the theorists discussed in Part 1 (e.g., Alfred Adler and Harry Stack Sullivan), Murray is primarily concerned with the dynamic aspects of personality functioning, and his concepts of "need" and "press," as we will soon see, are the most crucial of his theoretical formulations. These concepts, although essentially dynamic, do have considerable stability over time.

Murray probably comes closest to a structural view of personality in his concepts of id, ego, superego, and ego ideal, which he has borrowed from psychoanalytic theory and which he uses much as did Freud. His own formulations, however, of proceedings, serials, serial programs, schedules, abilities, and achievements are unique to his system of thought, and we will explore these latter phenomena next.

BEHAVIORAL UNITS: PROCEEDINGS AND SERIALS

The basic unit of behavior is the **proceeding**, which is a time-limited interaction between a person and one or more others or between a person and an object. A proceeding is "a temporal segment" that lasts long enough for a "dynamically significant pattern of behavior" to be completed (Murray, 1951a, p. 269). There is a certain amount of variation in the length of proceedings. For example, a proceeding may be as lengthy as an interview with a prospective employer or as brief as greeting a friend.

The proceeding is not as small a unit of behavior as that used by some other investigators, notably learning theorists. It embodies Murray's belief, however, that a person's behavior must be considered within its context. Thus, it is the smallest unit possible in his framework.

The **serial** is a series of proceedings and thus a longer unit of behavior. Because "no one proceeding . . . can be understood without reference to those which have led up to it and without reference to the actor's aims and expectations, his design for the future" (Murray, 1951a, p. 272), it is important and often necessary to study behavior over a longer period of time. For example, to understand the full meaning of a particular job interview, we might need to look at the serial of the person's entire career (see Fig. 9.1).

ORDINATION, ABILITIES, AND ACHIEVEMENTS

Ordination is Murray's term for the higher mental processes by which a person selects and puts into operation a plan of action that has a desired end state. Ordination has two components: **serial programs** and **schedules**. Serial programs are orderly arrangements of subgoals that stretch into the future and are designed to lead to some major goal. Thus, a person who wises to become president of a corporation may have as subgoals obtaining promotions, joining a club, and buying a home in which he or she can entertain.

People use schedules to time the actions they take in satisfying their needs so as to avoid conflict between competing needs and wishes; that is, people plan their time. If a person wants, for example, to put in long hours at her job because of an ambition to rise to the top but also wants to attend concerts because of a deep love for music, she may decide to buy tickets for events on the weekends only or to work over a weekend when a particularly good concert is being given on a Wednesday evening.

The **abilities** and **achievements** of the person are to Murray an extremely important part of the personality. Murray's research appraises subjects in terms of such areas of functioning as mechanical skills, leadership, intellectual achievements, and sexual behavior. Abilities and achievements indicate both what a person is capable of doing and what he or she actually does with knowledge gained. Thus, they illuminate the nature of a person's creative and plan-making processes.

Murray has been sharply critical of psychology for projecting a negative image of human beings. For Murray, what a person can and does do is just as significant as what he or she cannot do. In this connection, it is interesting to note Murray's criticism of Freud's (1910) exploration of the personality of Leonardo da Vinci. Murray (1968a) takes Freud to task for having totally ignored the healthy, joyous, and creative aspects of da Vinci's life and work.

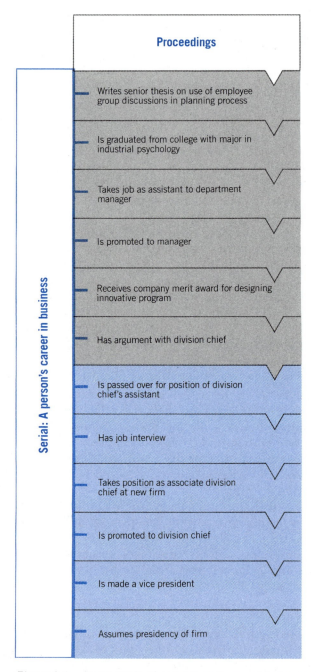

Figure 9.1   An example of a serial and some of its proceedings. Clearly, each proceeding here may also be a serial—that is, it may include a number of other, shorter proceedings. (Based on Murray, 1951a.)

PERSONALITY DYNAMICS

For Murray (1951a), the most important thing to discover about a person is the overall **directionality**, or goal orientation, of the person's activities, whether the latter are internal, as in thought, or external, as in speech and physical action. This concern with the intent of the person has led Murray to evolve a complex and very carefully worked out system of motivational constructs.

Although the trend in psychology has been to use a minimal number of concepts in explaining motivation (in Adler's system, for example, striving for superiority is the one, overarching motive), Murray has insisted that the complexity of human motives requires us to consider a large number of variables. His attempts to provide empirical definitions of these variables go beyond any other efforts in the area of motivation.

Let us begin by considering Murray's view of the notion of tension reduction and then examine his concept of need, by far the most influential of his motivational concepts and the one that represents essentially internal motivation. Then we can explore Murray's concept of press, which represents the environmental determinants of behavior, as well as several other constructs that elaborate need, press, or both.

TENSION REDUCTION

Like Freud and others, Murray says that in general, when a need is aroused, we are in a state of tension, and satisfying that need reduces the tension. Gradually, as the child develops, he or she learns to attend to objects and to perform actions that in the past have seemed to reduce tension.

For Murray, however, this is not the whole story. In the first place, people often actively seek to develop or increase tension in order to heighten the pleasure that follows upon **tension reduction**. For example, the pleasure of sexual intercourse is enhanced by affectionate and erotic stimulation (foreplay) before the sex act itself. In the second place, in some kinds of needs, such as those involved in play or artistic activity, pleasure accompanies the activity involved in satisfying the need; thus, pleasure is not necessarily a function of increasing or decreasing tension.

NEED: THE TERMS OF THE PERSON

According to Murray, **need** is a construct that stands for ''a force . . . in the brain region'' that organizes various processes such as perception, thinking, and action so as to change an existing and unsatisfying condition. A need can be provoked by internal processes, but more often it is stimulated by environmental factors. Typically, a need is accompanied by a specific feeling, or emotion, and it has a particular way of expressing itself in seeking resolution (Murray, 1938, pp. 123–125).

There are six criteria for inferring the existence of a need. Five of these are observations that can be made by an investigator; the sixth requires the participation of the person being studied:

1. The end result of the person's behavior
2. The particular pattern of the behavior
3. The fact that the person attends and responds to a particular class of stimuli
4. The person's expression of a particular emotion
5. The person's expression of satisfaction or dissatisfaction at the end result
6. The person's subjective report of feelings, intentions, and goals

Using all these criteria and studying a small group of subjects intensively, Murray (1938) and his colleagues at Harvard arrived at a tentative list of 20 needs that appeared to them to be the most significant. Table 9.1 lists 8 of these needs, as well as the emotions typically associated with them and the environmental factors, or press (see next section), that trigger or contribute to their presence. The table also gives examples of questionnaire items that, when answered by a person affirmatively, suggest that a given need is characteristic of the person.

Note that all the needs listed in Table 9.1 are **psychogenic**; that is, they are not connected with any specific organic processes and thus are assumed to be of psychological origin. In fact, with the exception of the need for sex, which has important physiological components, all 20 of the primary needs established by Murray and his group are chiefly psychogenic in nature; that is, insofar as they are physiological, they are of the brain, not the body. As you can see, in his concept of need, Murray has traveled far from the classical psychoanalytic approach to motivation, which traces all motives to the basic, organically related "life" and "death" instincts.

Of the 20 needs, 2 in particular have been the focus of a good deal of research. The **need for achievement**—or *n Ach*, as it is commonly abbreviated—has been examined extensively by John Atkinson (e.g., Atkinson, 1958; Atkinson and Feather, 1966; Atkinson and Raynor, 1974), David McClelland (e.g., McClelland, 1961; McClelland, Atkinson, Clark, and Lowell, 1953; McClelland and Winter, 1969), and others, and the **need for affiliation** has been explored by such investigators as Atkinson and Veroff (e.g., Atkinson, Heyns, and Veroff, 1954; Shipley and Veroff, 1952) and Schachter (1959). In addition, the power motive has been explored by McClelland (1975) and

TABLE 9.1   *Some Needs, Emotions, and Press*

NEED	BRIEF DEFINITION	ASSOCIATED EMOTIONS	CONTRIBUTING PRESS	SOME QUESTIONNAIRE ITEMS FOR MEASURING THE NEED
Abasement (n Aba)	To submit passively to external force; to admit inferiority, error, defeat; to blame or harm the self	Shame, guilt, inferiority	Aggression, dominance on part of others	I am more apt to give in than to continue a fight. I feel nervous and anxious in the presence of superiors. When something goes wrong I am more apt to blame myself than someone else.
Achievement (n Ach)	To accomplish something difficult; to master; to overcome obstacles and attain a high standard; to rival and surpass others	Zest, ambition	A task; a rival	I set difficult goals for myself that I attempt to reach. I work with energy at the job before me rather than dream about the future. I feel the spirit of competition in most of my activities.
Affiliation (n Aff)	To approach and enjoyably cooperate with someone; to win the affection of someone liked; to be a friend to someone	Trust, affection, love, empathy	Positive: a compatible person; negative: lack of friends	I like to hang around with a group of congenial people and talk about anything that comes up. I become very attached to my friends. I enjoy cooperating with others more than working alone.
Aggression (n Agg)	To overcome opposition forcefully; to fight; to revenge an injury; to punish, injure, kill another; to belittle, ridicule, curse, or slander someone	Anger, rage, jealousy, hatred	Aggression; superiority; rejection; a rival; a disliked other	I like physical competition, the rougher the better. When a friend annoys me, I tell him or her what I think. I often let myself go when I am angry. I try to get my own way regardless of others.
Autonomy (n Auto)	To get free; to resist coercion or restraint; to avoid domineering others; to be independent, unattached; to defy convention	Feeling restrained; anger	Positive: tolerance, open spaces; negative: physical restraint, dominance	I become stubborn and resistant when others attempt to coerce me; I go my own way regardless of the opinions of others; I try to avoid situations where I am expected to conform to conventional standards.

TABLE 9.1   (Continued)

NEED	BRIEF DEFINITION	ASSOCIATED EMOTIONS	CONTRIBUTING PRESS	SOME QUESTIONNAIRE ITEMS FOR MEASURING THE NEED
Dominance (n Dom)	To control one's human environment; to influence others by suggestion, persuasion, or command; to get others to do what one wants, admit one is "right"	Confidence	Inferior others; deference on part of others	I enjoy organizing or directing the activities of a group—team, club, or committee. When I am with someone, I am usually the one to make necessary decisions. I enjoy the sense of power I feel when I can control the actions of others.
Nurturance (n Nur)	To sympathize; to assist, protect, comfort someone who is helpless—a baby or anyone who is weak, disabled, tired, lonely, sick, confused; to help someone in danger	Pity, compassion, tenderness	Succorance, someone in need	I go out of my way to comfort people when they are in misery. I feel great sympathy for an "underdog" and usually do what I can for him or her. I enjoy putting my affairs aside to do someone a favor.
Succorance (n Suc)	To have one's needs gratified by a sympathetic person; to stay close to a protector; to be nursed, advised, forgiven, consoled	Anxiety of helplessness; insecurity; despair	Positive: nurturance; sympathy and help; negative: lack of support, loss, rejection, abandonment	I prefer to have some friend with me when I receive bad news. I am apt to rely on the judgment of someone else. I think of myself sometimes as neglected or unloved.

Source: Adapted from Murray (1938, pp. 151–187).
Note: Of Murray's 20 major needs, only 8 are presented here. The interested student is referred to Murray (1938) for information about the remaining 12: *counteraction, defendance, deference, exhibition, harmavoidance, infavoidance* (avoidance of humiliation or failure), *order* (neatness), *play, rejection, sentience* (sensuous expression), *sex,* and *understanding.*

Veroff (1957), and other variables, such as anxiety (Lindzey and Newburg, 1954) and aggression (Lindzey and Tejessy, 1956), have also been examined.

According to Murray, all needs are interrelated with each other in various ways. Certain needs demand satisfaction before others (Murray 1951b; see also the discussion of Maslow's hierarchy of needs, Chapter 6); for example, while a person is in pain or desperately hungry or thirsty, he or she will not be likely to try to satisfy needs such as those for understanding or play.

One need may conflict with another. For example, **autonomy**

This finalist in a race at the Wheelchair Olympics seems to exemplify Murray's much-studied need for achievement: setting high standards, overcoming obstacles, accomplishing difficult tasks.

may conflict with **affiliation**; a person may have a strong need to be independent and without ties, yet he or she may also need to share thoughts and experiences with someone else. Or one need may fuse with another; that is, one course of action may gratify more than one need. For example, **aggression** may fuse with **dominance**; a person may run for political office and wage a very hostile, ''mudslinging'' campaign.

In addition, one need may be subsidiary to another; that is, it may operate only to facilitate the other. For example, **abasement** may act in the service of **affiliation**, as when in order to preserve a friendship, a woman blames herself for some misunderstanding between her and her friend. Murray points out that tracing chains of subsidiation can be very helpful in revealing a person's basic motives.

PRESS: THE TERMS OF THE ENVIRONMENT

Murray's concept of press represents environmental determinants of behavior. A **press** is a property or attribute of another person, of an object, or of a condition of the environment that either helps or hinders the person's progress toward a given goal: ''The *press* of an object is what it can *do to the subject* or *for the subject*—the power that it has to af-

TABLE 9.2   Some Childhood Press

FAMILY INSUPPORT
  Family discord
  Inconsistent discipline
  Parental separation
  Absence of parent: father,
    mother
  Inferior parent: father, mother
  Poverty

DANGER OR MISFORTUNE
  Physical insupport, height
  Aloneness, darkness
  Accident

LACK OR LOSS OF
  Nourishment
  Possessions
  Companionship
  Variety

**PARENTAL WITHHOLDING
OF OBJECTS**

**PARENTAL REJECTION,
UNCONCERN, SCORN**

RIVAL
  Sibling (birth of)
  Other contemporary

AGGRESSION
  Maltreatment by elders: male,
    female
  Maltreatment by contem-
    poraries

**DOMINANCE, COERCION,
PROHIBITION**
  Discipline
  Religious training

DOMINANCE–NURTURANCE
  Parental ego idealism: mother,
    father
  Possessive parent: mother, father
  Oversolicitous parent: mother,
    father

NURTURANCE, INDULGENCE

**SUCCORANCE, DEMANDS FOR
TENDERNESS**

**DEFERENCE, PRAISE,
RECOGNITION**

AFFILIATION, FRIENDSHIPS

SEX
  Seduction: homosexual, hetero-
    sexual
  Parental intercourse

DECEPTION OR BETRAYAL

**PROLONGED OR FREQUENT
ILLNESS**
  Nervous, respiratory, cardiac,
    gastrointestinal

INFERIORITY
  Physical
  Social
  Intellectual

Source: Adapted from Murray (1938, pp. 291–292).

fect the well-being of the subject in one way or another'' (Murray, 1938, p. 121). A somewhat abbreviated list of a particular category of press—those of childhood—appears in Table 9.2.

It is important to distinguish two aspects of press: an **alpha** press is a quality of the environment as it exists in reality (to the degree that we can determine this); a **beta** press is an environmental quality as it is perceived by the person. For example, suppose a couple come home at the end of a day, and as the husband begins to tell his wife about a highly stressful meeting he has chaired, he perceives that she is not paying attention and decides that she is not supportive of his concerns: the husband's beta press is **insupport**. The wife has in truth been listening only partially, but not because she does not care about her husband and his well-being; she is preoccupied with the announcement, earlier that day, by the president of her company that she and other senior executives will have to take a pay cut. The couple had been counting on their combined income to make it possible for the husband to open his own firm; the wife is dreading having to break her unpleasant news to her husband. Thus, we might call the alpha press here one of **temporary inattention**.

People's behaviors are most closely correlated with their perceptions of the environment, or with beta press. Where wide discrepancies exist between objectively observable environmental phenomena and the phenomena to which someone appears to be reacting, we often infer some degree of psychological disturbance.

INTERACTION OF NEED AND PRESS: THE THEMA

To represent the dynamics of a behavioral unit, Murray proposes the **thema**, which deals with the interaction between need and press. In a sense, the thema is an aspect of the proceeding; the latter defines an observable and time-limited person–person or person–object interaction; the former describes the motives operating in that interaction.

As several proceedings can form a serial, so a number of themas can combine to form a **serial thema**. Say, for example, that an anthropologist presents his recent research to a group of colleagues. He hopes not only to impress his colleagues but to surpass them in his demonstrated knowledge of the field. He feels that they are critical of his methods and skeptical of his results; he is defensive about his methodology and conceals procedures that he feels are imprecise. Here we have a thema that includes an alpha press of **peer response**; a beta press of **peer criticism** and **skepticism**; and the needs of **achievement**, **dominance**, and **defendance**.

We see a similar thema when, discussing an exhibition at a new gallery with friends, the anthropologist evaluates the artist's work, tracing its inspiration to Toltec art in which he claims expertise. Someone else takes an opposing view, and the anthropologist defends his own by adding details of which he is not at all sure. These two themas could probably be added to others to form a serial thema that would revolve about this man's high degree of competitiveness, his uncertainty about his own competence, and his defensiveness when he feels challenged.

Related both to the notion of the thema and to the concept of the focal need is what Murray has called the **need integrate**—a need for a certain kind of interaction with a certain kind of person or object. It often happens that a person comes to associate particular objects with certain needs. An example of a need integrate would be a love of classical music as opposed to, say, rock, country, or other types of music. We will encounter the need integrate in another guise—that of the complex—a little later.

DIRECTIONALITY OF BEHAVIOR: VECTORS AND VALUES

Murray's **vector–value scheme** is his effort to represent the ultimate intent of behavior in his theoretical system. In arriving at this scheme, Murray notes that he was heavily influenced by the notions of Erik Erikson (Chapter 3), and Kurt Lewin (Chapter 8). According to Murray, everything that people do, they do in the service of some desired end state (desired to be either obtained or avoided). Thus, in pursuing any course of action, the person has some valued purpose in mind.

One of the shortcomings of his original conception of need, Murray (1951a) admits, is that information about specific needs and press does not ordinarily include information about a person's valued goals. Thus, knowing what a person's needs and press are does not necessarily tell us what the person will *do*. For example, a person may have a need for understanding, but what is the person's concept of her end goal and what does she do to attain it? Does the person read newspapers, news magazines, and the like voraciously in order to be well informed politically? Does she join a church with the goal of achieving spiritual understanding? And so on.

To represent the relation between action tendencies, or **vectors**, based on particular needs and the desired end states, or **values**, of such action tendencies, Murray (1951a) has tentatively proposed a system that we have depicted in Figure 9.2: each cell in the matrix represents a behavior that exemplifies a particular action tendency in the service of a particular goal. Row E and column 6 of the figure are filled in to indicate, first, how a particular person's goal, or value, of knowledge is served by various action tendencies and, second, how the person uses one action tendency, or vector, in the service of each of the values shown.

Murray suggests that it should be possible to use this scheme to represent not only the actions of one subject but specific subject–subject or subject–object interactions as well. For example, a person (*s*) may express (6) his or her theory (E) that high interest rates are desirable to a friend (*o*) who rejects (1) that theory (E); this interaction could be represented as $sE6 \rightarrow oE1$.

Murray notes that the vector–value system is incomplete. For example, the list of seven values is only tentative and needs to be augmented. And to describe a subject–subject interaction fully, additional variables (e.g., status of each person, role behavior, emotional investment in the idea being discussed) need to be represented.

Values (Goals)	Vectors (Action Tendencies)										
	1. Rejection	2. Reception	3. Acquisition	4. Construction	5. Conservation	6. Expression	7. Transmission	8. Expulsion	9. Destruction	10. Dependence	11. Avoidance
A. Body (physical well-being)						Skis, plays racquet-ball					
B. Property (useful objects, wealth)						Maintains comfortable home					
C. Authority (decision making, power)						Is chairman of physics department					
D. Affiliation (interpersonal affection)						Enjoys activities with spouse and children					
E. Knowledge (facts and theories, science, history)	Rejects material irrelevant to subject of paper	Absorbs information that comes to attention	Researches new idea in lab and library	Develops new theory	Stores new information in memory	Writes paper on new theory	Discusses paper with colleagues	Deletes incorrect ideas	Attacks others' erroneous ideas	Defends own conceptions	Avoids criticism by concealing some procedures
F. Aesthetic Form (beauty, art)						Attends concerts; paints landscapes					
G. Ideology (system of values, philosophy, religion)						Studies comparative religions					

Figure 9.2   An interpretation of Murray's vector–value system. Column 6 indicates the forms that a person's action tendency, or vector, of expression might take. Row E suggests how this person might pursue the goal (value) of knowledge, using all his or her action tendencies. (Based on Murray, 1951a.)

THE KEY TO UNIQUENESS: THE UNITY-THEMA

A person's **unity-thema** is the "key to his unique nature" (Murray, 1938). It is a usually unconscious compound of interrelated strong needs that are linked to press to which the person was exposed on one or more particular occasions in early childhood. The needs may be conflicting needs; the early experience may have been one of pleasure or of trauma. Whatever the nature of the thema, it repeats itself frequently during later life.

Consider, for example, a young man, studied by Murray (1938) and his colleagues, who was judged to have a unity-thema of **deprivation leading to an aggressive search for fulfillment**. This young man's mother had been an invalid and had died when he was young. The young man feared and hated his father, who was not a successful man, showed the son no affection, and actively discouraged him from attending school. The young man was determined to get a college degree and become an engineer. Study of his life by various methods, including the Thematic Apperception Test, or TAT (see Box 9.2), revealed unconscious feelings of great deprivation and support) and of a strong need to obtain what he had been denied.

REGNANCY: THE PHYSIOLOGICAL BASIS FOR BEHAVIOR

Murray has consistently emphasized the importance of keeping in mind the link between personality and the hypothetical variables that constitute the physiological underpinnings of all psychological phenomena. He christened these variables **regnant** (from the Latin *regnare,* "to reign" or "to rule") processes, writing that the discovery of "the physical nature of [these] processes and the proper way to conceptualize them" was not "to be expected in the near future" (1938, p. 47).

Murray (1938) also recognized the importance of unconscious processes. Citing a number of events and behaviors that support the notion of such processes (e.g., passing someone in the street and immediately thinking the person is anxious without being able to describe the phenomena that account for this impression; becoming a good driver and then being unaware of many intentions and motor movements involved in the activity), he declared that "all conscious processes are regnant but not all regnant processes are conscious" (Murray, 1938, p. 52). That is, every psychological event or process of which we are aware has a counterpart physiological process, but not all physiological processes are represented in awareness.

Like Freud and Jung, Murray recognizes different levels of the unconscious. Some things, he says, can come easily to awareness, but others are actively defended against. Thus, he accepts the Freudian concepts of repression and resistance (see Chapter 2).

BOX 9.2   Understanding Personality Through Fantasy: The TAT

The Thematic Apperception Test, or TAT, was developed by Christiana Morgan and Henry Murray on the basis of "the well-recognized fact that when a person interprets an ambiguous social situation he is apt to expose his own personality as much as the phenomenon to which he is attending" (Murray, 1938, p. 531). Morgan and Murray, who shared an extensive acquaintance with literature and literary criticism, also realized that through an author's work we get a feeling for him or her as a person.

On the assumption that stories anyone might tell would in the same way reflect the story-tellers' own views and characteristics and that such narratives might potentially reveal personality characteristics or trends in general, Morgan and Murray (1935) devised the TAT as a group of somewhat ambiguous pictures designed to stimulate a viewer's imagination and to suggest specific areas of motivational importance and possible conflict.

The TAT consists of 30 pictures and a blank card. Of the 31 cards, 11 (including the blank) are used with subjects of both sexes and all ages. The remaining 20 cards are designated as appropriate for males or females and adults or children, in various combinations, with the result that in any given administration, a total of 20 cards are shown to a subject. Following are descriptions of three of the pictures:

• A young boy is contemplating a violin that rests on a table

One of the pictures in Murray's original TAT series. Subjects often see the old woman on the right as a fantasied image; for example, as an image of oneself in old age.

in front of him.

• The portrait of a young woman. A weird old woman with a shawl over her head is grimacing in the background. (This picture appears in Figure 9.3.)

• The silhouette of a man (or woman) against a bright window. The rest of the picture is totally black. (Holt, 1951, pp. 202–203)

In the original TAT administration, a subject was given the following instructions:

This is a test of your creative imagination. I shall show you a picture and I want you to make up a plot or story for which it might be used as an illustration. What is the relation of the individuals in the picture? What has happened to them? What are their present thoughts and feelings? What will be the outcome? Do your very best. Since I am asking you to indulge your literary imagination you

may make your story as long and as detailed as you wish. (Murray, 1938, p. 532)

The examiner then handed the subject each of the 20 cards, one by one, writing down everything the subject said.

According to Morgan and Murray, "every subject almost immediately projects his own circumstances, experiences, or preoccupations onto the evocative object" (Murray, 1938, pp. 533). For example, a 24-year-old engineering student from a Middle Western state had hated the farm on which he was raised and, as a child, had felt that his often abusive father "was always trying to oppose my ambition [and] . . . keep me on the farm" (Murray, 1938, p. 673). This subject responded to the third of the TAT cards we have described as follows:

This young man is probably a farm hand. . . . He tells himself that he doesn't belong where he is. He wants to get away and lead the life that he feels he ought to lead. . . . He finds a way of getting ahead. (Murray, 1938, p. 676)

Although there is nothing in the card to suggest either farm or farm hand, the subject quite clearly has identified with the figure in the picture.

Our engineering student can be seen as having not only identified with the TAT picture but as having "projected" his own concerns onto it. The TAT is considered a **projective** test; it is based on the assumption that, given a somewhat vague stimulus that may be interpreted in various ways, a person will project his or her own needs, wishes, and fantasies and concerns—often those that remain below the level of consciousness—onto this stimulus. For example, the student said, *in interviews*, that "at times" he had hated his father but added that since his father had become an invalid, "I have lost the old feeling of fear and hate and now feel only kindliness and sympathy for him" (Murray, 1938, p. 633). In a number of this subject's TAT stories, however, an older male figure punished, exploited, or in some way used a younger man, and in one story the subject's apparently unconscious "parricidal fantasy is evident" (Murray, 1938, p. 677):

The younger man is a clerk in a bank who has been gambling—and he is in debt to the older man. The older man is trying to get him to engage in shady business with the bank. The younger man is objecting, not from conscience, but because he is running his neck into a noose. The young man is intelligent and will find a way . . . to get out of the man's power. It will be some drastic method. He might take the older man out in the dark and quietly throttle him and throw him over the brink.

Although the TAT continues to be widely used both as a clinical diagnostic device and as an instrument in personality research, some investigators have questioned whether it really taps unconscious material or reveals enduring characteristics of personality, as Murray and Morgan proposed. Holmes (1968), for example, found that subjects were aware of the traits that they projected. Holmes (1974) also showed that subjects could fake the possession of a specific trait when instructed to do so and, on request, could inhibit projections revealing of their personalities. McClelland and others (1953), however, did not find subjects to be successful in faking need achievement.

A substantial clinical and research literature suggests that attitudes and characteristics revealed by subjects in their TAT stories are significantly often confirmed by the results of other personality assessment devices. It would seem that, whether what subjects reveal is or is not accessible to consciousness, it is often material that they have difficulty discussing directly and openly. By attributing important needs and emotions to fictional characters, people not only may be enabled to express things they are reluctant to reveal but—in time—to regard such things more objectively and to be better able to deal with them.

THE DEVELOPMENT OF PERSONALITY

According to Murray, "the history of a personality *is* the personality" (1938, p. 604); studying people as they develop over time is crucial to understanding them. The combination of proceedings, serials, abilities, achievements, needs, press, themas, regnant processes, vectors, and values can be applied to understanding the person at any given point in time, but such a representation is not sufficient. Because the parts can be understood only with reference to the whole, the longitudinal study of persons is of great importance.

We will begin by considering Murray's conception of the complex, based on both Freudian and Jungian ideas. Then we will look at Murray's notion of how development and learning occur, including the important influences of genetic–maturational and experiential determinants. Finally, we will review his conception of how the person is socialized, or adapted to his or her environment.

INFANTILE COMPLEXES

Murray does not accept the Freudian and exclusively sexual interpretation of the child's enjoyment of sensations associated with specific zones of the body. He does find evidence, however, that children clearly take pleasure in certain bodily functions and activities—such as sucking, defecating, and genital manipulation—and that some children are unduly distressed by the frustration of these activities inevitable in weaning, toilet training, and other socializing procedures. Children may become fixated in respect to certain activities, Murray says, and these fixations may influence their later development.

Murray's concept of the complex is designed to represent the influence of the child's reactions to these early events in such a way as to tie the latter to specific developments in the person's life and behavior. You will recall that the need integrate is a need for a certain kind of interaction with a certain kind of object. When such a need involves one of these early events, or childhood press, and influences the course of later development, it is called a **complex**.

Following Freud and the psychoanalysts, Murray (1938) suggests several early conditions or activities—each of which is eventually terminated, frustrated, or limited by external forces—around which complexes are particularly likely to develop:

1. The secure and dependent existence in the womb (terminated by the painful experience of birth).
2. The sensuous enjoyment of sucking good nourishment from the mother's breast (or a bottle) while lying safely in her arms (brought to a halt by weaning).
3. The free enjoyment of the pleasurable sensations accompanying defecation (restricted by toilet training).
4. The thrilling excitations that arise from manipulating the genitals (prohibited by threats of punishment).

Presumably all people have complexes of varying severity; it is only in extreme cases that such complexes are considered abnormal. How is the existence of these complexes ascertained? Murray points out that because they develop for the most part before the child has the power of communication (language), their existence must be inferred, both by observing the child and by exploring these ideas with the adult, who must reconstruct what has transpired earlier.

DEVELOPMENTAL AND LEARNING PROCESSES

For Murray, the personality is the accumulated product of the interaction between **genetic–maturational** processes and **experiential** factors. It may be helpful at this point to reemphasize Murray's insistence on two things: (1) personality is linked to brain structure and function, and (2) all behavior is an interactive process between person and environment. The genetic–maturational determinants of personality are fundamental in the sense that they are given—they are coded in the cells' DNA (deoxyribonucleic acid). The environmental, or experiential, determinants strongly influence the way in which the products of the genetic–maturational determinants get expressed.

GENETIC–MATURATIONAL DETERMINANTS. Murray is greatly concerned with evolution and change, but he does not see development as occurring in definable stages. For him, the genetic program is "roughly divisible into three successive but overlapping temporal eras" (Murray, 1968b, p. 8) that are defined essentially by what Murray calls **psychometabolic** processes. Murray chooses the metabolic model because it enables him to emphasize process rather than structure and to represent the ideas of progression, construction, and creativity. He suggests that in the first era of life (roughly, infancy through early adulthood), **anabolic**, or building-up, processes are dominant. The person learns new things; new structures and functions in the brain are presumably laid down. In the second era (adulthood, or the middle years), anabolic and **catabolic** (breaking-down) processes more or less balance each other, and the chief emphasis is on preserving and reinforcing what one has already learned, through repetition, memory, and so on. In the third and final era (old age, or senescence), catabolic processes become dominant; the person learns much less new material, and memory is less reliable. Presumably, underlying structure and function begin to deteriorate. For example, it has been shown that, in general, the aging do not learn new things as rapidly as do younger people; they tend to have deficits in certain kinds of memory (notably "short-term memory," or memory for recent events).

Murray hypothesizes that the genetic program determines the earliest age at which various dispositions and aptitudes will emerge and be capable of development, given favorable conditions. That is, at a certain point, the program says, "Now is the time to learn to crawl"; at another, "Now comes the onset of puberty" (Murray, 1968b, p. 8). Murray also suggests that the genetic program determines the "limits of excellence to which a number of special skills (e.g., athletic, musical, mathematical, poetical) may be perfected under the most facilitating circumstances" (p. 8).

Genetic factors are also responsible for the presence, in the brain, of **delighters** and **distressors**, or centers of pleasure and displeasure. It is the process of discovering what generates pleasure and what generates distress that comprises learning.

EXPERIENTIAL DETERMINANTS. The experiential process is made up of a succession and recurrence of (1) events that occur in the person's environment; (2) the person's expressions of programmed dispositions ("instinctive outbursts"), triggered by specific environmental events; and (3) the person's efforts to do things, as well as the positive and negative effects of the person's actions, such as rewards or punishments. The foregoing phenomena interact with the person's genetically assigned potentials to determine what he or she will learn. Moreover, "what a person learns on one occasion will determine or modify his performance on a subsequent occasion of the same class" (Murray, 1968b, p. 9).

There are an almost unlimited number of delighters and distressors that reflect factors in the environment. In early infancy, when capacities for initiating behavior are fairly limited, delighters and distressors tend largely to involve the comfort the mother's presence brings and the distress caused by her absence. As the child grows, egocentric wants and fantasies (**central** determinants) and impressions of whether he or she is learning new skills and becoming more competent and independent (**achievement** determinants) become more and more important. And the person's interactions with others (**transactional** determinants) tend increasingly to constitute sources of delight or distress and thus to affect the person's development and learning.

Consistent with his emphasis on change, Murray points out that a great deal in life must be unlearned as well as learned. New learning often requires the reconstruction, if not the destruction, of old learning. Murray emphasizes the human being's "self-realizing, novelty-seeking, ambitious, proudful, imaginative, and creative" disposition and specifically rejects the concept of habit as of primary importance in personality development (1968b, p. 12). People get bored and seek new ventures, he says; they vary in their beliefs, codes, manners, political sentiments, and tastes; they try to accomplish things that are new, extraordinary, difficult, and hazardous; they are transformed by religious conversions; they discover that creating some form of culture—such as an original piece of writing—can be profoundly joyous. None of these things, Murray says, would happen if people were only creatures of habit. People "would stagnate with learned incapacities and a few enthralling memories of infantile attachments" (p. 12). Murray upholds Freud's "essential truth"—that early childhood experience has lasting effects—but insists that it be supplemented with "unlearning, . . . experimentation, courage, endurance, and constructiveness" (Murray, 1968b, p. 12).

THE SOCIALIZATION PROCESS

Murray resembles the socially oriented theorists (Chapter 5) and Kurt Lewin (Chapter 8) in assigning a major role in development to environmental factors and, specifically, to the interpersonal and social set-

For Murray, habit, or old learning, is not of prime importance in personality development. Human beings would not become bored and seek new ventures, he says, or try to accomplish extraordinary things if they were only creatures of habit.

ting in which development takes place. The central elements of Murray's theory—proceeding, need and press, thema—explicitly require an interactionist approach to human behavior.

For Murray, human personality is a compromise between the person's own impulses and the demands and interests of others. These demands and interests are represented collectively by the institutions and patterns of society. The process by which the person's own needs are compromised by society's demands is called the **socialization process.** Almost inevitably, conflicts between person and society are resolved by the person's conforming to the group in some way. In general, society's laws can be changed only if many persons together decide to change them; the individual alone can rarely succeed in altering cultural patterns.

For the person to become properly socialized, he or she must have developed an adequate superego. Thus the parents, as the most important authority figures and sources of superego components, are the chief agents of the socialization process. Their effectiveness in rewarding approved behaviors and punishing disapproved ones will largely determine the success of this process. In general, a mutually affectionate relationship between parents and children is the best facilitator; mere approval or disapproval can then suffice to control children's behavior.

Socialization can be overdone, Murray says. A person—even an entire society—can be debilitated by socialization processes that deny the fundamental biological nature of the human being and thus destroy the creative spontaneity and vigor essential to the most important kinds of human advances.

RESEARCH APPROACH AND METHODS

Murray's research has been characterized by the originality of its approach and methodology. He and his colleagues at Harvard devised a number of inventive instruments for measuring personality and undertook some groundbreaking research in the 1930s and 1940s. We will look first at some distinctive qualities of Murray's general approach and then at the methods and instruments he has used.

STUDYING THE INDIVIDUAL PERSON

Murray is convinced that an adequate understanding of behavior can be achieved only by complete and detailed studies of individual people. In some degree, this view reflects Murray's early training and experience in medicine, a field in which the case study has been indispensable in learning about the forms a given illness takes, their effects on the person, and appropriate treatments. Murray's approach also follows the tradition that derives from William James and William Stern (and represented also by Gordon Allport, Chapter 10), which considers the study of the individual person ''in depth and breadth'' (Epstein, 1979, p. 649) the only proper method of personality research.

Murray has also emphasized the need to study normal people; indeed, he has insisted that the so-called normal person should be the primary subject of personality research. Thus, his data provide a good complement to the case histories so many clinically oriented theorists have provided from psychotherapeutic settings. Because the personologist's ultimate aim is to predict the person's activities in everyday life, investigators not only must study normal people but must study them in natural settings. In recent years, there have been a few, somewhat delayed echoes of Murray's insistence on studying people in natural settings. It has been claimed that the laboratory experiment offers an inadequate sample of behavior and that the study of personality has ''somehow lost track of [its] subject matter'' (Epstein, 1979, p. 649; see also Carlson, 1971).

THE DIAGNOSTIC COUNCIL

Murray considers psychologists themselves primary instruments of psychological research. That is, whatever technical methods we use—rating scales, psychological tests, and the like—in the final analysis, it is the investigator who observes, interprets, analyzes, and, in general, translates the data into meaningful communication about the issue at hand. Thus, Murray feels, it is important to attend to the weak points of psychological investigators and to make efforts to improve their powers of observation; he and his colleagues were among the first to try to measure the effects of experimenter variables.

One of Murray's most innovative responses to the need to control for the influence of experimenters' own personalities on their assessment of their subjects was the **diagnostic council**. The council is a group of several observers, all of whom hold different points of view, all of whom study the same subjects. Here, Murray pioneered not only in the notion of having multiple observers of a given subject but in the idea of having investigators from different disciplines cooperate in personality research: the Harvard Psychological Clinic staff investigators typically included representatives of psychiatry, psychology, anthropology, sociology, and several other disciplines.

The diagnostic council method involves having each observer, using his or her particular disciplinary approach and measurement instruments, examine the subjects under study for a period of time. Then a meeting of all observers is convened, at which each presents his or her data and interpretations and every member of the council has an opportunity to react and to offer his or her own suggestions. One member of the group is responsible for coordinating the undertaking and for synthesizing the presentations at the end, but everyone has unlimited opportunity to contribute to the final product.

MEASURING PERSONALITY

No contemporary psychologist has made more significant contributions to personality assessment than Murray. He has devised many ingenious instruments for measuring personality (see, e.g., Murray, 1938; Office of Strategic Services Assessment Staff, 1948), only a few of which, however, have been used widely and systematically. One of these, the Thematic Apperception Test (TAT), which we discuss in Box 9.2, has become, "next to the Rorschach, the most widely used of all projective techniques" (Lindzey, 1961; see also Murstein, 1963; Zubin, Eron, and Schumer, 1965).

In the extensive research described in *Explorations in Personality,* Murray and his colleagues used interviews, questionnaires, problem-solving tasks, tests of skills, and a number of other devices to examine the thoughts, feelings, attitudes, and behaviors of 50 young men, most

BOX 9.3   Selecting Spies in Wartime: A Visit to "Station S"

The United States Office of Strategic Services (OSS) during World War II operated a three-day assessment program to evaluate candidates for the various espionage and intelligence jobs it carried out overseas. A group of psychologists and psychiatrists, including then Lt. Col. Henry A. Murray, developed and conducted the assessment program, which shared many features with Murray's Harvard studies. The results of the program are described in the book *Assessment of Men* (OSS Assessment Staff, 1948).

The purpose of the OSS program was to find out as much as possible in three days about the men being screened and to estimate how they would react in the variety of situations to which they might be subjected in the field. Would they respond quickly and coolly in situations of sudden danger? Would they be able to enlist the cooperation of others? Could they tolerate cheerfully the frustration, monotony, and loneliness inevitable in many overseas assignments?

To answer these questions, the OSS assessment staff undertook a multidimensional program. In addition to administering a variety of traditional tests and interviews focused on the candidates' abilities, personalities, interests, and life and medical histories, the OSS staff observed the candidates, individually and in groups, in a variety of situations designed to let them display positive or negative characteristics of potential importance in their eventual assignments.

After preliminary screening, a candidate for OSS duty—who might be an officer, an enlisted man, or a civilian—was ordered to report to a Washington headquarters building at a given date and time. There he was instructed to make up a fictitious name and to leave behind any letters, photographs, or other items that might provide clues to his real identity. He was asked to remove all outer clothing and to destroy any identifying marks on his underwear. He was issued two sets of army fatigue uniforms, one of which he was to put on. Thus, deprived of external signs of rank, status, or identity, he was trucked in the late afternoon with some 15 to 20 fellow-assessees to a converted estate outside Washington, called "Station S," where the men would stay for the three days of the assessment.

Upon arrival at S, each man was greeted by the assessment staff, assigned a bunk for his stay, and informed of the general schedule and procedures. Among other things, he was to develop a fictitious identity and maintain it at all times, except during certain specifically exempted interviews and questionnaires. He was warned that the staff might try to trick him at other times into revealing his true identity.

The three days that followed contained a heavy schedule of psychological tests, interviews, and situational tests, as well as observations of the candidate's behavior during meals, breaks, and informal interactions with staff members or fellow candidates.

One of the situational tests that the candidates confronted on the first day was designated "Construction."

For this task, each candidate reported individually to an isolated location on the estate, where a staff member met him. Various materials lay on the ground: 5- and 7-foot poles, wooden blocks with holes into which the poles could be fit, and pegs to hold them in place. The task assigned the candidate was to fit the pieces together into a simple structure, following a small model supplied. After explaining this, the staff member continued:

This is a construction problem, but even more important than that, it is a test of leadership. I say that because it is impossible for one man working alone to complete this task in the 10 minutes allotted to do it. Therefore, we are going to give you two helpers who work here on the estate. You are to be the supervisor, their boss. You are to guide them in their work, but as foreman, you will follow more or less of a hands-off policy. Let them do the manual labor. You can assume that they have never done such work before and know nothing about it. Any questions?

All right. It is now ten o'clock. You have just 10 minutes in which to do the job. I'll call your two helpers. (p. 103)

The helpers, however, were not the yokels they seemed, but two junior members of the staff whose task it was to make things as difficult and frustrating for the candidate as possible. They were traditionally known as Kippy and Buster. Kippy played a passive and sluggish role, standing around and doing nothing unless specifically ordered to, Buster was active, aggressive, critical of the candidate, and full of impractical suggestions. Although the two "helpers" were instructed not to disobey explicit orders from the candidate, they were free to misunderstand his intentions and to be as careless, critical, and stupid as they chose in carrying them out.

Kippy and Buster succeeded so admirably that no candidate ever managed to complete the construction within the allotted time, and the candidates' responses to the frustrating situation supplied the staff observers with rich material for their ratings.

Other situations calling on various physical, intellectual, and emotional capacities of the candidates followed over the next two days. Among other things, each candidate was given a "stress interview" in which he was subjected to intensive interrogation, and then, in the lull afterward, to an attempt to get him to break his cover story.

Following the three days, in a conference of the assessment staff, all the results for each candidate were reviewed, and a recommendation was arrived at concerning his fitness for his prospective assignment. On the basis of these recommendations, some candidates went off to dangerous or difficult or demanding intelligence assignments overseas, but some went home or back to their previous units.

It was never possible to evaluate exactly how successful the OSS assessment program was in screening out potentially unsatisfactory performers in difficult and sensitive jobs. For those who carried it out and for most of those who went through it, however, it was a memorable experience.

---

of whom were undergraduates or graduate students at Harvard. Subjects were rated, on a six-point scale, on needs, press, and other qualities, both by the experimenters and by themselves, and specific tasks were scored in appropriate ways.

The significance of this research is in large part the fact that it was the first major effort to study normal human beings intensively, by introspective means as well as by observation and by controlled experiment, and to form integrated characterizations of a stable group of people, based on data drawn not only from many different measures but assembled by observers of different disciplines. This kind of multidimensional approach to the study of persons as entities and in context was used by Murray in his wartime work with the United States Office of Strategic Services (see Box 9.3), and it has since been used in other investigations of personality, such as those undertaken at the Institute for Personality Assessment and Research (IPAR), at Berkeley.

By their nature, Murray's methods and instruments produce an enormous amount of material. Subjects are encouraged to provide as much information as they can, and imagination and fantasy are given free rein. The result is a wealth of a data that are richly promising but often difficult to analyze and interpret. Nevertheless, Murray is convinced that we will never understand human behavior by studying human beings in laboratories and certainly not by studying animals. He believes that among psychologists' great advantages is the fact that they are dealing with creatures that can talk: human beings can tell psychologists a great deal about such things as their own internal processes, their attention, and their reactions to external events and situations. Psychologists must assess subjective reports carefully and cannot take them at face value. Nevertheless, according to Murray, such reports represent a crucial beginning in the effort to unravel the secrets of human behavior.

EVALUATION

In developing his theory over time—sometimes modifying a concept, sometimes scrapping a notion, sometimes introducing a wholly new idea—Murray is not unlike many other personality theorists. He does differ from most theorists, however, in that his reexamination and modification have been incessant. Murray has insisted that new facts, new experience, new learning must continually be incorporated into any theory of personality. The title of his most recent major statement of his theory tells the story: "Components of an Evolving Personological System" (1968b).

Certain elements in Murray's theory do stand firm: his deep interest in the motivational process, including unconscious motivation; his conviction that all human behavior must be seen as an interactive process; his firm belief in the purposive, or goal-directed, nature of behavior; his insistence on the linkage between psychological and brain processes; and his concern with descriptive and taxonomic methods.

Probably the most distinctive component of Murray's work, and the most influential over the long haul, is his dedicated exploration of human motivation. He has taken a position between those who narrow motivation to a small number of master motives and those who assume so many motives that any effort to classify them is considered useless. Murray is convinced that motivation cannot be expressed adequately by 2 to 5 general motives. He finds that some 20-odd motives, however, are sufficiently general that they can represent the behavior of all or most people.

Second only in importance perhaps to his emphasis on motivation is Murray's insistence on considering behavior an interactive process—between a person and an object, between persons, and between a person or persons and the larger environment. His concept of alpha and beta press allows us to differentiate between the environment as it exists (insofar as it can be assessed objectively) and the environment as it is perceived by the person, a most important conception that some others (e.g., Sullivan, Lewin) have also underlined.

It is one thing to speak of the importance of the environment; it is quite another to characterize it in empirical terms. Murray is one of the very few theorists who have actually undertaken the exacting task of specifying categories (press) in terms of which significant aspects of the environment can be represented.

Murray's theory has been criticized for not providing a set of explicitly stated psychological propositions that can generate testable hypotheses. Perhaps his assumptions and concepts should be seen more as offering a general view of behavior that shapes the specific manner in which particular research problems are approached. He has done more than any other investigator to develop a set of variables that will do justice to the complexity of human behavior yet be specific enough to be used repeatedly by different investigators. As we have noted, his work has led to extensive studies of several specific motives.

Some critics think Murray's theory incorporates so much material that it loses distinctiveness. These critics suggest that the theory says so much that no single thing stands out, and the theory itself does not stand out from others. Other observers feel that Murray's classification schemes are unnecessarily detailed and tend rather to confuse than to resolve questions. Murray's insistence on constantly modifying his concepts has not helped in this matter.

Finally, critics point out that, although Murray has discussed the learning process, he has devoted relatively little attention to the specifics of how learning takes place. Thus, writers say, he cannot account for the way motives—his major concern—change and develop.

In any final appraisal of Murray's contributions, one must combine the theory, the man, and his research. There can be no doubt that this combination has introduced a note of vivid originality into an area of research sorely in need of such qualities. According to Donald MacKinnon, a former student of Murray, the two centers for the study of personality that Murray brought into being at Harvard "have been among the most creative environments in the history of psychology" (1982, pp. 7–8).

In the long run, one of the great enemies of empirical and theoretical progress is the fixation upon stable but trivial events. There has been no more ruthless critic of trivial investigation and formulation in personality research than Henry Murray.

SUMMARY

1. Personality theorists should study normal individuals in natural settings.

2. All behavior is interactive; thus the person must be studied in terms of his or her interactions with the environment.

3. The brain is the locus of personality. All psychological events and processes, conscious and unconscious, are linked to brain structures and functions that we do not as yet fully understand.

4. Personality comprises the person's central organizing and governing processes, whose function it is to resolve conflicts, satisfy needs, and plan for future goals.

5. To understand the **proceeding**, the basic unit of behavior, we must often examine the **serial** of which it is a part.

6. By means of **ordination**, a person chooses and enacts a plan with a specific end in mind. The person uses **serial programs** to set up systems of subgoals and **schedules** to time actions in order to avoid conflicts between competing needs.

7. **Need** stands for a force located in the brain that organizes various psychological processes so as to change an unsatisfying condition.

8. Two needs may be hierarchically related or in conflict; they may fuse together, or may be subsidiary to another.

9. **Press** are properties of objects, other people, or the environment that help or hinder the person in reaching his or her goal. **Alpha** press are properties as they exist in objective reality; **beta** press are properties as they are perceived by the person.

10. The **thema** describes the interaction of need and press within a behavioral unit, or proceeding; a **serial thema** is a sequence of themas that describes a person's tendency to behave in a particular way in situations involving certain needs and press.

11. Everything we do we do in the service of some desired end state; our action tendencies (**vectors**) are designed in some way to bring us closer to our goals (**values**).

12. The **complex** is a need–press combination that relates to one of five specific conditions of childhood and that strongly influences adult development.

13. Development and learning are determined by **genetic-maturational** and **experiential** factors. The genetic program determines the timing of events as well as the degree to which certain abilities can be developed in the best of environmental conditions. Environmental events and the results of the person's actions combine with genetic determinants to determine what a person learns.

14. **Socialization** very largely involves the person's conforming to the ways of society; personality is a compromise between the person's own impulses and the demands and interests of other people.

15. The **diagnostic council** method of personality research involves having a group of observers, of different views and varying disciplines, study the same subjects, share their impressions, and construct a final assessment based on a consensus.

16. The **TAT** is a projective test developed by Murray that is widely used both in research and in clinical settings.

17. Murray has been called to task for neglecting to specify how learning takes place and, in general, for not providing explicitly stated propositions that can generate testable hypotheses. Murray's theory has also been criticized as excessively detailed and as incorporating so much material that single elements can only with difficulty be teased out. Murray's intensive and extensive exploration of human motivation, however, and his explication of behavior as an interactive process are major contributions to personality theory, as are his effort to specify actual categories of environmental events that influence behavior, his insistence on the linkage between brain and psychological process, and his firm conviction of the goal-directedness of all behavior.

SUGGESTED READING

Explorations in Personality (1938), which summarizes the work of the Harvard Psychological Clinic staff at the end of its first decade of existence, is an excellent introduction to Murray's approach. This book presents Murray's concepts of need and press and gives fascinating excerpts from these depth studies of normal personality.

Assessment of Men (Office of Strategic Services, 1948), the account of Murray's work for the Office of Strategic Services in the 1940s, will give you a further appreciation of Murray's sensitivity and ingenuity in developing ways to appraise and analyze human capacities and motives. The TAT, used in both the Harvard and the OSS work, is best described in *Manual of the Thematic Apperception Test* (1943); you may also want to look at the article that introduced this test, written with Morgan: "A Method for Investigating Fantasies" (1935).

Some of the most helpful statements of Murray's frequent revisions of his theory and concepts are to be found in "Some Basic Psychological Assumptions and Conceptions" (1951a), "Preparations for the Scaffold of a Comprehensive System" (1959), and "Components of an Evolving Personological System" (1968b). You may also find interesting two discussions of Murray's thoughts on how personality research should be conducted: "Problems in Clinical Research: Round Table" (1947) and "Research Planning: A Few Proposals" (1949).

Some of the material we have cited is included in a recent collection of Murray's writings: *Endeavors in Psychology: Selections from the Personology of Henry A. Murray* (1981). This book presents many of Murray's major papers, his earliest proposals for a theory of personality (from his 1938 book), several autobiographical essays, and all his writings on Herman Melville; it also includes a complete bibliography of Murray's works. Together with *Explorations in Personality,* this volume will give you a solid acquaintance with Murray's thought.

The study of Herman Melville, the man and his novels, has been Murray's lifelong avocation, and Murray's unusual literary talents are particularly evidenced in his writing on this subject. To date, he has published only four pieces on Melvile, the most famous of which is "In Nomine Diaboli" (1973), a brilliant analysis of *Moby Dick* that has been reprinted many times and in various locations.

Lindzey (1979) has recently written a brief account of Murray's life and work, and Murray himself has written an autobiographical sketch that he has called "The Case of Murr" (1967), in which he has provided considerable data about his life and his intellectual influences and forebears. Additional biographical information can be found in "What Should Psychologists Do about Psychoanalysis?" (1940) and "Preparations for the Scaffold of a Comprehensive System." You may also enjoy reading an informal exploration of some of Murray's ideas in the *Psychology Today* interview, "A Conversation with Mary Harrington Hall" (1968a).

Chapter ten

10.

What drives behavior, drives now.
GORDON ALLPORT

The Uniqueness of the Person: Gordon Allport

With a certain brashness, the young man of 22 wrote to Sigmund Freud, announcing his presence in the eminent professor's city and suggesting that Freud might like to meet him. The year was 1920, and the young man, who had just completed a year of teaching in Istanbul, had stopped off in Vienna on his way home to the United States. Freud wrote back, inviting the young man to come to his office.

Soon after I had entered the famous red burlap room with pictures of dreams on the wall, [Freud] summoned me to his inner office. He did not speak to me but sat in expectant silence, for me to state my mission. I was not prepared for silence and had to think fast to find a suitable conversational gambit. I told him of an episode on the tram car on my way to his office. A small boy about four years of age had displayed a conspicuous dirt phobia. He kept saying to his mother, "I don't want to sit there—don't let that dirty man sit beside me." To him everything was schmutzig. *His mother was a well-starched* Hausfrau, *so dominant and purposive-looking that I thought the cause and effect apparent.*

When I finished my story Freud fixed his kindly therapeutic eyes upon me and said, "And was that little boy you?" Flabbergasted and feeling a bit guilty, I contrived to change the subject. While Freud's misunderstanding of my motivation was amusing, it also started a deep train of thought. I realized that he was accustomed to neurotic defenses and that my manifest motivation (a sort of rude curiosity and youthful ambition) escaped him. (Allport, 1967, pp. 7–8)

Gordon W. Allport said that he never quite got over his early encounter with Freud. It taught him, he said, that "depth psychology, for all its merits, may plunge too deep" and that psychologists should attend to "manifest motives before probing the unconscious." Clearly, Allport believed that he was simply trying to recount an interesting observation to Freud. Freud,

however, felt that other, more personal motives led to his young visitor's account.

Allport never listened to the proverbial drummer who set the pace for academic psychology in the early and middle years of this century; the drummer he marched to was different indeed. At a time when many of the best minds in psychology were either trying to uncover the secrets of the unconscious or attempting to develop an increasingly rigorous methodology, Allport calmly but persistently emphasized the importance of studying the individual person and of focusing on that person's conscious motivation.

From early on, Allport was convinced that amassing data about the "average person" would never inform us adequately about the individual human being, in whom he found both a dazzling complexity and an underlying unity, or consistency, of behavior. This unity reflected internal, "propriate" motives (see page 354) as much as if not more than external factors. Furthermore, Allport believed firmly that for the normal person, at least, conscious thoughts and wishes were far more important than unconscious needs and impulses. Consistent with his emphasis on rational factors, Allport proposed his famous concept of "functional autonomy," according to which the mature adult human being operates on the basis of factors in the present and the future, not the past.

Allport's primary inspiration came from such figures as William James, William Stern, and William McDougall and from Gestalt theory as it was developing in Germany in the early 1920s. It is largely from James that Allport traces his concern with the individual human being; indeed, if James was a precursor of the humanistic movement, Allport was one of its founding fathers. Many humanistic psychologists have found Allport a major source of ideas for their work. Allport's emphasis on motivational variables reflects the influence of Mc-

BOX 10.1 Gordon W. Allport (1897–1967)

The fourth and youngest son of a doctor, Gordon Allport early acquired a fundamental humanitarian attitude that was to characterize his entire adult life. He spent much of his youth helping to run his father's busy practice, learning from his father, he said, the value of hard work. From his mother, a former teacher, Allport learned the importance of "philosophical questing." Both lessons were to remain with him throughout his life.

At Harvard, Allport first focused on philosophy and economics and was preceded in the field of psychology by his older brother Floyd, with whom he collaborated in later years. After spending a postgraduate year as a teacher in Istanbul, Gordon Allport returned to the United States and began to study psychology, obtaining his Ph.D. in 1922. Degree in hand, Allport went abroad again, this time to spend a year each in Germany and England. According to Allport, these were

years of great intellectual awakening. He was particularly influenced by the German scientists with whom he studied— among them, Max Wertheimer, Wolfgang Köhler, William Stern, and Heinz Werner—and writes that "at that time, Gestalt was a new concept. . . . Here was the kind of psychology I had been longing for but did not know existed" (Allport, 1967, p. 10).

Returning to Harvard as an instructor in the Department of Social Ethics, Allport soon began teaching what was probably the first course in personality offered in an American college. After two years, he accepted an appointment at Dartmouth College, where he and his wife, Ada Lufkin Gould, a clinical psychologist, became the parents of a son (Robert Bradlee Allport, a pediatrician). In 1930, Harvard asked Allport to return, and he remained on the Harvard faculty until his death.

During World War II, Allport, like other psychologists, became involved in activities designed to apply the findings of psychological science to problems peculiar to wartime. With Henry Murray, Allport led a seminar in "morale research" in which students examined such things as wartime rumors, riots, and the character of Adolf Hitler. The seminar continued after the war, gradually coming to focus on the issues of group conflict and prejudice. Allport also wrote and spoke on wartime issues, and

throughout the war, he wrote a daily newspaper feature designed to quell harmful rumors.

In the summer of 1948, Allport attended a conference on international tensions held in Paris under the auspices of UNESCO and organized by one of his former students, Hadley Cantril. Harry Stack Sullivan was among the six others in attendance at this conference, and both Allport and Sullivan wrote chapters for the book that resulted from the meetings (Cantril, 1950). (Sullivan's editors took the title of one of his works from Allport's comment on Sullivan, "Sullivan, perhaps more than any other person, labored to bring about *the fusion of psychiatry and social science,*" Cantril, 1950, p. 135.)

Allport's awards and honors were many. In 1963 he received the Gold Medal Award of the American Psychological Foundation, and in 1964 he was presented with the Distinguished Scientific Contribution Award of the American Psychological Association. Allport was president of the APA, the Eastern Psychological Association, and the Society for the Psychological Study of Social Issues, an organization that grew out of wartime work. The society now awards an annual prize, named for Allport, for the best paper or article on the subject of intergroup relations.

A teacher for most of his life, Allport exerted a great deal of influence on his students for he was a provocative and dynamic lecturer. Allport encouraged students to tackle any significant problem they wished—not necessarily a problem in which he himself was interested—and in 1963, 55 of his former Ph.D.

students recognized this openness and concern for each person's special interests by presenting Allport with two volumes of their own writings, dedicated to him "from his stu-

dents—in appreciation of his respect for their individuality" (Allport, 1967, p. 24). Allport wrote that he prized this "intimate honor" above all others.

Dougall, and his belief that the individual possesses both uniqueness and consistency of behavior shows the influence of Stern and the Gestaltists. The influence of the latter may also be seen in Allport's distrust of the untamed application of natural science methodology to psychological research.

Allport's distrust of the methods of the physical sciences reflects his belief that these methods will be misleading in the study of complex human behavior. Unlike many other theorists, Allport sees a basic discontinuity between the nonhuman and the human animal; the behavior of the one, he insists, cannot inform us about the behavior of the other (Allport, 1947). Allport also sees a discontinuity between child and adult and as a result finds the child model as inappropriate as the nonhuman model to explain adult behavior. Finally, as we might expect, he finds the "abnormal" model totally inappropriate to the "normal" personality.

A curious blend of polemicist and eclectic, Allport often advanced unpopular views but at the same time argued for openness and the consideration of all relevant data. As a result, he has been both hotly criticized and greatly respected.

STRUCTURE AND DYNAMICS OF PERSONALITY

According to Allport, "the basic principle of behavior is its continuous flow" (1961, p. 333). In a sense, all of Allport's major personality concepts have to do with motivation—with what makes the person "go." At the same time, a person's "stream of activity" has both a "variable portion" and a "constant portion." Allport seeks to describe this constant portion with his concept of the trait, and he describes the variable portion with what he calls "functional autonomy," or the tendency for a behavior to continue to be performed for reasons that differ from the reasons that originally motivated it. Both conceptions—the trait and functional autonomy—are motivational; many traits have motive power, and functional autonomy specifically explains adult motivation. In Allport's theory, then, whether we are talking about traits or functional autonomy, we are talking about the dynamics of personality.

DEFINITION OF PERSONALITY

Consonant with his insistence on approaching any investigation with clear, rational guidelines, Allport was as serious about defining personality as he was about illuminating it. After studying half a hundred proposed definitions by other authorities in the field, he sought to combine their best elements in the following definition:

Personality is the dynamic organization within the individual of those psychophysical systems that determine his unique adjustment to his environment. (Allport, 1937, p. 48)

In this definition of personality, the term *dynamic organization* is carefully chosen to make two important points: not only is personality constantly developing and changing, but there is within the person some kind of central organization that holds the components of personality together and relates them to each other. The term *psychophysical systems* implies that personality is not just a hypothetical construct formed by the observer but a real phenomenon composed of both mental and neural elements, fused into "a personality unity" (Allport, 1937, p. 48). Eventually, Allport believed, we will discover the nature of the neural components of personality. For the moment we can only infer the existence of personality, but it is real—it is not something that exists only when there is another person to react to it. Finally, this definition's use of the word *determine* makes it clear that again "personality *is* something and *does* something" (Allport, 1937, p. 48)—it is not a conception devised simply to explain another's behavior but a functioning part of the individual that plays an active role in the individual's behavior.

In arriving at his definition of personality, Allport considered carefully the terms **character** and **temperament**, both of which have sometimes been used interchangeably with personality or confused with it. Traditionally, he points out, the word *character* has implied some code of behavior in terms of which people or their acts are evaluated: a person is often described as having a "good" or a "bad" character. *Temperament* ordinarily refers to those dispositions that are closely linked to biological or physiological determinants. Thus, says Allport, heredity plays a crucial role in temperament, which is the raw material, along with intelligence and physique, out of which personality is fashioned.

TRAITS AND PERSONAL DISPOSITIONS

What is a **trait**? We generally think of a trait as any enduring characteristic of a person that distinguishes that person from another. The trait, by definition, is a characteristic that is manifested consistently throughout a range of circumstances. For example, a person may have a trait of optimism that leads her to focus always on the most positive aspects of a situation and to expect the most favorable outcome.

Let us see how Allport defines trait:

> *A trait is . . . a neuropsychic structure having the capacity to render many stimuli functionally equivalent and to initiate and guide equivalent . . . forms of adaptive and expressive behavior. (Allport, 1961, p. 347)*

The first distinctive feature of Allport's definition is the specification that a trait is a "neuropsychic structure." Thus, like personality itself, a trait is not an abstract conception formed by an observer; it has objective reality. Allport admits that "no one ever *saw* a trait," but then no one has ever seen many of the phenomena with which psychology deals (e.g., drives, habits, attitudes). Allport was confident that "some day . . . neurophysiology will show us directly the processes of integration, gating, and phase sequence that correspond to our present hypothetical constructs" (1961, p. 337).

By "render many stimuli functionally equivalent," Allport means that a trait predisposes the person both to perceive various stimuli as having similar meaning and to respond to such stimuli with behaviors that are similar. For example, suppose a person leaves his home, having picked up the newspapers, taken out the garbage, and generally straigtened things up. He walks to the library and enters, carefully wiping his feet at the door and finds an empty carrel. He selects a number of books and sits down, placing the books in the order in which he will use them and setting out paper and pencils in careful array. This person's trait of neatness is leading him to perceive his home, the library, and his task as requiring a response of orderliness, and his various behaviors are all designed to effect such orderliness. According to Allport, these behaviors are not just a group of isolated habits, but neither are they tied together in some mechanical way. These behaviors "have the same essential social meaning" for the person (Allport, 1961, p. 323). Many situations evoke his disposition of neatness and lead to varied behaviors that all have the same meaning.

Allport (1961) distinguishes between the **common trait**, with respect to which most people in a given culture can be compared, and the individual trait, or, as he prefers to call it, the **personal disposition**, which is always unique to a given person. Allport gives almost the same definition for personal disposition as for trait, adding only that the disposition is "peculiar to the individual."

Suppose we measured our optimist, mentioned a few paragraphs earlier, on a scale of optimism–pessimism. We might confirm not only that she was more optimistic than pessimistic but that she was a great deal more optimistic than the average person. We would then say that this person has a common trait of optimism. If we now look at this person in depth, perhaps by interviewing her or by asking her to

For Allport, the trait is an essential component of personality that distinguishes one person from another.

write an autobiographical sketch, we might find that she has a personal disposition that we could describe as follows: "Mary has a penchant for looking on the bright side of things herself and for encouraging others as well to focus on the positive aspects of any situation." Notice that a common trait can be described by one word; to describe a personal disposition, we need several words or even an entire sentence. Moreover, as you can see, describing a personal disposition gives us a great deal more information about a person than does simply naming a common trait.

Trait-names, Allport points out, are range-names. That is, when we measure a group of people on a given trait and find that 20 of them, say, show the trait of aggressiveness, we are not saying that they manifest aggression in the same way. For example, one person may be assertive and competitive; another may be sarcastic and hostile; a third may be physically violent. As Allport says, verbal tags are really only categories, but they are all that we have at present with which to designate traits.

The distinction Allport draws between common traits and personal dispositions has failed to impress psychologists in general (Sanford, 1963), probably because the only real difference between the two is that the latter applies particularly to an individual. Essentially, the personal disposition is a subcategory, or a particularized aspect of a common trait; it describes the particular way in which a trait is manifested in a particular person. Why have these two categories? Why not just talk about traits? Allport says that it is important to distinguish the two types of traits as they evolve out of two quite different research approaches: the **nomothetic** approach, in which the way the same trait is manifested in different people or groups of people is studied, and the **idiographic** approach, in which the investigator studies one person and determines what Allport calls that person's "unique patterned individuality."

In nomothetic research, investigators start with some hypothetical but clearly delimited trait and seek to find it expressed or not expressed in a number of people. To some degree, each individual person studied is arbitrarily labeled by being given a score on such a trait, whether or not it applies to that person. In idiographic research, investigators let the data they collect about the individual person determine the trait categories they apply to the person. We will have more to say about these two approaches in the section on research.

HOW DO WE KNOW THAT TRAITS EXIST?   According to Allport a trait is inferred from "the repeated occurrence of acts that have the same significance following a definable range of stimuli having the same personal significance" (1961, p. 374). It may also be inferred from the endorsement of such acts in the presence of such stimuli. For example, when we observe a man repeatedly making sarcastic remarks in social situations, we may infer that he has a trait of hostility. Or when we find that people responding to a questionnaire endorse items that describe extraverted behavior in a variety of situations, we may infer that a trait of extraversion is being revealed.

BOX 10.2   Stinginess: From 350 B.C. to 1985 A.D.

Allport points out that for thousands of years, writers have been describing people, creating characters, by "defining the major dispositions" of a person: "Almost all the literature of character—whether [nonfiction] or fiction, drama or biography—proceeds on the psychological assumption that each character has certain *traits* peculiar to himself which can be defined through the narrating of typical episodes from life" (1960b, p. 8).

Consider the following character sketch, written by Theophrastus (Greek philosopher and naturalist; 371–287 B.C.) more than 2000 years ago, on "The Stingy Man":

Stinginess is economy carried beyond all measure. A stingy man is one who goes to a debtor to ask for his half-obol interest before the end of the month. At a dinner where expenses are shared, he counts the number of cups each person drinks and he makes a smaller libation to Artermis than anyone. If someone has made a good bargain on his account and presents him with the bill he says it is too much.

When his servant breaks a pot or a plate, he deducts the value from his food. If his wife drops a copper, he moves furniture, beds, chests, and hunts in the curtains. If he has something to sell he puts such a price on it

that the buyer has no profit. He forbids anyone to pick a fig in his garden, to walk on his land, to pick up an olive or a date. Every day he goes to see that the boundary marks of his property have not been moved. He will destrain on a debtor and exact compound interest. When he entertains the members of his deme, he is careful to serve very small pieces of meat to them. If he goes marketing, he returns without having bought anything. He forbids his wife to lend anything—neither salt nor lampwick nor cinnamon nor marjoram nor meal nor garlands nor cakes for sacrifices. "All these trifles," he says "mount up in a year." To sum up, the coffers of stingy men are moldy and the keys rust; they wear cloaks which hardly reach the thigh; a very little oil-bottle supplies them for anointing; they have hair cut short and do not put on their shoes until midday; and when they take their cloak to the fuller they urge him to use plenty of earth so that it will not be spotted so soon. (Allport, 1961, p. 43, quoted from Aldington, 1925)

Notice how Theophrastus traces the trait of stinginess through different situations—home, business, social settings, And the whole account rings true today—compare, for example, the following excerpts from an article entitled "He's

Stingy If . . . " in the popular magazine *Cosmopolitan* (September, 1976, p. 148):

Could a miser be lurking beneath that sensuous flesh and persuasive charm? Well, don't expect sapphires from him, dear, if he

- *Itemizes who owes what when you're out Dutch-treat rather than splitting the bill*
- *Washes plastic party cups to reuse them*
- *Steams uncanceled stamps from letters*
- *Serves only punch at parties*
- *Reshapes bent paper clips*
- *Looks hard for change he drops*
- *Has a dozen recipes for chicken wings*
- *Wears T-shirts with holes in them*
- *Cuts his own hair*
- *Travels only on business*
- *Burns only 25-watt bulbs in his apartment*
- *Wants rolls and butter included in his doggie bag*

In view of our strong, intuitive beliefs that traits exist and in view of the enormously real portraits drawn by writers and novelists, why may it be that researchers who attempt to demonstrate traits, or the consistency of behavior across situations, are often unsuccessful? For some answers, see Chapter 15.

Although writers have for centuries described people in terms of traits (see Box 10.2) empirical research has not been very successful in demonstrating the cross-situational consistency of behavior. Allport claims that when behavior appears inconsistent, we are often taking only a superficial view of that behavior. For example, Allport describes a professor who was always extremely neat about his person and his possessions; his lecture notes, outlines, and files were kept in perfect order; and all his belongings were kept under lock and key. The professor was in charge of his departmental library and, strangely, in that job he was totally careless—the door was not locked, books were lost, dust accumulated. Allport explains the seeming contradiction in this man's behavior by pointing out that underlying both types of behavior was a central disposition of self-centeredness, which allowed the professor to act always for his own interests but never for the interests of others (1961, p. 363).

THE NATURE OF TRAITS.   Traits, Allport argues, can be identified not by their rigid independence but by their tendency to have a center around which their influence operates. The behavior to which a given trait leads is influenced by other traits as well; no sharp boundary delimits one trait from another. For example, suppose that the optimistic person we have mentioned also has a trait of what we might call "ostrichism"—she tends to avoid difficulties by denying problems when they arise or to ignore them. It may sometimes be difficult to tell which trait is in ascendance: Is this person's Pollyanna-like approach due mainly to her insistence on cheerfulness in the face of disaster, or is it a sign that she has hidden her head in the sand?

Although a trait is inferred on the basis of certain consistencies in a person's behavior, Allport is quick to point out that his theory does not require complete consistency. In the first place, the very fact that traits overlap suggests that one may see inconsistencies from time to time. Moreover, if we look at personal dispositions, which are uniquely and individually organized, we may see inconsistencies between such dispositions and the corresponding, broader traits seen from the normative viewpoint. More than consistency, Allport says, a subtle congruence unites the various behavioral manifestations of the individual, although it is often difficult to detect just how this occurs.

WHAT IS THE FUNCTION OF THE TRAIT?   The trait not only guides behavior, it may also initiate behavior. Not all traits are equally impelling; some play a more crucial motivational role than others. For example, the person who has a trait of sociability will seek the company of others; such a person is unlikely to sit at home waiting for others to call. A trait of politeness may not initiate a person's behavior, but it will lead him or her to behave politely when a situation calls for, or provides the opportunity for, such behavior. And a trait of gracefulness will have relatively little motivational power; it will simply characterize a person's expressive movement. (For Allport's definition of expressive behavior and a discussion of some of his research in this area, see "Studies of Expressive Behavior," pages 365–366.)

In a sense, a trait is never the original motivator of behavior; some stimulus, external or internal, must precede its operation. For example, a sociable man may decide to go to a disco because in general he likes to be with people, but this particular behavior may have been set in operation by hearing some good music on the radio, realizing that it is Friday night and that he does not have to work the next day, receiving a telephone call from a friend who plans to go, and so on.

CARDINAL, CENTRAL, AND SECONDARY DISPOSITIONS.   Personal dispositions vary considerably in the degree of generality they possess. The **cardinal disposition** is so general that almost every act of a person seems to reflect it. For example, we may use the term *Machiavellian* to describe the person whose ruling passion is the manipulation of others; the *narcissistic* person is intensely and continually concerned with his or her own needs and interests. Not everyone can be said to have a cardinal disposition; indeed, the latter is, according to Allport, rather rare.

In general, a person can be fairly accurately described by 5 to10 **central dispositions**, tendencies that are highly charactristic of a person. For example, we might describe Shakespeare's Hamlet as introspective, obsessive, melancholy (depressive), revengeful, dramatic, indecisive.

Finally, the **secondary disposition,** like the cardinal disposition, is less common. It is also less crucial to a description of the personality, for it is more focalized than either of the other two. For example, a normally agreeable person might become intensely, even

explosively, angry when on occasion someone makes a derogatory re-
mark about the particular ethinic group to which he or she belongs.
Allport suggests that when a secondary disposition is ''aroused by
only a narrow range of stimulus situations it is more properly called an
attitude than a trait'' (1937, p. 341).

RELATIONS AMONG TRAITS, HABITS, ATTITUDES, AND TYPES.   Traits,
habits, and attitudes are all predispositions, they may all be unique,
they are all the product of both genetic factors and learning, and each
may initiate and/or guide behavior. These three phenomena differ in
certain ways from each other, however, and from types.

In a sense, the trait is the outcome of combining two or more
habits. A **habit**, like a trait, is a determining tendency, but the trait is
more general; it applies to more situations, and it leads to a greater variety of responses. For example, a woman may have a *habit* of hanging
the car keys on a hook next to the back door when she comes in. Her
trait of orderliness, however, may lead her not only to perform this
action repeatedly but to keep several ''in'' boxes of different categories
on her desk and to put reference books in the library in order when
others have left them in disarray.

The **attitude** is more general than the habit but less general
than the trait. Indeed, an attitude can range from the highly specific to
the very general, whereas a trait must always be general. The attitude
also differs from both the habit and the trait in that it is evaluative in
nature; thus, for example, a man's attitude toward equality of opportunity for both men and women may be positive—he may favor such
equality and seek to promote it—or negative—he may disapprove of
such equality and either ignore the efforts of those who support it or
actively seek to thwart them. (Table 10.1 summarizes the characteristics of traits, habits, and attitudes.)

The **type** is a nomothetic category and a much broader concept
than any of the three we have discussed. Indeed, it subsumes them all:
it describes certain combinations of traits, habits, and attitudes that,
theoretically, we can find in a number of people. However, when we
assign an individual to a type, we lose sight of his or her unique characteristics. And because no one fits any given type perfectly, the type is
an artificial distinction that blurs reality.

INTENTIONALITY
The two most distinctive characteristics of Allport's theory of motivation are his refusal to admit the past as a significant element in motivation and his insistence on the importance of cognitive processes, such
as intention and planning, in human adult motivation. Allport insisted
on regarding the human being as a primarily conscious, rational creature who acts on the basis of what he or she hopes to accomplish, not

TABLE 10.1   *Traits, Attitudes, and Habits*

	CHARACTERISTICS SHARED BY TRAITS, ATTITUDES, AND HABITS	FOCUS	GENERALITY	EVALUATIVENESS	EXAMPLE
Trait	Predisposition	Aspects of the self	Most general	Somewhat evaluative	Sociability
Attitude	Product of genetic factors and learning	Facets of the environment	Somewhat general	Most evaluative	Dislike for the Republican party
Habit	May initiate or guide behavior — May be unique	Particular response to particular stimulus	Least general	Least evaluative	Humming along when listening to music

Source: Based on Allport (1961, pp. 345–349).

on the basis of primitive desires or the residue of early traumatic experience.

For Allport, what people are trying to do—and by and large people can tell us what they are trying to do—is the best indicator of how they will behave in the present. Many other theorists, as we have seen, turn to the past for the key to the riddle of behavior, but Allport finds that people's hopes, wishes, ambitions, aspirations, and plans, all of which are subsumed under their intentions, are of primary importance in understanding people's motivation.

Motivation is a crucial aspect of Allport's theory of personality. For Allport (1961), a theory of motivation must acknowledge the contemporaneity of motives: "Whatever moves us must move now." Such a theory must be pluralistic: it must allow for motives of many types—transient, recurring, conscious, unconscious, pressing for basic need satisfaction or for the ambitions and interests of the normally developing adult. A theory must ascribe dynamic force to cognitive processes such as intention and planning, Allport insists, and it must allow for the concrete uniqueness of motives. That is, it is not enough to know that a person has a motive shared by others, as in "John has a need for achievement." We must know how that motive is given expression by that particular person; for example, "John worked very hard to become leader of his high school band."

THE PROPRIUM

The **proprium** (from the Latin *proprius*, meaning "own") is Allport's term for those aspects of personality that many other theorists subsume under *self*, or *ego*. Allport describes the self as "something of which we are immediately aware," something that we think of "as the warm, central, private region of our life" and thus "some kind of core in our being" (p. 110). At the same time, he says, the self is not a constant core—it seems at times to take command of all behavior and consciousness, at others to "go completely offstage." Allport felt that "this difficult problem of the subjective (felt) nature of the self" opened up "profound philosophical dilemmas concerning the nature of man, of 'soul,' of freedom and immortality" (1961, p. 111).

The proprium is the self as object—it includes the sense of bodily self; the sense of continuing self-identity; self-esteem, or pride; the extension of self (relatedness to the external world); the self-image; the self as rational coper; and propriate striving, which includes intentionality, long-range purpose, and distant goals. These seven aspects of the proprium evolve gradually, and we will have more to say about them in the section on personality development.

There is another aspect of self, however—the self as knower—whose place in the totality of the personality is variously described by philosophers and other theorists (see Allport, 1955, especially Sections 10 and 11): "Who is the I who knows the bodily me, who has an image of myself and sense of identity over time, who knows that I have propriate strivings? I know all these things and, what is more, I know that I know them. But who is it who has this perspectival grasp?" (Allport, 1961, p. 128). Allport feared that if we were to postulate a self as a separate agent that "knows, wills, wants and so on," we would be in danger of creating a personality within a personality, a homunculus, or "little man," who cannot really be studied. It is for this reason that he chose to use the term *proprium* rather than *self* or *ego*, which could too easily, he felt, create the presumption of such an inaccessible inner agent. In some way that he does not make quite clear, Allport admits the self-as-knower to the proprium; whether it is an eighth aspect, or the sum total of the seven aspects, or a shadowy phenomenon difficult to pinpoint we cannot tell.

FUNCTIONAL AUTONOMY

According to Allport, **functional autonomy** "regards adult motives as varied, and as self-sustaining contemporary systems, growing out of antecedent systems, but functionally independent of them" (1961, p. 227). By this, Allport means that a given activity or form of behavior may become an end or goal in itself, even though it was originally engaged in for some other, specific reason. And this is true whether or not it has derived from physiological tensions; even in the absence of biological reinforcement, the behavior may be capable of sustaining itself indefinitely.

According to Allport (1961), there are two levels of functional autonomy: perseverative functional autonomy skirts close to what are

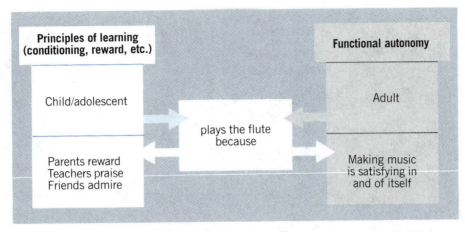

Figure 10.1   Motivation according to Allport.

(and may be assumed to be) "simple neurological principles" (1961, p. 230). Propriate functional autonomy "depends upon certain philosophical assumptions regarding the nature of human personality . . . [that] reach beyond present knowledge of the way the nervous system operates" (Allport, 1961, p. 230).

Allport illustrates **perseverative functional autonomy** with some accounts of experiments in which rats continued to perform certain behaviors in the absence of reinforcement or reward. As instances of such functional autonomy in human beings, Allport cites the child's repetitive behaviors (e.g., repeatedly throwing a toy on the floor until an adult wearies of picking it up); the tendency of people to work at or think about uncompleted tasks (this tendency has also been discussed as the Zeigarnik effect; see, e.g., Baddely, 1976; Deutsch, 1968); and the tendency of both child and adult to seek or prefer the familiar, the routine.

Propriate functional autonomy is found at "the highest levels of organization in personality" (Allport, 1961, p. 237). This type of functional autonomy has to do with the "complex propriate organization that determines the 'total posture' of a mature life system." A prominent ingredient of this propriate organization "is the sense of responsibility one takes for one's life" (Allport, 1961, p. 237).

As examples of propriate functional autonomy, Allport cites a number of events: a student may undertake a field of study, at first, because it is required, but in time, because he has become totally absorbed in the work, perhaps for life. The original motive is lost, and what was a means has become an end (see Figure 10.1). Similarly, the genius finds in his or her creative passion itself the motivation for behavior: Louis Pasteur, Marie Curie, and many others received little or no reward for their work during their lifetimes, yet they persevered, often against great odds.

The young Jascha Heifetz may have played his violin largely at his parents' urging, but it is propriate functional autonomy, according to Allport, that motivates the mature artist.

HOW DOES PROPRIATE FUNCTIONAL AUTONOMY COME ABOUT? It is not easy to determine how functional autonomy develops, partly because we lack sufficient knowledge of the underlying neurological processes that are involved and partly because we have as yet no consistent theory of the nature of man (Allport, 1961, p. 245). Some of the "quasi-mechanical" considerations Allport cites are delayed extinction and partial reinforcement, principles derived from learning theory; a basic neural property he labels "self-maintenance," as seen in what today we call "feedback"; and blending the novel with the familiar. By the last, Allport means that the human being continually incorporates new data into existing frameworks; for example, one may add new, more difficult formulas and theorems as one studies advanced mathematics. Finally, Allport cites the notion that "adaptation is sustained by many mechanisms": because "nature does not put all eggs into one basket," it is likely that functional autonomy is aided by any or all of the principles mentioned.

Allport also cites some "propriate considerations" that "taken together . . . [suggest] that functional autonomy comes about because it is the essence or core of the purposive nature of man" (1961,

p. 250). First, the human being is a creature of energies: "there must be motives to consume one's available energies; and if existing motives do not suffice, new ones will develop" (p. 251). Second, Allport refers to notions of mastery and competence advanced by other theorists, pointing out that "many authors reject the 'reactive' view of man" and that "man has energies to use that reach way beyond the need to react" (p. 251).

The essential nature of man . . . presses toward a relative unification of life (never fully achieved). In this trend toward unification we can identify many central psychological characteristics. Among them are man's search for answers to the "tragic trio" of problems: suffering, guilt, death. We identify also his effort to relate himself to his fellow men and to the universe at large. We see that he is trying to discover his peculiar place in the world, to establish his "identity." . . . We note that man's conduct is to a large degree proactive, intentional, and unique to himself. In the total process the sense of selfhood . . . is involved. . . . Selfhood is [the] reflection of this fundamental human process of becoming. (Allport, 1961, p. 252)

From this point of view, Allport concludes, functional autonomy is merely a way of stating that people's motives grow and change throughout the course of life "because it is the nature of men that they should do so" (1961, p. 252). Readers may find in Allport's position echoes of Jung's unity archetype, Adler's creative power of the self, and Horney's and Maslow's self-actualization.

THE RELATION BETWEEN FUNCTIONAL AUTONOMY AND PAST MOTIVATION.   The fact that the proprium—which is the seat, so to speak, of motivation and functional autonomy—is a developmental phenomenon (see next section) and thus has evolved out of primitive states and past experience would seem to suggest that in motivation there is indeed some link with the past. It is the proprium that determines what forms of behavior will become autonomous. Allport would probably say that the proprium itself is constantly evolving and that, by the time it reaches the last phase, of propriate striving, it has acquired motivational forces that are rooted in the present and the future and has, to a greater or lesser degree, discarded motivations from the past. For Allport, maturity is measured by the extent to which a person's motivations are autonomous.

One of the most useful attributes of the concept of functional autonomy is the fact that it permits a relative divorce from the past of the organism. The history of the person becomes a matter of relative indifference if present behavior is now driven by desires and intentions totally independent of those that served as motivators at earlier periods. In addition, the principle of functional autonomy effectively requires that we see in the person the great, dazzling, unique individuality that

Allport saw in every human being. If any form of behavior is capable of becoming an end in itself (though not all do, as we have seen), there is a sufficient heterogeneity of behavior to lead, with infinitely varied environmental demand, to a bewildering complexity and uniqueness of motives.

THE UNITY OF PERSONALITY

We began this chapter by saying that Allport finds both complexity and unity in the personality. We have discussed many of the complex elements and processes; now let us see how Allport manages to put all of these together.

Actually, Allport says that unity may never be achieved. What unity exists may be only a matter of degree; the human being is always in the process of becoming (more) unified. Nevertheless, several phenomena promote unification. First there is a dynamic unity in the infant's behavior: the baby responds in a sort of all-or-nothing, global manner. As the baby grows, it learns, through differentiation, to make part responses, to respond differentially to different stimuli. As it continues to mature, however, it also learns to integrate many of its acts and behaviors in order to accomplish particular tasks. For example, the baby may first wave its arms and legs when an interesting toy is held near it; gradually, it learns to move its hand toward the toy and then to grasp the toy with its fingers—ever-finer movements enable the infant to get what it wants. Then, as the child matures, he or she learns to put grasping movements together with many other movements in order, for example, to ride a bicycle.

Homeostasis, Allport says, is also an evidence of a tendency toward unity. Insofar as the organism attempts to maintain a steady state, it can be said to be seeking a single, unified condition. In addition, the fact that to carry out any integrated behavior or course of conduct one must mobilize one's energies suggests a unity in at least the functioning of personality.

Cardinal dispositions, by definition, confer unity on the personality, as does the fact of the interlacing of traits and dispositions. Often, when we seem to see inconsistency in the expression of a trait, we can find an underlying unity if we examine the individual's personal dispositions: recall the professor whose habit of neatness was subordinate to his self-centeredness.

The most important unifying forces, Allport says, are the propriate functions, most particularly the notions of the self-image and goal striving. The latter is "perhaps the most useful concept of all. . . . It is the pursuit . . . of major goals that configurates a life" (Allport, 1961, p. 391).

PERSONALITY DEVELOPMENT

It is clear from our discussion of functional autonomy that Allport's theory proposes significant changes between infancy and adulthood. In fact, one might almost say that Allport offers two separate theories of personality: a simple, biological, tension-reduction model of motivation is adequate to explain the infant's behavior, but a much more complex model is required to explain the behavior of the adult. Somewhere along the line between infancy and adulthood there is a complete—though not necessarily sudden—transformation. The mature, or healthy, adult is qualitatively different from the infant; the reasons for the adult's behavior are totally different from the baby's reasons.

INFANCY

Allport sees the newborn child as a creature of heredity, primitive drive, and reflex behavior. The infant does not have a personality. It is endowed with certain potentials, such as those for physique and temperament, but fulfillment of these potentials waits on growth and maturation. Much of the baby's behavior can be described as mass action, or a collection of gross undifferentiated responses in which most or all of the muscular apparatus seems to be involved. The baby is able to respond, however, with some highly specific reflexes, such as sucking and swallowing.

What is the original source of motivated behavior? Allport assumes that a general stream of activity sets the infant into action. Because at this point in development the child is largely a creature of segmental tensions and pleasure–pain feelings, Allport finds a biological model, or one that rests heavily on the law of effect or the pleasure principle, perfectly acceptable for the earliest years of life.

"In a sense," Allport says, "the first year is the least important year for personality, assuming that serious injuries to health do not occur" (1961, p. 78). Thus, although by the second half of this first year of life the infant begins to show distinctive qualities that may foreshadow enduring personality attributes (such as differences in movement or emotional expression), in general the infant at birth is a creature of biology. The baby does not know that it is hungry, wet, or in pain—the baby just *is*. The baby is, as Allport puts it, "solo centered," not ego centered, for ego requires a sense of self. It is only gradually that a growing awareness of the self leads the child to develop motives that bear no close relation to those that motivated his or her behavior originally.

PROPRIATE DEVELOPMENT

Allport's theory of the **development of the proprium** may at first seem at odds with his notion of discontinuity in the evolution of the personality. The proprium develops over a period that stretches from birth to adolescence, and the development of self-awareness and various other attributes of self occurs gradually. However, Allport also says that there is

no single transformation during the course of life so momentous as the gradual passing from the stage of utter solo-centeredness to the stage where the child knows himself to be different from others, to be separated from the environment, and to be able to perceive events as significant for himself as an independent being.'' (1961, p. 112)

Thus, although the transformation occurs gradually, it is total. There is something inexplicable about the transformation; it cannot be described as a moment in time or as a specific action or movement. It is simply accomplished, and the change wrought is radical.

Allport accepts many principles of learning theory as applicable to infant development, but he finds such principles as conditioning, reinforcement, and habit hierarchy quite inadequate to account for adult, or propriate, learning, which requires such mechanisms as cognitive insight. In addition, Allport accepts the explanatory role of psychoanalytic mechanisms only in the development of the nonnormal, or neurotic, personality.

During the first three years of life, as Table 10.2 outlines, three aspects of **self-awareness** develop. First to appear is the **sense of a bodily self**, the recognition of a bodily ''me.'' In developing the **sense of a continuing self-identity**, language is an important factor; naming objects and naming oneself gives the child its first sense of a continuing ''I'' that interacts with what is in the environment. At the same time, the toddler is not completely clear about his or her self—for example, the young child is often unaware of cold or of the need to eliminate. Last to develop during this first period is **self-esteem**, or **pride**. Children want to do things, to make things happen, to control their worlds.

Between the ages of 4 and 6, two more aspects of the proprium come into being: extension of self and the self-image. The extension of self—the relation between the self and those aspects of one's environment with which one is importantly linked, such as one's parents, house, church, country—is rudimentary at this point: the little girl feels that her daddy, her brother, her car are parts of her self, but she is not yet able to include more remote entities within her self-extension.

The **self-image**, or picture of the self as one is, wants to be, and should be, gets a start during this period. The little boy begins to know that his parents want him to be ''good,'' and he understands that at times he is ''naughty,'' but he has only begun to ''lay the foundations for the intentions, goals, sense of moral responsibility, and self-knowl-

TABLE 10.2 *Development of the Proprium*

AGE	EMERGING ASPECT OF THE PROPRIUM
0–3	The sense of bodily self; the physical body as ''me''
	The sense of continuing self-identity; awareness that ''I'' have continuity in time and place
	Self-esteem; pride in one's ability to do things, to control one's world
4–6	Extension of self; feeling of connectedness with people and things that are important in one's life
	Self-image; a sense of who one is, who one wants to be; who one should be
6–12	Self-awareness; recognition of one's ability to cope with problems by reason and thought
Adolescence	Propriate striving; plans and goals for future development: intentions, long-range purposes, distant goals

Source: Based on Allport (1961, pp. 113–127).

edge that will later play a prominent part in his personality'' (Allport, 1961, p. 123).

During the rather long period from 6 to 12 the sixth aspect of the proprium begins to evolve—the **self as rational coper**. Moving out from the family and into the world, children meet new and confusing demands—peer standards, for example, are quite different from parental standards—and they discover a new power, the ability to bring rational thought to bear on problems.

The seventh and last aspect of the proprium to develop, **propriate striving**, is made up of **intentions, long-range purposes**, and **distant goals**. When the person enters adolescence, he or she must again face the issue of self-identity; the central issue now is, Am I a child or an adult? The core of the problem is selecting an occupation or other life goal. It is the recognition that the future requires a plan that causes the adolescent to go beyond the child's wanting to be a firefighter or a pilot or whatever and to make a purposeful, integrated effort to achieve what he or she wants over a relatively long range.

ADULTHOOD

The major determinants of the behavior of the mature adult are a set of organized and congruent traits that initiate and guide behavior according to the principle of functional autonomy. Just how these traits have developed is not important to Allport, for in adulthood they derive their motive power from current sources. The past is not important unless it can be shown to be dynamically active in the present

TABLE 10.3   *Qualities of the Mature Personality*

Extension of the sense of self	The ability to participate in and enjoy a wide range of activities; the ability to identify oneself and one's interests with others and their interests; the ability to project into the future—to hope and to plan.
Warm relating of self to others	The capacity for both intimacy and compassion: intimacy involves loving relationships with family and friends; compassion is expressed in respectful and appreciative relations with all people.
Emotional security (Self-acceptance)	The ability to avoid overreaction to matters pertaining to specific drives (e.g., to accept one's sex drive, do one's best to satisfy it, and be neither inhibited nor promiscuous) and to tolerate frustration; self-control; sense of proportion.
Realistic perceptions, skills, assignments	The ability to see people, objects, and situations for what they are; a capacity for and interest in problem solving; having the necessary skills for accomplishing one's chosen tasks; being capable of "losing oneself" temporarily in one's work; being able to meet the economic demands of life without giving in to panic, self-pity, or other self-destructive behaviors.
Self-objectification: insight and humor	The ability to be objective both about oneself and about others. One needs insight—the ability to understand oneself and others—and humor—not only finding enjoyment and laughter in the world but being able to relate positively to self and others at the same time that one sees incongruities and absurdities in self and others.
Unifying philosphy of life	There should be an underlying thread of complete seriousness that gives purpose and meaning to everything one does. Religion is one of the most important sources of such a philosophy, though it is not the only one.

Source: Based on Allport (1961, pp. 283–304).

In general, the functioning of traits is conscious and rational. Moreover, this functioning follows a pattern at the core of which lie the propriate strivings we have just discussed. Thus, to understand the adult, we need a picture of his or her goals and aspirations.

Not all adults, of course, achieve full maturity. Some disturbed people act without knowing why they act; the behavior of such adults is more closely linked to childhood events than to present or future events. The degree to which conscious thoughts and wishes take precedence over unconscious motivation and the degree to which traits are independent of childish origins is a measure of a person's normality and maturity. Allport was much more interested in normal than in neurotic behavior, and he considered at some length the qualities that make for maturity of personality; Table 10.3 describes some of these qualities.

In his classic study The Nature of Prejudice *(1954), Allport traced the roots of the kind of mutual mistrust that this Laotian refugee woman and native New Englander seem to be expressing.*

RESEARCH EMPHASES AND METHODS

Interestingly, despite Allport's emphasis on the importance of idiographic research, which, you will recall, focuses on the individual, much of his own work falls into the category of nomothetic research, which compares many individuals. Allport's continuing concern with societal issues led him to devote considerable time as well to research on such matters as racial and ethnic prejudice, the formation and spread of rumor, and the psychology of mass communication.

The two primary methods Allport developed for measuring personality—the **A–S (Ascendance–Submission) Scale** and **A Study of Values**—were constructed essentially by nomothetic techniques, but they have both nomothetic and idiographic characteristics and applications (Allport and Allport, 1928; Allport, Vernon, and Lindzey, 1960). For example, the Study of Values examines the degree to which a person favors each of six ideal values—theoretical (truth), economic (usefulness), esthetic (harmony), social (altruistic love), political (power), and religious (unity)—by forcing the subject to rank these values in successive pairings; each value is paired an equal number of times with each of the other five. The resulting profile is idiographic in nature, inasmuch as it reflects only the relative importance of these values for a given individual. Because all rankings are fixed and comparative, as the score on one value rises, the score on another must decrease. But, Allport points out, the test also yields norms that have been broken down by such categories as sex and occupation, so that it combines advantages of both idiographic and nomethetic methods.

We will begin this section by comparing the nomothetic and idiographic approaches to the study of personality. Then we will look at two areas of Allport's work in which he has endeavored to use idiographic methods: his studies of expressive behavior and his study of a single individual—a woman called "Jenny"—through her letters.

IDIOGRAPHIC VERSUS NOMOTHETIC METHODS

Allport believed that there was a place in psychology for both idiographic and nomothetic approaches, but he also felt that American psychology had so overwhelmingly emphasized the nomothetic approach that our understanding of the individual and our ability to predict behavior have suffered. For Allport, it is only by knowing the person as a person that we can predict what he or she will do in any given situation.

Allport and his collaborators have developed several methods of idiographic investigation. The **matching technique** is described in the section on expressive behavior, and **structural** and **content analysis** are discussed in the section on "Jenny." We have already encountered some idiographic investigative techniques—the Q-methodology, described in Chapter 6, and the REP test, discussed in Chapter 8—and others have been developed (see, e.g., Shapiro, 1961; Kilpatrick and Cantril, 1960). Allport (1942) was a very early advocate of the usefulness of personal documents in the study of behavior and consistently emphasized the need for new and better idiographic techniques. Only a beginning has as yet been made in developing such methods. (For a recent effort in this direction, see Lamiell, 1981.)

Allport was critical of what he considered the excessive and inappropriate use of projective tests in measuring the individual personality. (Projective tests, like the Rorschach and the Thematic Apperception Test, or TAT, present ambiguous stimuli, asking subjects to describe what the stimuli remind them of or seem to mean, on the theory that unconscious thoughts and wishes will be "projected" onto the stimuli presented and thus brought into awareness.) Consistent with his belief in the overriding importance in the normal person of conscious, rational determinants of behavior, Allport insisted that projective, or indirect, measures of personality could contribute significantly to one's knowledge about a person only if the person were neurotic, or nonnormal. Because such people are ruled significantly by unconscious needs and desires, their responses on direct and indirect measures may be quite discrepant. In normal people, however, both types of measure should produce a consistent picture. Suggesting that one can often obtain just as much information by asking a direct question as by asking an indirect one, Allport tells the story of the man who remarked that a Rorschach card made him think of sexual relations. "The clinician, thinking to tap a buried complex, asked him why. 'Oh, because,' said the patient, 'I think of sexual relations all the time'" (Allport, 1953, p. 108).

STUDIES OF EXPRESSIVE BEHAVIOR

Insofar as it holds that all of the person's behavior is congruent and interrelated, Allport's theory suggests that even simple, inconspicuous acts will be related in some way to central aspects of the person's makeup. As a way of obtaining information about these central aspects of behavior, Allport and his collaborators began in the early 1930s to look at expressive behavior.

Expressive behavior includes such things as facial expression, quality of voice, gait, speed of movement, and style of handwriting. Every human response, Allport says, has at least two components: the **adaptive component**, which reflects the function, or purpose, of the act, and the **expressive component**, which reflects the manner or style in which the act is performed. For example, driving a car involves such adaptive behaviors as turning the ignition key, shifting gears, and steering. These same responses are performed by hundreds of people every day, but they are performed differently by each person: one person may flip the key as she jumps into the seat, whereas another may seat himself comfortably and then calmly turn the key; one person may shift gears abruptly, another with care; one person may sit up rigidly, both hands on the wheel, whereas another may sit and manipulate the steering wheel in a totally relaxed manner, almost one with the machine.

The expressive portion of conduct results . . . from deep-lying determinants functioning, as a rule, unconsciously and without effort. The adaptive portion . . . is a more limited system, circumscribed by the purpose of the moment. . . . The reason for a present act . . . is to be sought in the . . . intentions of the individual; . . . but the style of execution is always guided . . . by deep and lasting personal dispositions. (Allport, 1937, p. 466)

Thus, Allport found in expressive behavior not only confirmation of other aspects of the personality but information about important sources of motivation and conflict.

Allport points out that expressive behavior is also determined by sociocultural factors, by temporary moods, and by other variables. Like personality itself, expressive behavior may have many contributors, and many kinds of expressive behavior may be revealing of important information about the person.

Allport has carried out a number of studies of expressive behavior, the most extensive with Philip Vernon in the early 1930s. Allport and Vernon found not only a basic consistency among a person's various forms of expressive behavior but "a congruence between expressive movement and the attitudes, traits, values, and other dispositions of the 'inner' personality" (Allport and Vernon, 1933, p. 248).

Not long after his work with Vernon, Allport collaborated with Hadley Cantril (1934) in a study of subjects' ability to judge personality on the basis of voice alone. These researchers found that subjects were in fact able to relate voices heard both with lists of personality characteristics and with descriptions of physical characteristics with better than chance accuracy. Interestingly, Allport and Cantril also found that subjects were more consistent and more accurate in matching people's voices with their interests and traits than with their physical features or handwriting. The fact that traits, which can only be inferred, were judged more accurately than such obvious things as facial appearance, age, or height lends support, the authors suggest, to the central importance of traits and dispositions.

Summarizing his discussion of the foregoing and other studies, Allport (1961) writes that the evidence justifies three conclusions. First, expressive features of the body are not independently activated; any one of them may be affected in much the same way as any other. Second, the congruence is never perfect, for one feature is not an exact replica of another. If it were, we would be justified in diagnosing the personality from any one feature—from handwriting or from the eyes, hands, or limbs. Finally, the unity of expression, like the unity of personality, is a matter of degree.

THE PERSONAL DOCUMENT: "JENNY'S" LETTERS

As we have seen, Allport believed firmly that personality should be studied from many points of view. One of these views is that of the personal document—for example, the letter, the diary, the autobiography. When in the 1940s he was given 301 letters written by a middle-aged woman (fictitiously named "Jenny Masterson") to a young couple over a period of 12 years, Allport recognized the usefulness of this personal record in studying personality, and he used the letters for many years in his classes at Harvard, encouraging students to analyze the letters to determine "Jenny's" outstanding traits.

Allport himself, in a structural analysis (1965) of the letters, asked 36 people to read Jenny's letters and to characterize Jenny in terms of her traits. The judges came up with a total of 198 trait-names, most of which Allport was able to group under eight central trait categories. (Table 10.4 lists these categories as well as those derived by a computer analysis that is discussed a little later.) Almost all the judges felt that Jenny's most prominent traits were suspiciousness, self-

TABLE 10.4 *Jenny's Central Traits*

COMMONSENSE APPROACH	AS DERIVED BY COMPUTER ANALYSIS
Quarrelsome–suspicious } Aggressive }	Aggression
Self-centered	{ Possessiveness { Martyrdom
Sentimental	{ Need for affiliation { Need for family acceptance
Independent–autonomous	Need for autonomy
Aesthetic–artistic	Sentience
Cynical–morbid	(No parallel)
Dramatic–intense	(No parallel)[a]
(No parallel)	Sexuality[b]

Source: Based on Allport (1965, pp. 193–202).
[a]Computer analysis did reveal, however, that Jenny was much more given to overstatement (based on words indicating exaggeration such as *always, never, impossible*) than to understatement (words indicating caution and qualification).
[b]Sexuality is not of course a trait. What the computer picked up here, primarily, was Jenny's "romantic descriptions of her relationship with her son." Interestingly, in the commonsense analysis, an unclassified category of trait-names does include the term *incestuous*, which would seem to reflect judges' impression that Jenny's relationship with her son—and perhaps her sexual adaptation in general—was not completely normal.

centeredness, and independence–need for autonomy, but almost all of them also remarked on the importance of the other five categories. At the same time, Allport notes, there is considerable overlap between the categories; for example, quarrelsomeness is linked with aggressiveness. When Allport asked the judges whether they could perceive any one unifying theme (cardinal trait), however, no one such theme emerged. Allport admits that such a theme, or themes, may "lie completely buried" in the unconscious realms not given expression in the letters. At the same time, he points out that

after reading the first few letters we find ourselves forecasting what will happen next. . . . The predictability of Jenny, as with any mortal, is the strongest argument for insisting that personality is a dependable hierarchy of sentiments and dispositions, possessed of enduring structure. (Allport, 1965, p. 196)

Acknowledging that his analysis of the letters had used an essentially intuitive procedure, Allport describes two studies that used the method of **content analysis** to produce a more quantitative description of Jenny's communications. Baldwin (1942) used what he called "personal structure analysis" to select prominent topics and themes and to plot the frequency of their coexistence in the same context of thoughts as well as to connect these topics with Jenny's basic attitudes and value judgments. For example, when she spoke of her son, Ross, in a favorable light, she often discussed nature, art, and past experiences of these in Ross's company; when she spoke of Ross unfavorably, she tended to harp on his selfishness, her own self-sacrificing qualities, and the unfavorable qualities of Ross's women friends. (Box 10.3 presents selected letters that revolve particularly around Jenny's intense and unhappy relationship with her son.)

More than 20 years after Baldwin's work, Paige (cited in Allport, 1965) used computer methods to perform a similar content analysis that produced eight factors considered to be Jenny's most important traits. As you can see, from Table 10.4, these factors are very similar to those derived by Allport from his "commonsense" analysis. Although the correspondence between the two lists is not exact, the lists are very similar. Moreover, the objective analysis confirmed a number of the 198 trait-names included under the eight major categories of the commonsense analysis. Allport concludes that content analysis, although it "provides no golden key to the riddle of Jenny," does objectify, quantify, and to some extent purify commonsense impressions. "By holding us close to the data (that is, to Jenny's own words), it warns us not to let some pet insight run away with the evidence. And it brings to our attention occasional fresh revelations beyond unaided common sense. In short, by bringing Jenny's phenomenological world to focus, it enables us to make safer first-order inferences concerning the structure of personality that underlies her existential experience" (Allport, 1965, p. 204).

EVALUATION

Throughout his professional career, Allport maintained his allegiance to his theories of traits and of functional autonomy. At the same time, he argued to the end for what he called a "systematic eclecticism" or a "true synthesis of theories" (Allport, 1965, p. 211). He recognized the contradictory nature of this phrase—"a system is more than an eclectic assemblage. . . . It offers . . . a superordinate principle" (Allport 1968, p. 24)—but insisted that "by striving for system *in an eclectic manner*, we may actually achieve a comprehensive metatheory" (1968, p. 24). "Any investigator," Allport said, "has the right to restrict his variables and neglect, momentarily, irrelevant aspects of behavior, *but he has no right to forget what he has decided to neglect*" (Allport, 1967, p. 23). He believed that psychology must maintain an open system, and he justified his preference for a guiding theory by his conviction that "significant, not trivial questions must be posed before we lose ourselves in a frenzy of investigation" (Allport, 1967, p. 3).

Allport never developed a school of followers, as many personality theorists have done, although traces of his influence may be found in the work of former students such as Jerome Bruner, Gardner Lind-

BOX 10.3   Hell Hath No Fury, or, a Woman Scorned

The letters reproduced here are taken from *Letters from Jenny* (1965), a collection of 301 letters written by "Jenny Masterson" (all names are fictitious) to her son's college roommate and the latter's wife over a period of 12 years. The five letters reproduced include four from Jenny to "Glenn" and "Isabel" and one from Jenny's son, "Ross," to Glenn and span a period of only two and a half years. This period witnessed perhaps Jenny's most acute distress over the behavior of her son as well as his death at the age of 32, and they contain some of her most intense expressions of her feelings about Ross and their relationship. Ross's letter suggests frustration over the situation and a certain hopelessness.

March 9, 1928
My dearest Boy and Girl [Glenn and Isabel]:
    . . . . The only *real thrill* I have ever experienced in my whole life was when I held Ross's tiny hand in mine and knew him to be *mine*.

Jenny

May 31, 1929
My dearest and Best [Glenn],

No, things have not improved for me. Ross's chip-lady [Ross's friend Vivian] is all settled down in their apartment, about 15 minutes walk from our house, and Ross spends most of his time there—most of his nights certainly for he is seldom in this apt. until *4 or 5 AM*. . . . Ross is so unbelievably unprincipled, unfeeling and al-

most inhuman . . . Ah! Glenn, my dear, Ross is not a good son, nor is he a decent fellow. Ross is sex-mad. . . .

I am trying to save myself from a Lunatic Asylum, and so am reading my dear books over again—am almost through with Hugo—am fond of him, and then I think I'll "do" some poetry, and mythology—have always been interested in the Gods.

You have my best love, and my sincere gratitude. . . . I don't forget how you have always been my stand-by.

Jenny

July 6, 1929
[From a letter written by Ross to Glenn]:
I am sorry not to have something cheerful to say about Mother and me. Our lives seem constant problems—so constant that I am lost in their maze and see neither right nor wrong nor any solution. . . .

Ever since last summer I have returned home to be nagged about Marie [Ross's former wife]. The artist friend, Vivian Vold, whom Mother adopted for four months, helped for a while to dampen the recriminations about Marie. Then Mother decided I stayed out too late with Vivian. Then Vivian moved into a flat, and Mother began throwing my meals at me. "Hell hath no fury," etc. She never talked. . . . Whenever she broke silence at all it was to call Vivian a whore, prostitute, rat, etc. . . .

Meantime I am worried about my job which seems shaky and my life which seems futile. . . . I am the assistant to the General Manager. Politics are trying to oust him. If he leaves, I have no job.

If anything except the passage of time were being accomplished, I would not object. But I get nowhere, have no fun, do nothing, live in struggle of preserving enough sanity to continue supporting Mother and me, and trying to think out a means of living. . . .

Ross

In September 1929 Ross underwent surgery for a mastoid condition and "an abscess on the outer covering of the brain."

November 6, 1929
My dearest [probably Glenn]:
You must try and be patient with me for writing so often and so much—it is quite an imposition—but I am in great trouble, *and alone*.

First about Ross:—On hearing that he is living with that woman [Vivian], and eating her bread—lying in bed mornings while *she* hustles out to work—I was in despair. Of course anyone (except Ross) could see why she does it. She must cajole him into a marriage ceremony—merely to protect *herself*—and *then*—well! then she will tell him what she thinks of him (and who could blame her), just as his first wife did. *She* gains any benefit that is in the dirty business—he loses. . . . I would save him if I could.

... My plan is this—Ross acknowledged that he would not marry the chip at this time only that is under a financial obligation to her, and feels that he *owes* her a marriage ceremony. I say, all right, marry her, but *not now.* Today he has nothing at all to offer her. Leave her but announce to her Father and friends that she is his fiancée, and that he is going away to *make a home* for her. Then get a job—get himself in good physical condition, insure his life *for her*—have some money ahead and then say ''now here's the home I have made for *you*'' and return to N.Y. and marry her. By that time all bills are paid.

I will provide the money—I will pay his expenses [to any city he chooses] and give him $150 or $200 to start. In the meantime he is not to trouble about me at all—I'll get a job and get along somehow, and *be glad* to do it.

Lady M.

Telegram received by Glenn November 8, 1929:
ROSS DIED IN RELAPSE. CAN YOU COME? JGM

October 23, 1930
My dearest Girl [Isabel]:

This month has been pretty hard on me—I had to move—it cost a lot—then came Ross's birthday, October 16. Last Oct. 16 Ross spent with me—I watched for him all morning, my heart in my mouth. Then early in the afternoon he came, carrying a lovely bunch of red roses—my favorites—he always got red roses for me. I was in Heaven. He had not forgotten—he chose to have dinner with me—not with the Chip [Vivian]. He took me to a nice place up here on Broadway, and then to a show—a splendid show—he came to my room on the roof, and kissed goodnight under the stars—how little we dreamed of what the next year would bring! I am always thinking of him—always wishing that I had done something I did not do—or left something undone, or unsaid, that I did do, and said.

Lady M.

---

zey, Thomas Pettigrew, and Brewster Smith. Allport continued to modify his theory so as to place increasing emphasis on intentionality and on ego, or propriate, functions. Indeed, Allport was probably as influential as any psychologist in breathing life into the concept of ego, which had fallen out of favor in the early years of this century. He persistently emphasized the need for such a concept to represent normal, complex human behavior. This emphasis on ego functions was highly congruent with developments then beginning to occur in psychoanalytic ego psychology. As a result, despite the fact that he was an unremitting critic of Freudian theory, Allport became one of the more popular psychological theorists in psychoanalytic circles.

Allport's emphasis on the primary importance of the conscious determinants of behavior led, of course, to his advocating direct methods of assessing motivation, a position that has been distinctly unpopular among many contemporary psychologists. Allport's insistence that the present and the future are vastly more important than the past in determining the motivation and behavior of the person initially met similar resistance from psychologists, but, as the situational determinants of behavior have been emphasized more and more by theorists and researchers, Allport's position has gained in acceptance.

Allport's ardent plea for the detailed study of the individual case, his focus on current motives, and his emphasis on conscious motivation all serve to make him one of the few theorists who effectively bridges the gap between academic psychology on the one hand and the fields of clinical and personality psychology on the other. This open channel of communication not only enriches each subdiscipline with the insights of the other but helps to maintain an intellectual continuity that is important for the long-term development of psychology.

A final novelty in Allport's position lies in his emphasis on the future and the present to the relative exclusion of the past. Because psychoanalysis has been so influential, it has often been easy for the investigator or practitioner to bypass current and situational determinants of behavior in favor of determining factors that lie in the past. As a result, it has been helpful to have Allport's writings as a constant reminder that the past is not the whole of the functioning person.

Despite all these contributions to the body of knowledge and theory in personality, Allport's theory has been widely criticized (e.g., Bertocci, 1940; Coutu, 1949; Seward, 1948; and Skaggs, 1945). The formal inadequacy of the theory has given rise to many questions: What are the precise assumptions of this theory and what is open to empirical test? How are the theory's assumptions interrelated? Where are the careful empirical definitions that permit the investigator to translate concepts into operational terms?

These central issues have been debated by Allport and others. A particularly good example of such debate can be found in two articles by Holt (1962) and Allport (1962), published side by side in the *Journal of Personality*. Holt (1962) criticizes Allport's use of idiographic methods to study individual personalities, claiming that these special methods are not necessary for the study of personality. Allport (1962) argues for their necessity, however, and suggests several research techniques.

Allport's hope was that by studying an individual case by means of idiographic methods, personality psychologists could come "to do justice to the fascinating individuality that marks the personalities of Bill, John and Betty" (1962, p. 421). The result, he believed, would be a better theory of personality than could evolve from an exclusive focus on general features rather than those that are unique.

In large part because Allport embraces the idiographic approach to personality, his theory fails to specify a set of dimensions for studying personality. Personal traits or dispositions, for example, cannot be stated in any general form, so the investigator must devise new variables for each subject studied. This can be very discouraging for any investigator.

Although it is true that clinicians are more concerned with the individual's unique expressions of behavior than most other psychologists, even clinicians, Sanford (1963) points out, attempt to discover general principles in analyzing an individual case. Indeed, some clinicians, such as Harry Stack Sullivan, insist that the individual cannot be understood except in relation to others. (Sullivan agreed with Allport that there is an inner, private aspect to personality, but he believed that that can never be known by anyone but the individual himself or herself.)

Perhaps part of the problem here is that Allport, by his own admission, failed to give sufficient consideration to "the variability induced by ecological, social, and situational factors" (1968, p. 63). Allport stated that this oversight needs "to be repaired through an adequate theory that will relate the inside and outside systems more accurately" (1968, p. 63), but his death left this as a task for others.

Despite this concession, Allport firmly maintained that traits cannot be accounted for in terms of interaction effects. Environmental situations and sociocultural variables may be causal forces, but the intervening factor of personality is always the primary cause of human conduct. Allport summed up his approach to the person-in-situation as follows:

The personality theorist should be so well trained in social science that he can . . . cast the behavior of an individual properly in the culture where it occurs, in its situational context, and in terms of role theory and field theory. At the same time he should not lose sight . . . of the fact that there is an internal and subjective patterning of all these contextual acts. (1960a, p. 306)

One of the theory's biggest problems is its inability to demonstrate functional autonomy empirically. Allport tells us that the phenomenon occurs, but he provides no satisfactory explanation of how or why. As a result, opponents of his theory have attacked its simple premise—that given responses do not extinguish, or drop out, but continue even without reinforcement—by arguing that the investigator should simply watch longer to observe extinction or that what appears to be autonomous response is actually a manifestation of some underlying motivation not adequately understood by the investigator.

Another feature of Allport's theory that has come under fire is its assumption of discontinuity between animal and human being, infant and adult, normal and abnormal. Most psychologists are so firmly convinced that we have gained increased knowledge about normal adult human behavior from the study of the abnormal person, the infant, and the nonhuman animal that Allport's position seems nothing short of heretical.

For some, Allport's theory paints too pretty a picture of the human being. He has been criticized, as was Adler, for excessive optimism and for overemphasizing the positively valued aspects of human behavior. Allport never denied the importance of unconscious motives, and he frequently confronted the need to explain abnormal, or at least mildly neurotic, behavior in his work (see, e.g., Allport, 1965;

evaluations of ''Jenny's'' personality). Nevertheless, his eagerness to give the proper place in personality to socialized motives and rational processes has resulted in a position that to many appears out of balance.

In an area where there are so few well-established regularities and where the major variables almost certainly are not yet clearly identified, it seems important to maintain a healthy diversity in the theoretical positions guiding research. Allport's views give persuasive emphasis to problems and concepts often neglected in contemporary psychological theory. Perhaps the most remarkable characteristic of Allport's work is that, in spite of his somewhat unfashionable views and his continuing eclecticism, it has exerted a broad influence not only on the study of personality but on the general field of psychology.

SUMMARY

1. The normal adult human being is a rational creature governed largely by conscious intentions that are rooted in the present and the future, not in the past.

2. Personality is a dynamic phenomenon that has both psychological and physiological elements; as it grows and changes, it plays an active role in the functioning of the individual.

3. **Traits** are neuropsychic structures that lead the person to behave in ways that are consistent over time and space—to make similar responses to similar classes of stimuli.

4. The **common trait** is a characteristic shared by many people; the **personal disposition** is the manifestation of the common trait in a particular individual.

5. Traits have motive power, but some serve only to guide behavior already set in motion; others initiate behavior, leading the person to seek out certain situations and to behave in certain ways.

6. In rare instances, a person manifests a **cardinal disposition** that characterizes his or her entire life-style. More commonly, a person can be described by 5 to 10 **central dispositions**. The person is also characterized by **secondary dispositions**, but these are less common and less crucial to a personality description.

7. **Functional autonomy** holds that given activities or behaviors become ends or goals in themselves, even though they were originally engaged in for other reasons. Although many behaviors continue in adulthood to operate on the basis of simple learning principles, a measure of maturity is the degree to which one's motives have become functionally autonomous.

8. The best indicators of how people will behave in the present and the future are people's **intentions**—their plans and goals.

9. Somewhere in the course of development between infancy and adulthood, a complete transformation takes place. The motives that guide the adult's behavior are totally different from those that guide the baby's behavior.

10. The **proprium** is the self as object; how the self as knower is to be represented is not completely clear. The proprium is composed of seven aspects that evolve over the period that stretches from birth to adolescence: the **sense of bodily self**; the **sense of continuing self-identity**; **self-esteem**, or **pride**; **extension of self**; the **self-image**; the **self as rational coper**; and **propriate striving**, which subsumes **intentions**, **long-range purposes**, and **distant goals**.

11. The healthy adult is characterized by a set of organized and congruent traits whose functioning is largely conscious and rational. These traits derive their motive power from the propriate strivings; thus, to understand the adult, we must understand his or her goals and aspirations.

12. The person is always in the process of becoming more unified. The most important unifying forces are the propriate functions; among these, it is goal striving that configurates the personality.

13. Although both **idiographic** and **nomothetic** approaches to research are important, work is needed to develop better techniques of idiographic research.

14. The work of Allport and his collaborators on expressive movement has revealed a consistency among expressive behaviors as well as a congruence between expressive movement and traits, attitudes, and other aspects of the ''inner'' personality.

15. Several idiographic studies of 301 personal letters agreed essentially on six to eight central traits that characterized the writer of the letters, a woman called ''Jenny.''

16. Allport bridged academic and clinical psychology with his emphasis on the study of the individual case, the importance of conscious motivation, and the governing power of present and future motives. He was influential in restoring the concept of ego to favor in academic psychology, and his views have found favor with many ego psychologists and psychoanalysts.

17. Critics take Allport to task for offering a theory that lacks formal adequacy and that has thus not generated much research; for failing to demonstrate his central concept, that of functional autonomy; for assuming discontinuity between animal and human, infant and adult, normal and abnormal; for insisting on the uniqueness of the personality; for giving far too little attention to the influence of social and situational factors; and for painting the human being in too positive a light.

SUGGESTED READING

Allport's most formal presentation of his theories is contained in *Pattern and Growth in Personality* (1961), the revised edition of his first major work, *Personality: A Psychological Interpretation* (1937). In *The Person in Psychology* (1968), Allport offers a collection of essays that range over a number of topics, from his model of the trait and his views on eclecticism to his work on religion and prejudice. This book also includes a series of essays on important figures in psychology, such as William James and Kurt Lewin, as well as a copy of the autobiographical statement Allport wrote for Boring and Lindzey's *History of Psychology in Autobiography* (1967).

To understand Allport's position with respect to the detailed study of the individual case, you may find it helpful to look also at Allport's article on ''The Use of Personal Documents in Psychological Sciences'' (1942) and to study *Letters from Jenny* (1965), which we discussed briefly in the section on research.

Two papers Allport himself felt were important expressions of his views are ''The Ego in Contemporary Psychology'' (1943) and ''The Trend in Motivational Theory'' (1953). The former essay was instrumental in reintroducing the concept of self into academic psychology. The latter expresses Allport's anti-psychoanalytic views and argues for a theory of motivation that distinguishes sharply between what is infantile and what is strictly contemporary.

To appreciate Allport's views on nomothetic and idiographic research and to appreciate his ability to combine these approaches in personality measurement, you should look at one or both of the two personality tests for which Allport is well known: the *A–S Reaction Study* (1928), which he developed in collaboration with his brother Floyd Allport, and A *Study of Values*, originally developed in collaboration with Philip Vernon (1931) and later revised by Allport, Vernon, and Lindzey (1960).

Allport's *The Nature of Prejudice* (1954) is considered a classic study of racial and ethnic issues, and the student interested in this area would do well to examine it.

Chapter eleven

11.

Perhaps only two things count in human life; the influence you have upon others' minds, and what has delighted you—lighted up your imagination.

WILLIAM H. SHELDON

Constitutional and Genetic Views:
William Sheldon and Others

Many of us think of fat people as jolly and without much willpower, thin people as nervous and sometimes shy, redheads as hot-tempered and hard to get along with. For centuries, lay persons and many scholars shared the belief that behavior is related in important ways to a person's physical makeup. From the fifth century B.C. to the present day, investigators have described such relations and have tried to demonstrate them empirically.

Psychologists, particularly American psychologists, have been generally reluctant to consider the possibility of an intimate tie between body and behavior. Probably the primary reason for this has been our resistance to the notion of genetic determinism—the idea that behavior is innately determined and thus presumably unchangeable. American democracy, the Protestant ethic, and the dogma of the self-made person all have led us to reject such notions and to embrace an environmentalism that holds that nothing is given or predetermined. Anything and everything can be learned or achieved by anyone given the right environment.

In addition, some of the early efforts to explain behavior by reference to physical aspects of the person, such as phrenology (see page 379), were so poorly conceived and so exploited by those who sought only to defraud and deceive that the basic premises of the field of constitutional psychology—an assumption of a close relation between physique, or body build, and behavior—became generally suspect.

Today, as we extend the range of what is observable to submolecular levels, the importance of genetic transmission becomes increasingly clear, and, as the second major section of this chapter points out, some of the past speculations may eventually have a hard scientific basis. For example, obesity may not be caused by a lack of willpower; both obesity and so-called lack of willpower may derive from a physiological mechanism that regulates caloric intake and the expenditure of energy (see, e.g., Bennett and Gurin, 1982; Katahn, 1982). And, as we will see in this chapter and in Chapter 12, introversion, commonly associated with thin people, has been linked to a high level of cerebral excitability, a hyperresponsiveness. Thus, both thinness and ''shyness'' might reflect a supersensitivity to stimuli and a consequent overexpenditure of (caloric) energy.

In virtually all empirical disciplines, at one time or another, ideas have been advanced that are ''ahead of their time.'' Galileo's struggles to convince others of the accuracy of his conception of the universe are a case in point. Whether constitutional psychology will prove to be such a case, we cannot say. It does seem very likely, however, that the subject matter of this ancient field of study is closely related to that dealt with in such contemporary fields as psychophysiology, neurophysiology, psychopharmacology, and behavior genetics.

To help you understand these various fields and their interrelations, we focus, in the first part of this chapter, on the work of William H. Sheldon. (For a capsule history of constitutional psychology prior to Sheldon, see Box 11.1.) The second part of the chapter introduces you to the work that is being carried out in behavior genetics to advance our knowledge of the inherited underpinnings of human psychological functioning. Chapter 12, on the work of Raymond Cattell and Hans Eysenck, describes the thinking of two important personality theorists who derive a number of their formulations from genetically framed postulates.

WILLIAM H. SHELDON: FIRST MODERN PROPONENT OF CONSTITUTIONAL PSYCHOLOGY

For William H. Sheldon, psychologist, physician, philosopher, and naturalist, the physical structure of the body was a primary determinant of behavior. Sheldon (1949b) believed that psychology requires ''. . . a physical anthropology couched in terms of components or variables which can be measured and quantified at both the structural and behavioral ends—the anthropological and psychological ends—of the structure–behavior continuum which is a human personality.'' (p. xv).

Although Sheldon is sometimes referred to as a type theorist because his theory classifies people according to three primary kinds of physique, he argued against such typing, insisting that his variables were ''continuous.'' By this he meant that these variables were to be applied not categorically but in terms of degree. No one person represents this or that type. Everyone comprises, within his or her makeup, some portion of each of three basic components. Sheldon's theory

BOX 11.1   The Venerable Discipline of Constitutional Psychology

The Greek physician Hippocrates (ca. 460–377 B.C.) is generally considered the founder of the discipline of constitutional psychology. (He is also considered the father of modern medicine.) Hippocrates proposed a twofold classification of human physiques: those that were thick, muscular, and strong, and those that were delicate, linear, and weak. The first type were particularly subject to stroke (cerebrovascular accident, thrombosis), the second to tuberculosis.

In the medieval theory of the ''humors,'' derived from a concept of Hippocrates, the sanguine man (far left) had plenty of blood, the melancholy man (left) had a surplus of bile, the hot-tempered man (right) had excessive choler, and the sluggish man (far right) had too much phlegm.

Hippocrates also classified people according to four temperament types that corresponded to the four basic elements proposed by Empedocles, a contemporary Greek philosopher: air, water, fire, and earth. Hippocrates proposed that his temperament types were determined by four ''humors,'' or liquid substances, contained in the body.

According to Sheldon (1944), over the centuries a number of typologies were put forward, all of them rather similar to that proposed by Hippocrates. Galen, for example, a second-century Greek physician, proposed a typology of humors based on Hippocrates' system. But it was not until the eighteenth century that typologies based on observable physical characteristics were again suggested. In the late 1700s, Franz Joseph Gall (1758–1828), a German physician, together with his associate, Johann Friedrich Spurzheim (1776–1832), began to develop the ''science'' of **phre-** **nology**, which held that specific regions of the brain were actually the organs of the various faculties of mind, such as hopefulness, cautiousness, or self-esteem, and that as a result the configuration of the head (literally, bumps and indentations in the skull) revealed which of these faculties were strongest in a given person (Gall and Spurzheim, 1809). Phrenology itself has long been discredited, but neuroscientists continue to explore the question of the localization of behavior (feelings, thoughts, actions) in the brain.

In the early nineteenth century, several French writers, including Rostan (1824), devised threefold typologies of the human being. These generally described a digestive, a muscular, and a respiratory–cerebral type of person. In the early twentieth century, Viola (1909), in Italy, formulated another twofold classification that measured the linearity of a human body as compared with its mass. Viola's categories, you will note—the ''microsplanchnics,'' or small-bodied, and the ''macrosplanchnics,'' or large-bodied—resembled Hippocrates' two types.

It was Ernst Kretschmer (1888–1964) who launched constitutional psychology on its modern course. A German psychiatrist who made many contributions to European psychiatry, Kretschmer is known in this country for his studies of the relation between physique and mental disorder and for the typology that resulted from this work.

In his practice, Kretschmer became convinced that there were important relations between physique and behavior, particularly the type of behavior displayed in the two major forms of mental disorder, **manic-depressive psychosis** (characterized by excessively wide, intense mood swings) and schizophrenia (characterized by disordered thought, emotional unresponsiveness, withdrawal, and sometimes delusions, or false beliefs, and hallucinations, or false perceptions). On this theory, Kretschmer (1921) undertook a painstaking study of the body build of a large number of patients—an elaborate checklist representing major body parts was filled out as a subject stood naked before the investigators—and arrived at a conception of three fundamental types of physiques: the **asthenic**, or frail, linear physique; the **athletic**, or muscular and vigorous physique; and the **pyknic**, or plump physique. In a fourth, **dysplastic**, type, portions of the body might be of one type while other portions were of others.

With this typology in hand, Kretschmer studied another group of 260 patients, both manic-depressive and schizophrenic (85 manic-depressives, evenly divided between men and women; 125 schizophrenic men and 50 women). Table 11.1 presents Kretschmer's findings as to the percentages of each body type found among the two psychiatric classifications. As you can see, there was a clear association between manic-depressive psychosis and the pyknic type and between schizophrenia and the asthenic type. Among schizophrenic patients, however, the athletic and dysplastic types were also represented (about 20 percent each) as well as a mixed asthenic–athletic type; there seemed to be greater variability in body type among schizophrenics than among manic-depressives.

Kretschmer's contribution to constitutional psychology is considerable, but his work has been criticized on several bases. It has been suggested that because manic-depressive psychosis typically occurs later in life than schizophrenia and because most people have a tendency to become heavier and thus more "pyknic" as they age, Kretschmer's findings may have been spurious.

allows for a very large number of potential combinations of variables and hence for a very large number of possible physique types, or what Sheldon called "somatotypes."

Before we examine Sheldon's specific concepts and variables, we need to be quite clear as to what he meant by the term "constitutional." In the general field of psychology this term is often used to refer to those factors that are present at birth, hence, both to genetic factors and to influences present in the uterine environment. Sheldon's use of the term is closely related, but he was particularly concerned with these factors as they function or are observed or measured in the developed individual. Constitutional psychology for Sheldon, therefore, is "the study of the psychological aspects of human behavior as they are related to the morphology and physiology of the body" (1940, p. 1). "Constitution" embraces aspects of the person that are relatively unchanging, such as morphology (form and structure of living beings) and endocrine function, as contrasted to aspects that are relatively more susceptible to change by environmental pressures, such as habits and social attitudes (Sheldon, 1940). As this definition makes clear, Sheldon considered factors at the glandular and cellular levels of bodily function significant in determining behavior. In his empirical work, however, he focused chiefly on the directly observable, structural aspects of the body—the overall physique.

It is important to understand that Sheldon did not intend his

TABLE 11.1   Kretschmer's Correlations of Physique with Psychological Disorder

| | PERCENTAGE OF PATIENTS IN EACH PHYSIQUE CATEGORY | |
PHYSIQUE CATEGORY	MANIC-DEPRESSIVE	SCHIZOPHRENIC
Asthenic	5	50
Athletic	4	19
Asthenic–athletic mixed	2	7
Pyknic	72	1
Pyknic mixed	17	2
Dysplastic	0	21
Total	100	100

Source: Adapted from Kretschmer, (1921, p. 35).
Note: Figures are based on 243 patients and almost twice as many men as women. (The total group studied numbered 260, but 17 patients were excluded from the final correlations, being labeled "deformed and uncategorized"; 13 of these were among the schizophrenic group.)

theory to represent more than one "side of the structure as a whole" (1942, p. 438). He regarded constitutional psychology as "only a contribution to general psychology," one that was "possibly comparable to the description of the skeleton in anatomy" (p. 438). Quite intentionally, he deemphasized the influence of the environment in order to present the neglected genetic–physiological side of the picture, and he left the problem of synthesis for those who would come later. As a result—and because he showed little interest in formalizing or systematizing his viewpoint—Sheldon's theory is much less elaborate than many others.

THE STATICS OF PERSONALITY

According to Sheldon (1942), the study of the size and shape of human beings constitutes the **statics** of psychology—the nature of the balance among the components of human form and structure, or **morphology**. When we understand how the human being, at rest, is constructed, we can go on to examine human dynamics—how the person, in motion, feels, thinks, and behaves.

Underlying the observable structure, or physique, of the human being, Sheldon hypothesized a biological structure that he called the **morphogenotype**. Just as the **genotype**, the genetic constitution of an individual, is distinguished from the **phenotype**, the visible properties of an organism that are produced by interaction of genotype and environment, so the morphogenotype is distinguished from the visible body structure. The phenotype is what we see, but it is the morphogenotype that, according to Sheldon, is crucial not only in determining physical development but in molding behavior.

BOX 11.2   William Herbert Sheldon (1898–1977)

William Sheldon was raised on a farm in Rhode Island. Under the tutelage of his father—with whom he had a close relationship—he gained an early familiarity with the ways and breeds of animals. This atmosphere had a lasting effect on Sheldon's values and views of human behavior, and throughout his life, his writings gave frequent evidence of his understanding of and interest in the animal world.

Another very important influence on Sheldon was his godfather, William James (1842–1910), the eminent psychologist and philosopher. Sheldon's thinking shows clear traces of the pragmatic philosophy of James, and Sheldon's first book, *Psychology and the Promethean Will* (1936), was as much a philosophical as a psychological treatment of the sources of conflict in modern life.

With degrees from Brown University (A.B. 1919), the University of Colorado (A.M. 1923), and the University of Chicago (Ph.D. in psychology, 1926), Sheldon became an instructor in psychology, first at the University of Chicago and later at Northwestern University and the University of Wisconsin. Deciding to study medicine, Sheldon obtained his M.D. from the University of Chicago in 1933 and interned at a Chicago children's hospital. A fellowship then enabled him to study psychiatry in Europe for two years. He spent much of his time in Europe with Jung but visited also with Freud and with Kretschmer.

Returning to the States in 1936, Sheldon took up a professorship in psychology at the Chicago Theological Seminary but two years later moved to Harvard, where he met and began a long-time collaboration with S. S. Stevens, a well-known experimental psychologist. Sheldon was also a contemporary at Harvard of Gordon Allport, Henry Murray, and Raymond Cattell.

After serving in the army during World War II, Sheldon, in 1947, became director of the Constitution Laboratory of Columbia University's College of Physicians and Surgeons and remained in that position for a number of years. Concurrently, he held research appointments at Berkeley's Institute of Human Development, the University of Oregon, and Rockland State Hospital, in Orangeburg, New York. Upon retiring formally from Columbia, Sheldon returned to Cambridge, where he continued until his death to study human constitutional variation.

Widowed in his second marriage, Sheldon had no children. He devoted much of his time to his work but also found room to pursue several avocations. Throughout his life, he was a recognized expert on old coins; as a young man, he bought and sold collections in order to support himself in his studies, and in later years he wrote two books on the subject (1949a, 1976). He was an authority on the classification and natural history of moths, and, according to Osborne (1979), Sheldon was also a "romantic": he was an authority on the Age of Chivalry and had an extensive collection of literature on the Knights of the Round Table.

How can we assess the morphogenotype? We cannot do this directly; all we can see, touch, or measure is a phenotype. Thus, Sheldon proposed the somatotype (from the Greek *somato* meaning "body"), or body type. The somatotype relies heavily on measurement of the actual body, or phenotype, but it attempts to get at the underlying causal patterns of the morphogenotype by trying to deduce common denominators among the many visible characteristics of the human physique.

THE SOMATOTYPE: ENDOMORPHY, MESOMORPHY, AND ECTO-MORPHY.   What is a **somatotype**? In concrete terms, it is a quantitative statement of the degree to which a given physique possesses the three primary components of endomorphy, mesomorphy, and ectomorphy. The somatotype is a series of three numbers; the first always refers to the degree of endomorphy, the second to the degree of mesomorphy, the last to the degree of ectomorphy. Thus, a somatotype of 7-1-1 describes a person extremely high in endomorphy and extremely low on both other components (each component is ranked on a scale of 1 to 7); a somatotype of 4-6-1 describes a person who is about average in endomorphy, high in mesomorphy, and very low in ectomorphy.

And what are endomorphy? mesomorphy? ectomorphy? **Endomorphy**, the first component of body structure, is the relative predominance of the vegetative system, that is, those body portions that are involved in the assimilation and digestion of food. The endormorphic body tends to put on fat easily, and it is characterized by softness and roundness. Bone and muscle are relatively underdeveloped, and the physique is not generally suited to hard physical activity. The endomorphic body has more mass relative to its surface area, and it has a low specific gravity—it floats high in water.

Mesomorphy, the second component of physique, is the relative predominance of bone, muscle, and connective tissue. Primarily mesomorphic bodies are characterized by hardness and rectangularity; they are strong, tough, and generally resistant to injury. Such physiques are equipped for strenuous physical demands, such as those made on an athlete or an explorer.

Ectomorphy, the third body component, is the relative predominance of the skin and the nervous system. Primarily ectomorphic bodies are thin and lightly muscled. They are delicate and linear and have more surface area relative to mass than the other two body types. In proportion to overall size, the ectomorphic body has the largest brain and central nervous system. This type is overexposed to external stimulation and poorly equipped for competition and persistent physical activity.

Figure 11.1 presents examples of the extreme endomorphic, mesomorphic, and ectomorphic types of (male) bodies as well as examples of several more common body types. In the next section we will discover how Sheldon evolved his conception of the somatotype, and we will discuss his various techniques for assessing it.

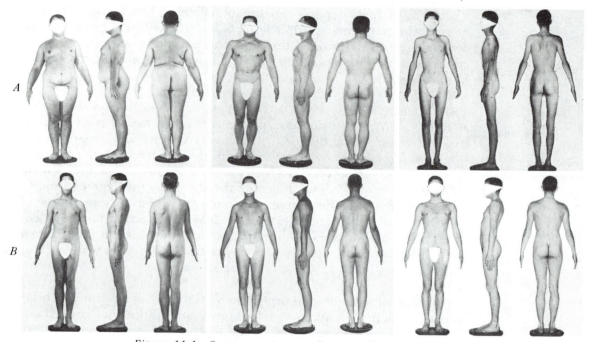

Figure 11.1 Some somatotypes. Panel A shows the three extreme types—the pronounced endomorph, mesomorph, and ectomorph, respectively. Panel B shows, first, the precise average (4 being the midpoint of the 1-7 scale); second, the most common somatotype found by Sheldon in his initial study—a mesomorphic ectomorph; and third, another common type. (Selected from Sheldon, 1954)

Sheldon derived his names for the three components of physique from the terms for the three layers of the embryo that give rise to varying portions of the body: from the **endoderm**, the innermost layer, arise major portions of the digestive system; from the **mesoderm**, the intermediate layer, come such portions of the body as the muscular, skeletal, and circulatory systems; and from the **ectoderm**, or outermost layer, arise, among other things, the brain, spinal cord, and outer layer of skin. Sheldon hypothesized that each of his three primary components of physique represented a relative overemphasis on the development of one of these basic embryological components.

For Sheldon, as you can see, the somatotype is a kind of compromise between the morphogenotype and the phenotype. It provides more information than a person's current physique does because it suggests something about presumed original—and continuing—influences. On the other hand, it offers considerably more ambiguous information than would the genotype, if we were only able to decipher the latter from the material coded in a person's genes.

ASSESSING THE SOMATOTYPE. Sheldon began his studies of physique by measuring subjects' bodies directly. He found, however, that these measurements produced inconsistent results despite careful specifications and laborious techniques. In addition, he discovered that it was impossible to tease out the important variables affecting physique without being able to see a great many physiques at one time, to see all sides or aspects of a given body at the same time, and, often, to see the same physique repeatedly. Thus, he devised a technique that involved taking carefully standardized photographs of each subject. Subjects were asked to stand, naked, in a specified position in front of a plain, light-colored background, and three photographs were taken: one of the front, one of the left side, and one of the back. This procedure came to be called the Somatotype Performance Test (Sheldon, 1954), and the photographs became Sheldon's raw data; they could be filed and reexamined at any time. (As you can see from Figure 11.1, to ensure confidentiality, subjects' faces were concealed and genitalia were also hidden.)

Sheldon derived his three primary components of physique by inspecting the photographs of some 4000 male college students and subjecting the principal variables that emerged from that inspection to three criteria:

1. Can every subject be ranked in terms of this variable?
2. Can different judges, working independently, agree on the rank assigned each subject on this variable?
3. Does this variable represent a characteristic that cannot be accounted for by any combination of other variables already identified?

Once a variable was accepted as significant, subjects were ranked, on a scale of 1 to 7, as to the degree to which they exhibited that characteristic.

When the three basic components of endomorphy, mesomorphy, and ectomorphy had been winnowed out from the 4000 sets of photographs, Sheldon and his collaborators took numerous "physical" measurements of the photographed bodies. That is, using dividers, they measured distances on the photographs corresponding to the diameters of various body parts. They then reduced the number of these measures to those that effectively differentiated between subjects who were high or low in judges' rankings on each of the three basic components. Eventually, they discovered that 17 of their physical measurements accurately differentiated subjects. Moreover, they found that these measures could be taken at least as accurately from photographs as from subjects' bodies.

Having assigned the 4000 subjects ranks on the three primary components and having rated them on the physical measurements, Sheldon was able to compile statistical tables linking the two sets of ratings. It was then possible to rank a new subject on the three primary components by taking the 17 physical measures of the subject's three photographs, plus his height and weight. However, the procedures used for arriving at the somatotypes from the measurements required either a great deal of experience or rather laborious searches through a number of tables. Indeed, at one point, Sheldon and his colleagues constructed a "somatotyping machine" to aid them in this task.

Over the years, Sheldon modified his procedure for somatotyping several times. In his first refinement, having gathered data on some 46,000 subjects, he devised a new set of tables, divided into five-year age groups from 18 to 65, into which he could enter a subject's age and **ponderal index**—the ratio of height to the cube root of weight—to determine the four or five somatotypes that were most typical for the age and index given. Then, by examining the actual physical measurement he had taken, by inspecting the photographs, and by comparing these data with the file of somatotype photographs in the *Atlas of Men* (Sheldon, 1954)—which contains over 1000 representative somatotype photographs—he could select the appropriate somatotype.

Eventually, Sheldon found that the somatotype could be derived most efficiently and with the greatest precision with the use of just three measures: the ponderal index; the subject's mature height, or greatest height attained over time; and the trunk index (Livson and McNeil, 1962; McNeil and Livson, 1963; Sheldon, Lewis, and Tenney, 1969); the last needs a little explanation.

Largely for the purpose of assessing dysplasia, a secondary component of physique that we will discuss in the next section, Sheldon had divided the body into five regions. In addition to giving the overall body rankings on each of the three primary components, he assigned rankings on these components within each of five regions: head–neck; chest–trunk; arms; stomach–trunk; and legs. The **trunk index**, or **TI**, was expressed as a ratio of the sizes of the second and fourth of these regions; it was obtained as the area of the trunk above the waist divided by the area of the trunk below the waist, as measured on the front or rear view standard photograph. In a later section, we will see that Sheldon was able to base his claim for the constancy of the somatotype to a great extent on the unchanging nature of this trunk index.

SECONDARY COMPONENTS OF PHYSIQUE. It may have occurred to you that the somatotype does not offer any way of describing such aspects of the body as odd combinations of the three basic components. You may know a woman, for example, who is generally quite sylphlike but has "piano legs." Or you may know a man who has rather soft contours, wide hips, and long, curly eyelashes. You have hit on two of

Somatotypes by the masters: Picasso's ectomorphic ''Actor,'' a Roman mesomorph, and a gently endomorphic Venus, by Titian.

Among this group of teenagers we can certainly find a few of Sheldon's 343 possible somatotypes.

the most important of Sheldon's secondary components of physique—dysplasia and gynandromorphy. **Dysplasia** (recall Kretschmer's fourth body type, Box 11.1) is the extent to which the three primary components appear in an inconsistent fashion in different parts of the body. **Gynandromorphy** (from the Greek **gyne**, referring to ''woman,'' and **andros**, meaning ''male'') is the degree to which body parts exhibit both male and female characteristics. Gynandromorphy is a term similar to one you are more likely to have encountered—*androgyny*. In current usage, however, the latter refers mainly to psychological characteristics.

Another secondary component of considerable importance is **textural aspect**, described as a measure of the coarseness or fineness of body characteristics. This component refers essentially to attractiveness, or beauty, and it is difficult to assess objectively, as you may imagine. It reflects, to some considerable degree, Sheldon's naturalist and animal-breeding background. Indeed, he suggests that it is a judgment of the ''quality of human stock,'' or the degree to which people, like horses, are ''thoroughbreds'' (Sheldon, 1940, pp. 75–76).

DISTRIBUTION OF SOMATOTYPES.　How many somatotype patterns are there? Theoretically, as you could easily calculate, 343 are possible (7^3). At first, Sheldon (1940) was able to identify only 76 distinct patterns, and even after he had examined many thousands of physiques, he still reported a total of only 88 different somatotypes (Sheldon, 1954). With the final revision of his somatotyping procedure, however, and with a wider range of ages and populations, Sheldon was

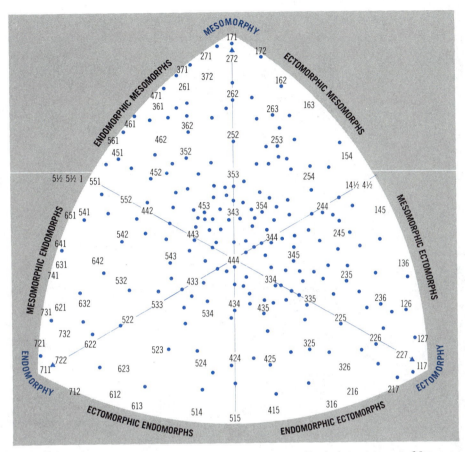

Figure 11.2   Distribution of 4000 male somatotypes. Each dot represents 20 cases. (From Sheldon, 1954, Figure 1, p. 12.)

able to report a total of 267 somatotypes (Sheldon, Lewis and Tenney, 1969).

Figure 11.2 shows the distribution of somatotypes among 4000 male college students. Although the distribution covers the entire "map" (Sheldon referred to this rounded triangular diagram as a "map" and to its regions as "northwest," "southeast," and so on), there is a clear tendency for the somatotype to concentrate in the mesomorphy and mesomorphy–ectomorphy regions. It is interesting to compare this distribution with that for 4000 female subjects (see Figure 11.3): males exhibit a wider range of variability than do females and they are also clearly more mesomorphic; females are more endomorphic.

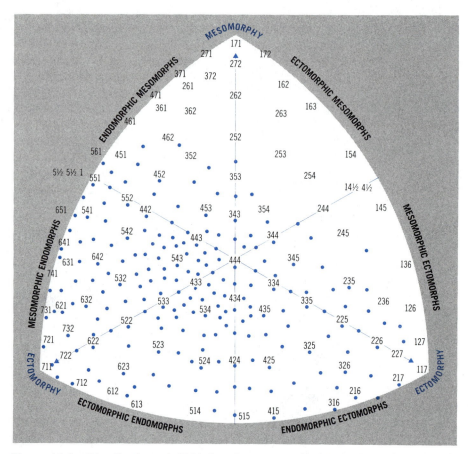

Figure 11.3   Distribution of 4000 female somatotypes. Each dot represents 20 cases. (From Sheldon, 1954, Figure 2, p. 13.)

CONSTANCY OF THE SOMATOTYPE.   Originally, Sheldon said that in following the cases of several hundred individuals over a dozen years, "we have discovered no case in which there has been a convincing change in the somatotype" (1940, p. 221). Nutritional factors might change specific measurements, but the resulting changes would simply appear as deviations from the basic somatotype. Sheldon suggested that "for the somatotype to change the skeleton must change, as well as the shape of the head, the bony structure of the face, the neck, wrists, ankles, calves, and forearms, and the relations of stature to measurements made at places where fat does not accumulate" (p. 221).

Later, however, Sheldon conceded that the constancy of the somatotype might be somewhat more of an idealized concept than an

According to Sheldon, the morphogenotype should be reflected in both our ancestors and our descendents. The resemblance between this man and his 18th-century forebear is indeed striking.

empirical fact. When he published his monumental *Atlas of Men* in 1954, he proposed that the somatotype held firm over time unless substantial change took place either in the person's nutritional intake or in his or her physical health: the somatotype was a ''trajectory or pathway through which the living organism will travel under standard conditions of nutrition and in the absence of grossly disturbing pathology'' (Sheldon, 1954, p. 19). (For example, starvation or a muscle-wasting disease can change the important relations among skeletal, muscular, and mass areas of the body.)

Ideally, Sheldon said, to obtain the best estimate of the underlying morphogenotype, we should have not only a complete history of the person but a record of his or her ancestors and descendants as well. In addition, somatotype photographs should be taken at regular intervals throughout the person's life, and various biological measures should be taken as often as possible.

In 1969 Sheldon, on the basis of his new method of assessing the somatotype, again asserted that the somatotype does not change. This assertion was based largely on his finding of remarkable stability over time, in a number of studies, in the trunk index, which we have already described (Sheldon, Lewis, and Tenney, 1969).

Although Sheldon (1940) said that more skill is required to assess the somatotype before than after the age of 30, he hypothesized that the somatotype could be accurately measured at ages as young as 6, and he speculated that eventually it would be possible to predict the somatotype at least approximately almost from birth. Parnell (1958), however, states that although children can be assessed at the age of 7, fully satisfactory estimates of the somatotype cannot be calculated at that age level. Parnell points out that an important factor in the difficulty in assessing children is the fact that in boys, at least, "muscularity does not reach its most prominent phase of development until late puberty" (1958, p. 34).

PERSONALITY DYNAMICS

When structure, the static aspect of personality, takes on function—when the person "gets up and moves around," expressing desires and motivations and interacting with others—the person becomes a **dynamic** organism. The behavior that this organism exhibits reflects what Sheldon described as **temperament**, or "the level of personality just above physiological function and below acquired attitudes and beliefs," the level "where basic patterns of motivation manifest themselves" (Sheldon, 1942, p. 4).

Sheldon felt certain that these two aspects of the person—physique and temperament—were connected in important ways. Indeed, he suggested that they could be seen as two aspects of the same thing. Thus, he said, we should not be surprised to find that "the dynamics of an individual should be related to the static picture he presents" (Sheldon, 1942, p. 4).

DIMENSIONS OF TEMPERAMENT.   Like Raymond Cattell, whose work is described in the next chapter, Sheldon began with the assumption that a relatively small number of basic factors underlay and accounted for the enormous surface variability and complexity of human behavior. Reviewing the personality literature, particularly that having to do with human traits, Sheldon extracted a list of 650 traits. Many of these were related to extraversion or introversion, the widely popular concepts introduced by Carl Jung (see Chapter 4).

Sheldon also deliberately selected traits that were likely, in his estimation, to have biological, or somatic, roots. Unfortunately, however, he did not explain this fact clearly until after the study was originally reported, and this failure contributed to the skepticism with which the high correlations he found between physique and temperament were greeted. But we are getting ahead of our story.

After combining overlapping traits, eliminating others that seemed unimportant, and so on, Sheldon and his co-workers arrived at a list of 50 traits that seemed to them to reflect all the ideas represented in the original 650. Sheldon then studied a group of 33 men—graduate students, instructors, and others—for a year, both by observing his subjects in their daily routines and interpersonal interactions and by talking with them in a clinical interview setting. Using a five-point rating scale (later expanded to a seven-point scale, to conform to the scale used in the studies of physique), Sheldon rated each man repeatedly on all 50 of the traits. At the end of the year, he subjected all these ratings to correlational analysis with the intent of discovering clusters of traits that could be considered to represent a few underlying variables. To be included in a cluster, a variable had to correlate positively at least .60 with other traits in the same cluster, and it had to correlate negatively at least .30 with traits in other clusters.

Sheldon's analysis revealed three major clusters of traits that included 22 of the original 50. He then proceeded to improve and enlarge the list for each variable in order to increase the reliability and validity of his measuring instrument. Eventually, he arrived at a total of 60 trait descriptions, 20 in each of three clusters labeled viscerotonia, somatotonia, and cerebrotonia.

In people who score high on **viscerotonia**, "the digestive tract is king, and its welfare appears to define the primary purpose of life" (Sheldon, 1944, p. 543). Such people show a general love of comfort and a kind of gluttony for food, other people, and affection. They are relaxed in posture, react slowly, and are quite even-tempered. They are sociable and tolerant of others and generally easy to interact with.

People who score high on **somatotonia** generally love physical adventure and risk taking and have a strong need for vigorous and muscular physical activity. They are aggressive, often insensitive to the feelings of others, and noisy. They are also courageous, and action, power, and domination are of prime importance to them. For people scoring high on **cerebrotonia**, being inconspicuous is a paramount concern. Such people are restrained and inhibited and tend to conceal both themselves and things that concern them from others. Secretive and self-conscious, these people are often afraid of other people and prefer to be alone, particularly when they are troubled. They react with excessive speed, sleep poorly, and are most comfortable in small, enclosed areas.

ASSESSING TEMPERAMENT.   The basic instrument for rating subjects on temperament is the Scale for Temperament (see Table 11.2). In using the scale, Sheldon said, the investigator should "observe the sub-

TABLE 11.2 *Items on the Scale for Temperament*

VISCEROTONIA	SOMATOTONIA	CEREBROTONIA
Relaxed posture and movement	Assertive posture and movement	Restrained, tense posture and movement
Love of physical comfort	Love of physical adventure	Physiological overresponsiveness
Slow reactions	Energetic quality	Overly fast reactions
Love of eating	Love of exercise	Love of privacy
Dating enjoyed as social experience	Love of dominating; lust for power	Mental overintensity; hyperattentiveness
Pleasure in digestion	Love of risk, chance	Emotional restraint
Love of social ritual and polite ceremony	Bold directness of manner	Intentness of gaze; alertness
Love of being with others	Physical courage for combat	Fear of social involvement
Indiscriminate amiability and goodwill	Competitive aggressiveness	Lack of poise and self-assurance
Greed for affection and approval	Insensitivity to needs and wishes of others	Resistance to forming habits and routines
Orientation to people	Hatred of being shut in (claustrophobia)	Hatred of unprotected places (agoraphobia)
Evenness of emotional flow	Ruthlessness; freedom from squeamishness	Unpredictability of attitude and behavior
Tolerance for people	Absence of vocal restraint	Restraint of voice and noise in general
Complacency; smugness	Indifference to pain	Hypersensitivity to pain
Deep, undisturbed sleep	General noisiness	Poor sleep; chronic fatigue
Lack of purpose, intensity, "fire"	Appearance of being older	Appearance of being younger
Lack of inhibition; exposure of innermost feelings to "public gaze." Extraversion of feeling	Separation from deeper levels of awareness; attention and actions oriented to "outward scene." Extraversion of action	Orientation toward own inner awareness; less concern with adaptation to environment. Introversion of both feeling and action
Sociability and emotional warmth exaggerated by alcohol	Aggressiveness and need for power exaggerated by alcohol	Strain, fatigue, depression increased by alcohol and other depressants
Need of people when troubled	Need of action when troubled	Need of solitude when troubled
Orientation toward childhood and family relationships	Orientation toward goals and activities of youth	Orientation toward the later periods of life

Source: Modified from Sheldon (1942, Scale for Temperament, p. 26 and pp. 31–94).
Note: Some sets of items constitute two-way dimensions (e.g., the second set for viscerotonia and somatotonia) and some three-way dimensions (e.g., the next-to-last set in all three columns). Sheldon commented that, ideally, the 60 items should constitute 20 three-way dimensions.

TABLE 11.3   Correlations (r) between Physique and Temperament Components (n = 200)

PHYSIQUE COMPONENT	TEMPERAMENT COMPONENTS		
	VISCEROTONIA	SOMATOTONIA	CEREBROTONIA
Endomorphy	+ .79	− .29	− .32
Mesomorphy	− .23	+ .82	− .58
Ectomorphy	− .40	− .53	+ .83

Source: Adapted from Sheldon (1942, p. 400).

ject closely for at least a year in as many different situations as possible'' (1942, p. 27). The investigator should conduct a series of at least 20 ''analytic interviews'' with each subject over this period of time and rate the person on as many of the traits as possible after each interview, continuing this process until he or she is ''reasonably satisfied that all of the sixty traits have been adequately considered and evaluated'' (Sheldon, 1942, p. 27). At the end of this process, a total score for each of the three components can be computed by adding the individual ratings. An average can then be taken, or a table consulted, to obtain an overall rating on each component for the person.

RELATION BETWEEN PHYSIQUE AND TEMPERAMENT.   The combination of static and dynamic elements to produce the moving, functioning person formed Sheldon's principal research interest. In his initial study of the relations between physique and temperament, he found, to his surprise, that the correlations between these two aspects of personality not only existed but were much stronger than he had thought.

Sheldon's Initial Study.   Over a period of five years, Sheldon (1942) studied 200 white males who were either college students or graduates involved in academic or professional activities. After careful observation, following the procedures already discussed, he assigned these subjects temperament ratings, using the Scale of Temperament (see Table 11.2), and somatotyped them by his original method.

The results of this first major study were surprising. Based on some earlier studies in which he had attempted to correlate Viola's morphological index with several aspects of mental ability and temperament (Sheldon, 1927a, b, c), Sheldon had expected only low correlations. He found strikingly high correlations, however, between physique and temperament, as you can see in Table 11.3. The correlations between endomorphy and viscerotonia, mesomorphy and somatotonia, and ectomorphy and cerebrotonia, respectively, were all in the neighborhood of +.80, a very high correlation. (This correlation indicates that the two might share as much as 80 percent of their causal influences.)

Note also that the correlations between other pairings of the six components under scrutiny in the present study are all negative and that some are, again, quite substantial. Some investigators have confirmed the kinds of relationship between physique and temperament that Sheldon found (see Box 11.3), but none have found such high correlations as he.

Sheldon (1942) concluded that correlations of the order of +.80 would suggest that "morphology and temperament, as we measure them, may constitute expressions at their respective levels of essentially common components." "If we *have* already reached basic factors in personality," he remarked, "the correlations are not higher than should be expected, for then with the two techniques we are but measuring the same thing at different levels of its expression" Sheldon (1942, p. 401). In that event, he suggested, these basic variables might provide a frame of reference in terms of which psychology could contribute to the study of individual differences in all areas of behavior, including the biological and social sciences.

Explaining the Correlations.   There are a number of possible reasons why correlations—large or small—might be found between physique and temperament. First, it may be that people with certain kinds of physiques find that particular behaviors are more often rewarded, whereas others are more often punished. For example, a person who is strongly ectomorphic may find the sport of distance running more congenial to his physique than, say, basketball and, hence, may use running to build self-esteem and win praise from others. But running is also a rather solitary sport, and this may reinforce or even create a tendency to become a "loner," to prefer to work and be alone. A person who is predominantly endomorphic, on the other hand, may find herself handicapped in studying dance or engaging in other physical pursuits and, hence, come to prefer various social and gregarious activities that can be carried out in relative physical comfort. A primarily mesomorphic person may find that in confrontations he or she is frequently at an advantage because of superior strength. As a consequence, such a person may develop a bold manner and a liking for dangerous and challenging adventures.

A second possibility is that people with certain kinds of physiques are stereotyped in certain ways by their culture; people tend to expect certain behaviors from such individuals. For example, as we said earlier, many of us have a tendency to expect thin people to be nervous and fat people to be jolly. We also rather expect thin people to be poets or scholars and fat people to be cooks or comedians. And we expect muscular types to be athletic; we may also expect, however, to find them in positions of power, such as political office or board chairmanships of large corporations. It may be that people who have certain

BOX 11.3   Physique and Temperament in Nursery School Children

There are several reasons for being curious about the relationships between somatotype and temperamental dimension in young children. If we were to find in 3- and 4-year-olds the sorts of relationships Sheldon reported for young adults, Sheldon's theory of a common constitutional basis for somatotype and temperament would gain some support. Such young children would have been exposed to many fewer years of the sorts of experiences that might tend to make an endomorph sociable, a mesomorph tough, or an ectomorph introspective. Such relationships would also be interesting in their own right to teachers and others who deal with young children.

Richard N. Walker (1962) carried out a study on body build and behavior with 125 nursery school children. The children, who were white and ranged in age from 2 years 6 months to 4 years 11 months, attended a nursery school that drew primarily from well-educated, affluent families. The study sample, of 73 boys and 52 girls, did not include any children with mental or physical handicaps.

Walker was careful to avoid the methodological difficulties of Sheldon's original study. Each child was rated on each of Sheldon's dimensions of physique by three judges, from standard somatotype photographs. Two of the judges had never seen the children and thus could not possibly have

been biased in rating the children's physiques by a knowledge of their temperaments. Each child was also rated by four or five teachers, using a list of 63 terms describing behavioral traits; for example, "self-assertive," "tense," "social in play," "quarrelsome," "given to daydreaming," "noisy," and "accident-prone." Most of the teachers who did the behavior ratings had no knowledge that the study had anything to do with physique. The raters of the physique dimensions agreed quite well with one another on their ratings of endomorphy and ectomorphy but had some difficulty with mesomorphy, especially for the girls. The raters of the behavioral traits showed moderate consistency, enough so that the average of four or five raters was reasonably reliable for most of the traits.

Before beginning the study, Walker had predicted which behavioral traits would be related to which somatotypes, based on Sheldon's theory. Altogether, 292 such predictions were made, out of a possible total of 378 (63 traits × 3 somatotypes × 2 sexes).

When the data were gathered, the results were compared with the predictions. About 73 percent of the relationships were in the predicted direction (50 percent would have been expected by chance). The strongest of the observed relationships were in the predicted direction nearly 90 percent of the time. On the whole, predictions were considerably more

often borne out for boys than for girls. Perhaps this is not so surprising, in view of the fact that the predictions were based on Sheldon's studies of adult males. Interestingly, predictions involving mesomorphy were most often supported, even though this had been the most difficult physique component to judge. Predictions involving ectomorphy were intermediate in their success, and predictions involving endomorphy were borne out at only about a chance level.

Although in Walker's study the *directions* of association between physique and temperament traits tended to be as predicted by Sheldon's theory, the *degree* of association—the size of the observed correlations—tended to be much weaker. In general, an individual child's behavior was not very predictable from his or (particularly) her somatotype. Only at the level of averages were the trends noticeable.

Why were Walker's associations weaker than Sheldon's? There are several possibilities:

1. In children this young, physique and temperament may not yet have settled down into their final form.
2. Temperament may be expressed differently in young children than in adults, in girls than in boys; these differences may not have been taken sufficiently into account in deriving the initial predictions.
3. Exposure to the responses of others—as yet minimal in

Walker's young subjects—may in fact be an important element in the consolidation of physique–behavior relationships.
4. Walker's well-controlled study avoided some of the conditions that could have inflated the correlations between ratings of physique and temperament in Sheldon's original study.

Despite the foregoing qualifications, the results of Walker's research do offer testimony that there seems to be ''something there'' in the physique–temperament relationships that Sheldon reported and that that something is detectable at a fairly early age.

physical characteristics are led to adopt patterns of behavior that match common expectations. Of course, we do not know where such stereotypes have come from nor can we explain, by this theory, the behavior of the person who fits no convenient physical stereotype—say, someone whose somatotype is close to 4–4–4.

Yet a third way of explaining the high correlations between physique and temperament is in terms of some unitary biological factor. It may be, for example, that among certain hereditary factors, there are associative links that result in particular kinds of physical characteristics being connected with particular behavioral tendencies. Two major twin studies (studies of twins raised separately; see secton on page 404) have found strong evidence for the role of genetic factors in determining physique (Newman, Freeman, and Holzinger, 1937; Osborne and DeGeorge, 1959). Inasmuch as a number of studies have supported the role of genetic variation in behavior (see Fuller and Thompson, 1978), it seems reasonable to suppose that genes, either alone or in combination, will have multiple effects that include both behavior and physique.

Finally, it is possible that environmental influences tend to produce particular kinds of physique and at the same time particular behavioral tendencies. Suppose, for example, that an overindulgent mother insists that her child eat continually, whether or not the child is hungry. This could lead the child to become obese, and, at the same time, the mother's protectiveness could lead the child to an excessive need for the affection and support of others. This line of thought assumes that because certain events influence the development of both physical and temperamental characteristics, we tend to see the two as linked. As you may imagine, Sheldon and constitutional psychologists in general are less enthusiastic about this essentially environmental explanation than about the other hypotheses as to the cause of the correlations between physique and temperament—hypotheses in which the constitution of the individual plays a direct or indirect causal role.

SOME THOUGHTS ON HEREDITY,
ENVIRONMENT, AND DEVELOPMENT
As we have indicated, Sheldon was convinced that genetic factors play a highly significant role in behavior and personality. He is not the first

of the theorists we have studied to hold this view; Freud and Murray both emphasized the psychobiological nature of human behavior, and, as we will see, so do Cattell and Eysenck, as well as investigators in the field of behavior genetics. But Sheldon is perhaps the only contemporary theorist whose primary methodology involved the direct measurement of physical–biological characteristics and whose view of personality was directly centered on the at least hypothesized somatic origins of behavior. Indeed, Sheldon even suggested that the **unconscious**— which he accepted as one determinant of behavior—*is* the body; our great difficulty in verbalizing the contents of the unconscious is due quite simply, he said, to the fact that our language is not geared to reflect what goes on at all levels in our bodies.

Sheldon's strong belief in the biological determinants of behavior led him to downplay the importance of early childhood events. Indeed, he was not at all certain that childhood played a role in adult behavior. It may well be, he suggested, that biological predisposition leads not only to particular kinds of infantile or childhood experiences but to certain forms of adult behavior; the apparent relation between early events and later behavior may be largely a reflection of the consistent operation, over a long period of time, of biological factors.

Sheldon did suggest that growing up could be made a great deal more efficient and less frustrating if parents or others who guide the child would consider the child's somatotype. In this way, he suggested, one could encourage the child to form aspirations and expectations more or less consistent with its physical and temperamental potentials. But Sheldon did not consider development completely fixed by biological inheritance. He saw the person as endowed with potentials that both mold the possibilities for future growth and set certain limits on them. The particular experiences a person has will have a crucial role in determining whether he or she eventually realizes the full extent of these potentials.

CHARACTERISTIC RESEARCH

Sheldon was convinced that constitutional psychology not only could shed light on normal behavior but could alleviate or prevent various psychological and social ills. After reviewing the existing system of psychiatric diagnosis, he concluded that to study the relations between physique and mental disorder, he would have to devise better measures of the latter. Consistent with his stress on continuous variables, Sheldon conceptualized mental disorder in terms of three primary dimensions rather than discrete, fixed categories. Admittedly, these dimensions correspond closely to three typical psychiatric diagnoses. They are applied, however, in the same way that Sheldon applied his other components, that is, in terms of degree, and, again, it is the patterning of the components that is crucial.

The first, or **affective**, component of mental disorder represents, at its extreme, manic-depressive psychosis. The second, or **paranoid**, component, represents paranoid psychosis. The third, or **heboid**, component represents the hebephrenic form of schizophrenia.

Each of these three components was postulated to represent a deficiency in one of Sheldon's three temperament components. Difficulties that involve wide swings of emotion and exaggerated accompanying behavior, as in manic-depressive disorders, reflect, Sheldon suggests, a lack of the kind of restraint and control typical of the strongly cerebrotonic person. Paranoid suspicion and delusions of being persecuted by hostile others reflect a lack of the kind of outgoing, sociable, trusting nature the viscerotonic person possesses. Finally, the schizophrenic person, who cannot seem to make sense of things and who withdraws in fear and desperation, lacks the bold, assertive, active qualities of the somatotonic person (Sheldon, Lewis, and Tenney, 1969).

Sheldon and his co-workers used a numerical scheme for assigning scores on the psychiatric components. Again, there are three components, each scored on a scale of 1 to 7. But although the psychiatric ratings superficially resemble the somatotype and temperament ratings, there are important differences. First, the psychiatric dimensions do not line up on a one-to-one basis with the somatotype–temperament dimensions. The first psychiatric component falls between the first and second temperament components (because it reflects the absence of the third), and the others are similarly offcenter.

The second important difference is that in the psychiatric dimensional scheme, 1–1–1 represents normality, whereas in the somatotype–temperament scheme, combinations like 1–1–1 are never seen—a balanced physique or temperament is represented by 4–4–4. In the psychiatric scheme, departures from 1 represent increasing degrees of disturbance on the corresponding dimension. Ratings of 2 represent a very mild level of disturbance. A person whose psychiatric ratings add up to a total of 5 or less—say, a 2–2–1 or 1–2–1—is probably judged to be normally adjusted by his friends, though perhaps as having a few problems. Rating totals that are a little higher, between 6 and 8, mark personality disturbance falling in the neurotic range. And a total of 9 or higher represents a disturbance likely to be labeled psychotic by a psychiatrist. Of course, the particular pattern—that is, which component is high—indicates what sort of personality disturbance it is.

Sheldon's theory of abnormal psychology holds that the distinction among normality, neurosis, and psychosis is primarily one of degree. The more serious personality disturbances are merely farther out on the same dimensions as the minor eccentricities we all learn to adjust to in friends and acquaintances. And the underlying basis of any such disturbance is a defect in the development of one or more of the temperament dimensions.

Sheldon attempted to relate these conceptions of mental disorder to his components of physique and to apply all these variables—physique, temperament, and mental disorder—to the study of nonnormal populations: a group of young delinquents and several groups of psychiatrically disturbed adults.

DELINQUENCY: SOMATOTYPES AND PSYCHIATRIC RATINGS. For eight years, Sheldon and his collaborators studied a group of delinquent boys, residents of a rehabilitation home in Boston, assigning them somatotype ratings as well as ratings on the secondary components of physique and on the three psychiatric components. In addition, Sheldon gathered detailed life histories that included information about mental and educational performance, family background, medical history, delinquent behavior, and other characteristic behavior.

The principal findings of this research were that the delinquents tended to be much more strongly mesomorphic than the college student population and to be low on the ectomorphic dimension. Their somatotypes bunch up strongly in the ''northwest'' region (see Figure 11.4), whereas somatotypes for the normal male population are distributed more evenly over the entire map (see Figure 11.2).

Among the delinquent boys, the most common rating for the psychiatric components was 3-2-1. This represents a psychiatric profile in the neurotic range of severity, with the first psychiatric component dominant. That is, the basic problem is a defect in cerebrotonia, which produces a disturbance of an impulsive kind. The secondary disturbance in the second psychiatric dimension reflects a defect in viscerotonia, a lack, perhaps, of sympathy and social interest, a callousness about the feelings of others. There was a considerable variety of patterns of psychiatric ratings among individual delinquents, ranging from several 1-1-1's, apparently perfectly well-adjusted personalities, to a definitely psychotic 5-2-3 and 4-3-3.

Sheldon's major findings with regard to physique and delinquency have received some support from subsequent studies. Glueck and Glueck (1950, 1956) compared 500 delinquents with 500 carefully matched nondelinquent young men and found that roughly 60 percent of the delinquent youth were primarily mesomorphic whereas only about 30 percent of the nondelinquent subjects were so classified. In addition, almost 40 percent of the normal subjects were primarily ectomorphic whereas fewer than 5 percent of the delinquents showed such a tendency. And, again, the delinquents seemed to be characterized by ''northwest'' physiques. Several other investigators (Cortes, 1961; Epps and Parnell, 1952; Gibbens, 1963) have also found high relative degrees of mesomorphy in delinquent subjects, whether male or female, British or American. Epps and Parnell (1952) also confirmed Sheldon's finding that delinquents tended to exhibit more affective than paranoid or heboid characteristics.

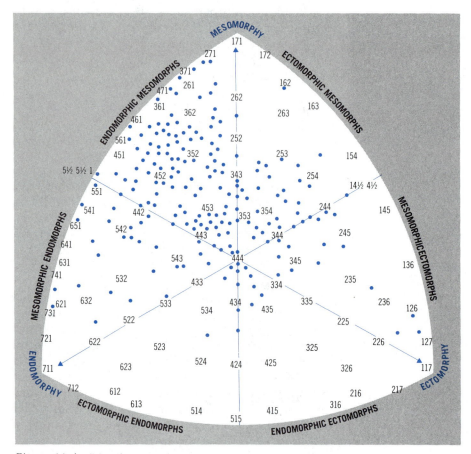

Figure 11.4   Distribution of somatotypes for 200 delinquent boys. Each dot represents 20 cases. (From Sheldon, 1949b, Figure 20, p. 729.)

Most of Sheldon's 200 subjects have been followed up over a 40-year period, first by Sheldon and subsequently by his collaborators. A recent account of the subsequent lives of these young men (Hartl, Monnelly, and Elderkin, 1982) documents some changes; for example, a few of the boys thought to have fairly serious problems at the time of the initial study have wound up leading reasonably normal lives in society. But the great majority of cases (86 percent) continued to suffer mild to severe difficulties of a variety of kinds, including neurotic and psychotic disturbance, alcoholism, criminality, and other problems. For the boys who were in military service in World War II, roughly 60 percent of the original group, the best single predictor of continuing difficulty in life was a low score on a rating of "value to the service" (Horn, 1983).

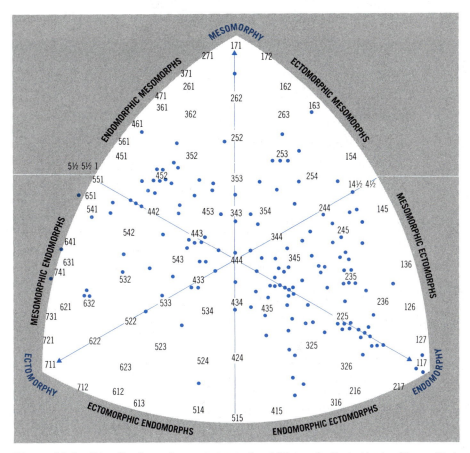

Figure 11.5   Distribution of somatotypes for 155 psychotic patients. (From Sheldon, 1949b, Figure 7, p. 70.)

MENTAL DISORDER AND PHYSIQUE.   Collaborating with Phyllis Wittman, Sheldon (Sheldon, 1949b; Wittman, Sheldon, and Katz, 1948) undertook to explore the problems of measuring mental disorder, particularly with the assistance of the somatotyping procedure. From the files of a state hospital, Wittman developed a list of 221 behavioral items that appeared to be important in the psychiatric description of patients and classified these items in terms of Sheldon's three psychiatric components. The resulting list was called the Check List of Psychotic Behavior. Then a group of 155 psychotic male patients were independently somatotyped by Sheldon (see Figure 11.5) and rated on the checklist by Wittman and C. J. Katz, a psychiatrist. Neither Wittman nor Katz saw Sheldon's somatotype ratings before rating subjects on the checklist, and neither saw the other's checklist ratings before

TABLE 11.4   *Correlations (r) between Physique and Psychiatric Components (n = 155)*

PHYSIQUE COMPONENT	PSYCHIATRIC COMPONENTS		
	AFFECTIVE	PARANOID	HEBOID
Endomorphy	+ .54	− .04	− .25
Mesomorphy	+ .41	+ .57	− .68
Ectomorphy	− .59	− .34	+ .64

Source: Adapted from Sheldon (1949b, p. 69).

carrying out his or her own. (The interrater reliability correlations between Wittman's and Katz's ratings were quite high.)

Table 11.4 shows the results of correlating the ratings for the psychiatric components and the physique components. As you can see, many of the correlations are fairly substantial.

The prediction from Sheldon's theory is that the affective psychiatric component should be negatively correlated with ectomorphy, because a defect in cerebrotonia is involved, and indeed there is a substantial negative correlation of − .59. The third (heboid) component should be negatively correlated with mesomorphy, and this is also the case (− .68). However, the second component, paranoia, which supposedly reflects a defect in viscerotonia, shows only a trivial negative correlation of − .04 with endomorphy. The remaining correlations in the table are sometimes in agreement with Sheldon's theory (the four positive correlations) but sometimes not (the two remaining negative correlations). Thus, the data clearly suggest that there are relations among specific somatotypes and psychiatric diagnoses, but these relations may be more complex than those between somatotype and temperament.

HEREDITY AND PERSONALITY: BEHAVIOR GENETICS

Many theories of personality hold that differences in the style, tempo, and direction of human behavior have at least some basis in constitutional factors. Sheldon's theory, considered in this chapter, and the theories of Cattell and Eysenck, described in the next, give biological variations among individuals a fairly central role.

To the extent that biology is important to a personality theorist, developments in the several scientific subdisciplines that are concerned with the relationships between body and behavior become relevant. Examples of such scientific fields are **behavior genetics**, which studies the influence of the genes in shaping behavior; **psychopharmacology**, which examines how chemicals affect mood and action; and the **neurosciences**, which look at how the structure and physiology of the nervous system relate to the behavioral patterns that the system serves.

In this section we will consider the first of these fields, behavior genetics, as an example of how the study of biology–behavior relationships may bear on the concerns of the personality theorist.

Many investigations, both those with human beings and those with other species, have been carried out by students of genetics and behavior (Fuller and Thompson, 1978). The fact that behavioral as well as bodily characteristics can be bred for in animals has long been known to professional breeders and animal fanciers. The differences in temperament among different dog breeds, for example, are well known.

One could not deliberately carry out such a study with humans, for obvious ethical reasons. Behavior geneticists investigating human personality and temperament must proceed somewhat less directly. Nevertheless, researchers have obtained results of considerable relevance to personality theory, as we shall see.

Consider three truisms: (1) Every individual differs in his or her behavior from every other individual. (2) Every individual (except members of identical multiple births) differs genetically from every other individual. (3) Every individual differs environmentally from every other individual.

To what extent is (1) a result of (2) and to what extent of (3)? This is one of the central questions of behavior genetics. In general, this is not an easy question to answer. One reason is that genes and environments are often correlated: if the son of a criminal grows up to be a delinquent, is it because the son was early exposed to a criminal milieu, or is it because the son shares his father's genes? Facile answers one way or the other have given rise to endless (and usually fruitless) controversy. The proper reply is that if the facts we have stated are the only information we have, we do not know.

But there *are* ways of answering questions like this one, at least for groups of individuals. Behavior geneticists use several different methods. The methods most applicable to answering questions about personality traits in human beings depend on locating groups for whom the correlations of genes and environments differ from the usual. Identical twins separated at or near birth and reared in different families provide one such group.

IDENTICAL TWINS REARED APART

Identical twins raised in separate families have identical genes, but these genes are exposed to different family environments. If these twins show greater resemblances to one another than typical members of these families do, we have evidence of the influence of genes. On the other hand, if these same twins differ in personality, we have evidence of the effects of environment.

Although these identical twins, Jim Springer and Jim Lewis, were separated when they were very young and reunited only years later, they are amazingly alike. Among other things, in their homes they each have workshops in which they build furniture.

Now identical twins separated at birth and reared apart in different families are fairly rare (for an example of such a pair, see Box 11.4). Nevertheless, there have been at least three studies in the past 50 years in which diligent investigators have tracked down a number of separated identical twin pairs and have administered some standard

BOX 11.4   A Pair of Identical Twins Reared Apart

Olive and Madge (not their real names), British identical twins, were among 44 such pairs studied by James Shields (1962). Separated seven days after birth because of the serious ill health of their mother, the twins were raised and grew to adulthood essentially apart. Madge was reared by a childless aunt and uncle, and Olive remained with her mother. Until they were 3 years old, the twins were taken to visit each other once a week, but then a quarrel arose between the families: Olive's mother wanted Madge back, but the aunt insisted on keeping her. Thereafter, the aunt refused to let Madge see Olive. Later she sent her to a new school and passed her off as her own child. Olive and Madge did not meet again until Shields separately interviewed and tested them when they were 35 years old.

Shields describes many striking resemblances between the personalities and life histories of the two women:

An initial shyness revealed itself in their remaining standing for a few minutes at the beginning of the interviews in their own homes. They both had much to say spontaneously about their shyness, but the impression they made was not a reserved one. . . . Their speaking voices were much alike and both used short, telling phrases. . . . They made the same kind of face when given the Dominoes [a psychological test] to do. . . . The twins describe similar tastes in clothes, books (especially the dramatic and imaginative) and music. One mentions Tchaikovsky's first, the other Rachmaninov's second piano concerto as among her favorite compositions. Olive likes the Messiah *best of all. On top of a pile of music in Madge's room was a copy of the* Messiah. *Although she plays only very little herself, Olive says "music is a big influence in my life." [Madge was a piano teacher.] Both are of good intelligence, but found they could not settle down to learning shorthand and typing. At about the time that Olive took up nursing, Madge had the wish to be a missionary. They both describe moods of irritability and tenseness in which they feel they want to cry or scream. (1962, p. 199)*

There were, of course, also differences between the two women. Olive was married and had been a nurse; Madge, the piano teacher, was single. Madge was more vivacious and light-hearted than Olive and was thought perhaps to be less mature.

Subsequent to Shields's interviews, the twins met briefly on two occasions between the ages of 35 and 39, by which time Olive was divorced and Madge's "mother" had died. When Shields contacted them a few years later, Madge had given up her piano teaching, and both worked as assistant nurses in the same hospital ward, one on day duty, the other at night.

Which of these resemblances between Olive and Madge were due to the fact that they had identical genes? Which were due to the fact that they were young women growing up at the same time in the same country in generally similar surroundings? Which were sheer coincidences that happened to catch James Shields's eye? In one particular case history, we can never know. But a particular case history can suggest hypotheses to be explored by some of the more systematic methods outlined in this chapter, and dramatic "coincidences" in identical twins reared apart can help motivate a search for answers.

personality questionnaires to the pair members. In each of the three studies, a comparison group of identical twins reared together was also available. The average correlation over the personality scales administered in each study is given in Table 11.5 for the twins reared apart in separate families and for the twins reared together in the same family.

Two interesting facts are represented in this table. First, the resemblance between identical twins on personality measures is substantial but far from complete; correlations lie in the .40 to .60 range. Sec-

TABLE 11.5   *Average Correlations on Personality Inventory Scales for Identical Twins Reared Together and Apart*

STUDY	CONDITION OF REARING		NO. OF SCALES	NO. OF PAIRS
	APART	TOGETHER		
Newman et al.	.58	.56	1	19 & 50
Shields	.57	.40	2	42 & 43
Bouchard	.56	.54	11	23 & 108

Source: Bouchard (1981); Newman, Freeman, and Holzinger (1937); Shields (1962).

ond, being reared together in the same family doesn't appear to make identical twins more alike. There is certainly no evident tendency for the separated twins to show lower correlations. If these samples were not so small, we might even conclude the opposite.

Correlations near .50 mean that members of identical twin pairs tend to be similar in respect to about half the factors contributing to variation in personality and to be different in respect to the other half. Inasmuch as such twin pairs' genes are identical (there are rare exceptions that need not concern us here), any differences between the twins of a pair beyond sheer errors of measurement must be due to environmental factors of some sort, and therefore environment must make a large contribution to personality variation.

The second fact, however, the finding of equivalent correlations for identical twins reared together and apart, says something interesting and perhaps surprising about the nature of the environmental factors that affect personality. Twins growing up in the same family apparently do not share such factors to any greater degree than do twins growing up in separate families. If they did, they should be more alike.

If this line of reasoning is correct, it suggests a powerful criterion for screening any environmental factor proposed as influencing personality development: if such a factor is more alike for two individuals growing up in the same family than for persons growing up in separate families, it is probably *not* a major influence. If it were, it should tend to make identical twins reared together more alike than identical twins reared apart. Many variables often considered to be important influences in personality development would fail this test. The set of older and younger siblings, for example, is the same for two twins reared together, but it may differ for twins reared apart. Twins reared together are exposed (pretty much) to the same parental personalities and the same child training philosophies and methods. Twins reared apart may not be. Twins reared together will typically share the same neighborhood environment, the same schools, and the same peer associations to a much greater degree than will twins reared apart.

For various reasons, including the small sample sizes on which the figures in Table 11.5 are based, one would not wish to base such far-reaching conclusions solely on studies comparing identical twins reared together and apart. But behavior geneticists studying human personality have been reporting rather similar results from two other methods (Rowe and Plomin, 1981). One of these compares the resemblances of members of ordinary identical and fraternal twin pairs. The other examines the resemblances among unrelated individuals brought up together in families via adoption.

IDENTICAL AND FRATERNAL TWINS

The **identical–fraternal twin comparison** depends on the fact that even though members of both kinds of twin pairs tend to be treated pretty much alike, especially in their early years, identical twins share all their genes, whereas fraternal twins share only about half of theirs. Thus, if both sorts of twins are observed to be decidedly and about equally similar on some personality characteristic, it is most likely as a result of their similar treatment, whereas if on some other characteristic identical twins are much more alike than fraternal twins, this may be reflecting the large difference in the degree to which the two kinds of twins share genes. If one wishes to make certain simplifying assumptions (which are often made by workers in this field, although they are subject to some debate), one can obtain a quantitative index of the importance of shared family environment for a given trait by subtracting twice the difference between the identical and fraternal twin correlations from the identical twin correlation. If both correlations are high and similar, say, .80 and .80, the result will be $.80 - 2(.80 - .80) = .80$, an indication that shared family environment is having a large effect on the trait. If, on the other hand, the identical twin correlation were .60 and the fraternal twin correlation were .30, the result would be $.60 - 2(.60 - .30) = 0$, an indication of little or no shared effect of environment. The quantity that is subtracted, twice the difference between the two types of twin correlation, can likewise be taken, under the same assumptions, as an index of the size of the genetic effect: that is, zero in the first example, $2(.80 - .80)$, and .60 in the second, $2(.60 - .30)$.

Table 11.6 shows some representative identical and fraternal twin correlations on two personality dimensions in three recent good-sized twin studies. The two personality dimensions are extraversion-introversion and emotional maladjustment, or neuroticism, as these traits are defined by H. J. Eysenck (see Chapter 12). Slightly different questionnaires were used in the three studies, but they were intended to measure the same two Eysenckian dimensions.

Consistent with the separated identical twin studies, none of the six rows in the table shows any evidence of a common family environmental effect, when twice the identical–fraternal difference is sub-

TABLE 11.6   *Correlations of Identical and Fraternal Twins on Measures of Extraversion–Introversion and Neuroticism in Three Twin Studies*

STUDY AND TRAIT	IDENTICAL TWINS	FRATERNAL TWINS	NO. OF PAIRS
Floderus-Myrhed et al. (Sweden)			
Extraversion	.51	.21	4987 & 7790
Neuroticism	.50	.23	
Loehlin and Nichols (United States)			
Extraversion	.60	.25	481 & 312
Neuroticism	.52	.24	
Young et al. (Britain)			
Extraversion	.51	.17	301 & 170
Neuroticism	.45	.05	

Source: Floderus-Myrhed, Pedersen, and Rasmuson (1980); Loehlin and Nichols (1976); Young, Eaves, and Eysenck (1980). The Swedish and British twins were adults; the Americans were high school juniors. Fraternal twins are same-sex pairs only. Correlations for males and females averaged.

tracted from the identical twin correlation. In fact, the estimate of shared family environmental effect is actually slightly negative in each case. The identical twin correlations lie in the .40 to .60 range, as in Table 11.5, and the differences between the identical and fraternal twin correlations are quite compatible, with all the resemblance being genetic in origin. Again, a large fraction of the personality trait variation apparently reflects the influence of environmental factors, but these seem not to be factors shared by twins of a pair.

ADOPTION STUDIES

The logic of the **adoption study** is very simple. If the environmental factors that family members share are important determiners of personality, then adopted children should grow up showing family resemblances to their adoptive parents, to each other, and to any natural-born children in these families. If such shared environmental factors are not influential, then adoptive family members should not show personality resemblance, although biologically related family members, on the basis of their shared genes, might do so.

The results from two recent U.S. adoption studies are shown in Table 11.7. The typical correlations among family members related only by adoption are very low in both studies, averaging about .05. They are about the same for parent and adopted child and for biologically unrelated children reared together as brothers and sisters. This is not quite the zero degree of resemblance predicted by the twin studies, but it is close to it. According to these data, about 5 percent of the causal influences on personality might be shared family environmental

TABLE 11.7   *Average Correlations on Personality Inventory Scales in Two Adoption Studies*

STUDY AND RELATIONSHIP	MEDIAN CORRELATION	NO. OF SCALES	NO. OF PAIRINGS
Scarr et al., adoptive			
Parent–child	.04	9	347
Sibling	.07	9	86
Loehlin et al., adoptive			
Parent–child	.06	25	594
Sibling	.03	25	123
Scarr et al., biological			
Parent–child	.15	9	477
Sibling	.20	9	150
Loehlin et al., biological			
Parent–child	.12	25	105
Sibling	.22	25	15

Source: Scarr, Webber, Weinberg, and Wittig (1981); Lochlin, Willerman, and Horn (in press). Age of children: late adolescent or young adult. Numbers of pairings for Scarr et al. study are estimates.

factors. The biological sibling correlations are not too dissimilar from the fraternal twin correlations in Table 11.6, which is what would be expected if they are due predominantly to the genes. The biological parent–child correlations are a little lower. A possible interpretation would be that somewhat different genes may affect a given trait at different points during the life span.

Thus, adoption studies support the studies of identical twins reared apart, and the studies comparing identical and fraternal twins, in two major conclusions. First, the genes appear to make a considerable contribution to personality—accounting for about one-half of the personality variation, according to the twin studies. (The adoption studies suggest a somewhat smaller genetic contribution, but still an appreciable one.) And, second, only at most a small fraction of the remaining environmental influences on personality are of the sort that family members share. Growing up together in the same family does not make people alike in personality. The moderate degree of personality resemblance seen in families seems to be largely a contribution of their shared genes rather than their shared environments.

Behavior genetic studies of personality offer, then, an interesting challenge. The personality theorist must specify environmental determinants of personality largely from among variables that family members do *not* share. Or, alternatively, the theorist must emphasize intrafamily variables that tend to differentiate family members, so that they can offset shared environmental influences. Either of these alternatives, seriously pursued, could make substantial changes in the face of tomorrow's personality theories.

EVALUATION

Few psychologists have shown greater dedication than William Sheldon in pursuing the empirical testing of hypotheses generated by a core idea. Sheldon's research, in turn, has led to many related investigations, both by people favorably disposed to his position and by those who were skeptical. Lindzey (1973) and Rees (1968, 1973) have summarized much of this research.

One very important service Sheldon performed was to remind American psychologists that the human being has a body and that this body may provide clues to underlying factors that may be quite as significant in understanding human behavior as environmental factors.

One may question the extent or degree of relationship between physique and personality, but the work of Sheldon and others seems to demonstrate that any comprehensive view of human behavior must include consideration of dimensions of physique. Moreover, Sheldon's insistence on the use of continuous variables rather than discrete categories represents an important advance in measurement. Sheldon's insistence on looking at patterns rather than at a few simple categories has provided for many an attractive alternative to the arbitrariness and rigidity of discrete categories or types.

On the negative side, probably the most common criticism of Sheldon's theory is that it is not a theory. In fact, it consists largely of one general assumption—that physique and temperament are closely related—and a set of descriptive variables for assessing each domain. Sheldon himself said that he was offering not a general theory but rather a "skeleton" conception to which others must add.

Some investigators have accepted Sheldon's basic premise that physique and temperament are related, but they have devised other methods of measurement or have suggested other variables as being more important than those advocated by Sheldon. Parnell (1958), for example, has used a three-variable system (fat, muscularity, linearity) quite similar to Sheldon's but insists that measurements taken from photographs be supplemented with actual, physical measurement of the body.

Some researchers (Ekman, 1951a, b; Humphreys, 1957) have claimed that Sheldon's three physique components are not independent of each other and that Sheldon's own findings indicate the existence of only two components, not three. To the extent that one can adequately represent somatotypes in a two-dimensional diagram— such as those in Figures 11.2 to 11.5—one could in principle get by with defining only two basic dimensions of physique instead of three, say, an endomorphy-to-ectomorphy scale as the horizontal dimension and mesomorphy as the vertical one. Sheldon's most recent version of the somatotyping procedure has something of this two-dimensional character, with the trunk index providing a mesomorphy-to-endomorphy dimension and stature–ponderal index an ectomorphic one at right angles to it. However, the fact that a two-dimensional representation is *possible* does not mean that it is necessary or even desirable. A Sheldon proponent might well argue that the endomorphy–mesomorphy–ectomorphy triad provides a more natural and compelling representation of the relationships among somatotypes and among temperaments than would any of the possible two-dimensional alternatives. Nature does not always proceed with maximum possible parsimony.

One of the most serious criticisms of Sheldon's work revolves around the extremely high correlations he reported between the components of physique and temperament. Humphreys (1957), among others, points out that because in Sheldon's initial study he himself made both physique and temperament ratings, his results could have been contaminated by his own beliefs. Sheldon has defended his methods at some length (1942), insisting, for example, that he made his temperament ratings before rating subjects on physique. It stands to reason, however, that Sheldon, experienced in somatotyping, could probably assess a person's somatotype at least approximately, even if unconsciously, while he was making temperament ratings. Thus an implicit physique rating could well have influenced his judgments of temperament.

A further objection is that correlations of the magnitude Sheldon reports between physique and temperament are just not consistent with all that is generally known about human behavior. For one thing, measurement error, inevitable in the construction and use of rating scales, would make such high correlations very unlikely. More basically, it seems improbable that aspects of physique alone could have such a strong influence on behavior; there are just too many other factors that must have some determining role.

There is also the question of whether the somatotype is constant over time. At first Sheldon said it was; then he suggested that constancy depends on consistent nutrition and physical health. Later he again asserted the constancy of the somatotype, claiming that his new ways of defining it were "constant through life" (Sheldon, Lewis, and Tenney, 1969). Obviously, if the somatotype is *not* constant, it loses some power as a predictive measure.

Certainly Sheldon's work has provoked many related studies. And it has helped to encourage a growing interest in the biological aspects of human personality. This stimulation of research may prove to be a very important contribution, whether or not some of the particular details of Sheldon's theory and findings stand the test of time.

SUMMARY

1. Factors that have inhibited the study of constitutional psychology are poor conceptualization and exploitation of early systems as well as the dominance of environmentalism in American psychology.

2. Predecessors of William Sheldon's theory of physique and temperament include Hippocrates' twofold typology and Kretschmer's three-fold system that related body types to forms of mental disorder.

3. Personality comprises the cognitive, affective, conative, physiological, and morphological—or structural—aspects of the individual. **Constitutional psychology** studies the relatively unchanging aspects of the person and focuses on the structure of the body.

4. Genetic factors are important determinants of human structure and function.

WILLIAM H. SHELDON

5. The **somatotype** attempts to represent the **morphogenotype**, or underlying biological structure of the individual; both are differentiated from the **phenotype**, which comprises the visible properties of the human being. The somatotype assesses the degree to which a person possesses the three primary components of physique: endomorphy, mesomorphy, and ectomorphy. These components are **continuous variables** and not discrete categories; no one is ''a mesomorph'' or ''a viscerotonic.''

6. In **endomorphy**, the vegetative system predominates, and the body is soft and rounded. In **mesomorphy**, bone and muscle predominate, and the body is hard and rectangular. In **ectomorphy**, skin and nervous system predominate, and the body is thin and delicate.

7. Somatotype ratings are calculated by inspecting and taking certain measuements from three standard photographs. Age, height, the **ponderal index** (height divided by the cube root of weight), and the **trunk index** (the ratio between two of the five body regions—chest-trunk divided by stomach–trunk) are the basis for the somatotype rating.

8. Secondary components of physique include **dysplasia**, or disharmony between the three physique components in different body regions; **gynandromorphy**, the combination of male and female characteristics in the same person; and the **textural aspect**, the physical attractiveness of the body.

9. The **constancy** of the somatotype over time has been strongly indicated but has not been definitively established. Weight gain or loss and diseases that cause muscular atrophy may affect the somatotype. The somatotype can be measured in children, but it is most clearly recognized in the adult.

10. The **Scale of Temperament** is used to determine the degree to which a person possesses each of the three components of temperament: viscerotonia, somatotonia, and cerebrotonia. **Viscerotonia** includes the qualities of relaxation and love of physical comfort; **somatotonia** includes energetic and aggressive qualities and love of physical activity; **cerebrotonia** includes qualities of tension, inhibition, and self-consciousness.

11. The relationships between endomorphy and viscerotonia, mesomorphy and somatotonia, and ectomorphy and cerebrotonia, respectively, have been confirmed by a number of investigators, although correlations are usually much smaller than Sheldon's.

12. Physique and temperament may be related because persons with certain builds tend to be rewarded for certain behaviors and punished for others; because cultural stereotypes lead people to expect those with certain builds to behave in certain ways; because some unitary biological factor influences both body build and temperament; or because environmental factors cause a person to develop related physique and behavioral characteristics.

13. The average male is more mesomorphic, the average female more endomorphic. Male delinquents tend to be more strongly mesomorphic than the average male, and female delinquents may also be more mesomorphic than the average female. Male delinquents may exhibit more of the **affective psychiatric** component than of the **paranoid** or **heboid** components. Among mental patients, the physique and psychiatric components were found to be moderately highly correlated: the affective component went with a lack of ectomorphy and the heboid component with a lack of mesomorphy, as predicted. However, the predicted relation between paranoia and lack of endomorphy was not found.

BEHAVIOR GENETICS

14. **Behavior genetics** is one of several scientific subdisciplines—two others are **psychopharmacology** and the **neurosciences**—that treat of the relations between body and behavior.

15. One of the central questions behavior genetics seeks to answer is, To what extent is the fact that everyone differs in his or her behavior from everyone else a result of (1) the fact that everyone differs genetically from everyone else and (2) the fact that everyone also experiences a different environment from everyone else.

16. Studies of **identical twins reared apart** suggest that such twins resemble each other greatly but not entirely—correlations range from .40 to .60—and that being raised in the same family does not make identical twins more alike.

17. Whatever the environmental factors are that significantly influence personality development, they are not factors that are more alike for people growing up in the same family than for people growing up in separate families—that is, they are not such things as same parental personalities, same neighborhoods, same schools.

18. Identical and fraternal twin comparison studies and **adoption studies** support the notion that shared family environmental factors do not significantly affect personality development.

19. Whereas genes appear to account for about half of personality variation, only a small fraction of environmental influences on personality are of the sort that family members share. The challenge to personality theorists is to discover environmental determinants of personality that family members do not share or to discover variables within families that somehow offset the shared environmental influences.

20. Sheldon and others have demonstrated that any comprehensive view of human behavior must include considerations of body build or physique. Sheldon's work has helped to encourage the growing interest in the biological aspects of personality. Also, his emphasis on patterns rather than on rigid categories or types is an important contribution to the study of personality. Sheldon's theory has been criticized on the grounds that it is not a theory but only one general assumption—of a relation between physique and temperament. The unusually high correlations Sheldon reports have been attributed to deficiencies in the methods he employed. The constancy of the somatotype, Sheldon's basic conception, raises problems; if it is not constant over time, it cannot serve as a predictive measure.

SUGGESTED READING

To get to know Sheldon's work, you should probably start with *The Varieties of Human Physique* (1940), which presents his basic theories and initial research on the somatotype. Following close upon this book was *The Varieties of Temperament* (1942), in which Sheldon presents his findings with respect to the relations between physique and temperament.

The *Atlas of Men* (1954) describes the technique of somatotyping and presents representative somatotype photographs of over 1000 men, derived from an original population of 46,000. In "Psychotic Patterns and Physical Constitution: A Thirty-Year Follow-up of Thirty-Eight Hundred Psychiatric Patients in New York State"(Sheldon, Lewis, and Tenney, 1969) and "The New York Study of Physical Constitution and Psychotic Patterns" (Sheldon, 1971), Sheldon deals with the relations between somatotype and mental disorder as well as with refinements of his method of somatotyping.

Varieties of Delinquent Youth (1949b) applies Sheldon's findings and methods to a study of boys remanded to a residential rehabilitation home near Boston.

To date no one has written a biography of Sheldon, but a brief biographical sketch by Osborne (1979) appears in the *International Encyclopedia of the Social Sciences*.

Chapter twelve

12.

When measurement is ready the real investigation of psychology as a science can begin.
RAYMOND B. CATTELL

I have usually been against the establishment and in favor of the rebels.
HANS J. EYSENCK

The Factor Analysts: Raymond Cattell
and Hans Eysenck

Raymond B. Cattell and Hans J. Eysenck have two fundamental beliefs in common: they believe in the existence of enduring dimensions of personality, and they believe that the sophisticated statistical technique of **factor analysis** (see Box 12.1) offers the best means of isolating these variables. There are other personality investigators who share these beliefs, J. P. Guilford (see page 441) among them. Cattell and Eysenck, however, have raised important and troubling issues in the area of personality, and each has labored mightily to bring this maverick field of study into the corral of true scientific endeavor. Both men are enormously prolific; from their separate laboratories have come a total of around 80 books and over 1000 journal articles and chapters in books edited by others. Athough not every one of these publications has aroused strong interest among the psychological community, as a body of work they have certainly been noticed. Whether or not their concepts and theories will ultimately prove valid, Cattell and Eysenck—who are often in disagreement with each other—have earned their place in the continuing endeavor to understand human personality.

RAYMOND B. CATTELL

Because he believes that we cannot define personality until we have fully specified all the concepts we plan to use in our endeavor, Raymond B. Cattell offers only the very general statement that "Personality is that which permits a prediction of what a person will do in a given situation" (Cattell, 1950, p. 2). He does, however, add that personality is concerned with all behavior, both overt and "under the skin," and he reminds us that the meaning of small segments of behavior can be fully understood only when seen within the framework of the entire functioning person. Like Gordon Allport, Cattell grounds his theory on the concept of traits; like William Sheldon, he strongly emphasizes the biological basis of behavior; and like Henry Murray, he explicitly gives a formal place in his scheme to both person variables and environment variables.

PERSONALITY AS A STRUCTURE OF TRAITS

Cattell views personality as a complex structure of traits of various categories. The trait, an inferred mental structure that accounts for the consistency of observed behavior, comes in several varieties and accounts for both structural and dynamic aspects of personality.

Cattell began his research with the 4500 or so trait-names that Allport and Odbert (1936) had garnered from an unabridged dictionary. He condensed this list to fewer than 200 items by grouping near-synonyms and by eliminating rare and metaphorical terms. He then intercorrelated and further reduced the resulting group of terms (by **clustering** procedures, similar to factor analysis but less complicated) to 35 surface traits.

The **surface** trait, one can say, is the first stage in Cattell's research. As we have just seen, it can be derived by grouping phenomena that seem to go together. If we were to work from observed behavior, for example, we might infer a surface trait of cheerfulness if we repeatedly observed a woman taking small mishaps in her stride, encouraging and comforting others, and planning her activities in anticipation of favorable outcomes. We might infer a depressive trait in another woman seen constantly criticizing others, predicting dire outcomes, and often pleading fatigue when invited to join in activities.

Cattell divides traits in several ways, and one of the most important distinctions is that between the surface and the source trait. The **source** trait cannot be inferred directly from observable behavior; it can be identified only by using the technique of **factor analysis,** in which many surface traits are intercorrelated and **factored** in order to determine the unitary influences that underlie them. According to Cattell, source traits, whose interaction produces surface traits, are the most useful in accounting for behavior. Because they are fewer in number than surface traits, source traits offer economy of description. Moreover, Cattell says, "as research is now showing, . . . source traits correspond to real unitary influences—physiological, temperamental factors; degrees of dynamic integration; exposure to social institutions" (1950, p. 27).

For Cattell it is also important, though difficult, to distinguish between traits in terms of the relative contribution made to them by hereditary and environmental factors. Every surface trait reflects a mixture of both heredity and environment, Cattell says, but some source traits may derive solely from factors within the person, others from environmental factors. Labeling the first type of source trait

BOX 12.1   Stalking the Alligators: The Technique of Factor Analysis

Imagine that you are hacking your way through a dense, tropical forest. Strange cries reach your ears from every side. The sun's brilliance is heavily shaded by the green mass above you, and you can see only dimly. As you reach to cut through the next tangle of lianas, your eyes focus on three dark blobs a few yards away. You stop. What are they? Three rotting logs? You wait. Suddenly the blobs move—together. As the alligator approaches, you also move. (Adapted from Cattell, 1966a)

Cattell's analogy serves nicely to introduce the purpose and general approach of factor analysis: in the jungle of human behavior, we need to sort out what is important. One way to reduce the numbers of things we must deal with is to assign them to broad general categories, and to do this, we need to know what "moves" with what.

The factor analyst begins with a set of scores from many different measures—questionnaires, observers' ratings, performance tasks, and the like—for a large number of subjects. To make sense of all these scores—to identify a small number of basic factors whose operation accounts for most of the variation in them—the factor analyst tries to see which ones "move together," or are correlated with each other. The factor analyst's findings are rarely as dramatic as yours when you correctly identify the alligator, for scores rarely correlate perfectly. However, factor analysis can produce very strong evidence of covariation and, thus, very suggestive evidence about basic factors that influence behavior.

Let us take a very simple example of how factor analysis works. Suppose we have grades for seven different exams—calculus, chemistry, English, fine arts, history, philosophy, and physics. We want to know if there are factors that explain why some people get high grades in one subject and low grades in another and so on. Look at Table 12.1, which shows hypothetical correlations obtained by comparing grades, or scores, on all these measures—English with fine arts, English with chemistry, fine arts with chemistry, and so on. (Note that these correlations are completely fictional and do not reflect an actual comparison of scores.) As you can see, the first four measures are highly correlated (correlations between +.70 and +.90) and the next three measures are also highly correlated (correlations of +.80 and +.90). On the other hand, the first four measures are only moderately correlated with the next three (correlations between +.30 and +.50). (You will remember from introductory psychology that in the statistical method of correlation, .00 indicates that there is no relationship between scores compared and +1.00 indicates that sources are perfectly corelated.) These findings suggest that there is some unitary factor that influences the ability to do well in English, fine arts, history, and philosophy; that another, second factor affects expertise in calculus, chemistry, and physics; and

TABLE 12.1 *Hypothetical Correlation Matrix*

EXAM	ENGLISH	FINE ARTS	HISTORY	PHILOSOPHY	CALCULUS	CHEMISTRY	PHYSICS
English	+ 1.00	+ .70	+ .80	+ .80	+ .30	+ .40	+ .40
Fine Arts		+ 1.00	+ .80	+ .70	+ .40	+ .40	+ .50
History			+ 1.00	+ .90	+ .30	+ .30	+ .50
Philosophy				+ 1.00	+ .50	+ .30	+ .50
Calculus					+ 1.00	+ .80	+ .90
Chemistry						+ 1.00	+ .80
Physics							+ 1.00

Note: The triangles will help you to see that the first four measures are all strongly correlated with each other, the last three measures are also strongly correlated with each other, but the first four are correlated only moderately with the last three.

that these two factors are moderately (not highly) correlated with each other.

In applying the technique of factor analysis, the investigator not only isolates the fundamental factors that control variation in the surface variables but estimates the extent to which each revealed factor contributes to each measure. This estimate is called the **factor loading,** or **saturation,** of the measure. The nature of the measures that have high loadings on a particular factor generally determines the psychological meaning—and the label—given to the factor. For example, the fact that chemistry, calculus, and physics all make heavy use of mathematical formulas and computations might lead us to call the factor underlying these three measures "mathematical skill." And because English, fine arts, history, and philosophy all require the clear articulation of thoughts, we might decide to call a factor underlying

these measures "verbal skill." Note, however, that even in this sophisticated statistical technique, objectivity is not absolute. Someone else might feel that "toughmindedness," in the sense of a dispassionate approach to things, might better describe the first factor and "tendermindedness," or a more feeling, intuitive approach, might best describe the second.

There is a tendency to regard the factor analyst's factors as some sort of mysterious phenomena, probably because many people are put off by complicated mathematical operations. In fact, however, these factors are simply conceptions of personality variables, not unlike the conceptions of personality theorists who do not use this particular technique. Factors are just efforts to formulate the significant variables that account for the complexity of human behavior. It is the techniques by which they are

derived that distinguish them from other theorists' conceptions.

Like any field of endeavor, factor analysis has its controversies. One issue on which factor analysts differ is that of the relative usefulness of two systems of factoring—the orthogonal and the oblique. Orthogonal factors are so defined as to be uncorrelated with each other. Oblique factors, on the other hand, are correlated with each other to some degree.

Factor theorists disagree as to whether correlated or uncorrelated factors should be extracted in their analyses. J. P. Guilford (see Box 12.5) and others prefer an orthogonal technique as more efficient, but Cattell argues for the oblique approach on the grounds that causal influences in the realm of personality may well be intercorrelated and that only by use of an oblique method can an undistorted picture emerge.

---

constitutional, Cattell suggests that its origin is "physiological and *within the organism,* which will mean inborn only in a certain fraction of cases" (1950, p. 34). **Environmental-mold** source traits, he says, "spring from the molding effect of social institutions and physical realities which constitute the cultural pattern" (p. 34).

A third important subdivision of traits reflects the particular aspects of behavior with which traits are concerned. **Dynamic** traits are concerned with setting the person in action toward some goal. **Ability** traits represent the effectiveness with which the person reaches that goal. **Temperament** traits have to do largely with the way in which the person moves toward his or her goal—that is, with such things as speed, energy level, and emotional reactivity.

Let us look first at temperament and ability traits, which have a somewhat less complex structuring. Then, with a better idea of how Cattell derives his trait concepts, we can examine the important cate-

BOX 12.2   Raymond Bernard Cattell (1905–   )

Raymond B. Cattell was born in Staffordshire, England, where his father and grandfather were owner–managers of several industrial plants and squarely "in the stream of Victorian, middle class liberalism" (Cattell, 1974, p. 61.). Cattell was the second of three sons, and he felt fiercely competitive with his older brother who, though apparently less intellectually gifted than he, had a "strong" personality and "power" that Cattell could not overcome.

At age 15, Cattell passed the university exam, and he was graduated from the University of London at 19 with a major in chemistry. At a time when he was struggling to find "a road through human irrationalities to the solution of social problems," he heard a lecture by Sir Cyril Burt (Burt is discussed in Box 12.7) on the work of Francis Galton and decided to study psychology.

By the time he obtained his Ph.D., in 1929, Cattell was a lecturer at Exeter University, and in 1932 he became director of the City Psychology Clinic at Leicester, a post he held for five years. Having studied at London with Charles Spearman, the originator of the technique of factor analysis, Cattell had become convinced that "the only proof of structure and causal relation lies in covariation," and he felt certain that the new technique could be used to find "the dynamic roots of behavior" (Cattell, 1974).

Opportunities in England in the 1930s were limited, however, for there was no money for research, and all the important chairs were filled by professors who were quite "hale and hearty." Thus, when in 1937 E. L. Thorndike invited Cattell to come to the United States to serve as his research associate for a year, Cattell accepted with alacrity. The following year, he was offered the G. Stanley Hall professorship at Clark University, and in 1941 he became a lecturer at Harvard. There he met Allport, Murray, and Sheldon, among others, and enjoyed many lunchtime discussions with these colleagues.

In 1944 Cattell was offered a research professorship at the University of Illinois, and he remained there, directing the Laboratory of Personality and Group Behavior Research, until his formal retirement in 1973. Then he founded the Institute for Research on Morality and Adjustment in Boulder, Colorado and, somewhat later, accepted a professorship at the University of Hawaii School of Professional Psychology, where he continues to engage actively in writing and research.

In 1960 Cattell helped to found the Society of Multivariate Experimental Psychology—which publishes the journal *Multivariate Behavioral Research*—and he served as the society's first president. Among Cattell's awards are a D.Sc. from the University of London for contributions to personality research (1937), the Wenner-Gren prize of the New York Academy of Science for work on the psychology of the researcher (1953), and the Educational Testing Service's citation for Distinguished Contributions to Psychological Measurement (1982).

Factor analysis and "the dynamic calculus," the system of mathematical formulas Cattell has devised to assess motivational factors in behavior have, Cattell admits, frightened off many psychologists. But he disagrees with instructors who hold that students are not equipped to handle these complex techniques: according to Cattell, students are quite as able to handle these techniques as they are to handle the computations required in physics and chemistry. Cattell's challenge to the student of personality is clear: "He has chosen proudly to study the most complex phenomenon in the universe: he must be prepared to think hard or be overwhelmed" (1983, p. 219).

Joan Benoit, gold medal winner of the first women's Olympic marathon, August, 1984. Cattell might find Benoit's dynamic, ability and temperament traits highly effective in moving her toward her goals.

gory of the dynamic traits, Cattell's formulation of the motivational aspects of personality. After that, we will explore some mathematical techniques for assessing both motivation and the degree of conflict generated by opposing traits. And we will close the section with a brief look at the ways in which state, role, and set, factors limited in time and space, influence personality.

TEMPERAMENT AND ABILITY TRAITS.   Three primary methods are used to derive information about personality traits: the life record, the questionnaire, and the objective test. In this section we will be talking primarily about **L data,** which are derived from the life record, and **Q data,** which are derived from the questionnaire. (We will discuss T data, derived from the objective test, in the following section.) The L data theoretically include actual records of a person's life, such as school grades or number of jobs held. Because such data are difficult to come by, however, in actual practice L data usually comprise ratings of a person by others who know him or her well. Q data are provided by the person in question, rating himself or herself on a variety of behaviors and characteristics by filling out a questionnaire form.

Theoretically, if we subject L, Q, and T data to factor analysis and find that the same factors emerge as important in all three types of data, we will have strong evidence that such factors represent true functional unities and thus can be considered source traits. In fact, the research carried out by Cattell and his associates over a period of several decades has revealed that whereas L and Q data tend to produce rather similar sets of factors, T data produce a rather different set. A possible explanation for this situation is that the three types of measures are sampling data at different levels of generality—but let us not get ahead of our story.

Some 35 personality factors tend to emerge from L and Q data. Of these, 16 have been incorporated into an instrument called the 16 Personality Factor Questionnaire (16 PF, for short). Table 12.2 lists the 16 factors included in the questionnaire; as you can see, most are temperament traits, describing the person's style of behavior. Factor B, intelligence, is considered an ability factor; factors Q_1–Q_4 represent more dynamic qualities.

Many of Cattell's formal names for his factors (see Table 12.2, column 2) are terms he has coined, based on his hypotheses about the origins or underlying nature of the factors. For example, factor H—in common language, boldness–shyness—is called "parmia–threctia." "Parmia" reflects Cattell's hypothesis that in people we would call bold and venturesome, the parasympathetic nervous system—which is generally associated with the state of relaxation—is dominant. Such people, he finds, do not startle easily and welcome new experiences. "Threctia" reflects his idea that people at the opposite pole of this dimension are highly susceptible to threat, tending to be timid, aloof, and slow or reluctant to make new friends or to speak up among strangers or before groups.

DYNAMIC TRAITS. Dynamic traits are derived primarily from **T data**, or the information produced by the objective test. The latter is a kind of "miniature situation" in which behavior can be quantitatively scored: for example, one may measure the electrical resistance of the skin (galvanic skin response), ask a subject to choose which of a list of books he or she would prefer to read, or test the subject's ability at a game involving risk taking. Cattell and his associates have devised more than 400 such tests.

There are three basic types of dynamic traits: the attitude, the sentiment (a kind of attitude structure), the erg (rhymes with *berg*). As we will see, these three kinds of traits are interrelated with each other through what Cattell calls chains of subsidiation: ergs—roughly, drives—are served by attitudes and sentiments. (In his most recent writings, Cattell has introduced the term "sem" in place of "sentiment," but we will continue here with his long-term usage.)

Attitudes. An **attitude** is an interest of a certain intensity in a particular course of action with respect to a particular object. Thus if a man

TABLE 12.2 Cattell's 16 Personality Factors

HIGH SCORER	LETTER SYMBOL AND FACTOR NAME	LOW SCORER
	A	
Outgoing	Affectia–Sizia	Reserved
	B	
More intelligent	Intelligence	Less intelligent
	C	
Stable	Ego strength	Emotional
	E	
Assertive	Dominance–Submissiveness	Humble
	F	
Happy-go-lucky	Surgency–Desurgency	Sober
	G	
Conscientious	Superego strength	Expedient
	H	
Bold	Parmia–Threctia	Shy
	I	
Tenderminded	Premsia–Harria	Toughminded
	L	
Suspicious	Protension–Alaxia	Trusting
	M	
Imaginative	Autia–Praxernia	Practical
	N	
Shrewd	Shrewdness–Artlessness	Forthright
	O	
Apprehensive	Guilt proneness–Assurance	Placid
	Q_1	
Experimenting	Radicalism–Conservatism	Traditional
	Q_2	
Self-sufficient	Self-sufficiency–Group adherence	Group-tied
	Q_3	
Controlled	High self-concept–Low integration	Casual
	Q_4	
Tense	Ergic tension	Relaxed

Source: Adapted from Cattell (1966a, Table 30, p. 365).

says, "I want very much to marry Rita," he is expressing an intense interest ("want very much") in a course of action ("to get married") toward a particular object ("Rita").

The result of experiential rather than hereditary factors, an attitude is an environmental-mold source trait. It is also the observable expression of underlying dynamic structure: ergs and sentiments and their interrelations must be inferred from attitudes. An attitude, however, need not be expressed verbally or even overtly. Indeed, Cattell would prefer to measure the strength of an attitude by a variety of indirect methods. For example, the seriousness of our man's interest in marriage might be assessed by measuring his rise in blood pressure as he looks at a picture of a wedding party, his tendency to remember more positive or more negative items from a list of the consequences of marrying, the accuracy of his information about the probabilities of making a successful marriage in our society, and so on.

Sentiments.   An organized structure of attitudes, the sentiment is also an environmental-mold source trait. Sentiments are an important origin of motivation, inasmuch as they tend to be organized around significant social institutions (e.g., career, religion) or people (e.g., parents, spouse, self). The self is an especially important sentiment, because it is linked to the expression of most or all of the ergs or other sentiments and because almost all attitudes tend to reflect the self-sentiment in some degree.

Ergs.   The erg corresponds roughly to what other theorists have called "drive." An **erg** is a constitutional source trait, "an innate psychophysical disposition which permits its possessor to acquire reactivity . . . to certain classes of objects more readily than others, to experience a specific emotion in regard to them, and to start on a course of action which ceases more completely at a certain specific goal activity than at any other." (Cattell, 1950, p. 199). Thus, for example, the erg of fear will lead one to develop special alertness to events and objects that endanger one's existence. Recognizing the funnel of an approaching tornado, one may feel fear and gather the family together in the cellar as quickly as possible.

    Cattell places particular emphasis on ergic (rhymes with *allergic*) motivation, in part, because of his belief that contemporary American psychologists have underestimated the importance of the hereditary determinants of behavior. (Of this, more later.) Cattell (Cattell and Child, 1975) considers the following 10 ergs to have been reasonably well established by his research: hunger, sex, gregariousness (sociability), parental protectiveness, curiosity, security (fear), pugnacity (aggressiveness), acquisitiveness, self-assertion, and narcistic sex (general self-indulgence).

Subsidiation: The Dynamic Lattice.   According to Cattell, ergs, sentiments, and attitudes are interrelated by chains of **subsidiation**; that is, one type of trait is subsidiary to another, or serves to facilitate the other.

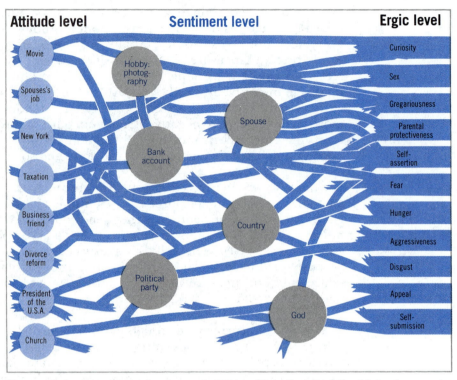

*Figure 12.1   Fragment of a dynamic lattice. Note that 8 of the 10 basic ergs are shown here (*acquisitiveness *and* self-indulgence *are excluded) as well as less well-established ergs—*disgust, appeal, *and* self-submission. *(Adapted from Cattell, 1950, Diagram 27, p. 158; Cattell and Dreger, 1977, Fig. 5, p. 450.)*

   Figure 12.1 illustrates some chains of subsidiation for a hypothetical person. Ergs appear at the right; the objects of sentiments appear in large circles in the middle; the objects of attitudes appear in smaller circles at the left. As you can see, any particular attitude (the channels show interrelations) may serve one or more sentiments or one or more ergs, and it may serve ergs directly or indirectly, through the sentiments. In addition, one sentiment may be subsidiary to another. Suppose, for example, that you want to see a new film on a political figure. By so doing you may satisfy not only your interest in photography but your concern for your country. Seeing the film may satisfy your ergs of curiosity (both through the photography hobby sentiment and directly), sex (because there is a subplot involving a sexual relationship between the main characters), gregariousness (if you go to the movie with a friend), protection (via interest in your country), and disgust (you may be strongly opposed to a political philosophy expressed in the film).

The diagram in Figure 12.1 is incomplete. Some connections have been merely suggested (see broken-off paths), and many more attitudes—and sentiments—could be represented. Cattell admits that because of the myriad connections that may exist among attitudes, sentiments, and ergs, the analysis of a dynamic lattice presents a considerable challenge. Yet, he says, "this is how human dynamic traits are structured, and we shall get ahead most quickly by admitting it. To the clinician, who may spend a year tracing the dynamic entanglements of a neurotic patient, the truth of the lattice concept will be immediately evident" (Cattell, 1950, p. 159).

FACTORING THE FACTORS.   The basic factors derived from L, Q, and T data are called **first-order**, or **primary**, factors. When you subject these variables to factor analysis, or **refactor** them—in short, find broad categories under which to group them—you derive **second-order**, or **secondary**, factors. We have mentioned the discrepancy that exists between the kinds of factors revealed by L and Q data, on the one hand, and T data, on the other. Interestingly, Cattell and his associates report that in a number of cases, T data first-order factors align themselves rather well with second-order factors derived from L and Q data. Thus, some primary T data factors appear to describe the same influences that some secondary Q data factors describe. According to Cattell, this difference of order, or stratum, comes about

presumably because the questionnaire items are, as it were, smaller particles than the sub-tests in an objective test battery. The questionnaire is like a higher-powered microscope. This same difference in the level of the unities perceived exists between an optical microscope, in which cells may be the recognized units, and the electron microscope, in which large molecules can be perceived. It is not that one is true and the other false: they are just views of unities at different levels of organization. (1966a, p. 119)

Whether Cattell's initial hope of finding identical factor structures in all three data sources will be realized remains to be seen. At this point, the factors derived are more different than alike, and only certain ones seem to match up.

THE BEHAVIORAL SPECIFICATION EQUATION.   Consistent with his general approach to identifying and classifying the elements of personality, Cattell proposes a mathematical technique of putting information about different kinds of traits—ability, temperament, dynamic—together in order to predict how a person will behave or respond in a particular situation. He suggests that we can do this by means of a **behavioral specification equation** of the following form:

$$R = s_1 T_1 + s_2 T_2 + s_3 T_3 + \cdots + s_n T_n$$

The first female park ranger to be stationed in a remote area, Linda Brown rests her horse along a river in Olympic National Park. Cattell's behavioral specification equation might have been used to predict Ms. Brown's success in this rather demanding job.

In this equation, R stands for response or behavior, T stands for trait, and s stands for situational characteristic. The last is an index of the extent to which a particular trait (the s's accompanying T) is involved in the particular situation. Thus, the way in which a person will respond in a particular situation may be predicted by adding the person's various traits (T_1-T_n), each weighted by its situational index (s_1-s_n). If a particular trait is highly relevant to a situation, its s will be large; if the trait is totally irrelevant, its s will be zero; if the trait detracts from or inhibits the response, the sign of s will be negative.

Suppose, for example, that a young man who is applying for a job as a forest ranger has traits of intelligence, emotional stability, dominance, and sociability. The first two traits may help him to respond appropriately to the requirements of the job, such as making what must often be rapid decisions and taking sole responsibility. The third trait may have little bearing on the situation. The fourth trait, however, may actively prevent this person from performing optimally on a job that will require him to spend much time alone.

The specification equation is, in a sense, a multidimensional version of Kurt Lewin's formulation of behavior $B = f(P, E)$, in which the properties of the person, P, are the traits, and the properties of the environment, E, are the situation indices. For example, if an applicant for the job of forest ranger has trait scores of 6, 7, 8, and 2 on the traits intelligence, stability, dominance, and sociability, and the corresponding situational indices for the position are .5, .7, 0, and $-.8$, the applicant's overall response in this situation will be a very favorable 6.5: $.5 \times 6 + .7 \times 7 + 0 \times 8 + (-.8) \times 2$. If he is more sociable, say, a 7, his score will be a less favorable 2.3: $.5 \times 6 + .7 \times 7 + 0 \times 8 + (-.8) \times 7$. And if he is highly sociable but neither very smart nor very stable, a misfit for the job, he may wind up with an unfavorable minus score: $.5 \times 4 + .7 \times 3 + 0 \times 8 + (-.8) \times 7 = -1.5$.

CONFLICT AND ADJUSTMENT.   A behavioral specification equation can also be used to assess conflict among ergs and sentiments. Let us go back to the young man who wants to get married. In the following equation, I stands for strength of desire to marry, the E's stands for ergs, and the M's for sentiments. The degree to which an erg or sentiment is involved in the attitude of wanting to get married is represented by a positive or negative number somewhere between 0 and 1.

$$I_{marry} = .2E_{curiosity} + .6E_{sex} + .4E_{gregariousness} - .3E_{fear} + .3M_{parents} - .4M_{career} + .5M_{self}$$

For this young man, marrying promises to reward his ergs of sex, sociability, and curiosity and to be compatible with his self-sentiment (self-esteem) and with his desire for parental approval. At the same time, he is a little frightened of the prospect. He also thinks marriage may hamper his career, which is just getting underway and demands a great deal of his time.

Motivational factors change constantly, of course, but in general, one can say that if the terms in a specification equation are more positive than negative, the attitude examined will tend to be a fairly stable feature of the person's motivational structure; if the terms are more negative than positive, the attitude will generally be abandoned. Moreover, the more negative terms in an overall positive equation, the more conflicted the person is likely to be about the attitude represented.

STATES, ROLES, AND SETS.   Certain patterns within the personality are less stable than others: your **state**, or mood, may change frequently; you may step in and out of a particular **role**, such as student or lab assistant; you may adopt a temporary mental **set** toward some aspect of the environment, (for example, when you start a new, multiple-choice section of an exam, having just finished a true–false section). To represent this variability, Cattell says, the specification equation must include terms representing state, role, and set, and each of these terms, like the trait terms, must be weighted by its appropriate situational index, defining its relevance to the behavior or response we are trying to predict.

Most of Cattell's work in this area has focused on states, particularly the state of anxiety (Cattell and Scheier, 1961). Anxiety is also a trait (it is a primary T data factor that matches up with a secondary

Q data factor). Thus, a person who is characteristically more or less anxious will vary in state from this normal level depending on situational and organismic influences. Cattell has studied other factors, such as depression, stress, fatigue, and general autonomic activity, and he indicates that a dozen or more state factors may be identifiable (Cattell, 1973).

THE DEVELOPMENT OF PERSONALITY

In an effort to develop measures that can assess the same personality factors at different ages and thus to map developmental trends in personality traits, Cattell and his associates have studied children and adolescents as well as adults. In general, Cattell finds similar factors at ages ranging from four years to adulthood. Behavior does vary at different age levels, however, and it is difficult to be sure that a given device is actually measuring the same thing in different age groups. To deal with this problem, Cattell has carried out bridging, or **boundary,** studies in which two tests designed for adjacent age-group levels are both given to members of an intermediate age group. When the corresponding scores on the two tests correlate highly, it is possible to infer that the same factor is indeed being measured. For a number of factors, especially at older ages, the results have been highly satisfactory. In other instances, such matches are not yet entirely compelling (Cattell, 1973).

HEREDITARY–ENVIRONMENT ANALYSIS. Cattell is much concerned with analyzing the relative effects on personality of genetic and environmental factors. Cattell's claim that certain traits—among them, intelligence, toughmindedness and impulsiveness—are heavily influenced by genetic factors involves him with the behavior genetic methods discussed in the last chapter.

For his own research in this area, which he continues to pursue, Cattell (1960) has devised a new statistical technique called **multiple abstract variance analysis,** or **MAVA**. MAVA, according to Cattell (1982), offers a great deal more information than typical heredity–environment research studies have been able to provide.

According to Cattell (1966a), the usual twin study tells us only whether heredity has any significant action at all. MAVA, Cattell says, tells us "*how much* of the environmental influence on a trait is typically due to differences in treatment within the family and how much to social differences between families. Similarly, it tells us the typical magnitude of the hereditary difference within families and between families" (p. 36). The MAVA technique provides for including nontwin siblings, both natural and adoptive, along with twins, thus combining in a single study several of the groups discussed in the section on behavior genetics in the preceding chapter.

One interesting finding of Cattell's work in this area is that, although we might expect heredity and environment to be positively correlated—that is, we might suppose that bright children would be given better educations—in fact these factors are often negatively correlated. Especially in the case of personality traits, there is a tendency for environmental factors to oppose the effects of heredity, as when parents or others attempt to encourage the bashful child and restrain the obstreperous one. This phenomenon results in what Cattell has labeled a **law of coercion to the biosocial mean**.

LEARNING.   For Cattell there are three main kinds of personality learning: first, the simple **association** of simultaneous cognitions; second, instrumental or **means–end** learning; and a third principle that represents essentially an elaboration of means–end learning and that Cattell calls **integration** learning. For Cattell, associative learning is important in providing a basic foundation for other kinds of learning; for example, the baby learns that the appearance of mother goes with relief of discomfort. It is by means–end learning that the person develops ways of satisfying basic, ergic goals. Thus, the baby may learn that crying will fetch mother to relieve its distress. Instrumental conditioning plays a substantial role in building up the dynamic lattice, for it forms means–end relationships whereby attitudes and sentiments serve to achieve, or are subsidiary to, ergic goals. For example, a person may learn that by lunching with a business associate, she may make a contact that will lead to her getting a new account, which will increase her bank account, which will increase her sense of security. Cattell points out that by a special form of instrumental conditioning, which he calls **confluence learning**, the person learns to satisfy more than one goal with a given behavior or attitude. Our earlier discussion of how attitudes, sentiments, and ergs may be interrelated in the simple act of going to a movie illustrated this type of learning.

In **integration learning**, the person learns to maximize total long-term satisfaction by, so to speak, selecting certain ergs for expression at any given moment and suppressing or sublimating others. This type of learning is a key aspect of the formation of the self and superego sentiments. For example, a child may learn to temporarily suppress his erg of self-assertion and to help his parents make needed repairs around the house, thus satisfying his ergic goal of parental love and protection.

THE SOCIAL CONTEXT.   Just as we must have a "true science of personality measurement" before we can study the individual, we must devise and test proper methods of measurement before we can explore important issues in social psychology: "The solution of the vital practical and theoretical social problems now clamoring for attention requires scientific workers to restrain themselves from superficial 'research' until a correct foundation for the meaningful description and measurement of groups has been achieved'' (Cattell, 1948, p. 48). When we have described, measured, and classified both groups and individual personalities and can talk about the nature and functioning of each, Cattell says, we can begin to talk about the effects of the one upon the other and particularly about the sociocultural determinants of behavior.

Cattell suggests that the same basic method, of factor analysis, can be used to study what he has called the syntality of the group. **Syntality**, which represents the characteristics of the group, is inferred from group action just as personality is inferred from the individual's action.

RESEARCH TECHNIQUES

Cattell has developed four primary research techniques for gathering the personality data that are subjected to factor analysis. In **R-technique**, a large number of people are compared in terms of their performance on a number of specific measures. What we are interested in here is how people who score high on one measure tend to score on the other; that is, we want to know whether the two measures are positively or negatively correlated or not correlated at all.

In **P-technique**, one person's scores on a number of measures are compared across situations and times, in order to discover both how consistent the person's behavior is and what different aspects of the person's behavior tend to go together. Box 12.3 describes Cattell's use of this technique in studying a young graduate student.

In **Q-technique**, two people are correlated on a large number of different measures. This technique produces a measure of the similarity between two people, and if such correlations are calculated for many pairs of people, we can analyze them to see if certain people cluster together, so as to produce ''types.'' For example, if 50 out of 100 people tend to appear sociable, bold, and impatient, whereas the other 50 appear reserved, cautious, and painstaking, we might conclude that we had found two clusters that we might choose to call extraversion and introversion.

Differential R-technique is a variant of R-technique in which measures are repeated on different occasions and the changes between them correlated. This procedure tells us not only whether certain traits are correlated on the average, but whether they appear to vary together over time. This method is particularly useful in the study of psychological states.

These four research designs are the ones Cattell has used most often. Cattell has proposed a number of other approaches, however, and if you are interested in research design, you may want to look at some of them (see, e.g., Cattell, 1966b, on the ''data box'').

BOX 12.3   The Play's the Thing: Six Weeks in the Life of a Drama Student

Cattell and Cross (1952) set out to test whether P-technique—measuring the same variables in one person on many repeated occasions—would reveal the same factors that R-technique—comparing many people on several variables on one occasion—uncovers. To do this, they needed a subject who was willing to devote the necessary time to the task, and they needed to work with variables on which they could expect to see a reasonable amount of variation in the time period covered.

A 24-year-old graduate student in drama, who was rehearsing a leading role in a play, not only had the requisite time but was willing to sit for twice-daily sessions. During the period of testing, the student kept a diary, which made it possible to relate fluctuations in the various traits measured to actual events in his life. His concern both with his imminent performance and with the well-being of his father, who suffered an accident during the time of the study, contributed to these fluctuations.

The 20 attitudes that the experimenters sought to explore represented 8 of the 10 established motivational variables, or ergs (see page 427), as well as the self-sentiment. These attitudes—expressed in statements such as "I want to make love to a woman I find beautiful" (sex erg) and "I want to increase my salary" (self-assertion erg)—were selected from the sample of attitudes used in earlier R-technique studies, and they

were measured in three ways. First, in a **preference** task, the subject was asked to choose between pairs of statements, each attitude being paired with every other for a total 190 pairs, indicating which of the two indicated behaviors or actions he would prefer.

Second, in a **fluency** task, each of the 20 attitudes was reexpressed in 40 separate statements. Each of these 40 was read to the subject, and he was then given 30 seconds to write down all the possible satisfactions that might be derived from that behavior or action.

Third, in a **retroactive inhibition** test, before the subject responded to some of the same statements used in the fluency task, he was asked to engage in a memory-for-digits task in which three-digit numbers were briefly exposed. He then had 15 seconds in which to write down all the numbers he could remember. After presentation of the attitude statements, the subject was again asked to write down all the numbers he could recall. The theory here was that the keener the subject's interest in the attitude statements presented, the more that interest would interfere with his second attempt to recall the numbers.

The subject's scores on each attitude, measured three ways, were combined to produce a single score for each attitude on each occasion. These combined scores were intercorrelated over occasions and then factored. Of the resulting eight factors, seven were judged to correspond to six ergs and one senti-

ment, which had been found in earlier R-technique studies: sex, self-assertion, parental protectiveness, fear (anxiety), appeal, narcism, and the self-sentiment. The extra factor was identified as fatigue, which has since emerged as a state factor in other studies from Cattell's laboratory.

In this study, then, the common traits identified earlier by R-technique appeared to describe a particular person rather well. Some of the loadings for this person differed somewhat from those found for a large sample by R-technique and may have represented unique features of this individual's traits.

Figure 12.2 illustrates the variation over 40 days in the drama student's scores on the six ergs, the self-sentiment, and fatigue. Some of the significant events in the subject's life are indicated along the top, and you can see, among other things, the sharp peaks in fatigue (1) during rehearsals for the play, (2) when he had a cold, and (3) just prior to and during his performances. You can also see the drop in fear-anxiety just after the play; the rise in the sex erg at the same time, when the student again had the time for dates; the rise in parental feelings at the time of his father's accident; and the rise in self-sentiment and self-indulgence during the play. Interestingly, a reproach by an aunt for not giving up his personal interests to help the family at the time of his father's accident caused a temporary drop

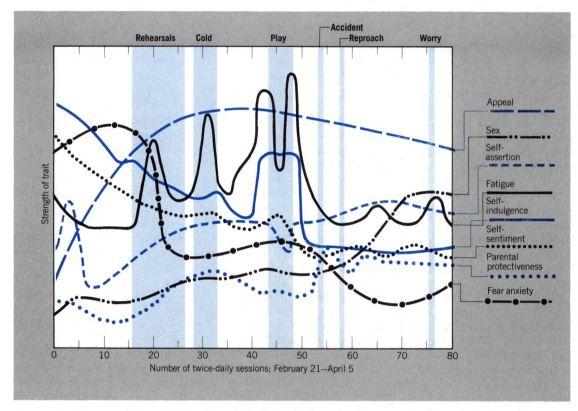

Figure 12.2 *Fluctuations in strength of dynamic source traits in 24-year-old drama student over period of 40 days. (From Cattell and Cross, 1952, Diagram II, p. 268.)*

in parental feelings—perhaps a sign of avoidance or rebellion.

The elevation of the fear–anxiety curve about the tenth to fifteenth sessions reflected an event that had occurred prior to the testing. The nights of the actual performance of the play are marked by significant variations in several drive strengths: narcism rises greatly, self-senti-ment parallels it, on a lesser scale, and self-assertion, which has been rising, drops sharply at about the last performance and then rises again.

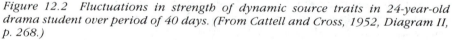

HANS J. EYSENCK

Hans J. Eysenck is something of an anomaly. His firm belief that the most fundamental personality characteristics are largely inherited supports a model of personality characterized by types and traits. His equally strong conviction that all behavior is learned supports his advocacy of learning theory and the behavior therapies. Having a foot in two camps, so to speak, Eysenck is not easy to classify. Placing him at the close of this third part of the book, on the enduring aspects of personality, allows him also to herald the fourth part, on learning theories and the influence of the environment.

Eysenck not only refuses to be neatly categorized as a theorist, he refuses to keep his nose to only one grindstone. In addition to personality theory and behavior therapy, he has concerned himself with such topics as the heritability of intelligence, educational theory and practice, sexual behavior, criminality, the effects of psychotherapy, the relation between smoking and health, and even astrology. These wide-ranging interests have contributed to a productivity that rivals Cattell's: Eysenck's most recent bibliography (1982) lists around 40 books and over 600 articles and chapters.

Eysenck shares with Cattell not only a view of the person as a creature with lasting and measurable qualities but a belief that measurement is fundamental to all scientific advance. Because in psychology we are not yet sure what we should be measuring, Eysenck says, taxonomy, or the classification of behavior, is a crucial first step. And factor analysis is the most useful instrument with which to take this step.

From the beginning of his career, Eysenck was convinced that most personality theories are too complex and too loosely formulated. He has attempted to derive conceptions of behavior that are simple and maximally operational, and as a result, his system is characterized by a very small number of major dimensions that have very thorough empirical definition. At the same time, his conceptions reflect his study and absorption of the thought of many different figures in our intellectual history: Hippocrates, Galen, Kretschmer, Jung, Pavlov, Hull, Spearman, and Thurstone.

Eysenck has used questionnaires, or self-ratings; ratings by others; objective behavioral tests; assessments of physique; physiological measurements; and biographical and other historical information as means of obtaining personality data. He believes that because each method of data collection has its weaknesses (e.g., self-ratings are biased by subjects' views of themselves; objective tests carried out in a traditional experimental manner may tap too little of the total organism they are intended to understand), one should assemble "all and every type of factual and objective information which can be used to support or refute [an] hypothesis under investigation" (Eysenck, 1953, p. 319).

DEFINITION OF PERSONALITY

Expanding on the definitions of Allport and Murray, Eysenck suggests that personality is

the sum-total of the actual or potential behavior-patterns of the organism, as determined by heredity and environment; it originates and develops through the functional interaction of the four main sectors into which these behavior-patterns are organized: the cognitive sector (intelligence), the conative sector (character), the affective sector (temperament), and the somatic sector (constitution). (1947, p. 25)

BOX 12.4   Hans Jürgen Eysenck (1916–   )

Hans J. Eysenck was born and raised in a Germany beset with economic hardship and the political upheaval wrought by Hitler's rise to power. Eysenck rarely saw his parents, both of whom were actors—his mother in films, his father on stage and in cabarets—and was raised entirely by his grandmother.

Known in school as a "white Jew," a term given to those who sympathized with the Jews, Eysenck hated the Nazi regime and refused, when he became 18, to join the military forces. Instead, he left his homeland for England where, at the University of London, he came to the study of psychology rather by accident: he lacked the prerequisites for physics, which he had intended to study, and someone suggested the (relatively) new science of psychology.

At London Eysenck studied under Sir Cyril Burt—"proba-bly the most gifted psychologist of his generation [but] . . . highly neurotic" (Eysenck, 1982, p. 290) and, after obtaining his Ph.D. in 1940, became research psychologist at the Mill Hill Emergency Hospital, a temporary psychiatric institution established during World War II. When the war ended, Eysenck was made director of the psychology department of Maudsley Hospital's new Institute of Psychiatry, a position he holds to this day. He is also a professor of psychology at the University of London.

From the beginning, Eysenck was highly skeptical of Freudian theory, and one of his first research efforts, aborted by his superiors, was an examination of inconsistency in psychiatric judgments. He persisted in his beliefs, and fairly early in his work at the institute, he was able to establish a program in behavior therapy, in spite of the objections of some of the psychiatric faculty. A little later he also organized a behavior genetics division in his department at a time when this topic was not fashionable.

As we have already noted, Eysenck fairly matches Cattell in productivity; both theorists have an enormous body of written works. Eysenck's output is perhaps the more catholic; a glance at a recent bibliography (1982) reveals a long list of topics, including introversion-extraversion, neuroticism, psychoticism, the autonomic nervous system, the reticular activating system, behavior therapy, conditioning, intelligence, traits, smoking, crime and violence, sex and sexuality, genetic studies of many of the foregoing variables, and cross-cultural explorations of a number of them. Eysenck has often written in collaboration with Sybil B. G. Eysenck, his second wife, and he has coauthored several publications with Michael W. Eysenck, his son, who is a well-known psychologist in the field of memory.

Eysenck loves a good fight—perhaps his brief early fling with boxing should tell us something about this—and at one time or another he has been called many names, "gadfly," "autocrat," and "racist" among them. He maintains that he has always sought, and will always seek, the "truth," even when it is, in the Greek sense, "tragic"—that is, when it involves two opposing rights. For example, it is "right" (or true) that people are born unequal, but it is also "right" that people should have every opportunity to overcome disadvantages due to their differences from others. Eysenck has always been for the underdog, he says, but he believes that we can change things only when we know what is there to be changed.

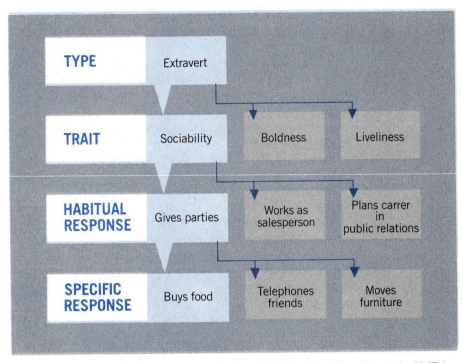

Figure 12.3   A sample of the hierarchy of personality. (Based on Eysenck, 1947.)

By including the role of heredity and environment in this definition, Eysenck calls attention to a proposition to which many of the theorists discussed in this book would subscribe—that we are creatures of both our inheritance and our experience. No theorist, however, with the possible exception of Cattell, has focused as much specific research effort on this proposition as Eysenck.

Eysenck's inclusion of the "somatic sector" underlines his interest in relating the behavioral aspects of personality to underlying physiological structure and function. Although like Sheldon he has given some attention to the relations between physique and personality, Eysenck's major effort has gone into probing the possible relations between observable behavior and the functioning of various parts of the brain.

ENDURING ASPECTS OF PERSONALITY

For Eysenck, personality consists of acts and dispositions organized in a hierarchical fashion in terms of their level of generality. As you can see from Figure 12.3, the **specific response** is the least general; it is an act or response that occurs in a single instance. For example, a person may buy food, telephone a friend, or move furniture. At the next level of generality is the **habitual response**, an act, made up of several specific responses, that characteristically recurs in the same or similar circumstances. For example, a person may give a lot of parties, and each time he does so he may go shopping for food and drinks, telephone friends to invite them, and rearrange his furniture to accommodate a crowd.

At the next level is the **trait**, "an observed constellation of individual action-tendencies." The trait is a collection of habitual responses that are in some way related to each other, that have some consistency. Suppose that someone not only gives parties frequently but is often seen with groups of people, is the campus salesperson for *The New York Times,* and is planning a career in public relations. We might hypothesize that this person has a trait of sociability, inasmuch as he appears to choose activities that involve him with other people.

The **type**, "an observed constellation or syndrome of traits," is at the most general level. Again, traits that are related to each other combine to make up a type. Note that Eysenck's use of "type" is quite particular: by "type" he means a broad dimension of personality, not a kind of person. Thus, if a person's sociability is combined with tendencies to be venturesome, lively, and the like, we might further hypothesize that he is on the extravert side of the **extraversion–introversion** dimension.

At the level of the type, Eysenck proposes three other broad dimensions: **neuroticism**, **psychoticism**, and **intelligence**. He is careful to point out that no one is ever a pure anything—a neurotic person is not neurotic all the time, for example, and quite clearly one cannot be intelligent and nothing else. Still, our typical levels of behavior do differ, so that each of us reflects a distinctive combination of these four dimensions and their many subdimensions. Thus Figure 12.3, if it were to represent the person described properly, would have to be greatly expanded so as to include each type that contributes to this individual's personality, together with each type's subsidiary traits and habitual and specific responses.

J. P. Guilford, a pioneer in the technique of factor analysis, has also represented personality traits or dimensions in a hierarchical fashion. A brief look at his work is presented in Box 12.5.

How did Eysenck derive his types, or dimensions, according to which people vary? He began, during World War II, by studying some of the many soldiers who were treated at the hospital where he served as staff psychologist. Eysenck's (1947) first major work studied some 700 male military psychiatric cases, and it led to the isolation of the two variables of introversion–extraversion and normality–neuroticism. These two factors were extracted from the analysis of a large number of variables, many of which were traits (e.g., anxiety, depen-

BOX 12.5   Guilford's Factor Analytic Approach

J. P. Guilford (1897–   ), professor of psychology at the University of Nebraska from 1928 to 1940 and at the University of Southern California from 1940 until his formal retirement in 1967, is probably best known for his work on intelligence and creativity and his textbooks on statistics and psychometric methods. Guilford (Guilford and Guilford, 1934) was also one of the first to use the technique of factor analysis to measure personality traits.

An outgrowth of Guilford's early work was the personality inventory called the Guilford–Zimmerman Temperament Survey (Guilford and Zimmerman, 1949), which measures 10 factorially defined traits. A number of these traits are quite similar to traits included in Cattell's 16 Personality Factor Questionnaire, and in fact when both inventories are given to the same subjects, they appear to cover much of the same general territory, although they do not match up individually, scale for scale.

Like Eysenck (see page 438) Guilford uses a hierarchical model to represent personality, with general types at the top, primary traits below, and the most specific actions at the bottom. Guilford divides primary traits into several categories, three of which are quite like Cattell's ability, temperament, and dynamic traits. Guilford organizes his dimensions, however, into two- or three-dimensional tables, or matrices.

Consider, for example, Guilford's matrix of temperament factors, shown in Figure 12.4. Guilford writes that "the temperament factors fall into three major groups of dispositions, depending upon the spheres of behavior in which they apply. Some of them seem to apply to many kinds of behavior, or to behavior in general, while others are more restricted to emotional aspects of behavior and still others to social behavior" (1959, p. 409). In the matrix, five bipolar traits are listed in each of the three areas of behavior. There is one example in each area from each of the five general categories of traits shown to the left.

KIND OF DIMENSION	AREAS OF BEHAVIOR INVOLVED		
	GENERAL	EMOTIONAL	SOCIAL
Positive versus negative	Confidence versus inferiority	Cheerfulness versus depression	Ascendance versus timidity
Responsive versus unresponsive	Alertness versus inattentiveness	Immaturity versus maturity	Socialization versus self-sufficiency
Active versus passive	Impulsiveness versus deliberateness	Nervousness versus composure	Social initiative versus passivity
Controlled versus uncontrolled	Restraint versus rhathymia	Stability versus cycloid disposition	Friendliness versus hostility
Objective versus egocentric	Objectivity versus hypersensitivity	Poise versus self-consciousness	Tolerance versus criticalness

FIGURE 12.4   A matrix of temperament factors. (From Guilford, 1959, Table 16.1, p. 409)

TABLE 12.3   Some Characteristics of Esysenck's Three Major Personality Dimensions

INTROVERSION-EXTRAVERSION

Introversion: tendermindedness; introspectiveness; seriousness; performance interfered with by excitement; easily aroused but restrained, inhibited; preference for solitary vocations; sensitivity to pain

Extraversion: toughmindedness; impulsiveness; tendency to be outgoing; desire for novelty; performance enhanced by excitement; preference for vocations involving contact with other people; tolerance for pain

NEUROTICISM

Below-average emotional control, willpower, capacity to exert self; slowness in thought and action; suggestibility; lack of persistence; tendency to repress unpleasant facts; lack of sociability; below-average sensory acuity but high level of activation

PSYCHOTICISM

Poor concentration; poor memory; insensitivity; lack of caring for others; cruelty; disregard for danger and convention; occasionally originality and/or creativity; liking for unusual things; considered peculiar by others

Source: Based on Eysenck (1947, 1952).

dency) but some of which were factual data (e.g., age, marital status). Much of Eysenck's initial data base consisted of ratings by psychiatrists and life-history information. Subsequent explorations, however, employed other kinds of data sources such as questionnaires and performance tasks.

Table 12.3 describes some components of introversion (I), extraversion (E), and neuroticism (N), and Figure 12.5 depicts combinations of these dimensions and accompanying sets of traits. As you can see, for example, the normal extravert tends, among other things, to be lively and responsive, the normal introvert reliable and thoughtful. The neurotic extravert may be touchy and aggressive, whereas the neurotic introvert may be anxious and pessimistic.

The third major dimension along which people vary, Eysenck proposes, is normality–psychoticism. Note that psychoticism (P) is not equivalent to psychosis as, for example, in schizophrenia—although a schizophrenic person would be expected to score high on psychoticism. The high-P person tends to be hostile and unconventional and considered ''peculiar'' by acquaintances (see also Table 12.3).

Eysenck has devoted a great deal of study to intelligence. One of

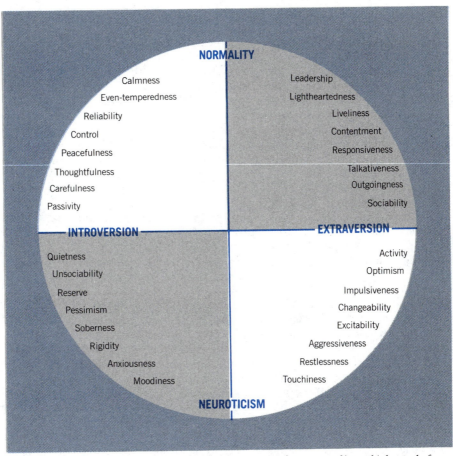

Figure 12.5 Two-dimensional classification of personality. (Adapted from Eysenck, 1982.)

his major concerns, the heritability of intelligence, is discussed in Box 12.6, which focuses on the controversy surrounding this topic.

PHYSIOLOGICAL CORRELATES OF PERSONALITY DIMENSIONS

Eysenck postulates that people differ by heredity in terms of the way in which their brains and central nervous systems react to and process stimulation from the environment, and he relates these differences to his dimensions of personality.

In this area Eysenck has drawn particularly on the work of Ivan Pavlov and Clark Hull. Recall, from introductory psychology, that Pavlov demonstrated the conditioned reflex, in animals; he also proposed that in his subjects certain kinds of temperamental, or ''person-

BOX 12.6   Heredity, Environment, Intelligence

As both common and scientific observation tell us, individual people tend to differ in their levels of intellectual ability. To what extent do differences in intelligence among people reflect differences in the genetic potential with which they began life? To what extent do they reflect differences in the educational and other environments that they have since encountered? Over the years, differing views on these questions have often led to acrimonious debates among both psychologists and lay persons.

A flurry of controversy on this topic was touched off in 1969 by an article published in the *Harvard Educational Review* by the educational psychologist Arthur R. Jensen. Jensen surveyed evidence suggesting that intelligence is highly heritable—Jensen's estimate was that about 80 percent of differences in IQ among people were due to genetic differences among them. Jensen also speculated that differences in IQ test performance between U.S. blacks and whites might be partly genetic as well.

Hans Eysenck early became embroiled in the argument. Jensen had visited Eysenck's department on a postdoctoral

fellowship in the late 1950s. Eysenck himself had been a Ph.D. student of the British psychologist Sir Cyril Burt, who held strongly hereditarian views. Soon after the publication of Jensen's article, Eysenck brought out a book, *The IQ Argument*, which was principally a presentation of Jensen's views to the British public. Eysenck's penchant for controversy ensured that the debate would proceed vigorously on both shores of the Atlantic.

Shortly, a new development shifted the focus of the IQ controversy away from racial differences. The American psychologist Leon Kamin, an ardent environmentalist, pointed out some suspicious regularities and irregularities in the publications of Cyril Burt on the heritability of intelligence, publications that supported Burt's view that individual and social-class differences in IQ were strongly influenced by the genes. Burt had by then died, and investigation was hampered by the fact that many of his scientific papers had been destroyed in the bombing of London in World War II and others thrown out after his death by an overzealous landlady. Nevertheless, after careful

study of Burt's remaining letters and diaries, his biographer L. S. Hearnshaw (1979) concluded that in Burt's later years, old and ill, he had indeed made up figures and data, most notably concerning a purported series of identical twins reared apart in separate families who continued to resemble one another strikingly in IQ.

Doubtless, the argument will continue as to just how important heredity and environment are in accounting for differences in intellectual performance. One reviewer (Henderson, 1982) has summarized recent estimates as falling mostly in the range of 40 to 70 percent of IQ differences being due to genetic differences among individuals, well below Jensen's estimate of 80 percent, but well above the figure of zero percent suggested by Kamin.

Behavior genetic studies, like those described in the last chapter, plus direct studies of neural and psychological development, should eventually narrow the uncertainty on questions such as these. But in the meantime, it seems safe to predict that the "IQ controversy" will continue.

---

ality," characteristics were associated with either ease or difficulty of conditioning. Broadly, Pavlov found that dogs who were generally "friendly" and "outgoing" were poor conditioners, whereas dogs who seemed timid and fearful were good conditioners.

Pavlov hypothesized that underlying these observed differences were differences in the dogs' nervous systems, and Eysenck has applied a similar suggestion to the understanding of introversion–extra-

TABLE 12.4   *Introversion–Extraversion, Neuroticism, and Physiological Arousal*

	CORTICAL EXCITATION LEVEL	LEVEL OF AUTOMATIC NERVOUS SYSTEM REACTIVITY
INTROVERT		
Normal	High	Low
Neurotic (e.g., anxiety neurotic)	High[a]	High
EXTRAVERT		
Normal	Low	Low
Neurotic (e.g., antisocial personality)	Low[a]	High

Source: Based on Eysenck (1952).
[a]Neuroticism raises cortical excitation level in both introvert and extravert: in the neurotic introvert, this level is highest of all; in the neurotic extravert, though it is higher than in the normal extravert, it is still lower than in the normal introvert.

version in human beings. In general, he finds, extraversion is correlated with a tendency not to condition easily, whereas introversion is correlated with a tendency to condition readily. Eysenck suggests that differences in **cortical excitation levels** are responsible for these findings. In the extravert, cortical excitation levels are generally low. Such people, Eysenck says, tend to seek stimulation, and it takes more stimulation to arouse them than it does to arouse other people. In the introvert, excitation levels are high; such people tend to avoid additional stimulation, and it takes much less stimulation to arouse them.

Eysenck also finds a correlation between his dimension of normality–neuroticism and **autonomic nervous system reactivity**. He suggests that the person whose autonomic nervous system (ANS) is highly reactive is likely, given the right environmental conditions, to develop a neurotic disorder. Thus, the tendency to respond very emotionally to stimuli is seen as a predisposing condition that is conducive to the development of psychological disorder.

Eysenck further suggests that when a person is both highly emotionally reactive (neurotic on the normality–neurotic dimension) and highly cortically excitable (introverted on the introversion–extraversion dimension), he or she is particularly prone to develop strong neurotic symptoms such as conditioned fears, phobias, compulsions, obsessions, and so on. Such people, Eysenck suggests, are suffering from **disorders of the first kind**. An example of this type is the anxiety neurotic.

People who are also highly emotionally reactive but who have low levels of cortical excitation (extraverted on the introversion–extraversion dimension) are suffering Eysenck says, from **disorders of the second kind**. The psychopath or antisocial personality is an example

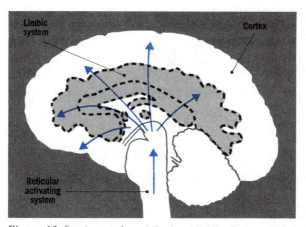

*Figure 12.6   Arousal and the brain. The figure shows the brain's cortex and the re-
ticular activation system (RAS). The RAS is a formation of nerve fibers that receives
input from sensory tracts and influences cortical and limbic system functioning;
the latter system is associated with the autonomic nervous system (ANS) and with
emotional behavior. (The structures generally included in the limbic system are indicated by dotted lines.) Eysenck believes the RAS to be important in extraversion–
introversion and the ANS to be important in neuroticism.*

of this second type; people who manifest antisocial behavior, such as
delinquents or criminals, have not acquired sufficiently strong fear (or
guilt) reactions about their own destructive impulses and thus fail to
inhibit the expression of such impulses. Table 12.4 shows the relations
among introversion–extraversion, cortical and ANS arousal, and type
of neurotic disorder.

Figure 12.6 shows the primary brain structure—the reticular
activating system—that Eysenck invokes in explicating his notions of
cortical excitation and ANS reactivity. Eysenck's hypotheses are very
appealing, and his findings to date certainly argue for continuing research in this area. However, it is important to keep in mind that his
work is hypothetical with respect to what is actually going on in the
brain. We do not as yet have direct empirical data connecting properties of central nervous system functioning to Eysenck's dimensions of
personality.

Eysenck's identification of the physiological basis of this third
dimension, psychoticism (P), is even more speculative. He concludes,
first, from behavior genetic studies of the heritability of psychoticism,
that this dimension has at least as strong a biological basis as the other
two. His tentative guess as to the physiological connection is based on
the fact that men both score higher on the psychoticism scale than
women do and are much more frequently found in jails, reform
schools, and other institutions frequented by high-P types. He suggests that it is therefore possible that male sex hormones provide some
part—though not all—of the biological basis of psychoticism.

HOW ARE PERSONALITY CHARACTERISTICS ACQUIRED?

Eysenck is firm in his conviction that heredity is the primary determining factor in intelligence. He also postulates a strong role for heredity in extraversion–introversion, neuroticism, and psychoticism. He bases this position in part on the correlations he has demonstrated between these personality dimensions and behaviors that presumably reflect differences in ANS reactivity and cortical excitation, and in part on direct behavior genetic studies (e.g., Young, Eaves, and Eysenck, 1980).

Despite this insistence on an inherited tendency to develop neurotic characteristics, Eysenck also maintains that neurotic behavior—indeed, all behavior—is learned. Moreover, neurosis does not develop out of (unconscious) conflict between instinctual forces and ego-defensive processes, as Freud argued. According to Eysenck, the core phenomenon in neurosis is a conditioned fear reaction. Such reactions are set in motion when on one or more occasions an initially neutral stimulus is paired with a physically or psychologically painful event. If the trauma is intense enough, and the person is particularly vulnerable—for example, by virtue of having an inherited tendency to neuroticism—only one such experience may be needed to establish an anxiety reaction of great strength and persistence.

Once they have been learned, conditioned fears or anxieties come to be elicited not only by the original object or event that triggered them but by other stimuli that either resemble the original ones or that just happen to be linked with the latter. (The learning principle of stimulus generalization, which explains the first effect, is discussed in Chapters 13 and 14.) Every time the person encounters some such stimulus and makes further responses in an effort to avoid or reduce anxiety, Eysenck says, he or she may become conditioned to even more stimuli that just happen to be present. Thus, the person's propensity to respond with neurotic behavior is expanded many times, and he or she may come to react with fear to stimuli that bear little or no resemblance to those involved in the original situation.

According to Eysenck, just as new stimuli that are in no way related to the original one(s) can become linked with the latter, so the person may develop ways of responding that have no real functional purpose but are simply behaviors that happened to be going on at the time the stimuli were encountered. By this point, Eysenck underlines his disagreement with the psychodynamic view that neurotic behaviors are developed for the explicit purpose of reducing anxiety. On the contrary, Eysenck says, neurotic behaviors are often developed for no clear reason at all and in fact are frequently counterproductive, raising anxiety instead of lowering it.

If behaviors are learned, it would seem logical that they can be unlearned. Eysenck is an ardent advocate of behavior therapies, or methods of treating psychological distress that focus on changing maladaptive behavior rather than on developing insight into presumed inner conflict. As you may well imagine, Eysenck is strongly anti-Freudian in his view, and in fact he holds that psychoanalytic and psychodynamic therapies are usually quite ineffective ways of treating neurotic symptoms.

We will have more to say about behavior therapy in the next part of this book, where we will be discussing theorists who have taken an exclusively learning theory approach to the study of personality.

RESEARCH TECHNIQUES

Like Cattell, Eysenck has relied very extensively on the technique of factor analysis in analyzing and interpreting his data. However, in response primarily to the frequent criticism that factor analysis is largely descriptive and that the decision as to what factor to derive from a given matrix of correlations is quite arbitrary, Eysenck has developed a method he calls **criterion analysis**. This method requires that an investigator not just start out with a set of measures that cover the domain, hoping that the factor analysis will reveal the nature of the underlying order. Rather, Eysenck says, one must begin with a more or less well-developed hypothesis about a specified underlying variable and then secure a set of measures that are presumably related to this hypothesized factor. Most important, this method requires that the investigator secure these measures for two groups that are contrasted in terms of the degree to which they can be presumed to possess the variable under investigation. In other words, the factor analyst using this method must not only secure multiple measures on a number of subjects in the conventional manner; he or she must also secure **criterion groups**, groups that possess discriminably different degrees of the hypothesized variable. Each of the individual tests is then correlated with the difference between the two groups in order to obtain a measure for each test that indicates how closely it is associated with the distinction implied by the criterion groups, that is, how sensitive the test is to the particular variable. The criterion groups impose a restriction on the factor analysis and imply that the factor ultimately derived will lean most heavily on those tests that discriminate most effectively between the criterion groups.

Eysenck differs from Cattell also in preferring to extract a rather small number of factors from an analysis. And Eysenck, like Guilford, prefers orthogonal factors; recall that Cattell chooses to extract oblique factors. Eysenck believes that his major dimensions correspond quite well to some of the higher-order factors that Cattell obtains when he factors the correlations among his basic factors.

EVALUATION

Although Raymond Cattell has grounded his theory of personality in an impressive array of empirical data, reviews of his work have been mixed. One reason for the uneasiness with which many have greeted Cattell's research and theorizing may be that he has tried to map "the whole domain of personality structure" rather than focus in careful detail on any one portion of the total task (Goldberg, 1968). The same criticism, of course, could be lodged against many personality theorists who, in formulating their theories, have drawn outlines long before being able to fill in the exact colors. Specialists in subtopics of psychology may find Cattell's rapid sweep across their particular corner of the field not doing full justice to the fine points as they know them.

Cattell (and other personality theorists) might well reply that it is unreasonable to expect a new perspective to bring everything into focus right away. Our impatience for detailed answers and our need for security, he might say, can conflict with our pursuit of proper scientific research. Only when our methods are perfected and extensively applied will we be able to picture the human being accurately. In all sciences,

periods and kinds of uncertainly, while ideas stand in a descriptive limbo, occur. . . . Typically, the discovery of a new vitamin, a new galaxy or a new sub-atomic particle has to be followed by a long inquiry in which the scientist knows where or who the entity is; but not what it is. Psychiatrists and psychologists, because of their infancy in the glib clinical school, like to have their explorations all at once. Consequently, theory is only slowly adjusting to the scientific discipline of entertaining these real but only partially explained patterns. (Cattell, 1966a, p. 77)

With Cattell, as with Hans Eysenck, J. P. Guilford, and others using factor analytic methodology, there is scarcely any clear separation of theory and experiment. Indeed, one sometimes feels that there is more experiment than theory. Cattell seems to have reversed Allport's approach: Allport said you must have a clear theoretical outline before you start collecting a lot of possibly meaningless data; Cattell says you must collect a lot of data and hone your empirical methods before you can honestly devise a theory. On the face of it, these two views seem irreconcilable. Are they?

Skeptics claim that factor analysts have a tendency to elevate what is only a technique to the status of theory. They point out that factor analysis can produce meaningful results only if the original material to which it is applied is appropriate. For example, a good deal of Cattell's research on dynamic traits was based on the factoring of an initial set of somewhat arbitrarily chosen attitudes. One can wonder whether a different initial choice of attitudes might have led to a somewhat different set of ergs and sentiments.

In the current climate of growing fascination with and reliance on computerized methods of processing data, Cattell's and Eysenck's approaches may generate increasing interest. Certainly such advances have made the extensive calculations required by the factor analytic method much easier to do. On the other hand, this greater interest in quantitative methods may be balanced in some quarters by a view that science has become too technical, too segmental, and that matters of the human mind and emotions cannot be accounted for entirely by mathematical formulas.

One of the most significant attributes of Cattell's and Eysenck's theories—and of factor theories in general—is their continuing effort to define their terms in the simplest and clearest way possible. Theorists who make use of this methodology are concerned to make their concepts operational and, thus, to work toward clear and unambiguous empirical definitions. In a field long dominated by the clinically based, subjective, inferential approach, the factor theorists' insistence on precision and testability has introduced a welcome aura of toughmindedness. Even if the factor analytic method retains some subjectivity, its supporters would say, it is far less subjective than traditional techniques of personality investigation.

Allport (1937) and others have criticized factor analytic methodology for describing only the "average personality," which is, of course, a complete abstraction. The technique, it is suggested, produces a system of artifacts that have no true relation to any single human being. As we have seen (Box 12.3), however, factor analysis *can* be used to compare one person with group averages and to examine the daily life patterns of that person, even though this is not its most common application.

One criticism that has been leveled against Hans Eysenck's personality theory is that it is too limited in its scope. It deals with three major personality dimensions, exploring their biological bases and their implications for various kinds of social and personal pathology extensively, but it does not emphasize a number of the concerns that have seemed central to many personality theorists. For example, it contains no theory of motivation in the traditional sense of drives, needs, wishes, or impulses. Its theory of development is also very sketchy. Eysenck does discuss the role of early conditioning in developing anxieties and the conscience, but his theory has not addressed psychological development along any very broad front. Of course, the concern with heredity and environment is, in a very generalized sense, a concern with development issues.

Now Eysenck can quite properly reply that it is no reflection on a theory of personality that it does not deal with every aspect of behavior. Indeed, he might well claim this as a virtue: better a theory that is simple enough to be explicit and testable than an elaborate and fuzzy verbal hodgepodge that vaguely touches on everything without being clear enough about anything to allow the unambiguous deduction of concrete predictions. (Some critics might say that even Eysenck's theory has a way to go before the deductions from it are unambiguous, but clearly it has a head start on some of the others.)

A different line of criticism does not object to the general form of Eysenck's theory, but takes exception to his particular choice of dimensions. Jeffrey Gray (1981a), for example, has suggested using a somewhat different alignment of two major dimensions, in place of Eysenck's extraversion–introversion and neuroticism. One of these, an anxiety dimension, would run from neurotic introversion to stable extraversion in Eysenck's scheme. The other, an impulsivity dimension, would run from neurotic extraversion to stable introversion. In short, Gray's dimensions would run at roughly a 45-degree angle to Eysenck's, in a figure such as 12.5. Gray argues that this arrangement fits better with underlying physiological mechanisms than does Eysenck's and nicely handles some experimental results that are awkward for Eysenck's version. Eysenck (1981) concedes that Gray's proposal is interesting and deserves research attention but still feels that his own scheme offers a better fit for the bulk of the evidence.

Other theorists dealing with basic temperament dimensions, such as Buss and Plomin (1975), have chosen to emphasize slightly different basic dimensions: in their case, they add an activity dimension and split extraversion into what Eysenck would consider two of its subfactors, sociability and impulsivity. Despite these variant positions, however, one is tempted to conclude with Gray that "the biological basis of personality, while it may not be quite as Eysenck now sees it, will remain profoundly Eysenckian for a long time to come" (1981b, p. 251).

SUMMARY

RAYMOND B. CATTELL

1. Personality allows us to predict what a person will do in a given situation. It is concerned with all behavior, including what is concrete and observable and what may only be inferred.

2. Personality is made up of **traits**, inferred mental structures that account for the consistency of behavior. **Surface** traits can be inferred from observed behavior. **Source** traits can be identified only by means of **factor analysis**, a statistical technique for detecting underlying order in a number of variables.

3. Source traits are **constitutional**, residing within the person, or **environmental-mold**, deriving from experience.

4. **L data**, ratings by others, **Q data**, self-ratings, and **T data**, objective test results, provide the material from which three types of source traits are derived. **Dynamic** traits are concerned with setting the per-

son in motion toward a goal. **Temperament** traits describe the manner in which the person moves toward a goal. **Ability** traits describe the effectiveness with which the person moves toward the goal.

5. Chains of **subsidiation** link the three types of dynamic traits: attitudes serve sentiments and ergs; sentiments, organized structures of attitudes, serve ergs and other sentiments. **Ergs** are constitutional source traits and correspond roughly to drives. **Attitudes** and **sentiments** are largely environmental-mold source traits.

6. The **16 Personality Factor Questionnaire** assesses people on 16 factors, or traits, most of which are temperament factors.

7. Traits derived by factor analysis from raw data are known as **first-order factors**. Refactoring a group of these factors can produce **second-order factors**, broader and more inclusive categories under which the first set are grouped. Some first-order factors derived from T data align with second-order factors derived from L and Q data, which may suggest that the different sets of data tap different levels of organization in the personality.

8. A **behavioral specification equation**, which incorporates trait variables and situational variables, makes it possible to predict how a particular person will behave in a particular situation. Accuracy in prediction may be enhanced by including variables for **state**, **role**, and **set** in the equation. A specification equation can also be used to assess conflict among ergs and sentiments.

9. Boundary studies compare personality factors at different age levels. In general, similar factors are found from 4 years of age to adulthood.

10. MAVA (multiple abstract variance analysis) is a statistical technique designed to examine the relative contributions of heredity and environment to particular personality variables. MAVA studies twins and nontwin and adoptive siblings and tells not only whether the influence of heredity is present but to what extent it is expressed within and between families.

11. Negative correlations between heredity and environment suggest a **law of coercion to the biosocial mean** in the personality domain.

12. People learn by **associative** and **means–end learning, confluence learning** (satisfying several sentiments and ergs through one action), and **integration learning**; in the last, one learns to maximize long-term satisfaction by selecting certain ergs for expression at any given time and suppressing or sublimating others.

13. Syntality is essentially the personality of the group. It is inferred from group behavior, as personality is inferred from individual behavior.

14. Cattell's four primary research designs involve **R-technique**, **P-technique**, **Q-technique**, and **differential R-technique**, P-technique analyzes the scores of one person; in the other three methods, large numbers of people are studied.

HANS J. EYSENCK

15. The most fundamental personality characteristics are largely inherited, but both heredity and environment determine behavior.

16. The classification of behavior is an essential first step toward the measurement of behavior, and factor analysis is the best means of classifying behavior.

17. All kinds of data—self-reports, objective tests, biographical information, and so on—are useful in attempting to understand the organism.

18. Behavioral acts and dispositions have several levels of generality, going from the **specific response**, the least general, to the **habitual response**, the **trait**, and the **type**, the most general. At the type level are four dimensions: **extraversion–introversion**, **intelligence**, **neuroticism**, and **psychoticism**.

19. The major dimensions are independent of one another: for example, normal behavior may take introverted or extraverted forms, as may neurotic behavior.

20. Extraverts, who have low levels of cortical excitation, tend to condition with difficulty. Introverts, who have high levels of cortical excitation and thus resist stimulation, condition readily.

21. People with high **autonomic nervous system** reactivity are likely to develop neurotic disorders. People with high ANS reactivity who also have high levels of **cortical excitation** are particularly prone to develop neurotic symptoms or **disorders of the first kind** (anxiety neurotic). People with high ANS reactivity but low levels of cortical excitation tend to develop **disorders of the second kind** (antisocial personality).

22. Degree of psychoticism may be related to male sex hormones.

23. Neurotic behavior is learned: traumatic events can produce particularly strong neurotic reactions in people who have inherited tendencies to neuroticism.

24. Conditioned fears come to be elicited not only by the original events that triggered them but by similar events.

25. Learned neurotic behaviors can be unlearned, through behavior therapies.

26. Criterion analysis is a variation of factor analysis in which **criterion groups** enable the investigator to determine with some precision how sensitive a particular test is to a particular variable.

27. Cattell has been criticized for spreading himself too thin over too many areas of psychology—a characteristic he shares with many personality theorists.

28. Eysenck's choice of personality dimensions has been criticized, and several investigators have proposed other choices. Eysenck's theory has been considered too limited in scope; he offers no formal theory of motivation, and his theory of development is very sketchy. Eysenck might reply that it is better to have a simple, explicit theory than one that touches on everything but leads to ambiguous predictions.

29. Factor analysts are criticized for emphasizing experiment over theory, for elevating what is essentially a research technique to theory. Psychologists generally have difficulty with multivariate methodology, and the factor analysts themselves disagree as to proper procedures. Factor analysis is criticized for describing only the average personality, an abstraction. But factor analysts work toward clear and unambiguous empirical definitions; their toughmindedness is reflected in their insistence on precision and testability.

SUGGESTED READING

RAYMOND B. CATTELL

The simple statistics of Cattell's published output are staggering: a recent bibliography (Cattell, 1983) toted up 439 articles, 51 books and monographs, and 59 chapters in books. In addition, Cattell has created at least a dozen intelligence, personality, and clinical tests, with associated handbooks. And his productivity has shown little sign of slackening: the year 1983, for example, resulted in two books, three chapters, and seven articles. Even allowing for the fact that much of this work has been done in coauthorship, its abundance is amazing.

With such a wealth of material, it is hard to know where to begin. One good introduction to Cattell's theory and research is his semipopular *The Scientific Analysis of Personality* (1966a). Another good and up-to-date treatment is his *Structured Personality–Learning Theory* (1983). The first third of this book provides a semiautobiographical account of the development of the major strands of his work. Other particularly important statements of Cattell's approach are contained in *Description and Measurement of Personality* (1946), *Personality: A Systematic, Theoretical, and Factual Study* (1950), *Personality and Motivation Structure and Measurement* (1957), *Motivation and Dynamic Structure* (Cattell and Child, 1975), and the two-volume work *Personality and Learning Theory* (1979, 1980).

Objective Personality and Motivation Tests (Cattell and Warburton, 1967) lists over 400 of the "miniature situational" tests that according to Cattell are "the foundation of personality research with which psychologists should be most seriously concerned" (1973a, p. x). In *Personality and Mood by Questionnaire* (1973),

Cattell discusses the theory and practice of personality measurement by questionnaire and summarizes his more than 30 years' work with Q data. For a specific example, you should certainly examine *The 16 Personality Factor Questionnaire* (Cattell, Saunders, and Stice, 1950), the widely used personality test for which Cattell has become best known, and its *Handbook* (Cattell, Eber, and Tatsuoka, 1970).

Cattell's work in the controversial area of the genetic foundations of personality is summarized in *The Inheritance of Personality and Ability* (1982) and his statistical methodology in *The Scientific Use of Factor Analysis in Behavioral and Life Sciences* (1978).

No biography of Cattell exists as yet. Like a number of psychologists, however, Cattell has written an autobiographical sketch for the series, *A History of Psychology in Autobiography,* edited by Gardner Lindzey (1974).

HANS J. EYSENCK

The best place to begin reading Eysenck may be with the first and last chapters of *Personality, Genetics, and Behavior* (1982). The first chapter of that book sketches the broad outlines of Eysenck's theory, which is illustrated by selected papers in the body of the book; the last chapter is a brief autobiography.

Eysenck's earliest research on personality is described in *Dimensions of Personality* (1947), and subsequent studies, expanding on this initial work, are examined in *The Scientific Study of Personality* (1952). *The Structure of Human Personality* (1960) discusses some major theories of personality organization and presents a critical review of empirical research on these theories. *The Biological Basis of Personality* (1967) describes Eysenck's theories of the relations between personality dimensions and the brain. *A Model for Personality* (1980) presents an up-to-date statement of Eysenck's views on the extraversion dimension plus a review of the supporting evidence by various associates.

Eysenck's theory of neurosis is outlined in *The Causes and Cures of Neuroses* (Eysenck and Rachman, 1965) and is discussed further in *Case Studies in Behavior Therapy* (1976).

Eysenck has summarized his views on intelligence in *The Structure and Measurement of Intelligence* (1979). Recently, in *The Intelligence Controversy* (1981), Eysenck and Leon Kamin have debated their very different perspectives on the role of genetic inheritance in IQ.

Gibson (1981) has written a biography of Eysenck called *Hans Eysenck: The Man and His Work,* and Eysenck has written an autobiographical sketch for the series, *A History of Psychology in Autobiography* (Lindzey, 1980).

Part 4   Focus on Learning and the Environment

We have now come to the fourth and last group of theorists to be considered: B. F. Skinner (Chapter 13), Neal Miller and John Dollard (Chapter 14), and Albert Bandura and other social learning theorists (Chapter 15). As you read on from Skinner to Miller and Dollard and then to Bandura and others, you will note an increase in theoretical complexity and in the use of internal variables that are not directly observable.

The theorists in this fourth part of the book tend to focus on learning and the learning process. The environment, which sets the immediate conditions for learning, tends to play a central role in their theorizing.

All of these theorists are American born and educated. They were all born in this century, they are mostly still living, and they are, on the whole, chronologically the most recent of the four groups we have considered. They are primarily experimental psychologists who have spent their careers in universities and research institutes, although they all have had an interest in using the insights of learning theory to lead to the modification of disturbed behavior.

The intellectual roots of this group of theorists tend to lie more in the experimental psychology of Ivan Pavlov, Hermann Ebbinghaus, and Wilhelm Wundt than in the clinical, Gestalt, or psychometric traditions, although some of these theorists, notably Miller and Dollard, have been considerably influenced by psychoanalysis.

As Figure 4 shows, these theorists are committed to the view that learning and its processes critically determine human behavior. However, the attempt to describe broad and enduring acquisitions of learning tends to be of little interest to them. They generally see the situation as being of greater significance than the person in determining behavior; they emphasize environmental factors over hereditary ones. And they tend to be mechanistic and analytic rather than purposive and holistic in approach.

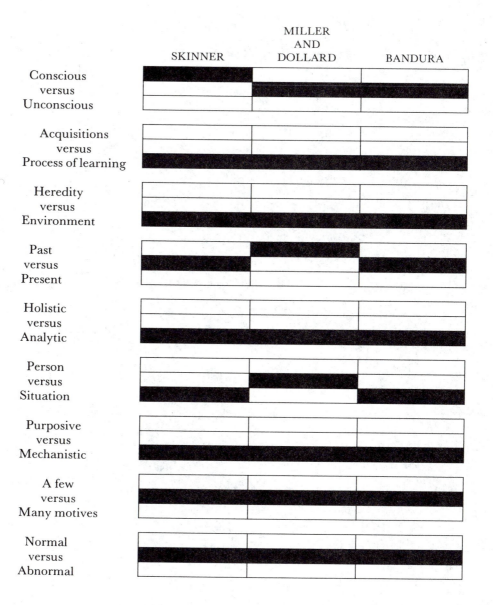

Figure 4   Learning–environmental theorists and the personality dimensions.

Chapter thirteen

13.

Twenty-five hundred years ago it might have been said that man understood himself as well as any other part of his world. Today he is the thing he understands least.

B. F. SKINNER

Operant Reinforcement Theory: B. F. Skinner

*"*I *can't swallow the system you've described because I don't see what keeps the motors running. Why do your children learn anything at all? What are your substitutes for our standard motives?"*

"Your 'standard motives'—exactly," said Frazier. "And there's the rub. An educational institution spends most of its time, not in presenting facts or imparting techniques of learning, but in trying to make its students learn. It has to create spurious needs. Have you ever stopped to analyze them? What are the 'standard motives,' Mr. Castle?"

"I must admit they're not very attractive," said Castle. "I suppose they consist of fear of one's family in the event of low grades or expulsion, the award of grades and honors, the snob value of a cap and gown, the cash value of a diploma."

"Very good, Mr. Castle," said Frazier. "You're an honest man. And now to answer your question—our substitute is simply the absence of these devices. We have had to uncover the worth-while and truly productive motives—the motives which inspire creative work in science and art outside the academies. No one asks how to motivate a baby. A baby naturally explores everything it can get at, unless restraining forces have already been at work. And this tendency doesn't die out, it's wiped out.

"We made a survey of the motives of the unhampered child and found more than we could use. Our engineering job was to preserve them by fortifying the child against discouragement. We introduce discouragement as carefully as we introduce any other emotional situation, beginning at about six months. Some of the toys in our air-conditioned cubicles are designed to build perseverance. A bit of a tune from a music box, or a pattern of flashing lights, is arranged to follow an appropriate response—say, pulling on a ring. Later the ring must be pulled twice, later still three or five or ten times. It's possible to build up fantastically perseverative behavior without encountering frustration or rage. It may not surprise you to learn that

461

some of our experiments miscarried; the resistance to discouragement became almost stupid or pathological. One takes some risks in work of this sort, of course. Fortunately, we were able to reverse the process and restore the children to a satisfactory level.

"Building a tolerance for discouraging events proved to be all we needed," Frazier continued. "The motives in education, Mr. Castle, are the motives in all human behavior. Education should be only life itself. We don't need to create motives. We avoid the spurious academic needs you've just listed so frankly, and also the escape from threat so widely used in our civil institutions. We appeal to the curiosity which is characteristic of the unrestrained child, as well as the alert and inquiring adult. We appeal to that drive to control the environment which makes a baby continue to crumple a piece of noisy paper and the scientist continue to press forward with his predictive analyses of nature. We don't need to motivate anyone by creating spurious needs." (Skinner, 1948, pp. 123–124)

The student who has had a course in experimental psychology may be surprised to find B. F. Skinner's viewpoint represented in this book. What do pigeons' pecking and reinforcement schedules have to do with personality? How can Skinner, a hard-headed experimentalist who acknowledges behaviorists like Watson and biologists like Ivan Pavlov and C. S. Sherrington as his most important influences, be concerned with the development and functioning of the most complex and subtle aspects of the human being? In fact, as the foregoing passage from Skinner's famous novel about a modern Utopia, *Walden Two*, reveals, Skinner is very much concerned with the forces that shape and direct human behavior. His behavioral principles, derived from experimentation with pigeons and other nonhuman species, are applicable, he believes, to many other organisms and situations. And in fact his approach, principles, and techniques have been applied to a broad range of practical human problems: some of these are education (Skinner, 1968), child development (Bijou and Baer, 1966), the treatment of mental disturbance (Krasner and Ullman, 1965), the development of experimental societies (Skinner, 1961a), missile control (Skinner, 1960), and space technology (Rohles, 1966).

Skinner's abiding concern is the understanding, prediction, and control of human behavior. Like many others, he believes that the progress humankind has made in understanding itself falls far short of the progress it has made in understanding other aspects of the natural world. Unlike many others, however, Skinner insists that human behavior (and personality) cannot be explained by "indwelling agents" such as an id or an ego. Behavior can be explained only by reference to observable antecedent situations and events. Skinner feels that too often in the study of human behavior, "the world of the mind steals the show" (1972, p. 12), behavior being regarded as merely the reflection or evidence of "fascinating dramas" that are staged within the mind.

BOX 13.1   B. F. Skinner (1904–   )

Burrhus Frederic Skinner was born and raised in Susquehanna, Pennsylvania, where his father practiced law. Skinner's eventual production of such things as the "Skinner box," the "baby box," and the programmed teaching machine was foreshadowed by his early efforts at building such things as scooters, wagons, sleds, rafts, see-saws, merry-go-rounds, slides, bows and arrows, blow guns, water pistols, and a steam cannon. Among his more ambitious constructions was a flotation system that separated ripe from green berries. For years, Skinner (1967) says, he tried to make a glider in which he could fly, and he labored long over an (unsuccessful) perpetual motion machine.

After graduation in 1926 from Hamilton College, where he majored in English, Skinner had a brief fling with the literary life. He tried short story writing, wrote for local newspapers, and read widely. Gradually he came to realize that he was intensely interested in human behavior but "had been investigating it in the wrong way" (Skinner, 1976, p. 291). In 1928 he became a graduate student in Harvard's department of psychology.

Skinner received his Ph.D. in 1931 and spend five years working in the laboratory of W. J. Crozier, the distinguished experimental biologist. Then in 1936, with his bride Eve Blue, Skinner moved to Minneapolis to join the faculty of the University of Minnesota's department of psychology. The nine years he spent at Minnesota were remarkably productive and established Skinner as a major experimental psychologist. In 1945 he moved to the University of Indiana, assuming the chairmanship of the psychology department.

While he was still at Minnesota, Skinner published his first major statement of his position, *The Behavior of Organisms* (1938), and he began work on his book on verbal behavior (1957). He also found time to write the novel, *Walden Two* (1948), during the years he spent in the Middle West.

In 1943, when his second daughter, Deborah, was born, Skinner designed his famous baby tender, or "baby box," as it was christened by the media. The baby tender was a "crib-sized living space" in which the air was climatically controlled so that, in a northern climate, the baby could wear minimal clothing, move freely, and never lie in wet diapers. Although much public interest was generated by the baby tender, Skinner was also roundly criticized for bringing his daughter up "in a cage," denying her social contact, and the like. Skinner pointed out that Debbie received just as much loving attention from her parents and her older sister, Julie, as any baby and added that she was extremely healthy and did not have a cold for many years.

In 1948 Skinner returned to Harvard's department of psychology, where he has remained ever since. Although he retired from active teaching in 1974, he has continued to write and lecture.

Skinner has received many honors in his long career, including the Distinguished Scientific Contribution Award of the American Psychological Association, the J. P. Kennedy, Jr., International Award for Outstanding Scientific Research, membership in the National Academy of Sciences, the William James Lectureship at Harvard, the Howard Crosby Warren Medal of the Society of Experimental Psychologists, the American Psychological Foundation's Gold Medal Award, and the President's Medal of Science.

Behavior per se has been studied only as the by-product of mental life, Skinner says, but in the final analysis, it is the behavior itself that matters and the antecedent conditions that allow us to predict and control it.

Before we examine some of the specific assumptions that underlie Skinner's work, let us look briefly at his overall approach as distinguished from those of other personality theorists. First, in spite of his influence on psychological theorists. First, in spite of his influence on psychological theory, Skinner (1950, 1956) not only does not regard himself as as theorist but has consistently questioned the contribution of most traditional theorizing to scientific development. It has been his hope to derive behavioral laws with no ''explanatory fictions'' at all.

Second, Skinner has derived his behavioral laws from precise experimentation, and as a result, his viewpoint is more firmly grounded in laboratory research than are most other approaches to the study of personality. For example, Skinner is not particularly interested in a description of which behaviors tend to go with which others, as a trait theorist might be. Skinner wants to know which antecedent conditions control the behaviors.

Third, Skinner, in common more with the clinician than with other experimental psychologists, reports his results typically in terms of individual records. He is not satisfied with findings that on the average support predictions. For Skinner, the behavioral law under investigation must apply to every subject observed under properly controlled conditions. Thus he attempts, by the inductive method, to deal with both the particular and the general case. He assumes that his findings have broad generality and that the same general principles of behavior will be uncovered regardless of what organism, stimulus, response, or reinforcement the experimenter chooses to study.

BASIC ASSUMPTIONS

In his work, Skinner makes three basic assumptions, at least two of which are commonly made by psychology in general—indeed, by the entire scientific community. First, Skinner, like other investigators, assumes that **behavior is lawful**: science is ''an attempt to discover order, to show that certain events stand in lawful relations to other events. . . . Order . . . is a working assumption which must be adopted at the very start'' (1953, p. 6).

Second, again like other investigators, Skinner (1953) assumes that **behavior can be predicted**: ''Science not only describes, it predicts. It deals not only with the past but with the future'' (p. 6). As we have said so often throughout this book, one of the criteria for a useful theory is that it must enable us to make predictions about future behavior and to test those predictions.

Skinner's third assumption, however, that **behavior can be controlled**, that "we can anticipate and to some extent determine" people's actions, is less enthusiastically received in some circles. Not only is Skinner curious about how behavior works; he is intensely interested in manipulating it, a possibility that he points out is "offensive" to many people: "It is opposed to a tradition of long standing which regards man as a free agent, whose behavior is the product, not of a specifiable antecedent condition, but of spontaneous inner changes. . . . It challenges our aspirations. . . . We simply do not want such a science" (Skinner, 1953, pp. 6–7).

Why does Skinner want so much to manipulate human beings' behavior? In part, because nothing tests the accuracy of our theories and predictions like successful control of circumstances, events, or behavior. More important, it is because he believes that human beings are destroying the world they inhabit by the very use of science and technology to combat their problems. Unhappily, says Skinner, "technology itself is increasingly at fault. Sanitation and medicine have made the problems of population more acute, war has acquired a new horror with the invention of nuclear weapons, and the affluent pursuit of happiness is largely responsible for pollution" (1972, p. 3). People must regulate their reproduction, adopt methods of industrial production that avoid the pollution of water and air, stop fighting wars, and so on. It is behavior that must be changed, says Skinner, "but a behavioral technology comparable in power and precision to physical and biological technology is lacking" (p. 5).

Skinner insists that a **functional analysis of behavior**—an analysis of behavior in terms of cause and effect relationships, where the causes themselves such as stimuli, deprivations, and so on, are controllable—will reveal that most of the causes of behavior lie in antecedent events occurring or located in the environment. Control of these events will let us control the behavior. There is no need to take the organism apart or to make any inferences about events going on inside it.

For example, suppose that a worker performs well when her supervisor is in the plant. There is a tendency to attribute the worker's good performance to the presence of the supervisor: the worker wants to be seen as efficient because she wants a raise or a promotion. Suppose, however, that the worker performs at the same high level when the supervisor is not present. Now we tend to give the worker more credit for her behavior—to say that she has initiative, is internally motivated, and so on. Skinner says that the worker's behavior is lawful whether or not its causes are obvious to the casual observer, and that giving credit or blame to people for their actions only impedes our search for the factors that actually control their behavior.

Here, for example, Skinner would say that on past occasions the worker has been reinforced in specific ways for efficient performance of her work in situations similar to that in which we now observe her. On past occasions, she has been given raises and promotions specifically described as due to her good work; also on past occasions, her supervisor, when present has praised her work. And this reinforcement has been intermittent, so that the worker's pattern of responding has become persistent (more about this shortly). Thus the supervisor's momentary presence or absence has little effect on the worker's current behavior.

TYPES OF BEHAVIOR

Skinner is not interested in structural variables of personality. We may have some illusion of explaining and predicting behavior on the basis of enduring factors in personality, but we can change behavior—control it—only by changing features of the environment. Thus Skinner is more interested in variable aspects of personality than in enduring ones.

The only thing about personality that Skinner sees as relatively enduring is behavior itself. He proposes two major classifications of behavior: operants and respondents. An **operant** is emitted; that is, an organism does something in the absence of any directly compelling stimulus. For example, a rat may run down the corridor of a maze; a person may walk out a door. A **respondent** is elicited; that is, an organism produces a respondent as a direct result of a specific stimulus. For example, a dog salivates at the sight and smell of food; a person blinks when a puff of air is blown into his eyes. We will have more to say about these two types of behavior a little later.

VARIATION IN THE INTENSITY OF BEHAVIOR

Motivational factors in behavior interest Skinner more than do structural elements. He recognizes that the same behavior in more or less the same situation does vary in terms of the strength and frequency of response. For example, eating does not always occur with the same intensity. We say that a person is not very hungry or is extremely hungry and postulate a level of drive to account for this variability. But Skinner says this is not necessary and that it is misleading to postulate an internal energizing force; we cannot know how the intensity of such a force is governed. Somewhere, says Skinner, we must have recourse to an **environmental variable** such as length of time since the person has last eaten. So why bother with a hypothesized internal state that itself depends on variation in the environment? Why not just deal with the environmental variable and account for the behavior directly? Thus, at a late lunch, a person may eat a lot because he has not eaten since the night before, but in the afternoon he may forgo a snack with

We might call this woman's behavior a respondent, inasmuch as her surprise is directly responsive to the stimulus of discovering the party in her honor. There is little question that this tournament golfer is emitting an operant response, as he expresses his elation at having sunk a difficult put to win an important match.

his coffee because he has only just eaten. The independent variable is food deprivation, or length of time since eating; the dependent variable is quantity eaten; and we have no need to deal with a hypothesized need or drive.

We can deprive a rat of water for a period of time; we can raise the temperature of the rat's cage, so that it sweats and loses water; or we can give the rat salty food. All these operations will increase another group of activities that lead to the rat's drinking water. Here again, Skinner says, we need not postulate a mysterious entity called "thirst" that makes the rat press a lever that releases a stream of water or run a maze to get water at the end. It is the several conditions that result in the rat's being deprived of water that cause the subsequent behaviors that lead to the rat's drinking water. For Skinner, terms like "hunger" and "thirst" are really only verbal devices that get their meaning by virtue of encompassing the relation between groups of independent and dependent variables.

So for Skinner, motivational concepts, which account for the variability of behavior in otherwise constant situations, are not equated with energy states, purpose, or any other causal type of condition. These concepts are simply convenient ways of relating groups of responses to groups of operations.

Emotions are handled by Skinner in much the same way. We may judge Emily to be angry, for example, because she speaks sharply, frowns, and slams the door. But Skinner would say that to offer ''anger'' as an explanation of these behaviors is not helpful. We need to look for the antecedent conditions. The promotion Emily was expecting was given to someone less competent than she (the boss's son); or she did not receive the raise she was due. We need also to look at her previous responses in similar situations, and their consequences, if we are to understand the particular form of her reaction.

PREDICTING AND CHANGING BEHAVIOR

As we have already said, Skinner's primary concern is behavioral change. He believes that an understanding of personality will develop from a consideration of the behavioral development of the human organism in continuing interaction with the environment.

Skinner does not offer a formal theory of development, and he does not deal with such notions as stages of development or developmental tasks. Recently, however, as you can see from Box 13.2, he has turned his attention to behavioral change in the aging adult.

PRINCIPLES OF CONDITIONING AND LEARNING

The most effective way to modify or control behavior, Skinner finds, is to reinforce it—that is, to carry out some operation that makes a particular behavior either more or less likely to occur in future. To understand Skinner's approach to this task, we need a basic understanding of the two principal forms of conditioning, classical conditioning and operant, or instrumental, conditioning. These types of conditioning are related to the respondent and operant forms of behavior mentioned earlier.

In **classical conditioning**, first described by Ivan Pavlov (Russian physiologist; 1849–1936), a stimulus that elicits a particular response from an organism is paired with another stimulus that comes in time to elicit the same kind of response; we say that the second operation and the second response have been ''conditioned'' to occur. For example, suppose we observe that a dog, when presented with a piece of meat, begins to salivate. Now suppose that just before we present the meat to the dog, we sound a bell. At first the dog salivates only when the meat appears, but after several such presentations, he salivates at the sound of the bell, before the meat is presented. The reinforcing agent here is the meat; its presentation strengthens the likelihood that salivation will occur when the bell is heard. The meat is a

BOX 13.2 Skinner on Aging

Aging should be the right word for how behavior changes as one grows older, Skinner says, but this word does not mean "development." To develop is "to unfold a latent structure, to realize an inner potential, to become more effective," Skinner points out, and aging "usually means growing less effective" (1983b, p. 239). There is an important difference, however, between the aging of an *organism* and the aging of a *person:* "The aging of a person . . . depends upon changes in the physical and social environments. . . . Fortunately, the course of a developing environment can be changed" (p. 239).

Thus, one way to cope with the inevitable biological changes of aging—changes that cannot be prevented but can only be compensated for, as by glasses and hearing aids—is to change the environment. What we need, says Skinner, is a "prosthetic environment" in which, even though biological capacities are reduced, behavior will continue to be effective.

Although in his 1983 article entitled "Intellectual Self-management in Old Age," Skinner addresses older people, many readers may be able to make use of his hints on how to remember better, how to avoid repetition in speech and writing, and so on. All people occasionally forget things like people's names or facts they need to know for work or study. And when people write, they sometimes forget that they have already made or discussed specific points. Skinner's prescriptions may help readers of all ages to behave more efficiently.

Skinner begins his advice with some "practical examples." Here is one: suppose, he says, that as you are eating breakfast you hear the radio say it will probably rain. You think, I must take my umbrella. When you walk out the door a half hour later, however, you forget the umbrella. The thought of the behavior of taking an umbrella occurred to you at a time when you were not yet able to execute that behavior. You can solve this kind of problem, Skinner suggests, by executing as much of the behavior as possible when it first comes to mind. Thus, you might hang your umbrella on the doorknob or put it through the handle of your briefcase.

Skinner is particularly concerned with the kind of problem that arises in intellectual work—reading, writing, studying. Although, he concedes, it does appear that older people forget more, repeat more, and are often somewhat less creative, "one *can* say something new. . . . Creative verbal behavior is . . . produced by skillful self-management" (1983b, p. 242). "The problem in old age is not so much how to have ideas as how to have them when you can use them," Skinner says; "in place of memories, memoranda" (p. 240). If one awakes in the middle of the night with an important idea, one should write it down or dictate it into a tape recorder.

What has often been called "lack of motivation" in the aging, Skinner says, is more likely to be lack of reinforcement. The aging person's world—his or her environment—has changed.

Skinner offers an analogy, pointing out that people who move to a new city often suffer a brief depression "which appears to be merely the result of an old repertoire of behavior having become useless" (p. 243). Old friends, familiar stores, restaurants, theatres are no longer there for one. This depression, however, is usually quickly relieved by acquiring a new repertoire of behavior. In the same way, when much of the aging person's repertoire has lost meaning, the solution may be to find a new repertoire—new friends, new activities, new interests. "Organize discussions, if only in groups of two. Find someone with similar interests. Two heads together are better than both apart. In talking with another person we have ideas that do not occur when we are alone at our desks" (p. 243).

Concluding his article, Skinner echoes Cicero's advice: " 'Old age is honored only on condition that it defends itself, maintains its rights, is subservient to no one, and to its last breath rules over its own domain' " (1983b, p. 242). When people turn over everything to the next generation, Skinner argues, whether their work or their material possessions, they may perhaps have no right to complain of neglect. And "beware," he says, "of those who are trying to be helpful and too readily flatter you. . . . Those who help those who can help themselves work a sinister kind of destruction by making the good things in life no longer properly contingent on behavior" (p. 244). In other words, one must keep doing things for oneself—one must keep behaving.

---

positive reinforcer because its presentation increases the chances of the response in which we are interested.

What happens, you may ask, if we stop presenting meat to the dog and simply sound the bell? For a while, the dog will still salivate to the bell, but less and less often until he will finally stop. This process is called extinction, and it demonstrates the necessity for continuing reinforcement; without reinforcement at least some of the time (see the next section), a behavior that is not automatic (reflexes, such as the knee jerk to a tap on the knee, are automatic behaviors) will eventually disappear.

Although Pavlov's work had "shown the way" to Skinner (Skinner, 1973, p. 383), Skinner was from the beginning much less interested in studying classical conditioning, which he came to call respondent behavior, than in exploring "the important business of the organism in everyday life" (p. 383). He believed that the same order or regularity could be found both at the level at which Pavlov worked and in the functioning of the organism as a whole in its environment.

Many early researchers thought that all learning was based on the process we have just described, classical conditioning. Skinner, however, saw that a great deal of behavior could not easily be fitted into this paradigm. For example, responses like painting a picture seem to be spontaneous and voluntary; they are not tied to a readily identifiable eliciting stimulus in the way that in the dog salivation is tied to the sight and smell of meat. Moreover, agents that appear to reinforce a behavior of this sort—say, critical acclaim or a large sum of money—typically follow, rather than precede, the behavior in question.

In **operant**, or **instrumental**, **conditioning**—first investigated systematically by E. L. Thorndike (American psychologist, 1874–1949)—the reinforcer is not associated with an eliciting stimulus; instead, it is associated with, and follows, the response. It is because the response itself is operational in bringing about the reinforcement that Skinner has labeled this response an **operant**. And it is to indicate that the response in classical conditioning is elicited by a specifiable stimulus that he has labeled that response a **respondent**.

A respondent is an automatic behavior that is within an organism's normal repertoire. In classical conditioning, we devise a way to elicit that response in a situation different from the one in which the response was originally elicited.

An operant response may or may not have been within an organism's original repertoire. It may be a behavior that has never, to our knowledge, been emitted before; for example, a rat in a cage may depress a bar, which leads to the delivery of a food pellet. The rat may never in its life have been presented with such a situation and may never have pressed a bar before. But when it does this, it is rewarded—its operant response is reinforced—by something desirable, here, food. As a result, the rat tends to repeat the response that led to the reinforcement; it will continue to press the bar as long as this action delivers food. (For a discussion of how very stable responding can be conditioned quite accidentally, see Box 13.3.) Again, as in classical conditioning, if we stop delivering the reinforcement, in time the rat will stop making the operant response; it will no longer press the bar except accidentally, as at the start.

The advantage of operant conditioning over classical conditioning is the former's greater flexibility. Because normally rare responses can be reinforced and thus made to recur dependably, we can build chains of responses so as to produce behaviors that an organism not only has never emitted before but would be highly unlikely to emit under natural conditions (see Fig. 13.1).

Although Skinner himself has done most of his experiments with rats, pigeons, and other nonhuman creatures, he believes that his principles apply to all living organisms. Let us look at an example of operant conditioning in a child. Suppose that a mother gives her little boy a cookie when, instead of dropping his jacket on the floor, he hangs it up neatly in the closet. If the next day he comes in and hangs his jacket up again and his mother again gives him a cookie, the likelihood that the hang-up-jacket–receive-cookie sequence will be repeated is greatly increased. Now if suddenly the mother stops giving the boy cookies, he may continue to hang up his jacket for a while, but unless or until there are other reinforcers for this particular behavior—such as his mother's smile or the internal reinforcement of self-praise—it may drop out.

What if we want to eliminate a behavior? One way to accomplish this is by means of punishment. If the little boy's mother were repeatedly to spank him for throwing his jacket on the floor, or to deprive him of something he likes, he might stop the undesirable behavior. On the other hand, the punishment may have unfortunate side effects, such as making the boy tend to avoid his mother when he comes home. In general, we can eliminate an unwanted behavior more effectively by finding and eliminating whatever is reinforcing it—not always an easy task—and then conditioning another, desirable behavior by the use of positive reinforcement, such as the cookie or the smile.

BOX 13.3   Superstitious Behavior

Superstitious behavior is a kind of conditioning in which a response and a reinforcer are accidentally connected. Although the response does not actually produce the reinforcement with which it is associated, the response acquires considerable strength.

Let us see how this sort of behavior comes about. Suppose we operate a food hopper in a Skinner box (see page 474) every 15 seconds, regardless of what the pigeon in the box is doing. When food first appears in the hopper, the bird will probably be engaged in some sort of movement—for example, it may have just started pacing in a circle in the center of the box. The fact that the food appears immediately after the bird begins pacing will enhance the likelihood that it will repeat this behavior—even though the two events occurred together by chance. And even though pacing will not always be followed by the appearance of food, if the pigeon keeps pacing, the response and the reinforcer will occur often enough together that the behavior may become extremely stable.

One can see this sort of behavior in the superstitious practices of primitive tribes or even of people in our own society. Some primitive tribespeople practice rain dancing in the belief that their dance produces rain. It is the fact that on some occasions rain does happen to follow this ritual that accounts for the persistence of the practice. The athlete who insists on continuing to wear the "lucky socks" that he happened to be wearing when his team won a crucial game would serve as another example.

The behavior that Skinner describes as superstitious is quite similar to the behavior Sullivan describes as parataxic (see pages 175–176). Parataxic distortion, as you will recall, refers to the tendency to connect things and events simply on the basis of temporal or spatial contiguity.

REINFORCEMENT AND THE SHAPING OF BEHAVIOR

It is not just the fact of reinforcement but the manner in which reinforcement is carried out that is crucial to the manipulation of behavior. Reinforcement, carefully administered, can enable us to **shape** an organism's behavior so that by operant learning processes, it will come to emit desired behaviors, often behaviors that it would never have emitted, left to its own devices.

Let us look at an experimental procedure for which Skinner has become famous—training a pigeon to peck at something other than food—in this case, a lighted disk. As we see how this behavior is shaped, we will see how various schedules of reinforcement—arrangements of the delivery of reinforcing stimuli according to different temporal schedules—can be employed to achieve the behavior we want.

We start with a hungry pigeon in a **Skinner box**, a small, well-illuminated chamber that has opaque, soundproof walls (see Fig. 13.2). The Skinner box (so-named by others) represents an important technical accomplishment. This chamber enables the experimenter to control for much environmental variation by shielding the subject

Figure 13.1   Barnabus, a rat trained in Barnard College's psychology laboratory, performed a chain of acts that led him to a one-minute feast of all he could eat. At a light flash he (a) ran up a circular mesh pathway from the bottom of a cage to a first landing, where he crossed a drawbridge and climbed a ladder to a second platform. There, with teeth and paws, he pulled a chain attached to a small car, climbed in and (b) pedaled across the platform. He then ran up a stairway to a third landing, squeezed through a 17-inch tube, stepped into an elevator, and (c) raised the flag of his university as he descended toward the lever he pressed for his reward.

from the external environment. The box also makes it possible to control both the occurrence and the recording of stimulus events.

Our hungry pigeon confronts little more than four smooth walls and a floor and ceiling—except that on one wall there is a translucent disk that can be illuminated from behind by a red light. The disk and the box are so wired that whenever the pigeon pecks the disk, a response is recorded and food is delivered to the pigeon in a hopper fixed to the wall just below the disk.

To get the pigeon to peck the disk for the first time, we have to shape its behavior; pecking at a red disk on a wall is not part of the normal behavioral repertoire of most pigeons. So we start by reinforcing behaviors that are closer and closer approximations to the disk-pecking

Figure 13.2 An example of operant conditioning. Here the hungry pigeon described in the text stands ready to peck at a lighted disk in the wall of a Skinner box. Below the disk is the hopper that delivers a food reward every time the pigeon pecks the disk.

behavior that we want: first, we train the bird to eat from the hopper; then, we present food only when the bird is near the disk (and the hopper); then, we reinforce the bird only when it raises its head as it stands near the disk; then, only when the beak is in a striking position with respect to the disk, and so forth. Eventually, the pigeon will peck the disk for a first time, and, of course, we deliver food immediately. From there on, the bird is more and more likely to peck the disk again, and each time it does we deliver food. Fairly soon, pecking will be occurring quite rapidly.

Thus, by a schedule of **continuous reinforcement**—an arrangement in which each correct response is reinforced—we have achieved the desired result. If we stop delivering reinforcement (food) at any time, the rate of pecking will decline and shortly will occur hardly at all; the response will have been extinguished.

Suppose, however, that we continue to deliver the reinforcing food but only occasionally. We may deliver the reinforcing food on a **fixed interval** reinforcement schedule, say, once every 5 seconds. Or we may use a **variable interval** reinforcement schedule—we may deliver food at intervals that vary randomly around a stated average. That is, we may reinforce the pigeon after 3 seconds, then after 6 seconds, then after 4 seconds, and so on, the average interval being 5 seconds. Under either condition, fixed interval or variable interval, the pigeon will typically respond with fairly continuous pecking. Although most of its pecks are not reinforced, those that are serve to maintain the overall response rate. With a variable interval schedule, the pecking rate is normally fairly steady. With a fixed interval schedule, it is likely to slow down immediately following a reinforcement and to pick up again as the time for the next reinforcement approaches. When we extinguish a response conditioned by interval reinforcement, such a

TABLE 13.1   Some Schedules of Reinforcement

Continuous	The organism is reinforced every time it correctly performs the desired response.
Interval	
Fixed	The organism is reinforced for correctly performing the desired response at specific intervals.
Variable	The organism is reinforced for performing the desired response at specified but different intervals that vary around a given average.
Ratio	
Fixed	The organism is reinforced for performing the desired response each time that it performs it a specified number of times.
Variable	The organism is reinforced for performing the desired response when it has performed it different numbers of times varying around a specified average.

response disappears much more slowly than does one conditioned by continuous reinforcement.

We can achieve a response that is even more resistant to extinction by using a reinforcement schedule in which reinforcement is a function of the organism's own behavior. For example, using a **fixed ratio** schedule, we may reinforce every tenth peck by the pigeon, or every twentieth, or some other number. Or we may use a **variable ratio** schedule, so that on average every fifth peck, say, is reinforced; we reinforce now the third peck, now the eighth peck, and so on.

Resistance to extinction is the greatest with the ratio schedules of reinforcement, first variable ratio and then fixed ratio. The interval schedules are somewhat less resistant to extinction, variable interval being more resistant and fixed interval less resistant. Least resistant of all to extinction is the continuous reinforcement schedule (see also Table 13.1 and Fig. 13.3).

Skinner and his associates (e.g., Ferster and Skinner, 1957; Skinner, 1969) have written extensively on the effects of a wide variety of reinforcement schedules. The student who explores this material will see that these different schedules correspond to many situations of interest to the personality investigator. For example, schedules can be set up to produce extremely persistent behavior that very rarely receives reinforcement.

It is important to note that undesirable behaviors can be reinforced quite inadvertently: it is the contingencies of reinforcement that matter, not the intentions of the controller. Consider a little girl in an institution who, when, the nurse or attendant pays attention to other

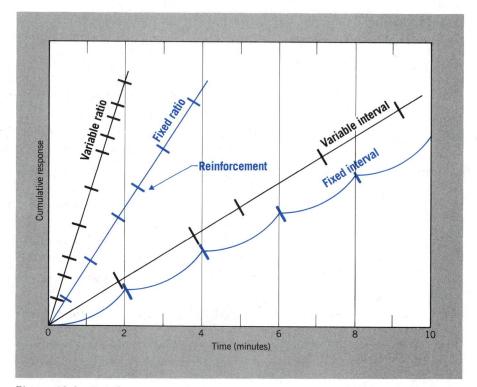

Figure 13.3 Reinforcement schedules. Number of responses per minute under four different schedules of reinforcement. The highest and most consistent responding occurs under a variable ratio schedule of reinforcement, wherein reinforcements are available only after a variable and unpredictable number of nonreinforced responses. Note that under the fixed interval schedule of reinforcement, rate of responding slows after each reinforcement and then increases rapidly as the time of the next reinforcement approaches. Under the other schedules, rate of responding is generally quite steady. (From Dember, Jenkins, and Teyler, 1983.)

children, begins to scream and bang her head against the wall. If the nurse drops what she is doing, rushes to the child, picks her up, cuddles her, and generally behaves in an affectionate manner, she may unintentionally reinforce the very behavior she wishes to eliminate. The problem is not the nurse's affectionate behavior, but its timing.

Let us return to the pigeon, who is still busily pecking away at the red-lighted disk and consuming food as it is presented. Food, says Skinner, is a **primary**, or **unconditioned**, **reinforcer**. It is easy to condition a response to such a reinforcer, in either a pigeon or a human being. However, not every action of a human being—at least in relatively affluent societies—is maintained by a primary reinforcer like food or water. Much of human behavior, according to Skinner, relies on **conditioned** reinforcement—**secondary reinforcers** that have

The powerful reinforcement of money in our society is illustrated by this line of people waiting to buy tickets in New York State's Lotto game when the jackpot prize for the first time reached $18.5 million.

been paired with primary reinforcers and have come to have reinforcing properties of their own. A good example of a conditioned reinforcer in human behavior is money. Let us see how such a conditioned reinforcer can evolve for a pigeon; then we can return to the human being.

Suppose that we make a new response available to the pigeon. We cover up the disk and insert a food pedal into the Skinner box, programming the apparatus so that one depression of this pedal causes the empty food hopper to be presented. We find that once having accidentally pressed the foot pedal and produced the food hopper, the pigeon will continue to press the foot pedal a good many times. The hopper, which was consistently associated with food in the first part of the experiment, has now become a conditioned, or secondary, reinforcer. Of course, this new conditioned response will not continue indefinitely unless the pigeon finds food in the hopper at least occasionally.

In the same way that for the pigeon the hopper is associated with food, for the human being, money is associated with the things it can buy—food, shelter, material possessions, and so on. Money is such an effective reinforcer because it is associated with so many other reinforcers. Money has no intrinsic value of its own—presumably it would lose its reinforcing effect in a society in which goods were distributed to everyone on some basis other than the payment of money.

GENERALIZATION AND DISCRIMINATION

Two phenomena are of great importance in Skinner's system, as they are in most personality theories that derive from learning theory. These phenomena are generalization and discrimination. By the process of **stimulus generalization**, an organism may come to make the response that it makes in one situation in other situations that are sufficiently similar to the first. By the process of **stimulus discrimination**, an organism may come to distinguish between situations in which a given response is or is not reinforced, thus making it in only certain situations.

Let us go back again to our pigeon in its original situation, pecking at the red-lighted disk. Suppose we manipulate the color of the lighted disk across the color spectrum. When the disk reflects colors that are very close to red, the bird's rate of pecking will be almost as high as when the disk is red. However, as the color of the disk moves further and further from the red portion of the spectrum, the rate of responding will decline. We say that the bird has generalized its responses to similar stimuli (the red colors) and discriminated its response from dissimilar stimuli (say, blues and greens). By appropriately reinforcing its behavior, we can change the organism's discriminations: for example, we could teach the pigeon to discriminate between similar colors, say, oranges and reds, for which stimulus generalization initially occurred.

Generalization and discrimination are enormously important tools of learning. If we could not generalize, we would never learn anything. If we had to learn everything we do from scratch, we would spend so much time every day learning new behaviors—because no person is ever in exactly the same situation twice—that we would be unable to function. On the other hand, if we could not discriminate among situations, we would constantly be making inappropriate responses in situations that are different from others, and our behavior would be chaotic.

SOCIAL BEHAVIOR

Although a great deal of human functioning is social in nature, Skinner, believes that the same principles determine the development of behavior whether it occurs in environments containing animate or inanimate objects. In either case, the organism interacts with the environment, receiving positive or negative reinforcement of its behavior.

Skinner grants that social responses and reinforcers are sometimes more difficult to identify than nonsocial ones, but in principle, he says, the same basic behavioral laws apply in the two cases.

When discussing social behavior, Skinner does not, as you may imagine, talk about personality traits or the way people characteristically behave. For Skinner, trait descriptions are ultimately reducible to groups of specific responses that tend to be associated in certain kinds of situations. Thus when we say a person is domineering, we mean that when we observe him in interaction with other people, we note that he is argumentative, interrupts others, talks more and louder than others, insists on his own views, and so on. It is the aggregate of these particular responses that tells us that this person is domineering. How did he get to be this way? In the past, Skinner would say, when interacting with others, the person was reinforced for the group of responses that he now emits and that are called dominance. These responses tend to go together because they are functionally similar in their social consequences and, hence, have been subject to similar histories of reinforcement. (Skinner would not exclude the possibility that behaviors might sometimes go together genetically, because of natural selection in the history of the species, but he tends to look first for a common basis in the history of the individual's development.)

Why does one person respond in what we call a dominant fashion to other people whereas another person responds with submissive behavior? Again, Skinner would go back to earlier reinforcements: the first person may have been reinforced earlier than the other for aggressive behavior and probably in a greater variety of situations. The second person may have been quite consistently reinforced for yielding to others or even punished for asserting himself.

Suppose that a dominant person applies for a job. She is very aggressive and presents herself as a self-starter who needs responsibility and the opportunity to lead others. She has been reinforced for these behaviors in the past. If she gets the job, she will again be reinforced, and these behaviors will be further strengthened. Even if she does not get the job, she will very likely not stop being aggressive. Most behavior outside the laboratory is reinforced only intermittently, and as we now know, such reinforcement generates very stable and persistent behavior.

ABNORMAL BEHAVIOR

Skinner assumes that abnormal behavior develops according to the same principles that govern normal behavior. Furthermore, he suggests that abnormal behavior can be replaced with normal behavior simply by manipulation of the environment. Repressed id impulses, inferiority complexes, anxiety, ego defenses, identity crises, ego-superego conflicts—these are all explanatory fictions for Skinner. For him, undesirable behavior can be eliminated simply by following the procedures of operant and respondent conditioning.

Suppose that a soldier is wounded in battle. When he recovers, after a hospital stay, he is sent back to the front line and immediately develops a paralysis in one arm. Physical examination reveals no physiological problem. Nevertheless, the soldier must be taken off active duty because he cannot use his arm.

How would Skinner analyze this situation? First, he would say that the soldier's wound was a **negative reinforcer**, an aversive stimulus, that the soldier will attempt to avoid in future. The front line, which is associated with the wound (that is where he received it) is a **conditioned negative reinforcer**, and the soldier will attempt to avoid it also. However, to refuse to go into battle will result, at the very least, in social rejection, at most, in a court martial and perhaps a long prison term or even death—all very aversive consequences. As a result, some behavior is likely to emerge that terminates both conditioned negative reinforcers, and this behavior will be reinforced and maintained. Because in most armies a soldier is not held responsible for paralysis, he will not be punished.

How do we cure the soldier? Theoretically, if he were to return to the front line (the conditioned reinforcer) but not to be wounded again (unconditioned reinforcer), his conditioned response (paralysis) would extinguish. However, the soldier is not likely to return to the battleground voluntarily. We could force him to return and hope that being in the aversive situation without the aversive consequences he experienced before would extinguish his response of paralysis; this sort of procedure is sometimes followed in behavior therapy. Called **flooding,** it involves encouraging a patient to go into an anxiety-arousing situation and "tough it out"—to stay there until he or she realizes that the expected disaster is not going to occur (see, e.g., Baum, 1970). In the situation of the soldier, of course, we can hardly guarantee that he will not be wounded again or suffer other negative reinforcers.

A second possibility is to shape some other response that is not considered abnormal but that also serves to terminate the conditioned negative reinforcer, being on the front line. For example, we might permanently discharge the soldier from the army without penalty; his paralysis would presumably disappear in due course (if we did not inadvertently reinforce it in other ways, such as disability benefits or a hero's welcome home). Another possibility would be a permanent career shift within the military service to a specialty in which the possibility of frontline duty would be remote. Again, the paralysis might be expected to disappear gradually once it no longer was required as justification for the job change.

One approach would probably *not* work: direct punishment. If we severely punished the soldier, his paralysis might well disappear, but it would be likely to be replaced by some other equally abnormal response. This is because what was reinforcing that response of paralysis—the aversive properties of the battleground—would not have been eliminated. As long as the soldier is liable to be sent to the front lines and the conditions are not fundamentally changed, he is likely to develop some other response that will remove him from the aversive situation.

Skinner's approach and that of behavior therapists in general has often been criticized for curing only symptoms and ignoring internal mental or physiological causes. Critics claim that **symptom substitution**—the appearance of a new symptom in place of one that has been eliminated—will often follow such treatment.

Skinner would deny the validity of such criticism—and, in fact, the literature does not support the notion of symptom substitution to any significant extent. Skinner would argue that conditions of treatment must be sufficiently analyzed: under certain conditions, we would expect the reoccurrence of symptoms; under other conditions we would not. In our example of the soldier, if we were to use punishment, we might expect a new symptom to appear; if we used formal discharge from the service, we might expect recovery.

RESEARCH METHODS AND EMPHASES

Skinner's work deviates from the contemporary norm for psychological research in several ways. First, Skinner focuses on the simplest of behavioral events. Second, he insists that experimental conditions be controlled and that subjects' responses be recorded automatically. And third, he undertakes the intensive study of one individual subject rather than the investigation of groups of subjects. For Skinner, the psychologist's aim is the control of behavior in the individual subject. Researchers who work with large groups of animals need be little concerned with uncontrolled variables, as long as these are randomly distributed. But Skinner believes that just like any other variables, uncontrolled variables must be carefully studied. If we are going to control behavior, we are going to have to find out what these other variables are so that we can control them too.

A Skinnerian researcher might well proceed along the following lines: After training a pigeon to peck at a disk and then maintaining the bird's responding with a variable reinforcement schedule, the researcher notices some minor fluctuations in the pigeon's behavior. He traces these to a possible uncontrolled condition in the pigeon's environment, say, transient traces of some odor in the air circulated to the box. Such a condition is then systematically varied, and if it is demonstrated that it has an effect on the pigeon's rate of pecking, one more variable that affects behavior has been brought under control.

EFFECTS OF DRUGS ON BEHAVIOR

Skinnerian methodology and the Skinner box have proved admirable tools for the study of the effects on behavior of various pharmacological agents. For example, a rat may be trained to press a bar in a Skinner box to the point where the rate of bar pressing very stable. At this point, a drug under investigation may be administered to the rat before the beginning of a new session. During the course of the new session, the time at which any effects of the drug begin to appear, the specific nature of these effects, and the duration of such effects may all be measured. The Skinner box allows the researcher to investigate drug effects on perception, fear, and approach and avoidance responding under very similar basic conditions. Indeed, no method of animal experimentation has even approached the Skinnerian in efficiency in isolating particular aspects of behavior and studying the effects on them of various drugs.

One drug that has been investigated extensively with Skinnerian methods is chlorpromazine, an antianxiety agent used in the treatment of psychosis. Under the influence of chlorpromazine, a rat will bar-press at a decreased rate, even though bar-pressing enables it to avoid electric shock. We might conclude from these results that chlorpromazine reduces fear—and it has generally been assumed that this drug, so often administered to persons diagnosed as schizophrenic, has just that effect. However, the same result—decreased bar-pressing—is found in rats under the influence of chlorpromazine when bar-pressing delivers food (Boren, 1966). Thus, it would appear that chlorpromazine acts as a general depressant, reducing all types of responding, not just responding that is a function of fear. The picture with this particular drug turns out to be more complicated, for effects differ at different dosage levels; at very low levels, the drug *increases* response rates. By using Skinnerian methods, we can locate and explore such complexities before producing unintended and possibly damaging effects in the use of the drug with human patients.

BEHAVIORAL INTERVENTIONS WITH PSYCHIATRIC PATIENTS

In the early 1960s, Ayllon and Azrin (1965, 1968) developed what has come to be known as the **token economy**, a technique based on the principles of operant conditioning. The token economy was designed to alter the behavior of mental patients—initially, chronic psychiatric patients who were long-term residents on a mental ward—in a desirable direction: conditioned reinforcers, in the form of tokens were provided to patients who emitted desired responses such as dressing themselves, eating without assistance, or completing work assignments adequately. These tokens could later be exchanged for primary reinforcers—things people want and enjoy—like new clothing, social interaction, cosmetics, attending a movie, and so on.

Since these early studies, token economies have been instituted in many different settings—with the developmentally disabled, the autistic child, the juvenile delinquent, and even the normal person. The technique has often proved successful in producing desirable forms of behavior (see, e.g., Ayllon and Azrin, 1968; Kazdin, 1977; Lovaas et al., 1973).

EVALUATION

Skinner's approach is strongly represented within American psychology. Operant reinforcement theory and research are the focus of the articles that fill the pages of the *Journal of the Experimental Analysis of Behavior* and the *Journal of Applied Behavior Analysis*. The American Psychological Association's Division for the Experimental Analysis of Behavior includes more than 1400 psychologists, and in a number of graduate training programs around the country, students are trained in the approach and techniques of various versions of operant reinforcement theory.

Not only has the Skinnerian approach produced a great deal of experimental research; it has been applied to a wide array of practical problems. We have discussed the use of behavioristic principles in the treatment and management of psychiatric patients and other people with psychological difficulties. And behavior therapy is widely used as a means of treating individual sufferers from such distressing symptoms as anxiety, compulsions, and phobias.

We have noted the use of Skinnerian techniques in an industrial setting—the pharmacological industry. Operant techniques have proven valuable in other areas as well. For example, in the field of animal training, whether the purpose is a scientific goal or entertainment, Skinnerian techniques clearly have no equal. Only Skinner and his associates and followers have been able to take untrained animals and shape their behavior in the view of the general public.

Yet it may turn out that it is in the area of education that Skinner's theory and research have had their most important influence. Teaching machines and programmed learning materials, based on the Skinnerian technique of building complex responses out of simple ones and associating reinforcement closely in time with the response to be learned, have become commonplace in educational settings, all the way from preschool to the world of postgraduate studies. Skinner

(1983a) personally devoted a great deal of his time and effort over a number of years to the development and promotion of teaching machines and programmed learning.

One accomplishment of Skinner and his colleagues is unmatched in the ranks of psychologists: their combination of elegant laboratory technique and precise experimental control with the study of the individual. The degree of lawfulness reported in the findings of Skinner and his students is virtually unparalleled in psychology and particularly among those who focus on the individual subject.

On the negative side of the ledger, one common criticism of Skinner and his associates is that Skinnerian theory is no theory at all. As we have already seen, Skinner himself agrees in part with this assessment. He insists that a science at the stage at which psychology finds itself is not likely to be helped by devoting time to building theories in the sense of explanations of observed facts that appeal "to events taking place somewhere else, at some other level of observation described in different terms and measured, if at all, in different dimensions" (Skinner, 1969, p. vii). He has suggested, however, that theory in the sense of "a critique of the methods, data, and concepts of a science of behavior" is not only acceptable to him but is "essential to the scientific understanding of behavior as a subject matter" (p. viii).

One problem with Skinner's tightly controlled experimentation, which avoids any inference of unobservable mechanisms or processes, is that Skinner has difficulty predicting what will happen in a situation where novel stimuli appear or where old ones combine in novel ways. He can predict only on the basis of the laws that he has established, and these can be extended only to instances of the type of behavior with respect to which they were formulated. In Skinner's system, there are no theoretical statements that one can use to make new empirical assertions.

According to Skinner (1950), even though theorizing based on inferred entities might lead us to novel expectations, unless such expectations are confirmed, such theorizing has no value. And, he says, although some day someone might come up with a valid theory of behavior—one that will provide the correct expectations for behavior in novel situations, by that time we could have spent years in unproductive research attempting to confirm unfruitful theories. Any important new situation will have to be investigated directly anyway, says Skinner, so there is really no need to theorize; sooner or later behavior in such a situation will be brought into the system whether we have a theory or not.

It will not surprise the reader to learn that holistic psychologists of all sorts find quite unacceptable Skinner's insistence that the whole is best understood as being just the sum of its parts. For these critics,

Skinner's approach is too simplistic and elemental to represent the full complexity of human behavior.

Clearly, Skinner experiments, for the most part, with relatively simple organisms that have relatively simple histories and that confront relatively simple environmental conditions. Subjects are rarely exposed to variation in more than one variable at a time. Critics point out that such simple situations never occur outside the laboratory and suggest that behavior is much more complex than Skinner would lead us to believe. Skinner replies that all science must proceed by starting with simple phenomena and then building up to the complex ones.

Skinner admits that it is difficult to be sure that in achieving the level of rigor he insists on we are not sometimes unduly simplifying conditions. Behavior examined in the laboratory may well appear less regular outside of it. Nevertheless, says Skinner (1957), we should remember that the same applies to physical phenomena. The fact that physical phenomena exhibit less order outside of controlled conditions does not mean that there is no order to these phenomena.

For example, suppose we observe the way a person drinks a cup of coffee. Many factors, such as the temperature of the coffee and events that take place at the breakfast table may intervene to affect the rate at which the person consumes the coffee; thus the behavioral curve graphed "will not be pretty." But, says Skinner, neither will the curve representing the physical cooling of the coffee in the cup. There are perfectly straightforward physical laws that govern the rate at which a liquid cools; the fact that in the everyday world many factors may affect the course of such a phenomenon does not mean that the physical rules do not apply.

A final criticism leveled at Skinner is that so much of his work has been done with pigeons and rats and, perhaps unjustifiably, extrapolated to other species, including human beings. The organism, these critics say, is not a *tabula rasa* whose final state is determined solely by Skinner's stimulus–response–reinforcement paradigm. These critics feel that there are at least some behavioral processes that do not fit into Skinner's model and cite work such as Harlow's (1962) work with social development in monkeys and the European ethologists' work with instinctive behavior. And some psychologists have emphasized the role of biological factors in learning, questioning whether "general laws of learning" are possible at all (Seligman and Hager, 1972).

As we have seen, however, Skinner does not really take a strong *tabula rasa* position. He is quite willing to allow in principle for the role of biological natural selection as well as for psychological operant conditioning in shaping behavior. He believes, however, that the latter process constitutes a very powerful and pervasive influence in animal and human behavior and provides the major means by which behavior can be brought under experimental and practical control.

As a personality theorist, Skinner is certainly unique. He is not much interested in individual differences, despite his focus on individual subjects; he is interested in general laws of behavior. He has done most of his experimental research with rats and pigeons, not the human species with which most personality theorists work. And he steadfastly refuses to invoke the sorts of internal entities that are the lifeblood of most personality theories. Perhaps we might say that Skinner's is a *theory of personality;* that is, it is a theory that attempts to explain the phenomena we call personality, but not a *personality theory*—that is, it does not use personality constructs to explain and predict behavior.

Despite his background in research with lower animals, Skinner has clearly been centrally concerned with human problems, both those of individuals and those of the societies and cultures individuals form and are formed by. He and his followers have been deeply involved in redirecting unsuccessful and maladaptive modes of behavior in order to let people live rewarding, rather than punished, lives. Very few theorists discussed in this book, with the exception of Freud, can claim to have had as much influence on contemporary life and thought as has B. F. Skinner.

SUMMARY

1. All **behavior is lawful**, and it can be both **predicted** and **controlled**. Control of behavior is important, both as a test of our hypotheses and because we will destroy ourselves and our world if we do not change our behavior.

2. **Respondents** are behaviors elicited by specifiable stimuli. **Operants** are behaviors emitted by the organism without specific stimulation.

3. Behaviors vary in intensity as a function not of inner needs or drives but of **environmental variables** such as deprivation of a given **reinforcer**.

4. In **classical conditioning**, a behavior elicited by a specifiable stimulus comes to be elicited by another, often totally different, stimulus. In **operant conditioning**, a behavior that an organism emits spontaneously is either encouraged to recur or eliminated by means of positive or negative reinforcers. By operant conditioning, we can encourage new, spontaneous responses to recur, thus building novel and complex sequences of behavior.

5. Punishment may eliminate an undesirable behavior, but eliminating the reinforcer of such behavior and substituting a desirable behav-

ior (by means of positive reinforcement) is more effective.

6. By **shaping** we can bring an organism to emit behaviors it would never have emitted, left to its own devices. Beginning with a spontaneous behavior, behaviors that are closer and closer to the desired behavior are successively reinforced until eventually the desired behavior appears.

7. The most common **schedules of reinforcement** are **continuous**, **fixed interval**, **variable interval**, **fixed ratio**, and **variable ratio**. Continuous reinforcement is least resistant to **extinction**; variable reinforcement is most resistant.

8. A behavior may be reinforced inadvertently or accidentally, as when a parent pays attention to a child only when it misbehaves, or when a pigeon develops **superstitious behavior**.

9. Primary reinforcers, like food and water, are reinforcing without any earlier training. **Secondary reinforcers**, by association with primary reinforcers, come to have a reinforcing effect.

10. By **stimulus generalization**, the organism learns to make a particular response in situations that are very similar to the situation in which the response was learned. By **stimulus discrimination**, the organism learns not to make a particular response in situations that are different from the one in which the response was learned.

11. Abnormal behavior can be treated by operant and respondent conditioning procedures. An example is **flooding**, which involves encouraging a person with, say, a phobia, to get into and stay in a situation that arouses fear until the fear subsides.

12. The **"Skinner box"** has been particularly useful in pharmacological research, where the effects on an animal of a particular drug can be closely controlled and monitored.

13. Behavioral techniques have been used with considerable success on mental wards and with the developmentally disabled and autistic child. In a **token economy**, good behavior earns people tokens, which they then exchange for desired goods or activities.

14. Skinner's approach has been applied to a wide variety of practical problems, in education, industry, the helping professions, and animal training. The lawfulness of his findings is unparalleled in psychology, and his schedules of reinforcement are important to both learning theorists and personality investigators. But because Skinner refuses to infer any unobservable mechanisms or processes, he has difficulty in extrapolating to completely novel situations. Holistic psychologists feel that Skinner's approach ignores the complexity of human behavior, and other critics point out that the simple situations Skinner studies never occur outside the laboratory. Other critics object to behavioral laws that do not explicitly take species differences into account.

SUGGESTED READING

Skinner's most important single publication is probably his first book, *The Behavior of Organisms* (1938), which continues to exert major intellectual influence in psychology despite the many years that have passed since its publication. For an introduction to the Skinnerian approach, however, the student might find it easier to start with Skinner's *Science and Human Behavior* (1953), which outlines Skinner's basic position and illustrates its application to a wide variety of practical problems, or his Utopian novel, *Walden Two* (1948). In *About Behaviorism* (1974), Skinner summarizes his views on the brand of psychology that has become practically synonymous with his name.

Skinner's *Verbal Behavior* (1957) contains a detailed analysis of language in terms of Skinner's concepts. Skinner's most important articles prior to 1961 are collected in *Cumulative Record* (1961a). An early example of programmed learning can be found in Holland and Skinner's *The Analysis of Behavior: A Program for Self-instruction* (1961), and in *The Technology of Teaching* (1968), Skinner details his approach to learning in the school setting.

Probably Skinner's most controversial book is *Beyond Freedom and Dignity* (1972), in which he argues that the concepts of freedom and dignity prevent us from improving society.

Skinner has written a very readable three-volume autobiography—*Particulars of My Life* (1976), *The Shaping of a Behaviorist* (1979), and *A Matter of Consequences* (1983a)—that by moving steadily forward in chronological fashion effectively melds his personal and professional lives.

Chapter fourteen

14.

To understand thoroughly any item of human behavior—either in the social group or in the individual life— one must know the psychological principles involved in its learning and the social conditions under which this learning took place.
NEAL MILLER AND JOHN DOLLARD

Stimulus–Response Theory: Neal E. Miller and John Dollard

As a graduate student of Neal Miller and John Dollard, you have just placed a laboratory rat in one compartment of a rectangular box that is divided in two by a low fence, or hurdle. You sound a buzzer; the rat perks up its ears but does nothing else in particular. Now you sound the buzzer again and immediately send an electrical charge through the grid floor of the rat's compartment. The rat exhibits signs of pain and distress; for example, it squeaks or shivers. Eventually it scrambles over the hurdle into the other compartment; immediately the buzzer and shock stop. You have arranged the "shuttlebox" apparatus so that as soon as the rat jumps the hurdle, the buzzer and shock are both terminated.

For the next hour you repeat these procedures, at regular intervals, and you see that the rat takes less and less time to jump over the hurdle after the onset of the buzzer–shock. Pretty soon, the rat is jumping the hurdle as soon as it hears the buzzer, even perhaps before the onset of the shock.

Next day you put the rat back in the shuttlebox for another hour. This time, however, instead of following the buzzer immediately with shock, you merely sound the buzzer; you deliver no shock at all. Nevertheless, the rat continues to hurdle the barrier whenever the buzzer sounds. It even improves its performance, jumping faster and with greater ease.

After several days of the buzzer-only procedure, you introduce the rat to a new condition: when it jumps the hurdle, the buzzer does not stop. Now the rat jumps back and forth a bit wildly, as the buzzer continues to sound. Eventually, by chance, the rat happens to press a lever that you have installed at the base of the hurdle. Immediately, the buzzer stops.

From this point on, hurdle-jumping begins to disappear. Instead, when the buzzer sounds, the rat tends to press the lever. Gradually, again, the time between buzzer and lever-press shortens, and eventually the rat is pressing the lever immediately the buzzer sounds.

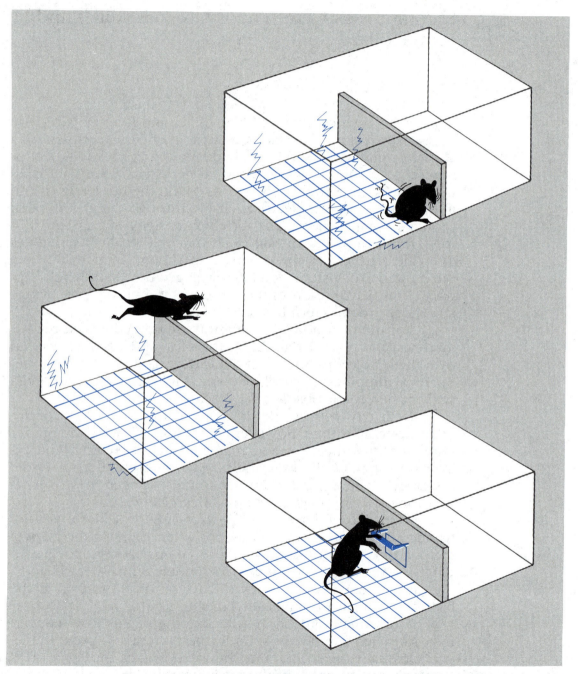

Figure 14.1   A hypothetical learning experiment. Electric shock paired with a buzzer arouses fear and emotional behavior in rat (a). The rat learns to jump a hurdle in order to terminate the buzzer–shock (b). When the buzzer (now without shock) continues despite the rat's hurdle-jumping, the rat learns a new response, of pressing a lever, to turn off the buzzer.

In this experiment you have demonstrated several learning principles: classical conditioning (the rat became *conditioned* to respond to the buzzer as it did initially to shock); instrumental learning (the rat learned to perform a specific act that was *instrumental* in effecting a certain result); and extinction (a behavior that the rat had learned—hurdle-jumping—ceased, or was *extinguished*). In addition, you have shown that a *primary drive*, of pain and distress, can give rise to a *learned*, or *secondary, drive*, of fear, which can then continue to motivate an organism's behavior even when the original source of pain and distress is no longer present.

As we will see, the core of Miller and Dollard's position is an analysis of the learning process. Moreover, for these theorists, a crucial factor in human learning is the secondary or learned drive of fear (anxiety). Much of what we learn we learn through fear, say Miller and Dollard, and thus their model, as reflected in our hypothetical experiment, is applicable to both normal and neurotic behavior. But we are getting ahead of our story. Let us start with a brief review of the history of the S–R, or stimulus–response, approach to learning.

HISTORICAL BACKGROUND

Elegant, economical, and closely linked to its natural science forebears, stimulus–response theory has evolved largely out of laboratory investigations. Thus it differs from many of the theories we have already discussed, in which the role of clinical or naturalistic observation is very important. S–R theory's explicitness and its efforts to provide empirical anchoring for its formulations are consistent with its origins.

Actually, there is no single S–R theory. Rather, there are a number of theories that share certain basic assumptions but differ in certain significant ways. All these theories began as attempts to explain how, with experience, human beings acquire and retain new forms of behavior. Not surprisingly, then, the theories emphasize the learning process. Although S–R theorists do not ignore innate factors, they are most interested in the processes by which people mediate between an array of possible responses and the tremendous variety of stimuli—both internal and external—to which they are exposed.

Among the many complex origins of S–R theory, the contributions of Ivan Pavlov, John B. Watson, and Edward L. Thorndike are particularly outstanding. Pavlov (1849–1936), the distinguished Russian physiologist, discovered the type of learning known as classical conditioning, to which you were introduced in Chapter 13. Watson (1878–1958), leader of the movement in American psychology called **behaviorism**, was the first to use the principles of classical conditioning to build an objective psychology that proposed to study behavior with the same types of objective techniques that the natural sciences used. Edward L. Thorndike (1874–1949) contributed the **law of effect**, according to which reward and punishment crucially affect the learning process.

Psychologists have devoted more thought and activity to the construction of learning theory than to any other contemporary theoretical enterprise. During the 1930s and 1940s, the ideas originated by Watson and Thorndike were explored, expanded, and elaborated by a number of investigators who gradually began to take sides in a controversy that is alive still today. Theorists such as Edwin R. Guthrie (1886–1959), Clark L. Hull (1884–1952), and Kenneth W. Spence (1907–1967) described the learning process as involving the associative linkage between sensory and motor processes. This viewpoint essentially embraces the position of classical empiricism, which held that experiences, or sense impressions, are the only source of knowledge; that all complex ideas are built up out of simple ideas and can therefore be reduced to such simple ideas; that ideas are connected by the association of experiences that occur close together in time; and that the mind is like a machine built from simple elements, with no mysterious components. B. F. Skinner, whose work we presented in Chapter 13, is probably the best known modern proponent of this classical, behaviorist approach.

The other side of the argument is represented by theorists who espouse cognitive views of the learning process. These views derive from the philosophical position of rationalism, which held that reason, rather than sense data, is the only valid basis for knowledge. Edward C. Tolman (1886–1959), one of the first ''cognitive'' learning theorists, agreed that the learning theorist must identify the environmental forces that shape behavior but conceived of learning per se as the development of organized cognitions about sensory or stimulus events. As we saw in Chapter 8, theorists such as Kurt Lewin and George Kelly greatly advanced the importance of cognitive factors in the formation and functioning of personality. In Chapter 15 we will see how several modern learning theorists have combined social and cognitive factors with the role of the environment to create a ''cognitive social learning'' theory of personality.

It is important to understand the rationale of the S–R theorists for the predominant use in their experiments of animals, particularly the laboratory white rat. Hull, who explicitly proposed to develop a general theory of human behavior, chose to develop his ideas through the study of lower organisms, not because he believed all behavioral problems could be solved in this manner but because he hoped the simplicity of the less developed organisms would permit the establishment of certain fundamental principles. Such principles, when elabo-

BOX 14.1   John Dollard (1900–1980)

Born in Menasha, Wisconsin, John Dollard received his bachelor's degree from the University of Wisconsin in 1922. He then served for several years as assistant to the president of the University of Chicago, where he took his master's degree in 1930 and his Ph.D., in sociology, in 1931.

Dollard spent the following year in Germany as a Social Science Research Council fellow in social psychology. During this year abroad, he underwent psychoanalysis with Hanns Sachs, a follower of Freud, and trained in analysis at the Berlin Institute, where one of his training analysts was Karen Horney (Chapter 5). Later, in the United States, Dollard became a member of the Western New England Psychoanalytic Society.

On returning home, Dollard accepted a position on the staff of Yale University's then new Institute of Human Relations, an interdisciplinary institution "founded to bring together eminent investigators from anthropology, sociology, psychology, and psychiatry" (Miller, 1982, p. 587). In 1933 Dollard became a professor of sociology in that Institute.

One of Dollard's first and most highly regarded works was his pioneering analysis of culture and personality, *Caste and Class in a Southern Town* (1937). This book, an illuminating study of the roots of black social immobility in a small Southern town, was considered a highly courageous effort; it was banned in Georgia and in South Africa (Miller, 1982, p. 587). Dollard's book was also important in breaking down the walls between the various social sciences, drawing, as it did, on the findings of several disciplines.

Shortly after his arrival at Yale, Dollard met Neal Miller, who was studying for his Ph.D. under Clark Hull. Their first joint effort, with Leonard Doob, O. Hobart Mowrer, and Robert Sears as well, was the now famous monograph, *Frustration and Aggression* (1939), the basic formulations for which grew, to some degree, out of Dollard's 1937 study. Subsequently, Dollard and Miller collaborated on two books—*Social Learning and Imitation* (1941) and *Personality and Psychotherapy* (1950)—and worked together on a number of other studies and projects.

According to Miller (1982), Dollard was one of the earliest psychotherapists to record psychotherapeutic interviews. He had "the courage to use unedited recordings" of his own cases in giving his students concrete illustrations of the therapeutic process, and he also included some of this material in a book (written with Frank Auld and Alice White), *Steps in Psychotherapy* (1953).

Throughout his professional career, Dollard's abiding concern was the integration of the social sciences. His ability to integrate several varying disciplines within his own life and work was particularly notable at a time when these disciplines were far less willing to cooperate than they are today. Dollard's contribution has been accented by Miller, who writes that "if trying to bring together contributions from sociology, anthropology, psychology, and psychotherapy no longer seems so novel it is because Dollard and other pioneers had the courage and tenacity to break through traditional barriers" (1982, p. 588)

rated by the study of more complex, human behavior, might become the core of a satisfactory theory of behavior.

MILLER AND DOLLARD'S APPROACH: AN OVERVIEW

This chapter focuses on the work of Neal Miller and John Dollard, whose theory, developed within the interdisciplinary approach of Yale University's Institute of Human Relations, brought together three traditions: the experimental study of learning, the psychoanalytic approach to personality development and functioning, and the insights into human behavior offered by the study of social anthropology. Miller and Dollard's theory stems from the Hull–Spence approach, which was particularly concerned with the role of motivation in behavior and the ways in which learned motives are acquired. Miller and Dollard have sought to explain the crucial psychoanalytic concepts—such as anxiety, conflict, and repression—by means of both the psychological principles and the social conditions of learning.

Dollard and Miller (1950) dedicated their book *Personality and Psychotherapy* to Freud and Pavlov and to the students of these great thinkers. Clearly, two more disparate traditions and sources of data could not be found. Nevertheless, Miller and Dollard's effort to bring the two together has had a significant impact on personality theory and research.

According to Miller and Dollard, learning theory, in its simplest form, "is the study of the circumstances under which a response and a cue stimulus become connected" (1941, pp. 1–2). The principles of association and of reward, or reinforcement, are essential to their position.

Let us begin by reviewing quickly what Miller and Dollard have to say about the structure and dynamics of personality. Then, returning to our experiment with the rat, we will explore Miller and Dollard's ideas about the development of personality, or the learning of behavior, which, for them, is the heart of the matter.

STRUCTURE OF PERSONALITY

Habit is almost the only element in Miller and Dollard's theory that has structural characteristics. A habit, which is simply a link or association between a stimulus and a response, does represent what is relatively stable and enduring in the personality. However, a person's configuration of habits depends on the unique events he or she experiences. Moreover, a habit configuration is only temporary: today's habits may change as a result of tomorrow's experience.

Miller and Dollard leave to others the task of specifying the par-

BOX 14.2   Neal Elgar Miller (1909–   )

Neal Miller was born in Milwaukee, Wisconsin, and grew up in Bellingham, Washington, where his father, also a psychologist, headed the Department of Education and Psychology of Western Washington State Teachers College. After receiving his bachelor's degree in 1931 at the University of Washington, Neal Miller studied for his M.A. (1932) at Stanford University under Lewis M. Terman, author of the Stanford–Binet IQ test, and for his Ph.D. (1935) at Yale, under Clark L. Hull.

While studying for his doctorate, Miller served as an assistant in psychology at the Institute of Human Relations. It was at that time that he met and began his long association with John Dollard, then an assistant professor of sociology at the Institute.

In 1935 Miller traveled to Europe on a Social Science Research Council fellowship. While in Vienna, he underwent eight months of psychoanalysis with Heinz Hartmann (see Chapter 3) at the Vienna Institute of Psychoanalysis. Miller says today that if he had known how many people would later ask him what Sigmund Freud was like, he would have secured at least an hour's time with the master. But as a young instructor on a tight budget, he found Freud's fee—$20 an hour, at that time—far too high!

Returning home in 1936, Miller joined the faculty of Yale's Institute of Human Relations, an association ended only in 1966, when he accepted an offer to establish and head Rockefeller University's Laboratory of Physiological Psychology. Currently, Miller is professor emeritus at Rockefeller University, where he continues to write and to maintain his high level of research productivity. Miller and his wife, the former Marion E. Edwards, live in New York City; the Millers have two children, Sara and York.

Miller has served as a consultant and on the boards and committees of many governmental and private institutions, including the National Research Council, the National Institute of Mental Health, and the American Institute of Research. During World War II, Miller served in the Army Air Force and was an advisor to the Office of the Assistant Secretary of Defense as well as to the Air Force Personnel and Training Research Center and the Army Department's Human Resources Research Office.

Miller has been honored many times both within and without his profession. In 1954 he was awarded the Howard Crosby Warren Medal of the Society of Experimental Psychology. The American Association for the Advancement of Science gave Miller (and James Olds) its Newcomb Cleveland Prize in 1957. In 1959 Miller received the American Psychological Association's Distinguished Scientific Contribution Award, and in 1965 he was awarded the President's Medal of Science, a distinction still somewhat rare among behavioral scientists. Miller received the American Psychological Foundation's Gold Medal in 1975.

A member of the National Academy of Science, Miller has served as president of the Eastern Psychological Association (1952–1953) and the American Psychological Association (1960–1961). In 1979 Miller was instrumental in inviting a representative from China to the APA's 87th annual meeting, and in 1980 he chaired the first official delegation of American psychologists to China. At the invitation of the Chinese Academy of Science's Institute of Psychology, the five-member delegation visited Beijing, Beijing Normal, and Shanghai Universities as well as other schools and institutions.

Miller's current research emphasizes biofeedback and behavioral medicine. He is particularly interested in stress and visceral learning.

ticular sets of habits that may characterize a person. Their concern is with understanding the *process* of learning, not its acquisitions. They do note, however, that for the human being an important class of habits is elicited by verbal stimuli, or words—the person's own or others'—and that responses are also frequently verbal in nature.

Miller and Dollard also consider secondary drives, such as the rat's fear of the buzzer, to be relatively stable portions of personality. Such drives often persist, as we saw, despite conditions that one might expect would bring about their extinction (absence of shock). Primary drives and innate S–R connections also contribute to the structure of personality. These latter phenomena, however, are generally less significant than habits and secondary drives, for they define only people's commonalities, not what makes a person unique.

DYNAMICS OF PERSONALITY

Miller and Dollard are very clearly concerned with motivation, or drive. They are not interested, however, in describing or classifying specific motives. They have focused on certain salient motives, such as anxiety, and in analyzing the development and elaboration of these, they attempt to illustrate the general process that presumably operates for all motives.

In human beings a great number of acquired, or secondary, drives eventually make their appearance, based on primary drives like hunger, thirst, and sex. "These learned drives . . . serve as a facade behind which the functions of the underlying innate drives are hidden" (Dollard and Miller, 1950, pp. 31–32). In fact, in modern Western society, the importance of primary drives is not often clear from casual observation of the socialized adult. Instead, what we see are the effects of such acquired drives as anxiety, shame, and the desire to please. It is only in the process of development or in periods of crisis that we see clearly the operation of primary drives.

Dollard and Miller go on to point out that not only are primary drives replaced by secondary ones; primary rewards are also replaced by secondary ones. For example, a parent's smile, by virtue of its being associated repeatedly with activities such as feeding, diapering, and other comfort-bringing activities becomes a powerful secondary reward for the infant.

It is important to note that the capacity of secondary reward to reinforce behavior is not sustained indefinitely. Unless secondary rewards occur on occasion in conjunction with primary reinforcement, they will cease to be effective. We will return to this idea in the next section.

DEVELOPMENT OF PERSONALITY

Miller and Dollard are among the personality theorists who find the transformation of the simple infant into the complex adult a fascinating process, and the bulk of their work has been concerned with developmental issues. In this section, we will see how psychoanalytic principles and the principles of formal learning theory come together to produce a theory of normal development. Later, we will see how the same basic processes can bring about neurotic personality development.

INNATE EQUIPMENT: SIMPLE RESPONSE AND PRIMARY DRIVE

The infant has a small number of **specific reflexes**, which are mostly distinctive responses to specific stimuli or classes of stimuli. For example, touching an infant's cheek typically causes the infant to turn its head in the direction of that cheek; this response is called the **rooting reflex**.

The infant also has a number of **innate hierarchies of response**, or tendencies for certain responses to appear in particular stimulus situations before certain other responses. For example, the infant tends to try to escape from an unpleasant stimulus before it cries.

Finally, the infant has a set of **primary drives**, or strong and persistent internal stimuli, that are usually linked to known physiological processes. These drives—for example, hunger, thirst, and pain—motivate the organism to act but do not determine what specific acts it will perform.

Given this initially rather limited repertoire, Miller and Dollard invoke learning principles to explain a number of phenomena: how the organism extends initial responses to new stimulus situations, how it develops new responses, how it eliminates old responses, and how it establishes new motives or drives.

A MODEL FOR DEVELOPMENT: SECONDARY DRIVE AND THE LEARNING PROCESS

Let us return now to the experiment described at the beginning of the chapter. This experiment (patterned after such pioneering studies as Miller, 1948, and Brown and Jacobs, 1949) illustrated the acquisition of a fear response through classical conditioning and the subsequent instrumental learning of particular behavioral responses, such as hurdle-jumping or lever-pressing, mediated by the learned drive of fear.

In addition to illustrating how the secondary drive of fear, or anxiety, is learned, our experiment demonstrates the operation of the four essential components of the learning process postulated by Miller and Dollard: drive, cue, response, and reinforcement (reward). We will review some elements of the experiment before discussing these four components in detail.

To begin with, in describing the experiment, we spoke only of one rat. Actually, in carrying out such an experiment, we would subject a number of rats to the procedures described. And we would assemble a group of control rats, each of whom would be placed in the box, like the experimental rats, but who would *not* experience shock. The buzzer would be sounded for these control rats so as to demonstrate that the simple buzzer, or buzzer-without-shock, had no particular effect. We would want to demonstrate, that is, that it was the learned drive of fear, acquired in response to the buzzer-with-shock, that stimulated the rats to learn hurdle-jumping and lever-pressing, behaviors that were rewarded with cessation of shock.

As predicted, the control rats would presumably show no systematic changes in their behavior in any of the experimental sessions. It would thus be clear that as a result of the buzzer–shock pairings, the experimental subjects would have learned responses that the control subjects would not have learned.

CLASSICAL CONDITIONING OF A FEAR RESPONSE. What has happened in our hypothetical experiment? As we said earlier, several kinds of learning have occurred. First, through **classical conditioning**, the rats have learned to fear the buzzer. The initially neutral buzzer was paired with the **unconditioned stimulus (US)** of shock, which regularly elicits a characteristic behavior pattern, called the **unconditioned response (UR)**. After the neutral buzzer was presented with the US a number of times, the neutral stimulus presented by itself came to elicit the response elicited by the US (or a very similar response); the neutral stimulus is now called the **conditioned stimulus (CS)**, and the response to it is called the **conditioned response (CR)**. The rat eventually responded with the anticipation of pain, or fear (CR), at the sound of the buzzer (CS), whether or not shock was presented.

In our experiment, the UR of pain and distress—which we infer from behaviors such as squeaking and shivering—gets transformed into the CR of fear as follows: the shock elicits a number of internal responses that are associated with pain (symbolized by "r_{emot}"), and these internal responses then give rise to an internal pattern of stimuli. These internal stimuli, like external stimuli, have the capacity to set off or "cue" still further responses; thus they are called **drive stimuli** (s_D). These drive stimuli set off the observable, external behaviors of the rat (squeaking and shivering, symbolized by "R_{emot}") that we have already described.

Now when the buzzer alone comes to elicit this same (or practically the same) sequence, the sequence is called the conditioned response (CR). The internal drive stimuli, because they are elicited by a learned response (r_{emot} is now occurring to a previously neutral stimulus), are considered to constitute a **secondary** or **learned drive**, which is called fear or anxiety.

What does it mean to say that a response—here, the response of fear—has been learned? In Miller and Dollard's—and Hull's—terms, a **habit**, a link between a stimulus (buzzer) and a response (r_{emot}), has been established. Now in Hull–Spence theory, in order for a habit to be established, not only must a stimulus and a response occur close to each other in space and time, but the response must be accompanied by a reinforcement, or reward. If this latter condition is met, the more often the stimulus and response occur together, the stronger the habit will become. In the next section, we discuss the important feature of reinforcement.

LEARNING AND EXTINCTION OF INSTRUMENTAL BEHAVIOR.   The rats in our experiment learned a good deal more than fear reactions. They learned to jump over a hurdle as soon as they heard a buzzer, and then they learned to press a lever in order to terminate that buzzer when hurdle-jumping was no longer effective in accomplishing that end. These two responses—hurdle-jumping and lever-pressing—are instances of **instrumental learning** (Skinner calls this ''operant conditioning'') because the responses are instrumental in producing a reinforcing event, that is, the cessation of buzzer–shock.

Recall that at the first presentation of buzzer–shock the rats squeaked and shivered. Why were none of these responses learned? Why only hurdle-jumping? Because only the latter was followed by **reinforcement**—cessation of shock. Although there are exceptions, events that reduce or eliminate drive stimuli typically increase the probability that any response they regularly accompany will appear; such events are, therefore, called reinforcers. Conversely, responses unaccompanied by events that reduce drive stimuli tend not to be repeated.

Now when we discontinued the shock and administered only the buzzer, we might have expected the response of hurdle-jumping—and theoretically the internal emotional sequence $(r_{emot} \rightarrow s_D)$ to discontinue or extinguish. If the reinforcement, which consisted of the cessation of the buzzer–shock, no longer occurred, the response that brought about such reinforcement should fade away. But it did not. Miller suggests that this failure of the response to extinguish is caused by the fact that the response actually *does* continue to be reinforced. The buzzer (CS) now elicits the learned fear sequence, and it is the latter that activates the instrumental response of hurdle-jumping. That response turns off the buzzer, thus reducing the intensity of the drive stimuli associated with fear. So the classically conditioned fear reaction and the instrumental hurdle-jumping both continue to be reinforced.

Extinction of the hurdle-jumping response did occur, however, when the response was no longer effective in stopping the buzzer and the fear it elicited. Still impelled by fear, the rats learned the new response of lever-pressing, which did turn off the buzzer. We will have more to say about the process of extinction in a little while.

Drive. A **drive** is a strong stimulus that impels action but does not determine the nature of that action. In our experiment, for example, the drive of pain impelled the rat to do *something* but did not specify *what* it would do. The latter function is performed by a "cue," as we will see in just a moment.

The strength of a drive depends on the intensity of the stimulus that arouses it. The stronger the drive, the more vigorous or persistent the behavior it produces. Suppose that in our experiment we had delivered only a mild shock to the rat: its efforts to escape a relatively painless stimulus might not be very vigorous. On the other hand, if we used a very strong shock, the rat's activity might become frantic.

Secondary, or learned, drives are acquired on the basis of the primary drives. In our experiment, the fear drive was built on the pain drive. Once acquired, learned drives motivate the learning of new responses just as primary drives do.

Secondary drive strength depends on the intensity of the primary drive on which it is built and on the number of reinforced trials involved in its acquisition. Again, in our experiment, if we used a very mild shock and a small number of trials, our rat would develop a much weaker fear of the buzzer than if we used a very strong shock and a long series of trials.

Cue. A **cue** is a stimulus that determines the exact nature of a response. Our rat's hurdle-jumping was responsive to several cues. Once the rat had been conditioned to respond to the buzzer as to the shock, the buzzer acquired a cue function. And once the responses of hurdle-jumping and, later, lever-pressing had been reinforced, the sight of the hurdle or of the lever served as a cue.

Cues may vary in kind or in intensity. Thus, for example, there are visual cues and auditory cues, of varying strengths. There are weak flashes of light and blinding ones, there are gentle bells and clanging ones. Although variation in kind generally provides a more distinctive cue than does variation in intensity, people do respond differently to stimuli of varying strengths. For example, you may turn your face to the morning sun but in the glare of noon put on sunglasses or go indoors. And stimuli may operate as cues not only singly but in combination: cue function may depend on a pattern of stimuli. For example, two songs may be made up of exactly the same notes yet be totally different because of the order in which the notes are played.

Response.   A **response** is simply any activity in which an organism engages. According to Dollard and Miller, before a response can be linked to a stimulus, that response must occur. For example, a child cannot begin to learn to read words until she actually starts trying to read; a person in therapy who is so afraid of other people that he cannot assert his own needs cannot learn to be assertive until he actually makes an assertive response.

In any given situation, certain responses are more likely to appear than others; this original order of preference is called the **initial hierarchy of response**. Learning may alter the individual's behavior and lead to a **resultant hierarchy**, which is usually more effective in obtaining desired goals. For example, Dollard and Miller asked a child to find a piece of candy hidden in a bookcase under a particular book. On her first try the child looked under more than 30 books, asked a number of questions, and engaged in various other behaviors before she located the candy. On successive trials the child made fewer and fewer wrong responses, until finally at the end of the experiment the response of looking under the correct book became the first, or dominant, response in her resultant hierarchy.

Reinforcement.   For learning to take place, Dollard and Miller say, reinforcement (reward) must occur, and reinforcement is best defined as drive reduction. Experiments typically demonstrate that the events that follow a response are very important to the fate of a stimulus–response connection. Miller and Dollard have proposed the drive-reduction hypothesis to explain why a given stimulus has reinforcing effects. In its ''weak'' form, this hypothesis states that an event that results in a sudden reduction in drive stimuli reinforces any response it accompanies; such an event is a *sufficient* condition for reinforcement. In its ''strong'' form, the hypothesis states that all reward is produced this way; drive reduction is not only a sufficient but a *necessary* condition for reinforcement (Miller, 1959). The drive-reduction hypothesis has generated a great deal of controversy, and Miller himself has questioned its ultimate correctness.

Sometimes no response an individual makes in a situation is successful, or a response that has been successful is no longer reinforced. Such **learning dilemmas**, Miller and Dollard suggest, lead to the extinction, or disappearance, of ineffective behavior and to the development of new responses. In our experiment, the rat stopped jumping the hurdle when that response was no longer reinforced and learned to press a lever instead. Miller and Dollard point out that if old

Reinforcement, or reward, is of great importance in Dollard and Miller's learning theory model of behavior. It is only by actually performing the response of riding that this little boy will be rewarded—by his mother's hug or his own feeling of satisfaction— and thus that he will learn to ride his new bike.

responses continued indefinitely to be successful, people would never need to produce new responses and would not learn.

Extinction.   **Extinction** is the disappearance of a particular response when that response is no longer reinforced. The apparent function of extinction is to eliminate unsuccessful responses so that other responses can occur. In our experiment, the hurdle-jumping response did not extinguish even though reinforcement (cessation of shock) had apparently stopped. It was only when hurdle-jumping was no longer successful in reducing the learned drive of fear that the response extinguished and the rat learned a new response.

Actual experiments have suggested that over time an instrumental response that allows a subject to avoid an anxiety-evoking conditioned stimulus may weaken. However, if the conditioned stimulus–unconditioned stimulus pair have been presented frequently during initial training, or if the noxious unconditioned stimulus has been intense, the response often continues over hundreds of trials (Miller, 1948). Fear is apparently such a powerful drive that responses associated with it are very resistant to extinction.

Dollard and Miller compare the rat who continues to fear a harmless event with the anxious human being. If we have seen the initial learning process, there is nothing mysterious about the animal's fear and its efforts to escape; if we could have seen what led to a neurotic person's anxieties, we would understand his or her behavior.

One method of eliminating a persistent response is called **counterconditioning**: a strong response that is incompatible with the first response is conditioned to the original stimulus. In a now famous experiment, Mary Cover Jones (1924) succeeded in getting a child's fear of furry objects to extinguish by gradually bringing a rabbit closer and closer to the child while the child was eating food that he liked. Thus, a response that competes with fear—most people have difficulty eating when they are really frightened—was conditioned to the stimulus of furry objects and became dominant.

Generalization.   **Stimulus generalization**, as we saw in Chapter 13, is the process by which a reinforced response comes to be made to stimuli other than the stimulus to which the response was originally made. The gradient of stimulus generalization states that the degree to which the response will be made varies as a function of stimulus similarity: the more similar the stimuli, the more likely the response. A child, bitten by a large black Great Dane, may not be distressed by a tiny white Schnauzer but a medium-sized black and brown German shepherd may terrify him.

By the related principle of **response generalization**, a stimulus comes to elicit not only the response that has typically followed it but a number of similar responses. For example, suppose that a child, intensely angry at her father for forbidding some much-desired activity, throws a tantrum. Her father punishes her severely. The next time her father scolds her, she is afraid to express her anger openly, but she may allow herself to look angry or to slam the door.

Generalization gradients depend not only on how similar new stimuli and responses are to old ones but on how much original learning took place and how intense the drives that underlie responses are. Generalization can be counteracted by **stimulus discrimination**. Suppose we varied the loudness of the buzzer presented to the rat. At first, the rat might jump the hurdle in response to buzzer intensities that were very close to the intensity of the original, thus exhibiting stimulus generalization. But if we continued to administer shock only with the buzzer of original intensity and omitted shock when the intensity was markedly reduced, we might soon have the rat hurdling the fence only in response to a sound that matched the original buzzer's intensity.

HIGHER MENTAL PROCESSES

According to Miller and Dollard, the individual's interactions with the environment are of two varietes. The first type of interaction generally has an immediate effect on the environment and is guided by a single cue or cue situation (for example, automatically braking an automo-

*Gestures, like words are cue-producing responses; their main function is to pro-
duce cues that are part of stimuli patterns leading to other responses. In what looks
like a rather serious discussion, this young couple's gestures seem clearly to have
cued each other.*

bile when one suddenly sees a child dart out into the street). The second type involves **cue-producing responses** that primarily lead the
way to other responses. Cue-producing responses are commonly mediated by a series of internal events we call a ''train of thought'' (for example, seeing a hardware store, remembering something you need,
thinking that you have enough money with you, and deciding to go
into the store).

''Language is the human example par excellence of a cue-producing response,'' say Dollard and Miller (1950, p. 122). Spoken language, thoughts, written words, and gestures all serve as cue-producing responses. Many such responses serve as communication to others,
as when you ask a friend to get you a glass of water.

Two of the most important functions of cue-producing responses are generalization and discrimination. By labeling two or
more events in the same way, we increase generalization between
these cue situations. For example, if we label two quite different situations ''threatening,'' say, the approach of a tornado and making a
speech in public, and the emotion we experience in each ''fear,'' it is
likely that we will respond in somewhat similar ways in both situations. On the other hand, if we label two rather similar situations so as
to distinguish them from each other, say, ''dinner with the family''
and ''dinner with guests,'' our behavior may be rather different in
each situation.

We can also make needed distinctions between stimuli. Sociocultural factors generally determine what kinds of distinctions people
will make. For example, the Cook Islanders, in whose economy the coconut plays an important and varied role, have 12 different words and

The sociocultural conditions under which people live determine how they distinguish between stimuli. The Eskimo, for example, whose lives are bound by the snowcovered land they live on, have many different words to describe the nature of snow. For Dollard and Miller, both the principles of learning and the cultural conditions under which learning takes place are important to an understanding of behavior.

phrases for the coconut, each of which describes a different stage in the nut's maturity and other characteristics of the nut.

Dollard and Miller place great emphasis on the role of language in motivation, reward, and foresight. They particularly stress the capacity of words to arouse drives (hearing the diagnosis ''cancer'' can arouse fear) and to reinforce or reassure (calling Melissa a ''good'' child for putting away her toys reinforces her behavior). And words can serve as time-binding mechanisms: we can reinforce present behavior by verbally describing future consequences. Johnny may do his homework on Monday if we remind him that it must be finished if he is to go on the ski trip on Saturday.

Clearly, it is the verbal intervention in the drive–cue–response–reinforcement sequence that makes human behavior so complex. Without words and thoughts to sustain motivation over time, we would be at once less consistent and less flexible in our behavior.

Reasoning, essentially the substitution of internal, cue-producing responses for overt acts, is a much more efficient way of attacking a problem than is overt trial and error. Reasoning shortens the process of choosing an action by enabling us to test alternatives without actually trying them out. And it facilitates planning, a variety of reasoning that emphasizes future action. Anticipatory responses, or responses that occur earlier than they might have in an original sequence, can occur more readily in internal processing than in reality and often crowd out useless acts. For example, if, as you leave the house to run an errand, you remember that the street you ordinarily take is under repair you can select an alternate route instead of starting out and then having to double back.

Language, Dollard and Miller point out, makes possible the transmission of wisdom from the past to the present:

The problem solutions painfully acquired during centuries of trial and error, and by the highest order of creative reasoning by rare geniuses, are preserved and accumulate as a part of the culture. Thus each new generation builds on the discoveries of the past. (Dollard and Miller, 1950, p. 116)

THE SOCIAL CONTEXT

The ability to employ language and other response-produced cues is greatly influenced by the social context in which the person develops. Much of the child's interaction with its environment is concerned with how to produce verbal cues, or the verbal symbols of communication, as well as with how to understand those cues when they are produced by others. Language is a social product, and if the language process is important, the social milieu must also be of significance in the development of personality.

Miller and Dollard (1941) stress the interdependence of the behavioral and sociocultural spheres. They point out that not only does the psychologist provide principles of learning that help the social scientist to account systematically for important cultural events, but the social scientist helps the learning theorist to fit these principles with the actual human experiences that constitute the conditions of learning. Both principles and conditions are essential to a full understanding of human development.

What, for instance, are the mechanisms by which culture is transmitted from one generation to the next? . . . It [must] be that social habits are taught to children by the adults of the culture and learned by children from their elders. The transmission of culture must follow the laws of learning. . . .

If social scientists find the knowledge of learning principles valuable in solving problems in their field, psychologists will find it no less useful to emphasize the conditions under which human learning takes place. . . . No psychologist would venture to predict the behavior of a rat without knowing on what arm of a T-maze the food or the shock is placed. It is no easier to predict the behavior of a human being without knowing the conditions of his "maze," i.e., the structure of his social environment. (Miller and Dollard, 1941, pp. 4–5)

Young boys of the Aboure tribe in Ivory Coast, Africa, learn about their culture from a tribal chief. For Dollard and Miller, both the principles of learning and the cultural conditions under which learning takes place are important to an understanding of behavior.

Miller and Dollard imply that their learning principles apply across cultures. At the same time, they clearly believe that a person's precise behaviors are greatly influenced by the society of which he or she is a member.

CRITICAL TRAINING SITUATIONS

Like psychoanalytic theorists, Dollard and Miller consider the first half-dozen years of life crucial in determining adult behavior. Highly significant for them is the extreme helplessness of the infant. The older child and the adult devise ways of getting out of severely frustrating situations. The infant, however, has very little ability to manipulate the environment and thus is at the mercy of impelling drive stimuli and overwhelming frustrations. The baby has not learned to hope and so to comfort itself; it has not learned to reason and plan and thus to escape present distress by constructing the future. ''Rather, the child is urgently, hopelessly, planlessly impelled, living by moments in eternal pain and then suddenly finding itself bathed in endless bliss. . . . These are the tumultuous circumstances in which severe unconscious mental conflicts can be created'' (Dollard and Miller, 1950, pp. 130–131).

TABLE 14.1   *The Genesis of Emotional Conflict: Critical Training Situations*

TRAINING SITUATION	CONFLICT LEARNED	POSSIBLE OUTCOMES
Feeding	Satisfaction of basic need versus fear, loneliness, helplessness	Apprehensiveness, apathy Fear of being alone, fear of being in the dark Lack of social feeling
Cleanliness	Enjoyment of things pertaining to self versus fear, anger, guilt	Anxiety and guilt about fecal material or anything connected with it Fear of loss of love Anger, defiance, stubbornness Timidity, conformity, feelings of unworthiness
Sexual behavior	Bodily pleasure versus fear, guilt	Repression of sexual thoughts and needs Problems about masturbation Homosexuality "Oedipal" problems, or parental attachments that hamper other heterosexual relations
Anger–aggression	Self-assertion versus disapproval, punishment, rejection	Sibling rivalry Lack of patience and foresight and the ability to comfort itself makes the child angry in frustrating situations "Devious" forms of aggression: gossip, deceit, creating confusion in others If severely inhibited, the person becomes dependent, unable to assert and maintain self; achievement is minimal and autonomy nonexistent

Source: Based on Dollard & Miller (1950, pp. 127–154).
Note: According to Dollard and Miller, many of these conflicts arise early in life because of poor labeling ability. The child whose language development is as yet insufficient has difficulty discriminating situations in which one or another emotion is appropriate.

Among the many demands our culture makes on the developing individual, Dollard and Miller identify four that are particularly likely to produce conflict and emotional disturbance: the feeding situation in infancy; toilet, or cleanliness, training; early sex training; and training in the management of anger and aggression. Noting that Dollard and Miller's analyses of all four of these critical training situations draw greatly on Freud's formulations, we will look briefly at the first—the **feeding situation** (see Table 14.1 for a sketch of the four situations).

Hunger involves some of the first strong drive stimuli the infant experiences. According to Dollard and Miller, the infant's handling of these stimuli provides a model for the way the adult will handle the reduction of other drives later in life. Thus the child who has learned to cry because it finds that this behavior leads to feeding has begun to manipulate its environment actively. The child who must "cry itself out," however, may be learning to react passively to strong drive stimuli. And if children are repeatedly ignored as hunger mounts, they may come to associate only mild hunger stimuli with the intensely painful, overpowering stimuli they have experienced on so many occasions. As a result, they may "overreact" to relatively mild drive stimuli; such stimuli may acquire a secondary drive strength that is equal to very intense drive stimulation.

Dollard and Miller believe that the feeding situation significantly affects future interpersonal relations. If in this first experience of intimacy the child experiences gratifying drive reduction, it will associate pleasure with its mother (or father or other caretaking person). And by generalization, such pleasure will come to be linked with other people also, so that being with others becomes a goal or a secondary reward. But if feeding is accompanied by anger and pain, the child may learn to avoid social interaction.

Harry Harlow's well-known studies of infant monkeys in the late 1950s (see, for example, Harlow, 1958; Harlow and Zimmerman, 1959) challenged Dollard and Miller's analysis. Harlow suggested that body contact is more critical than feeding in the development of the mother–child relationship. Infant rhesus monkeys were reared in isolation from all but two inanimate "mothers." One of these "mothers" was made of wire and held the infants' bottle; the other "mother" was padded with terrycloth and provided a soft, warm, comfortable surface to which the monkey could cling. Harlow found that the monkeys almost completely ignored their "wire" mothers, except during feeding. They behaved toward their terrycloth "mothers" as infant monkeys behave toward real mothers, playing near and clinging to them when frightened (see Fig. 14.2). Moreover, monkeys who had only a wire "mother" experienced many more problems in later social interactions than did monkeys who had also a cloth "mother."

Dollard and Miller themselves note that "if the child is properly held, cared for and played with, the blessed, relaxing quality of these experiences also will attach to those who care for it" (1950, p. 133). Although these investigators may have somewhat underestimated the significance of physical contact with the mother during feeding and may have exaggerated the importance of the reduction of hunger and thirst, it is important to note that Harlow's findings do not challenge the essential form of the Dollard and Miller account of the development of affectional attachments. These findings simply suggest that Dollard and Miller may have incorrectly identified the particular expe-

Figure 14.2   Monkeys and their "mothers." In Harry Harlow's well-known studies, infant rhesus monkeys clung to a cloth "mother" for comfort and security. They ignored a wire "mother," which provided their nourishment, except at feeding times. Even then they often clung to the cloth mother while "nursing" the wire mother.

riences in the mother–child interaction that affect learning—the conditions of learning.

UNCONSCIOUS PROCESSES

Dollard and Miller's theory is quite consistent with psychoanalytic formulations in acknowledging the importance of **unconscious** factors, but these theorists differ from Freud in their account of the origin of such factors. Dollard and Miller divide unconscious contents into what has never been conscious and what, once conscious, is so no longer. The first category includes stimuli, drives, and responses that the infant learns before it can speak and that therefore have no verbal labels. This category also includes some things that people learn nonverbally, such as the details of many motor skills. (Think how hard it can be to give a precise and wholly verbal explanation of how to ride a bicycle or swing a tennis racquet.) It is the second category of unconscious determinants that interests us here, however—that group that, through repression, has become unavailable to consciousness.

   We learn to repress, or to avoid certain thoughts, just as we learn any other response. Because "not thinking" of certain things that frighten us leads to a reduction of fear—and thus to reinforcement—**repression** can become a standard part of our repertoire. Initially, we think of the feared act or event, experience the fear, give up the thought—thus eliminating the fear—and so are reinforced for repression. Eventually, the response of "not thinking" becomes anticipatory. It occurs before we have actually reconstructed the feared thought. Repression also prevents the extinction of feared thoughts because it prevents the fear response from occurring. If a response that has been learned does not occur—and occur in the absence of reinforcement—it cannot extinguish.

The tendency to repression begins early. Children are often punished for using taboo words or even for just saying that they intend to do something their parents forbid. They are sometimes punished just for thinking certain things: parents often infer children's rebellious thoughts from their behavior. And often children are punished long after they have done something forbidden. These and other experiences can lead a child to generalize from a punished act to the thought of the act and thus to repress the thought. Fortunately, human beings learn to discriminate as well as to generalize: a child may also learn that it is all right to think about certain things even though it is not all right to do them.

Consciousness is crucially important, Dollard and Miller say, because verbal labels are so essential to the process of learning. As we have seen, generalization and discrimination are made much more efficient by the use of verbal symbols. If we could not label things we would be forced to operate at a primitive intellectual level. We would be much more concrete and stimulus-bound, and our behavior would far more closely approximate that of the infant or the nonhuman animal, in whom language is minimal or absent.

A MODEL OF CONFLICT

One of Dollard and Miller's best known formulations is their model of **conflict** behavior. No one, no matter how well adjusted, can escape the conflict of varying motives and tendencies, and severe conflicts often underlie the neurotic person's misery and symptoms. According to Dollard and Miller, such conflicts prevent the person from making the responses that normally would reduce high drives. An examination of these investigators' model will help us to understand the dynamics of conflict in both normal behavior and neurotic behavior.

Dollard and Miller (Dollard and Miller, 1950; Miller, 1944; Miller, 1951) make five basic assumptions about conflict behavior. First, a person's tendency to approach a positive goal becomes increasingly stronger the closer the person comes to that goal. This tendency, called the **gradient of approach**, is illustrated in Figure 14.3a.

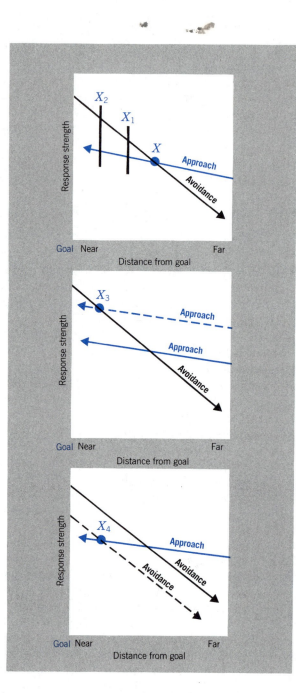

Figure 14.3 Approach–avoidance conflict. See text for discussion.

Second, the tendency to avoid a negative stimulus also becomes increasingly stronger as the person nears that stimulus. This tendency, called the **gradient of avoidance**, is also illustrated in Figure 14.3*a*.

These first two assumptions are derived in part from two, more basic principles: According to the **gradient of reinforcement**, the immediate effects of reward and punishment are greater than the delayed ones; the closer one is to a goal, the more immediate such effects will be. And, according to the principle of **stimulus generalization** (see also page 505), the making of a response to a particular stimulus is a function of the degree of similarity between that stimulus and the original one it resembles; the more similar the stimuli, the more likely the response. Because stimuli in the vicinity of a goal are more likely to possess such similarity than are stimuli at a distance, we can expect that approach or avoidance tendencies will be stronger nearer the goal.

Under their third assumption, Dollard and Miller also postulate that the gradient of avoidance will be steeper than the gradient of approach. That is, the rate at which avoidance tendencies increase as we near a negative stimulus is greater than the rate at which approach tendencies increase as we near a positive stimulus (see Fig. 14.3a).

The fourth assumption states that an increase in drive associated with either approach or avoidance will raise the level of the gradient. That is, increased motivation will cause either the approach or the avoidance tendency to be stronger at any given distance from the goal (see Figs 14.3b and c). Note also that decreasing the drive associated with either tendency will lower that tendency's gradient overall and thus weaken it, also at any distance from the goal (see Fig. 14.3c).

According to Dollard and Miller's fifth assumption, when two responses compete, the stronger will occur. For example, when there is competition between the tendency to approach and the tendency to avoid, it is the net result of the distance of the subject from each goal and the steepness of each gradient that determines which response will occur.

On the basis of these five assumptions, Dollard and Miller predict the ways in which people faced with various types of conflict will respond. The most common type of conflict is that created by the simultaneous occurrence of approach and avoidance tendencies toward the same object or situation. The resolution of such a conflict depends on whether the strength of one or the other tendency can be changed and on what actual moves the person makes.

APPROACH–AVOIDANCE CONFLICT.   Suppose that Bill, a computer systems manager, finds Susan, a colleague, very attractive but is afraid to ask her out because he sees her competence and self-assurance as aggressiveness. He is at point X in Figure 14.3a, where his tendencies to approach and to avoid are in equal balance. One weekend Bill imagines having a date with Susan, and he decides he will ask her out (X_1). But on Monday, when he stops by her office she is involved in a conference with another worker. She seems so poised and in charge that Bill's fear rises (X_2) and he goes back to his office. Until something happens to raise or lower one of Bill's tendencies, he may shuttle back and forth between points X_1 and X_2, unable to act.

Now suppose that Susan is assigned an office next to Bill's. As they begin to interact with one another more, Bill's interest grows; his approach tendency is raised, as he has more rewarded experience with her (see Fig. 14.3b). Now the point of equilibrium between his desire and his fear is much closer to the goal (point X_3). However, at that point, the strength of both tendencies is also much greater, so Bill's conflict is even more intense.

Suppose now that Susan and Bill are assigned to work together on a particular project. Bill finds Susan a good partner. He also observes that at times she is not clear about the next step in their work and asks for his suggestions. As Figure 14.3c shows, Bill's avoidance tendency is now lowered, again with the result that his point of equal pull (X_4) is closer to the goal. But now this point is lower on the strength axis: his fear of Susan has lessened. Bill's approach tendency is now likely to increase, and he will probably ask Susan out.

As this illustration suggests, it is generally easier to get a person to engage in behaviors he or she fears by decreasing an avoidance tendency than it is to try to increase the person's motivation to approach. This is why, Dollard and Miller point out, therapists have typically concentrated on reducing neurotic fears. Note, however, that although Bill's fear of Susan after working on the joint project (X_4) is less intense than his fear after occupying an office near her (X_1), it is still a little stronger than it was originally (X). Any change that produces movement toward a desired yet feared goal will increase the strength of the conflict. Thus a therapist may have to support a person strongly as he or she moves toward the goal.

AVOIDANCE–AVOIDANCE CONFLICT. In a second type of conflict, a person is faced with two competing avoidance responses. Avoiding one feared goal means confronting the other. Typically, the person facing such a conflict vacillates, approaching first one goal and then the other, turning back each time. If the tendency to avoid one goal becomes strong, the point at which the two tendencies conflict will be moved nearer the other feared goal (see Fig. 14.4, points Y_1 and Y_2) and fear of both will be heightened. If one avoidance tendency increases enough so that it is stronger than the other at the goal point, the person will simply continue to withdraw from the most feared goal until he or she is past the point of conflict.

Let us take another example. Suppose that Jessie, who is terrified of climbing but also very afraid of being called a coward, starts to climb a tree. Jessie's fear rises, her foot slips, and she climbs back

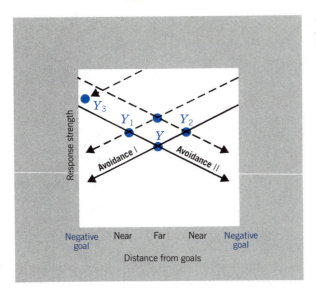

Figure 14.4 Avoidance–avoidance conflict. See text for discussion.

down. Then her friend Sara laughs and called her "chicken." The insult makes Jessie's need to avoid being labeled a coward increase in strength so that her gradient for that tendency is raised. When she starts to climb again, she will get farther up before she reaches the point where the two avoidance tendencies are equal (Y_1) and at which the fear of climbing begins to dominate. Now both tendencies are stronger, however, so Jessie's conflict is greater than before. Similarly, if her fear of climbing increases rather than her fear of being thought a coward, her point of equilibrium will again be at a level of greater intensity (Y_2).

If Jessie's fear of being called a coward intensifies sufficiently— as it may if Sara and she are joined by other friends who increase the pressure on Jessie to be brave—her avoidance tendency will rise to a point at which she will probably climb the tree (Y_3). Conversely, if her fear of climbing were to rise instead, she would probably climb down and accept being called a coward.

APPROACH–APPROACH CONFLICT. Competition between two approach responses is not a real dilemma, say Dollard and Miller. Even if a person begins exactly balanced between two goals, something will happen in this third type of conflict to move him or her toward one of the goals; the person will then continue toward that goal.

Suppose that Charlie has only enough money for one ride at an amusement park. He gets in line to buy a ticket for the roller coaster and then sees the parachute jump. Now he's in a quandary (point Z in Fig. 14.5). He may try to get more money from his parents, but unless

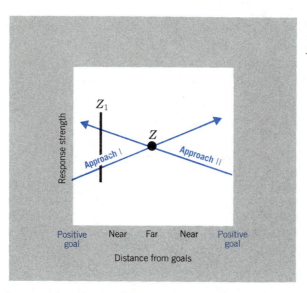

Figure 14.5 Approach–approach conflict. See text for discussion.

that works, eventually he will make a choice. Perhaps the delighted screams of horror from the roller coaster will make him take a step in that direction—he will move from point Z to Z_1. Once started, he will continue, for there is no negative gradient to stop him.

The Dollard and Miller conflict model has had considerable appeal to learning psychologists and personality theorists. In addition, clinical psychologists and other therapists have been attracted to these investigators' analysis of conflict because, as the next section indicates, it suggests intervention strategies.

NEUROTIC PERSONALITY DEVELOPMENT

Dollard and Miller's psychoanalytic orientation leads them to devote considerable attention to the development of neuroses and to methods of psychotherapy. Like a number of theorists, they see normal and neurotic behavior as occurring on a continuum rather than as distinct entities. Thus, neurotic behavior, for Dollard and Miller, is determined by the same learning principles that govern normal growth.

HOW NEUROSES ARE LEARNED

The core of every neurosis is a strong unconscious conflict that almost always originates in childhood. Often during one of the four critical training situations, children develop intense anxiety or guilt about the expression of basic needs, forming conflicts that continue into adulthood.

Just as the laboratory animal learns an instrumental response that allows it to escape a feared stimulus, so the human being may learn a response—such as repression—that permits escape from feelings of anxiety and guilt. But by "not thinking" about things, people prevent themselves from bringing problem-solving abilities to bear on conflicts and from recognizing that the conditions that created the conflicts are gone. For example, the woman whose parents threatened her, when she was a child, with loss of love whenever she showed anger may completely inhibit aggressive impulses. As a result, she may never discover that such feelings sometimes do require expression or that she need no longer submit to her parents. As long as conflicts remain unconscious, they are likely to continue (recall that something must occur in consciousness if it is to extinguish) and to produce **symptoms**—specific sensations or behaviors that the person experiences as unpleasant and not normal.

Symptoms often allow people temporary escape from fears and anxieties: "The symptoms do not solve the basic conflict, . . . but they mitigate it. . . . When a successful symptom occurs, it is reinforced because it reduces neurotic misery. The symptom is thus learned as a 'habit'" (Dollard and Miller, 1950, p. 15).

To understand Dollard and Miller's conception of the relationships among conflict, repression, symptoms, and reinforcement, let us look at some highlights from their "Case of Mrs. A":

Mrs. A, an attractive, twenty-three-year-old woman, consulted a psychiatrist when her many fears and phobias had led her to think she might be "going crazy." Mrs. A's most intense fear was that her heart would stop if she did not count its beats. In addition, she became anxious in public places and was increasingly fearful of leaving her apartment alone.

The therapist soon realized that Mrs. A's most severe conflict *concerned sex. Mrs. A had been raised by a foster mother whose training with respect to sexual matters was inflexible. Mrs. A grew up with so much guilt and anxiety that she repressed her strong sexual desires. Her foster brother had seduced her when she was 10 or 12, and she had had a number of other sexual encounters before marrying. Now she described sex as dirty and disgusting and was extremely shy in sexual activity with her husband.*

Analysis revealed that Mrs. A's phobic reaction to public places reflected fear and guilt over the possibility that she would be tempted to succumb to a sexual approach. Any stimulus with sexual connotations—including her own thoughts— would arouse her anxiety, but she could control that anxiety by counting her heartbeats, by staying at home, or by insisting that others accompany her. One or the other of these measures made her "feel better." Thus the habits—her symptoms—were reinforced by anxiety reduction. (Adapted from Dollard and Miller, 1950, pp. 17-22.)

Mrs. A's symptoms are seen here as learned behaviors. Now let us look at the way Dollard and Miller propose to help people change such behaviors by "unlearning" them.

PSYCHOTHERAPY

If neurotic behavior is learned, it should be unlearned by some combination of the principles by which it was taught. . . . Psychotherapy establishes a set of conditions by which neurotic habits may be unlearned and nonneurotic habits learned. . . . The therapist [acts] as a kind of teacher and the patient as a learner. (Dollard and Miller, 1950, pp. 7–8)

Despite some terminological differences, Dollard and Miller propose conventional therapeutic conditions and procedures: a sympathetic and permissive therapist encourages a patient to free associate and to express feelings. The therapist then tries to help the patient understand his or her feelings and how they developed. By way of contrast, consider the work of Joseph Wolpe, discussed in Box 14.3. Wolpe, also influenced by Pavlov and Hull, has evolved a learning model of behavior that specifically rejects psychoanalytic formulations.

Dollard and Miller's most novel contribution is their learning theory analysis of what occurs in relatively traditional psychotherapy. In the following paragraphs, brackets enclose examples taken from Mrs. A's story.

In the person who seeks therapy, Dollard and Miller suggest, anxiety and guilt have not extinguished because the person has developed techniques for avoiding anything that stirs up these emotions.

[Mrs. A avoided anxiety by counting her heartbeats and other means.]

Thus the therapist tries to set conditions that will lead to extinction of these troublesome emotions. The person is encouraged to express prohibited thoughts and emotions and to experience the fear and guilt they evoke. In the therapy situation, the feared consequences do not occur. Thus fear is lessened and repression need not be performed. Without reinforcement, fear gradually extinguishes.

At first the patient tends to discuss only moderately distressing problems.

[Although Mrs. A's therapist consistently encouraged her to say whatever came to her mind, for a long time she avoided topics that touched on her fundamental problems.]

But as the anxiety and guilt associated with these problems fades, the extinction effect generalizes to other, more disturbing problems, making it easier for the person to confront them.

[After telling of minor childhood scrapes, without being condemned by the therapist, Mrs. A was able to disclose her seduction by her foster brother.]

BOX 14.3   The Learning Theory Model of Joseph Wolpe

Joseph Wolpe (1915–   ), a psychiatrist and clinician, is one of the staunchest and best-known proponents of a learning theory model of behavior. Concerned principally with the treatment of behavioral problems, Wolpe has not written a great deal on the "normal" individual. He is interested in how maladaptive behaviors are acquired and, particularly, in how they may be altered.

Wolpe obtained his M.D. in 1948 from the University of Witwatersrand in South Africa, and until 1959 he lectured in psychiatry at the university, conducted research, and maintained a private clinical practice. After a year's research and study at the Center for Advanced Study in the Behavioral Sciences, in Stanford, California, Wolpe became professor of psychiatry at the University of Virginia Medical School in 1960. Five years later he accepted a professorship at Temple University's medical school, where he has remained.

For Wolpe, almost all behavior is learned. Some behavior, such as that of the developmentally disabled, is constitutionally determined, but in general, all that is needed for maladaptive behavior to occur, Wolpe says, is the pairing, on one or more occasions, of an initially neutral stimulus with a physically or psychologically painful event. Unlike Dollard and Miller, Wolpe does not call upon unconscious conflict or ego defenses to explain neurotic behavior.

CHANGING BEHAVIOR

If behavior is learned, then presumably it can be unlearned. For example, anxiety in social situations, or shyness, is for Wolpe a learned response that can be overcome by certain kinds of training. Even some behaviors that are not learned, Wolpe points out, can be unlearned. For instance, the self-mutilating autistic child can be taught not to bang his head against the wall or to scratch and tear his skin.

The methods by which Wolpe treats maladaptive behaviors, whether these behaviors are learned or constitutionally predisposed, constitute what is broadly known as behavior therapy. Such therapy concentrates on behavior itself rather than on presumed underlying causes. According to Wolpe, although occasionally patients are unaware of their "wrong habits of thought," much more commonly, anxiety is "triggered by situations that the patient *knows* to be harmless" (1978, p. 443).

Wolpe hypothesized that "if a response antagonistic to anxiety can be made to occur in the presence of anxiety-evoking stimuli so that it is accompanied by a complete or partial suppression of the anxiety responses, the bond between these stimuli and the anxiety responses will be weakened" (1958, p. 71). Wolpe saw this principle as a specific instance of the general principle of **reciprocal inhibition**, which he defines as the situation in which "the elicitation of the response appears to bring about a decrement in the strength of evocation of a simultaneous response" (1958, p. 29).

The response of eating, used successfully in counterconditioning with animals and children, proved not to be antagonistic to the adult anxiety response. Seeking another possible competing response, Wolpe eventually evolved the method for which he has become famous, that of **systematic desensitization**. In this method, a person is first taught relaxation (a response that *is* antagonistic to anxiety) and then enabled gradually to confront and deal with an anxiety-provoking object or situation. Let us suppose that a young woman has come to therapy with a terror of riding on escalators. Whenever she goes anywhere near an escalator, she becomes extremely anxious, experiences heart palpitations, breathes rapidly and shallowly, and so on. Treatment by systematic desensitization goes like this.

First, the person is taught to achieve deep muscle relaxation, or the complete relaxation of the voluntary skeletal muscles.

Next, therapist and patient together construct an **anxiety hierarchy**, which is a list of related situations that arouse emotional discomfort in the person, arranged in order of the amount of anxiety the situations elicit—see Figure 14.6.

The therapy itself then consists of having the person imag-

- Standing on the escalator while it moves
- Stepping onto the escalator
- Walking into the building and approaching the escalator
- Learning that an upcoming meeting will take place on a building's mezzanine, reachable only by escalator
- Hearing about a friend's chance encounter with a mutual friend on a department store escalator
- Reading the word *escalator* in an article on architectural design

Figure 14.6   An anxiety hierarchy. Note that the hierarchy starts, at the bottom, with the least frightening situation and proceeds to the most frightening, at the top.

ine, as vividly as possible, each scene on the hierarchy, while continuing to maintain relaxation. Our young woman would begin with the item lowest on the hierarchy in Figure 14.6—reading the word *escalator*. She would be instructed to stop imagining this situation immediately if she began to feel at all anxious, but she would keep trying with each item until she could picture it for a number of seconds and yet remain completely relaxed. She would then go on to the next item and follow the same procedure, and so on throughout the entire hierarchy.

BEHAVIOR THERAPY VERSUS PSYCHOANALYSIS

Wolpe (1981) claims that psychoanalysis does not work. He contrasts outcome studies of psychoanalysis and behavior therapy, pointing out that the latter show much higher rates of improvement—typically, 80 to 90 percent. The question of the relative efficacy of various psychological treatments is a complex one, and a very active research literature is devoted to

exploring comparisons of treatment modalities. Needless to say, many writers differ with Wolpe on this issue.

According to Wolpe (1981), behavior therapy has been wrongly accused of ignoring people's emotions, of failing to deal with cognitive processes, and of being suitable for only a very limited scope of problems, such as phobias.

Behavior therapy, says Wolpe, most certainly does take account of patients' thoughts and feelings; cognitive processes are in integral part of behavior therapy. The real problem, he maintains, is that there are simply not enough people trained in the proper conduct of behavior therapy. Many clinicians, according to Wolpe, have attempted to use these techniques without proper understanding. In particular, **behavior analysis** is rarely understood or applied. Without this process, which ''identifies and defines the stimulus sources of anxiety and establishes the causal connections between anxiety and any consequences it may have,'' the therapist cannot hope to make

accurate judgments, such as which anxieties are based on autonomic conditioning and which on cognitive errors. ''It is the therapist's skill in conducting this analysis that makes it possible for behavior therapy to succeed in even the most complex neuroses'' (Wolpe, 1981a, p. 162).

Since the late 1950s, many case studies reporting successful outcomes with behavior therapy techniques have been reported in the literature. Numbers of these studies not only confirm that desensitization can be used beneficially in treating many types of problems, but also that, in particular cases, the procedure may be superior to more traditional techniques. The arena of behavior therapy is currently characterized by healthy theoretical debate, and therapists have a number of techniques at their disposal, including systematic desensitization and flooding (see Chapter 13), each of which, singly or in combination, may be particularly useful with different individuals or in different kinds of complaints.

Wolpe has received a number

of awards and honors, including the APA's 1979 Distinguished Scientific Award for the Application of Psychology.

His major works are *Psychotherapy by Reciprocal Inhibition* (1958) and *The Practice of Behavior Therapy* (1982). Since 1969 Wolpe

has edited the *Journal of Behavior Therapy and Experimental Psychiatry*, which publishes experimental studies of behavior therapy.

The person becomes more and more able to face core conflicts and the meaning of symptoms. The therapist encourages the person to use verbal labels that help discriminate between inner fears and outer realities, between childhood and the adult world.

[When the therapist helped Mrs. A to discriminate between her childhood and the present, Mrs. A began to relinquish her dependent attitude and to take responsibility for her own ideas.]

As repressions lift and discriminations are developed, the person becomes able to use higher mental processes to solve problems constructively. Successful ways of behaving reduce fears still further, and symptoms disappear. Positive rewards reinforce new ways of responding, which replace the old symptoms that controlled anxiety.

[By helping Mrs. A label sexual thoughts and feelings and by failing to punish her for them, the therapist encouraged her to work on improving her sexual relationship with her husband. As her relationship improved, Mrs. A's fears decreased, and she became able to go out alone.]

CHARACTERISTIC RESEARCH

Miller and Dollard and their students have carried out a significant amount of empirical research to test derivations from their theory. To illustrate their research, we will examine two types of investigations. The first explores the psychoanalytic concept of displacement, relating it to the phenomenon of stimulus generalization. The second, representing Miller's current focus of attention, explores physiological bases of learning.

STUDIES OF DISPLACEMENT

Displacement is the redirection of impulses that one is prevented—either by external events or by self-imposed strictures—from expressing. Displacement can operate as a defense: one may be afraid to express anger, suppress or repress the emotion, and express it later in a different situation. For example, a woman who is afraid to tell her boss off may go home and start a fight with her husband. Note that in this form of displacement, a second response—usually fear—competes with the original response.

In what is considered an adaptive form of displacement—sometimes called **sublimation**—energies that cannot be expended in their original form are rechanneled. A man who is without a sexual relationship or who chooses to forgo one may displace his sexual energies into a drive for creative achievement, concentrating on his oil painting or building up his electronics business. Here the energy for one drive is displaced to another drive; in the first type of displacement, the energy of the same drive was directed to a different object.

Examining the first type of displacement, Miller and Bugelski (1948) gave a group of young boys who were attending a summer camp some questionnaires that assessed their attitudes toward several minorities. The boys did not know, at the time they filled out the questionnaires, that by doing so they were missing out on a very popular social event. After they completed the questionnaires, the experimenters told them about the event they had missed and then asked them to fill out another set of questionnaires.

What the investigators found was that the boys expressed significantly more negative attitudes toward the minorities *after* they learned about the event they had missed than they did before. In psychoanalytic terms, the investigators interpreted this apparent rise in hostility toward minorities as a displacement of the boys' anger at the researchers for keeping them from the event. In S–R terms, the boys were generalizing a response from one stimulus object (strangers—the experimenters who frustrated them) to another, similar stimulus (strangers—members of the minority groups).

AUTONOMIC NERVOUS SYSTEM LEARNING

Turning to a different area of study, let us look at some of Miller's research on the physiological mechanisms involved in the learning of symptomatic behavior. You will recall that Dollard and Miller saw Mrs. A's neurotic symptoms as learned responses, or habits, that, through psychotherapy, could be "unlearned." There are other symptoms, common in neurotic behavior, that are somatic in nature; for example, the rapid heartbeat often experienced in anxiety states. One does not have to learn to make one's heart beat or to increase or decrease its rate; this function is regulated by the **autonomic nervous system (ANS)**. For many years, it was believed that such autonomic responses were not subject to voluntary control, as are musculoskeletal responses like arm and leg movements, and thus could not be instrumentally conditioned. (In instrumental learning, remember, the organism must make a specific response for reinforcement to occur.)

For some time, Miller and Dollard accepted this traditional

view of psychophysiological, or psychosomatic, symptoms; if they could not be learned, presumably they could not be unlearned. Then, in a series of animal experiments in the 1960s, Miller challenged this view. In one of these experiments, Miller and Banuazizi (1968) monitored two types of internal responses in rats: heart rate and intestinal contractions. To ensure that the rats' responses were mediated by the ANS (and not the musculoskeletal system), the investigators injected the rats with the drug curare, which produces muscular paralysis by preventing motor nerve impulses from causing normal contraction of skeletal muscles. Then they divided the rats into two groups, In the first group, the rats were rewarded each time spontaneous intestinal contractions above or below a certain amplitude occurred. The rats exhibited significantly increased or decreased contractions over the training period, but showed no systematic change in heart rate, which was also monitored.

The second group of rats, rewarded for changes in heart rate, exhibited either fast or slow rates spontaneously in the appropriate directions but showed no changes in intestinal contractions. The fact that the conditioning effect in both animal groups was specific to the rewarded response suggests that the response was instrumentally conditioned.

These findings and others raised a number of intriguing possibilities. First, Miller (1969) suggested, it may be that we learn psychophysiological symptoms just as we learn other kinds of symptoms. And if that is so, perhaps instrumental conditioning techniques can be used to lessen the intensity of symptoms like high blood pressure, whether such symptoms were induced by psychological or physiological factors. These suggestions and others have contributed to the growing interest and research in the field of **biofeedback** training— providing a person with information, or "feedback," about some physiological process and reinforcing the person for altering this process.

As he has continued his work in this area, Miller has consistently attempted to demonstrate that what is being conditioned is in fact ANS responding. He points out, however, that although it is important for learning theory to know the answer to this question, we do not really need the answer to apply the principle of biofeedback in the treatment of specific illness.

Research on biofeedback by other investigators has indicated that some people can in fact learn to control their heart rates and other autonomic processes. However, such research has not shown definitively that the procedures can be used successfully with all people. And it has not demonstrated the effectiveness of these procedures in the treatment of actual disease states. Miller himself has had difficulties in replicating his earlier findings (Miller and Dworkin, 1974), and it seems clear that more work is needed in this complicated area.

EVALUATION

Since the early 1940s, several generations of psychologists have carried out a great deal of empirical research applying S–R learning principles to human behavior. This brand of personality theory is supported by a very vigorous group of adherents who are actively concerned with extending and modifying the concepts we have discussed.

Miller and Dollard's theory and research, in particular, has a number of virtues. First, its major concepts are clearly expounded and customarily linked to specific classes of empirical events. Second, it rarely appeals to such vague formulations as intuition; instead, it takes quite a hard-headed, positivist approach. Third, despite this approach, S–R learning theorists are ready to embrace a wide range of empirical phenomena; they show no hesitation about advancing upon highly complex behavioral phenomena with their conceptual tools. Fourth, Miller and Dollard's position specifically and carefully represents the learning process, a crucial consideration for any personality theory, yet one often overlooked or given short shrift. Thus, their theory provides a model for other theoretical positions. Finally, Miller and Dollard have made more explicit use of sociocultural variables than have many other theorists we have discussed. As a result, their theory has been applied—by cultural anthropologists, at least—more widely than has any other personality theory except psychoanalysis.

Within the learning theory camp itself, investigators are divided on the issue of whether to incorporate the hypotheses and speculations of other types of theories such as psychoanalysis. Psychologists like Eysenck, Skinner, and Albert Bandura (see Chapter 15) not only find little necessity to go beyond learning principles but often actively disagree with the views of more traditional theorists. Virtually all learning theorists (except Skinner) stress the necessity for a theory to guide investigations and the need to submit theoretical differences to experimental test. Among personality theorists, those who hold an S–R position tend to have a particularly good sense of the nature and function of theory in an empirical discipline.

S–R theory has been a prime target for the many psychologists who are convinced that an adequate understanding of human behavior must involve more than slavish application of the experimental methods of physical science. Such investigators feel that even though their own positions may not rest on adequately controlled observations, those observations are at least relevant to the matter they propose to study. The bulk of S–R studies, they point out, are concerned with simple, not complex, behavior and are carried out with subhuman animals, not human beings. What is the point, they ask, of doing vigorous, carefully controlled research with the laboratory rat if we then must make a shaky assumption of phylogenetic continuity in order to apply our findings to human behavior?

In a related vein, critics of S–R theory say that the relative formal adequacy of S–R theories is an illusion because it rests on applying the principles within a very limited scope—either to animal behavior or to very restricted domains of human behavior.

Perhaps the most important criticism of S–R approaches is that they do not adequately specify either stimulus or response. Learning theorists have traditionally been concerned with the process of learning; they have not attempted to identify or classify stimuli occurring in the natural environment or the particular responses of organisms.

Miller has remarked, somewhat humorously, that S–R theory might better be called "hyphen theory," because it has more to say about the connection between the stimulus and the response than about either the stimulus or response itself. On a more serious note, it can be argued that if psychologists cannot fully define the stimuli for human behavior and the responses that constitute that behavior, their task has barely begun.

The most frequently voiced criticism of S–R theory points to its simplicity and its insistence on studying behavior in a segmental, fragmented, and atomistic way. Holistic theorists claim that one cannot hope to understand or predict human behavior without considering the organism as a functioning whole and without looking at the patterning of the parts that the S–R theorists examine microscopically.

Finally, some criticize S–R theorists for having neglected language and thought processes. Such critics claim that S–R concepts are inadequate to explain the acquisition and development of complex cognitive functions. As we will see in the next chapter, in recent years theories of language and cognition have been incorporated into some learning theory accounts of personality development.

In many ways, S–R theory is a singularly American theoretical position. It is objective, it emphasizes empirical research, and it is only minimally concerned with the subjective and intuitive side of human behavior. It provides a rather striking contrast to many of the theories that we have discussed, which owe much to European psychology. Undoubtedly S–R theory's toughminded empirical strengths have made and will continue to make unique contributions to the study of personality.

SUMMARY

1. Objective and empirically based, S–R theory is concerned essentially with how human beings acquire and retain new forms of behavior.

2. From its beginnings, in the work of such investigators as Ivan

Pavlov, John Watson, and Edward Thorndike, to its present-day status, S–R theory has embraced a position derived from classical empiricism.

3. Convinced that only an approach integrating the views of the several social sciences could lead to an understanding of human behavior, Neal Miller and John Dollard have combined the learning theory of Clark Hull with psychoanalytic formulations and with knowledge from the fields of sociology and anthropology.

4. In Miller and Dollard's system, relatively enduring aspects of personality include the **habit** and the **secondary drive**.

5. Secondary drive is a crucial component in human motivation. The operation of **primary drives** is rarely seen in modern Western society. Most behavior reflects the operation of acquired drives such as anxiety, shame, and the desire to please.

6. Primary rewards are replaced by **secondary rewards**—like money—that become the reinforcers of most adult behavior.

7. The infant begins life with a repertory of **specific reflexes**, **innate hierarchies of response**, and primary drives.

8. A **drive** is a strong stimulus that impels action. A stimulus that determines the precise nature of such action is called a **cue**. A **response** is any activity in which an organism engages. A **reward** is thought to reduce or eliminate drive stimuli; thus, it **reinforces** any response it accompanies.

9. The secondary drive of fear (anxiety), often learned through **classical conditioning**, serves to motivate the **instrumental learning** of responses that reduce such fear. Responses that are no longer reinforced—that cease to eliminate a fear-producing stimulus—will extinguish and be replaced by new responses that successfully accomplish that goal.

10. Because the learned drive of fear is extremely strong and because, in the continued presence of a conditioned stimulus, this drive will continue to motivate responding, which reinforces the organism, learned emotional responses and instrumental behaviors will tend to persist, even when the original distressing stimulus is no longer present.

11. When a particular response is no longer reinforced, it tends to **extinguish**. Responses linked with the learned drive of fear are very resistant to extinction but may sometimes be eliminated by **counter-conditioning**.

12. By **stimulus generalization**, the organism learns to make the same, or a very similar, response in situations that are more or less like the original stimulus situation. By **response generalization**, the organism learns to make more or less different responses in stimulus situations that are the same or very similar. By **stimulus discrimination**, the organism learns to make appropriate responses in stimulus situations of varying degrees of similarity.

13. Cue-producing responses—in the human being, largely thought, spoken, or written language—facilitate generalization and discrimination. In **reasoning**, internal cue-producing responses are substituted for overt acts; **initial hierarchies of response** are transformed into **resultant hierarchies** more rapidly and efficiently than is possible in overt behavior.

14. Language, a social product, makes possible the transmission of habits (learning) from one generation to the next. Thus, both **language process** and **social milieu** are important in the development of personality.

15. Four **training situations** are critical in personality development: **feeding**, **cleanliness** training, **sex** training, and training in managing **anger and aggression**. For example, the feeding situation can have significant effects on future interpersonal relations; either drive reduction and the associated gratification of the infant or the comfort and security afforded the infant by bodily contact with its mother will tend to make being with others a positive and desirable situation.

16. Conflicts are of three basic types: **approach–avoidance**, **avoidance–avoidance**, and **approach–approach**. According to the **gradient of approach**, the tendency to approach a positive goal becomes increasingly stronger as one nears that goal. According to the **gradient of avoidance**, the tendency to avoid a negative stimulus also grows stronger as one nears that stimulus. The gradient of avoidance is steeper than the gradient of approach; and an increase in a drive may raise the level of the relevant gradient.

17. The core of every neurosis is a strong **unconscious conflict** that most often is learned in one of the four critical training situations of childhood. **Repressed** conflicts produce behaviors (**symptoms**) that persist because they allow temporary escape from fears and thus continue to be reinforced. Neurotic behavior can be unlearned by bringing conflicts into consciousness, where fears can be experienced without harmful consequences. With lessened fear, repression is not needed, and without reinforcement, fear gradually extinguishes.

18. Studies have demonstrated the **displacement** of hostile impulses.

19. Experimentation has shown that people and animals can, to some degree, learn to control the responses of their **autonomic nervous systems**; they can learn to raise or lower heart rate and to increase or decrease the amplitude of intestinal contractions. The field of **biofeedback** offers possibilities for treating specific illness-related problems, such as high blood pressure. Findings in this area are mixed, however, and more research is needed.

20. S–R theory has been criticized for emphasizing simple behaviors, primarily in subhuman animals, and for neglecting complex cognitive functions. Some suggest that because its learning principles can be applied on only a very limited basis, the theory's formal adequacy is illusory. S–R theory is more concerned with the process of learning than with specifying either stimuli or responses. Holistic theorists believe that S–R theory's segmental, atomistic approach cannot inform a true understanding of human behavior.

21. On the other hand, S–R theory, and Miller and Dollard's position in particular, offers a hard-headed, positivist, empirically oriented approach that embraces a wide range of phenomena. The S–R approach has a clear sense of the nature and function of theory in an empirical discipline, and with its emphasis on the learning process, it provides an excellent model for other theoretical positions.

SUGGESTED READING

The student who is interested in exploring the roots of S–R theory may want to read some of Pavlov's, Watson's, or Thorndike's original works; for example, Pavlov's *Conditioned Reflexes* (1927); Watson's *Behaviorism* (1925); or Thorndike's *The Fundamentals of Learning* (1932). Bower and Hilgard, *Theories of Learning* (1981), gives the reader an excellent summary of all the major types of learning theory.

The core of the Miller–Dollard S–R theory of personality is set forth in two books: *Social Learning and Imitation* (Miller and Dollard, 1941) and *Personality and Psychotherapy* (Dollard and Miller, 1950). Miller has summarized much of his experimental work in several handbook chapters, including "Liberalization of Basic S–R Concepts: Extensions to Conflict Behavior, Motivation, and Social Learning" (1959). In addition, in *Neal E. Miller: Selected Papers* (1971), Miller has collected from among his writings those that have most "current relevance, . . . historical significance at the time they were published, and . . . personal appeal to me."

Miller and Dollard collaborated with three other authors—Leonard Doob, O. Hobart Mowrer, and Robert R. Sears—in a famous monograph entitled *Frustration and Aggression* (1939). This was one of the earliest attempts to analyze personality phenomena in terms of S–R learning theory, psychoanalysis, and anthropological evidence. The book led to a host of related studies, although its basic postulate—that aggressive behavior invariably stems from frustration and that frustration always leads to aggression—was highly controversial. This idea has been a useful guideline for research, but it has been shown that many other factors besides frustration contribute to human aggression.

The reader interested in Miller's and other current investigators' work on biofeedback—the instrumental conditioning of bodily processes long thought to be involuntary—may want to look at Jonas, *Visceral Learning: Toward a Science of Self-control* (1973), a book written for the nonprofessional audience. Also, Miller and others have edited a book in this area—Miller, Barber, DiCara, Kamiya, Shapiro, and Stoyva, *Biofeedback and Self-control* (1973)—in which Miller has written an introductory chapter as well as a more technical article on clinical applications.

In his 1983, *Annual Review of Psychology* article on behavioral medicine, Miller has reviewed much of his work of recent years, connecting it with his earlier work with Dollard. Miller has spent more than 50 years as an active researcher, yet, as he turns his energies to the emerging challenges in psychology, his work is distinctly modern.

In addition to his work with Neal Miller, John Dollard wrote a number of books including his well-known *Caste and Class in a Southern Town* (1937), which we have already mentioned; *Children of Bondage* (1940, with Allison Davis); a related study; and *Victory over Fear* (1942) and *Fear in Battle* (1943), two psychological analyses of fear. Dollard's great interest in psychotherapy and its outcomes is reflected in his books, *Steps in Psychotherapy* (1953, with Frank Auld and Alice White) and *Scoring Human Motives* (1959, with Auld).

Chapter fifteen

15.

From a social learning perspective, human nature is characterized as a vast potentiality that can be fashioned by direct and vicarious experience into a variety of forms within biological limits.

ALBERT BANDURA

Helplessness is the psychological state that frequently results when events are uncontrollable.

MARTIN SELIGMAN

Progress in the area of personality psychology and assessment has been hindered by the failure to apply relevant principles about the conditions that produce, maintain, and modify social behavior.

WALTER MISCHEL

Personality as Social Learning: Albert Bandura and Others

Several weeks after being discharged from the hospital, a 35-year-old man consults his physician. When Mr. T. left the hospital he was told that his heart attack had left little permanent damage to the heart muscles and that he should begin gradually to resume his full range of activities—work, his weekly golf game, social events, and sexual relations with his wife. Now, however, Mr. T. is afraid to do any of these things and stays at home most of the time. He is constantly tired and he worries that any acceleration of his heartbeat signals another, this time fatal, heart attack.

The physician explains to Mr. and Mrs. T., who has accompanied her husband, that the physiological recovery of the damaged heart occurs more rapidly than the psychological recovery of the person. The physician recognizes that Mr. T. does not believe in his own physical efficacy; although Mr. T. is physically capable of resuming his normal routines without endangering his health, he does not believe this.

A few weeks later, at a routine follow-up visit, Mr. and Mrs. T. greet the physician warmly. With obvious pleasure, Mr. T. reports how low his golf score is, how well he is functioning at work and at home, and how his social and sexual lives have returned to normal. What has produced such a dramatic change in this man?

Mr. T. has been treated by a psychologist who used social learning techniques to modify Mr. T.'s perceptions of his cardiac robustness by increasing Mr. T.'s information about his physical status. The psychologist enabled Mr. T. to change his **efficacy expectations** by exposing him to four kinds of informative experience that enabled him to alter his perceptions and beliefs and thus to achieve a sense of **self-efficacy**. Mr. T. ran strenuously on a treadmill (**enactive** or **performance experience**). He talked to former cardiac patients who had resumed active life-styles (**vicarious experience**). He talked with his physician and physical therapist, who gave him factual information and encouraged him to engage in his usual activities (**persuasive experience**). And, finally, Mr. T. was taught the meaning of certain physical signs so that he would not misinterpret these events and become frightened: he was taught to distinguish fatigue, stress, and tiredness from the signs of a heart attack (**physiological information experience**). Because recovery from a heart attack is influenced by both interpersonal and individual factors, Mrs. T. underwent the same experience: she ran on the treadmill with her husband, and she participated in the vicarious, persuasive, and physiological components of the treatment as well.

The foregoing approach to changing a person's self-beliefs is a direct outgrowth of Albert Bandura's self-efficacy model of behavior change. As we review Bandura's personality theory, we will learn more about efficacy expectations and about how they can be modified so as to alter human behavior.

Social learning theory, as put forward by Bandura and others, shares two basic premises with other learning theories:

- Human behavior is largely acquired.
- Learning principles are sufficient to account for the development and maintenance of human behavior.

However, social learning theory insists that the social context in which much behavior arises is crucial to understanding such behavior. Moreover, this theory notes, a great deal of important learning occurs vicariously. That is, people often learn to do something simply by observing others do it.

Miller and Dollard (1941), you may recall, explored the role of imitation in learning and personality development, but their idea did not arouse much interest among psychologists. Bundura not only has sought to call others' attention to what he considers a crucial aspect of learning but has greatly extended the analysis of observational learning first undertaken by Miller and Dollard.

In this chapter we focus on the work of Albert Bandura, and we also consider the theory and research of Martin Seligman and Walter Mischel. Mischel, who has been a colleague of Bandura's, was a student of Julian Rotter, whose germinal theory of social learning is discussed in Box 15.1. All four of these theorists—Bandura, Seligman, Mischel, and Rotter—have grounded their concepts and principles firmly in learning theory, but they have also taken account of human beings' cognitive capacites and of our tendency to pursue our daily lives in a social context.

ALBERT BANDURA

For Bandura, although learning principles are sufficient to explain and predict behavior and behavior change, such principles must take ac-

BOX 15.1   Julian Rotter's Social Learning Theory

Julian B. Rotter's theory of personality, first set forth in 1954 in his important book, *Social Learning and Clinical Psychology*, was strongly influenced by such learning theorists as Edward Tolman, Clark Hull, and Edward Thorndike. Rotter's theory, however, included the complex variables of motivation and cognition, and it took into account variation among individuals and among the situations, or environments, in which people exist.

Born in 1916, Rotter was educated at Brooklyn College, where he majored in chemistry. An early interest in psychology kept him reading in that field, however, and eventually he obtained his M.A degree in psychology from the University of Iowa (1938) and his Ph.D. from Indiana University (1941). After serving as a military psychologist in World War II, Rotter joined the faculty at Ohio State University, where, with George Kelly (Chapter 8), he designed and administered the clinical psychology training program. In 1963 Rotter moved to the University of Connecticut to direct another clinical training program. Throughout his career, Rotter has combined the work of clinician, researcher, and author. He has served as president of the Eastern Psychological Association, and he has served on many academic and professional committees.

Rotter describes social learning theory as

a molar theory of personality that attempts to integrate two diverse but significant trends in American psychology—the stimulus–response or reinforcement, theories on the one hand and the cognitive, or field, theories on the other. It is a theory that attempts to deal with the complexity of human behavior without yielding the goal of utilizing operationally definable constructs and empirically testable hypotheses. (Rotter, 1975, p. 57)

Rotter's own theory introduced the new concept of expectancy and focused on three other general classes of variables: behaviors, reinforcements, and psychological situations. Rotter gave a central role to **expectancy**, which is one's belief, or subjective judgment, that in a certain psychological situation a particular behavior will lead to reinforcement.

Rotter is particularly well known among psychologists for having developed three very useful psychometric instruments: the Incomplete Sentences Blank, a scale that measures internal versus external control of reinforcement (often referred to as the "I–E Locus of Control Scale"), and the Interpersonal Trust Scale.

Rotter's Incomplete Sentences Blank (Rotter and Rafferty, 1950; Rotter, 1951) was recently ranked twelfth in a list of assessment devices most widely used in clinical practice. In this test, subjects are asked to complete sentences that begin, for example, as "I like—," "I suffer—," "I wish—," "My father—" (Rotter, 1954, pp. 304, 306). This test is considered a projective device, inasmuch as it assumes that "the subject reflects his own wishes, desires, fears, and attitudes" in the sentences he or she composes, but in general it is most useful in providing information about topics that a subject is able and reasonably willing to discuss. (Rotter, 1951, pp. 295, 309).

Almost a decade ago, Rotter (1975) estimated that the I–E scale had been used in over 600 studies, and the number is considerably higher today. The personality variable that this scale measures—the tendency to attribute control over the events in one's life either to one's own actions or to the actions of other, external forces—has been studied by many researchers in many different settings. Investigators have correlated this variable with measures of other important personality variables, such as achievement motivation and anxiety. Examples of items from the I–E Scale, which subjects mark either true or false, are "People's misfortunes result from the mistakes they make," and "This world is run by the few people in power, and there is not much the little guy can do about it" (Rotter, 1966).

Rotter's (1967, 1971, 1980) Interpersonal Trust Scale has also been used widely in research, but it is as yet not as well known as his other two scales. Sample items from this scale, also answered true or false, are "Parents usually can be relied upon to keep their promises," and "In dealing with strangers, one is better off to be cautious until they have provided evidence they are trustworthy'' (Rotter, 1967, p. 654).

Rotter's work has had a somewhat less direct impact on personality psychology than has the work of some of the other social learning theorists we discuss. The fruits of his work have come to play a very important role, however, both in the clinical setting and in social psychological research.

count of two very important phenomena neglected or rejected by approaches like that of Skinner. First, Bandura proposes, human beings can think and regulate their own behavior; thus they are not simply the pawns of environmental influence. Causality does not reside solely in the environment, for person and environment influence each other.

Second, Bandura points out, many aspects of personality functioning involve the interaction of the person with other people. As a result, an adequate theory of personality must take account of the social contexts in which behavior is originally acquired and in which it is maintained.

Bandura's **social learning theory** of personality, based on the foregoing formulations, ''approaches the explanation of human behavior in terms of a continuous reciprocal interaction between cognitive, behavioral, and environmental determinants'' (Bandura, 1977b, p. vii). By a process Bandura calls **reciprocal determinism** (see Fig. 15.1), people influence their destinies by controlling environmental forces, but they are also controlled by these forces.

As Figure 15.1 indicates, a reciprocal, or mutually interactive process occurs among behavior, the environment, and the person's

Perhaps nowhere do we see more clearly the reciprocal effects of human behavior and environmental forces than in the farmer's way of life.

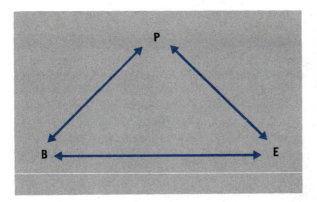

Figure 15.1 Reciprocal determinism. B = *behavior;* P = *the cognitive, perceptual, and other internal events that can affect people's actions;* E = *the external environment.* (Bandura, 1978, p. 345, Fig. 1.)

cognitions, perceptions, and other internal processes. Rather than person (P) and environment (E) causing behavior (B), as in Lewin's (Chapter 8) famous $B = f(P, E)$, any one of these three elements may have a causal influence on the other two. Thus, for example, a person's belief about what she is capable of doing and about what the outcome might be if she were to perform a specific action influences what she does, and her behavior then affects the environment, which, in turn, may alter her expectations. The three factors in each corner of the triangle in Figure 15.1 are interlocking and interdependent.

Another example of reciprocal determinism at work is television-viewing behavior. The potential televised environment, Bandura points out, is the same for everyone, but any individual's actual televised environment depends on what he or she chooses to watch. Viewer preferences, expressed through television ratings, partially determine the future televised environment. However, production costs and other industry requirements also determine what people are shown: the televised environment partly shapes viewer preferences. Thus, says Bandura, "all three factors—viewer preferences, viewing behavior, and televised offerings—reciprocally affect each other" (1978, p. 346).

Reciprocal determinism is a very important concept in Bandura's social learning theory; indeed, it is the cornerstone of Bandura's understanding of behavior: "Social learning theory treats reciprocal determinism as a basic principle for analyzing psychosocial phenomena at varying levels of complexity, ranging from intrapersonal development, to interpersonal behavior, to the interactive functioning of organizational and societal systems" (Bandura, 1978, p. 356).

THE SELF-SYSTEM

With a model like reciprocal determinism, one may feel a bit at sea. If everything is mutually interactive, is there a center, a beginning place,

BOX 15.2   Albert Bandura (1925–   )

Albert Bandura was born in Mundare in northern Alberta, Canada, and spent his elementary and high school years in that small village's one and only school. In 1949, after only 3 years at the University of British Columbia, Bandura was graduated with an award in his major field, psychology. Enrolling in graduate school at the University of Iowa, Bandura studied with Kenneth Spence, who had been an associate, at Yale, of Neal Miller and others. Although Bandura earned his doctorate in clinical psychology (1952), he was much influenced by learning theory approaches to the study of human behavior, and he was impressed with the value of experimentation.

In 1952 Bandura moved, with his wife, Virginia Varns, an instructor at Iowa's School of Nursing, to Wichita, Kansas, to take up a 1-year postdoctoral internship at the Wichita Guidance Center. Then, he was appointed an instructor at Stanford University, where he has since remained. Bandura was awarded the David Starr Jordan Professorship of Social Science in Psychology in 1974, and in 1976–1977 he chaired Stanford's psychology department.

On his arrival at Stanford, Bandura met Robert Sears, who in the 1950s was studying the influence of the family on social behavior and on the processes of identification. Influenced by this work, Bandura began to study the social learning of aggression, in collaboration with Richard Walters, his first doctoral student. In this early research, the role of modeling in human behavior was given special focus, and the efforts of these investigators led to a full program of laboratory research into the determinants and mechanisms of observational learning.

Bandura is active in scientific and professional affairs, having served on numerous advisory boards and panels of the federal government as well as on various committees and commissions of the American Psychological Association. He has served as president both of that association and the Western Psychological Association. He has also served on the editorial boards of about 20 journals, and for a period of 10 years he was series editor on social learning theory for Prentice-Hall.

Bandura has received many honors and awards, including the Distinguished Scientist Award of the APA's Division of Clinical Psychology, the California Psychological Association's Distinguished Scientific Achievement Award, the Distinguished Contribution Award of the International Society for Research on Aggression, and the Distinguished Scientific Contribution Award of the APA. Bandura is a Fellow of the American Academy of Arts and Sciences.

so to speak? Yes there is, says Bandura; this center is the self system.

The **self system** ''is not a psychic agent that controls behavior. Rather, it refers to cognitive structures that provide reference mechanisms and to a set of subfunctions for the perception, evaluation, and regulation of behavior'' (Bandura, 1978, p. 348). Unlike Skinner (Chapter 13), whose theory has no construct of the self, Bandura holds that ''self-generated influences cannot be excised from among the determinants of human behavior without sacrificing considerable ex-

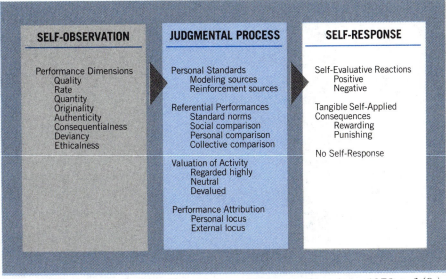

Figure 15.2   Processes in the self-regulation of behavior. (Bandura, 1978, p. 349.)

planatory and predictive power'' (1978, p. 351). Such influences are not automatic or autonomous regulators of behavior, however; they are part of the reciprocal interacting system.

It is one of the functions of the self system to regulate behavior by continuously engaging in self-observation, judgmental processes, and ''self-responses,'' or reactions to one's own behavior (see Fig. 15.2). We may observe ourselves in terms of such factors as quality of performance, originality of thought or work, and so on. We may judge our behavior according to personal standards, in comparison with the behavior of others, and in other ways. Finally, on the basis of our observations and judgments, we may evaluate ourselves positively or negatively, and we may reward or punish ourselves. We develop standards of behavior by observing models such as parents or teachers, by interpreting feedback on our own performances, and by following precepts given us by authority figures. Our evaluation and judgment of ourselves, as well as the consequences we apply to ourselves, also develop out of our experience.

A key component of the self system is **self-efficacy**, which Bandura defines as our self-perception of how well we can function in a given situation. The key to behavioral change, as we saw in the opening paragraphs of this chapter, is the alteration of expectations of personal efficacy. There are two types of expectation. **Efficacy expectations** are convictions that we can successfully execute the behaviors required to produce a particular outcome. For example, a student's ef-

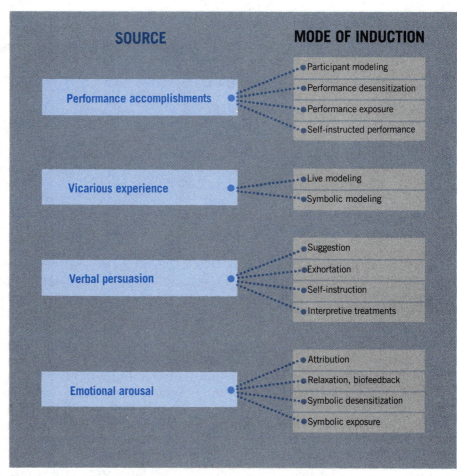

Figure 15.3   Major sources of efficacy information and the principal sources through which different modes of treatment operate. (Bandura, 1977a, p. 195.)

ficacy expectations are high if she has a strong conviction that she can successfully write the computer program for the problem assigned in class. **Outcome expectations** are our estimates that given behaviors will lead to particular outcomes. If the student does write the program, and if it runs on the computer, and if her outcome expectations are realistic, she will expect an ''A'' grade on the assignment. If efficacy expectations are high and outcome expectations are realistic, the person will work hard and will persist until a task is finished.

Efficacy expectations are an important part of coping and adaptive behavior, and Bandura (1977a, 1982) has reported many research studies that show how such expectations influence behaviors in various circumstances. ''Given appropriate skills and adequate incentives,

. . . efficacy expectations are a major determinant of people's choice of activities, how much effort they will expend, and how long they will sustain effort in dealing with stressful situations'' (Bandura, 1977a, p. 194).

A number of factors influence efficacy expectations. Recall Mr. T. Four different approaches were taken by Mr. T.'s treatment team (his physician, his psychologist, and his physical therapist) in promoting his sense of personal efficacy so as to change his expectations and enable him to cope more adaptively with his post-heart-attack status. The four primary sources of information about efficacy, as well as methods of transmitting such information, are indicated in Fig. 15.3. You can undoubtedly pick out, from among the various procedures listed in the right-hand column, the specific techniques that were used to help Mr. T.

Bandura and his colleagues have reported many experiments that demonstrate the effectiveness of changing personal efficacy expectations as a way of modifying behavior (see Bandura, 1982). In one experiment, when self-efficacy beliefs in severe agoraphobics (people who dread open spaces) were increased, there was a corresponding increase in the actual performance of such tasks as leaving the house alone and going shopping and to a restaurant by oneself (Bandura, Adams, Hardy, and Howells, 1980). Bandura (1982) has also offered some ideas about how to improve collective, or group, efficacy and about how group efficacy can lead to broad social change.

WHAT MOTIVATES HUMAN BEINGS?

Motivation, for Bandura, is a cognitive construct, and it has two sources. First, the "representation of future outcomes" can "generate current motivators of behavior" (Bandura, 1977a, p. 193). That is, the anticipation of future reinforcement motivates one to behave in one way or another.

Second, by setting goals, or desired levels of performance, and then evaluating their performance, people are motivated to perform at particular levels. An experiment reported by Bandura and Schunk (1981) showed that children who were deficient in mathematical skill were more likely to improve their performance when they set and strove to achieve a series of subgoals that led to immediate self-evaluation than when the goals were more distant and took longer to reach. Thus, continually perceiving, thinking about, and judging our behavior provides "self-incentives" to persist in achieving predetermined standards.

Like other learning theorists, Bandura sees reinforcement as the "cause" of learning. However, Bandura qualifies this statement in several ways. Not only can we learn by observing someone else, rather

Learning certain standards of dress is part of this young boy's socialization.

than perform the behavior in question ourselves; we can learn by **vicarious** reinforcement, and we can learn without any reinforcement at all. This acquisition of learning, however, may not always lead to performance. The crucial element, Bandura claims, is expectation.

Performance, Bandura suggests, is brought about not by reinforcement per se but by the **expectation of reinforcement**. By noting how others are rewarded or punished for their actions, we develop cognitive expectations about behavioral outcomes and about what we must do to achieve desirable outcomes or to avoid undesirable ones. Thus reinforcement comes to guide behavior primarily through the anticipation of its future occurrence.

We also develop expectations about future reinforcement from noting the consequences of our own behaviors. Through interaction with parents, peers, and other socializing agents—people who reward and punish—we develop personal standards of behavior, which generally reflect those of the socializing agents. We then come to reward and punish our own behavior, by **self-approval** or **self-criticism**, just as others have rewarded and punished us. And it is our anticipation of such self-approval or self-criticism that very largely guides our behavior. It is also in this way that our behavior achieves consistency; we do not change our behaviors constantly, "like a weathervane," every time a social influence changes.

In a study that supports these propositions, Kanfer and Marston (1963) found some suggestion that people who as children are praised and admired for relatively low levels of accomplishment may grow up to administer self-rewards more generously than people who are held to higher standards of excellence. And apparently self-evaluative standards can be acquired by simply observing others. Bandura and Kupers (1964) had children watch a model who set either a high or a low standard of achievement for self-reward. When the children were later observed performing the same task that they had watched, it was observed that those who had watched the model who set low standards rewarded themselves more indulgently than did those who watched the model who set higher standards.

Bandura's social learning theory places considerable emphasis on observational learning. Whether a child or adult will learn by observation depends, from the social learning theory perspective, on whether the observer has attended to and accurately perceived what the model did, remembered it correctly, and transferred the coded memory into new responses, and on whether the observer is sufficiently motivated to perform (anticipates reinforcement for performing) the model's acts.

LEARNING BY OBSERVATION: THE DEVELOPMENT OF BEHAVIOR

For Bandura, much learning occurs without any actual reinforcement. In a well-known study, Bandura (Bandura, Ross, and Ross, 1961) showed not only that children can learn novel responses merely by watching others, but that children can learn such responses without having had the chance to make them themselves and even when the model they observe receives no reinforcement for the response.

LEARNING NOVEL RESPONSES.   A group of nursery children, tested one at a time, watched an adult model perform a series of aggressive acts, both physical and verbal, toward a large inflated rubber doll (see Fig. 15.4). Another group of children—again, one at a time—watched an adult model who sat quietly in the experimental room, paying no particular attention to the doll. Then each child was subjected to mild frustration and placed in the room, alone, with the doll he or she had seen before.

The behavior of each group of children tended to conform to the behavior of the particular adult model the group had observed: the children who had watched the adult behave aggressively toward the doll tended to perform more aggressive acts toward the doll than did either the children who had watched the adult sit quietly or a group of control children, who saw no model. As a matter of fact, the children

Figure 15.4   After watching a film of the female model pictured here and then being subjected to mild frustration, these children reproduced the model's behavior almost exactly. It is this kind of finding that fuels the continuing concern over the effect on children of television violence.

who had watched the adult sit quietly made even fewer aggressive responses than did the control subjects.

The lesson here, according to Bandura, is that the performance of novel responses on the basis solely of having watched someone else perform them is made possible by the human being's cognitive abilities. The stimuli provided by the model's actual behavior are transformed into mental images—of what the model did or looked like—and even more important, into verbal symbols that can be recalled later.

These symbolic, **cognitive skills** also allow people to transform what they have learned or combine what they observe in a number of situations into new patterns of behavior. They can then develop novel, innovative behaviors instead of simply imitating what they have seen. For example, a little boy may have observed that when his mother is angry she refrains from expressing her anger and speaks very slowly and in an especially low voice. He may also have observed that when his father gets angry, he makes critical, sarcastic remarks in a very loud tone of voice. When this little boy becomes angry, he may express himself by combining the behaviors that his parents have modeled to produce an expression that is his own. Thus, he may bring his little sister to tears by ridiculing her in a very quiet voice.

OTHER EFFECTS OF MODELING.   Modeling behavior may have effects other than the learning of novel behavior. First, a model's behavior may draw out responses that are already in the observer's repertoire. This sort of effect is particularly likely when the behavior modeled is socially acceptable. For example, suppose that a teenager who frequently runs errands for her grandmother watches an adult help an elderly person cross the street. Watching this model may reinforce the young person's tendency to perform helping behaviors in future.

Second, models who perform behaviors that may or may not be in the observer's repertoire and that are socially unacceptable, or deviant, may also influence observers. Depending on whether the model is rewarded or punished, observers' inhibitions about performing a behavior may be either strengthened or weakened. Rosekrans and Hartup (1967), for example, showed that children who watched a model's aggressive behavior consistently being rewarded later displayed a high degree of imitative aggression, whereas children who saw the same behavior consistently punished showed practically no imitative behavior.

SYMBOLIC MODELING. In present-day society, of course, much of the modeling of behavior takes place in symbolic form. Movies and television present innumerable instances of behavior that may influence observers. And, in fact, such presentations are potent sources of modeled behavior. Bandura, Ross, and Ross (1963a) found that live models, movies, and even animated cartoons were equally likely to bring about imitative behavior in the child who watched them.

IMPORTANT FACTORS IN LEARNING. Of course, just watching someone else do something does not necessarily enable one to learn that response or, having learned it, to perform it in an appropriate situation. A very important factor in learning is **attention**: the observer must attend carefully to the cues provided by the model. What induces someone to attend to a model? There are two primary factors: **reinforcement**, or the **consequences** the model's behavior is seen to have for the model, and the **personal characteristics** of both model and observer.

If a model's behavior is rewarded, imitation is far more likely than if that behavior is punished (Bandura, Ross, and Ross, 1963b; Walters, Leat and Mezei, 1963). Imitation of a model's behavior may occur, however, even if the observer does not observe any response consequence or reward for the model. This is said to be because the observer sees the model as possessing the positive attributes indicative of a successful life-style and thus believes that the model has generally been rewarded.

Characteristics of the model, such as age, social status, sex, warmth, and competence, are equally important in determining the degree to which he or she will be imitated. Bandura, Grusec, and Menlove (1967b) found, for example, that children were more likely to model themselves after peers than after adults. Bandura and Whalen

Parents who are warm and nurturant are particularly likely to be imitated. This little fellow seems to have copied his father from head to toe!

(1966) found that children tended to imitate models whose achievement standards were within reach rather than models who set standards beyond the children's capacity.

Characteristics of the observer as well as of the model determine imitation. For example, in one study (Jakubczak and Walters, 1959), highly dependent children were found to be more influenced by the behavior of a model than were less dependent children.

As we might expect, characteristics of both model and observer often interact to determine whether behavior will be imitated and to what extent. Hetherington and Frankie (1967) investigated the effects of parental warmth, nurturance, and dominance on the imitative behavior of children of both sexes. A group of parents of young children were first assessed in respect to these characteristics. Then the children watched their parents play with various toys and games. The investigators found that both boys and girls were far more likely to imitate parents who were warm and nurturant, and that this was even more true of girls than of boys. Dominant parents generally commanded more imitative behavior, as well, although when the dominant parent was the father, there was a tendency for girls to imitate their mothers.

LEARNING AN EMOTIONAL RESPONSE.   Another interesting kind of learning is the vicarious, **classical conditioning of an emotional response**. An observer can learn to respond with a particular emotion to a particular situation simply by watching a model respond in the same way. In a study that illustrates this process, Bandura and Rosenthal

(1966) had models simulate painful reactions (they were not actually in pain) that observers then later exhibited themselves. The models were presented to the observers as subjects in the experiment, just like themselves. The observers then watched while the models reacted to a series of buzzers in a variety of ways indicating that they were experiencing pain. The observers were told that the sound of the buzzer was followed immediately by an intense shock. (This, of course, was not true. The models were what are known in psychology as "confederates" of the experimenters—they were paid to simulate the reactions required for the experiment and were not administered any shock at all.)

After these initial sessions, in which the subjects "witnessed" buzzer, shock, and pain, subjects themselves came to exhibit a conditioned emotional response to the buzzer even in sessions when the model was absent and despite the fact that subjects never directly experienced the painful stimulus supposedly administered to the model.

CHANGING UNDESIRABLE BEHAVIOR.   The realization that emotional responses can be acquired not only directly but vicariously, by simple observation, led Bandura to assume that such responses can also, under the right circumstances, be both directly and vicariously extinguished. Thus, people with unrealistic or exaggerated fears should be able to modify their exaggerated emotional reactions by watching models interact fearlessly with the objects of their fears. And by having people practice the models' behaviors with the latter's guidance, it might even be possible to eliminate fear responses.

In one of his most important publications, *Principles of Behavior Modification* (1969), Bandura discusses the modification of undesirable behaviors by means of techniques based on learning theory. He describes one interesting study (Bandura, Blanchard, and Ritter, 1969) that incorporated the behavior therapy technique called **desensitization** into the modeling condition. (Desensitization involves inducing relaxation in a person and then helping the person learn to tolerate an anxiety-producing object; see also Box 14.3, on Joseph Wolpe.) A group of adolescents and adults, all of whom suffered severe snake phobias, were assigned to three treatment conditions. In the first, **desensitization** group, subjects were helped to achieve a state of deep relaxation. Then, the investigators asked subjects to imagine a series of scenes involving snakes that depicted increasingly greater involvement with the animals. For example, subjects might begin by imagining looking at a toy snake in a store window. When they could imagine that scene without fear they were asked to imaging playing with that toy, then looking at a real snake in a case, then touching the snake while wearing gloves, and so on, until they could imagine holding a live snake in their bare hands.

In the second, **symbolic modeling** group, subjects in whom re-

Drawing by S. Gross: © *1974 The New Yorker Magazine, Inc.*

laxation had also been induced watched a film in which models interacted more and more closely with a large snake. In the third, **participant modeling** group, subjects watched a live model perform various behaviors with a live snake. After each such interaction, the subjects in this third group were asked to perform the same behaviors, at first with the model's assistance and later alone.

Both before and after the various treatments, all subjects in this experiment were asked to try to perform a graded series of tasks involving live snakes. Members of a fourth, control group were subjected to only these two test sessions; they received no intervening "treatment."

The control group showed essentially no change in behavior. Both the desensitization and symbolic modeling groups, however, showed a marked increase in tendency, after treatment, to approach and interact with a snake. The most successful treatment was that of participant modeling, the one in which subjects saw an actual model and then were guided in copying the model's behavior.

Apparently, neither fear reduction nor vicarious experience are enough to bring about an adequate sense of personal mastery. A subject must perform successfully in an actual situation involving the feared object if he or she is to achieve this aim. We are far more likely to try to perform a difficult or new behavior when, by our own effort, we have had some success at it than when we have been enabled to do it by the intervention of some outside agency.

Bandura points out that participant modeling not only allows a person to actually perform tasks that lead to a desired goal. This technique includes other helpful devices that encourage people to keep at a task until they do achieve a sense of mastery: these include the observation of a model; the performance of a graded series of tasks, at carefully spaced intervals and with the assistance of the model; and the gradual phasing out of such assistance, so that people become progressively more and more dependent on their own efforts (Bandura, Jeffery, and Wright, 1974).

WHAT CAUSES UNDESIRABLE BEHAVIOR?   Bandura (1977b) agrees with Eysenck (Chapter 12) and Wolpe (Chapter 14) that behavior therapies effectively reduce anxiety reactions. He does not believe, however, that the key element that causes exaggerated fear reactions and that must be eliminated in order to change behavior is emotional distress. Rather, says Bandura, the basic problem is the person's belief that he or she cannot cope effectively with a particular situation. The change that behavior therapies bring about results from people's development of a sense of self-efficacy—the expectation that they can, by their personal effort, master situations and bring about the results they want. For some impressive evidence that procedures that bring about behavioral change do so by increasing self-efficacy, see Box 15.3.

RESEARCH METHODS AND EMPHASES

Because for Bandura, theory is so closely linked to research, we have already discussed some of the chief foci of his investigations and several of his methods of study. In this section, we will briefly summarize Bandura's research approach.

Bandura is dedicated to exploring real-world problems in the laboratory. In that setting, he has studied such problems as aggression, phobias, recovery from heart attacks, and children's acquisition of mathematical skills. Although at times, his work may seem to focus more on demonstrating a theoretical point than on learning about the phenomenon under examination, Bandura's goal "is to provide a unifying conceptual framework that can encompass diverse modes of influence known to alter behavior. In any given activity, skills and self-beliefs that ensure optimal use of capabilities are required for successful functioning" (Bandura, 1982, p. 127).

Bandura (1982) has proposed a **microanalytic approach** in research. Such an approach entails making detailed assessments over time so that congruences—for example, between self-perception and behavior—can be achieved for each step of task performance.

BOX 15.3   Self-Efficacy: The Key to Emotional Health

In a study by Bandura, Adams, and Beyers (1977), people gave evidence that their expectations of success at a difficult task—and their actual success at it—were strongly influenced by the particular treatment technique to which they had been exposed. Subjects given vicarious experience only were less likely than those who engaged in participant modeling of specific behaviors to have gained in their sense of self-efficacy.

The subjects were a group of adults who had severe fears of snakes that adversely affected their lives. Subjects were assigned to one of two experimental conditions, a **participant** **modeling** group and a **vicarious experience** group, or to a third group that served as a control condition. The participant modeling group subjects were helped by the experimenter to perform a number of tasks, including holding a boa constrictor and letting it crawl on their laps. The vicarious experience group watched the experimenter perform the foregoing and other acts but did not engage in any behavior of their own with the snake.

As a result of the treatment, the participant modeling group were more successful on the post-treatment test in interacting with an unfamiliar snake than were the vicarious experience group. Moreover, when asked at the conclusion of the treatment sessions how sure they were that they would be able to perform each of the tasks in the test series, as the latter was described to them, subjects in the participant modeling group indicated stronger expectations of success (and later were actually more successful) than subjects in the vicarious experience group. The strength of each person's efficacy expectations predicted with a high degree of accuracy the actual behavior in which the person later engaged.

Throughout a continuing experimental endeavor, Bandura says, periodic attempts should be made to measure hypothesized mediators, which often are cognitive processes. Bandura's research strategy is thus to track changes over time, that is, to assess the process and not just the end goal.

Bandura's laboratory-based research reflects his early allegiance to experimental psychology and learning theory, but his training as a clinical psychologist has often led him to use analogs of behavior and situations commonly found in the clinical setting. The areas of Bandura's most intense interest continue to involve ideas such as self-efficacy, modeling, and observational learning. His work in exploring these and other ideas is all directed at understanding the learning conditions under which people change their behavior or acquire new behaviors. Other important areas focused on by Bandura and his colleagues are imitation and identification (Bandura and Huston, 1961; Bandura, Ross, and Ross, 1963b), social reinforcement (Bandura and McDonald, 1963), and self-reinforcement and monitoring (Bandura, Jeffery, and Wright, 1974; Rosenthal and Bandura, 1978).

MARTIN SELIGMAN

Martin Seligman is probably best known for his studies of the phenomena of learned helplessness and depression. In his work, Seligman has studied a variety of subjects—animals, children, college students,

BOX 15.4   Martin Seligman (1942–   )

Martin Seligman obtained his B.A. at Princeton University in 1964 and did his graduate work in experimental psychology at the University of Pennsylvania, receiving his doctorate in 1967. He began his academic career that year as an assistant professor at Cornell University and in 1970 returned to the University of Pennsylvania, where he is now professor of psychology.

Seligman has been awarded several visiting fellowships. In 1975 he was a visiting fellow at Maudsley Hospital, University of London. In 1978–1979 he was in residence at the Center for Advanced Study in the Behavioral Science, and later he accepted a fellowship at the Max-Planck Institute in Berlin.

Like many of the other personality theorists discussed in this book, Seligman is engaged in the practice of clinical psychology where he can apply the principles of his theory in helping people with real-life problems. Drawing on his clinical work and his teaching experience, Seligman has recently collaborated on a textbook in abnormal psychology, (Rosenhan and Seligman, 1984).

In 1976, in recognition of his research and writing, the American Psychological Association presented Seligman with its Early Career Award.

psychotherapy patients—in a number of settings—the laboratory, the psychotherapy session, the interview, and others. Seligman has shown a willingness to modify his theory as a function of input from a variety of data sources.

LEARNED HELPLESSNESS

In the natural world, Seligman observes, traumatic events that a person or an animal can do little or nothing to control may occur. When the organism discovers that it can do nothing to escape or ward off such an event—when it learns that reinforcement and behavior are not contingent on each other—it may acquire a reaction that Seligman calls **learned helplessness**. Learned helplessness has three components: emotional, motivational, and cognitive. First, Seligman says, the organism experiences **emotional disruption**, an intense experience peculiar to the situation of having no control over unpleasant events. Second, the organism experiences **reduced motivation**; it behaves passively and appears to "give up," making little effort to escape a noxious stimulus. Third, and most serious of all, is a **cognitive deficit** that interferes with the organism's capacity to perceive the relation between response and reinforcement in other, similar situations in which control *is* possible.

In the original formulation of this theory, Seligman proposed that learned helplessness and the psychopathological phenomenon of depression have similar origins. The behaviors of the depressed person strikingly resembled behaviors associated with learned helplessness. More important, methods that reduced experimentally induced learned helplessness were shown to be effective also in treating depressive reactions. As we will see, this proposal of Seligman's was rather widely criticized, and he has since revised his conception of the relations between learned helplessness and depression. To understand his current formulation, let us first look at his model of how learned helplessness is acquired.

THE ACQUISITION OF LEARNED HELPLESSNESS.   Seligman (Overmier and Seligman, 1967) demonstrated in an early experiment how the reaction of learned helplessness is acquired. A dog was placed in a shuttlebox. Periodically, a tone was sounded, and shortly after the tone the dog experienced a painful but physically harmless shock. At the onset of the shock, the dog whined and ran about. At one point, while the shock was still being administered, he happened to jump the barrier in the middle of the box. Immediately, both shock and tone ceased. With successive trials, the dog jumped the barrier more and more quickly. Eventually, he waited quite calmly in front of the barrier, nimbly jumping over it as soon as the tone sounded and thus avoiding the shock. So far, the experiment sounds like Miller and Dollard's (Chapter 14) demonstration of the acquisition of a fear response. But, as we will see, there is a difference.

In the next phase of Seligman's study, another dog was first placed in a restraining device, so that it could not move, and given a number of brief shocks. There was nothing the dog could do to escape or avoid these shocks. When this second dog was put into the shuttlebox a day later, initially it acted much like the first dog. Quickly, however, differences became apparent. Even if the second dog accidentally jumped the barrier, it never learned specifically to cross the barrier to escape or avoid shock. Instead, it sat or lay passively, whimpering, until the tone and shock ended.

Like the first dog in this study, almost all dogs learn the barrier-jumping response to escape or avoid aversive stimulation. In contrast, like the second dog, most animals who are given uncontrollable shock experience respond passively to the shock in the shuttlebox situation and show little or no learning of the barrier-jumping response. This learned helplessness effect has been demonstrated not only in dogs but in cats (Thomas and Dewald, 1977), fish (Padilla, 1973), rats (Seligman and Beagley, 1975), and human beings (e.g., Hiroto and Seligman, 1975; Klein, Fencil-Morse, and Seligman, 1976).

LEARNED HELPLESSNESS IN HUMAN BEINGS.   Learned helplessness can be induced in human subjects by uncontrollable unpleasant events that are not, however, necessarily physically noxious. Hiroto and Se-ligman (1975) presented three groups of college students with a shut-tlebox arrangement in which a subject could escape or avoid a loud noise by moving his or her hand from one side of the box to the other. Before confronting this situation, one group of students were given discrimination learning problems that they could and did solve. The second group were given problems that were insoluble, though the stu-dents did not know this. The third group were given no problems at all. Subjects who had been given problems they could solve or no prob-lems at all quickly learned how to escape the noise in the shuttlebox sit-uation. Subjects who had been given insoluble problems and thus sub-jected to failure did not learn. Seligman (1976) suggests that these results reveal primarily a motivational deficit in the second group of subjects; for some reason, these students were not motivated to initiate responses that would ward off undesirable outcomes.

Another experiment highlighted the cognitive deficit that is one of the symptoms of learned helplessness. Miller and Seligman (1975) subjected groups of students to an unpleasant noise that sounded peri-odically. The first group of students were allowed to discover a re-sponse that terminated the noise. The second group, however, were led to believe that nothing they did would affect the noise, that it would terminate for reasons out of their control. A third group of students re-ceived no pretreatment. Then, all groups were given a series of ana-grams to solve. The group that had experienced inescapable noise reached fewer solutions than did the other two groups.

The emotional disturbance typical of learned helplessness has also been demonstrated. For example, Glass and Singer (1972) found that human subjects who were forced to endure noxious stimulation passively reported more emotional distress and physical upset than subjects given the same stimulation and allowed to terminate it by per-forming some instrumental act. Animal subjects similarly forced to en-dure noxious stimulation are more likely to develop ulcers and to show weight loss, loss of appetite, and other symptoms of severe emotional stress than are subjects whose responses control the duration of nox-ious events (e.g., Weiss, 1971).

LEARNED HELPLESSNESS AND STRESS.   If subjects have been exposed only briefly to inescapable stress, learned helplessness is a transitory phenomenon that wears off quickly. Investigations with animals show, however, that repeated exposure to stressful conditions may lead to se-vere emotional reactions and to prolonged motivational and cognitive deficits. Animals that have been brought up in laboratory settings and thus have had no opportunity to learn to cope with the rough and tum-ble of the natural world are far more prone to exhibit learned helpless-ness after exposure to unavoidable stress than are animals raised in natural settings (Seligman and Maier, 1967; Seligman and Groves, 1970).

Human beings tested in the laboratory also differ in susceptibility to the helplessness syndrome. The life experiences that make some people particularly likely to become helpless are not known, but differences have been shown to be related to people's answers on the Rotter I–E Scale (Rotter, 1966; see also Box 15.1), which measures belief in internal versus external control of reinforcement (Hiroto, 1974; Dweck and Repucci, 1973). "External" people, who believe that what happens to them in life is a matter of luck and beyond their control, are more likely to become helpless after exposure to inescapable stress than are "internal" people, who believe that their destiny is largely in their own hands.

There is a rather simple "cure" for the fleeting kind of helplessness induced in human subjects in the laboratory. We can give such people experience in successfully mastering some task soon after they have been exposed to inescapable aversive stimuli (e.g., Klein and Seligman, 1976). "Curing" people in real-life situations is a little more complicated. In one study, Dweck (1975) tested "treatment" procedures with a group of young children. In the estimation of their teachers and principals, these children expected to fail, and they did badly in their school work when failure threatened. In addition, they were found more likely than other children to attribute their intellectual successes and failures to forces outside themselves and their failures to lack of ability (both of these causes are *not* controllable) rather than to their own lack of effort (a cause that *is* controllable).

Dweck divided her young subjects into two groups and, in an extended program, gave them problems to solve in each of a large number of sessions. In one group, the children were taught to take responsibility for their failures and to attribute them to lack of sufficient effort. In a second group, the children were given only success experiences. Then, in a post-treatment test, all the children were given difficult problems and, inevitably, were unable to solve a number of them. The subsequent performance of the children who had had only success experience deteriorated, but the performance of children trained to take personal responsibility held up or improved.

LEARNED HELPLESSNESS AND DEPRESSION.   As we have said, in his early work, Seligman noted striking parallels between learned helplessness, induced in the laboratory, and the phenomenon of depression, specifically, reactive depression. **Reactive depression** gets its name from the common hypothesis that this state is a reaction to some emotionally upsetting event such as the loss of one's job, the death of a loved one, or failure in some valued activity. Most of us suffer mild depression from time to time—we are "blue," or "down"—but for some people the state may be severe and long lasting and even carry with it the possibility of suicide. People who are depressed are typically slowed in speech and movement. They generally indicate that they feel unable to act or to make decisions. They may appear to have "given up"—to suffer from what one writer (Beck, 1967) describes as a "paralysis of will." When asked to perform some task, depressed people are likely to insist that it is hopeless to try because they are incapable of success and to describe their own performance as much worse than it actually is.

All the foregoing behaviors are seen also in the learned helplessness syndrome, and Seligman originally proposed that underlying depression "is not a generalized pessimism, but *pessimism specific to the effects of one's own skilled actions*" (1975, p. 122). This belief, that reinforcement is not contingent on one's actions is, of course, the core of learned helplessness. Thus, Seligman proposed, depression represents a type of learned helplessness and is triggered by the same causes: experiencing traumatic events that one's best efforts cannot ward off and and that one feels powerless to control.

In a test of this model of depression, Miller and Seligman (1975) had groups of mildly depressed and nondepressed students perform two series of tasks; one involving skill and the other involving chance. Before each task, these investigators had the student state his or her expectation of success. On the skill task, the nondepressed students adjusted their expectations up and down, depending on whether they had succeeded or failed on the preceding problem; on the chance task, their expectations showed little change. The depressed students also showed little change in expectations on the chance task, but they showed the same pattern on the skill task. Moreover, nondepressed students who had been subjected to the inescapable noxious stimulus situation discussed earlier behaved like the depressed students. Thus in this study, helplessness that was induced in the laboratory and naturally occurring depression were shown to have the same effect, of reducing the expectation that one's own efforts can influence outcomes.

We have already noted that Seligman's ideas about the relationship between learned helplessness and depression did not go unchallenged. As a matter of fact, his early work was criticized by a number of writers, (see, e.g., Blaney, 1977). One important criticism was that Seligman's theory did not account adequately for the fact that depression and helplessness each may be either chronic or transitory, general or specific. Another observation was that the theory did not address the drop in self-esteem seen often in people who are feeling helpless as well as in people who are depressed.

In a reformulation of his theory, Seligman (Abramson, Seligman, and Teasdale, 1978) proposes that learned helplessness is one risk factor (among others) in depression. By this he means that

TABLE 15.1   *Factors That Reflect Explanatory Style*

FACTOR	MANIFESTATION
Internal–external	Internal: My car is stuck in three feet of water because I am careless about where I park it.
	External: My car is stuck in three feet of water because the rainwater exceeded the dam's capacity and the street is flooded.
Stable–transient	Stable: This bad event happened because I am careless and always will be.
	Transient: This bad event happened because of a temporary environmental condition; the rain will stop and the floodwaters will recede.
Global–limited	Global: This bad event will affect everything else in my life; I may lose my job because I have no car in which to get to work; without an income I will be evicted from my apartment; and so on.
	Limited: This bad event may cost a little money, in terms of replacement parts for my car and perhaps a new carpet.

people who are extremely helpless are at a greater risk than others for developing depressive symptoms.

EXPLANATORY STYLE

Seligman has undertaken a number of studies to evaluate his reformulated theory of learned helplessness and depression (these studies are summarized in Peterson and Seligman, 1984), and the new theory has received its share of criticism too (see, e.g., Coyne and Gotlieb, 1983; Wortman and Dintzer, 1978). Notable in the new theory, however, and of particular interest to us is the personality variable that Seligman calls *explanatory style*, or the characteristic manner a person uses to explain events that occur in his or her life. Seligman is particularly interested in the way explanatory style enables people to handle bad things that happen in their lives, and he argues that explanatory style determines whether a person is at risk for feeling helpless and depressed.

Explanatory style is reflected in three crucial factors: internal–external, stable–transient, and global–limited (see also Table 15.1). According to Seligman, the depressive explanatory style is observed in people who use internal, stable, and global explanations for bad events in their lives. These are the people who say, "It's me; it's going to last forever; and it's going to affect everything I do" (Peterson and Seligman, 1984, p. 350). Such people feel that they have no control over events and that no action of theirs will control life in the future. They are, according to Seligman, at risk to develop symptoms of helplessness and possibly depression.

In one study, Seligman and his co-workers examined college students' reactions to low midterm grades (Metalsky, Abramson, Seligman, Semmel, and Peterson, 1982). The investigators predicted that students who used a depressive explanatory style—students who would explain a low midterm grade by thinking they were stupid, that they would always be stupid, and that they would never be graduated, get a good job, get married, have children, have a nice house, a nice car—would be likely to react to such grades with feelings of depression. Students who believed they received low grades because the test was poorly constructed and who also thought that the final would have better questions, that the midterm was only 25 percent of the semester grade, and that this one course was not all that important to the future would be less likely to react in this manner.

Students in an introductory psychology course answered an explanatory-style questionnaire, indicating what their aspirations for midterm grades were—that is, what grades would make them happy and what grades would make them unhappy. Before the midterm and again after it, each student also filled out a checklist that assessed mood, including depressed mood. In line with what they had predicted, the investigators found that students who received ''bad'' midterm grades (defined as grades that were lower than or equal to the grades they had initially said would make them unhappy), and who used internal, stable, and global explanations gave evidence of increased depressive moods after they received their midterm grades.

In reformulating his theory, Seligman seems to have made it more central to personality theory. He has begun to use personality variables such as internal versus external control, and he has introduced a cognitive component—that is, what people think about the events that occur in their lives—that is useful in the analysis of personality. Seligman is also interested in how personality variables may be changed, so that persons with particular explanatory styles may be helped to respond to ''bad'' events in more adaptive ways.

WALTER MISCHEL

Walter Mischel has for many years explored both the consistency and the variability of human behavior. In 1968, in his controversial book *Personality and Assessment,* Mischel challenged some of personality psychologists' most fundamental beliefs about the consistency of personality and social behavior. This critique of psychoanalytic theory, trait theory, and current personality research methods generated considerable debate and stimulated some significant research contributions on the part of other investigators.

BOX 15.5   Walter Mischel (1930–   )

A native of Vienna, Mischel fled with his family from the Nazis in 1938 and settled in New York City. Although he began by studying art at New York University—painting and sculpture have been a lifelong interest—in 1951 Mischel began the study of clinical psychology at what is now the City University of New York. At the same time he became a social worker, spending a great deal of time on New York City's Lower East Side. He soon moved on to Ohio State University, where he came in contact with Julian Rotter (see pages 535–536) and George Kelly (Chapter 8). Impressed with both theorist's work, Mischel has attempted to integrate social learning theory and cognitive theory into his own research and theory construction.

After obtaining his Ph.D. at Ohio State, Mischel taught first at the University of Colorado and then at Harvard University, where his colleagues included Henry Murray (Chapter 9) and Gordon Allport (Chapter 10). In 1962 Mischel moved to Stanford University, where he undertook some research in collaboration with Albert Bandura. In 1983, returning to the city of his youth and early education, Mischel became professor of psychology at Columbia University.

In 1982, Mischel received the Distinguished Scientific Contribution Award of the American Psychological Association; in 1978 he had received a similar award from the APA's Division of Clinical Psychology. He has been a Fellow at the Center for Advanced Studies in the Behavioral Sciences and has served on many scientific and professional committees.

Mischel's initial proposal that the situation might be more important than the person in determining behavior arose out of his experience in attempting to assess the personality characteristics of, and thus predict the success of, Peace Corps teachers assigned to Nigeria. Using existing methodology, Mischel found that in spite of his best efforts, involving multiple assessments, he could *not* predict teacher performance very well. He was also discouraged to find that his psychology training did not help him as he had expected it would in his then current job as a social worker. Somehow, the theory he was learning did not seem to have useful applications.

PREDICTION OF BEHAVIOR

Mischel argued initially that traditional trait and psychodynamic conceptions did not lead to useful predictions about human behavior. Global conceptions of dispositions, like aggression, anxiety, or dependency, were not helpful, Mischel asserted, because measures of these variables were not found to be highly correlated with behavior as it occurred in many diverse situations. Many psychologists—and Mischel includes himself in this group—seemed to assume that an accepted sign of, say, aggression, on a personality test like the Rorschach or the Thematic Apperception Test (TAT) or in an interview could and did predict aggressive behavior in other situations. But Mischel's research with Peace Corps volunteers showed, to his surprise, that the correlations between assessment data and real-life performance were nonsignificant.

Reviewing his early search for an answer to these puzzling findings, Mischel observes that he

was guided by a commitment to attend more to what people would actually do, to their actions and cognitions in the particular situations central to the theoretical or clinical problem of interest. [The search] was not undertaken to rejuvenate an atomistic behaviorism, nor to elevate situations into the prime causes of behavior. (Mischel, 1984a, p. 352)

Nevertheless, Mischel was accused of "advocating extreme situationism" and "taking the person out of personality psychology." Mischel feels that his work has been seriously misunderstood. Global dispositional and trait approaches to the personality have actually done a disservice to the individual he claims, by neglecting the individual person's uniqueness. Mischel explains that he

construes the individual as generating diverse behaviors in response to diverse conditions; the emitted behaviors are observed and subsequently integrated cognitively by the performer, as well as by others who perceive him, and are encoded on semantic dimensions in trait terms. Thus, while the traditional personality paradigm views traits as the intrapsychic causes *of behavioral consistency, the present position sees them as the* summary terms *(labels, codes, organizing constructs) applied to observing behavior.* (Mischel, 1973a, p. 264)

Many researchers have responded to Mischel's challenge to do a better job in personality assessment. Some recent efforts are summarized in Mischel (1984a) and Mischel and Peake (1982).

THE CONSISTENCY PARADOX

The **consistency paradox** refers to the fact that although "intuition seems to support a belief that people are characterized by broad dispositions resulting in extensive cross-situational consistency, the research in the area has persistently failed to support that intuition" (Mischel, 1984a, p. 357). Several approaches have been taken in attempts to resolve this paradox. Some have focused on improving the methods used to measure and study traits, on the assumption that up to now, research data have been unreliable or in other ways faulty.

Based on his belief that even the best methods have failed to demonstrate behavioral consistency, Mischel has taken a different approach. He has chosen to question the premises of trait theory, to view the person as proactive and cognitive, and to make very careful analyses of the person–situation interaction. Some highlights of an important study along these lines by Mischel and his collaborators are presented in Box 15.6.

Questioning trait theory, Mischel says, leads to the recognition of "the limitations of traditional global trait and state theories [but it] does not imply that people have no dispositions" (1984a, p. 356). Dispositions must be characterized in such a way as to allow for the fact that people are not totally consistent. They do discriminate, and their behavior changes as a function of the discriminations they make. Pursuing this notion, Mischel has studied how people construe, or categorize themselves, other people, and situations. A problem in attempting to resolve the consistency paradox, he suggests, is that researchers and their subjects may use different categories. People in general are likely to use loose, or what Mischel (1979) calls "fuzzy," categories.

Suppose that you observe a child's behavior with his peers at school and note that he frequently gets into fights, pushes other children, calls them names, and the like. You may label this behavior "aggressive" and, on the basis of the consistency-of-disposition model, expect the child to be aggressive in other settings; you may even call him "an aggressive child." But, suppose, you then find that this child is *not* aggressive at home, either with his siblings or with neighborhood friends. Investigating still further, you discover that the child is "aggressive" in Sunday school classes. Clearly, if you predict the child's aggressive behavior at home on the basis of his aggressiveness at school, you will not predict very well, but you may make very successful predictions if you predict the child's aggressive behavior at Sunday school on the basis of his aggressiveness at public school.

Mischel suggests that the observer's cognitive prototype of a given behavior affects his or her prediction. The **cognitive prototype** is what an observer, or rater, takes to be a typical defining characteristic of a disposition. Thus if for you a prototypical feature of aggression is hitting another person, when you see one child hit another you will infer aggression, even in the absence of other defining characteristics of aggression. "Consistency judgments rely heavily on the observation of the central (prototypic) features so that the impression of consistency will derive not from average levels of consistency across all the possible features of the category, but rather from the observation that some central features are reliably (stably) present" (Mischel, 1984a, p. 357).

Mischel would point out that the child uses cognitive constructs to categorize situations—to discriminate among environmental conditions—and may be aggressive only when he perceives that the likelihood of detection is low. Thus he may display aggressive behavior only in group settings where, he may feel, his behavior will be "lost in the crowd." Thus you could predict the child's aggressive behavior much more accurately if you assessed his perceptions and his thoughts about the various situations in which he finds himself, instead of basing your predictions on the assessment of just one aspect of the child's behavior

---

BOX 15.6 Behavioral Consistency: Hobgoblin or Human Nature?

Mischel and his collaborators undertook a four-year study of behavioral consistency at Carleton College in Northfield, Minnesota. These researchers studied 63 college students extensively and intensively assessing them, by means of various measures, on the two characteristics of conscientiousness and friendliness. Assessments by the subjects themselves, as well as by their parents and one close friend, were included. The subjects were also systematically observed over time, and behaviors that had been preselected—on the basis of students' views as well as those of experimenters—as reflecting these two characteristics were recorded.

Let us look briefly at the findings with respect to conscientiousness. Some of the behaviors measured included attending class, turning in assignments, and keeping one's room neat (or not keeping it neat). Repeated measures were made for each of these variables over a series of days. All subjects also rated themselves on self-perceived consistency of behavior.

Some of the many findings of this extensive study provided support for Mischel's current views of the person–situation controversy. Here we will discuss just a few of the study's results.

Temporal stability, or the stability of the same behavior over occasions, was found to be rather high (the mean correlation coefficient was .65). Thus, if a student attended class on day 1, it was likely that she would also attend class on day 6. When correlations were computed for cross-situational consistency, however, they were relatively low (the mean correlation coefficient was .13). Thus, for example, getting to lectures on time was not highly correlated with how neat a student's class notes were.

When correlational *patterns* were looked at, however, some interesting findings emerged. For example, when data are pooled, class attendance turns out to be highly correlated with appointment attendance, assignment punctuality, completion of class readings, and the amount of time spent studying. Mischel and Peake observe that "These coherences once again testify that behavior is patterned and organized rather than random." They go on to note, however, that these results clearly indicate that "behavior is also highly discriminative" and that broad cross-situational consistencies remain elusive with reliable measures (Mischel and Peake, 1982, p. 735).

---

as it appears in different settings and at different times. And if you wanted to change the child's behavior, you could develop a more useful intervention strategy if you knew that an important variable in his aggressiveness was likelihood of detection.

Concluding their 1982 article on the consistency of behavior, Mischel and Peake write

The consistency paradox may be paradoxical only because we have been looking for consistency in the wrong place. If our shared perceptions of consistent personality attributes are indeed rooted in the observation of temporally stable behavioral features that are prototypic for the particular attribute, the paradox may well be on the way to resolution. Instead of seeking high levels of cross-situational consistency— instead of looking for broad averages—we may need, instead, to identify unique bundles or sets of temporarily stable prototypic behaviors—key features—that characterize the person even over long periods of time, but not necessarily across many or all possibly relevant situations. (Mischel and Peake, 1982, pp. 753–754)

DELAY OF GRATIFICATION

In his work on **delay of gratification**, Mischel focuses on a process that is central to personality development and functioning: "the ability to purposefully defer immediate gratification for the sake of delayed, contingent but more desired future outcomes" (Mischel, 1984a, p. 353). Rewards for one's behavior are not always immediately forthcoming, and the ability to persevere in an endeavor in anticipation of later gain is an important component of psychological maturity.

In order to examine how the capacity for delaying gratification develops, Mischel has studied young children, publishing a number of papers on this topic. A typical experimental situation in Mischel's research is the following: A preschool child is told that the experimenter must leave the room for a few minutes and that if she will wait for him to return she will be given two marshmallows. If, however, she rings a bell to call him back sooner, she will be given only one marshmallow. Mischel has shown, in a series of studies, that children can delay for longer periods of time (1) if rewards are not in view (Mischel and Ebbesen, 1970), (2) if they play with a toy or think about "fun" things (Mischel, Ebbesen, and Zeiss, 1972), (3) if they avoid thinking about the consummatory features of the reward, such as the taste of the marshmallow (Mischel and Baker, 1975), and (4) if they shift their attention from the reward and occupy themselves with thoughts about other things (Mischel, 1981a).

Mischel (1961) also showed, in an early study in Trinidad, that delinquents will more often choose an immediate, though smaller, reward than they will defer such a reward and wait for a larger one at a later date. And, working together, Mischel and Albert Bandura (Bandura and Mischel, 1965) showed that delay behavior can be affected by exposure to a model, whether live or symbolic (described to, but not seen by, the subject): a child who has not delayed gratification may do so on subsequent trials if exposed to a model who does delay rewards.

Recently, Mischel and Harriet Mischel (Mischel and Mischel, 1983) have studied children's strategies in delaying gratification. In this study the Mischels were interested in what children knew about the factors that helped them delay reward, at what ages this knowledge was present, and what strategies the children used to delay gratification and maintain self-control. Working with children who ranged in

If this 5½ year old can stop thinking about the possible contents of the package and instead can concentrate on the old rule ''do not open before Christmas,'' she may be able to wait for her gift.

age from preschool to sixth grade, the Mischels were able to use a developmental perspective in evaluating children's understanding of the rules for effective delay. They found, for example, that by the age of 5 children understood that if you cover the marshmallows and think about the task of waiting—but not about the taste of marshmallows—you can wait longer.

RESEARCH METHODS.   Mischel prefers systematic research programs that rely on carefully controlled, experimental methods. Nevertheless, he tries to make his research fit into natural settings such as nursery schools or college campuses; he avoids highly contrived, artifical research settings. Mischel has studied children, adolescents, and adults, and he prefers to conduct studies of nonclinical populations.

Mischel employs a wide variety of data sources, from the number of seconds a child will wait in a delay-of-gratification setting to what preschoolers and elementary school children will tell experimenters about their thoughts and beliefs. Thus, as you can see, Mischel uses not only direct measures of behavior but subjects' self-reports as well. Mischel says he is often impressed by how "smart" his subjects are; indeed, he says, it is very useful for experimenters to listen to what subjects have to say!

EVALUATION

The social learning theorists have made a major and significant impact on current personality psychology. Indeed, at present, the contributions of these theorists seem to be enjoying greater popularity than some of the other personality theories we have discussed in this book. Bandura's work appears to be the most widely recognized today, but all the social learning theorists, especially insofar as they have become more cognitive in orientation, have had wide appeal to personality psychologists.

One of the strengths of social learning theory is that it has remained faithful to its experimental origins. Thus, the research stimulated by these theories is usually distinctive in its use of controlled experimentation and careful data analysis, and it has an overall scientific orientation that is absent in some personality theories. At the same time, Bandura, as well as Seligman and Mischel, have successfully introduced into their experimental settings conditions more analogous to real-life social environments. This has encouraged other personality researchers to take an experimental approach to their work. As a group, the social learning theorists have displayed considerable creativity as they have moved from theory construction to the experimental evaluation of their ideas.

Although all of the theorists discussed in this chapter have had some clinical experience and training, in general, they tend to deemphasize clinical phenomena and to select nonclinical subjects for study in their experiments. Seligman's concern with depression is an exception to this general trend, as is Bandura's work with phobics. For the most part, social learning theorists of personality have more to say about normal personality functioning than about disturbed functioning, or psychopathology.

Critics of the learning theory approach have often complained—particularly in respect to Skinner's (Chapter 13) work—that learning theorists (1) study nonhuman animals, who are far simpler than human beings, and (2) study these animals in such carefully controlled circumstances that experimental findings cannot reasonably be extrapolated to ordinary life. Contemporary social learning theorists rarely use animals in their work (Seligman is an exception), and as these theorists have studied human beings in more complex and real-life analogs, they have shifted to a much greater emphasis on cognition. Mischel, for example, has been able to make creative use of findings from the very active research area of cognitive science in evolving increasingly sophisticated cognitive variables.

The social learning theorists have also produced some useful assessment instruments, and they have developed research methods or paradigms, such as Bandura's modeling studies and Mischel's work on delay of gratification, that have positively influenced the research of others.

Social learning theory, with its current emphasis on cognition, is a very active area of theorizing and research on the landscape of contemporary personality psychology. Theories of this school are open to change and responsive to data. Not surprisingly, then, they have often been modified as a result of experimentation.

The most comprehensive of the social learning theories is that of Bandura, yet even his theory falls short of being an all-encompassing, grand theory. The other social learning theories discussed in this chapter appear to be even more limited in scope. Mischel, for example, has produced less than a general theory of personality, although his work has had a significant impact on one of the most difficult and persistent issues the personality psychologist has to face—the consistency and variability of behavior.

In sum, the social learning theory approach, especially with its modern emphasis on cognition, holds considerable promise for the field of personality. The contribution of these theorists and their research marks significant progress in personality. Yet, there is much to come before we can assess the enduring impact of these approaches on personality theory. One thing does appear certain: we can expect continued research activity from this group of theorists and their adherents.

SUMMARY

1. Social learning theory holds that human behavior is largely acquired and that learning principles are sufficient to account for the development and maintenance of human behavior.

ALBERT BANDURA

2. Human beings think and regulate their own behavior; they are not simply pawns of the environment.

3. A theory of personality must take account of the social contexts in which behavior is acquired and maintained.

4. **Reciprocal determinism** is the continuous reciprocal interaction

among the cognizing person, the person's behavior, and the external environment.

5. The **self system** refers to cognitive structures and subfunctions involved in perception, evaluation, and the regulation of behavior. The self system regulates behavior through **self-observation**, **judgmental processes**, and **self-response.**

6. Self-efficacy is the perception of how well one can function in a given situation. Strong **efficacy expectations** and realistic **outcome expectations** lead to persistence and hard work.

7. The key to behavior change is altering the expectation of personal efficacy. Efficacy expectations can be altered by four kinds of experience: **enactive**, or **performance**; **vicarious**; **persuasive**; and **physiological information** experience.

8. Changing personal efficacy expectations has been found to improve coping and adaptive behaviors in persons with a variety of behavioral problems.

9. Motivation has two sources: the anticipation of future outcomes and the expectation of success based on experience in setting and reaching successive subgoals. Performance tends to improve when subjects have an opportunity to set such subgoals and to evaluate their performance.

10. Observation and **vicarious reinforcement** or no reinforcement at all may lead to the acquisition of learning. It is the **expectation of reinforcement** that leads to the performance of learning.

11. The expectation of reinforcement can develop from observing the consequences either of others' behaviors or of our own behaviors.

12. Human behavior is guided largely and is kept consistent by anticipation of **self-approval** or **self-criticism**, both of which evolve out of personal standards of behavior that are based on the standards of socializing agents, like parents and peers.

13. Novel responses can be learned vicariously and without either actual or vicarious reinforcement.

14. Human beings' **cognitive skills** enable them not only to reproduce observed behaviors but to create innovative behaviors out of combined observations.

15. Modeled behaviors may strengthen responses already in an observer's repertoire. They may also strengthen or weaken an observer's inhibitions against performing socially unacceptable behavior, depending on whether the model is rewarded or punished.

16. Symbolic modeling, as in television and movies, can have strong effects on observers' behavior.

17. The observer's **attention**, an important factor in learning, is determined by the **consequences** of a model's behavior for the model and the **personal characteristics** of both model and observer. Personal characteristics of model and observer often interact to determine whether a model will be imitated.

18. An emotional response can be classically conditioned by vicarious means.

19. Undesirable behaviors can be extinguished both directly and vicariously.

20. The basic problem in anxiety or fear reaction is not emotional distress but the belief that one cannot cope effectively with a particular situation.

21. Participant modeling, the most effective technique for extinguishing undesirable behavior, enables people to become progressively more and more dependent on their own efforts, increasing their sense of **self-efficacy.**

22. The **microanalytic approach** in research entails making detailed assessments over time so as to achieve congruence between self-perception and behavior at each step of task performance.

MARTIN SELIGMAN

23. Learned helplessness encompasses **emotional disruption, reduced motivation**, and **cognitive deficits**.

24. When an animal is prevented from escaping from noxious stimulation, like shock, it typically fails to learn a way of escape even when that possibility is made accessible.

25. Human subjects, when subjected to inescapable noxious stimulation, show a similar inability to learn adaptive responses, and they exhibit other cognitive and emotional deficits.

26. Laboratory-induced learned helplessness may be ''cured'' by giving people experiences in successfully mastering tasks; similar techniques have been found helpful in improving actual school performance in children.

27. Many behaviors are common to both laboratory-induced learned helplessness and depression, and both phenomena have similar effects in reducing expectations of personal efficacy. Learned helplessness is seen as a risk factor in depression; people who tend to exhibit learned helplessness are more likely to become depressed than other people.

28. Explanatory style is person's characteristic manner of explaining events in his or her life. A depressive explanatory style—**internal, stable**, and **global**—may be associated with depressive reactions to the occurrence of ''bad'' events.

WALTER MISCHEL

29. Global dispositional and trait approaches to the personality neglect the individual person's uniqueness.

30. Measures of commonly accepted traits, like aggression or dependency, have not been found to predict behavior accurately.

31. The **consistency paradox** refers to the fact that although intuition supports a belief in broad dispositions that lead to cross-situational consistency, research fails to substantiate this notion.

32. The **cognitive prototype** is what someone judging another's behavior takes to be a typical defining characteristic of a particular disposition.

33. Consistency may lie in smaller, more discrete sets of behaviors that are temporarily stable but not necessarily stable across many or all possibly relevant situations.

34. Delay of gratification refers to the ability to forgo immediate gain for future reward. Studies have shown that children learn to postpone rewards by avoiding thinking about the desired reward and by shifting their attention to other things.

35. Critics complain that learning theorists study only nonhuman animals and use experimental laboratory settings that are not capable of extrapolation to real life. But although social learning theory has remained faithful to its experimental origins, social learning theorists usually study human beings, and they attempt to introduce conditions analogous to real-life social environments into their experimentation. Social learning theorists are willing to modify their theories as new data are acquired, and they have developed some important research models and assessment instruments. Their increasingly cognitive orientation makes their theories attractive to the personality researcher.

SUGGESTED READING

ALBERT BANDURA

Bandura's first major statement of his theory was presented in his book written with Richard Walters, *Social Learning and Personality Development* (1963). In this book, Bandura and Walters presented their social learning principles and the evidence on which their theory was based. Six years after this book appeared, Bandura published his *Principles of Behavior Modification* (1969), in which he outlined how techniques based on learning principles could be applied to the modification of behavior.

Bandura has for many years been concerned with the study of aggression. His first significant study of this subject was an exploration, again with Walters, of aggression in middle-class delinquent boys: *Adolescent Aggression* (1959). His more recent work on this topic has been described in *Aggression: A Social Learning Analysis* (1973) and "Psychological Mechanisms of Aggression" (1979).

Bandura's theoretically ambitious book, *Social Learning Theory* (1977), attempts "to provide a unified theoretical framework for analyzing human thought and behavior" (p. vi). Most notable of Bandura's recent papers are "self-efficacy: Toward a Unifying Theory of Behavioral Change (1977a), "The Self System in Reciprocal Determinism" (1978), and "Self-efficacy Mechanism in Human Agency" (1982). In a chapter written with Rosenthal, "Psychological Modeling: Theory and Practice" (1978), Bandura returned to a theme that has occupied his attention from the earliest years of his career: how social learning theory can help clinicians effect behavior change so that their clients can live realistic and effective lives.

MARTIN SELIGMAN

Seligman's theorizing and extensive experimental work on learned helplessness and depression are summarized in his books, *Helplessness* (1975) and *Human Helplessness: Theory and Applications* (with Garber, 1980), and in many articles. Most notable among the latter are "Learned Helplessness and Depression in Animals and Man" (1976), "Learned Helplessness: Theory and Evidence" (with Maier, 1976), "Learned Helplessness in Humans: Critique and reformulation" (with Abramson and Teasdale, 1978), and "Causal Explanations as a Risk Factor for Depression: Theory and Evidence" (with Peterson, 1984).

WALTER MISCHEL

In Mischel's most important book, *Personality and Assessment* (1968), he established a research agenda that he has pursued consistently over the years. Mischel has also published a personality textbook entitled *Introduction to Personality* (1981), and he has co-authored, with Harriet N. Mischel, a general textbook entitled *The Essentials of Psychology* (1980).

One of Mischel's most important papers is "Toward a Cognitive Social Learning Reconceptualization of Personality" (1973). Here Mischel reassesses his 1968 challenge to trait and global disposition theorists and discusses the work of other psychologists in reaction to that challenge. He also affirms his belief that theoretical advances will occur when cognititon becomes a more central part of personality theory. Mischel's paper entitled "On Empirical Dilemmas of Psychodynamic Approaches: Issues and Alternatives" (1973b) was clearly an attack on psychodynamic theories, and it stirred up considerable debate; see, for example, Wachtel, "On Fact, Hunch, and Stereotype: A Reply to Mischel" (1973b).

In "Beyond Déjà Vu in Search for Cross-situational Consistency" (with Peake, 1982), Mischel introduces new data from his own research and reviews the efforts of others to resolve the "consistency paradox." Mischel's most recent summary of the issues and relevant data on this central, hotly debated issue of behavioral consistency can be found in his 1984 article on "Convergences and Challenges in the Search for Consistency."

Representative examples of Mischel's recent work on self-control and delay of gratification can be found in a paper on "The Development of Children's Knowledge of Self-control Strategies" (with Harriet Mischel, 1983) and a chapter entitled "Delay of Gratification as Process and as a Person Variable in Development" (1983).

Part 5　Perspectives on Personality Theory

In the four preceding parts of the book we have grouped theorists according to certain general tendencies—an interest in internal psychodynamics, a concern with conscious experiencing, a focus on the more or less stable aspects of personality, and a view of the person as a learning organism, responding to many and varied environmental stimuli. We have also viewed each theorist's position against the framework of nine dimensions of personality theory.

In the last chapter of the book we will look back over the entire group of 20 major theories to see if any central tendencies offer a hint as to where personality theory may ultimately find its most fruitful avenues of pursuit. And we will consider trends in current personality theorizing with an eye, again, toward divining what directions will be most productive as new personality theorists appear on the scene and as we move ahead toward the twenty-first century.

Chapter sixteen

16.

And there's an end.
KING HENRY THE FIFTH

Personality Theories: Current Status and New Directions

We now have completed our tour through four broad classifications of personality theory and have studied in some detail the work of 20 major theorists. These theorists are listed in the order in which they appear in the book in the left-hand column of Figure 16.1. We have found in each of the theories features that distinguish it from others, and we have found in each something that makes it attractive. In this final chapter of the book, it seems useful to consider as well some of the similarities that exist among these theories in spite of their great differences. Students should be aware that although each viewpoint is unique, it also shares important common qualities with other theories.

THE THEORIES COMPARED

In the introductions to each part of the book we have previewed the comparison we now propose to make of the 20 major theories, sketching there the positions taken by the theorists discussed in each part on the dimensions of personality theory and summarizing this information in four charts (Figs. 1–4). Figure 16.1 combines the information presented in each of these charts.

DIMENSIONS OF PERSONALITY

In general, the **conscious** versus **unconscious** issue no longer revolves around the question of whether unconscious factors exist. Today, concern generally focuses around the related questions: To what degree do unconscious factors determine behavior, under what conditions, and how strongly? Freud's and other psychoanalytically oriented positions—such as Jung's and Murray's—give the heaviest weight to the importance of unconscious factors, and we find theories like Rogers's, Allport's, and Lewin's near the other end of the continuum, where unconscious motives are thought to be significant only in the determination of psychopathology, or disturbed behavior.

Clearly, most modern personality theorists accept the responsibility for dealing with both the **acquisitions** and the **process of learning**. Miller and Dollard, for example, have incorporated into their learning theory the structural concepts of psychoanalysis. Bandura's

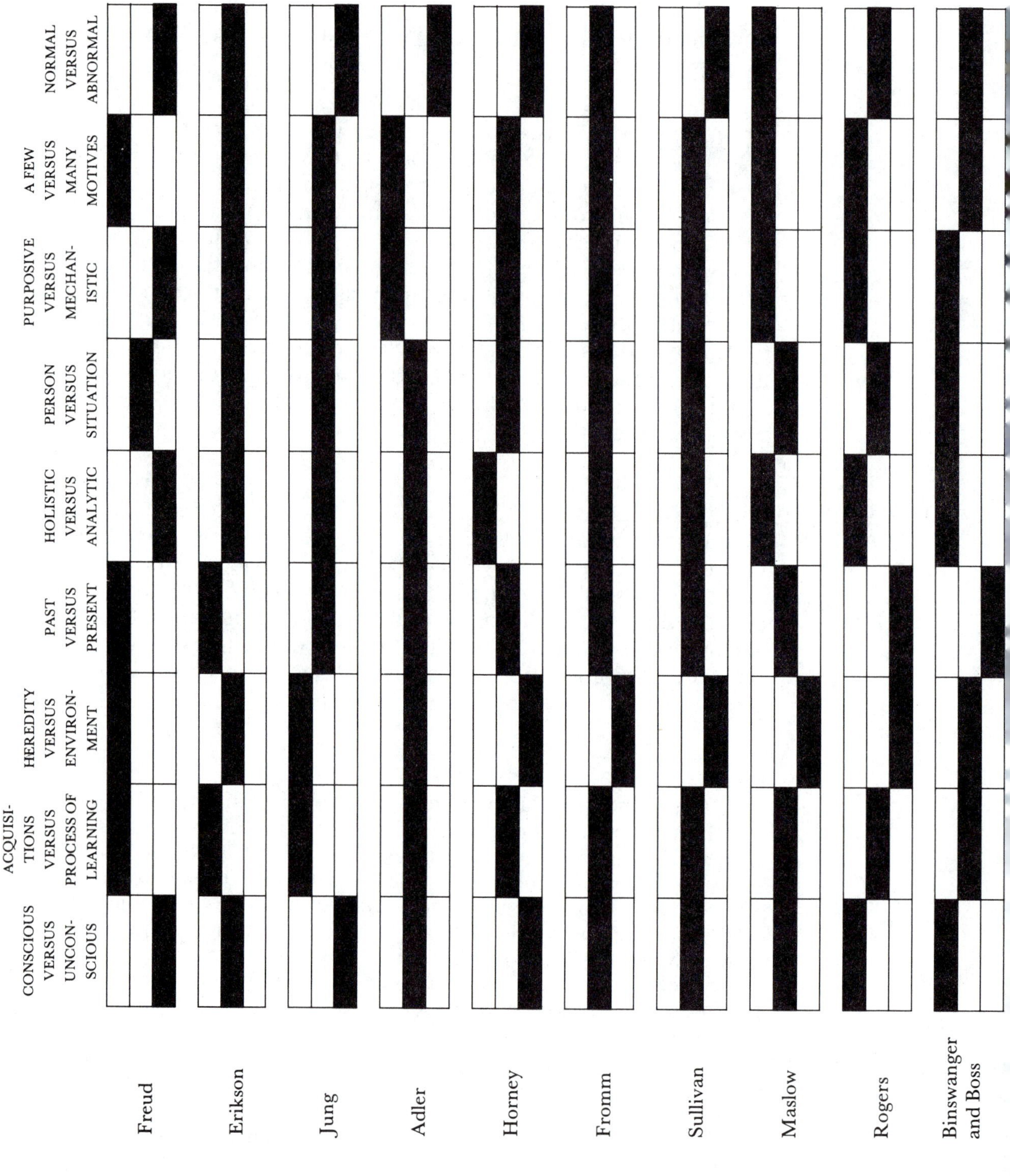
CONSCIOUS VERSUS UNCON- SCIOUS
ACQUISI- TIONS VERSUS PROCESS OF LEARNING
HEREDITY VERSUS ENVIRON- MENT
PAST VERSUS PRESENT
HOLISTIC VERSUS ANALYTIC
PERSON VERSUS SITUATION
PURPOSIVE VERSUS MECHAN- ISTIC
A FEW VERSUS MANY MOTIVES
NORMAL VERSUS ABNORMAL
Freud
Erikson
Jung
Adler
Horney
Fromm
Sullivan
Maslow
Rogers
Binswanger and Boss

Figure 16.1   The theorists and the dimensions of personality.

Lewin

Kelly

Murray

Allport

Sheldon

Cattell

Eysenck

Skinner

Miller and
Dollard

Bandura

theory includes features of the learning situation that facilitate observational learning. Skinner has shown the least interest in the acquisitions of learning, or indeed in structural concepts of any kind; his position revolves around his own interpretation of the learning process.

Some theorists, such as Adler, Rogers, and Kelly, offer little specific treatment of learning. Most personality theorists, in fact, have been content to conceptualize development by means of rather global principles such as maturation, individuation, or self-actualization, rather than provide a detailed picture of the learning process.

The most detailed treatments of the acquisitions of personality are to be found in the work of Freud, Murray, and Allport. As we have pointed out before, it is important to keep in mind that in general these acquisitions, or structures, of personality are not to be thought of as objects having existence in time and space. They are aspects of the personality that have a more enduring character than other, more changeable, qualities.

American psychologists, as a group, have tended to minimize the role of hereditary factors in the determination of behavior; Sheldon may be the only American-born theorist who is thoroughly convinced of the centrality of genetic determinants. Two other American theorists—Murray and Allport—take a somewhat middle-of-the-road position on the **heredity** versus **environment** issue. Theorists, on the other hand, who have come out of Europe—for example, Freud, Jung, and Cattell—more frequently emphasize the importance of hereditary factors.

Theorists are no longer sharply divided on the question of whether it is principally **past** or **present** factors that determine human behavior. The issue today is whether all factors that influence present behavior can be assessed adequately by observing that behavior or whether knowledge about past events provides special information of a crucial nature. Freud, Erikson, and Miller and Dollard all emphasize the importance of early experience, whereas Rogers and the existential theorists, Lewin, Kelly, and Allport, stress contemporary factors. None of the latter suggests that the past has no meaning; these theorists do hold, however, that the past can be of significance only through the operation of present factors.

For most contemporary personality theorists, the individual is a total functioning unit. An element of behavior may not be understood in isolation from the rest of the functioning person, including the person's biological makeup. Thus in the **holistic** versus **analytic** debate few theorists would totally reject the holistic approach. Some theorists, however, like Cattell, Eysenck, Skinner, Miller and Dollard, and Bandura, question, to a greater or lesser degree, the importance of studying the total individual.

In general, those who adopt a holistic position suggest that a successful theory must be complex and multivariate and that it must include reference to the situation within which a behavioral event occurs as well as to other behavioral events of the actor. Although some theorists, like Maslow, Rogers, and Allport, do insist that all aspects of the individual and his or her situation must be given their due before progress can be made, these theorists are willing to analyze behavior somewhat segmentally as long as the parts are put back together again.

With respect to the **person** versus **situation** issue, all theorists, even those most committed to the importance of environmental factors, assume at least a minimal degree of constancy in the personality at different times and in different situations. Trait theorists, like Allport and Sheldon, and situational determinists, like Skinner and Bandura, are no longer at loggerheads, or at least the sharpness of their debate has dissipated in the face of a new, interactionist position, according to which individuals' dispositions or traits help to determine the situations in which they find themselves as well as the stimuli in the environment to which they attend. On this view, both traits and situational variables play a significant role in determining behavior (Endler, 1981; Magnusson and Endler, 1977).

The interactionist position was foreshadowed by Murray's conceptions of need and press and by Lewin's conception of the psychological environment. Despite the insistence by such theorists as Skinner that behavior is elicited solely by stimuli in the physical environment, it is probably fair to say that personality theorists are more impressed with the significance of the psychological environment than of the physical environment.

There is a growing tendency for personality theorists to give explicit attention to the sociocultural context within which behavior occurs. Erikson, Adler, Horney, Fromm, Sullivan, Lewin, and Miller and Dollard have all been influenced by the findings of sociology and anthropology, and all of these theorists, except Miller and Dollard, may be considered field theorists. Lewin is the only theorist who has attempted to work out specific formulas for the interactions between person and environment, but Erikson and the interpersonal theorists—Adler, Horney, Fromm, and Sullivan—have based much of their theorizing on the ways in which they perceive people interacting with their social and cultural worlds.

Early in this century the question of whether human behavior is primarily goal seeking and purposive or whether it is determined largely by forces external to the organism—the **purposive** versus **mechanistic** issue—was a hotly debated topic. Today, although some personality theorists, such as Skinner and Eysenck, do not consider purpose a crucial consideration in understanding behavior, most theorists conceive of human beings as creatures with purposes and goals. Some theorists, such as Adler, Rogers, Binswanger and Boss, Kelly, and Allport, strongly emphasize a purposive view.

Another dimension of importance in our review is the issue of **a few** versus **many motives**. The majority of theorists choose to represent motivation in terms of a relatively small number of variables. Some theorists, however, such as Adler, Maslow, Rogers, and Kelly, suggest that human beings are driven essentially by one overarching motive; for Maslow, for example, this notion is the drive toward self-actualization. A few other theorists—Lewin, Murray, Allport, and Cattell—call upon a large number of motivational variables to explain behavior.

As we have seen, a good many personality theories have evolved out of a clinical concern with changing behavior that reflects psychological distress of one sort or another. A majority of the theorists discussed in this book are or were primarily psychotherapists, had training in psychotherapy, or conducted research in which subjects were patients or persons with behavior problems. Most of the theorists, however, fall somewhere in the middle of the **normal** versus **abnormal** continuum. Toward one end of this continuum we find Freud, Adler, Horney, and Sullivan, whose theorizing and writing strongly emphasize the psychologically distressed, and toward the other, Maslow, Lewin, Kelly, Allport, and Cattell, who are concerned primarily with the normal person.

The judgments we have offered in the preceding paragraphs are reflected in Figure 16.1, which indicates how our 20 major personality theories fall on the dimensions of personality. The reader is cautioned that this chart, like those in the part introductions, can make only the broadest and most approximate of statements in comparing theories on the personality theory dimensions. In the first place, the nine dimensions themselves are broadly stated. In the second place, most of the theories are sufficiently complex that it is difficult to say with certainty just where a particular theorist stands on a given issue. Readers are encouraged, therefore, to examine the chart critically.

Despite their many differences, all the theorists discussed in this book would agree that the human being develops and matures over time, and none would deny that rewards are important incentives to learning.

GENERATION OF RESEARCH

We have agreed that the most important criterion in evaluating personality theories is their capacity to generate research. Unfortunately, this is also the most difficult judgment to make with assurance. All the theories we have discussed here have stimulated some investigation, but the studies they have produced have varied a good deal, not only in quantity but in quality and in relevance to the theory in question. The relation between the theories and the research they have generated is so complicated—that is, the hypotheses derived and the methods used to test them rarely represent a direct and unambiguous derivation—that, at present, more than a rough assessment is beyond our reach.

With this caveat in mind, let us divide the theories into three groups in terms of their fruitfulness as generators of research (Table 16.1 sketches this division briefly). In the first group we place those theories that have led to a great quantity of investigation in a variety of areas by a diverse group of researchers. In this group are the theories of Freud, Lewin, Eysenck, Skinner, and Miller and Dollard. In the case of each of these theories, issues related to the important concep-

TABLE 16.1 *Personality Theories as Generators of Research*

Much research in many areas by diverse groups of investigators	Freud, Lewin, Eysenck, Skinner, and Miller and Dollard
Considerable research in limited areas largely by theory's followers	Erikson, Adler, Rogers, Kelly, Murray, Allport, Sheldon, Cattell, and Bandura
Some research in limited areas largely by theory's followers	Jung, Horney, Fromm, Sullivan, Maslow, and Binswanger and Boss

tions of the theory have been explored in a variety of different settings and by people who represent rather heterogeneous backgrounds. Perhaps the best example is psychoanalytic research, which has been carried out not only by people in the mainstream of the medical–psychoanalytic tradition, but also by persons who belong to an experimental tradition. In addition, psychoanalytic theory has had great impact on research in anthropology and sociology, as well as in the other social sciences and in literature, the fine arts, and religion.

Lewin's work has also led to a great deal of research, primarily within the field of psychology. Lewin's theories have had particularly great impact in social psychology. The study of group dynamics—which bridges such fields as social and industrial psychology, sociology, and the clinical disciplines of clinical psychology and social work—evolved out of Lewin's theory and research on the small group, as did some expressions of the human growth movement, such as the T-group (''T'' for training) and the encounter group.

Much Skinnerian investigation has been conducted by experimental psychologists, but there has been an increasing tendency for researchers in the clinical and personality areas to undertake research based on Skinner's conceptions. The *Journal of the Experimental Analysis of Behavior*, which publishes studies in the Skinnerian tradition, is evidence of Skinner's wide influence.

Stimulus–response theory, as modified by Miller and Dollard and others, has been applied in the study of social behavior, in psychopathology, and in educational psychology, as well as within the usual areas of animal and human learning. Many experimentally oriented clinical psychologists have found Miller and Dollard's formulations very useful in their research on complex phenomena such as anxiety and fear.

Eysenck's theory has also been very influential among personality researchers, to a considerable extent because of the clarity of his ideas and the apparent ease with which these ideas can be translated into experimental designs. Because the scope of Eysenck's theory is so broad, it has had implications for a variety of behavioral problems, including smoking, substance (alcohol and other drug) abuse, and criminality.

The second group of theories includes those that have stimulated considerable work but work that is somewhat limited in scope and has been carried out essentially by people intimately involved with a particular theory's development. In this group, we place the theories of Erikson, Adler, Rogers, Kelly, Murray, Allport, Sheldon, Cattell, and Bandura. Cattell's factor analytic studies, for example, have stimulated a good deal of research, but much of this work has been conducted by students of Cattell or by persons associated with the institute he founded.

A similar example can be found in the work of Erikson. A small group of active researchers who have been engaged in studying the concept of ego identity have made a considerable contribution to understanding this important aspect of personality development that takes place in late adolescence and early adulthood. And Erikson's own psychological studies of historical figures have initiated what is now a sizable body of work by others in psychohistory, or psychobiography.

In the third group of theories, which includes Jung, Horney, Fromm, Sullivan, Maslow, and Binswanger and Boss, there seems to be less evidence of high research productivity. In the case of some theories, such as Jung's, research has been somewhat limited in quantity and rather narrowly focused; to date, much Jungian research has focused on the concepts of introversion–extraversion and the psychological type. A somewhat similar situation obtains with respect to Maslow and his notions of self-actualization and the peak experience.

Among the small group of clinicians who are adherents of the Horney school of psychoanalysis, Horney's concepts continue to be the subject of theoretical essays and lively debate. Fromm's conception of social character is one of his most researchable formulations, but it apparently has not appealed to many investigators. Sullivan's theory enjoys widespread influence on the thinking and practice of clinicians, especially in psychiatric circles, but somehow his concepts have not stimulated a great deal of research interest among academic psychologists. Finally, the theories of the existential theorists are so often stated in philosophical and thus less empirically testable ways that research activity on these ideas has been sparse.

As a group, the personality theories discussed in this book have stimulated a considerable quantity of research. Even though some of this research is limited in scope and application, its existence demonstrates the interest these theories have aroused and the readiness of researchers to examine the theories, using empirical data. It seems reasonable to expect that such interest and concern will in time bring about the progressive change needed to produce more effective theories.

HOW CAN PERSONALITY THEORY BE IMPROVED?

The field of personality study would benefit greatly from an increased sophistication on the part of psychologists concerning the nature and function of theoretical formulations. The issue here is the understanding of the central importance of theories as a means of stimulating research. It is not sufficient to develop formulations that do no more than organize or make consistent what is already known in a given empirical area. Theories must continually be evaluated in terms of their capacity to generate new research. Theorists would be well advised to focus their attention on formulations that permit specific predictions to be made and that state explicitly what data should be collected and in what manner so as to permit accurate testing of the theory's derivations.

Personality theory and research need to be both more imaginative and more evaluative. Theorists must be willing not only to question but to challenge long-held assumptions about human behavior and to innovate—to create theories that are not tied to existing conceptions. Once having created new formulations, however, theorists must be persistent and patient and willing to devote painstaking attention to detail in order to explore fully the implications of their new concepts. Only careful, steady empirical investigation will demonstrate the usefulness of a new theory or conception, and only freewheeling, creative imagination will bring such a new conception into being. Thus personality theorists need not only creativity and flexibility but precision and discipline (Rorer and Widiger, 1983).

It is exciting to create something new and to gather preliminary findings that suggest the new conception may be valid. It may not be so exciting, however, to keep diligently examining the consequences of a theory. Much patience is required to devise appropriate experiments to test a particular notion, examining it minutely from all sides. Many studies and replications are required to confirm or disconfirm a given conception at a high level of probability.

Scientific entrepreneurs are like entrepreneurs in any field: they must have good ideas and they must be risk takers in advancing their ideas; they must also be willing to persevere in the implementation of their ideas, either until they have succeeded or until the accumulated evidence seems clearly to suggest that the ideas will not work and must be abandoned.

Theorists must be free to develop formulations that depart from normative or customary views of behavior. Often a theory has been criticized because it places what the average citizen thinks is undue emphasis on, say, sexual behavior—for example, Freud's theory—or because it fails to accord people some trait that we are all sure we possess, such as the ability to make choices—for example, Skinner's theory. Such criticism is nonscientific, for it rests on sociocultural or philosophical beliefs and attitudes, the accuracy of which has not been demonstrated. Freud or Skinner may be wrong, but until their theories are disconfirmed, they are as potentially useful as any others.

In the final analysis, the only telling criticism of a theory is an alternative theory that works better. It is a truism that it is much easier to criticize someone else's idea than to come up with viable ideas of one's own. We need to evaluate theories critically, but we cannot throw out a theory simply because it offends us. It is quite possible that the most fruitful theories of human behavior may be offensive to an average member of our society. It is equally possible that what is most useful will turn out to be what we most hope for. Only time and diligence and openmindedness will tell.

Theoretical formulation is a free enterprise if there ever was one. Theoretical certainty does not exist, and no theorist has the right to tell fellow theorists their business. Yet some contemporary personality theorists exhibit what we might call theoretical imperialism. Having developed a particular theoretical position, they try to persuade the reader that this position is the only defensible mode of representing human behavior. It is admirable to have the courage of one's convictions, but it is not very scientific to insist that one has the revealed truth. Theorists must state their theories and present their evidence in the most convincing way possible, but at the same time, they must allow the reader the freedom to make his or her own judgments.

CURRENT ISSUES AND RESEARCH TRENDS

It must be admitted that in recent years there has been less of an effort to develop comprehensive, master theories. There has been perhaps some reluctance to evolve a paradigm for personality. Some researchers question whether such a grand theory will be useful at this time, whether we are ready for it.

More typical of modern theorists is the effort to develop **minitheories**, formulations that, generally to the relative exclusion of other areas of study, focus on a particular kind or complex of behavior, such as decision making, learned helplessness, or moral development;

on a particular type of model, such as the mathematical model of learning; or on particular aspects of personality functioning, such as the neurophysiological substrates of mood. At some point and in some way, minitheories that are confirmed will need to be incorporated into any general theory of behavior.

There has been a broadening and deepening of our knowledge of the manner in which biological factors influence and are influenced by behavior (Fuller and Simmel, 1983; Henderson, 1982; Manosevitz, Lindzey, and Thiessen, 1969), and this information is beginning increasingly to inform accounts of human personality. It seems clear that biology is going to have much more to say about personality than it has had in the past, and theorists will have to incorporate the findings of the biological sciences into their formulations. Research in the neurosciences has been growing rapidly, and there have been some well-publicized efforts to extend evolutionary theory to areas of complex human behavior such as aggression, altruism, competition, cooperation, and sexual activity (Barash, 1977; Emlen and Oring, 1977; Wilson, 1975). As the reader can easily see, these are behaviors that are squarely in the domain of the personality theorist.

Developmental psychology has been exerting increasing influence on personality theory. Contemporary research on the developing human being, from infant to adolescent, has made important contributions to psychology and to personality theory (Hoffman, 1977). Research on social development, or the evolution of such behaviors as empathy, altruism, and role taking, has produced a very useful body of knowledge. And as more research on late adulthood and aging is conducted, information on personality change in the later years will increasingly be incorporated into personality theories. Thus it appears that personality theories will come in time to provide, in much greater detail, ideas about development throughout the life cycle.

Cognitive development is also an important focus of research interest that has had and will doubtless continue to have great influence on personality theory. Cognitive factors are of special interest to those theorists who are concerned with the self or the ego (Loevinger and Knoll, 1983).

Cognitive science in general, that area of psychology concerned with how people learn and use what they learn in their behavior, has become a very active area of research. Clearly, one can anticipate that research in cognitive science and personality psychology will continue to influence each other. Recently, in a diagram of the human cognitive system, Bower (Bower and Hilgard, 1981) has included goals and values; here is an instance of personality variables entering into cognitive science. Similarly, as more is learned about cognitive processes, personality theories that use cognitive formulations will benefit.

Behavioral medicine, or health psychology, is another research area that is currently active and that has considerable importance for personality psychology (Miller, 1983). Behavioral factors are significant in several major health problems, for example, obesity, smoking, and substance abuse. And considerable research has been conducted on the relation between the risk of heart attack and the personality types known as Type A and Type B.

Research in health psychology is advancing along a number of dimensions. For example, issues of disease prevention, compliance with treatment regimens, and post-illness health-promoting behavior have become the focus of considerable study. Personality theory quite clearly contributes to this work; ideas from a variety of theories have found their way into health psychologists' thinking and practice.

A promising trend among personality psychologists is what appears to be a lessening of polarization on specific issues. For example, as we have seen, the "either/or" argument between the trait theorists and the situational determinists seems to be resolving itself into an interactionist position. This particular issue does continue to be discussed, however (see Helson and Mitchell, 1978; Phares and Lamiell, 1977; Rorer and Widiger, 1983), for it is at the heart of personality theory. If there were no consistency or generality to a person's behavior, how could we speak of "personality"? Of what would "personality" consist? Although extremism in this debate has been significantly reduced, research and theorizing continue, as personality psychologists grapple with resolving these perplexing matters of human behavior.

The computer, now an established component of the scientific laboratory, has made possible quantitative analysis of hitherto undreamed of depth. Theories like Cattell's, for example, have been greatly enhanced in terms of the scope and power of the analyses they can carry out. Many other theories that use laboratory experimentation or large field studies have been facilitated by the ready availability of computerized means of controlling experiments and of collecting and analyzing data.

Factor analysis, as we have seen, involves locating a small number of hypothetical variables that could underlie and explain the interrelations that appear to exist among many observed variables. A new group of methods, variously called "causal modeling," "path analysis," or "structural equation analysis" (Bentler, 1980; Jöreskog and Sörbom, 1979) take the methods of factor analysis a step further. These new methods involve not only locating hypothetical variables A, B, C, D, and so on, but specifying causal relations among them, say, that A and B cause C, which in turn causes D. A statistical test can then be carried out against the observed data to see whether they are consistent with the relations the model would imply.

Because a number of causal relations can be specified among

The computer's capacity to handle extensive computations makes it indispensable to modern research techniques such as factor analysis and related methods.

the variables in such models, including feedbacks and reciprocal influences, these models alter the somewhat static picture presented by traditional factor analysis in the direction of a more dynamic representation of events. As a result, these methods have considerable appeal for personality, developmental, and social psychologists, in whose theories many such dynamic relations among unobserved variables may be found. These new methods involve extensive computation; hence, modern computers have played an essential role in their development and use.

The field of artificial intelligence essentially involves the use of computers to perform the kinds of cognitive tasks usually thought to be evidence of human thought or intelligence. Some psychologists see computer programs and the simulation of human behavior as the theoretical path of the future (Simon, 1969). But because human behavior involves more than cognitive functioning, the study of artificial intelligence is not likely to produce any general theories of behavior.

The assumption underlying artificial intelligence research is that to produce the equivalent of human reasoning we must first understand the processes that underlie human behavior. Clearly, this new field is going to continue to exert pressure on psychologists to produce ever more precise and explicit theories of human behavior and personality (Loehlin, 1968).

An important recent trend in reseach methodology will certainly have an effect on personality theory; subjects currently being studied are quite heterogeneous. From the infant to the octogenarian, from the normal person to the person who is seriously disturbed, from the college sophomore to the alienated youth, people of many different characteristics and backgrounds are providing, as research subjects, a broader and more robust data base for the evaluation and construction of personality theory.

ONE THEORY OR MANY?

Although, as we have seen, there are many similarities among the personality theories we have discussed in this book, these similarities are in general quite broad. The numerous diversities and disagreements are admittedly somewhat more striking. We are still a long way from a single, comprehensive theory.

It is good to have so many conflicting perspectives in a single empirical area? Would it not be useful to construct a single viewpoint by combining all that is good and effective from each of the theories we have reviewed? Could we combine the strengths of each of these theories into one really powerful theory that would improve our insight into human behavior and enable us to generate predictions that would be more comprehensive and verifiable than any currently generated by single theories?

A fair number of contemporary psychologists support this line of thought. There are, however, a number of serious objections to it; let us consider a few of these points. First, to combine elements of different theories we would have to be quite clear about the exact nature of such elements. As we now know, this is not possible, for many theories are stated imprecisely.

Second, to combine important elements of various theories, we would need either to be able to ascertain that there are no major conflicts between the theories involved or to be able to resolve any such conflicts. There are many points where theories are in flat disagreement. Further, these points of disagreement are often related to empirical phenomena that have not been adequately studied. Thus there is no quick and easy way to resolve conflicts.

Third, combining the best of each theory assumes that all or most of these theories have something positive to contribute to an integrated personality theory. The truth of the matter is that some of these theories have not as yet been shown to be useful. The amount of research that has been conducted on the derivable hypotheses of some theories has been minute, compared to the range of issues with which such theories propose to deal.

Fourth, the integrationist point of view assumes that at this point, theoretical agreement and harmony are healthy. When so little is known with certainty about human personality, when relevant empirical findings are so scanty and focused on so many divergent points, why place all of the future's hopes in one basket? It seems far more desirable to let theoretical development follow a natural course, with the reasonable expectation that as stable empirical findings multiply and individual theories are more precisely and adequately stated, an integration may evolve naturally. This seems preferable to prematurely imposing an artificial synthesis that inevitably will reflect personal taste and belief.

Finally, we must point out that a number of the theories we have discussed are highly eclectic. For example, Allport's final position incorporates much from other theories. Maslow's theory draws on a number of conceptions first introduced by others. Bandura's social learning theory has come to display much in common with cognitive approaches, which were once considered the very antithesis of the S–R tradition out of which Bandura's theory first evolved. All this natural merging and intermixing has not produced any single position of consensus, so how can we reasonably impose such a position at this time?

All right, some readers may say, but would it not be easier for the student to examine one organized view of personality than the welter of contradictory ideas we have presented in this book? It might indeed be easier for the student, but it would certainly give him or her a false sense of harmony and poor preparation for serious work in the

Much continuing investigation will be needed to produce a single, comprehensive theory of personality.

field of personality—indeed, for serious work in any academic field. To suggest to readers that there is only one useful theory when in fact no such thing has been demonstrated would deceive them as to the nature of science and as to the current status of the psychology of personality.

Readers should be aware that the challenges in this field are still there to be met and that, as a consequence, there is excitement ahead for the student of human personality. The importance of empirical study and the possibility that theoretical changes may be imposed by the outcome of such study must not be overlooked. It is also important to realize that the many different theorists making different assumptions, focusing on different empirical problems, and using different techniques are united in their common interest in human behavior. They expect empirical data to make the final decisions concerning theoretical usefulness.

Another problem with a general synthesis or integration is that it tends to make people cautious in approaching theory building and testing. One feels one must take all points of view into consideration and avoid emotional involvement with a particular position. As we said in Chapter 1, we feel strongly that once students have surveyed available theories of personality, they should adopt a given theory wholeheartedly and without reservation, giving it every possible chance to work for them. Only in this way can they examine the full potential of the theory.

The ultimate answer to any theoretical issue lies in well-controlled empirical data, and the nature of such data will be adequately defined only as the theories themselves are better developed. Giving each theory its fair opportunity seems the best way to ensure that such improved theories will produce the data we need to resolve the significant theoretical issues and to evolve the master theory for which psychology has so long been searching.

SUMMARY

1. Although the notion of **unconscious** as well as **conscious** factors in behavior is generally accepted, many theorists question the degree to which such factors operate—under what conditions and how strongly.

2. Even though most theorists accept the importance of both the **acquisitions** and the **process of learning**, only a few provide a detailed picture of the learning process.

3. Interest in the **hereditary** determinants of behavior is growing rapidly, but American-born theorists still tend to focus most of their attention on **environmental** factors.

4. Both **past** and **present** factors are generally accepted as determining behavior, but many theorists hold that the past is significant only through the operation of present factors.

5. There is a strong tendency for theorists to emphasize the **holistic** rather than the **analytic** approach, stressing that theories must be complex and multivariate and refer to the situation as well as to behaviors of the person in other contexts.

6. Most common is an interactionist view of the relative importance of **person** and **situation**.

7. Most personality theorists view human beings as **purposive**, rather than **mechanistic**, creatures.

8. Most theorists call upon **a few** rather than **many motives** to explain the dynamics of behavior.

9. Although the majority of the theorists discussed either are psychotherapists or have worked with the psychologically distressed, most try to address issues of both **normal** and **abnormal** functioning.

10. In general, personality theories have stimulated a great deal of research of varied types, which has been carried out by many different investigators. Some theories have led to research of somewhat limited scope; this work is often carried out by followers of these theories.

11. Personality theory needs to improve its understanding of the role of theory in stimulating research. Theorists must be both boldly creative and patiently diligent, and they must be free to develop any formulation that seems fruitful, regardless of whether it offends or is contrary to general beliefs. The only true criticism of a theory is an alternative theory that works better.

12. Theoretical imperialism will only impede psychology's progress toward its paradigm, which will be attained only by allowing the empirical data to determine theoretical usefulness.

13. There are a number of currently important substantive issues in personality theory. A growing number of **minitheories**, if confirmed, must eventually be incorporated into a general theory of behavior. Biological factors in behavior are being given increasing attention. The findings of research in developmental psychology are increasingly influencing personality theory. Work on cognitive development is of particular interest to theorists concerned with the self or ego. Cognitive science and personality theory are beginning to have considerable influence on each other. Personality theory is contributing to work in the area of behavioral medicine, or health psychology. And there is a trend to less polarization among theorists on issues important to personality theory, such as the person–situation argument.

14. Some methodological innovations are facilitating research in personality. The computer has enhanced the scope of research that can be carried out. New variations of factor analytic methods are making it possible to represent events in a more dynamic manner. Studies of artificial intelligence are demanding more precise and explicit theories of human behavior. And an increasing use of heterogeneous subjects is providing a more robust data base for personality theory formulations.

15. It would be premature to create a synthesis of existing personality theories. Existing theories are imprecise, they conflict in many ways, their findings are still conjectural, and the merging that has already taken place has not produced a single consensus. To impose an artificial synthesis at this stage would preclude giving existing theories every possible opportunity to contribute to the understanding of personality.

SUGGESTED READING

Here we provide the reader with some suggestions for locating resource material on personality theory and research. These suggestions will help orient readers to sources of information about current issues in personality theory, to research articles on the concepts of a particular theorist, to surveys of literature on specific conceptions, and so on.

Some of the most important journals for personality psychology are the *Journal of Personality*, the *Journal of Personality and Social Psychology*, the *Journal of Abnormal Psychology*, and the *American Psychologist*. In these journals the reader will find primarily research articles. A good way to keep informed of new books on the subject of personality is to read *Contemporary Psychology*, a journal devoted to reviewing recently published books in psychology. By reading the reviews, you can decide what books on personality you wish to read. We have already mentioned, in Chapter 1, the *Annual Review of Psychology*, each issue of which generally contains at least one chapter that reviews theory, research, and current trends in some area of personality psychology.

In the journal *Psychological Abstracts* you will find short abstracts of articles published elsewhere. These abstracts can help you decide whether to read an entire article. When you are searching for material on a particular topic or theorist, you may want to consult the periodical and reference section of your library to see if a computerized search for abstracts on a particular topic can be made.

Glossary

The glossary defines selected terms used by the theorists discussed in this book, as well as some general terms relevant to the study of personality. In some cases, common definitions of terms that are in everyday usage are also offered. Theorists' names or chapter numbers are included to help students locate text discussions; see also the book's index.

ability trait A characteristic of the person that has to do with how effectively the person pursues his or her goals (Cattell).

abstract behavior Behavior in which the person not only perceives and reacts to stimuli but thinks about the meaning, interrelations, and potential usefulness of such stimuli (Goldstein).

acquisitions of personality The outcomes of learning; the enduring aspects of personality, such as habits or traits.

active imagination A technique of analysis in which subjects concentrate on dream and other images, reporting changes in them as they occur (Jung).

adoption study A research method that attempts to assess genetic influences on personality by studying resemblances among members of adoptive families (Chapter 11).

amplification A method of dream analysis in which a subject gives multiple, repeated associations to a particular dream element (Jung).

anima, animus See **archetype**.

anxiety In general, an unpleasant emotional state characterized by feelings of threat. For Freud, **realistic anxiety** is fear of a real danger, **moral anxiety** is fear of punishment by one's conscience, and **neurotic anxiety** is fear of punishment by others for one's instinctual impulses. For Horney, **basic anxiety** is the feeling of being alone and helpless in a threatening, hostile world. For Sullivan, anxiety is transmitted from mother to infant and is the first important learning experience.

anxiety hierarchy A list of objects or events that arouse a particular person's anxiety, ordered according to the degree to which each is anxiety provoking (Wolpe). See also **behavior therapy**.

archetype An image, or thought-form, that represents the possibility of a certain type of perception or action (Jung). Important archetypes are the **persona**, the role we play in society; the **anima** and **animus**, the representation within each person of the qualities of the other sex; the **shadow**, our animal instincts, spontaneity, and creativity; and the **self**, the achievement of integration among all aspects of the personality.

A–S (Ascendance–Submission) Scale A personality scale that assesses a person's tendency to be dominant or submissive in interpersonal relations (Allport).

attitude A consistent response toward a class of objects. For Allport, a characteristic of the person that may be specific or general and that is always evaluative; see also Table 10.1. Compare **habit**, **trait**. For Cattell, an interest of a certain intensity in a particular action regarding a particular object.

attitudes For Jung, two basic ways of orienting oneself toward the world; see **extraversion**, **introversion**.

authenticity An ideal state, in which all the possibilities of one's being have been fully realized (Binswanger and Boss).

autism Withdrawal into an inner, private world. Commonly used to refer to infantile autism, a disorder in which a child fails to develop normal communicative skills and is withdrawn, unresponsive, and extremely difficult to reach, either emotionally or intellectually (Chapters 13, 14).

autonomic nervous system (ANS)   A division of the nervous system that is important in emotional response; arousal and relaxation are regulated by its two subdivisions, the sympathetic and parasympathetic nervous systems, respectively (Eysenck, Miller and Dollard).

basic hostility   The predisposition to expect harm from other people and thus to distrust them; the companion of **basic anxiety** (Horney). See also **anxiety**.

becoming   The process of attempting to fulfill all the possibilities of being-in-the-world (Binswanger and Boss).

behavior analysis   An initial, evaluative procedure in behavior therapy in which the sources of anxiety are identified and appropriate therapeutic procedures are selected (Wolpe).

behavior genetics   A field of inquiry that studies the influence of the genes on behavior (Chapter 11).

behavior therapy   A form of psychotherapy that uses procedures based on learning principles—for example, extinction, reinforcement, or modeling—to help people unlearn undesirable behaviors and learn adaptive ones.

behavioral specification equation   A mathematical formula designed to predict behavior on the basis of information about specific traits and situations (Cattell).

behaviorism   In its classical form, this school of thought defined psychology as the study of behavior and restricted its data to observable activities (Skinner, Miller and Dollard).

being-in-the-world   The existentialist conception of human existence, in which human beings and the world have no existence apart from each other (Binswanger and Boss).

biofeedback   Information about one's own internal physiological processes—such as heart rate and blood pressure—that enables one to monitor and control such processes (Miller and Dollard).

birth order theory   The notion that place in the family constellation is an important determining factor in personality makeup and functioning (Adler).

B-realm   One of two modes of relating to the world (Maslow). In the *B* or *being realm*, people are concerned with the growth need of self-actualization, which includes such *meta-needs* as truth, goodness, beauty. Compare **D-realm**. See also **self-actualization**.

castration anxiety   Fear of being castrated, which assists the little boy in the resolution of his Oedipus complex (Freud). See also **Oedipus complex**.

cathexis, or **object cathexis**   An investment of psychic energy in a particular object that appears to satisfy a need of the organism (Freud).

character   According to Allport, "personality evaluated." Character usually implies an ethical judgment of "good" or "bad."

classical conditioning   A type of learning in which the pairing of a new stimulus with a prior stimulus leads the organism to respond to the new stimulus as it did to the first one, even when the initial stimulus is not present (Skinner, Miller and Dollard).

client-centered psychotherapy (Rogers)   See **person-centered psychotherapy**.

coercion to the biosocial mean, law of   The phenomenon in which environmental factors tend to oppose genetic ones; e.g., shy children are encouraged, boisterous ones restrained (Cattell).

cognition   A process by which an organism obtains knowledge of something; includes such things as perceiving, judging, reasoning.

cognitive prototype   A person's view of the typical, defining features of a category of behavior (Mischel).

collective unconscious   A portion of the mind composed of primordial images, or thought-forms, which derive from our human and animal ancestral past (Jung). See also **primordial image**.

common trait   A characteristic common to many people; one on which most people in a given culture can be compared (Allport). Compare **personal disposition**, **trait**.

compensation   The principle by which polar elements in the personality complement each other (Jung).

competence   The ability to meet the challenges of the external world successfully and to grow and mature (White).

complex   For Jung, a group of associated feelings, thoughts, and memories that have intense emotional content. For Murray, the combination of a need for interaction with a certain object or situation with a particular childhood press; see also **need integrate**, **press**.

concrete behavior   Behavior in which the person perceives and reacts to some stimulus object or event as it appears at the moment (Goldstein). Compare **abstract behavior**.

conflict   Opposition or struggle among varying motives and tendencies, either within the person or between the person and the external world (Horney, Lewin, Cattell, Miller and Dollard).

conflict-free sphere   An area or portion of functioning in which the ego is not in conflict with either id or superego but pursues its own objectives in adapting to its experience (Hartmann).

confluence learning   A type of learning in which a given behavior or attitude satisfies more than one goal (Cattell).

congruence   A match between a person's perceptions and interpretations of reality and that reality as it is perceived or interpreted by others (Rogers).

consciousness   That portion of the mind or mental functioning of which we are aware.

consensual validation   Achieving agreement about something with other people (Sullivan).

content analysis   For Rogers, a method of studying personality that involves recording, classifying, and counting a person's oral statements over a period of time. Allport has used this method in studying written records, such as letters and diaries, as well.

continuing valuing process   A process by which one continually reviews one's experience and adjusts one's values as the conditions of life change (Rogers).

cortical excitation level   The amount of electrical activity in the brain's cortex, as recorded in an electroencephalogram (Eysenck).

counterconditioning   Eliminating an unwanted response by conditioning, to the same stimulus, another, more desirable response that is incompatible with the first (Miller and Dollard, Wolpe).

creative power of the self   The force that, together with heredity and environment, determines human behavior; the person's unique way of interpreting and making use of his or her heredity and experience (Adler).

criterion analysis   A variant of factor analysis in which criterion groups make possible the identification of hypothesized factors (Eysenck).

cue   A stimulus that triggers a response (Miller and Dollard).

cue-producing response   A response that leads to or triggers another response (Miller and Dollard).

Dasein   See **being-in-the-world**.

death instinct   The presumed, unconscious wish of the organism to die that, although normally opposed by the life instincts, accounts for aggressive and destructive behavior (Freud).

defense mechanisms   Mental processes that operate unconsciously and distort reality with the aim of reducing anxiety (Freud). See Table 2.2.

defensiveness   The tendency to give answers, in a self-rating scale, that are designed to make one "look good" or to present oneself in a desirable manner (Rogers).

delay of gratification   The ability to forgo immediate reward for the sake of greater, future reward (Mischel).

desensitization   See **systematic desensitization**.

developmental line   A dimension of human functioning outlined as a sequence in a child's maturation, leading in general from dependence to self-sufficiency (Anna Freud).

diagnostic council   A group of investigators, of varying points of view and often representing several disciplines, who observe and study a human subject and subsequently integrate their separate findings (Murray).

differential R-technique   See **factor analysis**.

disorder of the first kind   Psychological disturbance in a person who is highly emotionally reactive and has high levels of cortical excitation; e.g., the anxiety neurotic (Eysenck).

disorder of the second kind   Psychological disturbance in a person who is highly emotionally reactive and has low levels of cortical excitation; e.g., the antisocial person (Eysenck).

displacement   For Freud, a process by which energy that is blocked from being invested in an object becomes invested in another object. For Miller and Dollard, the redirection of impulses that one is prevented from expressing.

D-realm   One of two modes in which people relate to the world (Maslow). In the D-realm, people are concerned with *deficiency* needs—physiological, safety, belongingness and love, and esteem needs. See also **B-realm**.

dream analysis   A process in which the actual contents of a person's dreams and the person's associations to those contents are explored (Freud, Jung; compare Chapter 7).

dream series method   A technique in which every dream recounted by a person is analyzed in the context of those that precede and follow it (Jung).

drive   A strong stimulus that impels action but does not determine the precise nature of that action. *Primary drives* include hunger, thirst, pain. *Secondary*, or *learned*, *drives*, such as the drive of fear, are acquired on the basis of primary drives (Miller and Dollard).

dynamic trait   An **erg**, **sentiment**, or **attitude** that is concerned with goal-seeking behavior (Cattell).

dynamism   A specific and recurrent pattern of behavior that characterizes a particular person, such as fear of the unfamiliar (Sullivan).

dysplasia   The appearance of the three primary components of physique in an inconsistent manner in different body parts (Sheldon). See also **somatotype**.

effect, law of   The principle that an organism learns more rapidly behaviors that are followed by a satisfying state of affairs (Chapter 14).

effectance motivation   An active tendency, or a motive, to put forth efforts to influence the environment with the aim of achieving competence (White). See also **competence**.

efficacy expectation   The conviction that one can successfully execute the behavior required to produce a particular outcome (Bandura). See also **self-efficacy**.

ego   That portion of the personality that is oriented toward reality and the external world (Freud). See also **id**, **superego**, Table 2.1.

ego psychology   A modification of psychoanalytic theory that sees the ego as independent and underlines the important influence of the external environment on the ego's development and functioning (Anna Freud, Hartmann, White). See also **object relations**.

ego quality   A quality of the personality achieved during a particular period of development as a consequence of meeting a particular challenge (Erikson). See also **stage theories of development**.

elaborative choice   The principle that the choices people make are those that move their personal construct systems in the direction of a greater ability to predict (Kelly).

epigenesis The embryological principle that a new organism develops out of an initially undifferentiated entity that is programmed to develop all the organism's parts in sequence. Adopted by Erikson to explain the evolution of the human being's psychological and social characteristics.

equalization The principle that when a stimulus changes an organism's average state of tension, the organism will try to return to that average state (Goldstein).

equivalence The principle that energy is conserved, never lost, from the personality system; if it disappears from one element, it appears in another (Jung).

erg An innate psychophysical disposition that predisposes a person to respond more readily and more intensely to certain events than to others and to take certain kinds of actions in respect to those events (Cattell).

event The result of an interaction between two or more facts, derived on the basis of the principles of *relatedness*, *concreteness*, and *contemporaneity* (Lewin). See also **fact**; Table 8.1.

existential dilemma The inherent conflict between our animal limitations and our human possibilities (Fromm).

existential guilt See **guilt**.

existentials Certain characteristics that are inherent in every human existence, such as *mood* and *existence-in-a-shared-world* (Binswanger and Boss).

expansion See **interpersonal style, model of.**

expectancy The person's belief that in a certain psychological situation a particular behavior will lead to reinforcement (Rotter).

expectation of reinforcement An expectation about the likely outcome of behavior and about how to achieve desirable and avoid undesirable outcomes (Bandura).

explanatory style A person's characteristic manner of explaining events in his or her life (Seligman).

externalization Attributing the origins of one's thoughts, feelings, and acts, whether positive or negative, to external sources rather than to factors within oneself (Horney).

extinction The disappearance of a particular response when it is no longer reinforced (Miller and Dollard).

extraversion For Jung, one of the two major attitudes, or orientations, of personality; predominantly extraverted people tend to be attuned to objective experience and to spend more time perceiving and responding to the external world than in thinking about their perceptions. For Eysenck, a type dimension characterized by such qualities as toughmindedness, the tendency to be outgoing, and the desire for novelty and excitement.

factor analysis A statistical research technique that, by correlating and analyzing measures of surface variables, can isolate the fundamental factors that control variation in surface factors and can estimate the extent to which the latter reflect fundamental factors. Techniques for gathering data for factor analysis include **R-technique**, which compares many people on several specific measures; **P-technique**, which compares one person's scores on several measures across situations and times; **Q-technique**, which correlates two people's scores on many different measures; and **differential R-technique**, a variant of R-technique, which repeats measures on different occasions and correlates the changes between them. See also **criterion analysis**.

facts Empirical, hypothetical, phenomenal, or dynamic elements, sensed or inferred, that occupy specific cells or regions in the **life space** (Lewin).

feeling See **functions**.

fictional final goals Ideal goals created by human beings on the basis of their subjective interpretation of reality and motivated by their primary drive to become superior (Adler). See also **superiority**.

fixation See **defense mechanisms**; Table 2.2.

flooding A behavior therapy procedure wherein a person is encouraged to encounter an anxiety-arousing stimulus and to maintain contact until he or she realizes that the expected disaster will not occur (Chapter 13).

foreign hull The objective world, the area beyond the life space (Lewin). See also **life space**.

free association The psychoanalytic method in which patients are required to relate to the analyst anything and everything that comes into awareness (Freud).

functional analysis of behavior An analysis of behavior in terms of the relations between controllable causes (stimuli, deprivations, etc.) and their effects (Skinner).

functional autonomy The notion that a given form of activity or behavior, originally engaged in for some specific reason, may become an end or a goal in itself (Allport). *Perseverative functional autonomy*, such as children's repetitive behaviors, may reflect neurological principles. *Propriate functional autonomy* is found at the highest level of the personality's organization; it reflects the human being's need to reach beyond pure reaction, to establish an identity, to find answers to the great problems of life, to achieve selfhood and uniqueness.

functions For Jung, four sets of processes by means of which the person perceives and responds to the world. **Thinking** seeks to understand the world and to solve problems; **feeling** gives subjective experiences of pleasure, pain, anger, love; **sensing** provides one's perceptions of oneself and the world; **intuiting** involves perceiving by way of the unconscious, or by "hunch."

fundamental postulate The core statement of Kelly's theory, which proposes that behavior is directed by the way people construe or interpret the events of their worlds.

genotype The genetic constitution of an individual (Chapter 11).

Gestalt psychology The system of thought that holds psychological phenomena to be undivided wholes, or Gestalts, and thus capable of being studied only as such, not as collections of elements.

ground of existence The particular life conditions into which one is born; also called **throwness** (Binswanger and Boss).

guilt The realization that one has violated ethical, moral, or religious principles. Guilt is often accompanied by a lessening of one's sense of personal worth and a feeling that one must atone for wrong done. For Kelly, guilt is the result of perceived failure in a core role; see also **role**. **Existential guilt**, for Binswanger and Boss, is the recognition of one's failure to fulfill all the possibilities of which one is capable in life.

gynandromorphy The degree to which body parts exhibit both male and female characteristics (Sheldon).

habit For Allport, a particular response to a particular stimulus; see also Table 10.1. Compare **attitude**, **trait**. For Miller and Dollard, a link between a stimulus and a response.

habitual response An act, composed of several specific responses, that typically recurs in the same or similar circumstances (Eysenck).

holism The view that the organism always behaves as a unified whole and that its dynamics can be understood only by discovering the laws that govern the whole, not just its parts (Chapter 6). See also Table 6.1.

holistic–analytic methodology A method of personality study that combines analysis of subparts with continual examination of the role of such subparts in the dynamics of the whole (Maslow).

humanism A philosophy that asserts the dignity and worth of human beings and their capacity for self-realization (Chapter 6).

hysteria Broadly, a psychological disturbance in which **repression** is the chief defense mechanism. In a common form, physical pain and disability may be experienced despite the absence of any clearly established organic disorder (Chapter 2).

id The original system of the personality

(Freud). The id's aim is to obtain pleasure and avoid pain. See also Table 2.1.

idealized self-image   An imaginary, largely unconscious picture of the self as having unlimited powers and superlative qualities (Horney).

identification   The mechanism by which the ego matches the id's mental image of a desired object with the actual perception of that object in reality (Freud). Also, the process by which the developing personality conforms its standards and behaviors to those of significant models.

identity status   J. E. Marcia's concept of the identity process in which he postulates four phases: identity achievement, foreclosure, identity diffusion, and moratorium (Chapter 3). See also Table. 3.4.

idiographic research   Research that focuses on the particular, or individual, case (Chapter 10).

I–E Locus of Control Scale   A personality scale that assesses the degree to which people feel in control of their lives (Rotter).

Incomplete Sentences Blank   A psychological instrument that elicits useful information about people's wishes, fears, attitudes (Rotter).

individuation   The analytic, differentiating process in the person's development toward a stable unity (Jung). See also **transcendent function**.

inferiority   Feeling weak and unskilled in the face of tasks that need to be completed (Adler). Compare **superiority**.

inferiority complex   A generalized and strong feeling of inferiority that often masks feelings of superiority (Adler). Compare **superiority complex**.

innate hierarchies of response   The tendency, in the infant, for certain responses to appear in a given situation before certain other responses (Miller and Dollard).

inner-personal region   The central part of the person, representing the motivational aspects of personality (Lewin).

instinct   The psychological representation of a bodily need; the wish to fulfill a physiological need, such as hunger, thirst, or sex (Freud). See also Figure 2.1.

instrumental learning   See **operant conditioning**.

integration learning   Learning to maximize long-term satisfaction by selectively expressing certain motives at a given moment and suppressing others (Cattell).

interactionism   The view that both person and situation are critically important in determining behavior.

interdependence   The relations between tension systems in the personality. In *simple interdependence*, systems are interchangeable; in *organizational interdependence*, independent actions are organized hierarchically and combined into wholes (Lewin).

interpersonal style, model of   The proposition that people relate to others in three basic ways: in **self-effacement**, seeking love; in **expansion**, seeking domination; in **resignation**, seeking to avoid relationships (Horney). See Table 5.2.

Interpersonal Trust Scale   A personality scale that assesses people's tendencies to trust or distrust other people (Rotter).

intersubjective validation   A phenomenological research technique that establishes validity by comparing several investigators' observations of the same phenomenon (Binswanger and Boss).

intrasubjective validation   A phenomenological research technique that establishes validity on the basis of consistency among several explications of the same behavior in a variety of situations (Binswanger and Boss).

introversion   For Jung, one of the two major **attitudes**, or orientations, of personality. Predominantly introverted people tend to be attuned to inner, subjective experience and to focus on their own perceptions of the external world. For Eysenck, a type dimension characterized by such qualities as tendermindedness, introspectiveness, and preference for solitary vocations.

iteration   A research technique in which investigators gradually refine a concept by repeatedly gathering and reassessing data (Maslow).

intuiting   See **functions.**

Jonah complex   Fearing to attempt to achieve self-actualization, in the belief that one is unlucky, insignificant, inferior (Maslow).

L data   Information about personality traits derived from the life record (Cattell).

learned helplessness   A behavioral reaction to unpleasant stimuli that is based on a belief in one's own helplessness to control the events in one's world (Seligman).

learning dilemma   A situation in which no response an individual makes is successful or in which a response that has been successful is no longer reinforced (Miller and Dollard).

libido   The energy of the life instincts (Freud).

life instincts   Instincts, such as hunger, thirst, and sex, that preserve both the individual and the species (Freud).

life space   The psychological representation of a person and his or her perceived environment (Lewin).

locomotion   The physical or psychological movement of the person from one region of the life space to another (Lewin).

malevolent transformation   The development by a child of hostile or antisocial behavior because of an expectation that others will respond negatively to the child's expressions of a need for affection (Sullivan).

manic-depressive psychosis   Broadly, a mental disorder characterized by extreme mood swings. The manic phase may include excitement, rapid and disconnected thought, overactivity, sometimes violence; the depressive phase may include feelings of inadequacy, anxiety, sadness, sometimes suicidal attempts.

masculine protest   The wish for the qualities and privileges regarded in our culture as male, such as strength, courage, independence, success (Adler).

mechanism   The view that events can be explained entirely in terms of their antecedents and, further, that behavior can be accounted for in terms of physical laws and principles comparable to those of the natural sciences.

microanalytic approach   A research approach that involves making detailed assessments of behavior and of hypothesized mediators over time (Bandura).

minitheory   A formulation that focuses on a particular kind or model of behavior or on a particular aspect of personality functioning.

mode   The expression of **being-in-the-world.** Two people may express a *dual* mode; people may maintain formal relations, in a *plural* mode; a person may remain aloof, in a *singular* mode, or lose himself in a crowd, in the mode of *anonymity* (Binswanger and Boss).

morphogenotype   The hypothetical biological structure that underlies the observable structure, or physique, of the human being (Sheldon).

multiple abstract variance analysis (MAVA) A statistical technique for determining the relative effects on a trait of hereditary and environmental factors (Cattell).

need   For Murray, a construct representing a force in the brain that organizes processes such as perception and action so as to change an unsatisfactory condition; see also Table 9.1. Maslow's theory of human motivation proposes two sets of needs that arise in hierarchical fashion: deficiency needs, including basic physiological needs, must be satisfied before growth needs (metaneeds); see also **B-realm, D-realm, self-actualization.** Fromm posits eight specifically human needs in addition to the animal, or physiological, needs; see Table 5.3.

need integrate   A need for a certain kind of interaction with a certain kind of object or event (Murray). A need integrate that involves an object or event associated with a childhood press becomes a complex. See also **complex, press.**

negative identity A sense of being potentially bad or unworthy sometimes developed by a young person facing the identity crisis (Erikson).

neurosciences Life sciences (e.g., anatomy, physiology, biochemistry) that deal with the characteristics of nerves and nervous tissue, especially with their relationship to behavior and learning.

neurosis A mental disorder in which a person functions normally in most areas of life but experiences various distressing symptoms such as excessive anxiety or depression, troublesome thoughts, or physical disturbances that may or may not have organic causes.

neuroticism A personality dimension characterized by a tendency to have below-average emotional control, to be slow in thought and action, to lack sociability, to repress unpleasant facts (Eysenck). See also Table 12.3.

nomothetic research A type of research that attempts to discover general laws by comparing many individuals (Allport). See also **idiographic research**.

nonproductiveness The negative, life-denying orientation to the world (Fromm). See also Figure 5.3.

Nothingness The constant threat that one will lose one's Being, or become nothing (Binswanger and Boss).

object relations In ego psychology, the person's relations with other people, who are termed "objects" (Chapter 3).

Oedipus complex The child's development, somewhere between the ages of 2 and 5, of a sexual attraction toward the parent of the opposite sex and hostility toward the parent of the same sex (Freud). See also Box 2.2.

operant A behavior that is performed in the absence of any directly compelling stimulus (Skinner).

operant conditioning A kind of conditioning in which the response itself is operational in bringing about reinforcement (Skinner).

operational definition An empirical definition that attempts to specify the operations or procedures employed in measuring a variable or distinguishing it from others.

ordination The higher mental processes by which a person selects and puts into operation a plan of action that has a desired end state (Murray). See also **serial program**, **schedule**.

organism The physical creature, with its physical and psychological functions; the locus of all experience (Rogers). See also **phenomenal field**, **self**.

outcome expectations People's estimates that given behaviors will lead to particular outcomes (Bandura).

pampered style of life The style of life that characterizes the person who does little or nothing for others and either manipulates or forces them into satisfying his or her own needs (Adler).

paradigm A grand theory or super model that offers a revolutionary yet compelling way of looking at problems and solutions for an entire area of scientific research.

paranoid psychosis A mental disorder in which delusions, or false beliefs—usually of being persecuted by others—seriously interfere with normal functioning.

parapraxis Freud's term for a behavior that betrays unconscious processes, such as a slip of the tongue.

participant modeling A technique for changing behavior in which subjects first observe a model perform a specific behavior and then perform the same behavior, first with the model's help and then alone (Bandura).

peak experience A mystical experience in which there are feelings of ecstasy, wonder, awe (Maslow). People often feel strengthened, even transformed, by such experiences.

penis envy The little girl's belief that she has been deprived of a penis and the wish to possess one; both phenomena lead her into the **Oedipus complex** (Freud).

perceptual-motor region The outer region of

the person, representing perceptual and motoric aspects (Lewin).

permeability   For Lewin, the relative ease with which cells or regions in the life space influence each other. For Kelly, the capacity of a personal construct to adapt to changing conditions.

person-centered psychotherapy   A school of therapy (formerly called **client-centered**) in which the therapist and client relate to one another as persons of equal worth (Rogers).

persona   See **archetype**.

personal construct   The primarily cognitive means by which people construe or interpret the events of their worlds (Kelly). The personal construct is dichotomous, or bipolar; it has a **range of convenience**, applying to some things and not to others; and it may have greater or less **permeability**, or flexibility.

personal disposition   An individual trait that is unique to a particular person (Allport). Most people can be described by 5 to 10 *central*, highly characteristic dispositions. Of more limited occurrence, *secondary* dispositions are aroused by a narrow range of stimulus situations. The rare, *cardinal* disposition is a kind of ruling passion. See also **common trait**, **trait**.

personal unconscious   That portion of the mind, generally within easy reach of consciousness, that contains traces of experiences that have been suppressed or forgotten or have simply failed to make a conscious impression (Jung).

personality syndrome   A hierarchically organized complex of perceptions, impulses, thoughts, and behaviors that have a similar dynamic meaning or purpose (Maslow).

personification   An image of a person that one builds up out of either positive experiences with need satisfaction or negative experiences with anxiety and deprivation (Sullivan). Some early personifications are the *good* and *bad mothers* and the *good-me, bad-me,* and *not-me.*

personology   The branch of psychology that studies individual human lives and the factors that influence them (Murray).

phenomenal field   The totality of the organism's experiences, both conscious and unconscious (Rogers).

phenomenology   The study of the data of immediate experience (Binswanger and Boss).

phenotype   The visible properties of an organism, produced by the interaction of genotype and environment (Chapter 11).

phylogeny   The racial history of a particular organism or genetically related group of organisms. For Jung, the phylogenetic origins of personality lie in the individual's inheritance, through **primordial images**, of the past experience of the human race. See also **collective unconscious.**

pleasure principle   The principle by which the id operates, aiming always to achieve pleasure and to avoid pain (Freud).

ponderal index   The ratio of an individual's height to the cube root of his or her weight (Sheldon).

press   A property of a person, object, or environmental condition that has either positive or negative effects on a subject (Murray). *Alpha press* represent such properties as they exist in reality; *beta press* represent a subject's perceptions of such properties.

pride system   The combination of **neurotic pride**, or pride in things that support the idealized self-image, and **self-hate**, or self-criticism for not living up to that image (Horney).

primal scene   The child's actual witnessing, and later recall, of its parents' sexual intercourse, or the child's fantasy of this scene (Freud).

primary process   The type of mental processing that characterizes the id (Freud). The primary process is concerned with satisfying the id's desires without regard to reality's constraints. See also **secondary process.**

primordial image   A memory trace or thought-form from the human being's ancestral—both human and animal—past (Jung). See also **collective unconscious.**

proceeding The basic unit of behavior (Murray). A time-limited interaction between a person and one or more others or between a person and an object.

productiveness The positive, life-affirming orientation to the world (Fromm). See also Figure 5.3.

projection See **defense mechanisms**; Table 2.2.

projective test A psychological test that presents subjects with relatively unstructured stimuli on the assumption that, when unrestricted by rules or directions, subjects will respond so as to reveal unconscious desires and wishes.

propriate striving Intentions, plans, goal setting (Allport). See also **proprium.**

proprium The self as object, including the sense of bodily self, the self-image, and propriate striving (Allport). See also Table 10.2.

pseudospeciation The tendency to think of the subspecies to which one belongs (e.g., family, nation) as ''the'' human species (Erikson). Can vary from loyalty to prejudice.

psyche The personality, embracing all thought, feeling, and behavior, whether conscious or unconscious (Jung).

psychic energy For Freud, the energy that powers psychological activities like thinking; can be transformed into physiological energy and vice versa. For Jung, the energy of the personality, manifested consciously as many sorts of striving and willing, as well as by such processes as perceiving and thinking; originates in one's experience.

psychic value A measure of the amount of psychic energy committed to a particular psychic element (Jung).

psychical energy The energy that performs psychological work, derived from an increase in tension in one part of the personality relative to the rest of the system and from the system's effort to equalize this tension (Lewin).

psychohistory The study of the lives of historical figures (Erikson). Employs both psychoanalytic and historical methods of analysis.

psychological environment The person's environment as perceived by the person; thus, the subjectively experienced environment (Lewin).

psychopharmacology The study of the effect of chemical agents, or drugs, on behavior (Chapters 11, 13).

psychosexual A term descriptive of Freud's theory of development, which focuses on the unfolding of the sex instinct as it influences and is reflected in both mental and physical functioning (Chapters 2, 3).

psychosis A mental disorder in which contact with reality is impaired and which seriously interferes with all areas of a person's life.

psychosocial A term applied to Erikson's theory of development, which incorporates Freudian psychosexual dynamics but elaborates the effect of interaction with the social environment on the developing person's mental and emotional functioning.

psychosocial moratorium A time during which some young people who are not ready to resolve their identity crises postpone adult commitments (Erikson). See also **identity status**; Tables 3.2, 3.4.

psychoticism A type, or broad dimension, of personality characterized by such things as poor concentration, poor memory, insensitivity to others, unconventionality (Eysenck).

P-technique See **factor analysis.**

purposivism In general, the view that purposes are effective determiners of behavior; that behavior can be explained by its being directed toward specific goals.

Q data Information about personality that is obtained by questionnaire (Cattell).

Q-sort A method of data collection by which people's notions about themselves can be studied systematically (Rogers).

Q-technique See **factor analysis.**

quasi-need A specific need that evolves out of a person's interactions with other people and with aspects of the culture (Lewin).

range of convenience The area of meaning within which the dichotomy of a personal construct is applicable; e.g., tall–short applies to people but not to time (Kelly).

reaction formation See **defense mechanisms**; Table 2.2.

reality principle The principle by which the ego delays need satisfaction until it can decide on an appropriate course of action (Freud). See also **secondary process**.

reciprocal determinism The continuous reciprocal interaction among cognitive, behavioral, and environmental determinants (Bandura).

reciprocal inhibition A phenomenon in which eliciting one response appears to bring about a decrease in the likelihood of another (Wolpe).

region A division of the **life space** (Lewin).

regnancy The notion that specific, albeit hypothetical, brain processes exist that exercise controlling influence on psychological phenomena (Murray).

regression For Freud, a defense mechanism; see Table 2.2. For Jung, the "backward movement" of psychic energy; the rise in value of processes concerned with inner, usually unconscious, needs.

reinforcement An operation that makes a particular behavior either more or less likely to occur in the future. In **operant conditioning**, or **instrumental learning**, commonly called a **reward** (Chapters 13, 14).

repression For Freud, a defense mechanism; the forcing out of conscious awareness of memories, thoughts, and ideas that arouse anxiety; see Table 2.2. (Also, Jung, Miller and Dollard.)

resignation See **interpersonal style, model of.**

respondent In **classical conditioning**, a response that is elicited by a specifiable stimulus (Skinner).

response generalization The principle that a stimulus will come to elicit not only the response that initially follows it but a number of similar responses (Chapter 14).

reward See **reinforcement**.

ritual An activity engaged in by a community of adults to mark an important event of a recurring nature (Erikson).

ritualism The distortion of a ritualization, in which a person's attention becomes focused exclusively on self (Erikson).

ritualization A somewhat playful, culturally patterned way of doing something in interaction with other people (Erikson).

role A socially expected behavior pattern usually determined by a person's status in a particular society, e.g., husband, daughter, police officer, scout leader. For Kelly, role is a process that is based on the role player's construction, or interpretation, of how other people with whom he or she interacts construe or interpret particular events or situations. A *core role*, such as that of parent, is basic to the maintenance of a person's identity.

Rorschach test A projective psychological test in which subjects' statements as to what they see in a series of inkblots are thought to reveal significant unconscious desires and fantasies.

R-technique See **factor analysis.**

schedule A plan for satisfying needs and avoiding conflict between competing needs and wishes (Murray).

schizophrenia A collective term for a group of mental disorders that share certain basic characteristics—disruption in daily functioning and serious disturbance in one or more of the following areas: perception, thinking, language and communication, emotional expression, sense of self, goal-directed activity, relations with other people, and motor behavior. See also **psychosis**.

search for glory The attempt to fulfill one's **idealized self-image** (Horney).

secondary process Realistic thinking, the process by which the ego operates (Freud). See also **reality principle**.

selective inattention Failing to notice what one does not want to, or cannot, cope with (Sullivan).

self For Jung, the center of the personality; see **archetype**. For Rogers, an organized yet changing Gestalt that may be in or out of awareness. The *self as it is* reflects the self's current structure, the *ideal self* the person's goals for development and achievement. For Horney, the *actual self* is the person one is in everyday life, and the *real self*, the force that impels growth and self-realization; see also **idealized self-image**.

self-actualization For Maslow, the need to develop and make use of one's capacities and talents and to understand and accept oneself. For Rogers, this need is the single motivating force in life.

self-effacement See **interpersonal style, model of.**

self-efficacy The person's perception of how well he or she can perform in a given situation (Bandura).

self system Sullivan's self-system is composed of two elements, the *personified self* and *security operations*. The self-system, whose purpose is to avoid or minimize anxiety, protects the personality but can also interfere with its functioning; see also Figure 5.4. For Bandura, the **self system** comprises cognitive structures and functions whose purpose is to provide for the perception, evaluation, and regulation of behavior; see also Figure 15.2.

sensing See **functions**.

sentiment An organized structure of attitudes and an environmental-mold source trait (Cattell). See also **source traits.**

serial A series of proceedings (Murray). See also **proceeding**.

serial program An orderly arrangement of subgoals leading to some major goal (Murray).

serial thema A combination of themas in

which similar dynamics are operative (Murray). See also **thema**.

shadow See **archetype.**

shaping of behavior Manipulating the behavior of an organism so that, by successive approximations, it comes to emit desired responses (Skinner).

shoulds A set of rigid and excessively difficult demands on the self, created to support the **idealized self-image** (Horney).

16 Personality Factor Questionnaire A personality test that assesses people on 16 primary traits. Used as a research device and in diagnostic, therapeutic, counseling, and industrial settings (Cattell).

Skinner box A small, soundproof chamber for use in experimentation with pigeons, rats, or other small animals (Chapter 13).

social character theory Fromm's theory that character develops on the basis of the social arrangements under which human beings live. Postulates four basic character dimensions that may be adaptive or maladaptive: accepting–receptive, preserving–hoarding, taking–exploitative, and exchanging–marketing. See also **nonproductiveness**, **productiveness**; Figure 5.3.

social interest A caring and concern for the welfare of others that, ideally, continues to guide people's behavior throughout life (Adler).

somatotype Sheldon's formulation (a series of three digits) of the degree to which a physique possesses the three components of *endomorphy*, *mesomorphy*, and *ectomorphy*. See also Figure 11.1.

somnolent detachment The baby's means of escape, through sleep, from anxiety (Sullivan).

source traits Underlying traits, identified through factor analysis, whose interaction produces **surface traits** (Cattell). Termed constitutional or environmental-mold, depending on whether they are attributable to hereditary or environmental factors, respectively. See also **ability**, **dynamic**, and **tem-**

perament traits.

specific response A single act or response (Eysenck)

stage theories of development Theories of the evolution of personality that view the individual as developing through a series of stages. Freud's psychosexual theory posits five stages, from infancy through adulthood, the first three of which are decisive in the formation of personality; see Table 2.3. Erikson's psychosocial theory posits eight stages of development, from birth to old age, during each of which a specific crisis or challenge must be met in order for a positive ego quality, such as trust, to emerge; see Table 3.2. Jung proposes four stages, from childhood through old age; see Box 4.4 Sullivan proposes seven stages, from infancy through maturity; see Table 5.4.

stereotypes Mental images, common to members of a group, that represent oversimplified, evaluative judgments based on emotional response rather than rational thought. For Sullivan, shared personifications handed down from generation to generation.

stimulus discrimination A process by which an organism comes to distinguish between situations in which a response is or is not reinforced, learning to make the response only in certain situations (Chapters 13, 14).

stimulus generalization A process by which an organism comes to make the response it makes in one situation in other situations that are sufficiently similar to the first (Chapters 13, 14).

Study of Values, A A personality measure that assesses an individual's attitudes toward six particular values (Allport).

style of life Our unique way of seeking the particular goals we have set in the particular life circumstances in which we find ourselves (Adler).

sublimation For Freud, a form of **displacement** that can produce social and cultural achievements. For Jung, the displacement of energy from processes that are less differentiated to those that are more differentiated and emphasize cultural and spiritual aims. For Miller and Dollard, an adaptive form of displacement in which energies that cannot be expended in their original form are rechanneled.

subsidiation A relationship among needs or motives in which one is subsidiary to another or serves to facilitate the other (Murray, Cattell). See also Figure 12.1.

superego For Freud, that portion of the personality that represents parentally approved behaviors (ego ideal) and disapproved behaviors (conscience). See also Table 2.1.

superiority The goal of every human being (Adler). Together with the feeling of inferiority, the superiority drive powers the person's overarching motive to become strong, competent, achieving, creative.

superiority complex An apparent belief in one's superiority to everyone else (Adler). Usually hides feelings of inferiority. Compare **inferiority complex**.

superstitious behavior A kind of conditioning in which a response and a reinforcer are connected by accident (Skinner).

surface trait A trait derived by grouping phenomena that appear to go together (Cattell).

symbol An outward expression of an **archetype** (Jung).

symbolic modeling A method of changing behavior in which subjects observe filmed models and then imitate the models' behavior (Bandura).

symptoms Specific sensations or behaviors that the person experiences as unpleasant and not normal (Chapter 14).

symptom substitution The appearance of a new symptom in place of one that has been eliminated through therapeutic measures (Chapter 13).

synchronicity The principle that holds that events may occur together in time and appear to be related but may neither cause nor be caused by each other (Jung).

syntax A theory's set of rules for the systematic interaction of its assumptions and concepts.

systematic desensitization   A behavior therapy method in which a person is first taught to relax and then is helped gradually to deal with an anxiety-provoking object or situation (Chapters 14, 15).

task substitution   A research procedure devised to study the relations among tension systems in the personality and involving the substitution of one task for another (Lewin).

temperament   For Allport, composed of those dispositions that are closely linked to biological or physiological determinants. For Sheldon, composed of three basic dimensions—*viscerotonia, somatotonia*, and *cerebrotonia*—all assumed to have biological or somatic roots. See also Table 11.2.

temperament trait   A **source trait** that has to do with the manner in which a person moves toward his or her goals (Cattell).

tension   In the person, the state of one inner-personal cell relative to the state of surrounding cells (Lewin).

tension reduction   Brought about by the satisfaction of a need, For Freud, behavior is activated by increases in tension and is quieted by actions that dispel tension. The notion of tension reduction is important also in the theories of Sullivan, Lewin, Murray, Miller and Dollard.

textural aspect   A measure of the coarseness or fineness of body characteristics (Sheldon).

thema   A combination of a particular need with a particular press (Murray).

Thematic Apperception Test (TAT)   A projective psychologial test in which subjects are asked to tell stories in response to a series of somewhat ambiguous pictures on the assumption that these stories will reveal important needs and motives (Murray).

thinking   See **functions.**

thrownness   See **ground of existence.**

token economy   A behavioral therapeutic technique based on the principles of operant conditioning in which appropriate behavior is rewarded with tokens, which are later exchanged for desired objects and events (Chapter 13).

topology   A branch of mathematics that focuses on the connections and relations among things (Lewin).

training situations, critical   Four early childhood training situations (feeding, cleanliness, sex, aggression) that often produce conflict and emotional disturbance (Miller and Dollard).

trait   For Allport, a hypothetical neuropsychic structure that predisposes one to perceive various stimuli as similar and to respond to such stimuli in similar ways; see also **common trait, personal disposition.** For Cattell, an inferred mental structure that accounts for the consistency of observed behavior; see also **ability, dynamic, source, surface, temperment traits.** For Eysenck, a collection of habitual responses that are in some way related and that have some consistency; see also **habitual response, specific response.**

transcendent function   The process by which different aspects of the personality, including its conscious and unconscious portions, are integrated into an effectively functioning whole (Jung). See also **individuation.**

type   Jung postulates eight psychological types, or dimensions of personality, composed of two **attitudes—extraversion** and **introversion**—and four **functions—thinking, feeling, sensing, intuiting;** see Box 4.3, Figure 4.3. For Allport, a type is a combination of certain **traits, habits,** and **attitudes** that, theoretically, can be seen in a number of people but actually fits no one person perfectly; see also Table 10.1. For Eysenck, a type is a broad dimension of personality made up of traits that are related to each other. Four such types are **extraversion–introversion, neuroticism, psychoticism,** and **intelligence;** see also Figure 12.5, Table 12.3.

trunk index (TI)   The ratio of the sizes of the

chest-trunk and stomach-trunk regions (Sheldon).

twin study Research that attempts to assess genetic influence on personality by studying resemblances and differences between identical twins and/or fraternal twins reared either together or apart (Chapter 11).

unconscious That portion of mental functioning of which we are not generally aware because its contents never were conscious or have been repressed, owing to their threatening character (Freud).

unity-thema A usually unconscious compound of interrelated strong needs linked to early childhood press that tends, in later life, to have a dominant influence on many areas of functioning (Murray).

valence The value for a person of a particular region of the psychological environment (Lewin).

value The desired end state of a **vector** (Murray).

vector For Lewin, a psychological force that impinges on the person, tending to make the person move in one direction or another. For Murray, an action tendency, based on a particular need.

verifiability A theory's capacity to generate predictions that are confirmed by data.

vicarious reinforcement Reinforcement that leads to learning but is experienced indirectly, by observing a model's reinforcement, or reward, for a given behavior (Bandura).

vicious circle A cyclical process in which **basic anxiety** and **basic hostility** lead to behaviors that serve to increase anxiety and hostility rather than to reduce them (Horney).

wish fulfillment The process of forming an image of a tension-reducing object; exemplified in the adult in dreams, daydreams, and hallucinations (Freud).

word association test A projective test in which subjects' responses (delayed reaction time, increase or decrease in physiological functions such as heart rate) to a series of words are said to reveal the presence of specific complexes (Jung). See also **complex**.

world-design The all-encompassing pattern of a person's modes of **being-in-the-world**; determines how people react in specific situations and the kinds of character traits they develop (Binswanger and Boss).

world-regions The three kinds of surroundings in which **being-in-the-world** finds expression—*Umwelt*, the biological and physical surroundings; *Mitwelt*, the human environment; and *Eigenwelt*, the psychological and physical self (Binswanger and Boss). See also Table 7.1.

References

Abramson, L. Y., Seligman, M. E. P., & Teasdale, J. D. Learned helplessness in humans: Critique and reformulation. *Journal of Abnormal Psychology*, 1978, *87*, 49–74.

Adams-Webber, J. R. *Personal construct theory: Concepts and applications*. New York: John Wiley, 1979.

Adams-Webber, J. R. Personal construct theory: Research into basic concepts. In F. Fransella (Ed.), *Personality: Theory, measurement and research*. London: Methuen, 1981.

Adelson, J. Against scientism. Review of *Endeavors in psychology: Selections from the personology of Henry A. Murray*. (E. S. Shneidman, Ed.). *New York Times Book Review*, August 9, 1981.

Adler, A. *Practice and theory of individual psychology*. New York: Harcourt Brace World, 1927.

Adler, A. *The neurotic constitution*. New York: Dodd, Mead, 1926. (First German edition, 1912; fourth edition, 1928.)

Adler, A. *Problems of neurosis*. London: Kegan Paul, 1929.

Adler, A. Individual psychology. In C. Murchison (Ed.), *Psychologies of 1930*. Worcester, Mass.: Clark University Press, 1930.

Adler, A. *What life should mean to you*. Boston: Little, Brown, 1931.

Adler, A. The fundamental views of individual psychology. *International Journal of Individual Psychology*, 1935, *1*, 5–8.

Adler, A. Co-operation between the sexes: *Writings on women, love and marriage, sexuality and its disorders* (H. L. Ansbacher & R. R. Ansbacher, Eds. and trans.). Garden City, N.Y.: Doubleday, 1978.

Adler, A. *Superiority and social interest* (H. L. Ansbacher and R. R. Ansbacher, Eds. and trans.) (3rd rev. ed.). New York: W. W. Norton, 1979.

Adler, G. *Studies in analytical psychology*. New York: W. W. Norton, 1948.

Allport, G. W. *Personality: A psychological interpretation*. New York: Holt, Rinehart and Winston, 1937.

Allport, G. W. Motivation in personality: Reply to Mr. Bertocci. *Psychological Review*, 1940, *47*, 533–554.

Allport, G. W. The use of personal documents in psychological science. *SSRC Bulletin* 49. New York: Social Science Research Council, 1942.

Allport, G. W. The ego in contemporary psychology. *Psychological Review*, 1943, *50*, 451–478.

Allport, G. W. Scientific models and human morals. *Psychological Review*, 1947, *54*, 182–192.

Allport, G. W. The trend in motivational theory. *American Journal of Orthopsychiatry*, 1953, *23*, 107–119.

Allport, G. W. *The nature of prejudice*. Cambridge, Mass.: Addison-Wesley, 1954.

Allport, G. W. Becoming: *Basic considerations for a psychology of personality*. New Haven, Conn.:

Yale University Press, 1955.

Allport, G. W. The open system in personality theory. *Journal of Abnormal and Social Psychology*, 1960, *61*, 301–310. (a)

Allport, G. W. *Personality and social encounter.* Boston: Beacon Press, 1960. (b)

Allport, G. W. *Pattern and growth in personality.* New York: Holt, Rinehart and Winston, 1961.

Allport, G. W. The general and the unique in psychological science. *Journal of Personality*, 1962, *30*, 405–422.

Allport, G. W. Imagination in psychology: Some needed steps. In *Imagination and the university.* Toronto: University of Toronto Press, 1964.

Allport, G. W. *Letters from Jenny.* New York: Harcourt Brace Jovanovich, 1965.

Allport, G. W. Traits revisited. *American Psychologist*, 1966, *21*, 1–10.

Allport, G. W. Autobiography. In E. G. Boring & G. Lindzey (Eds.). *A history of psychology in autobiography* (Vol. 5). New York: Appleton-Century-Crofts, 1967.

Allport, G. W. *The person in psychology: Selected essays.* Boston: Beacon Press, 1968.

Allport, G. W., & Allport, F. H. *A-S reaction study.* Boston: Houghton Mifflin, 1928.

Allport, G. W., & Cantril, H. Judging personality from voice. *Journal of Social Psychology*, 1934, *5*, 37–55.

Allport, G. W., & Odbert, H. S. Trait-names: A psycholexical study. *Psychological Monographs*, 1936, *47*, (Whole No. 211).

Allport, G. W., & Vernon, P. E. *A study of values.* Boston: Houghton Mifflin, 1931.

Allport, G. W., & Vernon, P. E. *Studies in expressive movement.* New York: Macmillan, 1933.

Allport, G. W., Vernon, P. E., & Lindzey, G. *A study of values* (rev. ed.). Boston: Houghton Mifflin, 1960.

Angyal, A. *Foundations for a science of personality.* Foreword by A. H. Maslow. New York:

Commonwealth Fund, 1941.

Ansbacher, H. L. Alfred Adler and humanistic psychology. *Journal of Humanistic Psychology*, 1971, 11, 53–63.

Ansbacher, H. L., & Ansbacher, R. R. (eds.). *The individual psychology of Alfred Adler.* New York: Basic Books, 1956.

Atkinson, J. W. *Motives in fantasy, action, and society.* Princeton, N.J.: D. Van Nostrand, 1958.

Atkinson, J. W. *An introduction to motivation.* New York: John Wiley, 1964.

Atkinson, J. W., & Feather, N. T. (Eds.). *A theory of achievement motivation.* New York: John Wiley, 1966.

Atkinson, J. W., Heyns, R. W., & Veroff, J. The effect of experimental arousal of the affiliation motive on thematic apperception. *Journal of Abnormal and Social Psychology*, 1954, *49*, 405–410.

Atkinson, J. W. & Raynor, J. O. *Motivation and achievement.* New York: V. H. Winston/John Wiley, 1974.

Ayllon, T., & Azrin, N. The measurement and reinforcement of behavior of psychotics. *Journal of the Experimental Analysis of Behavior*, 1965, *8*, 357–383.

Ayllon, T., & Azrin, N. *The token economy: A motivational system for therapy and rehabilitation.* New York: Appleton-Century-Crofts, 1968.

Bach, G. R., & Torbet, L. *A time for caring.* New York: Delacorte, 1982.

Baddely, A. D. *The psychology of memory.* New York: Basic Books, 1976.

Baldwin, A. L. Personal structure analysis: A statistical method for investigating the single personality. *Journal of Abnormal and Social Psychology*, 1942, *37*, 163–183.

Ball, E. D. A factor analytic investigation of the personality topology of C. G. Jung. *Dissertation Abstracts*, 1968, *28*, (10-B), 4277–4278.

Bandura, A. *Principles of behavior modification.* New York: Holt, Rinehart and Winston, 1969.

Bandura, A. *Aggression: A social learning analysis*. Englewood Cliffs, N.J.: Prentice-Hall, 1973.

Bandura, A. Self-efficacy: Toward a unifying theory of behavioral change. *Psychological Review*, 1977, *84*, 191–215. (a)

Bandura, A. *Social learning theory*. Englewood Cliffs, N.J.: Prentice-Hall, 1977. (b)

Bandura, A. The self system in reciprocal determinism. *American Psychologist*, 1978, *33*, 344–358.

Bandura, A. Psychological mechanisms of aggression. In M. VonCranach, K. Foppa, W. Lepenies, & D. Ploog (Eds.), *Human ethology: Claims and limits of a new discipline*. Cambridge: Cambridge University Press, 1979.

Bandura, A. Award for Distinguished Scientific Contribution: 1980. *American Psychologist*, 1981, *36*, 27–34.

Bandura, A. Self-efficacy mechanism in human agency. *American Psychologist*, 1982, *37*, 122–147.

Bandura, A., Adams, N. E., & Beyer, J. Cognitive processes mediating behavioral change. *Journal of Personality and Social Psychology*, 1977, *35*, 125–139.

Bandura, A., Adams, N. E., Hardy, A. B., & Howells, G. N. Tests of the generality of self-efficacy theory. *Cognitive Therapy and Research*, 1980, *4*, 39–66.

Bandura, A., Blanchard, E. B., & Ritter, B. The relative efficacy of desensitization and modeling approaches for inducing behavioral, affective, and attitudinal changes. *Journal of Personality and Social Psychology*, 1969, *13*, 173–199.

Bandura, A., Grusec, J. E., & Menlove, F. L. Vicarious extinction of avoidance behavior. *Journal of Personality and Social Psychology*, 1967, *5*, 16–23. (a)

Bandura, A., Grusec, J. E., & Menlove, F. L. Some social determinants of self-monitoring reinforcement systems. *Journal of Personality and Social Psychology*, 1967, *5*, 449–455. (b)

Bandura, A., & Huston, A. C. Identification as a process of incidental learning. *Journal of Abnormal and Social Psychology*, 1961, *63*, 311–318.

Bandura, A., Jeffery, R. W., & Wright, C. L. Efficacy of participant modeling as a function of response induction aids. *Journal of Abnormal Psychology*, 1974, *83*, 56–64.

Bandura, A., & Kupers, C. J. The transmission of patterns of self-reinforcement through modeling. *Journal of Abnormal and Social Psychology*, 1964, *69*, 1–9.

Bandura, A., & McDonald, F. J. The influence of social reinforcement and the behavior of models in shaping children's moral judgments. *Journal of Abnormal Psychology*, 1963, *67*, 274–281.

Bandura, A., & Mischel, W. Modification of self-imposed delay of reward through exposure to live and symbolic models. *Journal of Personality and Social Psychology*, 1965, *2*, 698–705.

Bandura, A., & Rosenthal, T. L. Vicarious classical conditioning as a function of arousal level. *Journal of Personality and Social Psychology*, 1966, *3*, 54–62.

Bandura, A., Ross, D., & Ross, S. A. Transmission of aggression through imitation of aggressive models. *Journal of Abnormal and Social Psychology*, 1961, *63*, 575–582.

Bandura, A., Ross, D., & Ross, S. A. Imitation of film-mediated aggressive models. *Journal of Abnormal and Social Psychology*, 1963, *66*, 3–11. (a)

Bandura, A., Ross, D., & Ross, S. A. Vicarious reinforcement and imitative learning. *Journal of Abnormal and Social Psychology*, 1963, *67*, 601–607. (b)

Bandura, A., & Schunk, D. H. Cultivating competence, self-efficacy, and intrinsic interest through proximal self-motivation. *Journal of Personality and Social Psychology*, 1981, *41*, 586–598.

Bandura, A., & Walters, R. H. *Adolescent aggression*. New York: Ronald Press, 1959.

Bandura, A., & Walters, R. H. *Social learning and personality development*. New York: Holt, Rinehart and Winston, 1963.

Bandura, A., & Whalen, C. K. The influence of antecedent reinforcement and divergent modeling cues on patterns of self reward. *Journal of Personality and Social Psychology*, 1966, *3*, 373–382.

Bannister, D., & Mair, J. M. M. *The evaluation of personal constructs*. New York: Academic Press, 1968.

Barash, D. *Sociobiology and behavior*. New York: Elsevier, 1977.

Barker, R. G. *Ecological psychology*. Stanford, Calif.: Stanford University Press, 1968.

Barrett, W. *Irrational man: A study in existential philosophy*. Garden City, N.Y.: Doubleday/Anchor, 1962.

Bash, K. W. Zur experimentellen Grundlegung der Jungschen Traumanalyse (On laying an experimental foundation for Jung's dream analysis). *Schweiz. Z. Psychol. Anwend.*, 1952, *11*, 282–295.

Baum, M. Extinction of avoidance responding through response prevention (flooding). *Psychological Bulletin*, 1970, *74*, 276–284.

Bennet, E. A. *C. G. Jung*. London: Barrie and Rockliff, 1961.

Bennet, W., & Gurin, J. *The dieter's dilemma*. New York: Basic Books, 1982.

Bentler, P. M. Multivariate analysis with latent variables: Causal modeling. *Annual Review of Psychology*, 1980, *31*, 419–456.

Bertocci, P. A. A critique of G. W. Allport's theory of motivation. *Psychological Review*, 1940, *47*, 501–532.

Bieri, J. Cognitive complexity–simplicity and predictive behavior. *Journal of Abnormal and Social Psychology*, 1955, *51*, 263–268.

Bijou, S., & Baer, D. M. Operant methods in child behavior and development. In W. Honig (Ed.), *Operant behavior: Areas of research and application*. New York: Appleton-Century-Crofts, 1966.

Binswanger, L. *Sigmund Freud: Reminiscences of a friendship*. New York: Grune & Stratton, 1957.

Binswanger, L. The case of Ellen West. In R. May, E. Angel, & H. F. Ellenberger (Eds.), *Existence: A new dimension in psychiatry*. New York: Basic Books, 1958. (a)

Binswanger, L. The existential analysis school of thought. In R. May, E. Angel, & H. F. Ellenberger (Eds.), *Existence: A new dimension in psychiatry*. New York: Basic Books, 1958. (b)

Binswanger, L. Insanity as life-historical phenomenon and as mental disease: The case of Ilse. In R. May, E. Angel, & H. F. Ellenberger (Eds.), *Existence: A new dimension in psychiatry*. New York: Basic Books, 1958. (c)

Binswanger, L. *Being-in-the-world: Selected papers of Ludwig Binswanger*. New York: Basic Books, 1963.

Binswanger, L. *Grundformen und Erkenntnis Menschlichen Daseins*. (4th ed.). Basel: Reinhardt, 1964.

Blanck, G., & Blanck, R. *Ego psychology: Theory and practice*. New York: Columbia University Press, 1974.

Blaney, P. H. Contemporary theories of depression: Critique and comparison. *Journal of Abnormal Psychology*, 1977, *86*, 203–223.

Blitsten, D. R. *The social theories of Harry Stack Sullivan*. New York: William-Frederick Press, 1953.

Boren, J. J. The study of drugs with operant techniques. In W. K. Honig (Ed.), *Operant behavior: Areas of research and application*. New York: Appleton-Century-Crofts, 1966.

Boring, E. G. *A history of experimental psychology* (2nd ed.). New York: Appleton-Century-Crofts, 1950.

Boring, E. G., & Lindzey, G. *A history of psychology in autobiography* (Vol. 5). New York: Appleton-Century-Crofts, 1966.

Boss, M. *The analysis of dreams*. London: Rider, 1957.

Boss, M. *Psychoanalysis and Daseinsanalysis*. New York: Basic Books, 1963.

Boss, M. *A psychiatrist discovers India*. London: Oswald Wolff, 1965.

Boss, M. *Existential foundations of medicine and psy-*

chology. New York: Aronson, 1977.

Boss, M. *"I dreamt last night . . ."*. New York: Gardner Press, 1977.

Bottome, P. *Alfred Adler: A biography*. New York: Putnam, 1939.

Bouchard, T. J., Jr. *The Minnesota study of twins reared apart: Description and preliminary findings*. Address to the American Psychological Association, Los Angeles, August 25, 1981.

Bower, G. H., & Hilgard, E. R. *Theories of learning* (5th ed.). Englewood Cliffs, N.J.: Prentice-Hall, 1981.

Breland, K., & Breland, M. The misbehavior of organisms. *American Psychologist*, 1961, *16*, 681–684.

Breuer, J., & Freud, S. *Studies in hysteria*. (A. A. Brill, transl.) Boston: Beacon Press, 1937. (First German edition, 1895.)

Brolyer, C. R. Review of Lewin's *Principles of topological psychology. Character and Personality*. 1936–1937, *5*, 251–258.

Brown, J. A. C. *Freud and the post-Freudians*. Baltimore: Penguin Books, 1961.

Brown, J. S., & Jacobs, A. The role of fear in the motivation and acquisition of responses. *Journal of Experimental Psychology*, 1949, *39*, 747–759.

Brown, N. O. *Life against death*. Middletown, Conn.: Wesleyan University Press, 1959.

Bruner, J. S. A cognitive theory of personality. *Contemporary Psychology*, 1956, *1*, 355–357.

Brunswik, E. Organismic achievement and environmental probability. *Psychological Review*, 1943, *50*, 255–272.

Buber, M. *I and Thou* (2nd ed.). New York: Scribner, 1958.

Bugental, J. F. T. *The search for authenticity: An existential–analytic approach to psychotherapy*. New York: Holt, Rinehart and Winston, 1965.

Burton, A. (Ed.). *Operational theories of personality*. New York: Brunner/Mazel, 1974.

Buss, A. H., & Plomin, R. *A temperament theory of personality development*. New York: John Wiley, 1975.

Butler, J. M., & Haigh, G. V. Changes in the relation between self-concepts and ideal concepts consequent upon client-centered counseling. In C. R. Rogers, & R. F. Dymond (Eds.), *Psychotherapy and personality change: Coordinated studies in the client-centered approach*. Chicago: University of Chicago Press, 1954.

Campbell, J. C. *The portable Jung*. New York: Viking, 1971.

Cantril, H. (Ed.). *Tensions that cause wars*. Urbana: University of Illinois Press, 1950.

Caplan, P. J. Erikson's concept of inner space: A data-based reevaluation. *American Journal of Orthopsychiatry*, 1979, *49*, 100–108.

Carlson, R. Where is the person in personality research? *Psychological Bulletin*, 1971, *75*, 203–219.

Carlson, R. Studies of Jungian typology: II. Representations of the personal world. *Journal of Personality and Social Psychology*, 1980, *38*, 801–810.

Carlson, R., & Levy, N. Studies in Jungian typology: I: Memory, social perception and social action. *Journal of Personality*, 1973, *41*, 559–576.

Cartwright, D. Lewinian theory as a contemporary systematic framework. In S. Koch (Ed.), *Psychology: A study of a science* (Vol. 2). New York: McGraw-Hill, 1959.

Cattell, R. B. *Description and measurement of personality*. New York: World Book, 1946.

Cattell, R. B. Concepts and methods in the measurement of group syntality. *Psychological Review*, 1948, *55*, 48–63.

Cattell, R. B. *Personality: A systematic, theoretical, and factual study*. New York: McGraw-Hill, 1950.

Cattell, R. B. *Personality and motivation structure and measurement*. New York: Harcourt Brace Jovanovich, 1957.

Cattell, R. B. The multiple abstract variance analysis equations and solutions: For nature–nurture research on continuous variables. *Psychological Review*, 1960, *67*, 353–372.

Cattell, R. B. Group theory, personality and role: A model for experimental researches. In F. A. Geldard (Ed.), *Defence psychology*. Oxford: Pergamon Press, 1961.

Cattell, R. B. *The scientific analysis of personality*. Chicago: Aldine, 1966. (a)

Cattell, R. B. (Ed.). *Handbook of multivariate experimental psychology*. Chicago: Rand McNally, 1966. (b)

Cattell, R. B. *Personality and mood by questionnaire*. San Francisco: Jossey-Bass, 1973.

Cattell, R. B., Autobiography. In G. Lindzey (Ed.), *A history of psychology in autobiography* (Vol. 6). Englewood Cliffs, N.J.: Prentice-Hall, 1974.

Cattell, R. B. *The scientific use of factor analysis in behavioral and life sciences*. New York: Plenum, 1978.

Cattell, R. B. Personality and learning theory (Vols. 1 & 2). New York: Springer, 1979, 1980.

Cattell, R. B. *The inheritance of personality and ability: Research methods and findings*. New York: Academic Press, 1982.

Cattell, R. B. *Structured personality-learning theory*. New York: Praeger, 1983.

Cattell, R. B., & Child, D. *Motivation and dynamic structure*. New York: John Wiley, 1975.

Cattell, R. B., & Cross, K. P. Comparison of the ergic and self-sentiment structure found in dynamic traits by R- and P-techniques. *Journal of Personality*, 1952, *21*, 250–271.

Cattell, R. B., & Dreger, R. M. *Handbook of modern personality theory*. Washington, D.C.: Hemisphere, 1977.

Cattell, R. B., Eber, H. W., & Tatsuoka, M. M. *Handbook for the 16PF*. Champaign, Ill.: Institute for Personality and Ability Testing, 1970.

Cattell, R. B., Saunders, D. R., & Stice, G. F. *The 16 Personality Factor Questionnaire*. Champaign, Ill.: Institute for Personality and Ability Testing, 1950.

Cattell, R. B., & Scheier, I. H. *The meaning and measurement of neuroticism and anxiety*. New York: Ronald Press, 1961.

Cattell, R. B., & Warburton, F. W. *Objective personality and motivation tests*. Urbana, Ill.: University of Illinois Press, 1967.

Chapman, A. H. *Harry Stack Sullivan: His life and his work*. New York: Putnam, 1976.

Chesler, P. *Women and madness*. Garden City, N.Y.: Doubleday, 1972.

Chodorkoff, B. Self-perception, perceptual defense, and adjustment. *Journal of Abnormal and Social Psychology*, 1954, *49*, 508–512.

Clark, R. W. *Freud: The man and the cause*. New York: Random House, 1980.

Cohen, E. D. *C. G. Jung and the scientific attitude*. New York: Philosophical Library, 1975.

Colby, K. M. On the disagreement between Freud and Adler. *American Imago*, 1951, *8*, 229–238.

Cole, C. W., Oetting, E. R., & Hinkle, J. E. Non-linearity of self-concept discrepancy: The value dimension. *Psychological Reports*, 1967, *21*, 58–60.

Coles, R. *Erik H. Erikson: The growth of his work*. Boston: Little, Brown, 1970.

Cortes, J. B. *Physique, need for achievement, and delinquency*. Unpublished doctoral dissertation, Harvard University, 1961.

Coutu, W. *Emergent human nature*. New York: Alfred A. Knopf, 1949.

Coyne, J. C., & Gotlieb, I. H. The role of cognition in depression: A critical appraisal. *Psychological Bulletin*, 1983, *94*, 472–505.

Dallett, J. O. *The effect of sensory and social variables on the recalled dream: Complementarity, continuity, and compensation*. Unpublished doctoral dissertation, University of California at Los Angeles, 1973.

Davis, A., & Dollard, J. *Children of bondage*. Washington, D.C.: American Council of Education, 1940.

De Rivera, J. *Field theory as human science: Contributions of Lewin's Berlin group*. New York: Halsted Press, 1976.

Deutsch, M. Field theory in social psychology.

In G. Lindzey & E. Aronson (Eds.), *Handbook of social psychology* (Vol. I.). Reading, Mass.: Addison-Wesley, 1968.

Deutsch, M. Field theory. In D. L. Sills (Ed.), *International Encyclopedia of the Social Sciences* (Vol. 5). New York: Macmillan, 1968.

Dicks, H. V. In search of our proper ethic. *British Journal of Medical Psychology*, 1950, *23*, 1–14.

Dollard, J. *Caste and class in a southern town*. New Haven, Conn.: Yale University Press, 1937.

Dollard, J. *Victory over fear*. New York: Reynal & Hitchcock, 1942.

Dollard, J. *Fear in battle*. New Haven, Conn.: Yale University Press, 1943.

Dollard, J., & Auld, F. *Scoring human motives*. New Haven, Conn.: Yale University Press, 1959.

Dollard, J., Auld, F., & White, A. *Steps in psychotherapy*. New York: Macmillan, 1953.

Dollard, J., Doob, L., Miller, N., Mowrer, O. H., & Sears, R. *Frustration and aggression*. New Haven, Conn.: Yale University Press, 1939.

Dollard, J., & Miller, N. E. *Personality and psychotherapy: An analysis in terms of learning, thinking, and culture*. New York: McGraw-Hill, 1950.

Domhoff, G. W. Two Luthers: The orthodox and heretical in psychoanalytic thinking. *Psychoanalytic Review*, 1970, *57*, 5–17.

Dry, A. M. *The psychology of Jung*. New York: John Wiley, 1961.

Dweck, C. S. The role of expectations and attributions in the alleviation of learned helplessness. *Journal of Personality and Social Psychology*, 1975, *31*, 674–685.

Dweck, C. S., & Repucci, N. D. Learned helplessness and reinforcement responsibility in children. *Journal of Personality and Social Psychology*, 1973, *25*, 109–116.

Dyer, R. *Her father's daughter: The work of Anna Freud*. New York: Aronson, 1983.

Ekman, G. On the number and definition of dimensions in Kretschmer's and Sheldon's constitutional systems. *In Essays in psychology dedicated to Daniel Katz*. Uppsala: Almquist, 1951 (as cited in Humphreys, 1957). (a)

Ekman, G. On typological and dimensional systems of reference in describing personality. *Acta Psychologica*, 1951, *8*, 1–24. (b)

Emlen, S. T., & Oring, L. W. Ecology, sexual selection, and the evolution of mating systems. *Science*, 1977, *197*, 215–223.

Endler, N. S. Persons, situations, and their interactions. In A. I. Rabin, J. Aronoff, A. M. Barclay, & R. A. Zucker (Eds.), *Further explorations in personality*. New York: John Wiley, 1981.

Epps, P., & Parnell, R. W. Physique and temperament of women delinquents compared with women undergraduates. *British Journal of Medical Psychology*, 1952, *25*, 249–255.

Epstein, S. Explorations in personality today: A tribute to Henry A. Murray. *American Psychologist*, 1979, *34*, 649–653.

Erikson, E. H. *Young man Luther*. New York: W. W. Norton, 1958.

Erikson, E. H. Identity and the life cycle. *Psychological Issues*. Monograph 1, 1(1). New York: International Universities Press, 1959.

Erikson, E. H. *Childhood and society* (2nd ed.). New York: W. W. Norton, 1963.

Erikson, E. H. *Insight and responsibility*. New York: W. W. Norton, 1964.

Erikson, E. H. Ontogeny of ritualization. In R. M. Loewenstein, L. M. Newman, M. Schur, & A. J. Solnit (Eds.), *Psychoanalysis— A general psychology: Essays in honor of Heinz Hartmann*. New York: International Universities Press, 1966.

Erikson, E. H. *Identity: Youth and crisis*. New York: W. W. Norton, 1968.

Erikson, E. H. *Gandhi's truth*. New York: W. W. Norton, 1969.

Erikson, E. H. *Dimensions of a new identity*. New York: W. W. Norton, 1974.

Erikson, E. H. *Life history and the historical moment*. New York: W. W. Norton, 1975.

Erikson, E. H. *Toys and reasons*. New York: W. W. Norton, 1977.

Erikson, E. H. *The life cycle completed: A review*. New York: W. W. Norton, 1982.

Erikson, K. T. (Introduction by K. T. Erikson). *In search of common ground: Conversations with Erik H. Erikson and Huey P. Newton*. New York: W. W. Norton, 1973.

Ernst, C., & Angst, J. *Birth order: Its influence on personality*. Berlin: Springer-Verlag, 1983.

Etzioni, A. *An immodest agenda: Rebuilding America before the 21st century*. New York: McGraw Hill, 1983.

Evans, R. I. *Carl Rogers: The man and his ideas*. New York: E. P. Dutton, 1975.

Eysenck, H. J. *Dimensions of personality*. London: Routledge & Kegan Paul, 1947.

Eysenck, H. J. *The scientific study of personality*. London: Routledge & Kegan Paul, 1952.

Eysenck, H. J. *The structure of human personality*. London: Methuen, 1953: rev. 1960.

Eysenck, H. *The biological basis of behavior*. Springfield, Ill.: Charles C. Thomas, 1967.

Eysenck, H. J. *The IQ argument: Race, intelligence, and education*. New York: Library Press, 1971.

Eysenck, H. J. *Case studies in behavior therapy*. London: Routledge & Kegan Paul, 1976.

Eysenck, H. J. *The biological basis of personality*. Springfield, Ill.: Charles C. Thomas, 1967; rev. 1977.

Eysenck, H. J. The structure and measurement of intelligence. 1979.

Eysenck, H. J. Autobiography. In G. Lindzey (Ed.), A history of psychology in autobiography (Vol. 7). San Francisco: W. H. Freeman, 1980.

Eysenck, H. J. (Ed.). *A model for personality*. Berlin: Springer-Verlag, 1981.

Eysenck, H. J. *Personality, genetics, and behavior*. New York: Springer-Verlag, 1982.

Eysenck, H. J. & Eysenck, S. B. G. *Manual of the Eysenck Personality Inventory*. London: University of London Press; San Diego. Educational and Industrial Testing Service, 1964.

Eysenck, H. J., & Kamin, L. *The intelligence controversy*. New York: John Wiley, 1981.

Eysenck, H. J., & Rachman, S. *The causes and cures of neuroses*. San Diego, Knapp, 1965.

Eysenck, H. J., & Wilson, G. D. *The experimental study of Freudian theories*. New York: Barnes & Noble, 1974.

Feldman, G. The only child as a separate entity: Differences between only females and other first-born females. *Psychological Reports*, 1978, *42*, 107–110.

Ferster, C. B., & Skinner, B. F. *Schedules of reinforcement*. New York: Appleton-Century-Crofts, 1957.

Festinger, L. *A theory of cognitive dissonance*. Stanford, Calif.: Stanford University Press, 1957.

Festinger, L. *Conflict, decision and dissonance*. Stanford, Calif.: Stanford University Press, 1964.

Fisher, S., & Greenberg, R. P. *The scientific credibility of Freud's theories and therapy*. New York: Basic Books, 1977.

Floderus-Myrhed, B., Pedersen, N., & Rasmuson, I. Assessment of heritability for personality, based on a short form of the Eysenck Personality Inventory: A study of 12,898 twin pairs. *Behavior Genetics*, 1980, *10*, 153–162.

Fordham, F. *An introduction to Jung's psychology*. London: Penguin Books, 1953.

Fordham, M. S. M. *The life of childhood*. London: Routledge & Kegan Paul, 1947.

Franck, I. *The concept of human nature: A philosophical analysis of the concept of human nature in the writings of G. W. Allport, S. E. Asch, Erich Fromm, A. H. Maslow, and C. R. Rogers*. Unpublished doctoral dissertation, University of Maryland, 1966.

Frankl, V. E. *The doctor and the soul*. New York: Bantam Books, 1969.

Fransella, F. Repertory grid technique. In F. Fransella (Ed.). *Personality: Theory, measurement and research*. London: Methuen, 1981.

Frazier, E. E. *Negro youth at the crossways: Their personality development in the middle states.* Washington, D.C.: American Council on Education, 1940.

Freud, A. *The ego and the mechanisms of defense.* New York: International Universities Press, 1946.

Freud, A. Normality and pathology in childhood: Assessments of development. In *Writings* (Vol. 6). New York: International Universities Press, 1965.

Freud, A. Introduction to psychoanalysis: Lectures for child analysts and teachers. In *Writings* (Vol. 1). New York: International Universities Press, 1974.

Freud, S. *The interpretation of dreams.* In *Standard edition* (Vols. 4 and 5). London: Hogarth Press, 1953. (First German edition, 1900.)

Freud, S. *Psychopathology of everyday life.* In *Standard edition* (Vol. 6). London: Hogarth Press, 1960. (First German edition, 1901.)

Freud, S. *Fragment of an analysis of a case of hysteria.* In *Standard edition* (Vol. 7). London: Hogarth Press, 1953. (First German edition, 1905.) (a)

Freud, S. *Three essays on sexuality.* In *Standard edition* (Vol. 7). London: Hogarth Press, 1953. (First German edition, 1905.) (b)

Freud, S. *Analysis of a phobia in a five-year-old boy.* In *Standard edition* (Vol. 10). London: Hogarth Press, 1955. (First German edition, 1909.) (a)

Freud, S. *Notes upon a case of obsessional neurosis.* In *Standard edition* (Vol. 10). London: Hogarth Press, 1955. (First German edition, 1909.) (b)

Freud, S. *Leonardo da Vinci and a memory of his childhood.* In *Standard edition* (Vol. 11). London: Hogarth Press, 1957. (First German edition, 1910.)

Freud, S. *Psycho-analytic notes on an autobiographical account of a case of paranoia (dementia paranoides).* In *Standard edition* (Vol. 12). London: Hogarth Press, 1958. (First German edition, 1911.)

Freud, S. *On the history of the psychoanalytic movement.* In *Standard edition* (Vol. 14). London: Hogarth Press, 1957. (First German edition, 1914.)

Freud, S. *Introductory lectures on psycho-analysis.* In *Standard edition* (Vols. 15 and 16). London: Hogarth Press, 1963. (First German editions, 1916, 1917.)

Freud, S. *From the history of an infantile neurosis.* In *Standard edition* (Vol. 17). London: Hogarth Press, 1955. (First German edition, 1918.)

Freud, S. Preface to Reik's *Ritual in psycho-analytic studies.* In *Standard edition* (Vol. 17). London: Hogarth Press, 1955. (First German edition, 1919.)

Freud, S. *Beyond the pleasure principle.* In *Standard edition* (Vol. 18). London: Hogarth Press, 1955. (First German edition, 1920.) (a)

Freud, S. *The psychogenesis of a case of homosexuality in a woman.* In *Standard edition* (Vol. 18). London: Hogarth Press, 1955. (First German edition, 1920.) (b)

Freud, S. *Group psychology and the analysis of the ego.* In *Standard edition* (Vol. 18). London: Hogarth Press, 1955. (First German edition, 1921.)

Freud, S. *The ego and the id.* In *Standard edition* (Vol. 19). London: Hogarth Press, 1961. (First German edition, 1923.)

Freud, S. *An autobiographical study.* In *Standard edition* (Vol. 20). London: Hogarth Press, 1959. (First German edition, 1925.)

Freud, S. *Inhibitions, symptoms, and anxiety.* In *Standard edition* (Vol. 20). London: Hogarth Press, 1959. (First German edition, 1926.)

Freud, S. *Dostoevsky and patricide.* In *Standard edition* (Vol. 21). London: Hogarth Press, 1961. (First German edition, 1928.)

Freud, S. *Civilization and its discontents.* In *Standard edition* (Vol. 21). London: Hogarth Press, 1961. (First German edition, 1930.)

Freud, S. *New introductory lectures on psycho-analysis.* In *Standard edition* (Vol. 22). London: Hogarth Press, 1964. (First German edition, 1933.) (a)

Freud, S. *Why war?* In *Standard edition* (Vol. 22).

London: Hogarth Press, 1964. (First German edition, 1933.) (b)

Freud, S. *Analysis terminable and interminable*. In *Standard edition* (Vol. 23). London: Hogarth Press, 1964. (First German edition, 1937.)

Freud, S. *Moses and monotheism*. In *Standard edition* (Vol. 23). London: Hogarth Press, 1964. (First German edition, 1939.)

Freud, S. *An outline of psychoanalysis*. In *Standard edition* ((Vol. 23). London: Hogarth Press, 1964. (First German edition, 1940.)

Freud, S. *Project for a scientific psychology*. In *Standard edition* (Vol. 1). London: Hogarth Press, 1966. (Written in 1895; first German edition, 1950.)

Freud, S. *The standard edition of the complete psychological works*. J. Strachey (Ed.). London: Hogarth Press, 1953–1974.

Friedman, I. Phenomenal, ideal and projected conceptions of self. *Journal of Abnormal and Social Psychology*, 1955, *51*, 611–615.

Fromm, E. *Escape from freedom*. New York: Rinehart, 1941.

Fromm, E. *Man for himself*. New York: Rinehart, 1947.

Fromm, E. *The sane society*. New York: Rinehart, 1955.

Fromm, E. *The art of loving*. New York: Harper & Row, 1956.

Fromm, E. *Marx's concept of man*. New York: Ungar, 1961.

Fromm, E. *Beyond the chains of illusion*. New York: Simon & Schuster, 1962.

Fromm, E. *The heart of man*. New York: Harper & Row, 1964.

Fromm, E. *The revolution of hope*. New York: Harper & Row, 1968.

Fromm, E. *The crisis of psychoanalysis*. New York: Holt, Rinehart and Winston, 1970.

Fromm, E. *The anatomy of human destructiveness*. New York: Holt, Rinehart and Winston, 1973.

Fromm, E. *To have or to be?* New York: Harper & Row, 1976.

Fromm, E., & Maccoby, M. *Social character in a Mexican village*. Englewood Cliffs, N.J.: Prentice-Hall, 1970.

Fuller, J. L., & Simmel, E. C. (Eds.). *Behavior genetics: Principles and applications*. Hillsdale, N.J.: Erlbaum, 1983.

Fuller, J. L., & Thompson, W. R. *Foundations of behavior genetics*. St. Louis: Mosby, 1978.

Funder, D. C. Constructing their own world. *Contemporary Psychology*, 1981, *26*, 467–468.

Funk, R. *Erich Fromm: The courage to be human*. New York: Continuum, 1982.

Fürtmuller, C. Alfred Adler: A biographical essay. In A. Adler *Superiority and social interest* (H. L. Ansbacher & R. R. Ansbacher, Eds. and trans.) (3rd rev. ed). New York: W. W. Norton, 1979.

Gall, F. J., & Spurzheim, J. G. *Recherches sur le système nerveux*. Paris: Schoell, 1809.

Garber, J., & Seligman, M. E. P. (Eds.), *Human helplessness: Theory and applications*. New York: Academic Press, 1980.

Gardiner, M. (Ed.). *Wolfman: With the case of Wolf-man by Sigmund Freud*. New York: Basic Books, 1971.

Garrett, H. E. Lewin's "topological" psychology: An evaluation. *Psychological Review*, 1939, *46*, 517–524.

Geen, G. *Personality: The skein of behavior*. St. Louis: C.V. Mosby, 1976.

Gibbens, T. C. N. *Psychiatric studies of Borstal lads*. London: Oxford University Press, 1963.

Gibson, H. B. *Hans Eysenck: The man and his work*. London: Peter Owen, 1981.

Glass, D. C., & Singer, J. E. *Urban stress: Experiments on noise and social stressors*. New York: Academic Press, 1972.

Glover, E. *Freud or Jung*. New York: W. W. Norton, 1950.

Glueck, S., & Glueck, E. *Unraveling juvenile delinquency*. New York: Harper, 1950.

Glueck, S., & Glueck, E. *Physique and delinquency*. New York: Harper, 1956.

Goble, F. G. *The third force: The psychology of Abraham Maslow*. New York: Grossman,

1970.

Goldberg, L. R. Explorer on the run. *Contemporary Psychology*, 1968, *13*, 617–619.

Goldstein, J., Freud, A., & Solnit, A. J. *Beyond the best interests of the child*. New York: Free Press, 1973.

Goldstein, K. *The organism*. New York: American Book, 1939.

Goldstein, K. *Human nature in the light of psychopathology*. Cambridge, Mass: Harvard University, 1940.

Goldstein, K. *After-effects of brain injuries in war*. New York: Grune & Stratton, 1942.

Goldstein, K. Autobiography. In E. G. Boring & G. Lindzey (Eds.), *A history of psychology in autobiography*. (Vol. 5). New York: Appleton-Century-Crofts, 1967.

Goldstein, K., & Scheerer, M. Abstract and concrete behavior: An experimental study with special tests. *Psychological Monographs*, 1941, *53*, (2).

Goldstein, K., & Scheerer, M. Tests of abstract and concrete thinking. Tests of abstract and concrete behavior. In A. Weidner (Ed.), *Contributions toward medical psychology*. New York: Ronald Press, 1953.

Gordon, T., & Cartwright, D. The effects of psychotherapy upon certain attitudes toward others. In C. R. Rogers, & R. R. Dymond (Eds.), *Psychotherapy and personality change: Coordinated studies in the client-centered approach*. Chicago: University of Chicago Press, 1954.

Gorlow, L., Simonson, N. R., & Krauss, H. An empirical investigation of the Jungian typology. *British Journal of Social and Clinical Psychology*, 1966, *5*, 108–117.

Gray, H., & Wheelwright, J. B. *Jungian type survey*. San Francisco: Society of Jungian Analysts of Northern California, 1964.

Gray, J. A. A critique of Eysenck's theory of personality. In H. J. Eysenck (Ed.), *A model for personality*. Berlin: Springer-Verlag, 1981. (a)

Gray, J. A. The psychophysiology of anxiety. In R. Lynn (Ed.), *Dimensions of personality*. London: Pergamon, 1981. (b)

Guilford, J. P. *Personality*. New York: McGraw-Hill, 1959.

Guilford, J. P., & Guilford, R. B. An analysis of the factors in a typical test of introversion-extraversion. *Journal of Abnormal and Social Psychology*, 1934, *28*, 377–399.

Guilford, J. P., & Zimmerman, W. S. *The Guilford-Zimmerman temperament survey: Manual of instructions and interpretations*. Beverly Hills, Calif: Sheridan Supply, 1949.

Haigh, G. Defensive behavior in client-centered therapy. *Journal of Consulting Psychology*, 1949, *13*, 181–189.

Hall, C. S. *A primer of Freudian psychology*. Cleveland: World, 1954.

Hall, C. S., & Lindzey, G. The relevance of Freudian psychology and related viewpoints for the social sciences. In G. Lindzey & E. Aronson (Eds.), *Handbook of social psychology* (Vol. 1). Reading, Mass.: Addison-Wesley, 1968.

Hall, C. S., & Nordby, V. J. *A primer of Jungian psychology*. New York: New American Library, 1973.

Hall, M. H. Abraham M. Maslow. *Psychology Today*, 1968, *2*, 35–37, 54–57.

Hannah, B. *Jung: His life and work*. New York: 1976.

Harding, M. E. *Psychic energy, its source and goal*. New York: Pantheon Books, 1947.

Harlow, H. F. The nature of love. *American Psychologist*, 1958, *13*, 673–685.

Harlow, H. F., & Harlow, M. K. Social deprivation in monkeys. *Scientific American*, 1962, *207*, 136–146.

Harlow, H. F., & Zimmerman, R. R. Affectional responses in the infant monkey. *Science*, 1959, *130*, 421–432.

Hartl, E. M., Monnelly, E. P., & Elderkin, E. S. *Physique and delinquent behavior*. New York: Academic Press, 1982.

Hartmann, H. *Ego psychology and the problem of adaptation*. New York: International Universities Press, 1958.

Hartmann, H. *Essays on ego psychology: Selected problems in psychoanalytic theory*. New York: International Universities Press, 1964.

Hartmann, H., Kris, E., & Lowenstein, R. M. Papers on psychoanalytic psychology. *Psychological Issues*, Monograph No. 14. New York: International Universities Press, 1964.

Havener, P. H., & Izard, C. E. Unrealistic self-enhancement in paranoid schizophrenics. *Journal of Consulting Psychology*, 1962, *26*, 65-68.

Hawkey, M. L. The witch and the bogey: Archetypes in the case study of a child. *British Journal of Medical Psychology*, 1947, *21*, 12-29.

Hearnshaw, L. S. *Cyril Burt, psychologist*. Ithaca, N.Y.: Cornell University Press, 1979.

Heidegger, M. *Being and time*. New York: Harper & Row, 1962.

Heider, F. *The psychology of interpersonal relations*. New York: John Wiley, 1958.

Heider, F. On Lewin's methods and theory. *Psychological Issues*, 1959, *1*(3), 123.

Heider, G. Kurt Lewin. In J. A. Garrety & E. T. Jones (Eds.), *Dictionary of American Biography* (Suppl. 4, 1946-1950). New York: Scribners, 1974.

Helson, R. Heroic and tender modes in women authors of fantasy. *Journal of Personality*, 1973, *41*, 493-512.

Helson, R. Critics and their texts: An approach to Jung's theory of cognition and personality. *Journal of Personality and Social Psychology*, 1982, *43*, 409-418.

Helson, R., & Mitchell, V. Personality. *Annual Review of Psychology*, 1978, *29*, 555-585.

Henderson, N. D. Human behavior genetics. *Annual Review of Psychology*, 1982, *33*, 403-440.

"He's Stingy If . . .," *Cosmopolitan*, September 1976, p.148.

Hetherington, E. M., & Frankie, G. Effects of parental dominance, warmth, and conflict on imitation in children. *Journal of Personality and Social Psychology*, 1967, *6*, 119-125.

Hiroto, D. S. Locus of control and learned helplessness. *Journal of Experimental Psychology*, 1974, *102*, 187-193.

Hiroto, D. S., & Seligman, M. E. P. Generality of learned helplessness in man. *Journal of Personality and Social Psychology*, 1975, *31*, 311-327.

Hoffman, M. L. Personality and social development. *Annual Review of Psychology*, 1977, *28*, 295-321.

Holland, J. G., & Skinner, B. F. *The analysis of behavior: A program for self-instruction*. New York: McGraw-Hill, 1961.

Holmes, D. S. Dimensions of projection. *Psychological Bulletin*, 1968, *69*, 248-268.

Holmes, D. S. The conscious control of thematic projection. *Journal of Consulting and Clinical Psychology*, 1974, *42*, 323-329.

Holt, R. R. The Thematic Apperception Test. In H. H. Anderson & G. L. Anderson (Eds.), *An introduction to projective tests*. Englewood Cliffs, N.J.: Prentice-Hall, 1951.

Holt, R. R. Individuality and generalization in the psychology of personality. *Journal of Personality*, 1962, *30*, 377-404.

Holt, R. R. Ego autonomy re-evaluated. *International Journal of Psychiatry*, 1965, *46*, 151-167.

Holt, R. R. Drive or wish? A reconsideration of the psychoanalytic theory of motivation. In M. M. Gill & P. S. Holzman (Eds.), *Psychology versus metapsychology: Psychoanalytic essays in memory of George S. Klein. Psychological Issues*, Monograph 36. New York: International Universities Press, 1976.

Horn, J. M. Delinquents in adulthood. *Science*. 1983, *221*, 256-257.

Horney, K. *The neurotic personality of our time*. New York: W. W. Norton, 1937.

Horney, K. *New ways in psychoanalysis*. New York: W. W. Norton, 1939.

Horney, K. *Self-analysis*. New York: W. W. Norton, 1942.

Horney, K. *Our inner conflicts*. New York: W. W. Norton, 1945.

Horney, K. *Neurosis and human growth*. New York: Norton, 1950.

Horney, K. *Feminine psychology*. New York: W. W. Norton, 1967. (a)

Horney, K. On the genesis of the castration complex in women. In K. Horney, *Feminine psychology*. New York: Norton, 1967. (b)

Horney, K. *The adolescent diaries of Karen Horney*. New York: Basic Books, 1980.

Hull, C. L. *Principles of behavior*. New York: Appleton-Century-Crofts, 1943.

Hull, C. L. *A behavior system*. New Haven, Conn.: Yale University Press, 1952.

Humphreys, L. G. Characteristics of type concepts with special reference to Sheldon's typology. *Psychological Bulletin*, 1957, *54*, 218–228.

Jacobi, J. *Complex, archetype, symbol in the psychology of C. G. Jung*. New York: Pantheon Books, 1959.

Jacobson, E. *Progressive relaxation*. Chicago: University of Chicago Press, 1938.

Jaffé, A. *From the life and the work of C. G. Jung*. New York: Harper & Row, 1971.

Jaffé, A. *C. G. Jung: Word and image*. Princeton, N.J.: Princeton University Press, 1979.

Jakubczak, L. F., & Walters, R. H. Suggestibility as dependency behavior. *Journal of Abnormal and Social Psychology*, 1959, *59*, 102–107.

James, W. *Varieties of religious experience*. New York: Modern Library, 1936.

James, W. T. Karen Horney and Erich Fromm in relation to Alfred Adler. *Individual Psychology Bulletin*, 1947, *6*, 105–116.

Jensen, Arthur R. How much can we boost IQ and scholastic achievement? *Harvard Educational Review*, *39*, 1–123.

Johnson, C. S. *Growing up in the black belt: Negro youth in the rural south*. Washington, D.C.: American Council on Education, 1941.

Jonas, G. *Visceral learning: Toward a science of self-control*. New York: Viking, 1973.

Jones, E. *The life and work of Sigmund Freud* (Vols. 1, 2, 3). New York: Basic Books, 1953, 1955, 1957.

Jones, E. *The life and work of Sigmund Freud* (L. Trilling & S. Marcus, Eds. and abridg.). New York: Basic Books, 1961.

Jones, H. E. Order of birth in relation to the development of the child. In C. Murchison (Ed.), *Handbook of child psychology* (Vol. 1). Worcester, Mass.: Clark University Press, 1931.

Jones, M. C. A laboratory study of fear: The case of Peter. *Pedagogical Seminary*, 1924, *31*, 308–315.

Jöreskog, K. G., & Sörbom, D. *Advances in factor analysis and structural equation models*. Cambridge, Mass.: Abt Books, 1979.

Jung, C. G. *Experimental researches*, In *Collected works* (Vol. 2). Princeton, N.J.: Princeton University Press, 1973. (First German edition, 1904–1937.)

Jung, C. G. The psychological diagnosis of evidence. In *Experimental researches*, *Collected works* (Vol. 2). Princeton, N.J.: Princeton University Press, 1973. (First German edition, 1905.)

Jung, C. G. The association method. In *Experimental researches*, *Collected works* (Vol. 2). Princeton, N.J.: Princeton University Press, 1973. (First German edition, 1909.) (a)

Jung, C. G. The family constellation. In *Experimental researches*, *Collected works* (Vol. 2). Princeton, N.J.: Princeton University Press, 1973. (First German edition, 1909.) (b)

Jung, C. G. *Symbols of transformation. Collected works* (Vol. 5). Princeton: Princeton University Press, 1956. (First German edition, 1911–1912.)

Jung, C. G. The theory of psychoanalysis. In *Freud and psychoanalysis*, *Collected works* (Vol. 4). Princeton, N.J.: Princeton University Press, 1961. (First German edition, 1913.)

Jung, C. G. The structure of the unconscious. In *Two essays on analytical psychology*, *Collected works* (Vol. 7). Princeton, N.J.: Princeton University Press, 1953. (First German edition, 1916.)

Jung, C. G. *The structure and dynamics of the psyche, Collected works* (Vol. 8). Princeton, N.J.: Princeton University Press, 1960. (First German edition, 1926–1958.)

Jung, C. G. *Psychological types*. In *Collected works* (Vol. 6). Princeton, N.J.: Princeton University Press, 1971. (First German edition, 1921.)

Jung, C. G. Child development and education. In *The development of personality*, *Collected works* (Vol. 17). Princeton, N.J.: Princeton University Press, 1954. (First German edition, 1928.)

Jung, C. G. The significance of constitution and heredity in psychology. In *The structure and dynamics of the psyche*, *Collected works* (Vol. 8). Princeton, N.J.: Princeton University Press, 1960. (First German edition, 1929.)

Jung, C. G. The stages of life. In *The structure and dynamics of the psyche*, *Collected works* (Vol. 8). Princeton, N.J.: Princeton University Press, 1960. (First German edition, 1931.)

Jung, C. G. A review of the complex theory. In *The structure and dynamics of the psyche*, *Collected works* (Vol. 8). Princeton, N.J.: Princeton University Press, 1960. (First German edition, 1934.) (a)

Jung, C. G. The meaning of psychology for modern man. In *Civilization in transition*, *Collected works* (Vol. 10). Princeton, N.J.: Princeton University Press, 1970. (First German edition, 1934.) (b)

Jung, C. G. Principles of practical psychotherapy. In *The practice of psychotherapy*, *Collected works* (Vol. 16). Princeton, N.J.: Princeton University Press, 1954. (First German edition, 1935.)

Jung, C. G. The concept of the collective unconscious. In *The archetypes and the collective unconscious*, *Collected works* (Vol. 9, Part I). Princeton, N.J.: Princeton University Press, 1969. (First German edition, 1936.)

Jung, C. G. *The archetypes and the collective unconscious*, *Collected works* (Vol. 9, Part I). Princeton, N.J.: Princeton University Press, 1969. (First German edition, 1936–1955.)

Jung, C. G. *Psychology and religion*. In *Collected works*, (Vol. 11). Princeton, N.J.: Princeton University Press, 1958. (Originally published in English, 1938.)

Jung, C. G. On the psychology of the unconscious. In *Two essays on analytical psychology*, *Collected works* (Vol. 7). Princeton, N.J.:

Princeton University Press, 1953. (First German edition, 1943.)

Jung, C. G. *Psychology and alchemy*, *Collected works* (Vol. 12). Princeton, N.J.: Princeton University Press, 1953. (First German edition, 1944.)

Jung, C. G. The relations between the ego and the unconscious. In *Two essays on analytical psychology*, *Collected works* (Vol. 7). Princeton, N.J.: Princeton University Press, 1953. (First German edition, 1945.)

Jung, C. G. Psychic conflicts in a child. In *The development of personality*, *Collected works* (Vol. 17). Princeton, N.J.: Princeton University Press, 1954. (First German edition, 1946.)

Jung, C. G. General aspects of dream psychology. In *The structure and dynamics of the psyche*, *Collected works* (Vol. 8). Princeton, N.J.: Princeton University Press, 1960. (First German edition, 1948.) (a)

Jung, C. G. Instinct and the unconscious. In *The structure and dynamics of the psyche*, *Collected works* (Vol. 8). Princeton, N.J.: Princeton University Press, 1960. (First German edition, 1948.) (b)

Jung, C. G. On psychic energy. In *The structure and dynamics of the psyche*, *Collected works* (Vol. 8). Princeton, N.J.: Princeton University Press, 1960. (First German edition, 1948.) (c)

Jung, C. G. The shadow. In *Aion, Collected works* (Vol. 9, Part II). Princeton, N.J.: Princeton University Press, 1959. (First German edition, 1948.) (d)

Jung, C. G. A study in the process of individuation. In *The archetypes and the collective unconscious*, *Collected works* (Vol. 9, Part I). Princeton, N.J.: Princeton University Press, 1969. (First German edition, 1950.)

Jung, C. G. *Aion, Collected works* (Vol. 9, Part II). Princeton, N.J.: Princeton University Press, 1959. (First German edition, 1951.) (a)

Jung, C. G. The psychological aspects of the Kore. In *The archetypes and the collective unconscious*, *Collected works* (Vol. 9, Part I). Princeton, N.J.: Princeton University Press, 1969. (First German edition, 1951.) (b)

Jung, C. G. *Collected works* (H. Read, M.

Fordham, & G. Adler, Eds.) Princeton, N.J.: Princeton University Press, 1953–1978 (20 vols.).

Jung, C. G. Flying saucers: A modern myth of things seen in the skies. In *Civilization in transition*, Collected works (Vol. 10). Princeton, N.J.: Princeton University Press, 1964. (First German edition, 1958.)

Jung, C. G. *Memories, dreams, and reflections*. New York: Random House, 1961.

Jung, C. G. Approaching the unconscious. In *Man and his symbols* (C. G. Jung, M.-L. von Franz, J. L. Henderson, J. Jacobi, & A. Jaffe, Eds.). New York: Dell, 1964.

Jung, C. G. *Analytical psychology: Its theory and practice*. New York: Pantheon Books, 1968.

Jung, C. G. *Letters* (Vol. 1, *1906-1950*; Vol. 2, *1951-1961*). Princeton, N.J.: Princeton University Press, 1973, 1975.

Kanfer, F. H., & Marston, A. R. Determinants of self-reinforcement in human learning. *Journal of Experimental Psychology*, 1963, *66*, 245–254.

Katahn, M. *The 200 calorie solution*. New York: W. W. Norton, 1982.

Katsoff, L. O. Review of K. Goldstein's human nature in the light of psychopathology. *Journal of General Psychology*, 1942, *26*, 187–194.

Kazdin, A. E. *The token economy: A review and evaluation*. New York: Plenum, 1977.

Kelly, G. A. *The psychology of personal constructs* (2 vols). New York: W. W. Norton, 1955.

Kelly, G. A. A summary statement of a cognitively-oriented comprehensive theory of behavior. In J. C. Mancuso (Ed.), *Readings for a cognitive theory of personality*. New York: Holt, Rinehart and Winston, 1970.

Kelman, H. *Helping people: Karen Horney's psychoanalytic approach*. New York: Science House, 1971.

Kilpatrick, F. P., & Cantril, H. Self-anchoring scale: A measure of the individual's unique reality world. *Journal of Individual Psychology*, 1960, *16*, 158–170.

Klein, D. C., Fencil-Morse, E., & Seligman,

M. E. P. Learned helplessness, depression, and the attribution of failure. *Journal of Personality and Social Psychology*, 1976, *33*, 11–26.

Klein, D. C., & Seligman, M. E. P. Reversal of performance deficits and perceptual deficits in learned helplessness and depression. *Journal of Abnormal Psychology*, 1976, *85*, 11–26.

Klein, G. S. *Psychoanalytic theory: An exploration of essentials*. New York: International Universities Press, 1976.

Kline, P. *Fact and fancy in Freudian theory*. London: Methuen, 1972.

Kluckhohn, C., Murray, H. A., & Schneider, D. M. *Personality in nature, society, and culture* (rev. ed.). New York: Alfred A. Knopf, 1953.

Köhler, W. *Gestalt psychology: An introduction to new concepts in psychology*. New York: Liverright, 1947.

Kohut, H. *The analysis of the self: A systematic approach to the psychoanalytic treatment of narcissistic personality disorders*. The Psychoanalytic Study of the Child, Monograph 4. New York: International Universities Press, 1971.

Krasner, L., & Ullmann, L. P. (Eds.). *Research in behavior modification*. New York: Holt, Rinehart and Winston, 1965.

Kretschmer, E. *Physique and character* (W. J. H. Spratt, trans.). New York: Harcourt, 1925 (originally published, 1921).

Kuhn, T. S. *The structure of scientific revolutions*. Chicago: University of Chicago Press, 1962.

Laing, R. D. *The politics of experience*. New York: Ballantine Books, 1968.

Lamiell, J. T. Toward an idiothetic psychology of personality. *American Psychologist*, 1981, *36*, 276–289.

Leeper, R. W. Lewin's topological and vector psychology: A digest and critique. *Univ. Ore. Publ. Stud. Psychol.*, 1943, no. 1.

Lewin, K. *A dynamic theory of personality*. New York: McGraw-Hill, 1935.

Lewin, K. *Principles of topological psychology*. New York: McGraw-Hill, 1936.

Lewin, K. *Resolving social conflicts: Selected papers on group dynamics* (G. W. Lewin, ed.). New York: Harper & Row, 1948.

Lewin, K. *Field theory in social science: Selected theoretical papers* (D. Cartwright, ed.). New York: Harper & Row, 1951.

Lindzey, G. Review of Lewin's *Field theory in social science. Journal of Abnormal and Social Psychology*, 1952, *47*, 132–133.

Lindzey, G. *Projective techniques and cross-cultural research.* New York: Appleton-Century-Crofts, 1961.

Lindzey, G. Morphology and behavior. In G. Lindzey, C. S. Hall, & M. Manosevitz (Eds.), *Theories of personality: Primary sources and research.* New York: John Wiley, 1973.

Lindzey, G. (ed.). *A history of psychology in autobiography.* (Vol. 6), Englewood Cliffs, N.J.: Prentice-Hall, 1973; (Vol. 7), San Francisco: W. H. Freeman, 1980.

Lindzey, G. Henry A. Murray. In D. L. Sills (ed.) *International encyclopedia of the social sciences* (Vol. 18, *Biographical supplement*). New York: Free Press, 1979.

Lindzey, G., & Aronson, E. (Eds.). *Handbook of social psychology.* Reading, Mass.: Addison-Wesley, 1968.

Lindzey, G., & Newburg, A. S. Thematic Apperception Test: A tentative appraisal of some "signs" of anxiety. *Journal of Consulting Psychology*, 1954, *18*, 389–395.

Lindzey, G., & Tejessy, C. Thematic Apperception Test: Indices of aggression in relation to measures of overt and covert behavior. *American Journal of Orthopsychiatry*, 1956, *26*, 567–576.

Lippitt, R. Kurt Lewin. In D. L. Sills (Ed.), *International encyclopedia of the social sciences* (Vol. 9). New York: Macmillan and Free Press, 1968.

Lissner, K. Die Entspannung von Bedurfnissen durch Ersatzhandlungen. *Psychologische Forschung*, 1933, *18*, 218–250.

Livson, N., & McNeil, D. Physique and maturation rate in male adolescents. *Child Development*, 1962, *33*, 145–152.

Loehlin, J. C. *Computer models of personality.* New York: Random House, 1968.

Loehlin, J. C., and Nichols, R. C. *Heredity, environment, and personality: A study of 850 sets of twins.* Austin: University of Texas Press, 1976.

Loehlin, J. C., Willerman, L., & Horn, J. M. Personality resemblances in adoptive families when the children are late-adolescent or adult. *Journal of Personality ad Social Psychology*, in press.

Loevinger, J., & Knoll, E. Personality: Stages, traits, and the self. *Annual Review of Psychology*, 1983, *34*, 195–222.

London, I. D. Psychologists' misuse of the auxiliary concepts of physics and mathematics. *Psychological Review*, 1944, *51*, 266–291.

Lovaas, O. I., Koegel, R., Simmons, J. Q., & Long, J. S. Some generalization and follow-up measures on autistic children in behavior therapy. *Journal of Applied Behavior Analysis*, 1973, *6*, 131–165.

Lowry, R. J. *A. H. Maslow: An intellectual portrait.* Monterey, Calif.: Brooks/Cole, 1973. (a)

Lowry, R. J. *Dominance, self-esteem, self-actualization: Germinal papers of A. H. Maslow.* Monterey, Calif.: Brooks/Cole, 1973. (b)

Lowry, R. J. (Ed.). *The journals of Abraham Maslow.* Monterey, Calif.: Brooks/Cole, 1979.

Lustman, S. L. The scientific leadership of Anna Freud. *Journal of the American Psychoanalytic Association*, 1967, *15*, 810–827.

McClelland, D. C. *The achieving society.* New York: Free Press, 1961.

McClelland, D. C. *Power.* New York: Irvington Publishers, 1975.

McClelland, D. C., Atkinson, J. W., Clark, R. A., & Lowell, E. L. *The achievement motive.* New York: Appleton-Century-Crofts, 1953.

McClelland, D. C., & Winter, D. G. *Motivating economic achievement.* New York: Free Press, 1969.

Maccoby, E. E. & Jacklin, C. N. *The psychology*

of sex differences. Stanford, Calif.: Stanford University Press, 1974.

McDougall, W. *An introduction to social psychology.* Boston: Luce, 1908.

McGuire, W. (Ed.). *The Freud/Jung letters: The correspondence between Sigmund Freud and C. G. Jung.* Princeton, N.J.: Princeton University Press, 1974.

MacKinnon, D. W. *Environments that favor creativity.* Henry A. Murray Award Address given at the annual meeting of the American Psychological Association, Division of Social and Personality Psychology, Washington, D.C., August, 1982.

MacLeod, R. B. Phenomenology: A challenge of experimental psychology. In T. W. Wann (Ed.), *Behaviorism and phenomenology: Contrasting bases for modern psychology.* Chicago: University of Chicago Press, 1964.

McNeil, D., & Livson, N. Maturation rate and body build in women. *Child Development,* 1963, *34,* 25-32.

Maddi, R. *Personality theories: A comparative analysis* (4th ed.). Homewood, Ill.: Dorsey Press, 1980.

Magnusson, D., & Endler, N. S. (Eds.) *Personality at the crossroads.* Hillsdale, N.J.: Erlbaum, 1977.

Maher, B. (Ed.) *Clinical psychology and personality: The selected papers of George Kelly.* New York: John Wiley, 1969.

Mahler, W. Ersatzhandlungen verschiedenen Realitätsgrades. *Psychologische Forschung,* 1933, *18,* 27-89.

Malcolm, J. Psychoanalysis: The impossible profession. New York: Alfred A. Knopf, 1981.

Manosevitz, M., Lindzey, G., & Thiessen, D. D. *Behavioral genetics: Method and research.* New York: Appleton-Century-Crofts, 1969.

Marcia, J. E. Identity in adolescence. In J. Adelson (Ed.), *Handbook of adolescent psychology.* New York: John Wiley, 1980.

Marmor, J. Comments on "Adlerian psychology: The tradition of brief psychotherapy." *Journal of Individual Psychology,* 1972, *28,* 153-154.

Marrow, A. J. *The practical theorist: The life and work of Kurt Lewin.* New York: Basic Books, 1969.

Maslow, A. H. A theory of human motivation, *Psychological Review,* 1943, *50,* 370-396.

Maslow, A. H. Eupsychia: The good society. *Journal of Humanistic Psychology,* 1961, No. 2, 1-11.

Maslow, A. H. *Religions, values, and peak experiences.* Columbus: Ohio State University Press, 1964.

Maslow, A. H. *Eupsychian management: A journal.* Homewood, Ill.: Irwin-Dorsey, 1965.

Maslow, A. H. A theory of metamotivation: The biological rooting of the value life. *Journal of Humanistic Psychology,* 1967, *7,* 93-127. (a)

Maslow, A. H. Neurosis as a failure of personal growth. *Humanitas,* 1967, *3,* 153-170. (b)

Maslow, A. H. *Toward a psychology of being* (2nd ed.). Princeton, N.J.: D. Van Nostrand, 1968.

Maslow, A. H. *Motivation and personality* (2nd ed.). New York: Harper, 1970. (1st ed., 1954).

Maslow, A. H. *The farther reaches of human nature.* New York: Viking, 1971.

Maslow, A. H. Self-actualizing and beyond. In G. Lindzey, C. S. Hall, & M. Manosevitz (Eds.), *Theories of personality: Primary sources and research* (2nd ed.). New York: John Wiley, 1973.

Maslow, B. G. (Ed.). *Abraham H. Maslow: A memorial volume.* Monterey, Calif.: Brooks/Cole, 1972.

May, R. (Ed.). *Existential psychology* (2nd ed.) New York: Random House, 1969.

May, R., Angel, E., & Ellenberger, H. F. (Eds.). *Existence: A new dimension in psychiatry.* New York: Basic Books, 1958.

May, R., & Basescu, S. Existential psychology. In D. L. Sills (Ed.), *International encyclopedia of the social sciences* (Vol. 13), New York: Macmillan, 1968.

Mayeroff, M. *On caring.* New York: Harper & Row, 1971.

Medinnus, G. R. & Curtis, F. J. The relation between maternal self-acceptance and child acceptance. *Journal of Consulting Psychology*, 1963, *27*, 542–544.

Mehrabian, A., & Russell, J. A. *An approach to environmental psychology*. Cambridge, Mass.: M.I.T. Press, 1974.

Meichenbaum, D. Cognitive behavior modification. In J. T. Spence, R. C. Carson, & J. W. Thibaut (Eds.), *Behavioral approaches to therapy*. Morristown, N.J.: General Learning Press, 1976.

Meier, C. A. Clinic and Research Centre for Jungian Psychology, Zurich. *Journal of Analytical Psychology*, 1965, *10*, 1–6.

Melhado, J. J. *Exploratory studies in symbolism*. Ph.D. dissertation. University of Texas, 1964.

Metalsky, G. I., Abramson, L. Y., Seligman, M. E. P., Semmel, A., & Peterson, C. Attributional style and life events in the classroom: Vulnerability and invulnerability to depressive mood reactions. *Journal of Personality and Social Psychology*, 1982, *43*, 612–617.

Miller, N. E. Experimental studies of conflict. In J. McV. Hunt (Ed.), *Personality and the behavior disorders* (Vol. 1). New York: Ronald Press, 1944.

Miller, N. E. Theory and experiment relating psychoanalytic displacement to stimulus–response generalization. *Journal of Abnormal and Social Psychology*, 1948, *43*, 155–178.

Miller, N. E. Comments on theoretical models: Illustrated by the development of a theory of conflict behavior. *Journal of Personality*, 1951, *20*, 82–100.

Miller, N. E. Liberalization of basic S–R concepts: Extensions to conflict behavior, motivation and social learning. In S. Koch (Ed.), *Psychology: A study of a science* (Vol. 2), New York: McGraw-Hill, 1959.

Miller, N. E. Learning of visceral and glandular responses. *Science*, 1969, *163*, 434–445.

Miller, N. E. (Ed.). *Neal E. Miller: Selected papers*. New York: Aldine, 1971.

Miller, N. E. Obituary of John Dollard (1900–1980). *American Psychologist*, 1982, *37*, 587–588.

Miller, N. E. Behavioral medicine: Symbiosis between laboratory and clinic. *Annual Review of Psychology*, 1983, *34*, 1–31.

Miller, N. E., & Banuazizi, A. Instrumental learning by curarized rats of a specific visceral response, intestinal or cardiac. *Journal of Comparative and Physiological Psychology*, 1968, *65*, 1–7.

Miller, N. E., Barber, T. X., DiCara, L. V., Kamiya, J., Shapiro, D., & Stoyva, J. (Eds.). *Biofeedback and self-control*. Chicago: Aldine, 1973.

Miller, N. E., & Bugelski, R. Minor studies in aggression: II. The influence of frustrations imposed by the in-group on attitudes expressed toward out-groups. *Journal of Psychology*, 1948, *25*, 437–442.

Miller, N. E., & Dollard, J. *Social learning and imitation*. New Haven, Conn.: Yale University Press, 1941.

Miller, N. E. & Dworkin, B. R. Visceral learning: Recent difficulties with curarized rats and significant problems for human research. In P. A. Obrist (Ed.), *Contemporary trends in cardiovascular psychophysiology*. Chicago: Aldine, 1974.

Miller, W. R., & Seligman, M. E. P. Depression in humans. *Journal of Abnormal Psychology*, 1975, *84*, 228–238.

Millet, K. *Sexual politics*. Garden City, N.Y.: Doubleday, 1970.

Mischel, W. Delay of gratification, need for achievement, and acquiescence in another culture. *Journal of Abnormal and Social Psychology*, 1961, *62*, 543–552.

Mischel, W. *Personality and assessment*. New York: John Wiley, 1968.

Mischel, W. Toward a cognitive social learning reconceptualization of personality. *Psychological Review*, 1973, *80*, 252–283. (a)

Mischel, W. On the empirical dilemmas of psychodynamic approaches: Issues and alternatives. *Journal of Abnormal Psychology*, 1973, *82*, 335–344. (b)

Mischel, W. On the interface of cognition and personality: Beyond the person-situation debate, *American Psychologist*, 1979, *34*, 740–754.

Mischel, W. *Introduction to personality* New York: Holt, Rinehart, and Winston, 1971; 3rd ed., 1981.

Mischel, W. Convergences and challenges in the search for consistency. *American Psychologist*, 1984, *39*, 351–364. (a)

Mischel, W. On the predictability of behavior and the structure of personality. In R. A. Zucker, J. Aronoff, & A. I. Rabin (Eds.), *Personality and the prediction of behavior*. New York: Academic Press, 1984, pp. 269–305. (b)

Mischel, W. Delay of gratification as process and as person variable in development. In D. Magnusson & V. P. Allen (Eds.), *Interactions in human development*. New York: Academic Press, 1983.

Mischel, W., & Baker, N. Cognitive appraisals and transformations in delay behavior. *Journal of Personality and Social Psychology*. 1975, *31*, 254–261.

Mischel, W., & Eddesen, E. B. Attention in delay of gratification. *Journal of Personality and Social Psychology*, 1970, *16*, 329–337.

Mischel, W., Ebbesen, E. B., & Zeiss, A. R. Cognitive and attentional mechanisms in delay of gratification. *Journal of Personality and Social Psychology*, 1972, *21*, 204–218.

Mischel, W., & Mischel, H. N. *Essentials of psychology*. (2nd ed.). New York: Random House, 1980.

Mischel, W., & Mischel, H. N. The development of children's knowledge of self-control strategies. *Child Development*, 1983, *54*, 603–619.

Mischel, W., & Peake, P. K. Beyond déjà vu in the search for cross-situational consistency. *Psychological Review*, 1982, *89*, 730–755.

Mitchell, J. *Psychoanalysis and feminism: Freud, Reich, Laing, and women*. New York: Pantheon, 1974.

Morgan, C. D., & Murray, H. A. A method for investigating fantasies. *Archives of Neurology and Psychiatry*, 1935, *34*, 289–306.

Mosak, H. H., & Mosak, B. *A bibliography for Adlerian psychology*. Washington, D.C.: Hemisphere Publishing Corp., 1975.

Mullahy, P. *The beginnings of modern American psychiatry: The ideas of Harry Stack Sullivan*. Boston: Houghton MIfflin, 1973.

Munroe, R. *Schools of psychoanalytic thought*. New York: Dryden Press, 1955.

Murphy, G., & Kovach, J. K. *Historical introduction to modern psychology*. (3rd ed.). New York: Harcourt Brace Jovanovich, 1972.

Murray, H. A. *Manual of the Thematic Apperception Test*. Cambridge, Mass.: Harvard University Press, 1943.

Murray, H. A. (with collaborators). *Explorations in personality*. New York: Oxford University Press, 1938.

Murray, H. A. What should psychologists do about psychoanalysis? *Journal of Abnormal and Social Psychology*, 1940, *35*, 150–175.

Murray, H. A. Problems in clinical research: Round table. *American Journal of Orthopsychiatry*, 1947, *17*, 203–210.

Murray, H. A. Research planning: A few proposals. In S. S. Sargent (Ed.), *Culture and personality*. New York: Viking Fund, 1949.

Murray, H. A. Some basic psychological assumptions and conceptions. *Dialectica*, 1951, *5*, 266–292. (a)

Murray, H. A. Toward a classification of interactions. In T. Parsons & E. A. Shils (Eds.), *Toward a general theory of action*. Cambridge, Mass.: Harvard University Press, 1951. (b)

Murray, H. A. Preparations for the scaffold of a comprehensive system. In S. Koch (Ed.), *Psychology: A study of a science* (Vol. 3). New York: McGraw-Hill, 1959.

Murray, H. A. Autobiography. In E. G. Boring & G. Lindzey (Eds.), *A history of psychology in biography* (Vol. 5). New York: Appleton-Century-Crofts, 1967.

Murray, H. A. A conversation with Mary Harrington Hall. *Psychology Today*, 1968, *2*, 56–63. (a)

Murray, H. A. Components of an evolving personological sytem. In D. L. Sills (Eds.), *International encyclopedia of the social sciences.* (Vol. 12). New York: Macmillan, 1968. (b)

Murray, H. A. In nomine diaboli. (Originally published in New England Quarterly, 1951, *24*, 435–452.) In G. Lindzey, C. S. Hall, & M. Manosevitz, (Eds.). *Theories of personality: Primary sources and research* (2nd ed.), New York: John Wiley, 1973.

Murray, H. A. *Endeavors in psychology: Selections from the personology of Henry A. Murray* (E. S. Schneidman, Ed.). New York: Harper & Row, 1981.

Murray, H. A., & Kluckhohn, C. Outline of a conception of personality. In C. Kluckhohn, H. A. Murray, & D. Schneider (Eds.), *Personality in nature, society, and culture* (2nd ed.). New York: Alfred A. Knopf, 1953.

Office of Strategic Services Assessment Staff. *Assessment of men.* New York: Rinehart, 1948.

Murstein, B. I. *Theory and research in projective techniques.* New York: John Wiley, 1963.

Myers, I. B. *The Myers-Briggs Type Indicator.* Princeton, N.J.: Educational Testing Service, 1962.

Newman, N. H., Freeman, F. N., & Holzinger, K. J. *Twins: A study of heredity and environment.* Chicago: University of Chicago Press, 1937.

Norcross, J. C., & Prochaska, J. O. A national survey of clinical psychologists: Affiliations and orientations. *The Clinical Psychologist,* 1982, *35,* 1, 4–6.

Olson, W. C. *The measurement of nervous habits in normal children.* Minneapolis: University of Minnesota Press, 1929.

Orgler, H. *Alfred Adler: The man and his work.* New York: Liveright, 1963.

Osborne, R. H., & DeGeorge, F. V. *Genetic basis of morphological variations.* Cambridge, Mass.: Harvard University Press, 1959.

Osborne, R. H. William H. Sheldon. In D. L. Sills (Ed.), *International encyclopedia of the social sciences,* Biographical supplement (Vol. 18). New York: Free Press, 1979.

Overmier, J. B., & Seligman, M. E. P. Effects of inescapable shock upon subsequent escape and avoidance learning. *Journal of Comparative and Physiological Psychology,* 1967, *63,* 28–33.

Padilla, A. M. Effects of prior and interpolated shock exposures on subsequent avoidance learning by goldfish. *Psychological Reports,* 1973, *32,* 451–456.

Parnell, R. W. *Behavior and physique: An introduction to practical and applied somatometry.* London: Arnold, 1958.

Pavlov, I. P. *Conditioned reflexes* (G. V. Anrep, trans.). London: Oxford University Press, 1927.

Perry, H. S. Commentary. In H. S. Sullivan, *The fusion of psychiatry and social science.* New York: W. W. Norton, 1964.

Perry H. S. *Psychiatrist of America: The life of Harry Stack Sullivan.* Cambridge, Mass.: Harvard University Press, 1982.

Peterson, C., & Seligman, M. E. P. Causal explanations as a risk factor for depression: Theory and evidence. *Psychological Review,* 1984, *91,* 347–374.

Phares, E. J. Rotter's social learning theory. In G. M. Gazda & R. J. Corsini (Eds.) *Theories of learning: A comparative approach.* Itasca, Ill.: Peacock, 1980.

Phares, E. J., & Lamiell, J. T. Personality. *Annual Review of Psychology,* 1977, *28,* 113–140.

Porter, E. H., Jr. The development and evaluation of a measure of counseling interview procedures. *Educational Psychological Measurement,* 1943, *3,* 105–126, 215–238.

Raimy, V. C. Self-reference in counseling interviews. *Journal of Consulting Psychology,* 1948, *12,* 153–163.

Rapaport, D. A historical survey of psychoanalytic ego psychology. Introduction to E. H. Erikson, Identity and the life cycle. *Psychological Issues,* Monograph 1, 1 (1). New York: International Universities Press, 1959.

Rapaport, D. The structure of psychoanalytic theory: A systematizing attempt. *Psychological Issues,* Monograph 6. New York: International Universities Press, 1960; also in S.

Koch (Ed.), *Psychology: A study of a science* (Vol. 3). New York: McGraw-Hill, 1959.

Read, H. E. *Education through art.* New York: Pantheon Books, 1945.

Rees, L. Constitutional psychology. In D. L. Sills (Ed.), *International Encyclopedia of the Social Sciences* (Vol. 13). New York: Macmillan, 1968.

Rees, L. Constitutional factors and abnormal behavior. In H. J. Eysenck (Ed.), *Handbook of abnormal psychology.* San Diego, Calif.: Knapp, 1973.

Richter, C. P. A behavioristic study of the activity of the rat. *Comparative Psychology Monographs*, No. 2, 1922.

Roazen, P. *Erik H. Erikson: The power and limits of his vision.* New York: Free Press, 1976.

Rogers, C. R. *Counseling and psychotherapy: Newer concepts in practice.* Boston: Houghton Mifflin, 1942.

Rogers, C. R. *Client-centered therapy: Its current practice, implications, and theory.* Boston: Houghton Mifflin, 1951.

Rogers, C. R. Intellectualized psychotherapy. *Contemporary Psychology*, 1956, *1*, 357–358.

Rogers, C. R. A theory of therapy, personality, and interpersonal relationships as developed in the client-centered framework. In S. Koch (Ed.), *Psychology: A study of a science* (Vol. 3). New York: McGraw-Hill, 1959.

Rogers, C. R. *On becoming a person.* Boston: Houghton Mifflin, 1961.

Rogers, C. R. (Ed.). *The therapeutic relationship and its impact: A study of psychotherapy with schizophrenics.* Madison, Wisc.: University of Wisconsin Press, 1967. (a)

Rogers, C. R. Autobiography. In E. G. Boring & G. Lindzey (Eds.), *A history of psychology in autobiography* (Vol. 5). New York: Appleton-Century-Crofts, 1967. (b)

Rogers, C. R. *Freedom to learn: A view of what education might become.* Columbus, Ohio: Charles W. Merrill, 1969.

Rogers, C. R. *Carl Rogers on encounter groups.* New York: Harper, 1970.

Rogers, C. R. *Becoming partners: Marriage and its alternatives.* New York: Delacorte Press, 1972.

Rogers, C. R. Client-centered psychotherapy. In A. M. Freedman, H. J. Kaplan, & B. J. Sadock, (Eds.), *Comprehensive textbook of psychiatry* (Vol. 2; 2nd ed.). Baltimore: Williams & Wilkins, 1975.

Rogers, C. R. *Carl Rogers on personal power.* New York: Delacorte Press, 1977.

Rogers, C. R. *A way of being.* Boston: Houghton Mifflin, 1980.

Rogers, C. R., & Dymond, R. F. (Eds.). *Psychotherapy and personality change: Coordinated studies in the client-centered approach.* Chicago: University of Chicago Press, 1954.

Rohles, F. H. Operant methods in space technology. In W. K. Honig (Ed.), *Operant behavior: Areas of research and application.* New York: Appleton-Century-Crofts, 1966.

Rokeach, M. *The open and closed mind.* New York: Basic Books, 1960.

Rorer, L. G., & Widiger, T. A. Personality structure and assessment. *Annual Review of Psychology*, 1983, *34*, 431–463.

Rose, D. Wake up to an eye opener. *New York Times*, July 27, 1980.

Rosenkrans, M. A., & Hartup, W. W. Imitative influences of consistent and inconsistent response consequences to a model on aggressive behavior in children. *Journal of Personality and Social Psychology*, 1967, *7*, 429–434.

Rosenberg, S. A theory in search of its Zeitgeist. *Contemporary Psychology*, 1980, *25*, 898–899.

Rosenhan, D. R., & Seligman, M. E. P. *Abnormal Psychology.* New York: Norton, 1984.

Rosenthal, T. L., & Bandura, A. Psychological modeling: Theory and practice. In S. L. Garfield & A. E. Bergin (Eds.), *Handbook of psychotherapy and behavior change* (2nd ed.). New York: Wiley, 1978.

Rostan, L. Cours élémentaire d'hygiene (2nd ed.). Paris: Béchet jeune, 1824.

Rotter, J. B. Word association and sentence completion methods. In H. H. Anderson & G. L. Anderson (Eds.) *An introduction to projective techniques.* Englewood Cliffs, N.J.:

Prentice-Hall, 1951, 279–311.

Rotter, J. B. *Social learning and clinical psychology.* Englewood Cliffs, N.J.: Prentice-Hall, 1954.

Rotter, J. B. Generalized expectancies for internal versus external control of reinforcement. *Psychological Monographs*, 1966, *80*, (1, Whole No. 609).

Rotter, J. B. A new scale for the measurement of interpersonal trust. *Journal of Personality*, 1967, *35*, 651–665.

Rotter, J. B. Generalized expectancies for interpersonal trust. *American Psychologist*, 1971, *26*, 443–452.

Rotter, J. B. Some problems and misconceptions related to the construct of internal versus external control of reinforcement. *Journal of Consulting and Clinical Psychoogy*, 1975, *43*, 56–67.

Rotter, J. B. Interpersonal trust, trustworthiness and gullibility. *American Psychologist*, 1980, *35*, 1–7.

Rotter, J. B. *The development and application of social learning theory: Selected papers.* New York: Praeger, 1982.

Rotter, J. B., Chance, J. E., & Phares, E. J. (Eds.). *Applications of a social learning theory of personality.* New York: Holt, Rinehart, & Winston, 1972.

Rotter, J. B., & Rafferty, J. E. *Manual for the Rotter Incomplete Sentences Blank, College Form.* New York: The Psychological Corporation, 1950.

Rowe, D. C., & Plomin, R. The importance of nonshared (E_1) environmental influences in behavioral development. *Developmental Psychology*, 1981, *17*, 517–531.

Rubins, J. L. *Karen Horney: Gentle rebel of psychoanalysis.* New York: Dial Press, 1978.

Rudikoff, E. C. A comparative study of the changes in the concepts of the self, the ordinary person, and the ideal in eight cases. In C. R. Rogers & R. R. Dymond (Eds.), *Psychotherapy and personality change: Coordinated studies in the client-centered approach.* Chicago: University of Chicago Press, 1954.

Russell, W. A. Kelly's contribution: Technique or paradigm? *Contemporary Psychology*, 1969, *14*, 430–432.

Salter, A. *Conditioned reflex therapy.* New York: Creative Age Press, 1949.

Sanford, N. Personality: Its place in psychology. In S. Koch (Ed.), *Psychology: A study of a science* (Vol. 5). New York: McGraw-Hill, 1963.

Sarason, S. B. *The psychological sense of community.* San Francisco: Jossey-Bass, 1974.

Schaar, J. H. *Escape from authority: The perspectives of Erich Fromm.* New York: Basic Books, 1961.

Schacter, S. *The psychology of affiliation: Experimental studies of the sources of gregariousness.* Stanford, Calif.: Stanford University Press, 1959.

Schafer, R. *A new language for psychoanalysis.* New Haven, Conn.: Yale University Press, 1976.

Schafer, R., Berg, I., & McCandless, B. Report on survey of current psychological testing practices. Supplement to *Newsletter*, Division of Clinical And Abnormal Psychology, 4(5). Washington, D.C.: American Psychological Association, 1951.

Scarr, S., Webber, P. L., Weinberg, R. A., & Wittig, M. A. Personality resemblance among adolescents and their parents in biologically related and adoptive families. *Journal of Personality and Social Psychology*, 1981, *40*, 885–898.

Sechrest, L. The psychology of personal constructs: George Kelly. In J. M. Wepman & R. W. Heine (Eds.), *Concepts of personality.* Chicago: Aldine, 1963.

Seeman, J. A study of the process of non-directive therapy. *Journal of Consulting Psychology*, 1949, *13*, 157–168.

Seligman, M. E. P. *Helplessness: On depression, development and death.* San Francisco: W. H. Freeman, 1975.

Seligman, M. E. P. Learned helplessness and depression in animals and man. In J. T. Spence, R. C. Carson, and J. W. Thibaut (Eds.). *Behavioral approaches to therapy.* Morristown, N.J.: General Learning Press, 1976.

Seligman, M. E. P., & Beagley, G. Learned helplessness in the cat. *Journal of Comparative and Physiological Psychology*, 1975, *88*, 534–541.

Seligman, M. E. P., & Groves, D. Nontransient learned helplessness. *Psychonomic Science*, 1970, *19*, 191–192.

Seligman, M. E. P., & Maier, S. F. Failure to escape traumatic shock. *Journal of Experimental Psychology*, 1967, *74*, 1–9.

Seligman, M. E. P., & Hager, J. L. (Eds.). *Biological boundaries of learning*. New York: Appleton-Century-Crofts, 1972.

Seward, J. P. The sign of a symbol: A reply to Professor Allport. *Psychological Review*, 1948, *55*, 277–296.

Shapiro, K. J., & Alexander, I. E. Extraversion–introversion, affiliation, and anxiety. *Journal of Personality*, 1969, *37*, 388–406.

Shapiro, M. B. The single case in fundamental clinical psychological research. *British Journal of Medical Psychology*, 1961, *34*, 255–262.

Sheldon, W. H. Ability and facial measurements. *Personality Journal*, 1927, 6(2). (a)

Sheldon, W. H. Morphological types and mental ability. *Journal of Personality Research*, 1927, *5*, 447–451. (b)

Sheldon, W. H. Social traits and morphological types. *Personality Journal*, 1927, 6(1). (c)

Sheldon, W. H. *Psychology and the Promethean will*. New York: Harper, 1936.

Sheldon, W. H. (with the collaboration of S. S. Stevens & W. B. Tucker). *The varieties of human physique: An introduction to constitutional psychology*. New York: Harper, 1940.

Sheldon, W. H. (with the collaboration of S. S. Stevens). *The varieties of temperament: A psychology of constitutional differences*. New York: Harper, 1942. (Reprinted in 1970 with minor corrections.)

Sheldon, W. H. Constitutional factors in personality. In J. McV. Hunt (Ed.), *Personality and the behavior disorders*. New York: Ronald Press, 1944.

Sheldon, W. H. *Early American cents, 1793–1814*. New York: Harper, 1949. (a)

Sheldon, W. H. (with the collaboration of E. M. Hartl & E. McDermott). *Varieties of delinquent youth: An introduction to constitutional psychiatry*. New York: Harper, 1949. (b)

Sheldon, W. H. (with the collaboration of C. W. Dupertuis & E. McDermott). *Atlas of men: A guide for somatotyping the adult male at all ages*. New York: Harper, 1954.

Sheldon, W. H. The New York study of physical constitution and psychotic pattern. *Journal of the History of Behavioral Science*, 1971, *7*, 115–126.

Sheldon, W. H. *Prometheus revisited*. Cambridge, Mass.: Schenckman, 1974.

Sheldon, W. H. *Penny whimsey* (new ed.). Somerville, Mass.: Quarterman, 1976.

Sheldon, W. H., Lewis, N.D.C., & Tenney, A. M. Psychotic patterns and physical constitution: A thirty-year followup of thirty-eight hundred psychiatric patients in New York State. In D. V. Siva Sankar (Ed.), *Schizophrenia: Current concepts and research*. New York: PJD Publications, 1969.

Shields, J. *Monozygotic twins: Brought up apart and brought up together*. London: Oxford University Press, 1962.

Shipley, T. E., & Veroff, J. A. A projective measure of need for affiliation. *Journal of Experimental Psychology*, 1952, *43*, 349–356.

Shlien, J. M., & Zimring, F. M. Research directions and methods in client-centered therapy. In A. E. Bergin & S. L. Garfield (Eds.), *Handbook of psychotherapy and behavior change*. New York: John Wiley, 1971.

Silverman, L. H. Psychoanalytic theory: "The reports of my death are greatly exaggerated." *American Psychologist*, 1976, *31*, 621–637.

Silverman, L. H. The subliminal psychodynamic activation method: Overview and comprehensive listing of studies. In J. Masling (Ed.), *Empirical studies of psychoanalytic theories* (Vol. I). Hillsdale, N.J.: The Analytic Press, 1983.

Simmel, M. L. (Ed.). *The reach of the mind: Essays in memory of Kurt Goldstein.* New York: Springer, 1968.

Simon, H. A. *The sciences of the artificial.* Cambridge, Mass.: M.I.T. Press, 1969.

Skaggs, E. B. Personalistic psychology as science. *Psychological Review,* 1945, *52,* 234–238.

Skinner, B. F. *The behavior of organisms.* New York: Appleton-Century-Crofts, 1938.

Skinner, B. F. Review of K. Goldstein's "The organism." *Journal of Abnormal and Social Psychology,* 1940, *35,* 462–465.

Skinner, B. F. *Walden two.* New York: Macmillan, 1948.

Skinner, B. F. Are theories of learning necessary? *Psychological Review,* 1950, *57,* 193–216.

Skinner, B. F. *Science and human behavior.* New York: Macmillan, 1953.

Skinner, B. F. A case history in scientific method. *American Psychologist,* 1956, *11,* 221–233.

Skinner, B. F. *Verbal behavior.* New York: Appleton-Century-Crofts, 1957.

Skinner, B. F. Pigeons in a Pelican. *American Psychologist,* 1960, *15,* 28–37.

Skinner, B. F. *Cumulative record.* New York: Appleton-Century-Crofts, 1961. (a)

Skinner, B. F. The design of cultures. *Daedalus,* 1961, *90,* 534–546. (b)

Skinner, B. F. Autobiography. In E. G. Boring & G. Lindzey (Eds.), *History of psychology in autobiography* (Vol. 5). New York: Appleton-Century-Crofts, 1967.

Skinner, B. F. *The technology of teaching.* New York: Appleton-Century-Crofts, 1968.

Skinner, B. F. *Contingencies of reinforcement: A theoretical analysis.* New York: Appleton-Century-Crofts, 1969.

Skinner, B. F. *Beyond freedom and dignity.* New York: Alfred A. Knopf, 1972.

Skinner, B. F. A case history in scientific method. In G. Lindzey, C. S. Hall, & M. Manosevitz (Eds.), *Theories of personality: Primary sources and research* (2nd ed.). New York: John Wiley, 1973.

Skinner, B. F. *About behaviorism.* New York: Alfred Knopf, 1974.

Skinner, B. F. *Particulars of my life.* New York: Alfred A. Knopf, 1976.

Skinner, B. F. *The shaping of a behaviorist.* New York: Alfred A. Knopf, 1979.

Skinner, B. F. *A matter of consequences.* New York: Alfred A. Knopf, 1983.

Skinner, B. F. Intellectual self-management in old age. *American Psychologist, 38,* 1983, 239–244.

Smith, M. B. The phenomenological approach in personality theory: Some critical remarks. *Journal of Abormal and Social Psychology,* 1950, *45,* 516–522.

Snyder, W. U., and others. *Casebook of nondirective counseling.* Boston: Houghton Mifflin, 1947.

Solomon, R. L., Kamin, L. J., & Wynne, L. G. Traumatic avoidance learning: The outcomes of several extinction procedures with dogs. *Journal of Abnormal and Social Psychology,* 1953, *48,* 291–302.

Sommerschield, H., & Reyher, J. Posthypnotic conflict, repression and psychopathology. *Journal of Abnormal Psychology,* 1973, *82,* 278–290.

Spence, K. W. The nature of theory construction in contemporary psychology. *Psychological Review,* 1944, *51,* 47–68.

Spence, K. W. *Behavior theory and conditioning.* New Haven, Conn.: Yale University Press, 1956.

Sperber, M. *Masks of loneliness: Alfred Adler in perspective.* New York: Macmillan, 1974.

Spiegelberg, H. *Phenomenology in psychology and psychiatry.* Evanston, Ill.: Northwestern University Press, 1972.

Stephenson, W. *The study of behavior: Q-technique and its methodology.* Chicago: University of Chicago Press, 1953.

Stern, P. J. *C. G. Jung: The haunted prophet.* New York: Braziller, 1976.

Storr, Anthony. *The essential Jung.* Princeton, N.J.: Princeton University Press, 1983.

Straus, E. W. *The primary world of senses: A vindication of sensory experience.* Glencoe, Ill.: Free Press, 1963.

Straus, E. W. *Phenomenological psychology: The selected papers of Erwin W. Straus.* New York: Basic Books, 1966.

Straus, E. W. Norm and pathology of I-world relations. In G. Lindzey, C. S. Hall, & M. Manosevitz (Eds.), *Theories of personality: Primary sources and research* (2nd ed.). New York: John Wiley, 1973.

Stringer, P., & Bannister, D. (Eds.) *Constructs of sociality and individuality.* London: Academic Press, 1979.

Sullivan, H. S. *Conceptions of modern psychiatry.* Washington, D.C.: William Alanson White Psychiatric Foundation, 1947.

Sullivan, H. S. *The interpersonal theory of psychiatry.* New York: W. W. Norton, 1953.

Sullivan, H. S. *The psychiatric interview.* New York: W. W. Norton, 1954.

Sullivan, H. S. *Clinical studies in psychiatry.* New York: W. W. Norton, 1956.

Sullivan, H. S. *Schizophrenia as a human process.* New York: W. W. Norton, 1962.

Sullivan, H. S. *The fusion of psychiatry and social science.* New York: W. W. Norton, 1964.

Suppe, F. *The structure of scientific theories.* Urbana: University of Illinois Press, 1974.

Thomas, E., & Dewald, L. Experimental neurosis: Neuropsychological analysis. In J. D. Maser & M. E. P. Seligman (Eds.) *Psychopathology: Experimental models.* San Francisco: Freeman, 1977.

Thompson, C., with Mullahy, P. *Psychoananalysis: Evolution and development.* New York: Grove Press, 1950.

Thompson, G. G. George Alexander Kelly (1905–1967). *Journal of General Psychology,* 1968, *79,* 19–24.

Thorndike, E. L. *The fundamentals of learning.* New York: Teachers College Press, 1932.

Tolman, E. C. Kurt Lewin, 1890–1947. *Psycho-logical Review,* 1948, *55,* 1–5.

Truax, C. B., & Mitchell, K. M. Research on certain therapist interpersonal skills in relation to process and outcome. In A. E. Bergin & S. L. Garfield (Eds.), *Handbook of psychotherapy and behavior change.* New York: John Wiley, 1971.

Turner, M. *Philosophy and the science of behavior.* New York: Appleton-Century-Crofts, 1967.

Van der Post, L. *Jung and the story of our time.* New York: Pantheon Books, 1975.

Van Kaam, A. *Existential foundations of psychology.* Pittsburgh, Pa.: Duquesne University Press, 1966.

Veroff, J. Development and validation of a projective measure of power motivation. *Journal of Abnormal and Social Psychology,* 1957, *54,* 1–8.

Viola, G. *Le legge de correlazione morfologia dei tippi individuali.* Padova, Italy: Prosperini, 1909.

Vockell, E. L., Felker, D. W., & Miley, C. H. Birth order literature, 1967–1972. *Journal of Individual Psychology,* 1973, *29,* 39–53.

von Franz, M-L. *C. G. Jung: His myth in our times.* New York: Putnam, 1975.

Wachtel, P. L. Psychodynamics, behavior therapy, and the implacable experimenter: An inquiry into the consistency of personality. *Journal of Abnormal Psychology,* 1973, *82,* 324–334. (a)

Wachtel, P. L. On fact, hunch, and stereotype: A reply to Mischel. *Journal of Abnormal Psychology,* 1973, *82,* 537–540. (b)

Walker, R. N. Body build and behavior in young children. Body build and nursery school teachers ratings. *Monographs of the Society for Research on Child Development,* 1962, *27,* Serial No. 84.

Walters, R. H., Leat, M., & Mezei, L. Inhibition and disinhibition of responses through empathic learning. *Canadian Journal of Psychology,* 1963, *17,* 235–243.

Wann, T. W. (Ed.). *Behaviorism and phenomenology: Contrasting bases for modern psychology.* Chicago: University of Chicago Press, 1964.

Waterman, A. S. Identity development from

adolescence to adulthood: An extension of theory and a review of research. *Developmental Psychology*, 1982, *18*, 341–358.

Watson, J. B. *Behaviorism*. New York: W. W. Norton, 1925.

Wehr, G. *Portrait of Jung: An illustrated biography*. New York: Herder and Herder, 1971.

Weigert, E. V. Dissent in the early history of psychoanalysis. *Psychiatry*, 1942, *5*, 349–359.

Weiss, J. M. Effects of coping behavior in different warning signal combinations on stress pathology in rats. *Journal of Comparative and Physiological Psychology*, 1971, *77*, 1–13.

Wesstein, N. Psychology constructs the female. In V. Gornick & B. K. Moran, (Eds), *Women in sexist society: Studies in power and powerlessness*. New York: Basic books, 1971.

Wexler, D. A., & Rice, L. N. (Eds.). *Innovations in client-centered therapy*. Boston: Houghton Mifflin, 1970.

White, R. W. Motivation reconsidered: The concept of competence, *Psychological Review*, 1959, *66*, 297–333.

White, R. W. Competence and the psychosexual stages of development. In M. R. Jones (Ed.), *Nebraska symposium on motivation*. Lincoln: University of Nebraska Press, 1960.

White, R. W. Ego and reality in psychoanalytic theory: A proposal regarding independent ego energies. *Psychological Issues*, Monograph 11. New York: International Universities Press, 1963.

White, R. W. *The enterprise of living: Growth and organization in personality*. New York: Holt, Rinehart and Winston, 1972.

White, R. W. *Lives in progress* (3rd ed.). New York: Holt, Rinehart and Winston, 1975.

White, R. W., & Watt, N. F. *The abnormal personality* (5th ed.), New York: John Wiley, 1981.

Whyte, L. L. *The unconscious before Freud*. Garden City, N.Y.: Doubleday, 1962.

Wilson, C. *New pathways in psychology: Maslow and the post-Freudian revolution*. New York: Ta-plinger, 1972.

Wilson, E. O. *Sociobiology*. Cambridge, Mass.: Harvard University Press, 1975.

Wittman, P., Sheldon, W. H., & Katz, C. J. A study of the relationship between constitutional variations and fundamental psychotic behavior reactions. *Journal of Nervous and Mental Disease*, 1948, *108*, 470–476.

Wolpe, J. *Psychotherapy by reciprocal inhibition*. Stanford, Calif.: Stanford University Press, 1958.

Wolpe, J. Cognition and causation in human behavior and its therapy. *American Psychologist*, 1978, 437–446.

Wolpe, J. Behavior therapy versus psychoanalysis: Therapeutic and social implications. *American Psychologist*, 1981, *36*, 159–164. (a)

Wolpe, J. The dichotomy between classical conditioned and cognitively learned anxiety. *Journal of Behavior Therapy and Experimental Psychiatry*, 1981, *12*, 35–42. (b)

Wolpe, J. *The practice of behavior therapy* (3rd ed.). New York: Pergamon Press, 1982.

Wortman, C. B., & Dintzer, L. Is an attributional analysis of the learned helplessness phenomenon viable? A critique of the Abramson-Seligman-Teasdale reformulation. *Journal of Abnormal Psychology*, 1978, *87*, 75–90.

Wylie, R. C. *The self-concept. Vol. 1: A review of methodological considerations and measuring instruments; Vol. 2: Theory and research on selected topics*. Lincoln: University of Nebraska Press, 1974, 1978.

Young, P.A., Eaves, L. J., & Eysenck, H. J. Intergenerational stability and change in the causes of variation in personality. *Personality and Individual Differences*, 1980, *1*, 35–55.

Zajonc, R. B., & Bargh, J. Birth order, family size, and decline of SAT scores. *American Psychologist*, 1980, *35*, 662–668.

Zubin, J., Eron, L. D., & Schumer, F. *An experimental approach to projective techniques*. New York: John Wiley, 1965.

PHOTO CREDITS

Chapter 11 Page 379: New York Public Library Picture Collection. Page 382 and page 384: Courtesy Dr. William H. Sheldon, from *Atlas of Men, A Guide for Somatyping the Adult Male At All Ages* by William H. Sheldon, Hafner Publishing Co., 1970. Page 387: (top left) Pablo Picasso, The Metropolitan Museum of Art, Gift of Thelma Chrysler Fox, 1952, (top right) Alinari-Art Reference Bureau, (bottom) Titian, "Venus of Urbino" Alinari-Art Reference Bureau. Page 388: Jean-Claude LeJeune/Stock Boston. Page 391: Elliot Erwitt/Magnum. Page 406: Enrico Ferorelli/DOT.

Chapter 12 Page 423: Courtesy Raymond Bernard Cattell. Page 438: Courtesy Hans Eysenk. Page 424: Ron Kuntz/UPI. Page 430: Calvin Larsen/Photo Researchers.

Chapter 13 Page 463: Photo by Hans-Peter Biemann. Courtesy B.F. Skinner. Page 467: (left) Midge Keator/Woodfin Camp, (right) Jose A. Fernandez/Woodfin Camp. Page 473: New York Times Photos. Page 474: Robert Epstein, Department of Psychology, Harvard University. Page 477: Tannenbaum/Sygma.

Chapter 14 Page 495: Courtesy Yale University. Page 497: Stella Kupferberg. Page 504: Alan Carey/The Image Works. Page 506: Richard Hutchings/Photo Researchers. Page 507: Alex Harris/Archive. Page 509: Marc & Evelyne Bernheim/Woodfin Camp. Page 512: Nina Leen/Life Magazine, © Time Inc.

Chapter 15 Page 536: Dick Hehrwald/Black Star. Page 538: Courtesy Stanford University. Page 542: Charles Harbutt/Archive. Page 544: Courtesy of Albert Bandura, Stanford University. Page 546: Alan Carey/The Image Works. Page 548: Drawing by S. Gross; © 1974 The New Yorker Magazine, Inc. Page 551: Courtesy Dr. Martin Seligman, University of Pennsylvania. Page 563: Alice Kandell/Photo Researchers.

Chapter 16 Page 577: © 1967: United Feature Syndicate, Inc. Page 579: Frank Siteman/Taurus Photos. Page 586: Courtesy DuPont Company/Public Affairs Department. Page 588: Thomas S. England/Photo Researchers.

Part Openers Part 1: Marcel Duchamp, "Nude Descending a Staircase, No. 2" Louise and Walter Arnsberg Collection, Philadelphia Museum of Art. Part 2: Pierre August Renoir, "Two Girls at the Piano," 1891, Joslyn Art Museum, Omaha, Nebraska. Museum Purchase. Part 3: Victor Vasarely, "Gotha" Serigraph, Collection, The Museum of Modern Art, New York. Transferred from the Museum Library. Part 4: Oskar Schlemmer, "Bauhaus Stairway" (1932), Collection, The Museum of Modern Art, New York. Gift of Phillip Johnson. Part 5: Fernand Leger, "Two Men," Hirshhorn Museum and Sculpture Garden, Smithsonian Institution. Joseph Martin/Scala/Art Resource.

Chapter 2 Box 2.3 J. Breuer & S. Freud. *Studies in hysteria* (A. A. Brill, Transl.). Boston: Beacon Press, 1937.

Chapter 3 Figure 3.1 E. H. Erikson. *Childhood and society* (2nd ed.). Reproduced by permission of W. W. Norton & Company, Inc. Copyright © 1963 by W. W. Norton & Company, Inc. Table 3.4 J. E. Marcia. Identity in adolescence. In J. Adelson (Ed.), *Handbook of adolescent psychology*. New York: John Wiley & Sons, 1980.

Chapter 6 Box 6.3 D. Rose. "Wake up to an eye opener." *The New York Times*, July 27, 1980, Op-ed page. Copyright © 1980 by The New York Times Company. Reprinted by permission. Figure 6.4 C. R. Rogers (Ed.). *The therepeutic relationship and its impact*. Madison: The University of Wisconsin Press, 1967. Copyright © 1967 by The Board of Regents of the University of Wisconsin System. Figure 6.5 C. R. Rogers (Ed.). *The therepeutic relationship and its impact*. Madison: The University of Wisconsin Press, 1967. Copyright © 1967 by The Board of Regents of the University of Wisconsin System.

Chapter 8 Figure 8.7 K. Lewin. *Field theory in social science: Selected theoretical papers* (D. Cartwright, Ed.). New York: Harper & Row, Inc., 1951. Table 8.3 G. A. Kelly. *The psychology of personal constructs* (Vol. 1). New York: W. W. Norton, 1955.

Chaper 9 Table 9.1 H. A. Murray (and collaborators). *Explorations in personality*. New York: Oxford University Press, 1938. Table 9.2 H. A. Murray (and collaborators). *Explorations in personality*. New York: Oxford University Press, 1938.

Chapter 10 Pages 344–346, 348–349, 351, 353–360, 362, 365 G. W. Allport. *Pattern and growth in personality*. Copyright © 1961, 1937 by Holt, Rinehart & Winston, Inc. Reprinted by permission of Holt, Rinehart & Winston, CBS College Publishing. Box 10.2 "He's stingy if . . . ." Excerpted from *Cosmopolitan*, September 1976. Box 10.3, Table 10.4 G. W. Allport. *Letters from Jenny*. New York: Harcourt Brace Jovanovich, 1965.

Chapter 11 Figure 11.2 W. H. Sheldon. *Atlas of men: A guide for somatotyping the adult male at all ages* (with the collaboration of C. W. Dupertuis & E. McDermott). New York: Harper & Row, Inc., 1954. Figure 11.3 W. H. Sheldon. Distribution of 4000 female somatotypes. *Atlas of men: A guide for somatotyping the adult male at all ages* (with the collaboration of C. W. Dupertuis & E. McDermott). Figure 11.4 W. H. Sheldon (with the collaboration of E. M. Hartl & E. McDermott). *Varieties of delinquent youth: An introduction to constitutional psychiatry*. New York: Harper & Row, 1949. Figure 11.5 W. H. Sheldon (with the collaboration of E. M. Hartl & E. McDermott). *Varieties of delinquent youth: An introduction to constitutional psychiatry*. New York: Harper & Row, 1949. Table 11.1 E. Kretschmer. *Physique and character*. New York: Harcourt Brace Jovanovich, 1925. Table 11.2 W. H. Sheldon (with the collaboration of S. S. Stevens). *The varieties of temperament*. New York: Harper & Row, 1942. Table 11.3 W. H. Sheldon (with the collaboration of S. S. Stevens). *The varieties of temperament*. New York: Harper & Row, 1942. Table 11.4 W. H. Sheldon (with the collaboration of E. M. Hartl & E. McDermott). *Varieties of delinquent youth: An introduction to constitional psychiatry*. New York: Harper & Row, 1949.

Chapter 12 Figure 12.1 R. B. Cattell. *Personality: A systematic, theoretical and factual study*. New York: McGraw-Hill, Incorporated, 1950. Adapted by permission of the author; R. B. Cattell & R. M. Dreger. *Handbook of modern personality theory*. Washington, D.C.:

Hemisphere Publishing Corporation, 1977. Figure 12.2 R. B. Cattell & K. P. Cross. "Comparison of the ergic and self-sentiment structure found in dynamic traits by R- and P-techniques. *Journal of Personality* **21**, 250–271. Copyright © 1953 by the Duke University Press, Durham, N.C. Figure 12.5 H. J. Eysenck. *Personality, genetics and behavior.* New York: Praeger Publishers, 1982.

Chapter 13 Pages 461–462 B. F. Skinner. From *Walden two.* Reprinted with permission of Macmillan Publishing Company. Copyright © 1948, 1976 by B. F. Skinner. Figure 13.3 W. N. Dember, J. J. Jenkins, & T. J. Teyler. *General psychology* (2 ed.). Hillsdale, N.J.: Lawrence Erlbaum Associates, 1984. Figure 8.12 p. 325.

Chapter 14 Pages 498, 508, 509, 519, 520 J. Dollard & N. E. Miller. *Personality and psychotherapy.* New York: McGraw-Hill, 1950.

Chapter 15 Figure 15.1 A. Bandura. The self system in reciprocal determinism. *American Psychologist*, 1978, *33*, p. 345. Copyright © 1978 by the American Psychological Association. Adapted by permission of the author. Figure 15.2 A. Bandura. The self system in reciprocal determinism. *American Psychologist*, 1978, *33*, p. 349. Copyright © 1978 by the American Psychological Association. Adapted by permission of the author. Figure 15.3 A. Bandura. Self-efficacy: Toward a unifying theory of behavioral change. *Psychological Review*, 1977, *84*, p. 195. Copyright © 1977 by the American Psychological Association. Adapted by permission of the author.

Author index

Subject index

THE THEORISTS: A TIMELINE

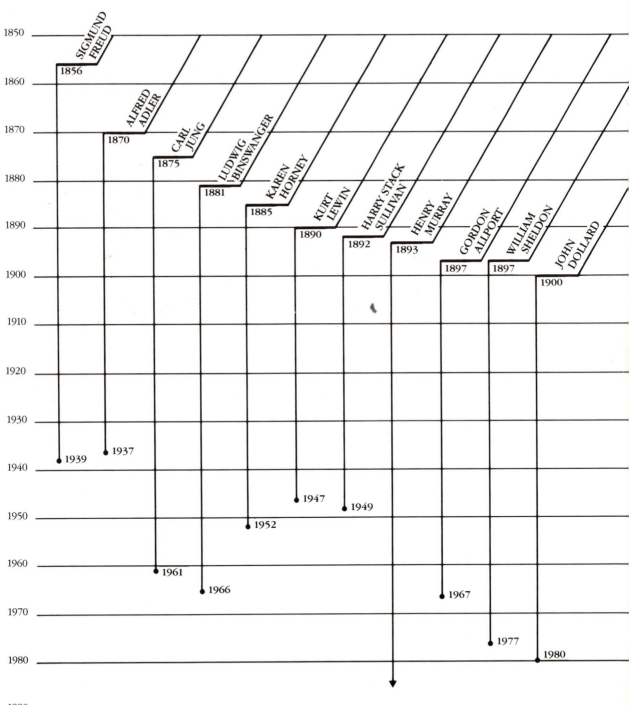